Y0-BBW-077

Protestantism and patriotism offers a fundamental reinterpretation of English political culture between 1650 and 1668. It is also both the most detailed study to date of the causes and consequences of the first two Anglo-Dutch Wars (1652–1654 and 1665–1667), and a reconfiguration of the English political nation which engaged in those two conflicts.

Professor Pincus argues that it is impossible to understand the making of English foreign policy in this period without a careful study of its ideological contexts, while at the same time suggesting that accounts of English domestic politics which ignore the ideological implications of England's place in European political culture are impoverished. Because of the broad context in which the Anglo-Dutch Wars are situated, the book will appeal not only to specialists in English foreign policy but to all those interested in seventeenth-century English and Dutch politics and culture.

Cambridge Studies in Early Modern British History

PROTESTANTISM AND PATRIOTISM

Cambridge Studies in Early Modern British History

Series editors

ANTHONY FLETCHER
Professor of History, University of Essex

JOHN GUY
Professor of Modern History, University of St Andrews

and JOHN MORRILL
Reader in Early Modern History, University of Cambridge, and Fellow and Tutor of Selwyn College

This is a series of monographs and studies covering many aspects of the history of the British Isles between the late fifteenth century and early eighteenth century. It includes the work of established scholars and pioneering work by a new generation of scholars. It includes both reviews and revisions of major topics and books which open up new historical terrain or which reveal startling new perspectives on familiar subjects. All the volumes set detailed reseach into broader perspectives and the books are intended for the use of students as well as of their teachers.

For a list of titles in the series, see end of book

PROTESTANTISM AND PATRIOTISM

Ideologies and the making of English foreign policy, 1650–1668

STEVEN C. A. PINCUS

University of Chicago

Published by the Press Syndicate of the University of Cambridge
The Pitt Building, Trumpington Street, Cambridge CB2 1RP
40 West 20th Street, New York, NY 10011-4211, USA
10 Stamford Road, Oakleigh, Melbourne 3166, Australia

First published 1996

Printed in Great Britain at the University Press, Cambridge

A catalogue record for this book is available from the British Library

Library of Congress cataloguing in publication

Pincus, Steven C. A.
Protestantism and patriotism: ideologies and the making of English foreign policy, 1650–1668 / Steven C. A. Pincus.
p. cm. – (Cambridge studies in early modern British history)
Includes bibliographical references.
ISBN 0 521 43487 4
1. Great Britain – Foreign relations – 1649–1660. 2. Christianity and politics – Protestant churches – History – 17th century. 3. Protestant churches – England – History – 17th century. 4. Great Britain – Foreign relations – 1660–1688. 5. Patriotism – England – History – 17th century. 6. Protestantism. I. Title. II. Series.
DA425.P56 1996 95–7666
327.41–dc20 CIP

ISBN 0 521 43487 4 hardback

CE

CONTENTS

Acknowledgments — *page* ix
List of abbreviations — xi

1 Introduction — 1

Part I The rod of the Lord: ideology and the outbreak of the First Anglo-Dutch War

2 Historiographical overview — 11
3 The attempt at unification — 15
4 The road to war — 40
Coda: the popular apocalyptic context — 76

Part II To unite against the common enemy: the 1654 Treaty of Westminster and the end of apocalyptic foreign policy

5 Historiographical overview — 83
6 The causes of the war stated — 87
7 Peace proposed — 101
8 Political upheavals and ideological divisions — 115
9 The rejection of apocalyptic foreign policy — 149
10 The Protectorate's new foreign policy — 168

Part III Popery, trade, and universal monarchy: ideology and the outbreak of the Second Anglo-Dutch War

11 Historiographical overview — 195
12 The establishment of an Orangist foreign policy — 199
13 The Anglo-Dutch treaty of 1662 — 214

14 The Northern Rebellion and the reestablishment of Anglican Royalist consensus 222
15 The April 1664 trade resolution 237
16 Popery, trade, and universal monarchy 256

Part IV The Medway, Breda, and the Triple Alliance: the collapse of Anglican Royalist Foreign Policy

17 Historiographical overview 271
18 The circulation of news and the course of the war 276
19 The popular understanding of the war 289
20 The government's war aims 318
21 An Orangist revolution 331
22 Victory denied and wartime consensus shattered 343
23 The rise of political opposition 369
24 The road to Chatham: the decision not to send out a battle fleet 379
25 The demise of Anglican Royalist foreign policy 407

Conclusion 441

Bibliography 453
Index 486

ACKNOWLEDGMENTS

The debts I have amassed in the production of this monograph are too vast to be given full notice here. Nevertheless many acts of generosity have been so great as to deserve special notice.

David Lagomarsino communicated his enthusiasm for history to me as an undergraduate and encouraged me to forego the temptations of a career in the law to attend graduate school in history. David Lagomarsino and the history and classics faculties at Dartmouth demonstrated to me the possibilities of combining first-rate scholarship with outstanding teaching.

Graduate school, extended research in England, and the opportunity to revise this manuscript were made possible by the generosity of the Mellon Fellowships in the Humanities, the Lord Harlech Trust, the Honda American Foundation, and the Harvard Society of Fellows.

The idea for this book arose from a paper produced for the seminar on Early Modern State and Society directed by John Brewer and Simon Schama, whose stimulating ideas, I hope, have significantly affected the finished product. Over the years Simon Schama has reminded me of the centrality of the Netherlands in early modern Europe, and made sure that I thought about the popular dimension of my project. John Clive taught me to look at my sources with a sense of humor, and to remember the importance of political culture in trying to understand politics.

My extended stay in Oxford convinced me of the vital importance of intellectual community in producing historical scholarship. Blair Worden, through his evening seminars and his own enthusiasm and generosity, made Oxford a wonderful place for an American to become acquainted with seventeenth-century English history. Toby Barnard went far beyond the call of duty in acting as my Oxford supervisor, listening patiently to my incoherent and often crazy ideas. He unfailingly pointed me in fruitful directions, carefully read and commented upon every poorly written and badly organized draft chapter. Perhaps most importantly, Toby Barnard constantly reassured me that this was a project worth undertaking.

I have benefited immensely from discussions with Sharon Achinstein, Bernard Bailyn, Jim Bjork, David Bush, Tony Claydon, Lee Davison,

Margot Finn, Adam Fox, Mark Goldie, Lije Gould, Tim Harris, Derek Hirst, Alan Houston, Mark Knights, Peter Le Fevre, Jim Livesey, Clair McEachern, John Miller, Peter Miller, Bill Novak, Nelly Oliensis, Cathy Patterson, Jenny Paxton, Katherine Penovich, Ben Polak, John Robertson, Craig Rose, Henry Roseveare, Paul Seaward, Nigel Smith, John Spurr, Nicholas von Maltzahn and Rachel Weil. The comments and criticisms of papers I read in Dr. Worden's seminar at Oxford, the Thursday Seventeenth Century seminar at the Institute of Historical Research, the Stuart seminar at Selwyn College, Cambridge, the 1660–1832 Colloquium held at Newcastle in 1989, and at the British History Colloquium at Harvard have done much to shape the finished product. I am greatly indebted to Sharon Achinstein, Kenny Bamberger, Jeremy Black, David Bush, Bernard Capp, Tom Cogswell, Ranu Dayal, Margot Finn, Lisa Freinkel, Tim Harris, Steve Maughan, Claire McEachern, Bill Novak, Cathy Patterson, Jen Poulos, John Robertson, Lynn Sanders, Simon Schama, Kevin Sharpe, Nick Souleles, John Spurr, Richard Strier, Nicholas von Maltzahn and Blair Worden for reading, criticising, and making suggestions on various sections of this book. My research assistant Jim Bjork has been indispensable in the final stages of production.

At different times I received much support and encouragement, as well as much prodding, from some very special people. My parents, though sometimes perplexed as to what I was doing, were invariably supportive and always quick to ask when the book would finally be done. Jen Poulos provided me with much warmth, support, and editorial assistance, never losing interest in the project or its author. Sharon Achinstein quickly made me feel at home in Chicago, provided me with much caring, support, and encouragement during those difficult last phases of manuscript production, and taught me many important things about the seventeenth century and much much more.

My final debt is my largest. Wallace MacCaffrey has been a kind, generous, and exacting supervisor. He not only kept up my spirits over the long haul, but also provided encouragement and critical advice at precisely the right moments. He has been for me, and for a whole generation of Harvard students, a model scholar and teacher.

ABBREVIATIONS

Add.	Additional Manuscripts
B.L.	British Library
Bod.	Bodleian Library, Oxford
Cal. EIC	Ethel Bruce Sainsbury (editor), *A Calendar of the Court Minutes etc. of the East India Company* (Oxford, 1913)
Carte	Carte Manuscripts, Bodleian Library, Oxford
Carte, *Collection*	Thomas Carte (editor), *A Collection of Original Letters and papers, Concerning the Affairs of England, From the Year 1641–1660* (London, 1739)
CJ	*Journal of the House of Commons*
CKS	Centre for Kentish Studies
Clar.	Clarendon Manuscripts, Bodleian Library, Oxford
CLRO	Corporation of London Record Office
Cov. MSS	Coventry manuscripts, Longleat House
CSPD	*Calendar of State Papers, Domestic*
CSPV	*Calendar of State Papers, Venetian*
CUL	Cambridge University Library
DNB	*Dictionary of National Biography*
Evelyn, *Diary*	S. R. Gardiner (editor), *Letters and Papers Relating to the First Dutch War 1652–1654* (London, 1899)
Houghton	Houghton Library, Harvard University
HL	Huntington Library, San Marino, California
HMC	Historical Manuscripts Commission
IOL	India Office Library, London
Josselin, *Diary*	Alan MacFarlane (editor), *The Diary of Ralph Josselin 1616–1683* (London, 1976)
LOC	Library of Congress, Washington DC
LRO	Leicestershire Record Office

Nickolls, *Original Letters*	John Nickolls (editor), *Original Letters and Papers of State* (Milton State Papers) (London, 1743)
NMM	National Maritime Museum, Greenwich
NRO	Norfolk Record Office
Orrey State Letters	*A Collection of State Letters of the Right Honourble Roger Boyle* (Dublin, 1743)
Pepys, *Diary*	Robert Lathham and William Matthews (editors), *The Diary of Samuel Pepys*, Vols. I–IX (London, 1970)
POAS	George DeF. Lord (editor), *Poems on Affairs of State*, Vol. I 1660–1678 (New Haven, 1963)
PRO	Public Record Office, Chancery Lane, London
PRO Kew	Public Record Office, Kew Gardens, London
Rawl.	Rawlinson Manuscripts, Bodleian Library, Oxford
Rep.	Repertory Books of the Court of Aldermen, CLRO
Scott, *Algernon Sidney*	Jonathan Scott, *Algernon Sidney and the English Republic, 1623–1677* (Cambridge, 1988)
SRO	Staffordshire Record Office
Steckley, *John Paige*	George F. Steckley (editor), *The Letters of John Paige, Merchant, 1648–1658* (London, 1984)
Thomason:	Thomason's dating of pamphlet, British Library Thomason manuscripts
TT	Thomason tract number, British Library, Thomason Manuscripts
Wood	Wood's dating of pamphlet, Woods Diaries Manuscripts, Bodleian Library, Oxford

Dates in the form 24–5 May refer to newspapers, etc., in which the publication covers numbers of days. Dates in the form 24/5 May refer for the most part to correspondence in which a continental calendar has been used: the two dates refer to the English and continental dates on which the letter was written.

1

Introduction

Seventeenth-century English foreign policy has more often been written off than written about. Domestic constitutional and social developments have dominated the recent historiographical headlines. Foreign policy's retreat from the stage of early modern English history has been so complete that one well-respected historian has recently challenged his readers to "ponder the question of how many English victories over continental powers you can name between the battles of Agincourt (1415) and Blenheim (1704)."[1] The lack of memorable English victories, John Brewer has implied, indicates the relative unimportance of seventeenth-century England on the European scene, and consequently the insignificance of the study of its foreign policy. Brewer's is not a unique assessment. "For three centuries before 1688, the English state had been unable to raise adequate revenues from taxes," Lawrence Stone has claimed in order to explain away the historiographical neglect of seventeenth-century foreign policy, "as a result of which [England] was no more than a marginal player in the European power game."[2]

Nevertheless seventeenth-century foreign policy was not always thought to be so marginal. Contemporaries thought of England as one of the great powers of Europe. Agents from Denmark, Sweden, Portugal, Spain, and France stood in line for favors from Oliver Cromwell.[3] "The sea is your own and now all nations greet / with bending sails each vessel of your fleet," bragged one panegyric to Cromwell, "your power extends as far as winds can blow / or swelling sails upon the globe may go."[4] This seventeenth-century national self-image was not soon forgotten. The English admiral

1 John Brewer, *The Sinews of Power* (London, 1989), pp. xiii–xiv.

2 Lawrence Stone, "England's Financial Revolution," in *New York Review of Books* Vol. 38 No. 3 (15 March 1990), p. 50.

3 Josselin, *Diary*, 24 January 1653, p. 295; Sagredo to Doge and Senate, 13/23 December 1653, *CSPV*, p. 160; Giacomo Quirini to Doge and Senate, 7/17 June 1654, *CSPV*, p. 224; John Thurloe to Bulstrode Whitelocke, 24 February 1654, in Sigismund von Bischoffshausen, *Die Politik des Protectors Oliver Cromwell in der Auffassung und Thätigkeit seines Ministers des Staatssecretärs John Thurloe* (Innsbruck, 1899), p. 168.

4 "A Panegyrick to Oliver Cromwell," in Bod., Rawl. Poet. 37, f. 119.

Robert Blake, for example, received high praise from many writers in the eighteenth and nineteenth centuries, including from Samuel Johnson.[5] Blake, insisted one of his nineteenth-century biographers, William Hepworth Dixon, was the man "who had humbled the pride of Holland, Portugal and Spain, who had laid the foundations of our lasting influence in the Mediterranean, and in eight years of success had made England the first maritime power in Europe!"[6]

Victorian historians universally looked to the mid-seventeenth century for the foundations of Britain's rise to greatness. "After half a century during which England had been of scarcely more weight in European politics than Venice or Saxony," pronounced Lord Macaulay in his magisterial and elegant *History of England*, "she at once became the most formidable power in the world."[7] Sir John Seeley, Professor of Modern History at Cambridge, insisted upon highlighting the contemporary political relevance of the history which he taught, comparing the age of Cromwell to that of Napoleon and that of Julius Caesar in its imperial importance. The Navigation Act which the Rump Parliament passed in 1651 – and which Seeley identified as the outgrowth of ideological rather than mercantile discontent with the Dutch – was "the act which laid the foundation of the English commercial empire." For Seeley the period from the Armada to the Glorious Revolution was critical in laying the groundwork for the growth of Britain; Elizabeth, Cromwell, and William III were his heroes.[8] Although English radicals of all classes in the mid Victorian era pointed to different heroes than did the liberal unionist Seeley, they too frequently recalled Cromwell's foreign policy with pride. For these radical men and women, the Cromwellian tradition committed England to defend liberty against tyranny in the international arena – a commitment which the radicals pressed upon successive British governments to fulfill in Hungary, in Italy, and in France.[9] No one can doubt that the Victorians had little trouble recalling seventeenth-century military heroes. In his *Child's History of England*, Charles Dickens used Cromwell's foreign policy as the yardstick by which to measure all future English statesmen. "Between you and me," Dickens remarked at the high water mark of England's informal empire, "England has rather lost ground in this respect since the days of Oliver Cromwell."[10]

5 Samuel Johnson, "Blake," in *The Works of Samuel Johnson* (London, 1825), Vol. VI, pp. 293–309.

6 William Hepworth Dixon, *Robert Blake* (London, 1852), p. 366.

7 Thomas Babington Macaulay, *The History of England*, edited by Charles Harding Firth, (London, 1913), Vol. I, pp. 120–122.

8 Sir John R. Seeley, *The Growth of British Policy* (Cambridge, 1922), *passim* and especially Vol. II, pp. 1–45.

9 Margot Claire Finn, *After Chartism: Class and Nation in English Radical Politics, 1848–1874* (Cambridge, 1993), *passim.*

10 Charles Dickens, *A Child's History of England and Miscellaneous Pieces* (New York, n.d.), p. 364.

In the recoil from Empire, however, the achievements of the seventeenth century have been made to look less grand. Far from being the progenitors of the Victorian Empire, English men and women of the seventeenth century have been presented as rarely looking beyond their own local communities. "The social and political life of the vast majority of Englishmen, even among the gentry," Alan Everitt has observed, "was lived almost wholly within the confines of their county – their 'country' as they significantly called it." Naturally enough, this outlook – an outlook which Everitt and others have insisted outlasted the temporarily centralizing forces of the Interregnum – was "insular and inbred," more interested in encroachments upon local communities than upon distant developments in Madrid, Paris, Vienna, or the New World.[11] This insularity was, according to Conrad Russell, reflected in the debates at Westminster. Members of the early Stuart House of Commons, he claims, "almost always put concerns for their own counties above any concept of the national interest." When pressed – and for Russell foreign policy was always pressed upon provincialist members of Parliament by more cosmopolitan courtiers – country gentlemen resisted involvement in continental politics because of the inevitable burden which extraordinary taxation would place upon their local communities.[12] This is not surprising, argues one prominent revisionist historian, because country gentlemen knew little and cared less about the international situation. They received and collected newsletters and pamphlets from London, to be sure, but the localist gentry were "almost invariably" more interested in "the success and failure of courtiers in their gambling enterprises, and the state of the London marriage market" than in great political questions or foreign policy.[13]

Foreign policy, in this reconstruction of seventeenth-century English history, is hardly worthy of study. The sense of purpose in England's foreign policies, the antagonism to Spain of the Elizabethan period, and the opposition to France of the Hanoverian period, "is lacking" in the international entanglements of the seventeenth century.[14] Most English men and women displayed a "conventional protestant nationalism" that only went skin deep.[15] Consequently England avoided war whenever possible. Though "by the end of the sixteenth century a popular consensus had been created in English politics that English foreign policy should be conducted to a

11 Alan Everitt, *The Community of Kent and the Great Rebellion 1640–1660* (Leicester, 1973), pp. 13, 18. This view is endorsed by Anthony Fletcher in "The First Century of English Protestantism and the Growth of National Identity," in Stuart Mews (editor), *Religion and National Identity* (Oxford, 1982), pp. 316–317; and by John Morrill in *The Revolt of the Provinces* (London, 1976), pp. 19–23.

12 Conrad Russell, *Parliaments and English Politics 1621–1629* (Oxford, 1979), pp. 8, 70–84.

13 Morrill, *Revolt*, p. 23.

14 G. M. D. Howat, *Stuart and Cromwellian Foreign Policy* (New York, 1974), p. 1.

15 The phrase is Morrill's in *Revolt*, p. 20.

greater or lesser degree in defence of the protestant cause on the continent," when the early Stuart monarchs resisted entering the Thirty Years War on the Protestant side, most people were unwilling to suffer the inconvenience of increased taxation required to support a Protestant crusade. Naturally the religious fanaticism which ultimately precipitated the Civil War, argue these revisionists, recast English neutrality in the Thirty Years War, a neutrality very much dictated by English insolvency, as part of the greater Popery of the court. In the minds of religiously committed men who directed the Parliamentary war effort against Charles I, the failure of the early Stuarts to assume the mantle of the Protestant cause was further evidence of their commitment to the cause of Rome. Consequently when the religious extremists, those aristocratic puritans who had opposed the government in the 1630s by forming the Providence Island Company, "moved into leadership, the goals of Providence Island Company investors finally became the goals of the national government."[16] Indeed, though there has been a spirited debate over the relative merits and demerits of Cromwell's foreign policy, all the participants have agreed that it was fundamentally Protestant.[17] Debates over foreign policy were really factional struggles within the aristocratic community, a community which was supposedly far more interested in religious issues than in foreign affairs. If English men and women outside Westminster pondered the world beyond their county communities at all, they thought about retreating farther away from it.

This understanding of foreign policy has carried over into the study of the Restoration. Politics in the Restoration, argues the most prolific commentator on later Stuart England, J. R. Jones, was based on "cynicism and opportunism."[18] The voluminous pamphlet debates of the Interregnum had little lasting effect upon ordinary English men and women. There was little politically informed public opinion. After the Restoration most members of Parliament "limited their mental and political horizons" once again to the "interests of their 'countries', that is their shires and neighborhoods." English political rhetoric after the Restoration, John Miller has contended,

16 Here I am summarizing the arguments of Simon Adams in "Spain or the Netherlands? The Dilemmas of Early Stuart Foreign Policy," in Howard Tomlinson (editor), *Before the English Civil War* (London, 1983), pp. 79–101; and "Foreign Policy and the Parliaments of 1621 and 1624," in Kevin Sharpe (editor), *Faction and Parliament* (London, 1978), pp. 139–171. The analysis of Cromwellian foreign policy comes from Karen Ordahl Kupperman, "Errand to the Indies: Puritan Colonization from Providence Island through the Western Design," in *William and Mary Quarterly* Vol. 15 No. 1 (January 1988), p. 88.

17 Menna Prestwich, "Diplomacy and Trade in the Protectorate," in *Journal of Modern History*, Vol. 22 No. 2 (June 1950), pp. 105–121; Roger Crabtree, "The Idea of a Protestant Foreign Policy," in Ivan Roots (editor), *Cromwell: A Profile* (New York, 1973), pp. 160–189; Michael Roberts, "Cromwell and the Baltic," in *English Historical Review* Vol. 76 No. 300 (1961), pp. 402–446.

18 J. R. Jones, "Parties and Parliament," in his *The Restored Monarchy* (London, 1979), p. 50. This is also the situation described by Ronald Hutton in *The Restoration* (Oxford, 1985) and *Charles II* (Oxford, 1989).

was "dominated by a violent and often hysterical anti-Catholicism."[19] Consequently when foreign policy was debated in Parliament "the quality of speeches rarely rose above the ventilation of prejudices and personal grievances."[20] When England did go to war between 1660 and 1688, it was because one court faction or another hoped to drum up support for its domestic political agenda. Only James II's bullheaded insistence on transforming the political structure of local communities to allow a larger political role for Roman Catholics brought England back onto the international stage on the Protestant side. And this was only because involvement in the war against Louis XIV was William III's price for intervention in English affairs.

In this construction of English history, then, little actually changed in the seventeenth century. Foreign policy remained the special preserve of the aristocracy. Few people cared about events outside their communities. When foreign affairs were debated in Parliament, it was usually because of the manipulation of a court faction. The majority of members of Parliament simply wanted to make sure that their localities would not have to pay higher taxes. Nevertheless it was easy enough for aristocratic troublemakers to stir up temporary waves of political sentiment by touching upon popular xenophobia. In times of crisis English men and women frequently rediscovered their Protestant nationalism. This has led Jonathan Scott to conclude that the "events, structures, and issues in the reign of Charles II ... are almost xerox copies of events, structures and issues of the early Stuart period." Political debates after 1660 occurred in "the same language" that had dominated earlier discourse, a language which was predominantly "religious" for "it is the problem of popery which gives the seventeenth-century English experience as a whole (1603–1688) its essential unity."[21]

Recently, perhaps influenced by the reintegration of Britain into the European community, historians – at least of the early Stuart period – have begun to question the insularity of English men and women. Richard Cust has demonstrated that far from being ignorant of, and unconcerned about, national and international political developments, men and women in the English provinces in the 1620s and 1630s were eagerly gathering and analyzing news from London.[22] Under the close scrutiny of Ann Hughes and Clive Holmes the county community has appeared less cohesive and self-contained; its gentry "encouraged broad participation in politics," enjoyed "broad social alliances" and generally "participated in a national

19 John Miller, *Popery and Politics in England, 1660–1688* (Cambridge, 1973), p. 1.

20 J. R. Jones, *Britain and the World 1649–1815* (Glasgow, 1980), pp. 12–13.

21 Jonathan Scott, "Radicalism and Restoration: The Shape of the Stuart Experience," in *Historical Journal* Vol. 31 No. 2 (1988), pp. 458, 460, 462. Scott has elaborated this claim in his *Algernon Sidney*.

22 Richard Cust, "News and Politics in Early Seventeenth-Century England," in *Past and Present* No. 112 (August 1986), pp. 60–90.

political culture."[23] Debates about foreign policy, Tom Cogswell has shown, were far from peripheral concerns to county communities but rather were conducted with enthusiasm, sophistication, and spontaneity outside of Parliament. Most English men and women were much more than lukewarm about English involvement in the Thirty Years War.[24] Caroline Hibbard's valuable study of court Catholicism in the years just before the outbreak of the Civil War has suggested powerfully that "antipopery as a political-religious phenomenon ought to be approached from an international and London perspective." It was precisely the awareness of English men and women of the successes of Counter-Reformation Catholicism which made Laudianism and court philo-Catholicism appear as the first steps down the slippery slope to Popery.[25] Finally Peter Lake has carefully unraveled the language of anti-Popery to show that it was an "ideological tool" rather than "a wholly irrational and unitary thing." Significantly Lake has suggested that "along with other fixed points on the polemical map, anti-popery was transformed by the turmoil of the interregnum and thus made available as a free-floating term of opprobrium."[26] It is precisely this variability of the language of anti-Popery that allowed English men and women to integrate concerns with the outside world with their own local experiences.

These important reassessments of early Stuart political culture seem to call for a reinvestigation of English foreign relations after 1650. Indeed the first two Anglo-Dutch Wars (1652–1654 and 1664–1667) seem to be the ideal testing ground for these various understandings of English political culture. If English men and women desired so desperately to avoid paying extraordinary taxes, why did England go to war so often after 1650? Why, if English national identity was so closely bound up with its Protestantism, did the nation go to war three times against the Protestant Dutch from 1652 to 1674? How could Englishmen who understood the world in terms of the binary opposites of Popery and Protestantism justify war, not once but three times, against a fellow Protestant nation?

Historians have offered two sorts of explanations. One group, building on nineteenth-century claims that the seventeenth century laid the foundations for England's commercial empire, has argued that, despite similarities in religion, the English and the Dutch were first and foremost economic

23 Ann Hughes, "Local History and the Origins of the Civil War," in Ann Hughes and Richard Cust (editors), *Conflict in Early Stuart England* (London, 1989), p. 249; Clive Holmes, "The County Community in Stuart Historiography," in *Journal of British Studies* Vol. 19 No. 2 (spring 1980), p. 73; Ann Hughes, *Politics, Society and Civil War in Warwickshire, 1620–1660* (Cambridge, 1987).

24 Thomas Cogswell, *The Blessed Revolution: English Politics and the Coming of War, 1621–1624* (Cambridge, 1989).

25 Caroline M. Hibbard, *Charles I and the Popish Plot* (Chapel Hill, 1983), p. 4.

26 Peter Lake, "Anti-Popery: The Structure of a Prejudice," in Richard Cust and Ann Hughes (editors), *Conflict in Early Stuart England* (London, 1989), p. 96 and *passim*.

competitors. Economic pressure groups ultimately pushed England to war. These pressure groups, it is claimed, were able to persuade regimes as different as the Rump and the Restored Monarchy to pursue the same policy because that policy represented the true national interest. A second group of scholars, by contrast, has suggested that the wars had little to do with any conception of national interest. Instead the wars were the outward reflection of power struggles at court. One faction or another would opportunistically become an advocate of an Hollandophobic foreign policy – in full confidence of the support of a xenophobic populace – in order to topple their rivals from the pinnacle of political influence.[27]

The best means to test these hypotheses is to construct a dense narrative based upon placing the diplomatic negotiations surrounding the outbreak and conclusion of the first two wars in the context of contemporary political and religious debates. The first part of the book, then, explores the causes of the first Anglo-Dutch War. The second part explains the complicated diplomatic maneuvers that put an end to that war in April 1654. The third part provides an explanation for the outbreak of the second Anglo-Dutch War, while the final part details the causes and consequences of the infamous and devastating Dutch raid on the Medway in June 1667. Despite their narrative structures, the discussions in each part explore larger questions about the nature of English political culture. Was English foreign policy created on the basis of an uninformed xenophobia or a sophisticated understanding of European politics? Did popular opinion matter in the making of English foreign policy, or did foreign policy remain the preserve of the king and the aristocratic factions? Did the language of political culture – the meaning of anti-Popery, for instance – remain unchanged throughout the seventeenth century or did the convulsions of the mid-century precipitate a series of political redefinitions? This study, then, aims not only to reexamine seventeenth-century Anglo-Dutch relations, but also to explore the content, meaning, and significance of English political ideologies in an age of revolution.

27 These interpretations are obviously oversimplified. They receive fuller, and fairer, treatment, I hope, in the introductory paragraphs of each section of the book.

Part I

THE ROD OF THE LORD: IDEOLOGY AND THE OUTBREAK OF THE FIRST ANGLO-DUTCH WAR

2

Historiographical overview

The victory at Dunbar on 3 September 1650 convinced the English in general and members of the Rump in particular that God had not forsaken England, making it possible for them to look beyond the problems of the British Isles. Since the days of Elizabeth the United Provinces of the Netherlands had appeared to many in England as their natural ally. Yet the foreign-policy wishes of the Stuarts and then the antagonistic attitude adopted by the Princes of Orange had dashed their hopes. By the end of 1650, however, the Stuart monarchy was ostensibly banished from England forever and William II, Prince of Orange, was dead leaving only a posthumous son to carry on the Orange line. The English Commonwealth consequently seized upon the opportunity, despatching two of its most eminent statesmen, Walter Strickland and Oliver St. John, to The Hague in the early spring of 1651. Their purpose, Oliver St. John told the General Assembly of the States General, was "to enter into a more intimate alliance, and nearer union" with the Dutch "whereby a more real and intrinsical interest of each other may be contracted for their mutual good."[1] The English people were kept informed of the initially triumphant progress of their extraordinary ambassadors by means of a variety of pamphlets and newspapers. These reminded the English of the variety of Dutch virtues, claiming for example that the United Provinces is "such a glorious State" which "for plenty, riches, and policy, hath preeminence of all the monarchies in Europe."[2] Unlike modern historians, contemporaries did not see the mission as a utopian fantasy. The Dutch were enthusiastic, "expressing their earnest desires in having an intimate correspondency with England and in all their discourses."[3] Indeed a correspondent to Marchamont Nedham's *Mercurius Politicus* claimed that "the alliance and amity of England is that which above all things is desired by the common sort of people" in the United Provinces: "They pray for it, and would think

1 Oliver St. John's speech, *Joyful Newes from Holland* (London, 1651), Thomason: 7 April 1651, p. 3.

2 *A Perfect Account*, 9–16 April 1651, p. 108.

3 Ambassadors to Council of State, 20 March 1651, Bod., Rawl. C129, f. 6.

themselves happy if they could see the day."[4] Although the rest of Europe was less excited about the prospect of an Anglo-Dutch alliance, it did not cavalierly dismiss the goings-on at The Hague. The *Weekly Intelligencer* may have exaggerated when it proclaimed that the prospect of "the firm union" between England and the United Provinces dominated "all the discourse, all the joy and grief of other nations," but it did not do so by much.[5] After all, the officers of the English Commonwealth were proudly proclaiming in the capitals of Catholic Europe that an Anglo-Dutch union "would awe the whole world."[6]

Yet the alliance was not to be. The ambassadors returned to England in June 1651 empty-handed. Four months later the Rump would pass the decidedly anti-Dutch Navigation Act. And, despite frenzied attempts by the Dutch ambassadors to prevent a breach, war between the two great republics had broken out by the next summer. What had happened?

Historians have offered two types of explanation.[7] The economic explanation was classically stated by Charles Wilson in his famous study of Anglo-Dutch relations in the seventeenth century. Wilson argues that the three wars against the Dutch were the inevitable outcome of half a century of bitter economic competition. What was new in the England of the 1650s, he claims, was a "heavier depression in trade, which sharpened men's demands for action, and the new circumstances of naval strength, which increased their confidence that the time had come to strike." The Navigation Act, then, was passed because "the belief was widespread that Holland was the source of England's balance of trade troubles." Although Wilson is not willing to argue that the Navigation Act led directly to war, he does claim that the catalyst for the war, the principle of the right to search, really involved economic disputes over "the fisheries and the unsolved question of maritime sovereignty."[8]

This explanation was supported in the 1960s and the 1970s by the work of two American scholars, J. E. Farnell and Robert Brenner. Farnell's prosopographic study, focusing heavily on Benjamin Worsley and Maurice Thompson, concludes that there was an intellectual consistency in the diplomatic initiatives of the Rump in 1651–1652, that for the Commonwealth leaders the plan of union with the Netherlands and the Navigation Act "were probably alternate approaches to the same end the establishment

4 *Mercurius Politicus*, 10–17 April 1651, p. 724.

5 *Weekly Intelligencer*, 18–25 February 1651, p. 65.

6 Basadona to Doge and Senate, 15 July 1651, *CSPV*, p. 192.

7 Here I am deliberately excluding the work of Blair Worden, whose important article "Classical Republicanism and the Puritan Revolution," in Hugh Lloyd-Jones, Valerie Pearl, and Blair Worden (editors), *History and Imagination* (London, 1981) is, as far as I know, the only serious attempt to unravel the ideological debates of the 1650s in relation to the outbreak of the first Anglo-Dutch War.

8 Charles H. Wilson, *Profit and Power* (London, 1957), pp. 56–59.

of England as the entrepôt of the Western European trade." It was in this context that he was able to affirm "a causal relationship" between the Navigation Act and the first Anglo-Dutch War.[9] Brenner accepts this analysis, adding only an ideological framework in which the actions of the Rump are to be understood. Brenner traces the rise of a "colonial-interloping group" of merchants whose economic interests determined their political and religious allegiance to the Independents, allowing them in December 1648 "to ride to power on the backs of the Army after many years in the political wilderness."[10] It was this grouping then, Brenner argues, that promoted the Navigation Act and the Anglo-Dutch War. The two most recent scholarly articles treating the first Anglo-Dutch War modify, but do not ultimately reject this view. Simon Groenveld, after a very thorough survey of Anglo-Dutch relations in the 1640s, concludes that "a combination of bellicosity and commercial self-interest" made it inevitable that the Rump's mailed fist would "be turned against the Dutch" in 1652.[11] Research into the economies of the United Provinces and the English Commonwealth has led Jonathan Israel to a similar conclusion. The cessation of the Eighty Years War, he points out, left the Dutch free to evict the English from the footholds they had established in the Mediterranean trade. The resulting tension leads Israel to insist "that the Anglo-Dutch wars of the seventeenth century were the outcome of 'commercial rivalry'."[12]

A second group of historians argues that the Anglo-Dutch conflict arose from strategic rather than purely economic motives. S. R. Gardiner, in his encyclopedic study of the Commonwealth and Protectorate, argues that the failure of the ideologically motivated plan of union radically transformed the nature of political discourse. The Navigation Act, then, "did not profess to have other than material aims." But, it was intended to make all England, not just a select group of merchants, richer. It is in this context that Gardiner

9 J. E. Farnell. "The Navigation Act of 1651, the First Dutch War, and the London Merchant Community," in *The Economic History Review* 2nd series, Vol. 16, No. 3 (1963–1964), pp. 439–454.

10 Robert Brenner, "The Civil War Politics of London's Merchant Community," in *Past and Present* No. 58 (February 1973), pp. 92–95. Brenner's monumental *Merchants and Revolution: Commercial Change, Political Conflict, and London's Overseas Traders, 1550–1653* (Princeton, 1993) appeared too late to be considered fully. However, much of his argument about the Navigation Act and the origins of the Dutch War seem to have changed little from his earlier work. I want to emphasize that while I differ in detail from Brenner, and want to prioritize political and religious concerns over economic ones, I absolutely endorse his initial critique of early-seventeenth-century historiography on pp. 647–648.

11 Simon Groenveld, "The English Civil Wars as a Cause of the First Anglo-Dutch War, 1640–1652," in *The Historical Journal* Vol. 30, No. 3 (1987), p. 566.

12 Jonathan I. Israel, "Competing Cousins: Anglo-Dutch Trade Rivalry," in *History Today* Vol. 38 (July 1988), p. 17. For reasons of brevity I have necessarily eliminated the subtleties of many of these arguments, and consequently many of the differences among them. But, since I am trying to advance an ideological interpretation of the events I don't feel that I have treated them unfairly.

could argue that although the Navigation Act did not lead ineluctably to war – he explains the actual outbreak of war by "the assertion in practice of the doctrine of the Plantagenets [of] the English sovereignty of the seas" – it did open a new era in which wars were precipitated by "questions of commerce" rather than "questions of religion."[13] More recently J. R. Jones has allowed an even smaller role for economic argument, insisting that "political and indeed personal motives were more important as causes of the Dutch wars than the economic and commercial reasons that were publicly proclaimed." The first war, then, was precipitated by a "tight knit republican faction" that wanted to preserve its own power in "a hostile world." Public opinion, in this scenario, has a very small role to play.[14]

Against these views I hope to show that the first Anglo-Dutch War was the result of an unusual political alliance between apocalyptic Protestants and classical republicans who dominated English political culture both inside and outside Parliament immediately after the execution of the king in January 1649. Initially these groups hoped to implement their long-cherished political alliance with the United Provinces – a goal which had been enunciated forcefully since the 1620s. However, once it had become clear to the Rump's ambassadors and then to a wide cross-section of the political nation that the Dutch were neither good Protestants nor committed republicans, the English felt compelled to deal with the Dutch as they had dealt with the Scots. While the political developments of the 1640s did vastly broaden the scope of the political nation, and while the membership of the Rump was in fact somewhat less socially exalted than pre-Civil War Parliaments, modern notions of national interest had not yet come to dominate political debate. While the Rump did pass the Navigation Act, I claim that this did not represent the first volley of a modern trade war, but rather a punitive move against a corrupt polity. The Rump went to war against the Dutch, I will argue, because its republican and apocalyptic leaders came to understand, indeed reimagined, the Dutch polity as materialistic and Orangist. Unfortunately neither the Rump nor the Dutch States General – both regimes which had come to power in recent revolutions – were able to control rising popular antagonisms or more importantly the animosities between their politically radicalized fleets, when the cooler heads of each regime's diplomats were successfully resolving their political differences.

13 S. R. Gardiner, *History of the Commonwealth and Protectorate 1649–1656* Vol. II, pp. 147–175.

14 J. R. Jones, *Britain and the World 1649–1815* (Glasgow, 1980), pp. 53–68.

3

The attempt at unification

In order to understand the ideological development of Anglo-Dutch relations 1650–1652, it is necessary to begin with the mission of Walter Strickland and Oliver St. John to the United Provinces in the spring of 1651. Why did the Council of State see fit to send the extraordinary ambassadors? What were their aims?

Despite Parliamentary professions of friendship , the Orangist-dominated States General had refused to recognize the English Republic. Although the provincial government of Holland had effectively prevented the Stadholder William II from aiding his brother-in-law Charles II, Parliament's ambassadors were refused audience by the States General, and one – Dr. Dorislaus – had been cruelly murdered in The Hague. The Rump was right to insist that "the fault hath not been in them" that closer relations had not been established.[1] In the summer and autumn William II began conducting an aggressive and largely successful campaign to compel the resistant provinces, especially Holland, to support his policies. Dutch pro-Stuart neutrality in the English war against Scotland looked as if it would soon become active hostility. In the wake of William's attack on Amsterdam, the *Mercurius Politicus* warned that it would not be long before the Dutch "show their teeth at England."[2] Fortunately for the Rump, William II suddenly died from smallpox just as he was poised to intervene in British affairs.

Immediately after William's death two Dutch pamphlets appeared in England – *A Faithfull Advertisement to all Good Patriots of the United Provinces, in the present Conjunctures Since the Death of the Prince of Orange* and *The Troubles of Amsterdam* – explaining the recent developments in the Netherlands. Dutch hostility to the English Commonwealth,

1 Stadholder in each province of the United Provinces was literally he who holds the place of the king. The constitutional role of the Stadholder was hotly contested in the period. Some saw him as akin to a monarch, others saw him as the servant of the States. Simon Groenveld, "The English Civil Wars as a Cause of the First Anglo-Dutch War, 1640," in *The Historical Journal* Vol. 30, No. 3 (1987), pp. 552–554; Rump to Gerard Schaep, 18 June 1650, Bod., Dep. C171N , Nalson Papers XVIII, f. 291.

2 *Mercurius Politicus*, 31 October–7 November 1650, p. 371.

the pamphleteers claimed, should not be blamed upon the Dutch people, but upon the tyrannical young Stadholder. William II "hath especially set himself against all the Lords and Cities of Holland," the last opponents of his design to "make himself absolute monarch of all the United Netherlands."[3] Like Charles I, he had employed the army and the clergy "who do write, preach, pray, and run for him as his vassals" to cow the people. The Dutch clerics, "like the Bishops, *quondam*, in England," were mere "abominable flatterers" who "covet authority" at the expense of the teaching of the Bible.[4] When William made policy, the *Faithfull Advertisement* asserted, "the State's interest came not once into consideration" his interests were solely dynastic. As "Lord and Master of all the United Provinces" William II would be poised "to assist his brother in law to invade the kingdom of England by force of arms." It was William who had in fact blocked the acceptance of Parliament's ambassadors, who had prevented the punishment of Dorislaus's murderers. Indeed "What plots were there not laid? What practices remained unattempted to engage us in a war against England?"[5] All this, the pamphlets made clear, was but the design of a party – a very small party – in the Netherlands. Most Dutchmen knew "that the true, and perfect sovereignty is in the Republic, which never dies."[6]

In this context, then, the English placed a special significance on the death of the Prince of Orange. "It is very observable," Joseph Frost told William Clarke, "that no sooner had [William II] espoused the quarrel of that wicked Scotch family and set himself to help to re-set up that tyranny which the Lord in his mercy had thrown down, but the Lord cut him off."[7] "That liberty which had been won by so many years of toil and battle would now have perished from your midst," John Milton told the Dutch, "had not the most providential death of that headstrong youth allowed it to breathe again."[8] Ralph Josselin, the vicar of Earls Colne, wrote in his diary that "God taketh away our enemies abroad viz the Prince of Orange, which is a great work as things stood there and here."[9] God "in season took from thence, that rash, and over-much intrusted prince, who had almost enslaved them" proclaimed the prolific poet George Wither.[10] "The death of William

3 *The Troubles of Amsterdam*, printed in Dutch, translated into English by L. W. (London, 1650), Thomason: 12 November 1650, pp. 7, 13.

4 *Troubles of Amsterdam*, pp. 7–8; *A Faithfull Advertisement to all Good Patriots of the United Provinces, In the present Conjunctures Since the Death of the Prince of Orange* (London, 1650), Thomason: 18 December 1650, pp. 13–14.

5 *Troubles of Amsterdam*, pp. 4–5; *Faithfull Advertisement*, pp. pp. 10–11.

6 *Faithfull Advertisement*, p. 6.

7 Joseph Frost to William Clarke, 9 November 1650, HMC, *Leyborne-Popham*, p. 77.

8 John Milton, *A Defence of the People of England* (24 February 1651). in Don M. Wolfe (editor) *Complete Prose Works of John Milton* (New Haven, 1966), Vol. IV, pp. 311–312.

9 Josselin, *Diary*, 17 November 1650, p. 220.

10 George Wither, *British Appeals, with God's Mercifull Replies, On the Behalfe of the Commonwealth of England* (London, 1651), p. 40.

the late Prince of Orange," John Moyle informed his friend Colonel Robert Bennet, was "a very great mercy to this commonwealth for he was the bitterest enemy that we had, and by reason of his nearness and power that he had got over that state, the most dangerous. I trust the Lord will in mercy look upon us, and make our work daily less difficult."[11] Even the Rump newspaper *Mercurius Politicus* later claimed that the United Provinces would have been reduced "under the yoke of kingly power" had William II not been killed by "a miracle of Providence."[12] The French agent Croullé was right to tell Mazarin that everyone in England saw William's death as a "coup du doigt de Dieu."[13]

Political developments in the United Provinces soon bore out English expectations. English newspapers informed their readers that the political dominance of the House of Orange was at an end. The States of Holland immediately decided to "assume to themselves all the power which the Pr[ince] of Orange had, as Governor of Holland, and all which did concern the civil state." By the middle of December 1650 it was well known that the States General had "resolved not to choose a State-holder in the room of the deceased Prince of Orange," his authority will instead be "divided in [the] Assembly."[14] High political maneuvers were pushed along by popular political sentiment. Political poems expressed relief at William II's "most timely death" which "hath sav'd" the United Provinces from "Royal tyranny." William's posthumous son, William III, would be "no rising sun." Few now would openly support the Orangist cause, a cause which now had precious "few worshippers." Even traditionally Orangist Zealand "seeing the ills they were formerly drawn into by the Prince of Orange, will for the future trade in the same steps with those of Holland."[15] Significantly for English audiences, the new regime appeared determined to adopt a sound religious policy. As soon as the Dutch General Assembly sat, it "unanimously agreed for the extirpation of Popery. And religion to be settled as it was determined by the Synod of Dordrecht in the year 161[8]."[16]

11 John Moyle to Colonel Robert Bennet, 16 November 1650, Folger MSS, Xd483(71).

12 *Mercurius Politicus*, 6–13 May 1652, pp. 1587–1588. When the Netherlands were ravaged by a series of unusually bad floods in March 1651 the English popular press was quick to proclaim it "a sad judgment" upon the Dutch for their "transgression against the Laws of God" in supporting William II. Cf. *Weekly Intelligencer*, 11–18 March 1651, p. 89; *Mercurius Politicus*, 6–13 March 1651, p. 654.

13 Croullé to Mazarin, 21 November 1650, PRO, PRO 31/3, ff. 357–358. For Royalist despair at this development see Richard Fanshaw to Richard Brown, 9/19 November 1650, Christ Church, Richard Browne Letters, Box D–L.

14 *Mercurius Politicus*, 5–12 December 1650, p. 451; *Mercurius Politicus*, 12–19 December 1650, p. 459; 19–26 December 1650, p. 476.

15 *Mercurius Politicus*, 5–12 December 1650, p. 447; *Mercurius Politicus*, 16–23 January 1651, pp. 542, 545.

16 *Weekly Intelligencer*, 28 January–4 February 1651, pp. 47–48. Clearly the Dutch were at pains to remedy the perception that "Statists were atheists," a perception based on the Orangist support of the Calvinist Synod of Dort against the republican party of Old-

The consequence in the realm of foreign policy was predictable. "The States of Holland; Zeeland, and Groningen, go on jointly in their resolutions to acknowledge the Parliament of England for a free State," *A Perfect Account* told its readers in January; "it's thought the rest of the seven provinces will agree upon the business." "It's most evident," wrote the Dutch correspondent to the *Politicus*, "that all things here are like to come to a nearer conjunction with you, and all men speak openly now, that they hope it will not be long before they see Strickland."[17] It was now the Royalist minister MacDowell who was left waiting at the doors of the provincial States. Indeed when the English Royalist exiles at The Hague tried to celebrate the second anniversary of Charles's martyrdom, "the great Hall sent one to command them silence, and to depart."[18]

In an important article, Dr. Blair Worden attributes the English response to this exciting news to a small group of classical republicans, both parliamentary and literary. It was one of the literary men, Marchamont Nedham, who first floated the idea of union with the Dutch. By correlating this proposal with Nedham's later encomiums of the Roman republican policy of incorporating defeated foes, Worden suggests that there was a republican impetus to union.[19] The testimony of both of the English ambassadors supports this conclusion. "It will be our interest to be fast friends with them, theirs to be so with us" now that the United Provinces are again a republic, Strickland wrote to Cromwell, "and that being, no foreign enemies could do you harm."[20] St. John told the States General that their treaty and alliance could be brought "to the nearest conjunction" because neither state "depended upon the uncertainties of the life, allegiance, change of affections, and private interest of one person."[21]

Nevertheless it would be wrong to insist on the purely secular nature of the republican language. Jonathan Scott, in his biography of Algernon

enbarnevelt. English newspapers, especially the *Mercurius Politicus*, implied that the roles had been reversed. The Orange party, so dependent on clerical flattery, allowed Catholic supporters of the regime to practice their idolatrous religion. Cf. *Mercurius Politicus*, 30 January–6 February 1651, pp. 577–579.

17 *A Perfect Account*, 22–29 January 1651, p. 19; *Mercurius Politicus*, 7–14 November 1650, p. 384. See the similar conclusion drawn by the English resident in Hamburg: Richard Bradshaw to Secretary Frost, 5 November 1650, HMC, *6th Report*, p. 433.

18 *Mercurius Politicus*, 13–20 February 1651, pp. 603–604; *Weekly Intelligencer*, 18–25 February 1651, p. 66.

19 Worden, "Classical Republicanism," pp. 198–199. Worden has since compellingly fleshed out this account in his "English Republicanism," in J. H. Burns and Mark Goldie (editors), *The Cambridge History of Political Thought 1450–1700* (Cambridge, 1991), pp. 443–475.

20 Strickland to Cromwell, 14 January 1651, Nickolls, *Original Letters*, p. 51. Admittedly this letter could be read to mean that security was the motive for negotiations with the Dutch. But, in that context the proposals for union would make little sense. I think it more likely that Strickland was, in fact, motivated by the sort of ideology outlined by Worden. However, as the following will show, Strickland's case was unusual.

21 St. John's speech in PRO, SP 103/46, f. 124.

Sidney, has claimed that many Rumpers – including Algernon Sidney and Sir Henry Vane – arrived at their republicanism through a sophisticated fusion of Platonism and Protestestantism. While Scott's reading of Sidney's thought remains controversial, there can be no question that in the early 1650s there were many who found it hard to accept the more aggressively secular philosophy of Henry Marten.[22] For these men, then, there was no contradiction between republicanism and their apocalypticism. In the heady early days of the Rump Parliament scrutiny of classical texts and eschatological readings of recent events led to similar political conclusions. Classical and apocalyptic republicans made common cause.[23]

Indeed in the wake of the victory at Dunbar it had become quite fashionable to preach an aggressive apocalyptic republicanism – a republicanism derived not only from an analysis of classical texts but from a conviction that God would replace the rule of earthly kings with that of Christ in the last days. God "is now coming to set up his prerogative kingly power," wrote Noah Banks, He "shall break in pieces the gold, silver, brass, and iron, and clay, *Dan.* 2 all former monarchical governments."[24] James Douglas argued that it was "unnatural, irrational, sinful, wicked, unjust, devilish, and tyrannical" for a king to "endeavor to appropriate and assume unto himself the office and sovereignty of God, who alone doth, and is to rule."[25] William Hughes knew that it was "natural for monarchy to degenerate into tyranny" which was why God told the people of Israel that He only gave them "a king in mine anger, and took him away in my wrath."[26] "Monarchs look upon all religions with love or disdain, as they

22 Jonathan Scott, *Algernon Sidney*, pp. 15, 23–29, 51, 94. While I think Scott has made a significant contribution by identifying an apocalyptic opposition to monarchy, I am inclined to agree with Worden and Alan Houston that Sidney's republicanism was more classical than apocalyptic. For an excellent discussion of the philosophy of the Christian republicans see Mark Goldie,"The Civil Religion of James Harrington," in Anthony Pagden (editor) *The Languages of Political Theory in Early Modern Europe* (Cambridge, 1987), pp. 203–204, 210.

23 My point is that while there were profound ideological differences between the classical republicans and the apocalyptic opponents of monarchy, those differences were of little *political* significance until 1653. It was only in the context of the Nominated Parliament, under the pressures applied by the Dutch War, that the two groups could no longer make common cause.

24 Noah Banks, *Gods Prerogative Power* (London, 1650), Thomason: 8 November 1650, pp. 10–11. Banks might well be the lay preacher, identified as Alan or Adam Banks, who appeared at the bar of the House of Commons in June 1641. See Murray Tolmie, *The Triumph of the Saints: The Separate Churches of London, 1616–1649* (Cambridge, 1977), pp. 37, 67–68.

25 James Douglas, *A Strange and Wonderful Prophesie* (London, 1651), Thomason: 22 January 1651, p. 4.

26 W. Hughes, *Magistracy God's Ministry: Or, A Rule for the Rulers and Peoples due Correspondence* (London, 1652), Thomason: 17 May 1652, pp. 11–12. William Hughes was a chaplain (and perhaps a fellow) of New College during the Interregnum. He was licensed as a Presbyterian after the Restoration. He then reappeared as the Whig chaplain of St. Thomas's hospital, and came under attack from Roger L'Estrange. I owe this

find them suit with their worldly concernments," argued another pamphleteer, therefore "the voice of Providence," "the approbation of God himself," had spoken against monarchies. "Monarchy," this pamphleteer insisted, "is a sacrilegious overcharging of a single person with more honor and power, then so frail a creature is able to bear, without falling into the distemper of excess."[27]

These were not merely the ideas of cranks and radicals. John Evelyn, in England in the summer of 1650, heard a sermon "at the Rolls" on the republican text 1 Samuel 12.[28] Ralph Josselin, who was asked to preach at St. Paul's by the Lord Mayor in 1651, knew that "god is casting down princes." "Parliament," Josselin wrote in his diary, "declare against Popery anti-Christianity in all things, and kings whom they call tyrants, and for liberty."[29] "God hath cursed that kingly race," George Bishop wrote to Cromwell. God informed another of Cromwell's correspondents that "a free commonwealth, as it is the original and best of human associations and societies, so it is the only government ... to be well settled in."[30] All claims that monarchy was divinely instituted, Cromwell's polemicist John Hall pointed out, "proceeded from misinterpretation of Scripture."[31] "God is no more the author of such a government," the Rump's solicitor-general at the trial of Charles I, John Cook, said of monarchy, "than he is the author of sin." "The statute law concerning kings" – 1 Samuel 8 – clearly demonstrates, Cook argued, "that the first generation of monarchs and the rise of kings, was not from above, not begotten by the word and command of God, but from the people's pride & ardent importunity." So important was this text that Cook thought that "it is a chapter that deserves to be written in capital letters of gold, and if it were convenient to appoint the reading of it but once a month in the public meeting places."[32] Although 1 Samuel 8 never became compulsory reading in English pulpits, one polemicist did

information to Craig Rose. See also John Patrick Laydon, 'The Kingdom of Christ and the Powers of the Earth' (Cambridge, Ph.D. thesis, 1977), pp. 70–71.

27 *A Persuasive to A Mutuall Compliance Under the Present Government: Together with a Plea For a Free State Compared with Monarchy* (Oxford, 1652), Thomason: 18 February 1652, pp. 24, 28–30, 37–39.

28 Evelyn, *Diary*, 4 August 1650, Vol. III, p. 15.

29 Josselin, *Diary*, 17 December 1650, p. 223; Josselin, *Diary*, 31 December 1650, pp. 227–228.

30 George Bishop to Oliver Cromwell, 14 January 1651, Nickolls, *Original Letters*, p. 50; Hickman to Cromwell, 16 November 1650, Nickolls, *Original Letters*, p. 32.

31 J[ohn] H[all], *The Grounds and Reasons of Monarchy* (Edinburgh, 1651), p. 10. For Hall's long-term commitment to the cause of republicanism and his role as a Cromwellian propagandist in Scotland, see J. Davies's account in John Hall (translator), *Hierocles upon the Golden Verses of Pythagoras: Teaching a Vertuous and Worthy Life* (London, 1657), sig. B3–B4.

32 John Cook, *Monarchy No Creature of Gods Making* (Waterford, 1652), pp. 1–2, 29. Edmund Ludlow, whose views had probably not changed significantly from the 1650s, expressed similar sentiments in his memoirs: "AVoyce from the Watch Tower," Bodl., English History MSS C487, p. 1104.

publish the popular republican tract *A Cat May Look Upon a King* so that "the common people of the kingdom" would "hereafter know for whom and for what they fight and pay."[33]

Two of the Rump's most important propagandists, Marchamont Nedham and John Milton, adopted a language which would appeal to both classical and apocalyptic republicans. Nedham for all his knowledge of Machiavelli, Tacitus, and the Roman histories justified his republicanism on religious grounds as well. "Guicciardini affirms," wrote Nedham in one of his editorials, "that Free States must needs be more pleasing to God than any other form." When the Israelites insisted on having a king, wrote Nedham citing the Christian republicans' favorite text, "God himself was displeased at it, and so was Samuel too." "My conscience tells me," the *Politicus* reported in July 1651, "being informed by those Scriptures which speak of the glorious state of believers in the last times, and by observing the passages of God's providence, in carrying on his truth through, and from form to form, that in the end he will dash all forms in pieces, that stand betwixt him and his glory. This is his great design now on foot in the world." So, when Nedham insisted that "all the western world" was "in *puris naturalibus*, in their first and foremost innocent condition, settled in the same form" previous to the establishment of monarchies, he was speaking both the language of a classical republican and that of a Christian apocalyptic.[34]

John Milton, who would play a large role in the negotiations with the Dutch in his capacity as Latin Secretary, published his *Defence of the People of England* on the eve of the departure of the English ambassadors to the United Provinces. Since the *Defence* was commissioned by the Council of State it provides a glimpse of the ideology of the Rump. John Milton, for all his classical learning, could still deploy language familiar to eschatological Protestants. The Israelites after having demanded a king, he therefore argued, "complained that it had been ruinous for them to have other kings than God." Since "Christ gave a warning to prevent a Christian people from having a master at all," Milton drew the clear inference that: "Among you there will be no haughty tyranny of kings." It was human corruption that explained the existence of kings among Christians and Israelites. They "were given a king by God in his wrath." Even now the English were not free from sin, Milton was forced to admit, but "their sins were taught them under the monarchy, like the Israelites, and have not been immediately unlearned in the desert."[35]

33 *A Cat May Look Upon a King* (London, 1652), pp. 32–33.

34 *Mercurius Politicus*, 24–31 July 1651, pp. 950–951; *Mercurius Politicus*, 18–25 September 1651, pp. 1078–1079; *Mercurius Politicus*, 15–22 April 1652, pp. 1538–1539.

35 Milton, *A Defence*, pp. 370–387. The most convincing account of Milton's republicanism, a republicanism which was not apocalyptic, is that offered by Blair Worden in "Milton's Republicanism and the Tyranny of Heaven," in Gisela Bock, Quentin Skinner, and

Of course, not all republicans rejected monarchy absolutely. John Milton was willing to accept a king so long as he "is the best of men and fully deserving of the crown."[36] Even the radical Thomas Harrison was willing to accept a godly monarchy as late as 1653.[37] Although the author of *Natures Dowrie* only claimed that "A king is not a necessary ingredient of the government of a state," he made it clear that for God's chosen people only divine government would do.[38] Consequently even those who believed that there was a proper place for monarchy could agree that absent a godly ruler – and there was no one in France, Spain, or Germany to fit that qualification – one should support republics.[39]

Significantly all republicans – whether classical or apocalyptic – advocated an aggressive foreign policy, a Protestant foreign policy.[40] Milton was careful to place his argument firmly within the traditions of the international Protestant cause. Salmasius, Milton was quick to point out, had condemned "the churches in France and Germany," in short "most Protestants," as being "hostile to kings." Milton had not lost the enthusiasm for a Protestant foreign policy which he had displayed in the early 1640s.[41] Marchamont Nedham castigated James I for neglecting the Protestant cause in Germany.[42] Ralph Josselin dreamed "that we of our nation were instrumentally employed about that work in France."[43] "The work that God hath

Maurizio Viroli (editors), *Machiavelli and Republicanism* (Cambridge, 1990), pp. 225–245. Perez Zagorin has also argued that "the apocalyptic strain had vanished" from Milton's post-regicide writings in his *Milton: Aristocrat and Rebel* (Rochester NY, 1992), p. 65. For other views see Hugh Trevor-Roper, "Milton in Politics" in his *Catholics, Anglicans and Puritans: Seventeeth Century Essays* (Chicago, 1987), and Jonathan Scott, *Algernon Sidney*, pp. 26–28. Richard Tuck has highlighted the anti-Orangist implications of Milton's republicanism: *Philosophy and Government 1572–1651* (Cambridge, 1993), pp. 252–253.

36 Milton, *A Defence*, p. 427.

37 Bernard Capp, *The Fifth Monarchy Men* (London, 1972), p. 137.

38 L. S. [Seaman, Lazarus?], *Natures Dowrie: Or, the Peoples Nature Libertie Asserted* (London, 1652), Thomason: 29 June 1652, pp. 7–8, 40.

39 Even conservative lawyers like Oliver St. John, who was known to support some form of monarchy, would agree that absolute monarchies – like those of Charles I, Louis XIV, and Philip IV – should be opposed. For St. John's views on monarchy see Whitelocke's *Annals*, BL, Add. 37345, f. 171: "It will be found, that the government of this nation, without something of monarchical power, will be very difficult to be so settled, as not to shake the foundations of our laws, & the liberties of the people." See also Gilbert Burnet, *History of His Own Time* (Oxford, 1823), Vol. I, p. 117.

40 Groenveld has thoroughly documented the history of English relations with the United Provinces in the 1640s in his article, "English Civil Wars," pp. 544–555.

41 Milton, *A Defence*, pp. 514–515; for an interesting discussion of the context of Milton's foreign policy views in the 1630s and 1640s see Martin Butler, *Theatre and Crisis 1632–1642* (Cambridge, 1984), pp. 34–35. At least one Anglican, Pierre du Moulin, well understood the full implication of Milton's claims. He consequently published a pamphlet in 1652 disputing that the continental Protestants supported tyrannicide. See the excellent discussion of this point in Mark Goldie's "The Huguenot experience and the problem of Toleration in Restoration England," in C. E. J. Caldicott, H. Gough, and J. P. Pittion (editors) *The Huguenots and Ireland* (Dublin, 1987), pp. 191–192.

42 *Mercurius Politicus* , 15–22 May 1651, p. 800.

43 Josselin, *Diary*, 13 November 1650, pp. 219–220.

begun in England," Noah Banks insisted, "shall go on till he hath made all his enemies his footstool."[44] Robert Parker, the friend of William Ames, knew that the "sixth angel" which shall destroy Spain and "her ancient friend, the Beast, and his followers" would be "England, or the Low Countries, or both jointly with their friends."[45] No wonder the French agent Croullé was convinced that Cromwell and his faction, with the support of other nations which would emulate the English, wanted "to destroy all monarchies."[46]

So, when the Dutch pamphlet *A Faithfull Advertisement to all Good Patriots of Holland* proclaimed that "the Scripture is plain, that republics are more acceptable or agreeable to God, then monarchies," the English thought they had discovered kindred spirits.[47] The Dutch commissioners knew very well whom they were dealing with when they pleaded that the English ambassadors remain in the Netherlands to continue "the intended work of overthrowing Popery and tyranny."[48]

It was in this ideological context that the Rump decided to respond to the new developments in the United Provinces. Initially, to be sure, not everyone in the Council of State was convinced that the Dutch had reformed. "Some think," George Bishop informed Cromwell, "that in regard they had disowned our agent, both before and since this change of government, that Amboyna formerly, and Dorislaus was lately there assassinated, and no suitable detestation manifested by them, that they have owned MacDowell as ambassador of the king of Great Britain; that we ought not to send one thither, till they acknowledge this Commonwealth." Significantly none of the objections were economic. Indeed these arguments were all criticisms of the treatment the English had received from the Orangist regime. "Their declaring to acknowledge the Commonwealth for the supreme power," Walter Strickland insisted, "is a reparation in honor for the delay received when I was there."[49] On the night of the debate, apparently, enough of the

44 Banks, *Gods Prerogative Power*, sig A3.

45 Robert Parker, *The Mystery of the Vialls Opened* (London, 1650), Thomason: 21 August 1650, p. 13.

46 Croullé to Mazarin 26 September 1650, PRO, PRO 31/3, ff. 305–306; 7 November 1650, PRO, PRO 31/3, f. 341.

47 *A Faithfull Advertisement*, p. 13.

48 Ambassadors' journal, 21 April 1651, Bod., Rawl. C129, f. 23.

49 George Bishop to Oliver Cromwell, 21 January 1651, Nickolls, *Original Letters*, p. 55; Walter Strickland to Oliver Cromwell, 14 January 1651, Nickolls, *Original Letters*, p. 55. Royalist rumors, the basis for much of the evidence for the economic self-interest of the Rump, added a number of economic grievances to Council debates. See the letter from Edward Nicholas to Marquis of Ormonde, 15 January 1651, in Carte, *Collection*, Vol. I, p. 402. There is, however, no corroborating evidence for this. Edward Nicholas was in The Hague, and internal evidence suggests that he was relying on Orangist sources. Ascribing economic self-interest as the sole motivation of one's enemies was the seventeenth century's most common form of opprobrium. The East Indian Spice Island Amboyna was the site of a spectacular massacre of the English by the Dutch in February 1623.

members of the Council of State were convinced of the reformation of the Dutch to recommend to the House that "an agent be sent to the Netherlands." On 21 January Parliament approved of the mission with no recorded opposition. The next day Bulstrode Whitelocke recorded that Holland, Zeeland, and Groningen acknowledged the English Commonwealth. Within a week the newspapers reported that the Dutch States General "have voted England a free Commonwealth, and that they will acknowledge them to be such, and receive any message from them as from a free State."[50]

The Council of State immediately formed a committee to review the history of the Rump's relations with the United Provinces and to draw up instructions for the ambassadors. Although it is true that the classical republicans Henry Martin and Thomas Challoner formed part of that committee, there is little evidence that they dominated.[51] Viscount Lisle, who inherited the Sidney family anti-Catholicism as well as its Platonism, reported to the Rump the Council of State's recommendation to send a public minister to the United Provinces. Bulstrode Whitelocke, who would later play a large role in both Rump and Protectorate relations with other Protestant powers, reported the Heads of Instructions for the ambassadors. Sir Henry Vane, perhaps the Rumper most ideologically committed to the Protestant cause, handled the Council of State's correspondence with the ambassadors once they had departed for the United Provinces.[52] Clearly those who played the largest role in formulating the Rump's foreign policy at this stage were committed to a godly and republican alliance.

Perhaps the best evidence of ideological motivation for the mission was the selection of the ambassadors. On the same day that the Council of State decided to send an embassy to the United Provinces they selected Oliver St. John and Walter Strickland to be their ambassadors extraordinary. St. John, who "was looked upon as the principal man," was perhaps an odd choice.

50 Bishop to Cromwell, 21 January 1651, Nickolls, *Original Letters*, p. 55; *CJ*, 21 January 1651, p. 525; Whitelocke's *Annals*, BL, Add. 37345, 22 January 1651, f. 122; *Weekly Intelligencer*, 21–28 January, 1651, p. 39; *A Perfect Account* 22–29 January 1651, pp. 17–18; *Mercurius Politicus*, 16–23 January 1651, p. 549. Groenveld's claim that "it was probably the moderates who gained a majority in favour of Strickland and St. John's mission, though at 42 and 29 it was not a large one" ("English Civil Wars," p. 555), is misleading. The issue at stake was not the mission, but whether St. John – who had petitioned to be removed from the mission – should be retained as the leader of that mission. *CJ*, 28 January 1651, p. 528; *CSPD*, 1651, 28 January 1651, p. 26.

51 *CSPD*, 1651, 22 January 1651, p. 19. The committee also included Sir Henry Vane, Bulstrode Whitelocke, John Lisle, Valentine Wauton, Oliver St. John, Sir Henry Mildmay, Viscount Lisle, William Purefoy, and Thomas Scot. Most of these men had records of commitment to the Protestant cause. English foreign policy was not being made exclusively by classical republicans. Rather it was the product of the current ideological alliance between the republicans and the apocalyptics.

52 *CJ*, 21 January 1651, p. 525; *CJ*, 14 February 1651, p. 535; *CJ*, 1 April 1651, p. 554. Similar evidence can be found in *CSPD*.

Whitelocke, who must have played an important role in his selection, admitted that he was "not much versed in foreign affairs or languages." But this does not seem to have been the main qualification. Valerie Pearl has shown how St. John rose to leadership of the parliamentary middle group in the 1640s largely because of his ability "to submerge minor differences for the greater good of the 'Protestant cause.'" His religious commonplace book, his patronage of Samuel Hartlib, and his letters to Oliver Cromwell leave little doubt that he was a Protestant apocalyptic. In the 1650s he was active in a circle which included James Ussher – now preacher at Lincoln's Inn – who had written more than anyone else about the importance of the Protestant cause. It was this background, no doubt, that led Whitelocke and the Council of State to conclude that "his disposition suited with such an employment." Despite some initial hesitation, St. John himself was convinced of the important role he would play in the eschatological drama, and was consequently "cheerful to undergo his embassage" on the eve of his departure.[53] Walter Strickland's selection to join St. John was less surprising; he was the Rump's expert on the United Provinces. Yet he too evinced a commitment both to the Protestant and the republican cause. Jonathan Scott has included him with Vane, Whitelocke Algernon Sidney, and Lord William Howard as men who continued the middle group political tradition into the 1650s.[54] His confidence in the new Dutch regime testifies to his republican sympathies.

The ambassadors' brief reflected the powerful and complex republican ideology of the Rump. No longer would England be satisfied with "the good correspondency that hath been anciently between the English nation

53 Valerie Pearl, "Oliver St. John and the 'Middle Group' in the Long Parliament: August 1643–May 1644," in *English Historical Review* 81 (July 1966), pp. 500–503; Capp, *Fifth Monarchy Men*, p. 40; Whitelocke's *Annals*, BL, Add. 37345, 1 February 1651, f. 122; John Harington's diary, BL, Add. 10114, *passim*, especially BL, Add. 46374 (this is the nineteenth-century transcript) 2 June 1650, f. 76; 30 October 1650, BL, Add. 10114, f. 27; 9 February 1651, BL, Add. 10114, f. 28; 11 February 1651, BL, Add. 10114, f. 28; Oliver St. John's religious commonplace book is at BL, Add. 25285. At least one Royalist observer bracketed St. John with Lord Wharton and Henry Vane as religious and political disciples of Lord Say and Sele, *Vox Veritatis*, Thomason: 16 November 1650, p. 9. This book makes clear that St. John's lingual difficulties were not in dead languages; his Latin, Greek, and Hebrew were quite up to snuff. *CSPD*, 22 January 1651, p. 19. It is very tempting to posit ties between the group surrounding Ussher at Lincoln's Inn and Hartlib's circle at this time. Certainly they were in close epistolary contact. That St. John was in control of the embassy is confirmed by Edward Hyde, who knew that St. John "had the whole trust of the embassy, being very powerful in the parliament, and the known confident of Cromwell." Edward Hyde, *The History of the Rebellion and Civil Wars in England* (Oxford, 1888), p. 784. Marvell in his poem "*In Legationem Domini Oliveri St. John ad Provincias Foederaratas,*" written in February 1651, claims that St. John was "cui soli voluit respublica credi." Significantly, for Marvell, the choices were already only union or war, "Foedera seu Belgis seu nova bella." Elizabeth Story Donno (editor), *Andrew Marvell: The Complete English Poems* (London, 1972), p. 61.

54 Scott, *Algernon Sidney*, pp. 80, 89. For evidence of Strickland's interest in religious matters in 1651 see *CJ*, 4 July 1651, p. 597 where he reports about scandalous ministers.

and the United Provinces." Instead St. John and Strickland were to seek "a more strict and intimate alliance and union with them whereby there may be a more intrinsical and mutual interest of each in other then hath hitherto been for the good of both."[55] Edward Hyde interpreted the mission as the Rump's plea for alliance with "their sister republic" hoping "to be as one commonwealth, and to have one interest."[56] The republican nature of the embassy seemed confirmed because "at the very instant" that St. John and Strickland entered "the great hall" at The Hague "the young Prince of Orange fell into shrewd convulsion fits."[57] An alliance between two republics, St. John told the Dutch in his opening speech, "would be more durable, and advantageous than formerly, when they depended upon the uncertainties of the life, alliances, change of affections, and private interest of one person."[58] The Protestant element of the proposed alliance and union was also evident from the outset. St. John and Strickland were instructed to remind the Dutch "how great an influence for good or for evil the union or disunion between them must needs have upon the true reformed religion, which this Commonwealth resolves through God's assistance to own and support by all due and just means to the utmost of their power."[59] Fully convinced that "the signal blessing of Almighty God, hath ever accompanied the actions" of both republics, St. John followed his brief, insisting upon the urgency of the mission. He told the Assembly that "the Protestant Religion was in great danger, the princes round about being enemies to it, and the peace of Germany altogether unsure, the Pope having absolved the emperor and others from what had been done therein."[60] In reemphasizing the special importance of this English embassy, St. John made clear the new ideology which underlay it. St. John distinguished between traditional Anglo-Dutch friendship which had been based on "the common interests of state" – defined as "the defense and aid against foreign enemies, and the free intercourse of trade, and traffic" – and his current hopes which were based on "the occasion sithence, of the profession of the true reformed religion, and of the just liberties, and freedoms of the people of equal concernment unto both" republics.[61] "Although their past and

55 "Heads of Instructions for the Ambassadors going into Holland presented for the debate of the Council," 14 February 1651, Bod., Dep. C171N, Nalson Papers XVIII, f. 192. These instructions were accepted, apparently with little alteration on 18 February. Whitelocke's *Annals*, BL, Add. 37345, f. 124.

56 Hyde, *History*, p. 784.

57 *Mercurius Politicus*, 10–17 April 1651, p. 722.

58 PRO, SP 103/46, f. 124.

59 "Heads of Instruction to the Ambassadors," 14 February 1651, Bod. Dep. C171N, Nalson Papers XVIII, f. 192.

60 PRO, SP 103/46, ff. 123, 126. St. John's speech is reprinted with slight variations in *Joyful Newes*, pp. 3–5. For more evidence of the nature of the first meetings with the Dutch see Bod., Rawl. C129, ff. 5–9.

61 PRO, SP 103/46, f. 123. Interestingly another copy of this speech suggests that the only alteration of Anglo-Dutch relations was the "addition ... of the just liberties and freedom

present endeavors have not hitherto produced that happy issue," on the eve of his departure a bitterly disappointed St. John reminded the States General of his Christian republican aims: "the safety and preservation of the true reformed religion, and of the due rights and liberty of the people."[62]

Unfortunately the expected Protestant and republican union never materialized. After three months of negotiations, St. John and Strickland returned to England having achieved nothing. Why did the mission fail?

The embassy certainly began in a promising fashion. Oliver St. John and Walter Strickland were granted every formal courtesy by the States General. Indeed the young Duke of York held "in great indignation the reception of his blessed father's murderers."[63] Yet once the negotiations commenced the Dutch were surprisingly reluctant to agree to English demands that they agree in principle to a more "strict union and alliance." The Dutch did concur that the "amity and league between the two nations [should] be continued and renewed," but this was insufficient for the English who were instructed to treat "the words in the proposals" as an ideological test.[64] The Dutch "had stood all this while upon a neutrality," the ambassadors later explained to their fellow Rumpers, "the question now was, whether they would depart therefrom, and until that were known, it would be vain and to no purpose to offer the particulars of such an alliance."[65] In response to the English insistence, the States General felt compelled to refer the wording back to the provincial estates, engendering long delays. Apparently unable to achieve their goals, the ambassadors secured their recall at the end of April, without having even begun to negotiate.

Why had the Dutch refused to accept the English proposal for a more intimate union and alliance, a proposal which in no way bound them to action? The answer lies in the nature of Dutch politics; in the existence of profound ideological divisions within the United Provinces.[66] The English ambassadors very quickly learned that their image of a Dutch people united against the tyranny of the House of Orange was naive. They soon distinguished between "the bad and disaffected party" and "the honest

of the people." St. John's speech to States General, March 1651, NMM, Clifford Papers, Vol. I, Dw2.

62 "Departing Paper," 20/30 June 1651, Bod., Rawl. C129, f. 51.

63 Nicholas to Ormonde, 19 March 1651, Carte, *Collection*, Vol. I, pp. 425–426.

64 Council of State to Ambassadors, 3 April 1651, PRO, SP 25/96, f. 102; Whitelocke's *Annals*, 14 April 1651, BL, Add. 37345, f. 129; *Weekly Intelligencer*, 29 April–6 May 1651, p. 148.

65 "Ambassadors' Narrative," 17 April 1651, PRO, SP 103/46, f. 130.

66 My description of Dutch politics necessarily stresses developments in the center of a notoriously decentralized state (a word which Simon Schama has taught us to use only with great caution in describing the United Provinces). Nevertheless my view is supported by the work of Herbert Rowen, *John De Witt, Grand Pensionary of Holland 1625–1672* (Princeton, 1978), p. 65.

party."[67] "Orange," the English learned, "(though dead) is still alive here in his faction." The Orangists, no doubt aided by the Cavalier exiles, were spreading pernicious rumors hoping "thereby to spread a mist before the eyes of the ignorant."[68] "We know who our enemies are," proclaimed the correspondent to the *Mercurius Politicus*, they are led by "the grand Architectress ... Mal. Tarquin, whom we call here by the name of the Princess Royal." Despite the death of her husband William II and the execution of her father Charles I, the Princess Royal's resources were not inconsequential. "Nothing can be said, or done, at my Lord's ambassadors," the English complained, "but it is presently known at the Queen of Bohemia and Princess Royal's courts." She maintained "a great deal of interest in some of the States General, who are her only favorites."[69]

The real strength of Orangism, however, lay in the provinces. Orangist support had always been strongest in the frontier regions, which depended for their protection upon the benevolence of one or another member of the House of Orange-Nassau. Within a week of their arrival in The Hague the ambassadors informed the Council of State that in Friesland and Zeeland "the party of the Prince of Orange will endeavor all ... to hinder this alliance with England and restore the prince to be Stadholder."[70] It soon became clear that the opponents of alliance with England were strong enough to block agreement in Gelderland, Friesland, Overijssel, and Groningen.[71] In the face of intense diplomatic pressure, the Orangist provinces felt their best hope lay in delays. "There are some that do much oppose any agreement," explained the *Mercurius Politicus*, "which is the cause why the business goes on so slowly." Though the States General might well have "inclined to make an alliance," their "knowing how much the hearts of the common people were bent to the family of the Prince of Orange," the historian Aitzema later recalled, they "durst not engage in such a treaty." The Dutch are "so chastely circumspect," commented one English correspondent, it is "as if they cared not to understand what intrinsical is, they will do nothing fully until further experience."[72]

67 *Mercurius Politicus*, 19–26 June 1651, p. 893. The *Mercurius*'s correspondent in the United Provinces was clearly a member of the ambassadorial entourage, indeed at times it seems as if Nedham was getting information direct from Thurloe. Consequently I have, at times, used reports in the *Mercurius* to indicate the attitudes of the English embassy as a whole.

68 *Mercurius Politicus*, 3–10 April 1651, pp. 714–715; *Mercurius Politicus*, 19–26 June 1651, pp. 892–893; *A Perfect Account*, 9–16 April 1651, pp. 108–109.

69 *Mercurius Politicus*, 10–17 April 1651, pp. 724–726.

70 "Ambassadors' Journal," 4 April 1651, Bod., Rawl. C129, f. 14. Zeeland had a schizophrenic relationship with England. It was the cradle of the Dutch Revolt, and hence intensely loyal to the memory of William the Silent. But it was also the most strongly Calvinist province, and the province most dependent upon trade links with England.

71 *Mercurius Elencticus*, 10–17 June 1651, p. 13; *Mercurius Politicus*, 19–26 June 1651, p. 822.

72 *Weekly Intelligencer*, 17–22 April 1651, p. 134; *Mercurius Politicus*, 24 April–1 May, 1651, p. 760; Aitzema, "Selections," Bod., Rawl. C734, f. 72r.

The reports of Dutch goodwill towards the English Commonwealth were, of course, not all chimerical. Holland, the richest and most powerful province, was very much in favor of alliance with England. Indeed it was said that in Holland the people "are as much against the Prince of Orange his faction, as we against the Cavaliers."[73] Amsterdam, the city which had resisted William II with the greatest determination, was also the city which was most "affectionately inclined to a conjunction of interest with us."[74] St. John and Strickland were confident that "if the treaty might be managed according to the desires and pace of those of Holland it would be with good effect and speedy."[75] Holland was willing and able to exert pressure upon "the rest of the United Provinces to join with [them] in the desired league." Apparently the arguments of the Holland deputies, in tandem with local States party supporters, eventually persuaded the provinces of Utrecht and Zeeland to support the proposed alliance with England.[76] It was no doubt the influence which Holland could exert in The Hague, which was after all very much a Holland town, which convinced the Orangist provinces that their best policy was delay.

In addition to diplomatic obstructionism, the English ambassadors were subjected to a variety of personal affronts, both physical and verbal. "Many of our gentlemen have been affronted by the English Cavaliers, who are very numerous in this place," the *Politicus*'s correspondent soon reported, "they called us traitors, rebels, and St. John's bastards ... some spit in our faces."[77] The English "found a general disgust in the people in whose minds the blood of the late king was fresh, calling them rogues and murderers of their king as they passed through the streets."[78] The Queen of Bohemia's youngest son, Prince Edward, was unable to restrain himself from publicly confronting the ambassadors. As he passed the ambassadorial coach in one of the parks in The Hague Edward "made monkey-like mouths at them; and with a squeaking voice called them dogs, rogues,

73 *Mercurius Politicus*, 27 March–3 April 1651, pp. 696–697.

74 *Mercurius Politicus*, 29 May–5 June 1651, p. 834. The hostile Edward Nicholas, then at The Hague, lamented that "very many (especially those of Holland, and particularly the Amsterdammers) incline to conclude such a league with the rebels of England." Nicholas to Ormonde, 14 May 1651, Carte, *Collection*, Vol. II, pp. 1–2. Amsterdam's support suggests that the Dutch did not oppose the union for economic reasons.

75 "Ambassadors' Journal," 11 April 1651, Bod., Rawl. C129, f. 19. see also Bod., Rawl. C129, f. 23. Rowen has shown the enthusiasm of Dordrecht for the treaty. *John De Witt*, p. 66.

76 Nicholas to Ormonde, 21 May 1651, Carte, *Collection*, Vol. II, pp. 11–12; Gentillot to Servien, 5 June 1651, PRO, PRO 31/3/90, ff. 441–442; "Ambassadors' Journal," Bod., Rawl. C129, f. 22; Whitelocke's *Annals*, 16 June 1651, BL, Add. 37345, f. 132; *Mercurius Politicus*, 5–12 June 1651, p. 857; 12–19 June 1651, p. 872; *A Perfect Account*, 30 April–7 May 1651, p. 135.

77 *Mercurius Politicus*, 27 March–3 April 1651, p. 696; *Weekly Intelligencer*, 1–8 April 1651, pp. 116–117.

78 Aitzema, "Selections," Bod., Rawl C734, f. 72r. See also Roger Whitely's Notebook, Bod., English History MSS, E308, f. 9.

traitors."[79] The insults soon turned into almost daily physical attacks on the ambassadorial train. Rumors of Cavalier plots to murder the ambassadors were confirmed when Colonel James Apsley called on St. John, and after informing him that some Scotsmen and Cavaliers "had taken a full resolution to murder" the ambassadors who had "so much strength and resolution that it would hardly be in our power to resist," proceeded to make an attempt himself.[80]

The ambassadors soon learned that the Cavaliers were not alone in their attacks. The French ambassador to the States General, Bellievre, having failed diplomatically to prevent the Anglo-Dutch negotiations had shifted his strategy. "It is known well enough that Monsieur Bellievre was one of those that set on his lackeys," wrote one correspondent clearly reflecting the views of the English ambassadors, "which is no great wonder; for, since he hath nothing to busy himself withal here, he must find work for the boys."[81] It was soon clear that an unholy alliance had been formed among "the English fugitives and malignants, the French ambassador's retinue, and other French men about this town, the Orange party, and other loose people here." The hostile Edward Nicholas concurred that the parliamentary retinue "cannot walk the streets, but they are by boys and women, as well as by men, especially Dutch, French, and Germans, affronted and railed at in the streets."[82] Orangist political power was clearly not dead.

Naturally the States General, and especially the States of Holland, did not fail to notice or act upon these affronts. But they were unable to prevent Prince Edward from fleeing to Germany or to capture those who had plotted the death of Oliver St. John. The ambassadors were furious "for the

79 *A Perfect Account*, 9–16 April 1651, p. 108; *Mercurius Politicus*, 3–10 April 1651, p. 713. The correspondents could report with satisfaction that when Edward "with his hat strook my Lord's saddle horse on the buttock, [he] returned it again with both his heels as high as his head, and missed not much of leaving the print of his shoes on his breast."

80 Ambassadors to States of Holland, 31 March 1651, Bod., Rawl. C129, ff. 12–13; *Weekly Intelligencer*, 8–15 April 1651, pp. 125–126; *Mercurius Politicus*, 3–10 April 1651, pp. 709, 716–717; *Mercurius Politicus*, 10–17 April 1651, pp. 725–729; *Mercurius Politicus*, 17–24 April 1651, p. 745. The miscellaneous attacks on the ambassadorial train were too frequent to be given full justice in this note. They are mentioned in all of the weekly newspapers, and in the "Ambassadors' Journal," Bod., Rawl. C129.

81 *Mercurius Politicus*, 17–24 April 1651, p. 746; Ambassadors to Council of State, 9 April 1651, Bod., Rawl. C129, f. 16. For the failure of the French diplomatic initiative see Croullé to Mazarin, 26 December 1650, PRO, PRO 31/3/90, f. 398; *Weekly Intelligencer*, 18–25 February 1651, p. 66; *Mercurius Politicus*, 5–12 December 1650, p. 453; *Mercurius Politicus*, 27 February–6 March 1651, p. 636; *Mercurius Politicus*, 17–24 April 1651, p. 745; *Mercurius Politicus*, 22–29 May 1651, p. 828.

82 St. John and Strickland to Council of State, 9 April 1651, Bod., Tanner MSS 54, f. 29; Nicholas to Ormonde, 19 March 1651, Carte, *Collection*, Vol. I, p. 427; Nicholas to Ormonde, 5 April 1651, Carte, *Collection*, Vol. I, p. 437; *Weekly Intelligencer*, 15–22 April 1651, p. 129; *Mercurius Politicus*, 10–17 April 1651, pp. 732–734; Edward Bill, *Certain Propositions Sent by the States of Holland to the Lords Ambassadors of the Common-wealth of England* (London, 1651), Thomason: 15 April 1651, pp. 1–2; Samuel Tuke to John Evelyn, 1651, Christ Church, Evelyn In-Letters, 1278.

affronts and indignities ... given to the Commonwealth of England." The *Mercurius Politicus* raised the issue to the level of ideology, insisting that "a violating of Ambassadors in any kind, is *Laesa Majestas*, an injury done to the majesty of that nation which they represent. It was England that received the affront done by the petty, paltry thing, called prince." The Council of State scoffed at the Dutch "examination of inferior judicatory and not securing the offendor[s], which we conceive expressed not a sufficient sense of that affront, nor was suitable to what was held forth in their place." The *Perfect Account* demanded that the Dutch "extend themselves beyond paper protection."[83] Ominously the English ambassadors were no longer willing to distinguish between the United Provinces of William II and the current regime. "[Parliament] had wasted here six or seven years and their resident could never have audience, they sent a second and he was murdered," St. John complained to the States General, "and now they had sent two extraordinary Ambassadors about matters which equally concerned them as well as England, who had been under so many indignities that were not to be endured, and yet no justice done upon any one, as in the case of Apsley and Prince Edward."[84]

"The many indignities and insolencies" combined with a conviction that the Dutch were "deliberating how to keep the ambassadors at The Hague, without declaring any thing touching the business came about" convinced St. John that there was "little hopes of dispatching the treaty with" the Dutch "especially to his proposal of coalition." Consequently St. John mustered "his private friends in Parliament, who swayed the house" to recall the ambassadors.[85]

The news of the arrival of the English boats sent to retrieve the ambassadors "took flight immediately into the great Assembly," where it "so startled the great Assembly that they laid aside all other business, and dispatched an eminent personage to attend our Ambassadors."[86] A flurry of Dutch activity – "nothing is now debated on by the States General and Provincial, but the more near alliance with England" – persuaded the English to remain in The Hague while the Dutch sent an express to Westminster which was accompanied by Holland's agent Schaep and St.

83 English Ambassadors to States General, 9 May 1651, in Thomas Birch (editor), *A Collection of the State Papers of John Thurloe, Esq.* (London, 1742), Vol. I, pp. 181–182; *Mercurius Politicus*, 3–10 April 1651, p. 715; Council of State to Ambassadors, 4 April 1651, PRO, SP 25/96, f. 107; *A Perfect Account*, 9–16 April 1651, p. 112.

84 "Ambassadors' Journal," 22 April 1651, Bod., Rawl. C129, f. 25.

85 "Ambassadors' Narrative," PRO, SP 103/46, 19 April 1651, f. 131; PRO, SP 103/46, 22 April 1651, f. 134; Council of State to Ambassadors, 12 April 1651, PRO, SP 25/96, f. 121; Whitelocke's *Annals*, BL, Add. 37345, 30 April 1651, f. 128. This is yet more testimony to St. John's continuing influence in the Rump, lending further credibility to the pivotal role which I claim he played in the passage of the Navigation Act.

86 *Mercurius Politicus*, 24 April–1 May 1651, p. 765; *Weekly Intelligencer*, 29 April–6 May 1651, p. 148.

John's secretary John Thurloe.[87] Parliament and the Council of State were persuaded to prolong the embassy for forty days upon Dutch promises and protestations that they would act with despatch. "Now no body doubted of a full agreement between these two States," Thurloe recorded in his narrative of the embassy, "the Dutch having obtained their desire of longer time for the treaty; and given such great assurances to the Ambassadors of their full compliance with England against all people ... so that now nothing seemed to be wanting for the completing the said alliance."[88]

The Dutch did begin, at last, to negotiate. But the alliance was never concluded. St. John and Strickland left The Hague in June no more satisfied than they had been at the end of April. Why did the negotiations break down?

It was certainly not because of economic differences. The economic centers of the United Provinces, and especially Amsterdam, the home of the Dutch East India Company, were most enthusiastic for a close alliance with England. The English Commonwealth was primarily interested in alliance and union, St. John and Strickland informed the States General, in return for which they were willing to "afford proportionable advantages" to the Dutch. Thurloe was at pains to emphasize that these advantages would be "in reference to trade, which the Dutch would be desirous of." "As for terms," the *Perfect Account* correctly concluded, "it concerns them more than us."[89] The Rump was naturally deluged with economic grievances against the Dutch as soon as it became clear that serious negotiations with the States General were under way. But one should not overestimate their importance. St. John and Strickland made it clear that concerns about the Danish Sound and the East India trade would be considered only "as soon as the other parts of the treaty will give us leave."[90] Edward Hyde's Dutch correspondent was correct to predict that with respect to economic issues "in the end, I am afraid [the English and the Dutch] will prove but birds of a feather."[91]

87 "Ambassadors' Journal," Bod., Rawl. C129, 21 April 1651, f. 24; "Ambassadors' Journal," Bod., Rawl. C129, 22 April 1651, f. 26; *Mercurius Politicus*, 24 April–1 May 1651, pp. 765–766; *Weekly Intelligencer*, 29 April–6 May 1651, pp. 148–149.

88 "Ambassadors' Journal," Bod., Rawl. C129, 3 May 1651, f. 27; "Ambassadors' Narrative," PRO, SP 103/46, f. 136.

89 Strickland and St. John to States General, 17 April 1651, Bod., Rawl. A2, f. 178; "Thurloe's Review," PRO, SP 103/46, f. 220; *A Perfect Account*, 7–14 May 1651, p. 141.

90 Ambassadors to Council of State, 17 May 1651, Bod., Rawl. C129, f. 31. Petitions of economic grievances were commonplace during any diplomatic negotiations; they should not be read as attempts to block those negotiations but as efforts to procure economic restitution as part of the political settlement package. It was very much in the petitioners' economic interest for a settlement to be reached.

91 Hugh Nathan to Edward Hyde, 12 December 1650, Bod., Clar. 41, f. 92. Nathan is suggesting that economic issues would not divide the two republics. I have found little evidence in the papers surrounding the Anglo-Dutch union proposals of 1651 to substantiate Robert Brenner's assertion that "it was apparently hoped that the threat posed by English naval power to Dutch trading operations would help to make the Dutch see the long-run economic advantages of politico-commercial cooperation." Brenner, *Merchants*

The failure of the negotiations must rather be attributed to Dutch reluctance to accede to English demands. After Thurloe's return to the United Provinces with the Rump's extension of the ambassadorial commission, negotiations again slowed down. St. John and Strickland proposed that "the two Comonwealths may be considered as old friends joined and allied together for the defense and preservation of the liberties and freedom of the people of each."[92] Five days later the States commissioners responded with a paper declaring the States General's "Resolution to renew all ancient treaties, and especially that fundamental and essential one, made for a perpetual confederation between the same two nations, in the year 1495" which established the principle of "mutual defense and conservation of the liberty and franchise of the two Commonwealths and of the commerce and navigation reciprocal, and of the common interests, against all that should endeavor the disturbance of either of them." This was exactly what the English wanted to hear. They quickly drew up a series of propositions, "which comprehended no new matter," and delivered them to the States commissioners.[93]

It was in the States General that the proposed treaty met with resistance. The delegates of the Orangist provinces insisted that the proposed articles be sent "down into their several provinces to have the advise, and directions of their superiors therein." The ambassadors were furious, knowing full well that the delay would be interminable. How could the Dutch "after so many professions made and assurances given" that all was well still need to appeal to the provinces? Indeed, St. John fulminated, the Dutch were merely seeking "authority to consent to the very thing that they themselves had offered."[94] As the news from the provincial debates began to filter into The Hague the results were all too predictable. "Some of the provinces" – we can only guess which ones – "will not consent."[95] The English ambassadors saw no alternative but to request that ships again be sent to bring them back across the North Sea.[96]

and Revolution, p. 601. Indeed neither the English nor the Dutch appear to have understood the proposed union in Brenner's terms; they saw the proposed union as politico-religious not politico-commercial. While Brenner's clever claim that the union proposals were seen as the only way to overcome the inexorable economic competition between the two "nations" seems initially plausible, there is no evidence to support the claim – and much to suggest otherwise – that St. John and Strickland thought in terms of a "zero-sum competitive commercial game" or that they were interested in national advantages. See Brenner, *Merchants and Revolution*, p. 621.

92 Paper to the Commissioners of the States General in "Ambassadors' Journal," Bod., Rawl. C129, ff. 28–29; another copy, incorrectly transcribed, is in Thomas Birch (editor), *A Collection of the State Papers of John Thurloe, Esq.* (London, 1742), p. 182.

93 Ambassadors to States General, 16 June 1651, "Ambassadors' Journal," Bod., Rawl. C129, ff. 46–47; Ambassadors to Council of State, 17 May 1651, "Ambassadors' Journal," Bod., Rawl. C129, f. 31.

94 "Ambassadors' Narrative," 15 May 1651, PRO, SP 103/46, ff. 141–142.

95 Ambassadors to Council of State, 13 June 1651, Bod., Rawl. C129, f. 37.

96 "Ambassadors' Narrative," PRO, SP 103/46, f. 144.

Again the arrival of the Parliament ships at Goree produced an "alarm at the Hague." The Dutch commissioners reappeared on the doorsteps of the English ambassadors, prepared with thirty-six propositions which they claimed "did contain in them both an answer to those propositions which their Excellencies had delivered unto them, and likewise several things of their desire on their part."[97] After reviewing the propositions the ambassadors found that the Dutch "say nothing" to the fifth English proposition dealing with the "declared enemies to the freedom and liberty of the people." The desired confederation was to be made "only in point of trade."[98]

The English were beside themselves with rage. By June 1651 it was clear that the Dutch pipeline to the Royalists in Scotland had not been severed with the death of William II. The attacks on the English ambassadors convinced them that the Orange–Stuart alliance was still very much alive. Information from intercepted Royalist correspondence and reports from well-affected Dutch men convinced St. John and Strickland that the Scots were receiving ships and ammunition from the Dutch provincial ports.[99] The Dutch, St. John and Strickland told the Council of State "had done little less hurt to the Commonwealth of England then if they had been declared enemies thereunto."[100]

St. John and Strickland insisted upon the *Intercursus Magnus* – the 1495 commercial treaty between England and Burgundy – particularly "the articles concerning the not aiding of rebels, and fugitives with arms, [and] victuals" as a minimum basis for negotiation. They reiterated that they "asked nothing but what was in the treaty of 1495 and there is the same occasion now as was at th[at] time." This demand "was very unwelcome to the commissioners," well cognizant of the limited powers they had from the provinces. They pleaded that it was "exceeding hard to banish all persons that are banished out of England, all men have refuge to us, and must not be banished."[101] This in no way satisfied the English ambassadors. "It is no

97 "Ambassadors' Narrative," 10 June 1651, PRO, SP 103/46, f. 144; "Ambassadors' Journal," 14 June 1651, Bod., Rawl. C129, f. 37; *Mercurius Politicus*, 5–12 June 1651, p. 857.

98 "Ambassadors' Journal," 14 June 1651, Bod., Rawl. C129, f. 45; 19 June 1651, f. 49. This confirms Thurloe's later gloss on the negotiations which declared that "the 36 Articles composed by them were somewhat in the nature of a League Defensive, but they did most principally relate to trade & commerce." "Thurloe's Review," PRO, SP 103/46, ff. 220–221.

99 Ambassadors to Council of State,"Ambassadors' Journal," 9 April 1651, Bod., Rawl. C129, f. 17; Bod., Rawl. C129, 18 April 1651, f. 20. Apparently the group around Christopher Love was sending their support to the Royalist cause via Holland. *Weekly Intelligencer*, 17–24 June 1651, p. 208.

100 Ambassadors to Council of State, 18 April 1651, "Ambassadors' Journal," Bod., Rawl. C129, f. 21.

101 "Ambassadors' Narrative," PRO, SP 103/46, ff. 156, 162; "Ambassadors' Journal," Bod., Rawl. C129, ff. 45–46.

answer to say, that you will look hither, that they doe no wrong," they fumed, "we have had experience of that already. We know ... the Scots king, the Scots and our rebels made a treaty here, and laid the foundation of that war which now the Scots make upon us." St. John and Strickland pointed out that there were two elements of the *Intercursus*, one which granted freedom of commerce and navigation, the other which guaranteed aid against each others' rebels. "You yourselves are in possession" when it "is for your advantage." "I would fain know which right we have by the treaty of 1495 if these articles be not granted to us," St. John demanded; "is the treaty of 1495 of force or not?" "If you expect we should perform with you," he threatened ominously, "you must perform with us, either the treaty is at an end for the whole, or of force."[102] The brief granted by the provincial assemblies was not sufficiently broad to leave room for maneuver. The Dutch commissioners could only plead that "they could not treat upon the old treaty without the inclusion of their new articles." Despite a flurry of Dutch diplomatic special pleading, the negotiations were at an end.[103]

The English dream of a Protestant and republican alliance between the two maritime commonwealths had turned into a nightmare for the ambassadors. The embassy failed not because of Anglo-Dutch economic differences, but because of Dutch reluctance to ally with the regicide republic, in short because of the lingering power of the House of Orange.[104] Just as important as the reasons of the failure of the St. John/Strickland mission in explaining the course of English foreign policy is their perception of the causes of that failure. The perception of St. John and Strickland was important not only because they were themselves influential Rumpers, but because it was their reports which so heavily influenced opinion in the Rump. From the ambassadorial reports, the Council of State affirmed, "we may take an estimate of what we may expect there; and from what principles [the Dutch] are moved."[105] How, then, did the ambassadors explain their returning to England empty-handed?

102 "Ambassadors' Journal," deals with the negotiations of 14 June 1651, Bod., Rawl. C129, ff. 45–46.

103 "Ambassadors' Journal," Bod., Rawl. C129, ff. 48–49.

104 Rowen, who has studied the Dutch archival material most closely, also concludes that the negotiations broke down over the English requirement that the Dutch expel the Royalists. *John De Witt*, p. 55. See also Morosini to Doge, 2 May 1651, *CSPV*, p. 180. Significantly, the Holland republican theorist Pieter de la Court also attributed the failure of the 1651 negotiations to "those that conceived themselves bound as slaves to the House of Orange." It was the Orangists who "did not only oppose the concluding of the foresaid desirable treaty, but also sent away those ambassadors with all manner of reproach and dishonour." [Pieter de la Court], *The True Interest and Political Maxims of the Republick of Holland and West-Friesland* (London, 1702), p. 458.

105 Council of State to Ambassadors, 6 June 1651, PRO, SP 25/96, f. 221; Cromwell was kept current of all the developments in the Netherlands, receiving copies of all the despatches from St. John and Strickland, e.g. Council of State to Cromwell, 29 March 1651, PRO, SP

The prolongation of the ambassadorial stay in the United Provinces, in the eyes of St. John and Strickland, removed any just grounds for the Dutch to complain "for want of time and opportunity."[106] Nevertheless, even after Thurloe's return to the United Provinces, the negotiations were plagued by delay. "To break off the treaty was as much against their will, as to conclude it suddenly," the ambassadors declared, "to procrastinate was their best interest." The English were kept in play with "some courtesies and fair words to delay the business," wrote the head of the traditionally pro-Dutch Sidney family in his journal. The Dutch, of course, pleaded that their constitution made delays inevitable. But the ambassadors' stay in The Hague had given them "sufficient appearances of the delusion of that pretense."[107] The Dutch were clearly hoping to "spin out the treaty until the Scots mist was over." "Like cunning foxes," the *Mercurius Pragmaticus* explained, the Dutch stand "gazing after the negotiations in Scotland, and according to the procedure of the designs there, they will compose a return." "That they would fain see the issue of the affairs in Scotland, before they come to a conclusion with the English Ambassadors is agreed by all," noted one of the Rump's foreign-policy specialists, Bulstrode Whitelocke.[108] This reflected the persistence of Orangism: "they cannot join with you against the Scots, and forsake the king utterly."[109] Clearly the English had "wise men to deal with, that can play their own game." "They be a cunning, and a deceitful people," opined one newsletter-writer. Even the hostile Marquis of Ormonde could not but conclude that the Dutch were "entirely governed" not by "honor or gratitude which are things now wholly lost in all nations," but by "the notion of reason of state."[110]

Dutch perfidiousness was made manifest in the negotiation process. They were not interested in "a nearer union," wrote the ambassadors, "but only for such an alliance as might tend to the increase of trade." The *Mercurius Elencticus* opined that "a League of amity and commerce happily at long running may not be denyed; but for any thing else (more than what relishes of apparent advantage to them) must not be expected." The departure of the English ambassadors allowed the world to see "what juggling sharks

25/96, f. 89. The "Ambassadors Narrative" which was prepared particularly for presentation to the Rump. It was read and approved of on 2 July 1651, *CJ*, 2 July 1651, p. 595.

106 *Mercurius Politicus*, 8–15 May 1651, p. 793.

107 "Ambassadors' Narrative," PRO, SP 103/46, f. 131; "Leicester's Journal," HMC, *DeLisle*, 25–26 June 1651, p. 601; "Ambassadors' Journal," 28 June 1651, Bod., Rawl. C129, f. 59.

108 "Ambassadors' Narrative," PRO, SP 103 46, f. 142; *Mercurius Pragmaticus*, 3–10 June 1651, p. 6; Whitelocke's *Annals*, 24 June 1651, BL, Add. 37345, f. 133. This version of events was also aired in the press. *Weekly Intelligencer*, 13–20 May 1651, p. 161; 2–10 June 1651, p. 187; 8–15 May 1651, p. 792; 29 May–5 June 1651, p. 834; *Mercurius Politicus*, 19–26 June 1651, p. 893.

109 *Mercurius Politicus*, 19–26 June 1651, p. 885.

110 *Mercurius Politicus*, 10–17 April 1651, p. 732; "Intelligence from Dort," 25 July 1651, Nickolls, *Original Letters*, p. 77; Ormonde to Nicholas, 6 June 1651, BL, Egerton MSS. 2534, f. 90.

they have met with; a pack of Machiavels which will hear of nothing but their own particular advantage."[111]

This policy of material self-interest was clearly contrary to the desires of God. Contemporary English polemics were especially virulent in their attacks on the worldly pursuit of profit. "Who'd dote on gold! a thing so strange and odd? / 'Tis most contemptible when made a God," ran one popular poem, "All sins and mischiefs thence have rise and swell: / One Indies more would make another hell."[112] It was in this context that the *Politicus*'s correspondent bemoaned Dutch policies which "take their rise and vigor only from the reflections of worldly interest, not considering the present motions of the great wheel of Providence; nor weighing the great design of God now in the world, to pull down all tyrranic-fleshly interests and principles in the kingdoms of men."[113] The English had come to the United Provinces in search of an alliance "for the good of the Protestant religion and the profession thereof against the growing interest of Popery," John Thurloe later recalled, "but without any effect, in respect the United Provinces always found it necessary to mingle therewith the considerations of trade."[114] "I fear these people could not obtain that interest and profit they looked for," concluded the *Perfect Diurnall*, "for take once away their gain, then life and religion and all is gone." Clearly the United Provinces is a place "where religion and policy, and all is servant to the great God Mammon; but there is a greater God than he will teach us better I hope."[115]

Not surprisingly a people motivated by an Orange-tinged self-interest were soon revealed to be bad Protestants. The Dutch predikants or preachers were found to be describing the English as "a company of heretics and schismatics, as the Church of Scotland styles you." "The ministers of this country are none of our friends," wrote the *Politicus*'s correspondent, "they work a world of mischief amongst the people for although they are forbidden to meddle with state affairs in their pulpits, yet they do nothing else but twaddle up and down the houses." Reports came in from all over the United Provinces, even from Holland, that the English were called "enemies to all Godliness," that "the Parliament of England are of a contrary religion."[116] These were dangerous claims, indeed, to make before

111 "Ambassadors' Narrative," PRO, SP 103/46, f. 126; "Thurloe's Review," PRO, SP 103/46, ff. 220, 223; *Mercurius Elencticus*, 17–24 June 1651, pp. 22–23; 24 June–1 July, 1651, p. 31.

112 *News from Newcastle* (London, 1651), Thomason: 3 February 1651, p. 1.

113 *Mercurius Politicus*, 19–26 June 1651, p. 882.

114 "Thurloe's Review," PRO, SP 103/46, f. 226. "The Dutch," Thurloe claimed in another retelling of these events, "had discovered in this and in other rancounters a fixed design to monpolize all trade into their own hands." "Concerning the Foreign Affairs in the Protector's Time," LRO, Finch Papers DG7/Box 4963/Folder 6, f. 13.

115 *A Perfect Diurnall*, 7–14 July 1651, p. 1151; *Mercurius Politicus*, 24–31 July 1651, p. 960.

116 *Mercurius Politicus*, 12–19 June 1651, pp. 870–871; *Mercurius Politicus*, 19–26 June 1651, p. 885; *Mercurius Politicus*, 26 June–3 July 1651, p. 897; *Weekly Intelligencer*, 24

a government convinced that the final eschatological struggle was now in progress.

Material self-interest, religious rigidity, and monarchical symapthies were a familiar set of traits to the English ambassadors. "I am confident they appear to be perfectly of the Scots mould," was how Thurloe described the Dutch to the Council of State, "by converse with whom and the French, they have learnt the art, of making huge professions ... and at the same time, intend to perform no more of them than apparently stands with their own advantage."[117] This description was ideologically charged. Oliver St. John had described the Scots as so "many doubtful persons and seeming friends" against whom God had delivered his "heavy judgment" at Dunbar. For William Hickman, another correspondent of Cromwell's, no people were "more deep in ingratitude and falsehood" than the Scots. Whitelocke noted approvingly in his *Annals* a letter which described the Scots as "a people, who delight to enslave others, yet are of a slavish and servile condition themselves ... a generation of very hypocrites and vipers, whom no oaths, or covenants can oblige, no courtesies or civilities oblige."[118] Like the Dutch the Scots were motivated only by "profit and preferment," their "own advance and private advantage," swayed only by "their own interests and ends."[119] Again like the Dutch, it was the Scots' ministers who were to be blamed for "the carrying on a worldly interest of domination and faction, to the extreme prejudice and danger of our nation."[120] It was this similarity to the Scots, then, which explained the Dutch reluctance to commit themselves to expel English enemies. "It was easy to be learnt from hence," the ambassadors informed the Rump, "what good intentions these people have to the Protestant religion."[121]

The ambassadors' experience in the Hague had shattered the English image of a United Provinces committed to the crusade against Popery and tyranny. Instead the Dutch were revealed as worshipping Mammon rather than God, as supporting the cause of Orange and Stuart rather than that of

June–1 July 1651, p. 210. These attitudes of the Dutch clergy are confirmed by the research of Keith Sprunger, *Dutch Puritanism* (Leiden, 1982), p. 365.

117 John Thurloe to Council of State, 6 June 1651, Bod., Rawl. A2, p. 217a (repaginated).

118 St. John to Cromwell, 26 September 1650, Nickolls, *Original Letters*, p. 25; Hickman to Cromwell, 16 November 1650, p. 29; Whitelocke's *Annals*, BL, Add. 37345, 16 September 1650, f. 99.

119 *Mercurius Elencticus*, 17–24 June 1651, p. 19; *Mercurius Politicus*, 17–24 April 1651, p. 735; *Mercurius Politicus*, 1–8 May 1651, p. 767; *Mercurius Politicus*, 12–19 June 1651, pp. 864–865; R. F., *The Scot Arraigned, and at the Bar of Justice, Reason, and Religion, Convinced, Convicted, and Condemned of a most Horrid and Odious Conspiracy and Rebellion against the Native Liberty and Birth-right of the Church and Free State of England* (London, 1651), Thomason: 16 June 1651, pp. 4–5.

120 The literature on this topic is vast. I only cite examples here which prove that this meaning was current at the time of Thurloe's statement. *Mercurius Politicus*, 12–19 June 1651, p. 863; *A Perfect Account*, 21–28 May 1651, p. 152.

121 "Ambassadors' Narrative," PRO, SP 103/46, ff. 129–130.

liberty. The Dutch, in English eyes, had confounded "divine Providence" which had created this opportunity to perfect an "alliance and union," an opportunity that "hath not heretofore been administered, nor is likely hereafter to be, if this be neglected." The onus was now on the Dutch to prove the English wrong. "England was as near to the Low Countries, as the Low Countries to England," St. John told the States General on the eve of his departure, "the Parliament was done going there and it now rested with them."[122]

[122] Ambassadors to States General, 17 May 1651, Bod., Rawl. C129, f. 33; "Ambassadors' Journal," Bod., Rawl. C129, ff. 49–50.

4

The road to war

The eschatological Protestant and classical republican contexts in which the ambassadors and the Rump placed the mission to the United Provinces makes it difficult to accept economic historians' explanation of the passage of the Navigation Act. Certainly it is hard to imagine that the calm, cool, and rational calculators of economic self-interest inhabited the same world as Walter Strickland, John Thurloe and Oliver St. John. Closer examination of the context of English politics in late 1651 makes it even harder to see the Navigation Act as the product of a group of merchant-interlopers.

The contemporary evidence which economic historians have adduced to demonstrate the political power of the colonial interlopers is of questionable quality. The material – a Royalist newsletter, the report of a Venetian ambassador based in Spain, and the account of the Dutch ambassadors to England in 1654 – all reflects the official Dutch and Royalist interpretation of English motivation. Not only does none of it come from sources who were in England in the summer and autumn of 1651, but it reflects the view of those who were unable and unwilling to understand the motivations for the English proposals to the Dutch in the spring of 1651.[1] In fact, there is a good deal of evidence that the merchant-interlopers had little support in the government. The East India Company retained its control over exports of bullion. The Leveller William Walwyn's attempt to break the Levant Company's monopoly failed. The Greenland Company retained most of its

1 Robert Brenner, "The Civil War Politics of London's Merchant Community," in *Past and Present* No. 58 (February 1973), pp. 104–105; repeated in his *Merchants and Revolution: Commercial Change, Political Conflict, and London's Overseas Traders, 1550–1653* (Princeton, 1993), p. 625; Thurloe's Review PRO, SP 103/46; Dutch account, August 1652, PRO, SP 103/46, ff. 207–211; *CSPV*, pp. 187–188. The Royalist newsletter in question is to be found at Bod., Clar. 45, f. 142. Hyde himself refused to trust the Royalist newsletter-writers. "It is very hard to make any conclusion from the intelligence we get from England," he explained to Lord Rochester, "which can be but the guesses of people there who though upon the place, must see at a great distance, and many untruths are purposely divulged to amuse the people." 9/19 December 1653, Bod., Clar. 47, f. 147r. Similar points have been made by Blair Worden, *The Rump Parliament, 1648–1653* (Cambridge, 1974), p. 257 and J. P. Cooper, "Social and Economic Policies under the Commonwealth," in G. E. Aylmer (editor), *The Interregnum: The Quest for Settlement 1646–1660* (London, 1972), p. 122.

exclusive rights. Dr. Loughead has shown that "there is no evidence" that even the East India Company "at any time" "suffered from political prejudice despite the personal disfavor with which some of its leading members were viewed."[2] Nor was the Navigation Act especially drafted in the interest of Maurice Thompson and his interloping interests. Indeed, Loughead has found that Thompson was hardly an economic radical. He "did not advocate an open trade at any stage" and in the period prior to the Dutch War "he appears to have had little difficulty in operating within the company's joint stock framework."[3] There is certainly no evidence that the big London chartered companies perceived the Act as an attack on their privileges.[4] Consequently there is little reason to reject Dr. Worden's assessment that although the "Rump worked closely with merchants who were prepared to assist it," those "negotiations were conducted strictly on the government's terms."[5]

There were, of course, economic grievances in 1651. The economic community was well aware of the "deadness of trade," a situation so bad that it "makes all trade at a stand."[6] Yet the merchant community, in

2 *CSPD*, 7 May 1652, p. 235; PRO, SP 105/144, ff. 35 ff; *CSPD*, 12 March 1652, pp. 177–178; *CJ*, 24 December 1650, pp. 513–514; Peter Loughead, 'The East India Company in English Domestic Politics, 1657–1688' (Oxford, D.Phil. thesis, 1980), pp. 12–13. All of this has been discussed perceptively by Cooper, "Social and Economic Policies," p. 132.

3 *CJ*, 17 February 1652, p. 90; Loughead, "East India Company," pp. 17–18, 20, 61; Cooper, "Social and Economic Policies," p. 135. Cooper and Loughead have both offered reasons why the Navigation Act ran counter to Thompson's interests. I am also skeptical of Brenner's characterization of Maurice Thompson's ideological convictions in a broader sense. The same Restoration report which Brenner quotes approvingly (*Merchants and Revolution*, [Princeton, 1993], p. 622) also reports that Thompson was "intimate with the Protector" – certainly something that could be said of very few republicans and even fewer of the religious radicals: L. Hugh Squire to Earl of Arlington, 24 June 1666, PRO, SP 29/159/108 I. While Thompson was able to make common cause with religious radicals and extreme republicans in the early 1650s (and might have been very close to them ideologically as well as politically) – and I am absolutely convinced that he was a bitter opponent of the Restored Monarchy – he seems to have followed Cromwell in his rejection of extreme religious and political radicalism in the later 1650s. It should also be noted that Thompson's willingness to aid the Dutch in the second Dutch War suggests that when his political or religious convictions came into conflict with his economic nationalism, he chose to follow the former rather than the latter.

4 Cooper, "Economic and Social Policies," pp. 134–135; Loughead, p. 62. The feeling that this was so comes from a reading of R. W. K. Hinton, *The Eastland Trade and the Common Weal* (Cambridge, 1959), pp. 90–92. Hinton has read the Levant Company papers in the PRO, and by claiming that "their only recorded desires were for privileges" means only that they did not argue for across-the-board restrictions of imports. Their petition for a prohibition of Dutch importation of Levant goods is at PRO, SP 105/44, f. 55. Apparently this petition was drawn up in response to a request from the Council of Trade which was concerned about "the prejudice likely to befall the Commonwealth by the importation of Turkey goods from Holland." PRO, SP 105/151, f. 50. This demand was probably aired before the mission to the United Provinces was approved.

5 Worden, *Rump*, p. 258; Hinton, *Eastland Trade* reached the same conclusion, p. 90.

6 Court minutes of Fishmongers Company, 26 May 1651, Guildhall, 5570/4, f. 271; Paige to Paynter and Clerke, 8 April 1651, Steckley, *John Paige*, p. 39; Paige to Paynter and Clerke,

private letters, pamphlets, and newspaper accounts, overwhelmingly blamed its troubles on Royalist pirates and the French, not on Dutch competition.[7] The situation in the Channel was so hostile that the French agent could "see no difference between a declared war, and that which they are now doing." The Spanish merchant John Paige moaned that the French "give commissions to take English ships, and our states give the like to take theirs" with the result that "the poor merchant suffers on both sides." "We find that [the Venetians] privately, as the French openly, have endeavored for a long time to destroy our trade," wrote the English ambassador Thomas Bendish from Constantinople, "and had very nearly attained their desires therein."[8] The Levant Company, whose ships were better suited to fight off the attacks of French men-of-war than most, declared to the Council of State "that this ample trade into Turkey and the Levant ... must needs be totally lost, unless some speedy redress be made."[9] The redress they envisaged was clearly not a Dutch war; for should such a war break out, at least one Levant merchant knew that it would mean "adieu to all trade."[10] The activities of Prince Rupert and other Royalist privateers, now armed with an entire fleet of revolted English ships, struck fear into the hearts of English merchants. The *Bloudy Almanack*, always a good gauge of popular opinion, predicted that in June 1651 "many pirates [would] range greatly abroad to the London merchants' damage." "The times are now very dangerous" because of privateering activities, wrote John Paige in 1649, so that "insurers will hardly underwrite upon any ship under sixteen or eighteen guns." Even Charles II's reverses did not put an end to privateering activities. The *Mercurius Bellonius* lamented in 1652 that the activities of the Royalists "causeth our merchants to cease trafficking except they have

6 May 1651, Steckley, *John Paige*, p. 40; Orders of court assistants, Grocers Company, Guildhall, 2 April 1652, 11588/4, f. 285; Thomas Merry, Edwin Pearce, and George Oxinden to East India Company, 24 October 1650, IOL, E/3/22, f. 49r; Cooper, "Social and Economic Policies," p. 123. In my survey of the court minutes of the London livery companies I found no evidence of anti-Dutch sentiment. They were not blaming their difficulties on the Dutch.

7 There were, of course, occasional pamphlets which mentioned the Dutch; but they were frequently reprinted pamphlets for political purposes or pamphlets which referred to Dutch successes as models for emulation.

8 Thomas Bendish to Council of State, 1 March 1651, PRO, SP 97/17, f. 64r.

9 Croullé to Mazarin, 19 September 1650, PRO, PRO 31/3/90, f. 299; Paige to Paynter and Clerke, 16 January 1650, Steckley, *John Paige*, p. 8; Paige to Paynter and Clerke, 22 March 1650, Steckley, *John Paige*, p. 18; Paige to Clerke, 20 September 1650, Steckley, *John Paige*, p. 27; Paige to Paynter and Clerke, 15 November 1650, Steckley, *John Paige*, p. 29; Morosini to Doge, 4 July 1651, *CSPV*, p. 190; Basadona to Doge, 15 July 1651, *CSPV*, p. 192; petition of Levant Company to Council of State, 17 September 1650, PRO, SP 105/144, f. 26. The number of notices of individual incidents of French attacks on English merchant shipping reported in the newspapers is too vast to be given full play here.

10 Thomas Banckes (Leghorn) to Sir Ralph Verney, 19 February 1652, HMC *7th Report*, p. 457.

convoys."[11] It was consequently "very dangerous for any ships to pass securely without a strong convoy."[12] It was this situation which many merchants blamed for their losing markets to the Dutch. The Levant Company knew that its Dutch competitors were "not so subject to those difficulties and surprisals which we are subject to, as well from the French fleet, as our own revolted ships." "Our trade is at present very small, and if we cannot get convoy the trade will be lost," wrote the Rumper and City merchant Edward Ashe to Colonel Popham, "for the Dutch have convoys to supply their markets daily."[13] While there was more direct competition with the Dutch in the East Indies, the East India Company refused to countenance belligerent means to ameliorate the commercial situation. Indeed the East India Company gave strict instructions to its factors never – even if they were at a comparative advatage – to molest the Dutch in the Indies.[14]

Far from attacking the Dutch, the English merchants soon realized that they alone could maintain their livelihoods. The work of Professor Knachel on Anglo-French relations during the Fronde has revealed that English merchants were using "Dutch carriers almost exclusively for trade" through the Channel. If anything, then, many merchants had powerful economic incentive *not* to want the Navigation Act.[15] The Dutch correspondent to *A Perfect Account* was apparently right to predict that "your London merchants ... will be great losers" from the Act.[16] It was probably opposition to the Navigation Act in certain sectors of the merchant community which prompted Benjamin Worsley to write "the *Advocate* in defense of it."[17] The veritable plethora of mercantile petitions demanding relief from the terms of the Navigation Act do not prove that the merchant community violently disapproved of the Act, but they do at least suggest that some merchants were unprepared for the measure.[18]

11 *The Bloudy Almanack: Or Englands Looking Glass* (London, 1650), Thomason: 18 November 1650, p. 4; Paige to Paynter, 25 May 1649, Steckley, *John Paige*, p. 2; Paige to Clerke, 22 January 1650, Steckley, *John Paige*, p. 10; *Mercurius Bellonius*, 25 February–3 March 1652, p. 26. There is also a vast amount of material in the newspapers dealing with particular incidents.

12 *Faithful Scout*, 26 March–2 April 1652, p. 491. The result was that a number of insurers were devastated and small mercantile shipping became impossible. Paige to Paynter and Clerke, 3 September 1650, Steckley, *John Paige*, pp. 24–25; Paige to Paynter and Clerke, 15 November 1650, Steckley, *John Paige*, p. 29.

13 Levant Company to Council of Trade, 30 December 1650, PRO, SP 105/144, f. 30; Edward Ashe to Colonel Edward Popham, HMC, *Leyborne-Popham*, 28 March 1651, p. 82.

14 East India Company to president and Council in Surat, 30 January 1650, IOL, E/3/84, f. 104v. Apparently they did not believe they were involved in a "commercial struggle with the Dutch." Brenner's phrase in *Merchants and Revolution*, p. 599.

15 P. A. Knachel, *England and the Fronde* (Ithaca, NY, 1967), p. 157.

16 *A Perfect Account*, 3–10 December 1651, pp. 385, 391; newsletter from Westminster, 30 December 1651, Worcester College, Clarke MSS 20, f. 79v.

17 Worsley to Lady Clarendon, 8 November 1661, Bod., Clar. 75, f. 300.

18 Whitelocke's *Annals*, BL, Add. 37345, 30 December 1651, f. 174; "Narrative ... of

Finally, the account provided by Farnell and Brenner cannot explain the timing of the Navigation Act. If the Independents gained control of legislation in 1649, and "placed commercial and colonial expansion near the top of [their] agenda," as Brenner asserts,[19] why did it take them until October 1651 to pass legislation so vital to their economic program? L. A. Harper has shown that it was not for want of effort. From December 1649 various proposals were advanced to exclude foreigners from English trade routes, but the Council of State denounced those propositions as "dishonorable in Council." It was only in the summer of 1651, after the attempt at Protestant republican union had ignominiously failed, that the Navigation Act began to move quickly through Parliament.[20]

Why then was the Navigation Act passed? Two well-informed contemporaries, from exactly opposite political perspectives, seemed to know quite well. Oliver St. John returned from The Hague with "extreme indignation," according to Edward Hyde, "which he manifested as he soon as he returned to the Parliament; who, disdaining likewise to find themselves undervalued (that is, not valued above all the world besides,) presently entered upon counsels how they might discountenance and control the trade of Holland, and increase their own."[21] The disappointment of the Dutch negotiations "sat so heavy upon the haughty spirit of the Lord Chief Justice St. Johns," the apocalyptic republican Edmund Ludlow recalled, "that he reported these transactions with the highest aggravations against the States and thereby was a principal instrument to prevail with the Council of State to pass" the Navigation Act.[22] Significantly, Sir Josiah Child, whose memory might well reflect that of the East India Company as a whole, recalled that

Councell for Trade," PRO, SP 18/16, f. 206 (dated 20 November 1651); minutes of Committee of Foreign Affairs, 7, 12 May 1652, PRO, SP 25/131, ff. 2–3; petition by Sam. Misselden, 18 November 1651, PRO, SP 46/96, f. 110; *CSPD*, 14 April 1652, pp. 217–218; *CJ*, 9 January 1652, p. 65; *CJ*, 3 February 1652, pp. 80–83; *CJ*, 17 February 1652, pp. 89–90; *CJ*, 2 March 1652, pp. 100–101; J. Ivemey (editor), *Life of Mr. William Kiffin* (London, 1883), pp. 24–25.

19 Brenner, *Merchants and Revolution*, p. 577.

20 L. A. Harper, *The English Navigation Laws* (New York, 1939), pp. 39–45. Certainly it is odd that the Act was passed at a time when the influence of the radicals in London city politics was on the decline. See Worden, *Rump*, pp. 290–291.

21 Edward Hyde, *The History of the Rebellion and Civil Wars in England*, pp. 784–785. Hyde came to this conclusion despite having read both the Royalist newsletter which Farnell and Brenner (*Merchants and Revolution*) make so much of, and despite having received Benjamin Worsley's letter in which he proclaims himself author of the Navigation Act. Another Royalist, Sir Philip Warwick, substantially supported this account. Although he did not specify St. John as the author, he did insist that the Navigation Act was passed out of resentment for the Dutch treatment of St. John and Strickland at The Hague. Sir Philip Warwick, "Memoirs," HL, HM 41956, p. 103.

22 Edmund Ludlow in C. H. Firth (editor), *The Memoirs of Edmund Ludlow* (Oxford, 1894), p. 267. John Toland would have little motive to rewrite this story. Obviously neither Hyde nor Ludlow were in fact in England in the summer of 1651; but, both had better information (especially Ludlow) about the goings on inside the Council of State than foreign ambassadors in hostile European cities.

"lord Chief Justice St. John ... was a principle engineer in the first Act of Navigation."[23] There is quite good reason to accept this interpretation. While still in the Netherlands St. John and Strickland complained that the Dutch were violating the terms of the *Intercursus Magnus*. The Dutch, they claimed, were "in the full possession of what is of greatest advantage by that treaty unto them [free trade]," while "the Commonwealth of England ... is out of possession of what they ought to enjoy by the treaty of 1495 [aid against and expulsion of rebels]."[24] The Navigation Act served to rectify the imbalance. It was only after the failure of English attempts at alliance, Thurloe later recalled, that "the considerations of preserving the commerce and navigation of the States as well in Europe as India were applied to."[25] In this context the complaints of Samuel Avery, the governor of the merchant adventurers and host of the English ambassadors while they were in the United Provinces, before the Council of State in July is surely significant. After cataloguing Dutch violations of the treaty of 1495 he recommended that England refuse to grant Dutch fishermen freedom of commerce on the English coast, which would surely "produce a fair treaty."[26]

St. John's newfound detestation for the Dutch, increasingly evident in the ambassadors' letters to the Council of State, was clear to all by late June. No one could misunderstand St. John's promise to the Dutch commissioners that "you will ... repent of having rejected our offers."[27] The idea of punishment for sin was not new to the thought of the Chief Justice. In the previous autumn he had told Oliver Cromwell that "we ought to seek God" because of the Scots' sins, so "that they may see the rod." The English, he said, "must not insult over them, but still endeavor to heap coals of fire upon their heads."[28] Punishment could only do the Dutch a deal of good.

Developments in the war against the Scots served to conflate the two English concerns about the *Intercursus Magnus*. The Dutch, the Council of

23 [Josiah Child], *A Treatise* (London, 1681), p. 1. It is surely damaging for the arguments of Farnell ("Navigation Act") and Brenner (*Merchants and Revolution*) that St. John was known to oppose mercantile involvement in the creation of national economic policy. According to Child, St. John was convinced "that trading merchants while they are in the busy and eager prosecution of their particular trades, although they be very wise and good men, are not always the best judges of trade, as it relates to the profit or power of a kingdom. The reason may be, because their eyes are so continuously fixed, and their minds intent upon what makes for their particular gain or loss, that they have not leisure to expatiate or turn their thoughts to what is most advantageous to the kingdom in general."

24 Ambassadors to States General, 28 June 1651, Bod., Rawl. C129, f. 59.

25 "Thurloe's Review," PRO, SP 103/46, f. 226.

26 Samuel Avery at Council of State, 16 July 1651, PRO, SP 46/76, ff. 57–58; Samuel Avery petition to Council of State, 30 July 1651, PRO, SP 46/96, f. 60.

27 Morosini to Doge and Senate, 18 July 1651, *CSPV*, p. 193; quoted in Samuel Gardiner, *History of the Commonwealth and Protectorate 1649–1656* (New York, 1965), Vol. I, p. 365.

28 St. John to Cromwell, 26 September 1650, Nickolls, *Original Letters*, p. 26.

State now knew, were causing "great inconveniences and mischiefs upon this Commonwealth." The Council of State informed Cromwell that the Dutch were sailing "with bills of lading from Leith, to show if they be examined at sea, but if they meet none of our ships, they easily put into the enemy's ports." They recommended prohibiting all trade in Dutch bottoms, whereby "all color will be taken away from them of giving supplies to the enemies of any provisions of war."[29] This was the same reasoning used the previous year when the Rump had prohibited trade with Barbados, Virginia, Bermuda and Antigua. Far from being intended to line the pockets of a favored group of interloping merchants, that precursor of the Navigation Act was passed because Lord Willoughby had inclined "to the lost Cavalier party." Willoughby was using commerce with the Dutch "to fortify himself against his enemies." Not surprisingly, then, the Council of State described the purpose of the Act to be for "settling, reducing, and governing the said islands." The reasoning behind the Act, the Canary merchant John Paige told his trading partners, was that "the Barbadians are proclaimed rebels to our State for revolting and not being subordinate to the present government."[30] The Dutch, it was becoming clear to the English, were seeking profit to the benefit of Royalists. Mammon, Charles Stuart and the Antichrist were working hand in hand.

In this context the legislative history of the Navigation Act becomes more easily explicable. The Council of Trade presented a report to the Council of State "concerning restraint of goods of foreign growth to be imported in foreign bottoms" on 31 July. Bulstrode Whitelocke, one of the Rump's specialists on Anglo-Dutch relations, then reported the bill to the Rump on 5 August. After this the bill was committed to a Committee of the Whole House, where it was extensively debated and presumably amended from 21

29 Council of State to Cromwell, 30 July 1651, PRO, SP 25/96, f. 317. The letter also mentions the economic advantages, but this might be less important given the ideological context. In fact, Parliament ships were capturing Dutch ships bringing supplies to the Scots. See Whitelocke's *Annals*, 20 August 1651, BL, Add. 37345, f. 143.

30 "Instructions for Captain Robert Davies, Mr. Richard Bennet, Mr. Thomas Stagge, and Captain William Clabourne," 26 September 1651, Thomas Birch (editor), *A Collection of the State Papers of John Thurloe, Esq.* (London, 1742), Vol. I, p. 197; A. B., *A Brief Relation of the Beginning and Ending of the Troubles of the Barbados* (London, 1653), Thomason: 29 July 1653, p. 1; Paige to Paynter and Clerke, 15 November 1650, Steckley, *John Paige*, p. 30; *CJ*, 27 September 1650, p. 474; *CJ*, 3 October 1650, p. 478; Whitelocke's *Annals*, BL, Add. 37345, 5 October 1650, f. 103. The merchant community, especially the New England merchant community, were not terribly happy about the Act. Their complaints are registered in the Admiralty Committee Book, Bod., Rawl. A.225, ff. 6, 13. There was also an Act passed prohibiting trade to Scotland for similar reasons. *CJ*, 18 September 1650, p. 470. Apparently as areas came under control of Cromwell's armies they were relieved of the restrictions on trade placed upon them by the Act. Brenner is certainly right to point out the involvement of Maurice Thompson and others in the formulation of the Act (*Merchants and Revolution*, pp. 591–592); this merely reinforces my point that their program could only be implemented insofar as it accorded with the government's political concerns.

August to 9 October. In any case, after a month of discussion and revision, the Act probably bore little resemblance to the draft originally presented by the Council of Trade.[31] It was probably in the committee stage that Oliver St. John made his contribution to the Navigation Act. The legal historian L. A. Harper has also found reason to suppose St. John's authorship. The language of the Act, he comments, "is characterized by a theoretical approach to problems of commerce, an attempt to evolve comprehensive formulae, a clarity of statement, and a disregard of the complexities of trade or practical consideration of administrability, which might be expected from a Chief Justice of the Common Pleas who had had a legal rather than a mercantile or administrative training."[32]

In all likelihood, a large group within the Council of Trade was not terribly happy with the final form which the Navigation Act had taken. The Council, as Dr. Cooper has shown, had a very large representation of provincial merchants. It was precisely these merchants who were most upset with the Act, proclaiming that it had "upon it only a London stamp." Here they were almost certainly mistaken. The *Journal of the London Common Council*, usually so full of debates regarding trading measures, records absolutely nothing about the Navigation Act. Indeed, that Thomas Challoner felt obliged to divide against the committed defenders of the Protestant cause, Carew Raleigh and Sir Henry Mildmay, in order to grant merchants relief from the penalties of the Act, shows just how little the merchant community, and the Council of Trade had to do with the final version of the Act.[33] These developments only become explicable if the measure was passed for political rather than economic reasons. Even the Masters of Trinity House knew that the Navigation Act "was made when there was inclination to have wars with the Dutch."[34]

Although Oliver St. John almost certainly wrote the final draft of the Navigation Act and used his political capital to maneuver the Act through Parliament, Benjamin Worsley did defend it. Can he be fitted into this ideological context? The pioneering work of Dr. Charles Webster on the "Spiritual Brotherhood" has done much to recover the intellectual milieu of the Commonwealth's economic theorists. Far from being the economically motivated imperialists described by Brenner, Webster has found that Worsley and his friends were devotees of Baconian eschatological science.

31 "Narrative of What Things Have Been Reported From the Councell of Trade," PRO, SP 18/16, f. 206; *CJ*, 5 August 1651, p. 617; *CJ*, 19 August 1651, p. 2; *CJ*, 21 August 1651, p. 4; *CJ*, 28 August 1651, p. 7; *CJ*, 4 September 1651, p. 11; *CJ*, 11 September 1651, p. 15; *CJ*, 18 September 1651, p. 19; *CJ*, 26 September 1651, p. 21; passed *CJ*, 9 October 1651, p. 27.

32 Harper, *English Navigation Laws*, p. 47.

33 Cooper, "Social and Economic Policies," pp. 133, 138; *CJ*, 3 February 1652, pp. 80–83. For more discussion of the Council of Trade see Worden, *Rump*, pp. 254–257.

34 Quoted in Harper, *English Navigation Laws*, p. 48.

Indeed, upon reading Worsley's imperial program, Sir Cheney Culpeper ecstatically praised this outline which would glorify God "throughout the whole world ... not the family, country, nation, but whole mankind."[35] Worsley himself claimed that the ultimate end of his colonial plans was "the endeavoring an union and reconciliation throughout all the Christian at least all the Protestant Churches."[36] Worsley's *Advocate,* which Hinton has suggested directly reflects the opinions of the Council of Trade, is another application of apocalyptic economics. Worsley wrote in the full confidence of "the breaking forth, very shortly, of [God's] Glory." Since we have now "recovered our liberties," Worsley explained, we can now "see the necessity of providing for the defense of this Commonwealth by shipping." The anti-Dutch nature of the Navigation Act Worsley explained in ominously familiar language. "The design of Spain," he reflected, "is, to get the universal monarchy of Christendom. Nor is it a thing less true (how little soever observed) that our neighbors [the Dutch] (after they had settled their liberty, and been a while encouraged by prosperity) have, likewise, for some years, aimed to lay a foundation to themselves by engrossing the universal trade, not only in Christendom, but indeed of the greater part of the known world."[37] For Worsley, then, the Navigation Act was necessary to prevent the Dutch from achieveing universal economic dominion – not an attempt to promote particular economic interests.

There is good reason to believe that Worsley truly was airing the ideas of a significant portion of the Council of Trade. Cooper has documented the extremely close links between the Council and the "Spiritual Brotherhood." Tom Challoner, for all his Socinianism, praised the very Protestant achievements of "worthy Hawkins and the famous Drake." Sir Balthazar Gerbier, by the 1650s a committed Protestant internationalist, mentioned the imperialist plans of the Rumper's ancestor "Baronet Challoner" in the same breath with those of Sir Walter Ralegh and the Earl of Warwick.[38] Richard

35 Quoted in Charles Webster *The Great Instauration: Science, Medicine and Reform 1626–1660* (London, 1975), p. 357. The argument of much of this paragraph is given substance by the exhaustive research which Webster has presented in his exciting book.

36 Webster has reprinted in its entirety Worsley's "Proffits humbly presented to the Kingdom," in Appendix V of his book. Webster, *Great Instauration*, p. 546.

37 [Benjamin Worsley], *The Advocate* (London, 1652), Thomason: 11 February 1652, sig. B1, pp. 1–2, 11. For Worsley one of the signs of the coming of Christ was to be, significantly, "the detection, by little and little, of all imposture, and the laying of all things low, naked, and mean before him; the stripping men of that honor, credit, and repute, that they had by several means been gaining with themselves (and by themselves with others, either through a not-knowledge, or through an artificial concealing of themselves." In this circumstance this almost certainly refers to the Dutch. Hinton, *Eastland Trade*, pp. 90–93.

38 Cooper, "Social and Economic Policies," pp. 125, 133–134; Worden, "Classical Republicanism," p. 195; Worden, *The Rump*, p. 254; Scott, *Algernon Sidney*, pp. 50–51; Balthazar Gerbier to Oliver Cromwell, 1 March 1652 [1653], BL, Add. 35838, ff. 306–307.

Salwey, another Rumper and member of the Council of Trade, was later proposed as ambassador to Sweden in order to carry out yet another aspect of England's Protestant foreign policy. He was sufficiently apocalyptic to be approved by the millenarian Colonel John Jones, and to describe English successes in the war against the Dutch as "miraculous workings" of God's power which pointed to "the more spiritual appearance of our Lord Jesus in his kingdom."[39] Hartlib himself might possibly have provided the links with the political ideas of his former patron Oliver St. John. Hartlib's circle was certainly in close contact at just this time with St. John's friend and fellow apocalyptic James Ussher.[40]

The similarity between Worsley's imperial plans and those of Maurice Thompson, so carefully described by Farnell, coupled with the similarity of their religious outlook, suggests that Thompson as well might have been motivated by an eschatological vision. He was after all quite involved in the activities of the vestry of St. Dunstan in the East, a vestry which apparently requested that the future fifth monarchist John Simpson be their lecturer.[41] Dr. Loughead has shown that Thompson's Assada scheme was "rested on a straight-forward revival of ideas current at court before the Civil War." The ideological context of those ideas, which centered on a proposal to colonize Madagascar, was that of the forward Protestant foreign policy advocated by the group surrounding Queen Henrietta Maria.[42] Significantly the Assada scheme was set up by a group known as the "Independent Brotherhood," with the intention, according to one hostile witness, of providing "shelter for traitors" in case of Charles II's "coming in a conqueror."[43] In fact, the first Governor of Assada, Lieutenant-Colonel Robert Hunt, described his own and his fellow adventurers' first priority as making "known the Lord Jesus Christ to the poor heathen in these Eastern parts of the world, and I shall much rejoice if the Lord shall please by me to open a door for that purpose."[44] But it was only after Oliver St. John and the rest

39 John Jones to Thomas Scot, 16 September 1651, in Joseph Mayer (editor), "Inedited Letters of Cromwell, Colonel Jones, Bradshaw, and other Regicides," in *Transactions of the Historic Society of Lancashire and Cheshire*, new series, Vol. 1 (1861), p. 188; Cromwell to Salwey, 11 August 1653, in Thomas Salwey, *Occasional Poems* (privately published, 1882), p. 123; Salwey to Cromwell, 13 August 1653, in Thomas Salwey, *Poems*, pp. 124–125; see also Worden, *Rump*, p. 128.

40 The occasion was a scheme to provide a new translation of the Bible. The contacts are fleshed out in Ussher's correspondence. See especially the letter from Arnold Boate to Ussher, 17 November 1650, in C. R. Elrington and J. M. Todd (editors), *The Whole Works of James Ussher with a Life of the Author* (Dublin, 1864), Vol. XVI, p. 168.

41 Tai Liu, *Puritan London* (Newark DE, 1986), pp. 107–108.

42 Loughead, "East India Company," pp. 50–52; Kevin Sharpe, *Criticism and Compliment* (Cambridge, 1987), pp. 94–97; Martin Butler, *Theatre and Crisis 1632–1642* (Cambridge, 1984), pp. 25–35.

43 Deposition of W. Fairfax, 13 October 1651, PRO, Kew CO 77/7, f. 87v.

44 Lieutenant-Colonel Robert Hunt, *The Island of Assada* (London, 1650), Thomason: 12 August 1650, pp. 1–2.

of the political nation became convinced that the Dutch were neither good Protestants nor good republicans that the Hollandophobe aspects of Worsley's economic vision could be adopted by the Rump.

The Navigation Act, then, was not the result of special pleading of merchants who were temporarily able to achieve power in the Rump. In fact, in the short term – in many ways the only economic planning possible for merchants in a period of deep depression – many merchants felt the Act ran contrary to their economic interests. Nor was the Act the result of purely pragmatic calculation. Instead the Rump passed the Navigation Act when it did in order to punish the Dutch for apostatizing, for abandoning the Protestant and republican cause, and consequently violating the terms of the *Intercursus Magnus*. If the Dutch were not prepared to join them, the Rump must have reasoned, they would have to prepare to carry on the ideological struggle without them.

Much of the recent scholarly debate about the Anglo-Dutch War has focused upon whether or not the Navigation Act made it inevitable. In light of the intense anti-Dutch feeling which developed in England after the failure of the St. John–Strickland mission, this question seems misguided. It was hostility to the Dutch which provoked the Navigation Act, not the Navigation Act which provoked hostility toward the Dutch.

The Dutch were at first only dimly aware of the increasing English Hollandophobia. Though the States General had decided to send ambassadors to England in July, it was not until December that Cats, Schaep, and Van de Perre sailed for England. The primary aim of the mission had not changed in the intervening months. The Dutch ambassadors wanted above all else to "return with an olive-branch in their mouths," believing that "the Low Countries cannot subsist without a peace established with England."[45] The knowledge that the Queen of Sweden was also sending an ambassador to Westminster no doubt encouraged haste at The Hague. In the context of increasing Anglo-Dutch hostility, rumors that "England and Sweden by joint force" intended to take control of the Danish Sound "and lay hold of those keys of our cupboard, which now we wear at our own girdle" were too plausible to be ignored.[46]

Although it is true that "repeal of the [Navigation] Act and related measures was the first point to be discussed" by the Dutch ambassadors, one should not overestimate the economic importance of the act. In the United Provinces the act was "little regarded." The Amsterdammers knew full well that it "would be more prejudicial to England than it can be to

45 Herbert H. Rowen, *John De Witt, Grand Pensionary of Holland, 1625–1672* (Princeton, 1978), pp. 55, 64–65; *Mercurius Politicus*, 4–11 December 1651, pp. 1267–1268; *Weekly Intelligencer*, 2–9 December 1651, pp. 277–278.

46 *Mercurius Politicus*, 27 November–4 December 1651, pp. 1250–1251; *Weekly Intelligencer*, 2–9 December 1651, p. 277; *French Intelligencer*, 2–9 December 1651, p. 19.

Holland." Although the Dutch preferred the repeal of the measure, they would not go to war over it, preferring to "shake hands with us upon some honorable design."[47] The Dutch were more concerned with what the Navigation Act revealed about the state of Anglo-Dutch relations than about its direct economic implications. The Dutch correctly perceived the Act as "a breach of the Eternal League made with them in the year 1605," as "a breach of commerce and amity, which could not consist with the peace between the two nations."[48] It was in this context that the Dutch ambassadorial team hoped to restore good relations between the two republics.

The Dutch arrived in a very hostile England. Members of the Rump were convinced that there had been no reformation since the death of William II. Old grievances against the Dutch were being unearthed and acted upon. The heirs of John Paulet, an English merchant whose ship the Dutch had seized in 1630, were granted letters of reprisal in July.[49] The Rump was entertained with accounts of the brutal Dutch massacre of English merchants at Amboyna as well as the more recent assassination of Dr. Dorislaus at The Hague.[50] Petitions from English merchants came pouring in complaining of Dutch commercial abuses. More importantly, perhaps, Thomas Scot's intelligence network chose this moment to reveal that the Dutch were sending ammunition to Catholic rebels in Ireland.[51] Even the great Protestant internationalist Hugh Peter "inveighed against the Dutch because of their pride."[52] The press was full of rumors that the Dutch ambassadors had come with "very high terms" and "bold propositions." "It is a great folly to lose what is our own, if we are able to keep it, as it as an offense to intrude upon others through too much ambition," commented the *Perfect Passages* reflecting the views of many Rumpers, "if the Hollander make not a peace, why should we any longer suffer injuries by them, seeing God hath put in our hands means to remedy the same." "The English and Dutch are

47 Simon Groenveld, "The English Civil Wars as a Cause of the First Anglo-Dutch War, 1640–1652," *The Historical Journal* Vol. 30 No. 3 (1987), p. 564; *Faithful Scout*, 17–24 October 1651, pp. 310–311; *Mercurius Politicus*, 16–23 October 1651, p. 1155; *Mercurius Politicus*, 30 October–6 November 1651, p. 1186; *A Perfect Account*, 21–28 April 1652, p. 550; G. N. Clark, "The Navigation Act of 1651," *History* Vol. 7 (1922–1923), pp. 283–284.

48 *Mercurius Politicus*, 25 December–1 January 1652, pp. 1312–1313; Hyde, *History*, p. 785; "States Declaration," August 1652, PRO, SP 103/46, ff. 205–206.

49 Committee of the Admiralty report, 8 October 1651, PRO, SP 46/96, f. 66; Dutch Ambassadors to States General, 30 January 1652, in Gardiner (editor), *Letters and Papers*, Vol. I, pp. 74–75.

50 *CSPD*, 13 November 1651, p. 16; *CSPD*, 9 January 1652, p. 95; petition of Thomas Billingsby, 6 January 1652, PRO, SP 84/159, f. 107; petition of Sarah Collins, 8 January 1652, PRO, SP 84/159, f. 109; see also Richard Bradshaw to John Bradshaw, 1 July 1651, PRO, SP 82/8, f. 116v.

51 *CJ*, 28 November 1651, p. 45; *CJ*, 30 December 1651, p. 59; *CSPD*, 1 December 1651, p. 42.

52 Hugh Peter in conversation with Mylius, 26 December 1651, quoted in Leo Miller, *John Milton and the Oldenburg Safeguard* (New York, 1985), pp. 118–119.

likely to quarrel and fight," the Guinea merchant Thomas Wall sensibly advised his brother John, "if matters be not composed between them by the interpositions of their ambassadors." It is hardly surprising that a large part of the merchant community "feared they will not agree."[53]

Nevertheless it would be wrong to assume that Rump foreign policy-making was motivated by a different set of ideological assumptions from those which had prompted the embassy to the United Provinces in March. Only the Rump's image of the Dutch had changed. For all of their expertise in commerce and diplomacy, the group centered upon Henry Marten, Herbert Morley, and Tom Challoner played a very small role in the negotiations with the Dutch. The negotiations were instead placed in the hands of men known to be committed to the Protestant cause. The ambassadors were initially received by the Protestant apocalyptic Earl of Pembroke, Milton's friend Sir Peter Wentworth, and Viscount Lisle. The Rump later added the religious radical Sir Henry Mildmay and two of Henry Marten's enemies, the Earl of Salisbury and Sir John Danvers, to the reception committee.[54]

After the Dutch ambassadors had arrived, the Council of State appointed Bulstrode Whitelocke, John Lisle, Thomas Scot, William Purefoy, Dennis Bond, and Viscount Lisle to handle the negotiations.[55] These men were no less committed to the Protestant cause than the reception committee. Bulstrode Whitelocke, who had played an important role in the earlier negotiations, was perhaps the most important figure. He was almost always present at the discussions with the Dutch, was the last man to proofread drafts of proposals, and frequently reported the results to the Council of State and the Rump. It was no exaggeration for him to claim that "my attendance and labor was not small or easy."[56] For all of his "moderation" Whitelocke was a committed Protestant. His only regret after Worcester – a battle which he thought was won because of God's "wonderful appearance for us" – was that "so many of our countrymen and Protestants" had been

[53] *A Perfect Account*, 3–10 December 1651, p. 391; *Perfect Passages*, 9–16 January 1652, p. 355; Thomas Wall to John Wall, 19 December 1651, BL Loan MSS 29/240 (unfoliated); Paige to Paynter and Clerke, Steckley, *John Paige*, 8 January 1652, pp. 57–58; 16 February 1652, p. 62.

[54] *CSPD*, 4 December 1651, p. 46; *CJ*, 18 December 1651, p. 53. This evidence, and that of the next paragraph would appear to be inconsistent with Brenner's claim that "the Commonwealth's imperialist republican leaders, most prominently Marten, Challoner, Neville, and Morley, bent on aggression, controlled overseas policy in the period of growing tension between mid-1651 and mid-1652, during which the Anglo-Dutch negotiations disintegrated and ultimately collapsed." *Merchants and Revolution*, p. 630.

[55] *CSPD*, 7 January 1652, p. 94; 14 January 1652, p. 102; 16 January 1652, pp. 105–106. John Bradshaw was originally named as well but withdrew. *CSPD*, 8 January 1652, pp. 94–95.

[56] *CSPD*, 28 April 1652, p. 228; *CSPD*, 10 May 1652, p. 236; Whitelocke's *Annals*, BL, Add. 37345, 25 March 1652, f. 188; 14 April 1652, ff. 198–199. Whitelocke's name appears at every stage of the negotiation process.

killed. John Dury, the most fervent ideologue of the international Protestant cause, later lauded the selection of Whitelocke for negotiations with German Protestants, an opportunity for Whitelocke's "excellent abilities" to be "most usefully and gloriously set a work."[57] At this point in time Whitelocke's Protestantism was at its most committed. George Cockayne, whom Bernard Capp has identified as one of the earliest fifth monarchists, lived in Whitelocke's house "and Mr. Cockayne constantly prayed twice a day in my family." It is just possible that Whitelocke was present at one of the meetings in which the fifth monarchists attempted to persuade Cromwell to accept their reading of Providence. If so, Whitelocke approved, commenting that they preached "excellently well." In any case, Whitelocke's religious views were quite pronounced. He supported lay preaching – "any man, whom God hath enabled thereunto by his spirit and gifts, may (if not ought) to preach unto and exhort his Christian brethren met together" – advocated gadding to godly sermons beyond one's own parish, sneered at ordination, and condemned Presbyterian discipline for "too too much invading the honor and authority of our great High Priest and Saviour."[58] Clearly there was an ideological element to Whitelocke's interest in Anglo-Dutch relations.

The other men involved in the negotiations with the Dutch were no less committed to the cause. John Lisle's views in this period are difficult to discern, but he had been a regicide, Professor Underdown has called him a "radical Independent," and he was murdered after the Restoration as he was leaving a Gathered Church in Switzerland.[59] Thomas Scot, though he would later celebrate English victories over the Dutch, would also later declare that the aim of the war had been to bring the Dutch "to oneness with us."[60] Dr. Worden has called called William Purefoy one of the Rump's "experts on religion."[61] Dennis Bond, despite his activity on numerous committees, remains a shadowy figure.[62] But Viscount Lisle's

57 Whitelocke's *Annals*, 7 September 1651, BL, Add. 37345, f. 153; Dury to Whitelocke, 15 April 1656, BL, Add. 32093, f. 341.

58 Whitelocke's *Annals*, BL, Add. 37345, 14 September 1651, ff. 156–158; 29 February 1652, f. 181; 12 June 1653, ff. 276–279; 18 June 1653, f. 280v; BL, Add. 4992, 20 August 1653, f. 28v; 25 September 1653, f. 36v; 23 October 1653, ff. 44–45; Bernard Capp, pp. 58–60; for a different view of Whitelocke's religious beliefs see Worden, *The Rump*, pp. 131–136.

59 David Underdown, *Pride's Purge: Politics in the Puritan Revolution* (London, 1971), p. 86; Edmund Ludlow, "A Voyce from the Watchtower," Bod., English History MSS C487, p. 1030. I am grateful to Blair Worden for pointing out Ludlow's discussion of Lisle's post-Restoration activities to me.

60 John Towill Rutt (editor), *Diary of Thomas Burton* (London, 1828), Vol. III, 7 February 1659, p. 111.

61 Worden, *Rump*, p. 126.

62 Though of his republican commitment there was little contemporary doubt. Anthony Wood knew him to be an "antimonarchist." See Andrew Clark (editor) *The Life and Times of Anthony Wood* (Oxford, 1891), 30 August 1658, Vol. I, p. 258.

anti-Catholicism and family relationship with the Dutch must have been well known. The negotiations, then, were left in the hands of men who were ideologically sound Rumpers, not in those of calculating capitalists.

The Dutch understood very well, if belatedly, the nature of the men they were dealing with. Lord Cats, the leader of the Dutch diplomatic team and former Pensionary of Holland, immediately sought to soothe English feelings. He emphasized that the Dutch very much wanted a "firm league of amity and union" which would include assisting each other "both in the offensive and defensive war, against any common enemy whatsoever." Just as importantly for the English he reiterated the religious nature of the mission. "Out of the band of religion," Cats pointed out, "deriveth the true soul of hearts for to keep society amongst men, so are confederacies made amongst those of differing religions very seldom stable or durable." In this case, both England and the United Provinces "have not only the profession of the true religion, but also that the same on both sides is confirmed with numerous martyrdoms."[63] Cats had struck the right note for on Christmas Eve the Rump declared "an ardent affection for the ent[er]ing into a league and unity, with the Lords, the Estates General of the United Provinces."[64] The ambassadors had done a great deal to reassert the image of the United Provinces as a Christian republic.

Appreciation for the Dutch attitude was soon reflected in English actions. The letters of marque awarded to the heirs of the merchant Paulet were called in, along with all other letters of marque granted against the Dutch.[65] The Council of State made certain that illegally seized Dutch prizes were released. Customs officers were reminded not to exceed the letter of the law, to seize salted but not fresh fish, the Council of State "being unwilling that there should be any just cause for dissatisfaction from any of the people of the United Provinces."[66] The *Mercurius Politicus* could again describe the Dutch as an example of a people that "ever grow magnanimous and gallant upon a recovery" of their liberty.[67]

63 Cats's speech before Parliament, 19 December 1651, Bod., Clar. Dep. C172, Nalson Papers XVIII, ff. 318–319; *A Declaration and Narrative of the Proceedings of the Parliament of England, Touching the Message and Letters of Credence, sent from the Estates General of the United Provinces; and Presented to the Parliament of the Lord Ambassador Cats* (London, 1651), Thomason: 29 December 1651, pp. 6–7; *Mercurius Politicus*, 13–20 November 1651, p. 1210; *Mercurius Politicus* 27 November–4 December 1651, p. 1251.

64 *French Intelligencer*, 23–31 December 1651, p. 43.

64 *French Intelligencer*, 23–31 December 1651, p. 43.

66 Council of State to Captain Boreman, 13 February 1652, *CSPD*, p. 142; Council of State to Thomas Bendish, 19 February 1652, *CSPD*, p. 148.

67 *Mercurius Politicus*, 15–22 January 1652, p. 1352; see also *A Perswasive to A Mutuall Compliance Under the Present Government. Together with a Plea For a Free State Compared with Monarchy* (Oxford, 1652), Thomason: 18 February 1652, p. 23. "I rather think we shall agree than fall out," wrote one army newsletter-writer at the end of January: newsletter from Westminster, 31 January 1652, Worcester College, Clarke MSS 22, f. 19v.

In this situation it was possible for serious negotiations to take place. By the end of January the Council of State had drawn up and delivered answers to the initial Dutch propositions, separating specific claims from the items of principle.[68] The Dutch, evidently pleased with the English answer, rehabilitated the 36 Articles which had been discussed while Strickland and St. John were in the United Provinces. The Articles clearly raised complicated legal issues, requiring over a month of debate before the Council of State could deliver an answer to the Dutch propositions. This delay should not, however, be read as an attempt to derail the negotiations. During this period the Council of State allowed the Dutch free access to the negotiating committee, a committee which was supplemented by the pro-Dutch Henry Vane and Cromwell's old friend Sir William Masham.[69] After a conference in early April, both sides spent the rest of the month fine-tuning the treaty. On 26 April "the business of Holland, France, and Ireland" were given top priority on the Council of State's agenda. "Equal liberty" was given to both sides "to make further propositions in carrying on the treaty." Finally on 5 May thirty copies of the 36 Articles, including the Dutch demands and English answers, were to be written out in English. The basis for a treaty had been reached.[70]

The terms debated clearly reveal that the economic problems were minimal. Although it is true that the English did not explicitly repeal the Navigation Act – that would have gone "against the grain of true Englishmen" – they did minimize its effect. The Dutch were allowed to "come by water or by land" into "towns or villages, walled or unwalled, fortified or unfortified" in "all dominions in England Scotland and Ireland ... with freedom and security" to "trade and traffic, and have commerce in any goods or commodities they please." The English emphasized that merchants "may not be seized or arrested in the lands, ports, havens, rivers of the other by virtue of any general or particular commands." Only the plantations and colonies were to be excepted because the "the people of the Commonwealth

[68] *CSPD*, 19 January 1652, p. 109; *CSPD*, 20 January 1652, p. 111; *CSPD*, 23 January 1652, p. 117; *CSPD*, 26 January 1652, p. 119; *CSPD*, 28 January 1652, pp. 121–122; *CSPD*, 29 January 1652, pp. 122–123; "Advice from London," [30 January] 1652, *CSPV*, p. 214; *Mercurius Politicus*, 1–8 January 1652, p. 1332; *French Intelligencer*, 13–20 January 1652, p. 60.

[69] *CSPD*, 12 February 1652, pp. 140–141; *CSPD*, 25 February 1652, p. 151; *CSPD*, 5 March 1652, p. 169; *CSPD*, 8 March 1652, p. 172; *CSPD*, 9 March 1652, p. 172; *CSPD*, 11 March 1652, p. 175; "Advices from London," 15 February 1652, *CSPV*, p. 215; *CJ*, 10 March 1652, p. 103; for evidence of friendliness toward the Dutch see *CSPD*, 24 February 1652, p. 151; *CSPD*, 2 April 1652, p. 205 (addition of Vane and Masham).

[70] *CSPD*, 5 April 1652, p. 209; *CSPD*, 7 April 1652, p. 212; *CSPD*, 12 April 1652, p. 215; *CSPD*, 14 April 1652, p. 217; *CSPD*, 15 April 1652, p. 218; *CSPD*, 22 April 1652, p. 224; *CSPD*, 26 April 1652, p. 227; *CSPD*, 27 April 1652, pp. 227–228; *CSPD*, 5 May 1652, p. 233; newsletter from Westminster, 16 March 1652, Worcester College, Clarke MSS 22, f. 52; newsletter from Westminster, 17 April 1652, Worcester College, Clarke MSS 22, f. 76.

of England hav[e] been always strictly forbidden to trade in all plantations and places belonging to the people of the United Provinces that are not within the United Netherlands."[71] The issues of fishing and reparations for Amboyna were settled separately. By February it was known that the English and Dutch had agreed upon "the yearly revenue for fishing." In May the Canary merchant John Paige was able to assert that the Dutch "proffer £700,000 to the state in satisfaction to the injuries they did us 30 years since at Amboyna."[72]

In other respects as well the negotiations of 1652 closely resemble those of 1651. In order to guarantee "a nearer union and confederacy between both Commonwealths than hath formerly been," any citizen of the United Provinces "being of the reformed religion" was allowed to "freely dwell and inhabit, exercise trade and commerce" in the British Commonwealth "as any of the native people of this nation may or ought to enjoy by virtue of their birth."[73] The English were still adamant that no citizens of the United Provinces "nor any abiding or being within their power, shall give any aid, counsel or favor to the enemies and rebels of either Commonwealth." Despite some resistance from the Dutch, both sides seem to have agreed to include non-military supplies in the list of prohibited goods.[74] In short, the treaty would have been the first step to a union of the Protestant republics. In the meantime potential areas of disagreement were settled. English "dominion of the sea will be acknowledged," wrote the Venetian agent in London; in return the English "will grant the Dutch free navigation."[75]

Everyone believed that an Anglo-Dutch alliance was imminent. By the middle of March the conveyers of political gossip were confident that an agreement would soon be reached. "Good results are expected from the negotiations of the Dutch ambassadors," wrote one correspondent of the Venetian ambassador in Paris. Ralph Josselin heard that there was "some likelihood of agreement with the Hollander." "After much tugging and struggling with the Dutch Ambassadors," reported the *Perfect Account*,

71 Paige to Paynter and Clerke, 16 February 1652, Steckley, *John Paige*, p. 62; "Response of the Councell to the 36 Articles," BL, Add. 4211, ff. 13, 14, 19. This document is almost certainly one of the thirty copies ordered to be written by the Council of State.

72 *French Intelligencer*, 23–31 December 1651, p. 48; 27 January–4 February 1652, p. 73; *The Faithful Scout*, 30 January–6 February 1652, p. 427; *Perfect Passages*, 9–16 January 1652, p. 602; Paige to Paynter and Clerke, 12 May 1652, Steckley, *John Paige*, p. 74.

73 BL, Add. 4211, f. 11; "Thurloe's Review," PRO, SP 103/46, f. 222.

74 BL, Add. 4211, ff. 3, 4, 11.

75 Paulucci to Morosini, 14 May 1652, *CSPV*, p. 234. It is true that Paulucci also believed the English would not allow the Dutch "to import foreign produce into England." But, this seems to be inconsistent with the English response to the 36 Articles. He probably misinterpreted the English reticence to explicitly repeal the Navigation Act. Paulucci later reported "that the Commonwealth will make some concessions and permit transit and shelter to Dutch bottoms freighted with foreign produce in the ports of England, Scotland and Ireland, whereas it had been originally intended to exclude them entirely." *CSPV*, 20 May 1652, p. 240.

"there are now fair hopes that the treaty will produce a happy conclusion."[76] Developments in the United Provinces appeared to confirm this assessment. The States of Holland released the English ships which had been embargoed, leading the *Mercurius Politicus* to conclude that the Dutch "(especially Holland) hath some good satisfaction in your answer to those proposals of their ambassadors, or else your ships had not been so freed and befriended with a convoy."[77] After considering the English answer to the 36 Articles, the vroedschap (town council) of Amsterdam "declared that they heartily desired peace with England." When the Dutch decided to send yet another ambassador to England to encourage "a firm league and amity between the two nations," there seemed no reason to doubt that the negotiations would "in due time draw forth the blessed plants of peace and amity, and open a way of trade and commerce, to the cheering of the hearts of many thousands in each nation."[78] Perhaps the surest sign that a treaty was about to be concluded is that merchants again delivered petition after petition to the Rump, hoping to have their particular grievances included in the general settlement.[79]

Diplomats were confident in May, the very month that the English and Dutch fleets under admirals Blake and Van Tromp clashed in the Downs, that a treaty would be concluded. Despite the differences between the English and Dutch, the Venetian agent Paulucci wrote, all "will be adjusted successfully because of interest and national sympathies." The Dutch ambassadors themselves were sure that a treaty was about to be concluded. "We were confident," they wrote angrily to Van Tromp after the battle with Blake, "of bringing our negotiations before long to a satisfactory conclusion." "Who should ever believe that so noble a work, and one desired with so many wishes of all honest men, and especially of all the churches of the reformed Christian religion," asked the ambassadors rhetorically, "should be cut off or hindered by any imprudent and turbulent man ... without the knowledge and against the will of the States of the United Netherlands?"[80]

The Navigation Act, then, did not make war between England and the

76 "Advice from Holland," 20 March 1'652, *CSPV*, p. 219; Josselin, *Diary*, 21 March 1652, p. 275; *A Perfect Account*, 17–24 March 1652, pp. 507–508.

77 *Weekly Intelligencer*, 30 March–6 April 1652, p. 414; *Weekly Intelligencer*, 13–20 April 1652, p. 430; *Dutch Spy*, 31 March - 7 April 1652, pp. 17–18, 22; *Faithful Scout*, 2–9 April 1652, p. 499; *Mercurius Politicus*, 8–15 April 1652, p. 1536; *Perfect Passages*, 9–16 April 1652, pp. 433–434.

78 *Perfect Passages*, 16–30 April 1652, p. [448]; *A Perfect Account*, 28 April–5 May 1652, p. 560; *A Perfect Account*, 12–19 May 1652, pp. 572, 575; *Mercurius Politicus*, 29 April–6 May 1652, p. 1578; *French Occurrences*, 10–17 May 1652, p. 107.

79 *CSPD*, 5 May 1652, p. 232; *CSPD*, 6 May 1652, p. 234; *CSPD*, 12 May 1652, p. 239; *CSPD*, 19 May 1652, p. 298.

80 Paulucci to Morosini, 8 May 1652, *CSPV*, p. 231; 13 May 1652, *CSPV*, p. 237; Dutch Ambassadors to Tromp, 23 May 1652, Gardiner, *Letters and Papers*, Vol. I, pp. 238–239; Dutch Ambassadors to the Council of State, 24 May 1652, Gardiner, *Letters and Papers*, Vol. I, pp. 230–232.

United Provinces inevitable. Instead it reflected an image of the Dutch as false Protestants and insincere republicans who were only interested in profit, an image which the Dutch ambassadorial team did much to eviscerate. Once the Dutch had reemerged as liberty-loving Protestants the English were quite ready to remove the teeth from the Navigation Act and to pave the way for a closer alliance between the two nations. That this treaty was not completed, that the Protestant cause was not advanced, must be explained by factors other than economic competition.

Why then were negotiations aborted? Why did two nations which had looked to be on the brink of concluding an offensive and defensive alliance in May end up fighting each other by the summer of 1652? In order to answer these questions one must examine developments in Anglo-Dutch relations at the popular level. What did the English think of the Dutch?

As soon as St. John and Strickland returned from the United Provinces in July 1651, the press began to spew forth anti-Dutch propaganda.[81] The Dutch, "from the Hogen to the Boor," were found to be the "greatest sticklers" in support of the young King of Scots. Not only was the Orangist party found hoping for a Stuart victory against the Rump's armies, but even the "truly honest" "were hurried away with the cry of the pack." There were recurrent rumors that the "Dutch butter-boxes" were about to appoint Charles Stuart their protector.[82] Each new rumor of a Royalist victory in England produced new celebrations in the United Provinces. "Swarms of hacksters flocked hither to give and receive news," reported the correspondent of the *Mercurius Politicus* from The Hague. The people were "in the heat and height of jollity, upon mere chimaeras of their own brains that the king had got victories, divided the spoil, and triumphed in the city and capitol of London, before ever a sword was drawn, or stroke struck."[83] Even after the battles which the pamphleteers had won for Charles at "Hereford, Gloucester, Bristol and all" were refuted by the reality of Worcester, the Dutch continued to "hide their shame, and their eyes from beholding the works and wonders of God." "After our good God had broke their swords, and [s]napt their spears in sunder," snorted one polemicist at

81 Relations between the press and the government during the Interregnum are quite murky. I think it quite likely that St. John, Strickland, and their political allies leaked information which spurred a reimagination of the Dutch polity. Indeed much of the material about the Dutch polity printed in Nedham's *Mercurius Politicus* is taken from correspondence now among Thurloe's papers. However, once the process of reimagination had begun it took on a life of its own – a life deeply informed by the political and religious convictions of the various newspapers and astrologers.

82 William Lilly, *Annus Tenebrous: or the Dark Year* (London, 1652), p. 36; *Mercurius Politicus*, 25 September–2 October, 1651, pp. 1100–1101; *A Perfect Account*, 17–24 September 1651, p. 292; *Faithful Scout*, 13–20 February 1652, p. 443; *French Intelligencer*, 30 March–6 April 1652, p. 150.

83 *Mercurius Politicus*, 25 September–2 October 1651, p. 1101; *Mercurius Politicus*, 2–9 October 1651, p. 114.

the Dutch, "you let the ribald pen vomit out floods of reproaches, in hope to destroy this nation, who was then in strong labor with peace, amongst a wilderness of distractions."[84] Of course Dutch support of Charles II came not out of any ideological commitment, "not out of any love to him, but for fear the Parliament grow powerful, and so obscure the future of Hoghen Moghen."[85]

Naturally, the English were convinced that the Lord did not take kindly to anyone who betrayed his people, who attempted to contravene Providence. "The Dutch may too late repent what they have done," threatened *The Diary*. "The Lord is to be feared for his judgments which he executeth," mused Ralph Josselin ominously, "when the Hollander rejoiced in the false news of our fall, the enemy fell at Worcester."[86]

Just before the arrival of the Dutch ambassadors, the English press rehabilitated the most sensational tale of Dutch perfidy: the massacre at Amboyna. The newspapers reprinted testimonies of the "English-men who lately suffered martyrdom at Amboyna."[87] Two pamphlets soon appeared retelling the atrocity in full. One of them, that written by the republican friend of Samuel Hartlib, Benjamin Worsley, and admirer of Milton, John Hall, was commissioned by the Council of State.[88] The bloody tale of torture and murder was written in the language of Foxe's *Acts and Monuments*, the "martyred" Englishmen were all extremely pious men conferring with the preacher provided by the Dutch in their last moments, demanding forgiveness for their sins. At the instant of the execution "there arose a great darkness, with a sudden and violent gust of wind and tempest" which tore two of the Dutch ships from their anchors. A few days later God made his displeasure evident to all. William Dunckin, who had invented the story of English betrayal and informed the Dutch, fell on the grave of the Englishmen, and only rose three days later having gone insane. "A new sickness" befell Amboyna "which swept away about a thousand people," a sickness predicted by one of the martyred English, which could only be interpreted as "a token of the wrath of God for the barbarous tyranny of the Hollanders."[89] John Hall demanded retribution. "The breach being so

84 *Mercurius Politicus*, 25 September–2 October 1651, pp. 1101–1102; *A Seasonable Expostulation with the Netherlands* (Oxford, 1652), Thomason: 12 June 1652, p. 7.

85 *Mercurius Politicus*, 28 August–4 September 1651, pp. 1036–1037; *Mercurius Politicus*, 11–18 September 1651, p. 1067.

86 *The Diary*, 13–20 October 1651, p. 132; Josselin, *Diary*, 21 September 1651, p. 257; *Mercurius Politicus*, 25 September–2 October 1651, pp. 1100–1101.

87 *French Intelligencer*, 16–23 December 1651, p. 39; *Faithful Scout*, 5–12 December 1651, pp. 364–365.

88 Wilbur Cortez Abbott, *The Writings and Speeches of Oliver Cromwell* (Cambridge MA, 1939), Vol. II, p. 547. These pamphlets probably reflect the anti-Dutch feeling in the Council before the negotiations began. My claim here is that their propagandistic effect lasted longer than the Hollandophobia of the Council of State.

89 Thomas Ramsey, *Bloudy Newes from the East-Indies* (London, 1651), Thomason: 12 December 1651, pp. 5–8; *A Declaration and Narrative of the Proceedings of the*

national, and to this day unsatisfied," Hall reminded his readers, "and the blood there spilt no doubt crying loud, it had been injustice to have buried it in silence." "Now, since that yoke of kingship is taken off our necks," he implored his readers using typically republican language, "we should like men, whose shackles are taken off them while they are asleep, [to] leap up nimbly and make use of our liberty."[90]

Confrontations at sea soon provided the press with new atrocity stories. The Dutch, reported one newspaper, "have stript, whipped, and then hanged on the main mast an English man who was master of a ship they took, and threw all the men over board."[91] But it was the unfortunate story of Captain Henry Greene which truly captured the popular imagination. After taking a French ship, for which he had letters of marque, Greene and his crew were captured by a Dutch man-of-war. Despite their official papers, the Dutch captain insisted on calling the English "rogues, villains, and pirates," "cruelly beat Capt[ain] Green and his company, and said he would throw them all overboard." The English sailors were eventually taken to Amsterdam where they were held "for the space of about seven weeks in fetters and chains and in that time suffered much misery and want both of food and lodging."[92] The newspapers added an element to the tale – an element serving no doubt as a parable – which did not appear in the judicial proceedings. In this version the ship was blessed with the presence of a first officer called Oliver. Faced with a horrible storm which threatened to wreck the ship on the rocks, almost certainly an allegory for the Civil War, the ship was saved "by the blessing of God, and the care of the said Oliver." It was only after the ship/England had survived this travail with divine intervention that it was set upon by the treacherous Dutch. Oliver was "turned a drift in the boat; but providence protected him to the harbor of Portsmouth, from the violence and bloodthirstiness of the barbarous Hollander."[93]

The Dutch were clearly "an unthankful people," a people whose "want of gratitude and civility" to a nation "who next to God, may justly be styled her maker" was fickle at best. "O horrible ingratitude!" wailed the *Faithful Scout*, "what have you forgotten the days of old?" "Though we have done

Parliament of England, pp. 7–8; *Faithful Scout*, 5–12 December 1651, pp. 364–366; *French Intelligencer*, 16–23 December 1651, p. 39. John Hall's pamphlet was advertised in *A Perfect Diurnall*, 15–22 December 1651, p. 1550; *Mercurius Politicus*, 20–27 November 1651, p. 1236.

90 [John Hall], *A True Relation of the Unjust, Cruel, and Barbarous Proceedings against the English at Amboyna In the East-Indies, by the Netherlandish Governour and Council There* (London, 1651), Thomason: 29 November 1651, pp. i–viii.

91 *Perfect Passages*, 2–9 January 1652, p. 349.

92 Judges of court of Admiralty to Council of State, 19 May 1652, PRO, SP 46/96, f. 178; Whitelocke's *Annals*, BL, Add. 37345, 30 December 1651, f. 174.

93 *French Intelligencer*, 30 December – 6 January 1652, p. 56; *Faithful Scout*, 2–9 January 1652, pp. 396–397.

both the Dutch and Scots so many civilities, and enriched both those unthankful people, and thereby have deserved so much at both their hands," England's most popular author, William Lilly, commented, "yet they never did, nor they ever will affect us, nor will be ever any perfect friendship or league betwixt us."[94] In the wake of Worcester this was an ominous comparison indeed.

The image of the Dutch full of "domineering pride" had become a commonplace. "It is the nature of the Dutchmen to strike sail for their own profit, to offer any kindness where they perceive they may be any way the gainer," commented the author of one of the popular chapbooks describing the exploits of the thief James Hind. "We are high, blown up with wealth," observed the Dutch correspondent of the *Mercurius Politicus*, "therefore we vapor, and love our money better then the remembrance of all those ancient courtesies that are received from England."[95] Dutch treachery, pride, and self-interest naturally had religious implications. Although the Dutch still spoke in the accents of the godly, this was not to be confused with real religiosity. For the Dutch "hold Popish ... all that help them not." The Dutch were "bred statesmen, none of them being so nice of conscience, but they can turn out religion, to let in policy." Balthazar Gerbier, whose imperial projects were treated seriously by the Council of State at this time, attributed the Dutch behavior to a "strategem (hatched by a[n] Italian Devil, fostered by the Antichristian Father the Pope, and fomented by a world of malignants to boot)" which aimed to divide the Protestant cause. "Thou growest proud, and hast forgotten thy God," the popular almanac writer Nicholas Culpeper warned the Dutch, "mindest thy self; thy God knows how to bring thee poor again."[96]

All of this demanded retribution. The calls for punishment were issued forth in the most violent terms and with the most frequency by astrologers, who were enjoying an unprecedented popularity. William Lilly promised that "the vengeance of Almighty God is ready to be poured forth upon the Dutch for their too too much unthankfulness." He predicted that the English would "be a scourge unto the Dutch, for their pride and injuries

94 William Lilly, *Merlini Anglici Ephemeris* (London, 1651), sig. B3 (unpaginated); *A Seasonable Expostulation with the Netherlands*, p. 3; *Faithful Scout,* 13–20 February 1652, p. 444.

95 *A Perfect Account*, 25 February–3 March 1652, p. 481; *A Second Discovery of Hind's Exploits: or a Fuller Relation of his Ramble, Robberies, and Cheats in England, Ireland, Scotland with his Voyage to Holland* (London, 1652), Thomason: 19 November 1651, pp. 12–13; *A Perfect Account*, 25 February - 3 March 1652, p. 481; *Mercurius Politicus*, 12–19 February 1652, p. 1422.

96 *A True and Exact Character of the Lowe Countreys; Especially Holland: Or, The Dutchman Anatomized and Truly Dissected.* (London, 1652), Thomason: 15 March 1652, pp. 11–17; Gerbier, *A Discovery of Certain Notorious Stumbling-Blocks Which the Devill, the Pope, and the Malignants have Raised to put Nations at Variance.* (London, 1652), Thomason, 12 March 1652, pp. 1–2; Nicholas Culpeper, *An Ephemeris for the Year 1652* (London, 1652), Thomason: November 1651, sig. C3.

offered us these many years." Should the Dutch "justly provoke our state," the English would soon be "taking down their pride in all parts of the world, and in time making Amsterdam a synagogue of sinners, and Flushing an habitation of herring fishermen."[97] "Let the Hollander beware how he meddles with us," warned Culpeper, "until such time as he longs to be beaten." A war against England would make the Dutch "sensible of an invasion to better purpose than that of Alva." "The Dutch will be troublesome this year at sea," predicted another prognosticator, "but we shall make them tame enough quickly." "A dreadful judgement I know is hanging over all their heads," prophesied William Lilly, "less than half an age will make them despicable."[98]

Despite these vituperative attacks upon the Dutch character, most in England did not want to give them up for lost. "Nor can it be forgotten," the *Mercurius Politicus* reminded its readers, "how much of monarchy of late crept into the United Provinces, the relics of which are not yet extinct." "A republic [cannot] decline sooner into a tyranny," explained another pamphleteer, "than by continuing that shadow which decency constrains free governments to retain of monarchy, too long in one family (as the Dutch did)."[99] The reports of Dutch officials being punished for embezzlement only served to confirm English suspicions. Someone merely needed "to play the physician, to administer a strong purge to evacuate the corrupted humors; and like a good surgeon, rather than the whole body should perish, to cut off those rotten members, that have laboured to fell and ruin the state." The possibility of such a reformation allowed Balthazar Gerbier to continue to hope for "amity between two such potent nations, who are of one profession in matters of religion; of one and the self same strength by sea; and who being in peace may counterpoise all other parts of Europe."[100]

It is always difficult to measure the effect of printed material on the ideas and actions of the general public.[101] Nevertheless there is good evidence to suggest that English antipathy for the Dutch was on the increase after the

97 Lilly, *Annus Tenebrous*, pp. 18–19; William Lilly, *Merlini Anglici Ephemeris* (London, 1653), (unpaginated).

98 Lilly, *Annus Tenebrous*, p. 12; Lilly, *Merlini Anglici Ephemeris*, "To the Reader," sig. B3 (unpaginated); Nicholas Culpeper, *Catastrophe Magnatum: Or The Fall of Monarchie* (London, 1652), Thomason: 31 March 1652, p. 56; *A New Remonstrance of the Free-Born People of England* (London, 1651), Thomason: 14 November 1651, p. 5.

99 *Mercurius Politicus*, 29 April–6 May 1652, p. 1573; *A Perswasive to A Mutuall Compliance*, p. 24.

100 *French Intelligencer*, 4–11 February 1652, p. 83; *Mercurius Politicus*, 2–9 October 1651, p. 1118; 8–15 January 1652, p. 1337; 29 January–5 February 1652, pp. [1392–1393]; Gerbier, *A Discovery*, p. 3.

101 I realize that I am finessing a thorny methodological problem. There is simply limited material with which to assess the reading habits of the English during the revolutionary period. However, I think that the temporal correspondence of the new-found popular animosity and the lingual similarity to the press campaign suggests that many in England were deeply influenced by its arguments.

failure of the embassy of Strickland and St. John. John Donne's assessment that "we are content to be assured that the Devil has got the Dutchman" is confirmed by a variety of tangible manifestations of Hollandophobia.[102] Dr. Groenveld has shown that in the year 1651 English seizures of Dutch shipping more than doubled those of the previous year. The English Admiralty courts and the Council of State were deluged with petitions from Dutch merchants demanding release of their ships. But instead of restoring the ships the English responded with praise for their privateers in the popular press. "Here is news that the English have taken a Dutch vessel or two," admitted the *Perfect Account*, "but what is that unto those they have taken of the English." "The English ... are very successful and victorious, and have taken sundry rich prizes," crowed *The Faithful Scout*, "Gallant news! 'tis richly worth a penny."[103] When the Dutch ambassador extraordinary Adrian Pauw took his leave of England in June 1652, he particularly complained about English seizures of Dutch ships under pretext of letters of reprisal awarded against the French.[104]

More telling, perhaps, than the numerical evidence of ship seizures, is the evidence of personal malice that English sailors had for the Dutch. "The English master and his crew uttered all manner of abusive words and insults against us," complained the Dutch vice-admiral Jan Evertsen. Each time he came across an English ship in the Channel he was greeted with "many insolent speeches."[105] Verbal harassment was only the beginning. There were rumors in the United Provinces that English seamen had "cast above seventy Zeelanders overboard." In February 1652 the Zeeland Board of Admiralty insisted that the "exorbitant excesses of the English have grown worse" and that they "increase daily." Things had become so bad that the judges of the English High Court of Admiralty encouraged the Dutch victims of "the many cruel and barbarous acts of punishment and torture" to bring in their complaints. The Council of State tried in vain to stop the"cruelty and inhumanity of the people of this nation inhabiting on the maritime coast."[106] This was almost certainly a response to the anti-Dutch

102 John Donne to Lord Conway, [July 1652], PRO, SP 46/95, f. 376.

103 Groenveld, "English Civil Wars," p. 561; Rowen, *John De Witt*, pp. 65–66; Bod., Clar., Dep. C.172, Nalson Papers XVIII, ff. 308–309; Bod., Tanner MSS 54, f. 122; Whitelocke's *Annals*, BL, Add. 37345, 20 December 1651, f. 172; 12 January 1652, f. 175; "Advices from London," 22 February 1652, *CSPV*, p. 216; *Faithful Scout*, 5–12 December 1651, p. 364; *A Perfect Account*, 6–13 February 1652, p. 440; 1–8 October 1651, p. 311; *French Intelligencer*, 23–30 March 1652, p. 141; *Weekly Intelligencer*, 10–17 February 1652, p. 357; *Mercurius Politicus*, 4–11 December 1651, p. 1267; 12–19 February 1652, p. 1421. The relevant Admiralty records are in the PRO, at HCA 30/495–500.

104 Adrian Pauw to Council of State, 27 June 1652, in Birch, *Thurloe State Papers*, Vol. I, p. 210.

105 Evertsen to States General, 29 March 1652, Gardiner, *Letters and Papers*, Vol. I, pp. 134–135.

106 Zeeland Board of Admiralty to States General, 4 February 1652, Gardiner, *Letters and Papers*, Vol. I, p. 76; *Mercurius Politicus*, 16–23 October 1651, p. 1145; "Declaration of

campaign conducted in the press. "We are told," averred the Dutch correspondent of the *Mercurius Politicus*, "yours do not only search our ships for French commodities ... and abuse our men, but they talk of torturing, and tying them up by the thumbs, to make them confess, *as if you meant to be even with us for Amboyna.*" After the attack on Captain Greene had received full play in the press, *The French Intelligencer* reported that "Cap[tain] Smith met with some of the Hollanders, and hath meted the same measure to them again."[107] Anti-Dutch feeling was reaching new heights at just the moment that the negotiators in Westminster were beginning to hope for a mutually agreeable settlement and a Protestant alliance.

It is not surprising that English seagoing men and the inhabitants of the maritime towns reacted so quickly to the press campaign. Bernard Capp has shown that religious enthusiasts tended to congregate in towns "close to or on the sea." The navy was a "center of millenarian enthusiasm." Admiral Robert Blake was a committed republican, reportedly having proclaimed in Cadiz that "with the example afforded by London all kingdoms will annihilate tyranny and become republics."[108] The most recent students of the Commonwealth navy have also concluded that "the navy was a highly politicized, partisan force."[109]

The Dutch could not help but react to the English insults, tortures, and ship seizures. The "daily reports" of attacks by the English at sea led the Dutch "to murmur and surmise the worst, that you have a mind to break with this state." "Owing to the constant reprisals of the English," the Venetian diplomat in Paris observed upon the arrival of the Dutch ambassadors at Westminster, "at present the Dutch are more disposed to a breach." The *Mercurius Politicus* was right to say of the Dutch maritime provinces that "if you touch their ships, you take away their lives."[110]

Seagoing men were especially angry. "Above and under deck among the shippers," observed the Dutch correspondent to the *Mercurius Politicus*, "the blood and humors begin to boil ... these testy men you have so much stirred by your proceed[ing]s, like as the vintner with a stick at the bottom

the High Court of Admiralty of England," 16 February 1652, PRO, SP 46/96, ff. 180–181; Judges of the Admiralty to Council of State, 19 May 1652, PRO, SP 46/96, ff. 178–179; Council of State to Vice Admiral of Cornwall, 13 February 1652, PRO, SP 25/97, f. 129.

107 *Mercurius Politicus*, 12–19 February 1652, p. 1422 (my emphasis); *French Intelligencer*, 6–13 January 1652, p. 54.

108 Bernard Capp, *The Fifth Monarchy Men* (London, 1972), pp. 77, 80–81; Basadonna to Doge, 8 February 1651, *CSPV*, pp. 169–170.

109 Bernard Capp, *Cromwell's Navy: The Fleet and the English Revolution 1648–1660* (Oxford, 1989), p. 2. William Bennet Cogar, "The Politics of Naval Administration, 1649–1660" (Oxford, D.Phil. thesis, 1983), p. 7.

110 *Mercurius Politicus*, 30 October–6 November 1651, p. 1185; 1–8 January 1652, p. 1327; 15–22 January 1652, p. 1359; 29 January–5 February 1652, pp. [1390–1391]; Morosini to Doge, 19 December 1651, *CSPV*, p. 207.

of the Rhenish wine barrel." The "Dutch capt[ains] talk much of a war ... and despise your sea capt[ains] as they do them again." By early 1652, when the negotiations in Westminster were going along well, a naval correspondent to the *Perfect Diurnall* could "observe a far rougher temper in these Dutch captains then formerly." Bulstrode Whitelocke noted that "the Dutch captains were rough against the English and demanded restitution of their ships taken by the English."[111]

The merchant community in the Dutch maritime provinces was no less agitated. "The people of this nation are generally extremely mad with you," observed one of the Rump's political informers in Rotterdam, "the more because of your granting letters of mart to take their ships. Hereupon, many Zeelanders, Amsterdammers, and Rotterdammers, have this week been with the States General to present their grievances." Demands for retribution were most frequent and most violent in Zeeland, formerly one of the provinces most sympathetic to England. Now "the communality of Zeeland are stark mad," claiming "that things were come to such a pass, that the States durst not any longer deny it." "The great excitement of the most respectable merchants" in Zeeland soon forced an official response. A petition from the merchants of the major Zeeland towns demanded that "before they treated of any other matters" the provincial government "would have letters of mart granted them to take upon the English." When the provincial government hesitated, at least some merchants took out their letters of marque in the name of the Duke of York.[112] When reports began to arrive that the English had seized many Dutch ships in the Caribbean, an attack planned long before the Dutch diplomats arrived in England, it provoked a "great rage." The English seizures, wrote Edward Nicholas from The Hague, "hath much incensed the merchants of Amsterdam. In Zeeland the people from there come in great numbers tumultuously to [get] letters of reprisal against the English."[113]

Dutch Anglophobia was not limited to those who had direct experience of English malice. Polemicists who "print and publish what they please against England" were to be found throughout the United Provinces. Even in Amsterdam a broadside was printed "and dispersed up and down the

111 *Mercurius Politicus*, 6–13 November 1651, p. 1200; 19–26 February 1652, pp. 1434–1435; *Perfect Diurnall*, 9–16 February 1652, p. 1671; Whitelocke's *Annals*, BL, Add. 37345, 11 February 1652, f. 178.

112 Intelligence from Rotterdam, 9 January 1652, Nickolls, *Original Letters*, p. 80; *Mercurius Bellonius*, 9–16 February 1652, pp. 9, 12; *A Perfect Diurnall*, 23 February–1 March 1652, p. 1705; *Faithful Scout*, 30 January–6 February 1652, p. 432; *Weekly Intelligencer*, 13–20 January 1652, p. 323; , 6–13 February 1652, p. 377; *Mercurius Politicus*, 23–30 October 1651, p. 1167; 29 January–5 February 1652, p. [1393]; 4–11 March 1652, pp. 1471–1472; *CSPD*, 21 April 1652, p. 223; Zeeland Board of Admiralty to States General, 4 February 1652, Gardiner, *Letters and Papers*, Vol. I, pp. 75–78.

113 *Mercurius Politicus*, 28 February–4 March 1652, pp. 1451–1452; Nicholas to Hyde, 12 February 1652, Bod., Clar. 42, f. 385.

city, full of invectives against the Parliament of England, calling them rebels, traitors and bloodsuckers."[114] The effect was tremendous. "The whole population clamor loudly," reported a Venetian observer. It was well known that "the Hollander[s] in general express great hatred against England." There were even rumors that the Dutch were planning a lightning strike against England in which they would block up the Thames. "They give out high Dutch," announced the *Faithful Scout*, "as if they intend to bring us to low English."[115] The Dutch were not content with mere words. "There is nothing but threatenings of fire and sword against the English," ran one frequently printed account, "that they go in danger of their lives." There were reports of physical assaults in many of the major Dutch cities. "So enraged are the boors against the English," wrote the *Faithful Scout*, "that they do nothing but grin and show their tusks in the open streets."[116]

It would, of course, be a mistake to see Dutch political culture as monolithic. In fact, Dutch politics in the early modern period was dominated by intense party divisions, party divisions at the national, provincial, and local level. While there were moments of party quiescence, it only took a small spark to rekindle the fires of party warfare. Relations with England was just such a spark, and 1652 was just such a time.

Naturally the English popular press simplistically distinguished between the "tumultuous rabble" and the "wisdom and prudence of the States," "the desperate unsettled brains" and the "grave and solid party," "the giddy sort" and "the more sage people," in short between those agitating for war against England and those in favor of peace.[117] In fact, of course, the coalitions were much less clear cut. But there was a good deal of truth in the *Faithful Scout*'s isolation of the Dutch "sea-towns and royal butter-boxes" as those who would "rather dissolve in heat and fury, then condescend upon terms of peace and unity."[118] Popular Orangist sentiment demanded a war against republican England.

English actions coupled with effective Orangist propaganda had done a great deal to destroy the support for an English alliance which had once existed in Zeeland. When the States of Holland declared their support for

114 *Perfect Passages*, 13–27 February 1652, p. 390; *The French Intelligencer*, 6–13 January 1652, p. 54.

115 Paulucci to Morosini, 19 June 1652, *CSPV*, p. 253; *A Perfect Account*, 18–25 February 1652, p. 480; 7–14 April 1652, p. 536; *Faithful Scout*, 20–27 February 1652, p. 454; *Faithful Scout*, 27 February–5 March 1652, [p. 464]; *French Intelligencer*, 2–9 March 1652, p. 118.

116 *Faithful Scout*, 5–12 March 1652, p. 468; *Faithful Scout*, 19–26 March 1652, p. 485; *Faithful Scout*, 26 March–2 April 1652, p. 494; *French Intelligencer*, 9–16 March 1652, p.122; *Faithful Scout*, 30 March–6 April 1652, p. 146; *A Perfect Account*, 24–31 March 1652, p. 513; *Mercurius Politicus*, 12–19 February 1652, p. 1417; *Mercurius Politicus*, 4–11 March 1652, pp. 1468–1469.

117 *Faithful Scout*, 9–16 April 1652, p. 509; *A Perfect Account*, 5–12 November 1651, p. 353; *A Perfect Account*, 25 February–3 March 1652, p. 487.

118 *Faithful Scout*, 28 November–5 December 1651, p. 346.

an English alliance in the States General in early April, "the States and merchants of Zeeland rose up in angry fury, dissolved the Assembly, and vowed revenge upon the English." Attacks on English merchants were at their most frequent in Middleburgh and Flushing. Indeed, in Orangist Zeeland the States of Holland were popularly called "little better than traitors" for pursuing negotiations with England.[119]

The States of Holland, and presumably the governments of other provinces as well, were also less committed in their support of an English alliance than they had been the previous year. But, perhaps because of the republicanism they shared with the English Commonwealth, perhaps out of a sincere desire for a Protestant alliance, or perhaps merely because they felt it was "almost impossible for Holland to subsist without the friendship of England" the States continued to support an English alliance. As a result of the powerful role that Holland played in national politics, it did seem as if there was a split between the attitudes of the governed and those of the governors. There were "divers that covet after war; justifying it to be both necessary and lawful." Yet "the care and industry of their governors" was also "remarkable," doing everything "almost beyond their power to suppress" the popular Anglophobia. "The States Gen[eral]," it appeared, were "more prudent and wise then to hearken to the ayes of the scum of their nation." Should there be a war between England and the United Provinces, the *Perfect Passages* predicted it would "set all at difference at Amsterdam, and other places of chiefest importance."[120] So deep was anti-English sentiment among the people that there was "evident danger of mutiny." "The people in all the sea towns continue very mutinous," reported the *Weekly Intelligencer*, "and are no less angry with their own Governors then with the English." There were actually "tumults and risings" in Zeeland and the Holland towns of Rotterdam, Delft, Dordrecht, and The Hague, in which the English were labeled "traitors and conspirators to their religion and liberties." It was in this context that William Lilly could predict that the "unruly multitude and giddy people" would "let loose the reins of government, and become disobedient unto authority."[121]

119 *A Declaration of the High and Mighty Lords, The States of Holland, Concerning the Parliament and Commonwealth of England*... (London, 1652), Thomason: 5 April 1652. TT: E659(3), pp. 3–4; *Faithful Scout*, 27 February–5 March 1652, pp. 459, [464]; *Mercurius Politicus*, 18–25 March 1652, p. 1488; *Mercurius Politicus*, 17–24 June 1652, p. 1683.

120 *Perfect Passages*, 2–9 January 1652, p. 349; *Perfect Passages*, 9–16 January 1652, p. 361; *Weekly Intelligencer*, 23–30 March 1652, p. 403; *Severall Proceedings*, 8–15 April 1652, p. 2076; *A Perfect Account*, 10–16 March 1652, p. 503; *Faithful Scout*, 23–30 April 1652, pp. 523–524; *Mercurius Politicus*, 30 October – 6 November 1651, p. 1186; 29 January – 5 February 1652, p. [1391]; 26 February – 4 March 1652, p. 1449.

121 *A Declaration of the High and Mighty Lords*, pp. 4–5; *Mercurius Politicus*, 29 January – 5 February 1652, p. [1393]; *Mercurius Politicus*, 26 February–4 March 1652, p. 1452; *Dutch Spy*, 17–25 March 1652, pp. 1–2; Lilly, *Annus Tenebrous*, pp. 4–5; *Weekly Intelligencer*, 9–16 March 1652, p. 384.

The death of William II had unleashed the full force of party play in the United Provinces. Naturally local factions attempted to gain support from more powerful national groupings. In the wake of William's death it was the republican States party – "Barnvelt's faction" – which had largely succeeded in gaining control in Zeeland and Holland. But its opponents, the supporters of the Prince of Orange, were actively using antipathy to the English to revive their political position. "Being troubled in mind" by the English attacks on Dutch shipping, the Dutch correspondent to the *Mercurius Politicus* explained, the Dutch "now reckon up all grievances, and say, the State is some millions in debt, which how it should come about, they do not understand; and therefore talk of having an account." The "good patriots and Republicans" were anxious for peace with England, "knowing that war would only bring misery and tribulation," the Dutch ambassadors in England were informed, but the Orangist "boutefeus" were doing all they could "to spark a war."[122]

Faced with English attacks on their shipping and violent criticism from their political opponents the governors of the United Provinces had to take action. They adopted two complementary strategies. First, they prohibited all commerce with England. This was done, presumably, to prevent Dutch ships being taken as a consequence of the English Navigation Act and as the least provocative way to register their official disapproval of the seizure of Dutch ships by English seamen. As a treaty of alliance with England began to look increasingly probable, the Dutch withdrew this embargo. But within a fortnight official reports came in of the English fleet's taking large numbers of Dutch ships off Barbados. Not only did the Dutch reinstate the embargo but "in retaliation" for the English attack they gave "strict charge and command, that all ships and goods whatsoever belonging to the English Nation, be forthwith seized upon." "There is nothing more to be feared, then a war," wrote the *French Intelligencer* echoing the sentiments of the merchant community.[123] Second, the States General decided to equip a large fleet of 150 men-of-war "to restore the freedom of commerce." Seamen had demanded such a fleet as early as December 1651. Given the frequency of riots in the Dutch sea towns there seems little reason to doubt that this move was in fact an attempt "to appease the common people." The preparation of this huge fleet, "their great Armada, which they say will be accounted, the world's wonder" accentuated national feeling in the United

122 Nicholas to Ormonde, 11 July 1651, Carte, *Collection*, Vol. II, pp. 44–45; *Mercurius Politicus*, 4–11 March 1652, p. 1472; intelligence from The Hague addressed to Dutch ambassadors, Longleat House, Whitelocke MSS XI, ff. 89–90.

123 *A Perfect Account*, 7–15 January 1652, p. 425; *Perfect Diurnall*, 12–19 January 1652, p. 1606; *French Intelligencer*, 30 March–6 April 1652, p. 151; *Mercurius Politicus*, 11–18 December 1651, p. 1184; *A Declaration of the High and Mighty Lords*, pp. 3–4; *Weekly Intelligencer*, 30 March–6 April 1652, pp. 407–408; Paige to Paynter and Clerke, Steckley, *John Paige*, 6 March 1652, p. 66.

Provinces. Despite official Dutch statements, "to prevent all misinterpretations, evil thoughts, and mistrusts," that "they would not act anything that should be prejudicial to the Commonwealth of England," the English could not but be apprehensive. Bulstrode Whitelocke was not alone in musing that the embargo and the huge Dutch fleet "raiseth thoughts that they intend a war against England."[124]

At the same time, then, that talks between English politicians and Dutch diplomats were inching towards a mutually acceptable treaty of alliance, popular polemics were fanning the flames of popular hatred.[125] Despite government-inspired pleas in the English press to leave foreign policy "to those that are in place, which stand upon giants' shoulders, see with many eyes, and hear with many ears," Anglo-Dutch maritime hostility was at its worst in the first half of 1652. While informed of the apparent success of the Westminster negotiations, the Venetian diplomat Michiel Morosini was sure that "the constant maritime aggressions" would lead ineluctably to "an open declaration of war later on." "The damages and indignities offered to each other," commented that always perceptive political observer Edward Hyde, "may possibly not be so easily reconciled as is apprehended."[126] Both sides were armed to the teeth, imbued with deep hatred for the other, only waiting for a spark to ignite a war.

What, then, was the catalyst which finally precipitated the war? What destroyed the negotiation process just as it was on the brink of succeeding? Ostensibly it was a revival of the age-old dispute over sovereignty of the sea. On 19 May the English and Dutch admirals, both supported by newly reinforced fleets, faced each other in the Downs. When Admiral Blake saluted the Dutch admiral Van Tromp in the customary manner,

124 *Weekly Intelligencer*, 23–30 December 1651, p. 304; 24 February–2 March 1652, p. 370; *Mercurius Politicus*, 25 December–1 January 1652, p. 1316; *Mercurius Politicus*, 29 January–5 February 1652, p. [1393]; *Mercurius Politicus*, 12–19 February 1652, p. 1422; *French Intelligencer*, 24 February–2 March 1652, p.112; *Perfect Passages*, 26 December–2 January 1652, p. 395; *Perfect Passages*, 13–20 February 1652, p. 385; *A Perfect Account*, 11–18 February 1652, p. 490; *A Perfect Account*, 17–24 March 1652, pp. 509–510; *Mercurius Bellonius*, 25 February–3 March 1652, pp. 26–27; *Faithful Scout*, 12–19 March 1652, p. [480]; Dutch Ambassadors to States General, 10 March 1652, Bod., Tanner MSS 55, f. 164; "Thurloe's Review," PRO, SP 103/46, f. 223; Whitelocke's *Annals*, BL, Add. 37345, f. 188.

125 Despite its military might, the Rump was a regime with limited political and cultural resources. Woolrych has pointed out that it was a regime which was unpopular among many in the political nation, and knew it. Austin Woolrych, *Commonwealth to Protecorate* (Oxford, 1982), p. 7. Many of its leaders were also committed to notions of providence which limited their will to attempt to stem the tide of events with which they might not have been completely sympathetic. As a result, the press campaign and the resultant popular hatred of the Dutch took on a force of their own, a force which other seventeenth-century English political regimes might have been able to limit.

126 *A Perfect Account*, 17–24 March 1652, p. 512; Morosini to Doge, 18 March 1652, *CSPV*, p. 217; Hyde to Nicholas, 29 March 1652, Bod., Clar. 43, f. 48.

requesting the usual striking of the topsail in deference to English sovereignty, "Van Tromp saluted with a broad side." The Dutch were denying that they were in a "private Channel belonging to England."[127] The ensuing battle ultimately ended the negotiations then on the verge of conclusion in Westminster, leading within a month to a declaration of war. The Dutch "have laid it as their settled design to obtain to themselves the dominion and sovereignty of those seas," declared the English Council of State, "thereby not only give what rules of commerce they please, but to destroy the trade and shipping of this Commonwealth, as inconsistent (in their apprehension) with absoluteness and command at sea which they aspire after."[128]

It is true, of course, that there had been repeated minor clashes between Commonwealth navy and Dutch seamen. The English press did reissue John Selden's *Mare Clausum*, newly translated by Marchamont Nedham, and John Boroughs' *The Soveraignty of the British Seas*. The Dutch admiralty courts did once again listen to legal arguments surrounding the classic dispute.[129] But this merely begs the question. Why did this dispute flare up into a war only in 1652?

Naturally the popular antagonism and the naval armaments race between the English and the Dutch greatly increased tensions at sea, making a confrontation all the more likely. But the battle seems to have been fought over an issue of principle, an issue that was quite new. Dutch seamen were being accused of exciting "contempt and disdain for the English nation and government." They were calling the Commonwealth navy "traitors." "If there was a king" in England they would strike sail, claimed Van Tromp, "but being the oldest States they would not." When one Captain Johnson required another group of Dutch naval vessels "to strike sail, in obedience and honor to the States of England," the Dutch admiral responded, "that although they never cut off a king's head yet they were the ancientest

127 *Mercurius Pragmaticus*, 18–25 May 1652, pp. 7–8; *Weekly Intelligencer*, 18–25 May 1652, p. 468.

128 Council of State to Levant Company, 23 July 1652, PRO, SP 105/144, f. 47.

129 For conflicts over the flag see: *Weekly Intelligencer*, 25 March–1 April 1651, p. 111; *Weekly Intelligencer*, 10–17 February 1652, pp. 358–359; *Weekly Intelligencer*, 23–30 March 1652, p. [406]; *Dutch Spy*, 24–31 March 1652, pp. 12–13; *The Diary*, 13–20 October 1651, p. 32; *Mercurius Politicus*, 16–23 October 1651, pp. 1148–1149; 27 May–3 June 1652, p. 1640; *Faithful Scout*, 17–24 October 1651, p. 310; *Faithful Scout*, 26 March–2 April 1652, p. 490; *Perfect Passages*, 28 November–5 December 1651, p. 341; *French Occurrences*, 17–24 May 1652, pp. 14–15; Whitelocke's *Annals*, BL, Add. 37345, 20 October 1651, f. 164; BL, Add. 37345, 27 March 1652, f. 188; Evertsen to States General, 29 March 1652, Gardiner, *Letters and Papers*, pp. 134–135. For the reprinting of the pamphlets see the advertisements in *Perfect Diurnall*, 26 January–2 February 1652, p. [1646]; *Mercurius Politicus*, 12–19 February 1652, p. 1424; and the comment in Oxenden's commonplace book, BL, Add. 54332, f. 38. For the Dutch Admiralty courts see *Mercurius Politicus*, 13 November 1651, p. 1200; *Faithful Scout*, 7–14 November 1651, p. 330; *Weekly Intelligencer*, 11–18 November 1651, p. 351.

States."[130] This attitude of the Dutch navy was not altogether surprising. Van Tromp, who "hath so great an influence upon the mariners and seamen, that what way soever he bears up his helm, they will steer after him," was a well-known Orangist. He "hath declared for the Royal-party," reported the *French Occurrences*, "and, its said, is much inclined to the cause of the K[ing] of Scots, who hath often times solicited him to the quarrel." By negotiating with the English, Van Tromp had long maintained, "we tread under our feet the lion and honor of our country." In this context, the rumors that Van Tromp wanted "nothing more then to beget a war betwixt the two States" is quite understandable.[131]

The ritual and symbolism of the Dutch fleet confirms that it had taken up the cause of monarchy. Dutch men-of-war were spotted with "the King of Scot's colors on their topsails." Despite demands from the States General that the colors of the House of Orange be withdrawn from all public places, Van Tromp insisted that his fleet fly the Orangist flag. At the battle of the Downs, the colors of the House of Orange were clearly visible on the "admiral's main-mast."[132] Apparently the Dutch admiralty had accepted the arguments of the Scots agent William MacDowell that "all contracts have been made betwixt the successive kings of England, their lawful heirs, and the High and Mighty States General, and not with England." "The respect they had formerly shewed upon those encounters [with English ships of war], was because the ships were the king's, and for the good intelligence they had with the crown," the admiralty instructed Van Tromp, "but they had no reason to continue the same in this alteration of government." Van Tromp had no objections, ordering his fleet "not to strike sail to the English, upon pain of death, unless they have the Scotch king's colors."[133]

130 Evertsen to States General, 29 March 1652, Gardiner, *Letters and Papers*, Vol. I, p. 133; *Bloudy Newes from Holland* (London, 1652), Thomason: 17 March 1652, pp. 3–4; *French Occurrences*, 17–24 May 1652, p. 16.

131 *A Declaration of the L. Admiral Vantrump Concerning The King of Scots, and the Parliament of England ...* (London, 1652), Thomason: 25 June 1652, p. 5; *Weekly Intelligencer*, 27 May–2 June 1651, pp. 182–183; *Weekly Intelligencer*, 22–28 June 1652, p. 506; *French Occurrences*, 24–31 May 1652, p. 24; *French Occurrences*, 7–14 June 1652, p. 35; *French Occurrences*, 21–28 June 1652, pp. 54–56; newsletter from London, 31 May 1651, Worcester College, Clarke MSS 19, f. 13v; Sir Philip Warwick, "Memoirs," HL, HM 41956, p. 103.

132 *Faithful Scout*, 19–26 March 1652, p. 488; *Mercurius Politicus*, 18–25 March 1652, p. 1487; Van Tromp's instructions to his fleet, 15 May 1652, Gardiner, *Letters and Papers*, Vol. I, pp. 167–168. See also Gardiner's perceptive comments on p. 167. For the decree against the Prince of Orange's colors and the popular response, see *Weekly Intelligencer*, 4–11 May 1652, p. 451; *Mercurius Politicus*, 29 April–6 May 1652, p. 1578, 1581; *Perfect Passages*, 7–14 May 1652, p. 264.

133 *Anglia Liberata: or, The Rights of the People of England Maintained Against the Pretences of the Scottish King, As They Are Set Forth in an Answer to the Lords Ambassadors Propositions of England* (London, 1651), Thomason: 4 October 1651, pp. 2–3; Hyde, *History*, p. 785 (he is quoting from an official document); Anthony Young to Lenthall, 14 May 1652, Gardiner, *Letters and Papers*, Vol. I, p. 181; *Faithful Scout*, 18–25 June 1652,

The issue then was not the old dispute over sovereignty of the sea, but an argument about whether the Commonwealth had the same rights as the English Monarchy had had. Selden and Boroughs, for all of their learned argumentation, were not relevant in this context. They had written under the monarchy, and were defending the rights of the kings of England. Even the republication of the Venetian tract *Dominium Maris* did not completely serve the purpose because the author of the preface had ineptly compared the claims to those of monarchies, failing to make an argument based on national sovereignty. Belatedly the Rump understood the issue at stake. "The late clash that broke out 'twixt us and Holland," explained the future poet laureate James Howell, occurred because "upon this change of government and devolution of interest from kingly power to a Commonwealth there may happen some question touching the primitive and inalienable right that Great Britain claims to the sovereignty of her own seas." Though Howell did not receive the commission to pen the new treatise as he would have liked, the Council of State did ask Bulstrode Whitelocke to do the job. Whitelocke soon found a case for "maintaining the right of the Commonwealth in the dominion of the British Seas." Not surprisingly he declared the sovereignty "to be in the nation of England."[134] The dispute between England and the United Provinces had returned to a question of recognition of the regicide republic.

As soon as the Rump heard of the battle between Van Tromp and Blake in the Downs it despatched the naval expert Dennis Bond and the pro-Dutch Cromwell to the Cinque Ports to investigate the situation. After interviewing Dutch prisoners of war as well as the English naval commanders Cromwell was convinced that the Dutch had precipitated the conflict. "The imperiousness of the Hollander was so great," he told the Rump on 25 May, "that satisfaction must be given for that unhappy breach."[135]

The battle in the Downs freed the English popular press to print all sorts

p. 588; *French Occurrences*, 14–21 June 1651, p. 40; *A Perfect Account*, 2–9 June 1652, p. 600.

134 *Dominium Maris: Or, the Dominion of the Sea. Expressing the Title, which the Venetians Pretend unto the Sole Dominion, and Absolute Sovereignty of the Adriatick Sea, Commonly called The Gulph of Venice* (London, 1652), Thomason: 15 May 1652. TT:E795(1), sigs. A4–B; James Howell to Council of State, May 1652, BL, Add. 35838, f. 370; Whitelocke's *Annals*, BL, Add. 37345, 23 June 1652, f. 206; BL, Add. 37345, 24 June 1652, f. 206. Howell's letter is also noticed by Daniel Woolf in his "Conscience, Constancy and Ambition in the Career and Writings of James Howell," in John Morril, Paul Slack, and Daniel Woolf (eds.), *Public Duty and Private Conscience in Seventeenth-Century England* (Oxford, 1993), pp. 270–271. Given that Whitelocke took up the proposal before the war broke out, I am not convinced by Woolf's claim that Howell made his proposal "at some point after the start of the first Dutch War in 1652."

135 Paulucci to Morosini, 8 May 1652, *CSPV*, p. 231; 27 May 1652, p. 243; *CSPD*, 24 May 1652, p. 256; examinations before Cromwell and Bond, 22 May 1652, Bod., Clar. Dep. c172N, Nalson Papers XVIII, f. 336; *French Occurrences*, 24–31 May 1652, p. 24; newsletter from Westminster, 22 May 1652, Worcester College, Clarke MSS 22, ff. 94–95; newsletter from Westminster, 25 May 1652, Worcester College, Clarke MSS 22, f. 17; Co. Thompson, "Notes Upon the Dutch War," Bod., Clar. 47, f. 178r. For Cromwell's earlier

of anti-Dutch propaganda. Dutch versions of the conflict at sea were quickly denounced as mere "legend" which could be easily contradicted by "the inhabitants in Dover, and hundreds of the country, then present on the shore."[136] Far from punishing the nefarious Van Tromp, the States General were said to have declared "that he had not done anything but what tended to the freedom of the people, and the honor of his country." He was ostensibly received in Amsterdam with such "abundance of solemnity and ceremony that Augustus Caesar himself never return'd more regally laden with victorious palms into the Senate of Rome." If there was any remorse, it was not for "what late was done, but rather for the ill success." "The boors begin to be much exasperated against the English," reported the *French Occurrences*, "belching forth many imprecations and oaths, for an open war with England." The only issue in dispute was "whether their fear and hate be greater towards us, or the Spaniard."[137]

News of the battle and the subsequent expositions of Dutch attitudes had an immediate effect. Concerned that "many people" were "highly incensed" the Council of State granted a protective guard to the Dutch ambassadors. Proposals to declare war immediately and to dismiss the Dutch ambassadors without allowing for any further audience were defeated in the Rump by only two votes. Most people suspected that "the orders of General Tromp were at variance with the instructions given to the Dutch ambassadors." The Venetian agent claimed that the Rumpers were "clamorous ... in their demands for satisfaction." "There has been a hot and sharp debate in Parliament on the late occurrence, which is regarded here as a settled design and undertaking," wrote the Dutch ambassadors, "they appear to be determined on a formal revenge."[138] In its official answer to the Dutch ambassadors, the Rump declared that the "Dutch have an intention by force to usurp the known rights of England in the Seas, to destroy the fleets that are under God, their walls and bulwarks, and thereby to expose the Commonwealth to invasion at their pleasure."[139]

pro-Dutch attitude, which was typical rather than exceptional, see Rowen, *John De Witt*, p. 65; Groenveld, "English Civil Wars," p. 557.

136 *Weekly Intelligencer*, 18–25 May 1652, p. 470; 8–15 June 1652, p.491; 22–28 June 1652, pp. 505–506.

137 *French Occurrences* 31 May–7 June 1652, p. 32; *French Occurrences*, 14–21 June 1652, p. 48; *Mercurius Pragmaticus*, 25 May–1 June 1652, pp. 15–16; *A Perfect Account*, 26 May–2 June 1652, pp. 591–[592]; *Weekly Intelligencer*, 8–15 June 1652, p. 487; *The Declaration and Resolution of the States of Holland, Touching the Parliament and Commonwealth of England* ... (London, 1652), Thomason: 28 May 1652, p. 8. The analogy between Van Tromp and Augustus captures his perceived anti-republican fervor.

138 Whitelocke's *Annals*, BL, Add. 37345, 22 May 1652, f. 203; *CSPD*, 20 May 1652, p. 250; Paulucci to Morosini, 27 May 1652, *CSPV*, p. 243; *CSPV*, 3 June 1652, p. 245; Dutch ambassadors to Van Tromp, 26 May 1652, Gardiner, *Letters and Papers*, Vol. I, pp. 239–240.

139 Whitelocke's *Annals*, 10 June 1652, BL, Add. 37345, f. 205; *French Occurrences*, 7–14 June 1652, p. 39.

There were of course some both within the Rump and outside it who wanted very much to avoid a war with the Dutch. The Amsterdam merchant Henry May was no doubt right to predict that "there will be many in this cause troubled in conscience." One should not, however, overestimate Protestant opposition to the war. Hugh Peter and Henry Vane did find it difficult to accept the conflict, but the more apocalyptic Thomas Harrison had opposed negotiating with the Dutch as early as March. Not everyone interpreted the workings of Providence in the same way. What is perhaps more significant is that a majority of Rumpers appeared willing to accept the terms set forth in the treaty before the battle in the Downs whereas after that battle most Rumpers demanded satisfaction from the Dutch.[140] Attitudes towards the Dutch polity were not monolithic, but in 1652 most Rumpers were firmly committed to a Protestant and a republican foreign policy.

As soon as Cromwell and Bond returned from the Cinque Ports the Rump began its preparations for war. Thurloe was ordered to prepare an official account of the battle between Van Tromp and Blake for the press. The Council of State instructed the Committee of Foreign Affairs to prepare for a general embargo of all shipping. The English navy was ordered "to lose no time" in attacking the Dutch fishery and in disrupting their Eastland trade.[141] Not surprisingly the press was soon filled with reports of new battles off the English coasts, of new seizures of huge numbers of Dutch ships.[142] The Dutch ambassadors were right to warn Van Tromp that "preparations and arrangements are being made as though an open rupture had taken place."[143]

It was in a situation full of "irritation and excitement" that the Dutch

[140] Violet Rowe, *Sir Henry Vane the Younger* (London, 1970), p. 147; R. P. Stearns, *The Strenuous Puritan: Hugh Peter 1598–1660* (Urbana, 1954), p. 389; Henry May, *XXX Christian and Politick Reasons Wherefore England and the Low-Countries May not have Warres with Each Other* (London, 1652), Thomason: 15 June 1652, pp. 3–5. There is, of course, a venerable tradition which claims that there was a peace party in the Rump (Worden, *Rump*, p. 302; Gardiner, *Letters and Papers*, Vol. II, pp. 192–193). Advocates of alliance with the Dutch obviously existed, but the discomfort which some Rumpers displayed was with the high terms demanded of the Dutch ambassadors not with the demands for satisfaction. See Whitelocke's *Annals* 1 July (BL, Add. 37345) in which he notes the displeasure of some that "so high terms were insisted upon by the Parliament," f. 208; and *CJ*, 24 June 1652, p. 145. But, the very next day, the Rump did vote for demands for satisfaction.

[141] *CSPD*, 20 May 1652, p. 249; *CSPD*, 24 May 1652, pp. 255–256; *CSPD*, 25 May 1652, p. 258; instructions to Blake, Bod., Clar. 43, f. 159.

[142] *Weekly Intelligencer*, 25 May–1 June 1652, p. 478; *Faithful Scout*, 4–11 June 1652, p. 572; *Mercurius Politicus*, 3–10 June 1652, p. 1645; 10–17 June 1652, pp. 1671–1672; *A Perfect Account*, 9–16 June 1652, p. 601; *Weekly Intelligencer*, 8–15 June 1652, p. 493; *Mercurius Pragmaticus*, 18–25 May 1652, p. 8; Whitelocke's *Annals*, BL, Add. 37345, 12 June 1652, f. 205.

[143] Dutch Ambassadors to Van Tromp, 23 May 1652, Gardiner, *Letters and Papers*, Vol. I, p. 239.

sent Lord Pauw as ambassador extraordinary. Though his words were soothing – he duly reminded the Rump of "the common religion and liberty" they shared with the Dutch – his mission was hopeless. It soon appeared that he was powerless to negotiate. Pauw was only able to provide "dilatory excuses" according to one hostile commentator. "It's conceived [Pauw] comes to spin out time, and thereby to gain advantages," warned one army newsletter. "Intelligent persons" knew "for certain there will be a war between the two states." After more than a month of fruitless diplomatic activity the Dutch found themselves unable to explain away the confrontation in the Downs. "War may now be considered as declared" was the Venetian agent's correct assessment as the Dutch ambassadors left London.[144]

War between England and the United Provinces broke out not because of their irreconcilable economic differences, but because popular images had been created on each side of the North Sea which made it impossible to negotiate a peaceful settlement. Algernon Sidney, who as a member of the Council of State was in a position to know, later recalled that the "war was not brought on by a contrariety of interests."[145] Dutch Orangists saw the English as perfidious regicides whose very state was illegitimate and whose religion was heresy. The English, by contrast, had come to see the Dutch as fallen brethren, men who had been seduced by Mammon and monarchy. Although the Dutch diplomats in Westminster were doing much to change the Council of State's image of the United Provinces, their negotiations were overtaken by events. Popular antipathy – Providence in the eyes of many Rumpers – was ultimately more powerful than diplomacy.

144 Paulucci to Morosini, 11 June 1652, *CSPV*, p. 249; 19 June 1652, *CSPV*, p. 253; 2 July 1652, p. 255; Dutch Ambassadors to Council of State, 3 June 1652, Gardiner, *Letters and Papers*, pp. 270–271; newsletter from Westminster, 12 June 1652, Worcester College, Clarke MSS 22, ff. 104v–105; *French Occurrences*, 7–14 June 1652, pp. 34–35; newsletter, 18 June 1652, Bod., Clar. 43, f. 190. Pauw apparently called the clash in the Downs "an accidental chance" and blamed the English for acting so precipitately: Edward Conway to George Rawdon, 30 June 1652, HL, HA 14355.

145 Algernon Sidney, "Court Maxims," Warwickshire Record Office, [f. 172].

Coda: the popular apocalyptic context

For the English political nation these were special times indeed; each event was replete with ideological significance. Apocalyptics were convinced they were witnessing the dawning of the last days. "All things conspire to shew that the end of the world is at hand," the editor of the *Weekly Intelligencer* told his readers, "for not only in Christendom, but beyond it the presages have manifested themselves." "Antichrist shall be destroyed by the brightness of Christ's coming," Culpeper knew from the stars, "neither shall you see the effects of that Eclipse [of] 1654 passed, before it be accomplished." This was no time to be lukewarm.[1] Naturally these shakings in the world were not compatible with earthly monarchy. "You shall shine forth to other nations," Cromwell told the Rump, "who shall emulate the glory of such a pattern" of Commonwealth "and through the power of God turn into the like." Nicholas Culpeper knew that the time had come to "bring a new Government into the world different from Kingly Government."[2] These opinions could easily be turned against the Dutch whose Protestantism was now seen to be lukewarm, whose republicanism was perceived to be nominal, for Englishmen had been taught to believe that before "God destroy the Pope, he shall pour out his vial on some Protestant or Lutheran

1 *Weekly Intelligencer*, 17–24 June 1651, p. 208; Nicholas Culpeper, *An Ephemeris for the Year 1652* (London, 1652), Thomason: November 1651, p. 19. See also John Owen, *The Advantage of the Kingdome of Christ in the Shaking of the Kingdomes of the World*, sermon preached to Parliament 24 October 1651. (Oxford, 1651), pp. 25–26; *A Perfect Diurnall*, 22–29 September 1651, p. 1326; ; Stephen Marshall, *A Sermon Preached To The Right Honourable the Lord Mayor, the Court of Aldermen of the City of London, at their Anniversary Meeting on Easter Monday April 1652* (London, 1653). Thomason: 11 May 1653, p. 19. All of these themes are commented on by a sermon of William Ames reprinted on 30 November 1651, *The Saints Security, Against Seducing Spirits*. (London, 1652). Thomason: 30 November 1651, p. 1.

2 Cromwell to William Lenthall, 4 September 1650, in *The Letters and Speeches of Oliver Cromwell with Olucidations by Thomas Carlyle*, edited by S. C. Lomas (London, 1904) Vol. II, pp. 108–109; Culpeper, *An Ephemeris for 1652*, p. 15. See also *Weekly Intelligencer*, 2–9 September 1651, p. 273; William Lilly, *Monarchy, or No Monarchy in England*. (London, 1651). Thomason: 6 August 1651, p. 55; memoranda to Hyde, Bod., Clar. 41, f. 28.

Church which made profession of the Gospel against Popery, but obeyed it not."[3]

Classical republicans also saw the urgency in combatting any who supported a restoration of the Stuarts. As a newly formed republic, England "must look to have all those for enemies, that were familiars and retainers to the tyrant." The Dutch, one pamphleteer explained, had shown just such "unnatural ingratitude" by "fomenting ... the Royal party against the Parliament of England." Clearly they were prepared to "become an Egyptian plague unto us."[4] Although the Dutch had once seemed like "the Israelites passing the Red Sea," they now appeared to be dominated by "imperiousness of spirit." William Lilly consequently predicted defeat for the "ambitious Hollander." "It is God's way," warned the *Mercurius Politicus* ominously, "to suffer the rabble of his enemies by seeming advantages to grow very insolent before their ruin."[5]

Certainly the navy did not see the war against the Dutch as a battle fought for economic gain. All indications serve to vindicate the claims of *Mercurius Politicus* that there was "a very great resolution in all the officers of our fleet, to stand up for the interest of the Common-Wealth." "The Lord (appearing mightily for his people in times of greatest danger)," wrote one naval man in the wake of the battle of the Downs, "wonderfully preserved the life of our admiral." Robert Blake himself invoked the blessing of "righteous God." "We had the strong God on our side," agreed Rear Admiral Nehemiah Bourne, "who would judge between the nations." "This is the first of God's appearing for us by sea," he ecstatically proclaimed, "giving us great boldness to believe that the war was his." "I am very confident upon very safe grounds of faith," wrote Bourne drawing the obvious corollary, "that [the Dutch] should be as driven stubble before the whirlwind of the Lord."[6] The entire fleet, joined by "some particular congregations in London," "kept several days of humiliation" to put them in the right frame of mind to do God's work.[7]

3 Robert Parker, *The Mystery of the Vialls Opened.* (London, 1650), Thomason: 21 August 1650, p.5. Much of this argument, indeed eschatological thinking in general, was refined in the two-year struggle against Charles II and Covenanting Scotland. That these arguments had been current for so long makes it exceedingly likely that these arguments were neither hard for Englishmen to understand nor believe. See for example Cromwell's letters in *Letters and Speeches to Cromwell*, Vol. II, pp. 109, 123, 137, 140–141, 151.

4 *Mercurius Politicus*, 10–17 April 1651, p. 719; *A Seasonable Expostulation with the Netherlands* (Oxford, 1652), Thomason: 12 June 1652, pp. 1–2.

5 *Faithful Scout*, 28 May–4 June 1652, p. 564; *Mercurius Politicus*, 23 September–1 October 1651, pp. 1099–1100; John Lilly, *Merlini Anglici Ephemeris* (1651), n.p.

6 *Mercurius Politicus*, 3–10 June 1652, pp. 1651, [1656]; *A Perfect Account*, 19–26 May 1652, pp. 578–579; Blake to Lenthall, 20 May 1652, Gardiner, *Letters and Papers*, p. 195; [Nehemiah Bourne], *The Copy of a Letter of the Reare-Admiral of the English Fleet for the Common Wealth of England, to an Eminent Merchant in London* (London, 1652), pp. 4, 6, 7.

7 *Perfect Diurnall*, 31 May–7 June 1652, p. 1927; *Several Proceedings*, 3–10 June 1652, p. 2207; *French Occurences*, 31 May–7 June 1652, p. 27.

The reaction of civilian society was similar. Retribution was the most common theme. "There is nothing like a bastinado to bring these poor Johns and pickled herrings to their senses again," opined the *Mercurius Bellonius*. John Owen lamented that the Dutch "should join with the great Antichristian interest." The Dutch had appealed to heaven to support their cause, "and so heretofore had the Scots" commented the *Weekly Intelligencer*, "but the event hath since taught them which is the cause that Providence will own." "The Lord will make them a rod of his wrath to be chastised" wrote another journalist. Ralph Josselin knew that Holland was the Tyre – the maritime city which was destroyed because of its inordinate materialism and its failure to aid its ally Jerusalem – described in Ezekiel. All of these themes were graphically displayed in a broadside published on the eve of the departure of the Dutch ambassadors. In *Dr. Dorislaus Ghost* all of the canonic tales of Dutch perfidy were retold, using powerful religious imagery. In the center of the print a pristine virgin is matched against a worldly Dutchman, whose pendant represents a Lion's Paw obscuring the sun, representing the efforts of Lord Pauw to obscure the truth of the Dutch attack in the Downs. The print's commentary describes the scene as "Dr. Dorislaus's Ghost representing truth, brought forth of the grave by time." In these last days of the world Dutch crimes would be revealed and punished.[8]

The outbreak of the Anglo-Dutch War, then, appears very different when evaluated in the context of the ideological debates which loomed so large during the Interregnum. The cause of the war was economic only in the sense that the English believed lingering Orangism to have led the previously virtuous Dutch Republic down the path towards a base materialism. Not only was the political language in which the war was justified not the language of economic interest, but every indication suggests that the English economic community was very unhappy with the outbreak of the war. The powerful London merchant John Greene knew that the war "will be fatal to all merchants and trade." A war with Holland, wrote the Canary merchant John Paige, would "give over our trade." "Our merchants will suffer" in war, the *Perfect Passages* admitted. Even the Earl of Leicester thought that a war with the Dutch "probably would ruin both

8 *Mercurius Bellonius*, 9–16 February 1652, p. [13]; Owen quoted in Blair Worden, *The Rump Parliament, 1649–1653* (Cambridge, 1974), p. 302; *Weekly Intelligencer*, 20–27 April 1652, p. 436; *French Occurrences*, 14–21 June 1652, p. 48; Josselin *Diary*, 15 January 1652, p. 268 – refers to the story in Ezekiel 26; *Dr. Dorislaus Ghost, Presented by Time to Unmask the Vizards of the Hollanders; And Discover the Lions Paw in the Face of the Sun, in this Juncture of Time: Or, a List of XXVII Barbarous and Bloody Cruelties and Murthers, Massacres and Base Treacheries of the Hollanders against England and English men* ... (London, 1652). Thomason: 29 June 1652. Broadside.

their state and this."[9] In light of the relatively small capital of the English merchants and the instant havoc that a war would wreak these were not unreasonable assessments.

Rather, the war began because the English political nation was profoundly disillusioned by the Dutch refusal to join them in a Protestant and republican alliance. The political and religious vocabulary then current left very few options. Indeed the similarities between the Dutch and the Scots seemed all too obvious to Englishmen, who called for a similar response to both crises. It was the English conviction that the Dutch were fallen Protestants, corrupted by their experience under Orangist tyranny into worshipping gold rather than God, that provoked them into passing the Navigation Act. Only by striking the Dutch where they could still feel the dagger, did the English think they could resuscitate the souls of the Dutch and restore them to a proper republican spirit. By the winter of 1651–1652 so many pamphlets, newsbooks, almanacs and sermons had proclaimed the Dutch to be lapsed Protestants and insincere republicans that even though the Council of State wished to pull back from the brink of war popular opinion pushed them over. This war was not fought for economic motives, because the economic arguments that were made were only a means to reach Protestant and Republican ends. A French newsletter writer was exactly right when he told Mazarin that the Rump acted only upon "motives of religion and principle."[10]

9 E. M. Symonds (editor), *The Diary of John Greene (1635–1657)* Pt. III, in *English Historical Review* Vol. 44 No. 173 (January 1929) pp. 106–117; Paige to Paynter and Clerke, 16 February 1652, Steckley, *John Paige*, p. 62; *Perfect Passages*, 4–11 June 1652, p. 393; Leicester's Journal, HMC, *DeLisle*, p. 613.

10 Newsletter to Mazarin, 13 February 1652, PRO, PRO 31/3/90, f. 451 (my translation).

Part II

TO UNITE AGAINST THE COMMON ENEMY: THE 1654 TREATY OF WESTMINSTER AND THE END OF APOCALYPTIC FOREIGN POLICY

5

Historiographical overview

The English, convinced that God had shown his favor towards them in demolishing the tyranny of Charles I and subsequently in defeating the invasion of his son at the head of a Scottish army, could not help but place a special significance on their struggle with the Dutch. The English could be certain that this was no minor squabble, after all the Dutch naval war hero Martin Van Tromp had proclaimed that "no quarter shall be given to the English and that [the Dutch] will revenge themselves with fire and sword." Indeed, the entire Dutch navy had "taken an oath and protestation to live and die together, and to fight it out to the last man."[1] Consequently the importance of the war against the Dutch was clear to a wide variety of observers. "Many eyes are on our breach with Holland," noted the Essex clergyman Ralph Josselin, "God is shaking the earth and he will do it." "So terrible a sea-fight hath not been heard of in the remembrance of any man," commented one pamphleteer after a minor skirmish in August 1652, "the discolored sea showing the effects of their wrath." After the battle of Portland in February 1653, observers had more reason to express wonder at the scale and ferocity of the conflict. "The battle of Lepanto was not comparable to this," thought the Canary merchant John Paige; "there was never the like battle fought upon the salt waters since the creation of the world." The Royalist exile Edward Hyde agreed that "it was the most bloody sea battle that hath been in these last ages." The apocalyptic admiralty secretary Robert Blackborne described the English victory as "that memorable and never to be forgotten appearance" of the Lord.[2]

There could be no doubt, the English thought, that the affairs of all the known world turned on the outcome of their epic struggle with the Dutch. One seaman described a battle with the Dutch as acting "the theater of Europe's tragedy." The battle of Portland, averred the *Weekly Intelligencer*,

1 *French Occurrences*, 5–12 July 1653, p. 66; *A Great Victory Obtained By his Excellency the Lord Gen: Blake* ... (London, 1652), Thomason: 1 July 1652, p. 7.

2 Josselin, *Diary*, 20 June 1652, p. 281; *Terrible and Bloudy Newes From Sea* (London, 1652), Thomason: 6 August 1652, pp. 3–4; John Paige to Paynter and Clerke, 1 March 1653, Steckley, *John Paige*, p. 86; Hyde to Rochester, 4/14 March 1653, Bod., Clar. 45, f. 153r; Robert Blackborne to Captain Badiley, 14 March 1653, CSPD, p. 213.

"will serve all Christendom for discourse." "All nations are at a stand," wrote one Europe-based observer, "and though working yet, the whole wheel of affairs lies on this business." Not surprisingly, then, when England and the United Provinces began negotiations to end the conflict, many were certain "all Christendom depends on how England and Holland may conclude."[3]

Why, then, did this struggle which contemporaries conceived in such monumental terms come to an end? Did the peace concluded by the Protectorate in April 1654 reflect an achievement of the goals which the Rump had established when it went to war in June 1652?

Historians, unable to agree as to why the war occurred, have similarly disputed its outcome. Even those who are sure the war was an economic struggle disagree as to its conclusion. "When the Dutch refused to allow their colonies to be peacefully incorporated in the British empire," argues Christopher Hill, "the Dutch war was another way to achieve the same end." While acknowledging that Cromwell had ideological differences with the more radical members of Barebones, Hill believes that he continued to support the war on the principle that "the commonwealth should do anything to preserve its trade." Not surprisingly, then, Hill asserts that the Cromwellian peace of 1654 was "not unfavourable to England."[4] Charles Wilson also thinks the war began because "a powerful element in the new government was materialist and anti-Dutch, and the parliamentary party could not ignore the demands of its supporters amongst the London merchants." Since the Rump viewed its conflict with the Dutch as a trade war, "it was sufficient ... to ruin Dutch commerce and thus bring the enemy to his knees." In Wilson's view, Cromwell had always opposed the war as an unChristian conflict against fellow Protestants and did his best to keep the treaty in play against the opposition of the religious radicals. So when he was proclaimed Protector in 1654 Cromwell's peace was "extraordinarily mild." Nevertheless Wilson posits that "the relative magnanimity of the terms could not ... disguise the magnitude of the defeat suffered by the Dutch." Since the war "had fulfilled in the main the prophecies of those who, since Thomas Mun's time, had spoken with confidence of England's chances of victory in a Dutch war," the English merchant community "could look back on the war with some satisfaction."[5] More recently

3 *The Last Bloudy Fight at Sea, Between the English and the Dutch, on Tuesday Last* (London, 1652), Thomason: 27 July 1652, pp. 3–4; *Weekly Intelligencer*, 22 February–1 March 1653, p. 751; newsletter from Dort, 3/13 June 1653, Bod., Rawl. A3, p. 164; Hugh Morrell to Oliver Cromwell, 20/30 December 1653, CSPD, p. 302.

4 Christopher Hill, *God's Englishman: Oliver Cromwell and the English Revolution* (New York, 1970), pp. 131, 155–157. It should be noted that Hill also acknowledges the importance of the Protestant cause in Cromwell's foreign policy, but sees the war primarily as an economic struggle. In many cases I find Hill's description of Cromwell's attitude towards the war more persuasive than that of any other modern scholar.

5 Charles H. Wilson, *Profit and Power* (London, 1957), pp. 61–77.

Jonathan Israel, in his massive study of the *Dutch Primacy in World Trade*, has taken a novel approach. The first Anglo-Dutch War, Israel agrees, "sprang from commercial and maritime conflict." But "Parliament in the end, to obtain peace, was forced to abandon every single one of its economic maritime and colonial demands on the Dutch." In the Baltic, in the Mediterranean, and in Asian Waters, Israel demonstrates, the Dutch were able to drive the English merchants from their trade routes. The result was a complete Dutch victory. "That a war which cost so much in men, ships, and trade should have ended without any tangible gains" for England, Israel concludes, "is the measure of England's failure."[6]

Historians of English domestic politics, who largely emphasize the political nature of the war, have found more ground for agreement. Samuel Rawson Gardiner, who in his magisterial history argues that the maritime conflict was in some sense the first commercial war, feels that its conclusion turned decisively on domestic developments. After the dissolution of the Rump, Gardiner describes Cromwell's position as analogous to "an opposition leader aiming at peace, whilst the recognized authorities were aiming at the continuance of war." It was Cromwell's ideological opposition to the war, coupled with "the financial strain upon the resources of the Commonwealth," which convinced him to conclude a peace with the Dutch as soon as he was named Protector. "The struggle for the command of the North Sea," Gardiner consequently insists, "had certainly not resulted in its complete domination by the English fleet." As a result the Treaty of Westminster reflected in political terms the military ambivalence of the war. But the end of the Dutch War did free Cromwell for more grand designs. Since there was no European power which threatened an "overwhelming predominance," Cromwell could initiate "a policy of aggression calculated on the weakness of one or the other of the leading states." Spain became the object of Cromwell's aggression, Gardiner argues, because it tried to block the Anglo-Dutch peace and because of its failure to tolerate English Protestant merchants within its territories.[7] Charles Korr has found evidence to support Gardiner's argument. Cromwell had always opposed the Anglo-Dutch War "on moral as well as political grounds." So, after the resignation of the Barebones Parliament, Cromwell was "in a position to end the war that he had been willing to accept as long as he was walking a political tightrope between factions in England." Following the Venetian ambassadors, Korr has added that Cromwell and his council were the more anxious for peace because "the war was costing a great deal of money" and because he hoped that putting an end to a long war would increase his own

6 Jonathan Israel, *Dutch Primacy in World Trade 1585–1740* (Oxford, 1989), pp. 210–213.

7 S. R. Gardiner, *History of the Commonwealth and Protectorate 1649–56* (New York, 1965), Vol. III, pp. 48–83.

popularity.[8] Austin Woolrych, in his magnificent study of the Nominated Parliament, has come to similar conclusions about the pattern of Anglo-Dutch relations in 1653. Cromwell "strongly desired" peace with the Dutch, but was frustrated in his aims by "an unbroken run of English naval victories, a lack of realism about the terms that the Dutch would accept, and latterly the fanatical lust for universal conquest that consumed the Fifth Monarchist faction." Indeed it was only the hope that Barebones would be dissolved that stopped the Dutch ambassadors from breaking off the treaty in December 1653.[9] Significantly all of these historians explain the conclusion of the war in purely English terms. Perceptions of Dutch politics had little or no effect on diplomatic proceedings because the English negotiators were "inept," lacked "experience," and were "amateurs in the area of foreign policy."[10]

Against these views, I claim that although the English politicians who conducted the negotiations with the Dutch diplomatic team in 1653 and 1654 may have been novices in international relations, they did not come to those negotiations without any conception of international politics. Indeed it was their perception of a decisive change in Dutch politics that prompted Cromwell and his political allies to turn against a war which they had initially supported. This new political insight brought them into direct conflict with the more apocalyptic members of the new Nominated Parliament, and in so doing prompted not only a political revolution in England, but an ideological one as well. The new English government, the Protectorate, was able to dictate the terms of peace with the Dutch because it was clear that the English had won the war. These terms, unsurprisingly, reflected the war aims of the now-triumphant Cromwellian moderates, war aims which had precious little to do with establishing English commercial supremacy. Once in power the Cromwellian moderates rejected notions of apocalyptic foreign policy, just as they had discarded their apocalyptic former colleagues. The Treaty of Westminster, then, represented the end of English apocalyptic foreign policy.

8 Charles Korr, *Cromwell and the New Model Foreign Policy* (Berkeley, 1975), pp. 76–78.
9 Austin Woolrych, *Commonwealth to Protectorate* (Oxford, 1982), pp. 277–279, 323–325.
10 These are the descriptions of Woolrych, *Commonwealth*, p. 279; and Korr, *Cromwell*, p. 78.

6

The causes of the war stated

Why, then, did the English think they were fighting their fellow Protestant republic from across the North Sea? How did they explain this conflict which had already taken on epic proportions in their imaginations?

There could be no question, argued Donald Lupton, that the "Dutch were the first offenders, so 'tis just and fitting on our parts to repulse the injuries and affronts offered us." The war had its origin in "the wicked thoughts" of Admiral Van Tromp, who as "a vassal of the Orange family" was "by consequence a Cavalier in grain, and enemy to the Commonwealth of England."[1] The English were sure that the Dutch had taken on the cause of the despised Stuart family. The official *Declaration of the Parliament* catalogued a litany of Orangist-inspired Dutch actions in favor of the House of Stuart. English newspapers frequently reported naval cooperation between the Dutch fleet and Royalist pirates. One Dutchman was even reported to have said that "the rod is growing in Holland to revenge that innocent blood of the king." A republican poet found "the Hogen of a royal mind / Inclin's to monarchy," advising him to "beware / thou dost not put thy foot into a snare."[2]

Not surprisingly, the Dutch martial aim was thought to be the subversion of the English state. "The States of the Netherlands have proclaimed open wars against England," reported the *French Occurrences*, "and utterly

1 [Donald Lupton], *England's Command on the Seas* (London, 1653), pp. 96–97; *Mercurius Politicus*, 11–18 August 1653, p. 2655. Richard Lyons, chaplain to the generals of the fleet, was sure the English had won the war when Van Tromp's Orange flag was destroyed in the battle of the Texel. *Mercurius Politicus*, 28 July–4 August 1653, p. 2627.

2 *A Declaration of the Parliament of the Commonwealth of England, Relating to the Affairs and Proceedings Between this Commonwealth and the States General of the United Provinces of the Low Countreys, and the Present Differences Occasioned on the States Part* (London, 1652), Thomason: 9 July 1652, p. 4. The literature on Royalist/Dutch cooperation is vast; see for example *French Occurrences*, 5–12 July 1652, p. 57; *Mercurius Politicus*, 15–22 July 1652, p. 1742; *Mercurius Politicus*, 10–17 March 1653, p. 2297; George Wither, *The Dark Lantern* (London, 1653), p. 29; J. W., *Brandy-Wine in the Hollanders Ingratitude* ([London], 1652), Thomason: 30 July 1652, p. 7; *The Examiner Defended, In a Fair and Sober Answer To the Two and Twenty Questions which Lately Examined the Author of Zeal Examined* (London, 1652), Thomason: 14 September 1652, p. 18.

disown it for being a commonwealth." The Dutch, Marchamont Nedham informed his compatriots, "have no other ground of quarrel but that you are a republic." The goal of the Dutch, agreed the poet J. W., could only be "to subvert our state." "Down with your Parliament they now cry," testified another pamphleteer, "this is the time to set their poor distressed Lord and master in his royal saddle and restore him to his disjointed throne." The States General were said to have "concluded upon a thundering, terrible, roaring, desperate, and uncharitable vote to do their utmost to ruin England, and not to be at peace with them, until they changed both the power and government." The Dutch "would with all their hearts help you to a monarch again," explained the *Mercurius Politicus*.[3] It seemed as if the Hollanders were indeed "foolishly charmed with the magical spells of monarchy." They had appealed to all the European "princely powers" for aid against the English, appearing in the guise of "lovers of monarchy."[4]

Why had the Protestant and republican Dutch suddenly taken on the cause of monarchy and tyranny? For Englishmen and women in 1653 the answer was not far to seek. Though the Dutch might once have been in the vanguard of the Protestant struggle against the forces of Spain and Popery, their early religiosity was now lost; they had succumbed to their own forms of idolatry.[5] The Dutch, it seemed, now worshiped "idols of gold and silver." This prompted the New Englander William Hooke to proclaim to Cromwell that "gain is their God."[6] It was this indifference to religion which made the United Provinces into a new Tower of Babel. "The Dutch," opined the *Mercurius Britannicus*, "are a mercenary rascality of Jews, Moors, and Spaniards." They are "in plain English a gallimaufry of all religions; except only what's true and pure," observed the author of *Amsterdam and her Other Hollander Sisters*, "they account the best religion which brings most gains to them, for toleration, were it the Turks' Alkoran,

3 *French Occurrences*, 16–25 August 1652, p. 96; J. W., *Brandy-Wine*, pp. 5–6; Marchamont Nedham, (translator and compiler), *Of the Dominion or Ownership of the Sea* (London, 1652), sigs. c1v–c2r, d2r; *The Parliament of England's Message to the Queen of Sweden*... (London, 1652), Thomason: 24 November 1652, pp. 6–7; *French Occurrences*, 7–14 September 1652, p. 124; *Mercurius Politicus*, 26 August–2 September 1652, p. 1835; Paulucci to Sagredo, 8/18 July 1653, *CSPV*, p. 99; [Marchamont Nedham], *The Case Stated Between England and the United Provinces in this Present Juncture* (London, 1652), pp. 14, 21. Many of these claims appeared verified with the publication of the Dutch tract *An Answer to the Declaration of the Imaginary Parliament of the Unknowne Common-wealth of England*... (Rotterdam, 1652), Thomason: 10 October 1652. The Rump immediately had it suppressed – see *Weekly Intelligencer*, 26 October–2 November 1652, p. 645.

4 *Faithful Post*, 1–8 April 1653, p. 697; *French Occurrences*, 12–19 July 1652, p. 80; *A Remonstrance from Holland*, (London, 1652), Thomason: 24 December 1652, p. 4.

5 *Amsterdam, and her Other Hollander Sisters put out to Sea, By Van Trump, Van Dunck, & Van Dumpe* (London, 1652), Thomason: 12 July 1652, pp. 8–9; *Flying Eagle*, 25 December–1 January 1653, p. 35.

6 *Mercurius Politicus*, 30 September–7 October 1652, p. 1924, William Hooke to Cromwell, 3 November 1653, Bod., Rawl. A8, p. 14. See also Abraham Woofe, *The Tyranny of the Dutch Against the English*, dedicated to Oliver Cromwell, (London, 1653), pp. 4, 41–42.

that's their best God that brings the most gold." The chief characteristic of the Dutch Church was that "it can sail with all winds, and wind and turn in what coast or port the mariners will have her." Andrew Marvell, who was at this time working for John Milton and the Rump, eloquently imagined Dutch religious culture using the language of worldly materialism. "Amsterdam, Turk–Christian–Pagan–Jew, / Staple of sects and mint of schism grew, / That bank of conscience, where not one so strange / Opinion but finds credit, and exchange / In vain for Catholics ourselves we bear; / The Universal Church is only there," sneered Marvell.[7]

The religious and ideological apostasy of the Dutch was naturally manifest in their political actions. The Dutch had "made Reason of State their God, and the rule of all their actions." Another pamphleteer denounced the Dutch for their "Machiavellian policy" and their "subtle and knavish" actions as befitted "Staten Heeren."[8] Although many Rumpers admired Machiavelli's republican pronouncements, very few advocated elevating Reason of State above the law of God and nations. Marchamont Nedham, who admired Machiavelli's "very solid judgement and most active fantasy," roundly condemned his advocacy of Reason of State as "many pernicious sprinklings, unworthy of the light" and as "contrary to the law of God, or the law of common honesty and of nations." "Violation of faith, principle, promises, and engagements upon every turn of time and advantage," concluded Nedham, "ought to be exploded out of all nations that bore the name of Christian."[9]

Repeated Dutch successes in employing their theory of Reason of State had made them into a proud and grasping nation. It was common parlance throughout Europe that the "Dutch are so ambitious that they would fain give laws to all the world," wrote one correspondent to the *Mercurius Politicus*, "but they hope now that they have met with a nation who will not be baffled by them." The Dutch, thought one naval correspondent, failed to salute the English because "their spirits [were] heightened with the presumption of their own strength." Consequently all England prayed before the war began that their fleets would "find a Providence with them, that can

7 *Mercurius Britannicus*, 26 July–2 August 1652, pp. 26–27; *Amsterdam and Her Other Hollander Sisters*, pp. 3–4; *Mercurius Democritus*, 23 February–2 March 1653, p. 362; Andrew Marvell, "The Character of Holland," in Elizabeth Storry Donno (editor), *Andrew Marvell: The Complete English Poems*, (London, 1972), lines 67–76, pp. 113–114.

8 *Mercurius Politicus*, 24 June–1 July 1652, pp. 1693–1694; *The Dutch-mens Pedigree: Or A Relation, Shewing How They Were First Bred, and Descended from a Horse-Turd, Which Was Enclosed in a Butter-Box* (London, 1653), Thomason: 8 January 1653; *French Occurrences*, 9–16 August 1652, p. 84; *Amsterdam and her Other Hollander Sisters*, pp. 9–10.

9 *Mercurius Politicus*, 24 June–1 July 1652, pp. 1690–1692; *Mercurius Politicus*, 22–29 July 1652, pp. 1758–1759; Thomas Peters, *A Remedie Against Ruine: A Sermon Preached at the Assizes in Lanceston Cornwall, March 17 1651* (London, 1652), Thomason: 17 July 1652, p. 12.

easily bring down [the Dutch] pride."[10] "The Lord hath a great controversy with Holland," argued the *French Occurrences*, "both for their pride, and blasphemous title of High and Mighty, which is only to be given to God." Indeed pride had made the Dutch into "the high and imperious States," making "Mr. Hans ... somewhat too imperious."[11] Each calamity which befell the Dutch, each English victory, was interpreted as God taming the Netherlandish pride. The loss of three Dutch ships in a Mediterranean storm convinced another writer that "the Lord is now stretching forth against that nation for their pride, their treacherous and bloody actions." Slingsby Bethel and his fellow Merchant Adventurers knew that the victory off Portland meant that it had "pleased the Almighty to restrain the enemy in his pride."[12]

This Dutch insolence was particularly insufferable in English eyes because the United Provinces owed their very existence to English benevolence. Poems, newsbooks, sermons, broadsides and almanacs all evoked the memory of Sidney and Vere and the heroic Elizabethan defense of the United Provinces against the ostensibly invincible Spanish army. "A foot of ground cannot be called yours," insisted the *French Occurrences*, "that owes not a third part to the expense valor, or counsel of the English." The Dutch are "of all mankind most unthankful to contend with us English," William Lilly told his readers in his almanac for 1653, "our very forefathers by their blood and valor having advantaged these Dutch men's progenitors from the condition of poor muddy fishermen and boores, into their present greatness of this time."[13]

It was the perceived ideological and religious lassitude of the Dutch, not the ineluctable law of supply and demand, which made the Dutch into dangerous economic rivals. It was a commonplace in the 1650s that only

10 *Mercurius Politicus*, 22–29 July 1652, p. 1749; *Mercurius Politicus*, 19–26 August 1652, p. 1824 (from Brussels); *Bloudy Newes from Sea* (London, 1652), Thomason: 6 July 1652, pp. 4–5.

11 *French Occurrences*, 12–19 July 1652, pp. 79–80; *Amsterdam and her Other Hollander Sisters*, 12 July 1652, pp. 4–5; *A Dangerous and Bloudy Fight Upon the Coast of Cornwall Between the English and the Dutch, On Thursday Last.* (London, 1652), Thomason: ca. 24 October 1652, p. 8; *A Remonstrance from Holland*, pp. 3–4.

12 *Mercurius Politicus*, 23–30 September 1652, p. 1907; *Mercurius Politicus*, 27 January–3 February 1653, p. 2203; petition of Slingsby Bethel, Alex Baron, Dan. Farrington, and Wm. Johnson for Merchant Adventurers, 24 March 1653, *CSPD*, p. 230. There are far too many examples of this rhetoric to be given full justice here.

13 *French Occurrences*, 19–26 July 1652, p. 69; *French Occurrences*, 26 July–2 August 1652, p. 75; *Mercurius Britannicus*, 19–26 July 1652, pp. 2–3; *Ad Populum: Or, A Low Country Lecture to the People of England* (London, 1653), Thomason: 27 August 1653, sig. A1v; J. W., *Brandy-Wine*, p. 2; *A Declaration of the Parliament of the Commonwealth of England, Relating to the Affairs and Proceedings of this Commonwealth and the States General of the United Provinces of the Low Countreys and the Present Differences Occasioned on the States Part* (London, 1652), Thomason: 9 July 1652, p. 3; *Amsterdam and her Other Hollander Sisters*, p. 7; William Lilly, *Merlini Anglici Ephemeris* (London, 1653), Thomason: 16 November 1652, sig. A5v.

true religion and good government served to tame man's natural insatiable desires. It is well known, observed William Sclater the preacher of St. Peter-le-Poer in London, that men are "full of savage and unreclaimable desires of profits, lust, of revenge; which as long as they give ear to religious precepts, and to good laws, sweetly teach'd with eloquence, and persuasion of the makers, so long is society and peace maintained." For Bulstrode Whitelocke, one of the Rump's foreign-policy specialists, and the Nominated Parliament's ambassador to Sweden, Dutch political and religious failings had made them guilty of the sin of Tyre. "The nature of man, being corrupted, is most apt to be high minded, most subject unto pride," Whitelocke wrote in January 1653 drawing the parallel between the Anglo-Dutch War and Ezekiel 28.5, "and nothing is more apt to puff up the mind of man in pride, than the abundance of worldly riches."[14] The negotiation process had proven beyond doubt that if the English were not wary they "should be wholly eaten out by the people of the United Provinces." This would not, of course, be the result of superior Dutch economic techniques but because "their whole trade is but defrauding."[15]

It was this corruption, this covetousness, the English believed, which led the Dutch to challenge English control of the Narrow Seas. "All in general are against the English," reported the *The Resolution of the Hollanders*, "swearing, that their former name and reputation as masters and lords of the sea must and shall have an end, and they must not think always to keep possession of that which ought to be free and common to all." The Dutch commander Witte De Witt was said to have taken an oath "to make the Netherlanders sole commanders of the Narrow Seas."[16] But, this was not a purely local struggle; Dutch ambition and covetousness was not limited to the North Sea. "The subject of the Dutch intentions and practices," explained the author of the *Seas Magazine Opened* was "to engross all trade through Europe and the other parts of the world into their own hands." The "unlimited desires" of the Dutch, Viscount Lisle was instructed to inform Queen Christina of Sweden, made it their "constant and first design" to "engross to themselves the trade of the world." Indeed once the Dutch had engrossed "the trade of Christendom into their own hand" they would not hesitate to "administer laws to the most kings thereof." There could be no question that the

14 William Sclater, *Civil Magistracy by Divine Authority*, Preached at Southampton Assizes, 4 March 1652 (London, 1653), Thomason: 30 October 1652, p. 8; Whitelocke, *Annals*, January 1653, BL, Add. 37345, f. 255.

15 Thurloe's "Review," PRO, SP 103/46, f. 239v; *Amsterdam and her Other Hollander Sisters*, 12 July 1652, pp. 6–7; Whitelocke, *Annals*, 7 May 1654, BL, Add. 4992, f. 85.

16 *The Resolution of the Hollanders* (London, 1652), Thomason: 20 July 1652, pp. 4–5; *Dutch Intelligencer*, 8–15 September 1652, p. 16; *French Occurrences*, 28 June–5 July 1652, pp. 57, 60; *Faithful Scout*, 10–17 June 1653 (hopelessly mispaginated).

unlimited desire of the Dutch was now making a fair bid to "be Masters of all."[17]

The epic nature of the Anglo-Dutch struggle and the manifest corruption of the Dutch led learned English to make a very telling comparison. "Reflecting upon the late affairs," wrote Marchamont Nedham, "methinks I see the old game betwixt Rome and Carthage (the two great commonwealths of the elder times) revived again." The English/Romans were of course "the more gallant people, such as in all their actions stood on points of honor," while the Dutch/Carthaginians were "base and sordid, such as steered all their counsels by the card of profit" and "crafty over-reaching wits, infamous for their breaches of faith and promise." The result of this new Punic War was historically predictable. "Carthage overcome," wrote Andrew Marvell, "would render fain unto our better Rome."[18]

Worshipping Mammon rather than God brought predictable results in both the antique and modern worlds. "If you trust in worldly riches," warned Whitelocke, "you will bitterly provoke God to anger against you." "Holland never knew when she was rich enough," crowed Nicholas Culpeper in his almanac for 1653, "and now she is beaten unto better manners." As soon as the Dutch "threatened Mare Clausum out of date / to make, and sacred rights to violate," one popular poet explained that "gaping after gain / themselves a prey unto the sea became." The moral was only too clear. "Do not wonder at their wicked and traitorous and unjust wringing of all trade out of other men's hands," advised one popular broadside distributed in London in the summer of 1653, "Nay do not wonder at their barbarous and inhumane cruelties, since from Hell they came, and thither without doubts they must return again."[19]

The most spectacular example of Dutch corruption and perfidy – the Amboyna massacre – still exercised the consciences of many in England. Pamphlet after pamphlet retold the tale of the horrible massacre of Englishmen in the Spice Islands. There could have been no motivation for

17 *The Seas Magazine Opened: Or, The Hollander Dispossessed* (London, 1653), Thomason: 15 August 1653, pp. 1, 9; instruction to Viscount Lisle, March 1653, Bod., Rawl. A2, pp. 367–368; *Mercurius Politicus*, 24 June–1 July 1652, pp. 1701–1702; newsletter from The Hague, 28 October/7 November 1653, Bod., Rawl. A7, pp. 263–264; *Amsterdam and her Other Hollander Sisters*, p. 7.

18 *Mercurius Politicus*, 25 November–2 December 1652, pp. 2053–2054; Marvell, "Character of Holland," p. 115, lines 141–142. It is important to note that the image evoked is that of the first Punic War, a war in which Carthage was tamed but not eviscerated. Nigel Smith is working on an annotated edition of this Marvell poem and has kindly let me see a draft of his introductory essay. The less classically minded Abraham Woofe compared the struggle to that against Spain in 1588. The actors were different, but the ideological stakes were the same: Woofe, *Tyranny of the Dutch*, p. 41.

19 Whitelocke, *Annals*, January 1653, BL, Add. 37345, f. 257r; Nicholas Culpeper, *An Ephemeris for the Year of Our Lord, 1653* (London, 1653), Thomason: 16 November 1652, sig. F1r; *Mercurius Politicus*, 10–17 March 1653, p. 2297; *Several Proceedings*, 15–22 November 1653, pp. 234–235; *The Dutch-mens Pedigree*.

this action but "a covetous desire to engross the whole East India trade to themselves." "Witness that bloody and unparalleled butchery of the English at Amboyna in the East Indies," one pamphleteer demanded of his readers, where the Dutch "torments upon the brave English did exceed those of Pizarro or any other Spaniard in the West Indies." This served as proof that the Dutch were still unrepentant and unreformed. Each new tale of Dutch atrocities, which were manifold indeed during the war, only confirmed the moral turpitude of the Dutch. A Dutch massacre of Englishmen in North America proved that "Amboyna's treacherous cruelty" was now "extending itself from the East to the West Indies." Dutch torture of a naval captain preparatory to an attack on Guernsey seemed "to forspeak some new Amboyna design."[20] Unfortunately the corrupt Caroline regime had never sought reparations for the bloody massacre. Now, however, God was calling in His debts. "The time is come," insisted *Mercurius Politicus*, "that God will reckon with the insufferable pride and cruelties of that society." "The ghosts of the slaughtered English at Amboyna call upon us of the commonalty to revenge their murder," proclaimed William Lilly in his extremely popular *Ephemeris*. After one English victory, *A Perfect Account* announced that "God is making inquisition for the innocent blood they shed at Amboyna."[21]

The English in the 1650s, then, were encouraged to believe that they were fighting the Dutch not because the Dutch were their economic rivals, but because they had ceased to be a bulwark against irreligion and tyranny. Although the Dutch still claimed to be a republic, they had taken on the cause of the English royal family. Although still claiming to be a Protestant nation, the Dutch had become the font of heresy, schism, and irreligion. As a result of this political and moral depravity, not because of the inevitable working out of the laws of supply and demand, the Dutch had sought maritime hegemony.

Despite the English confidence, the early phases of the war went badly. English fleets were defeated in the Baltic, in the Mediterranean, and in November in the Channel. Nevertheless the English interpreted this as a period of trial before the inevitable victory. "I see our enemies must deal with us a little at sea, as the old Cavalier did by land," argued the *Mercurius Politicus* in a telling comparison, but one could still be confident that God

20 *A Memento for Holland: Or a True and Exact History of the Most Villainous and Barbarous Cruelties used on the English Merchants Residing at Amboyna* (London, 1653), Thomason: 2 July 1653, sig. A3r; *Amsterdam and her Other Hollander Sisters*, p. 10; *A Declaration of his Excellency the Lord Admiral Vantrump Touching the Royal Fort of Monarchy ...* (London, 1652), Thomason: 21 July 1652, p. 5; *Declaration of Parliament*, 9 July 1652, p. 4; *The Second Part of the Tragedy of Amboyna* (London, 1653), Thomason: 8 August 1653, pp. 4–5; *Mercurius Politicus*, 6–13 January 1653, p. 2157.

21 J. W., *Brandy-Wine*, p. 6; *Mercurius Politicus*, 5–12 August 1652, p. 1793; Lilly, *Merlini Anglici Ephemeris*, 1653, sig. A6; *A Perfect Account*, 3–10 August 1653, p. 1078.

"hath some great design of grace in it to our poor nation." Significantly it was Dr. John Owen, one of the Rump's favorite preachers, who explained the reason for England's confidence in a Thanksgiving sermon. "The rejection of the Gospel by any people or nation to whom it is tendered," he preached in obvious reference to the Dutch, "is always attended with the certain and inevitable destruction of that people or nation."[22]

After a series of naval and administrative reforms, the English fleet soon justified the confidence of those who had stood by their interpretation of God's cause. "Our God in whom we trust hath appeared graciously for and by his servants in defeating this very great fleet of the Hollanders," gushed the *Mercurius Politicus* after the victory off Portland (18 February 1653). "It may well be said of England, as sometimes Moses said of Israel, who is like unto thee," that newspaper confirmed the following week, "O people saved by the Lord!"[23] Three months later the Three Days Battle (2–4 June 1653) confirmed God's intentions. "The signal victory which the Lord hath been pleased to give over our enemies," opined the author of *A Letter from the Fleet*, "may be recorded amongst the chief of those mercies that God hath bestowed upon his saints." "It is a mercy minding us, and sealing to us, all our former mercies," proclaimed an official broadside. Another pamphleteer could assert that "we have still large experience that God's time is best in all the issues of his designs for his people."[24] The final great set-piece battle of the war, the bloody struggle off the mouth of the Texel (31 July 1653) again revealed "God's hand lifted up." The victory, opined another pamphleteer, was but another of "so many eminent discoveries of the will and purpose of God, touching the establishment of our Commonwealth."[25]

How broadly based was this interpretation of the Anglo-Dutch War? How widespread was this view of the Anglo-Dutch War as an ideological struggle, rather than a struggle for lucre? It would have been very difficult indeed for any in England to be ignorant of the goings-on at sea. The sound of battle could be heard in all of the coastal towns. The army regiments stationed throughout England, Scotland, and Ireland were kept informed by official orders and newsletters. Every one of the proliferating number of printed newsbooks devoted a sizeable portion of its coverage to

22 *Mercurius Politicus*, 9–16 December 1652, p. 2065; *Moderate Intelligencer*, 22–29 December 1652, pp. 2623–2624; John Owen, *A Sermon Preached to the Parliament, Octob. 13. 1652* (Oxford, 1652), Thomason: 30 October 1652 p. 48.

23 *Mercurius Politicus*, 24 February–3 March 1653, pp. 2261–2262; *Mercurius Politicus*, 3–10 March 1653, p. 2285.

24 *A Letter from the Fleet* (London, 1653), Thomason: 13 June 1653, pp. 1–2; *A Declaration from the General and Council of State*, (London, 1653), Thomason: 12 June 1653, broadside; *A Perfect Account*, 8–15 June 1653, p. [1013]; *The Particulars of all the Late Bloody Fight at Sea* (London, 1653), Thomason: 6 June 1653, pp. 1–2.

25 *Several Proceedings*, 30 August–5 September 1653, pp. 79–80; *An Exact and True Relation of the Great and Mighty Engagement Between the English and Dutch Fleets* (London, 1653), Thomason: 6 September 1653, p. 1.

the great naval conflict. Pamphlet after pamphlet commented on the war and its ideological significance. Almanac writers consciously made an effort to explain the grounds of the controversy with the Dutch to their humbler readership. "I had not wrote thus much," averred William Lilly with only slight exaggeration, "but that I know this little *Anglicus* of mine shall pass into all the habitable parts of the world, whereas the Parliament's declaration of the Dutch proceedings against us sells slowly" thus helping to insure that "the body of this nation should know either the truth, or the true grounds of the present quarrel betwixt us and the Hollander."[26] Unsurprisingly the war and its causes had become "the only argument of discourse" in the Midlands.[27] So deeply had the war invaded the popular imagination that one Reading man could not but dream about the conflict.[28]

Fasts and Days of Humiliation were held in Parliament, City, and nation in order to celebrate victories and to entreat God to prevent defeats.[29] Each of these special days allowed preachers to disseminate the message to those who did not or could not read the newsbooks, newsletters, or pamphlets. Indeed all of the available evidence suggests that the clergymen did in fact expound upon the same themes as the printed commentaries. Early in the war John Donne informed Lord Conway, that "all their service by land would produce nothing but beans and peas, a reward fitter for their horses than them," ... "and that the spirit now was to move upon the waters." "Strange! that Ephraim should join with Syria to vex Judah their brother," John Owen preached in a widely disseminated sermon, "that the Netherlanders, whose being is founded merely upon the Interest you have undertaken should join with the great Anti-Christian interest, which cannot possibly be set up again, without their inevitable ruin." John Goodwin, the influential Independent divine, wrote a hymn on the subject of the Dutch War which both explained the outbreak of the war, and proclaimed that God had sided with England. "Mammon their God inflam'd their zeal / and set them all on fire," Goodwin wrote of the Dutch, but "the great spectator of the fight / and righteous judge of nations / at last gave sentence of the wrong / He gave large reparations." The Essex clergyman Ralph Josselin preached on Isaiah 24 and Daniel 4.37 at one public fast, informing his

26 Lilly, 1653, *Merlini Anglici Ephemeris*, sig. A6v.

27 John Langley to Sir Richard Leveson, 4 May 1653, SRO, D593/P/8/2/2.

28 Diary of George Starkey, 11 August 1652, Bod., English Miscellaneous MSS E118, f. 73r.

29 *CJ*, 1 September 1652, p. 173; *CJ*, 27 January 1653, p. 251; newsletter from Westminster, 26 February 1653, Worcester College Library, Clarke MSS 24, f. 121; *CJ*, 15 March 1653, p. 266; Whitelocke, *Annals*, 14 June 1653, BL, Add. 37345, f. 280r; Whitelocke, *Annals*, 23 June 1653, BL, Add. 37345, f. 280v; *Weekly Intelligencer*, 21–28 June 1653, p. 892; *Several Proceedings*, 23–30 June 1653, p. 3089; *CJ*, 6 August 1653, p. 297; Whitelocke, *Annals*, 9 August 1653, BL, Add. 4992, f. 25; Whitelocke, *Annals*, 17 August 1653, BL, Add. 4992, f. 28r.

parishioners that God was using the war to punish the Dutch for their pride and sin.[30]

It is necessarily difficult to assess how many people accepted this interpretation of the war; however, there is a fair amount of evidence to suggest that a wide variety did understand the Anglo-Dutch War as an ideological struggle. In London, where the pamphlets, newsbooks, and sermons almost certainly had their greatest effect, there was widespread support and interest in the conflict. The London magistracy and the Gathered Churches were successful in gathering voluntary contributions for the relief of maimed and wounded seamen. In the metropolis "immense applause is lavished on Cromwell" as a result of the victory off the Texel, reported the Venetian resident.[31]

The evidence on attitudes toward the war outside London is rather thinner on the ground; but, where it does exist, it suggests a similar worldview. "I perceive the Dutch affairs fly high," wrote one correspondent from Scotland, "the hand of our God is in all their revolutions, and he will bring forth his own glory." The Dutch "had a form and power of godliness at the time of the revolt from Spain, and when they were refuges to our English persecuted saints ... they were once a tom-hedge to keep out the Romish boar from England," admitted one West Country minister, "but the work is done, and the hedge is rotten, fit for the fire ... Their belly is their God, their godliness is their gain." In Bristol as in London, collections were taken for the relief of wounded seamen, in the confidence that they were advancing "the mighty work of God in the great deep against the insolent Dutch." "We joy exceedingly here at the news of our victory at sea," wrote one inhabitant of Manchester pleased that "we should overcome those insolent Hollanders that rely upon the arm of the flesh."[32]

There can be little doubt, then, that most in England who engaged in or supported the first Anglo-Dutch War explained this conflict as a continuation of the struggle against crass materialism and tyranny rather than as a struggle for trade routes. However, it is possible that these men merely adopted the language of liberty and godliness, while really pursuing worldly ends. Is there any evidence to support this proposition?

Certainly the ubiquity of the language of godliness in the declarations of

30 John Donne, Jr. to Lord Conway, [July 1652], PRO, SP 46/95, f. 376; Owen, 30 October 1652, p. [29]; *Moderate Publisher*, 8–15 April 1653, pp. 804–805 (prints Goodwin's hymn in full); Josselin, *Diary*, 13 October 1652, p. 287.

31 *Mercurius Politicus*, 3–10 March 1653, p. 2282; Paulucci to Sagredo, 12/22 March 1653, *CSPV*, p. 42 (this letter makes it clear that the contributions were viewed as a test of support for the war); Paulucci to Sagredo, 7/17 August 1653, *CSPV*, p. 110.

32 *Mercurius Politicus*, 1–8 July 1652, pp. 1715–1716 (Scotland); *Perfect Diurnall*, 7–14 March 1653, p. 2558 (Edinburgh); *Mercurius Politicus*, 5–12 August 1652, p. 1798 (West Country Minister); *Mercurius Politicus*, 24 February–3 March 1653, p. 2273 (Bristol); *The Moderate Publisher*, 25 February–4 March 1653, p. 743 (Bristol); *Mercurius Classicus*, 6 August 1653, p. 4 (Manchester).

government, in newsbooks, sermons, almanacs, and private correspondence makes it hard to accept that this was merely a rhetorical stance employed to obfuscate more material motives for fighting the Dutch. Indeed, if the war was fought for trade, it is hard to believe that the English would have castigated the Dutch for having forsaken God for Mammon. Closer examination of the evidence makes it even more difficult to believe that the English fought the Dutch for profit.

Bulstrode Whitelocke, who was the most active member on the Rump's committee for foreign affairs, was always reminding his children that the pursuit of wealth was far less important than seeking after God. None of the ancient philosophers valued wealth, Whitelocke reflected, and for good reason. "Riches are *Impedimenta Fortuna*, the baggage of fortune," he lectured during the Dutch War, "or rather the great removers to our voyage to eternity, they imp[ede] the wings of the soul from soaring heavenwards, and are as clogs and shackles to hinder men's race to everlasting happiness."[33] God has informed his people "not to look after merchants, as to grow great and rich by the wealth of other nations," the religious radical and one the greatest of Hollandophobic propagandists, John Canne, explained, "but to break their power and strength in pieces." "The Lord gave their men of war into our hands, not their merchant ships," Canne reminded his brethren after the Three Days Battle, "speaking here I say, as it were from heaven, that it is not prizes, of the enemy's goods, our hearts or hands should desirously be upon: But to destroy Babylon, stain the glory of kings and kingdoms, and lay low the high and great mountains of the earth."[34]

Not surprisingly an investigation of the strategy and tactics of the English Commonwealth, of the attitudes and concerns of the merchant community, during the war reveals that seventeenth-century Englishmen were more conversant with the ideas of John Canne than those of Robert Brenner and Charles Wilson. Immediately after the outbreak of hostilities in the summer of 1652, the Dutch ambassadors could report that English people "are all disobliged no care [is] taken for the increase of trade" – a strange mood indeed for the outset of a trade war. No doubt mercantile concerns were not assuaged when reports came in that General Blake had captured a whole fleet of Dutch herring busses but released them "in regard they are too low a subject for the resolution of our gallant navy."[35]

33 Whitelocke's sermons on the evils of the pursuit of wealth are scattered throughout his papers in the British Library and at Longleat. Here I have drawn on the following: Whitelocke, *Annals*, BL, Add. 37345, ff. 253v–254r (meditations on 1 Timothy 6.17); Whitelocke, *Annals*, 26 September 1652, BL, Add. 37345, ff. 224v–225v (on Psalm 4.2); Whitelocke, *Annals*, 12 November 1653, BL, Add. 4992, f. 55r (on Matthew 13.45, 46).

34 John Canne, *A Voice from the Temple to the Higher Powers* (London, 1653), Thomason: 13 June 1653, p. 39.

35 Newsletter from The Hague, 25 July/4 August 1652, PRO, SP 84/159, f. 127r (reporting the contents of the Dutch ambassadors' letter); *Mercurius Politicus*, 5–12 August 1652,

The records of two of the great trading companies – the Levant Company and the East India Company – reveal that the war was certainly not fought on their behalf. Before the war broke out, the Levant Company could proudly claim that they had achieved their economic goals. The Company's merchants "have managed their trade so warily, supplied the foreign markets so fully, and sold so cheap, as hath almost wholly beaten out their corrivals in trade (French, Venetians, and Dutch) who would not omit to supply our defects, if they could find any," the Levant merchants smugly informed the Rump's Committee on Trade and Foreign Affairs. The state's lack of interest in the Levant trade during the war, soon put an end to that prosperous state of affairs. It was the Rump which begged the Levant Company – unsuccessfully – to send out ships against the Dutch. By the end of the summer, Dutch and French attacks forced the Levant Company to report that it was "altogether incapable of setting out ships by letters of mart." The Company sent letter after letter to the Council of State begging for a convoy to allow them to maintain a presence in the Mediterranean. These complaints fell on deaf ears; the Council of State was concerned to humble the Dutch, not to seize their trade. Soon the Company gave up all pretences of maintaining its economic activities, and signed over its remaining ships for state service. This was not out of any hope to advance its own trade – it knew that it was the war which had "wholly disabled" it as Turkey merchants – but because the "war is national."[36]

The East India Company fared little better. Although it had loudly complained about Dutch unfair trading practices, the Company's merchants clearly hoped that the Rump would be able peacefully to negotiate for reparations. After the outbreak of the war, the directors of the Company were shocked that the Commonwealth expected them to give over trading in order to help the naval effort. "It is a national war," the Company's deputy protested, "not concerning them as the East India Company." Indeed Colonel Robert Thompson, whose brother Maurice was a director of the East India Company, later complained that the Council of State had done precious little to protect the Company's assets in the East.[37] If this was

pp. 1790–1791; *Mercurius Britannicus*, 26 July–2 August 1652, pp. 29–30; Whitelocke, *Annals*, 31 July 1652, BL, Add. 37345, f. 215.

36 Levant Company to committee on trade and foreign affairs, 21 May 1652, PRO, SP 105/144, f. 44; Court minutes of Levant Company, 24 July 1652, PRO, SP 105/151, f. 81r; Levant Company to Council of State. 6 August 1652, PRO, SP 18/24 Pt. II, f. 36r; Levant merchants' petition, 29 July 1653, *CSPD*, p. 58; Levant Company to Council of State 29 July 1652, PRO, SP 105/144, f. 48r; Levant Company to Council of State, 5 August 1652, PRO, SP 105/144, f. 49r; court minutes of Levant Company, 21 January 1653, PRO, SP 105/151, f. 93r. The Company ceased petitioning for convoys largely because it no longer made any pretence of sending out ships. I have profited greatly from discussions with Trevor Dickey.

37 General Court of the Fourth Stock of the East India Company, 28 July 1652, *Cal. EIC*, p. 181; Colonel George Thompson, "Notes Upon the Dutch War," Bod., Clar. 47, f. 184r. This suggests that it was not the Thompsons and their interloping friends who were directing the war effort.

a war fought to seize trade routes, the Council of State seems to have been kept in the dark.

The interdependence of European commerce in this period also makes it unlikely that this was a war fought for the benefit of merchants. London, Norwich, and Yarmouth all had sizeable Dutch communities, while Amsterdam and Rotterdam had large English communities.[38] There are numerous indications that merchantmen were seized by their former trading partners. Indeed there is every reason to believe that English merchants invested heavily in the Dutch East and West India Companies, making it unlikely that they had agitated for this war in order to increase their profits. It should come as no surprise, then, that when a Dutch merchant fleet evaded the English navy and returned safely to Amsterdam there was "on the Exchange and in the City generally" a "great appearance of joy for it."[39] It was precisely because this was not a war for trade that the English Commonwealth had such great difficulty in "trying to induce the richest capitalists and the wealthiest of the city companies to furnish a public loan" to finance the war.[40]

In fact, the Rump and Nominated Parliaments did everything possible to hurt trade during the war. Merchant ship after merchant ship was seized by the state and converted into a man-of-war.[41] Desperate for sailors to man their ships, the Rump was willing to resort to extreme measures. Henry Hatsell recommended "a general embargo until the ships which the state intend to set forth be manned," apparently unaware that the war was being fought to protect that trade he was proposing to stop. Fortunately this measure proved unnecessary as the Rump was able to press men from all imaginable places. "We have so fleeced this river," reported one observer, "that unless it be States-watermen or some others that be protected, there is not an able man to be found." Not surprisingly this activity made it very difficult to conduct trading voyages. As merchantmen approached London,

38 For one discussion of the close mercantile ties between the two nations see John Stoye, *English Travellers Abroad, 1604–1667*, revised edition (New Haven, 1989), pp. 172–173.

39 Newsletter from Yarmouth, 22 July 1652, PRO, SP 84/159, f. 125 (for indication of merchant familiarity); newsletter from London, 27 May 1653, Bod., Clar. 45, f. 439; Bordeaux to de Brienne, 24 February 1653, PRO, PRO 31/3/90, f. 615r (for another example of English merchants' concern for the safety of a Dutch merchant fleet). The case of the Bonnel family, with bases in Dublin, London, Stockholm, and Rotterdam was surely not unique. I discuss Toby Bonnel below.

40 Paulucci to Sagredo, 5/15 February 1653, *CSPV*, p. 25. Paulucci argues that this was in part because the capitalists could not be sure that they would receive a return on their investments. Surely if this had been a war for trade routes they would have been less reticent.

41 Newsletter from Westminster, 7 November 1652, Worcester College, Clarke 24, f. 47; Bordeaux to de Brienne, 20/30 December 1652, PRO, PRO 31/3/90, f. 535v; day's proceedings, 9 March 1653, *CSPD*, p. 204; Blake to Commissioners of the navy, 1 December 1652, BL, Loan 29/241, f. 169r (complaint about the quality of the merchantmen in the navy).

the pressgang raided the ships, leaving them "not as many men as would bring in their ships." "Here is such an extraordinary great pressing," wrote the Canary merchant John Paige to his trading partners, "that it's a difficult thing to get out a ship."[42] Nor did the navy make an attempt to protect English trade routes. Although it is true that the English did blockade the Dutch coast, the aim seems to have been to bring the United Provinces to its knees rather than to destroy its trading assets. No effort was made to send a great fleet to the Mediterranean, to the coast of India, or to the West Indies. Instead England concentrated on defeating the main Dutch naval force in set-piece battles.[43]

The Anglo-Dutch War, even the hostile Venetian resident Paulucci was forced to admit, reflected an English ideology "which made them consider themselves stronger than all the rest, from their successes in the civil war." This did not always follow a logical, rational course. He explained to the Venetian ambassador in Paris that "the English look at things in their own way not that of others."[44] For the English, the United Provinces had ceased to be a nation favored by God because they had forsaken the Lord for Mammon and had abandoned true republicanism for alliance with profane monarchy.

42 Henry Hatsell to William Rowe, 7 December 1652, PRO, SP 18/26, f. 12; newsletter from London, 18 March 1653, Bod., Clar. 45, f. 204r; Newsletter from London, 25 March 1653, Bod., Clar. 45, f. 205; Newsletter from London, 1/11 April 1653, Bod., Clar. 45, f. 223r; Paige to Paynter and Clerke, 12 March 1653, Steckley, p. 88; Paulucci to Sagredo, 9/19 April 1653, *CSPV*, p. 58

43 This point depends on my reading of a vast array of materials. This view is given some support by Bernard Capp's useful summary of the war, *Cromwell's Navy* (Oxford, 1989), pp. 78–83.

44 Paulucci to Sagredo, 31 December/10 January 1652/3, *CSPV*, p. 5; Paulucci to Sagredo, 10/20 November 1653, *CSPV*, p. 147.

7

Peace proposed

Why then did the Rump begin negotiations with the States General in March 1653? Why were the English willing to treat with a nation which had perfidiously attacked them less than a year previously while an alliance was being discussed in Westminster?

There were, of course, many in England, even many supporters of the Rump, who opposed the war against their Protestant brethren. Almost as soon as newsmongers heard that Blake and Van Tromp had fought in the Downs, they began disseminating stories of an Anglo-Dutch rapprochement.[1] Though these stories were certainly exaggerations and mere fabrications, there can be little doubt that there was a significant sector of the English population hostile to the war. "There be thousands who mutter at the business," conceded the Hollandophobic Donald Lupton, "and seem to bear affection to" the Dutch cause. In the Rump itself there were frequent murmurings of discontent. "Parliament never meets," the Venetian resident reported in February 1653, "without accusations and reproaches being heaped on the authors of this war."[2] Hugh Peter, one of Cromwell's favorite preachers, was known to have written to Sir George Ayscue "desiring him to forbear engaging the Dutch in this unjust quarrel." Peter, in fact, was quite anxious to tell anyone who would listen that many in the United Provinces were anxious for peace. Though Peter was fiercely attacked for his activities in the summer, his very public rehabilitation by the Rump in January 1653 reveals a good deal about the temper of the House.[3] The

1 Intelligence from London, 8/18 July 1652, Bod., Clar. 43, f. 205; newsletter from London, 16/26 July 1652, Bod., Clar. 43, f. 215; *A Message Sent to the L. Admiral Vantrump* (London, 1652), Thomason: 16 July 1652, p. 4; newsletter from The Hague, 25 July 1652, PRO, SP 84/159, f. 128; *French Occurrences* , 26 July–2 August 1652, p. 80.

2 Paulucci to Sagredo, 13/23 February 1653, *CSPV*, p. 30; Bordeaux to de Brienne, 6/16 January 1653, PRO, PRO 31/3/90, f. 558; Bordeaux to Servien, 17/27 January 1653, PRO, PRO 31/3/90, f. 570; Bordeaux to de Brienne, 24 January/3 February 1653, PRO, PRO 31/3/90, f. 584r. See also Thomas Papillon to David Papillon, 7 October 1652, CKS, U1015/C1/4.

3 Newsletter from Westminster, 28 August 1652, Worcester College, Clarke MSS 24, f. 17v; Bordeaux to de Brienne, 6/16 January 1653, PRO, PRO 31/3/90, f. 558v; *Weekly Intelligencer*, 7–14 September 1652, p. 596 (Peter preaching before Cromwell); newsletter

former Caroline courtier, and apocalyptic mystic, Sir Balthazar Gerbier was said to be plying "hard through the Provinces the business of accommodation; and tells them that the Lord General and soldiery are against a war with them." When rumors began to circulate that even Robert Blake was uncomfortable with the war, one of Whitelocke's correspondents complained "that too many faces here look towards [the Dutch] and are (I fear) too apt to take in an accommodation on base terms."[4] But these men and these sentiments had been unable to prevent war from breaking out; there was no reason to believe that they now had the political capital to compel the Rump to negotiate a peace.

Those who did support the war, however, must have been concerned by the early defeats of England's navy. By December Blake "was not able to do anything in opposition to the Dutch who range up and down the coast, land their men at pleasure for little plunders, and are entire masters now of the seas." There was talk that the Dutch had plans "to block up the English ships in the mouth" of the Thames. Van Tromp now claimed to be "Master of the Narrow Seas." Not surprisingly, the Dutch were said to "spurn at the least thoughts of any accommodation, unless it may be upon their own terms."[5] Hostile observers were convinced that the Rump would indeed now beg for peace. "They are at their wits' end, and ready to be overwhelmed by their own disorders and wants," the Royalist William Edgeman wrote gleefully. The knowledge that Providence was against them would surely make the Rump succumb to the inevitable. "It is the first signal loss they have undergone either by sea or land," Hyde explained after Van Tromp's devastating victory off Dungeness (30 November 1652), "and therefore likely to make a deep impression generally upon the people who are already alarmed and even half dead with prophecies."[6]

from Westminster, 29 January 1653, Worcester College, Clarke MSS 24, f. 112; for the most virulent attacks on Hugh Peter see *A New Hue and Cry after Maior General Massey and Some Others, Who by the help of Peters Keyes, Escaped from the Tower of London, August the 30, and is Thought to be Fled into Holland* (London, 1652), Thomason: 6 September 1652, especially p. 3. Hugh Peter's avid desire for peace suggests that though he might well have been "the new merchants' close collaborator" in some things, his commitment to the "quest for world power [and] the drive for commercial hegemony" was limited by other ideological concerns. The quotes are from Robert Brenner, *Merchants and Revolution* (Princeton, 1993), pp. 623, 639.

4 Letter to Bulstrode Whitelocke, 24 September 1652, Longleat, Whitelocke MSS XII, ff. 167–169.

5 William Edgeman to Sir Richard Browne, 21/31 December 1652, Christ Church, Richard Browne Letters Box D–L; Bordeaux to de Brienne, 23 December/2 January 1652/53, PRO, 31/3/90, f. 545r; *French Occurrences*, 6–13 December 1652, p. 224; *Mercurius Politicus*, 16–23 December 1652, p. 2102; *Mercurius Politicus*, 23–30 December 1652, pp. 2115–[2116]; newsletter from Amsterdam, 17/27 December 1652, Bod., Tanner MSS 53, f. 174r.

6 Hyde to Marquis of Newcastle, 8/18 January 1653, Bod., Clar. 45, f. 17r; *Mercurius Politicus*, 13–20 January 1653, pp. 2172–2173; *Mercurius Politicus*, 20–27 January 1653,

However, instead of begging for peace on bended knee, the Rump redoubled its war effort. In December, January, and February the Rump strained every nerve to improve the pay of its seamen, the quality of its naval supplies, and the quantity and appropriateness of its men-of-war.[7] Most importantly, the government felt it necessary to rid the navy of "those wasps and drones who serve not but for filthy lucre," or, in Blake's words, those suffering from "baseness of spirit." By early January, the Navy Commission had been reformed and the new commissioners were busily dismissing unreliable commanders and replacing them with "godly able persons."[8] All of the evidence suggests that the reforms were remarkably successful. "Both soldiers and sailors are punctually paid and kept in good humor," remarked the Venetian resident. "They were diligent in the business," noted Bulstrode Whitelocke with approval; "the preparations for the navy and the war at sea with the Dutch went on with great vigor, and the Parliament were quick in it."[9] Clearly, then, it was not the prospect of military defeat which compelled the Rump to initiate negotiations in the spring of 1653.

The English fleet's first great naval victory of the war off Portland in late February 1653 dramatically altered the situation. In fact, it was only after Blake's victory had made the English "masters of the sea again" that serious discussions for peace began. The English conviction that God wished them to humble the proud Dutch had allowed them to "display extraordinary endurance." It was this belief that they were fighting on the side of Providence coupled with a steadfast defense of "the honor of England" which convinced most observers "that the enemy must make the first overtures." "This prosperity," the French ambassador wrote in reference to the battle, "does not stop the general and the other principle men, who were

p. 2191 (for similar reports circulating in the United Provinces); William Edgeman to Sir Richard Browne, 14/24 December 1652, Christ Church, Richard Browne Letters Box D–L; Hyde to Newcastle, 14 December 1652, BL, Loan MSS 29/235, f. 327r.

7 Charles Longland to Robert Blackborne, 27 December 1652, PRO, SP 18/26, f. 96r; Bordeaux to de Brienne, 20/30 December 1652, PRO, PRO 31/3/90, f. 535; Bordeaux to Servien, 20/30 December 1652, PRO, PRO 31/3/90, f. 538r; Paulucci to Sagredo, 5/15 February 1653, *CSPV*, pp. 24–25; Bernard Capp, *Cromwell's Navy*, (Oxford, 1989) pp. 79–80.

8 Newsletter from Amsterdam, 17/27 December 1652, Bod., Tanner MSS 53, f. 174v; Blake to Commissioners of the Navy, 1 December 1652, BL, Loan MSS 29/241, f. 169r; Paulucci to Sagredo, 24 December/3 January 1652/53, *CSPV*, p. 2; Bordeaux to de Brienne, 23 December/2 January 1652/53, PRO, PRO 31/3/90, f. 545v; newsletter from Westminster, 15 January 1653, Worcester College, Clarke MSS 24, f. 104v. For summaries of the reforms see Whitelocke, *Annals*, January 1653, BL, Add. 37345, f. 253v; and *Weekly Intelligencer*, 28 December–4 January 1653, pp. [727–729].

9 Paulucci to Sagredo, 29 January/8 February 1653, *CSPV*, p. 20; Whitelocke, *Annals*, January 1653, BL, Add. 37345, f. 253r. For a belief that the reforms improved the quantity and quality of the seamen see T. Smith, P. Pett, and Francis Willoughby to Committee of the Navy, 21 March 1653, PRO, SP 18/34, f. 109r.

themselves the cause of the war with Holland, from speaking of sending ambassadors to treat for peace."[10]

Fortunately, the Dutch were well poised to take advantage of this change in English sentiment. Since the middle of December the constant entreaties for peace by both the English and Dutch merchant communities had been supplemented by the presence in London of Lieutenant-Colonel Dolman, an Englishman in Dutch service. His very presence in England struck fear in the hearts of Royalists. "Lieutenant-Colonel Dolman's going for England," Edward Hyde wrote to his close friend and fellow exile Sir Edward Nicholas, "troubles me more than Gerbier's coming into Holland and twenty knaves more." Not only was Dolman "a man of parts," but he was "a great Parliamentarian and friend of St. John's." It was almost certainly through Dolman's mediation that the States of Holland were persuaded to write the Rump indicating a willingness to treat for peace.[11] Nevertheless it is important to note that despite Dolman's powers of persuasion and his excellent connections, it was only after the English had received news of the victory off Portland that any move toward peace was made.

In the middle of March the Rump received a letter from the States of Holland, delivered by the secretary of the republican statesman Pauw. In it the Dutch were at pains to emphasize that they were "in no wise constrained by any other consideration" than their "pious zeal" and their concern for "the great effusion of blood of the Household of Faith" to approach the English. But they were sure that the war was "a remarkable punishment from the just judgement of God irritated by the many sins of the people." It was clear from their geographical proximity, their common religion and the many evidences of "divine grace" towards both nations, that they ought to be obliged to "love, unity, and reciprocal care, to procure each other's good at home, and mutual luster abroad."[12]

10 *Mercurius Politicus*, 10–17 March 1653, p. 2301; Paulucci to Sagredo, 29 January/8 February 1653, *CSPV*, p. 21; Paulucci to Sagredo, 5/15 February 1653, *CSPV*, p. 25; Paulucci to Sagredo, 20 February/2 March 1653, *CSPV*, p. 33; Paulucci to Sagredo, 27 February/ 8 March 1653, *CSPV*, p. 35; Paulucci to Sagredo, 12/22 March 1653, *CSPV*, p. 42; Paulucci to Sagredo, 19/29 March 1653, *CSPV*, p. 48; Bordeaux to de Brienne, 24 February/6 March 1653, PRO, PRO 31/3/90, f. 615r; Bordeaux to de Brienne, 3/13 March 1653, PRO, 31/3/90, f. 620r.

11 Bordeaux to de Brienne, 23 December/2 January 1653, PRO, PRO 31/3/90, f. 545 (on mercantile entreaties for peace); Hyde to Nicholas, 10/20 December 1652, Bod., Clar. 44, f. 146v; Hyde to Nicholas, 1/11 January 1653, Bod., Clar. 45, f. 10v; Hyde to Lord Rochester, 18/28 February 1653, Bod., Clar. 45, f. 103v; Aitzema, "Selections," Bod., Rawl. C734, f. 74r (Dolman's friendship with St. John); newsletter from London, 13 May 1653, Bod., Clar. 45, f. 382v. One Royalist newsletter-writer credited Dolman and Hugh Peter as being "the instruments wholly employed" in initiating the discussions: newsletter from London, 15 April 1653, Bod., Clar. 45, f. 293.

12 I have located two copies of this document: States of Holland and West Friesland to Parliament, 8/18 March 1653, Bod., Tanner MSS 53, f. 226; and States of Holland and West Friesland to Parliament, 8/18 March 1653, PRO, SP 105/98, f. 1; *Moderate Publisher*, 18–25 March 1653, p. 771.

As soon as this letter from the States of Holland was received it was referred to the Council of State. Significantly, the men who considered the letter – Henry Marten, Algernon Sidney, Walter Strickland, Thomas Scot, Dennis Bond, and Bulstrode Whitelocke – were men who had played large roles in the decision to go to war in the summer of 1652. That they decided to refer the letter to the full Rump for debate reflects a change in sentiment among some of the Council.[13]

The subsequent debate in the Rump was fierce indeed. Although it was eventually decided that the letters received from the States of Holland were "plausible" and that "there should be a speedy and civil answer returned," this did not reflect any consensus. Marchamont Nedham, while admitting that the letter indicated that Dutch "stomachs are not so high," complained that "it speaks not at all in direct terms any desire of peace, nor any acknowledgment of wrong done, or the like." Bulstrode Whitelocke "saw little hopes to effect" the peace. Edward Hyde, always a keen political observer even though observing from a great distance both ideologically and physically, thought the peace "should be no easy matter."[14] Consequently, that the Rump responded at all to the letter from the States of Holland represents a victory for conservative Protestant opinion in the House. Although the Venetian resident Paulucci may have been too precise when he credited "the Presbyterians, who are of the same creed as the Dutch" with persuading the Rump to act, he probably captured the tenor of the debate. It is certainly not insignificant that the Rump selected Toby Bonnel, a merchant with Presbyterian sympathies and Dutch family connections, to deliver their response to the States of Holland and the States General.[15]

Nevertheless the letters sent to the United Provinces do not reflect a complete victory for the peace party in the Rump. Although the Rump did

13 *CJ*, 22 March 1653, p. 270; *CJ*, 24 March 1653, p. 271; *CJ*, 29 March 1653, pp. 272–273; Whitelocke, *Annals*, March 1653, BL, Add 37345, f. 268; newsletter from Westminster, 22 March 1653, Worcester College, Clarke MSS 24, f. 129v; Paulucci to Sagredo, 2–29 January/February 1653, *CSPV*, p. 21 (claiming continuity of ploicy-making personnel).

14 Bordeaux to de Brienne, 14/24 March 1653, PRO, PRO 31/3/90, f. 627r; Bordeaux to de Brienne, 24 March/3 April 1653, PRO, PRO 31/3/90, f. 631v; *A Perfect Account*, 9–16 March 1653, p. 912; Robert Blackborne, to Captain Badiley, 14 March 1653, *CSPD*, p. 213; newsletter from London, 18 March 1653, Bod., Clar. 45, f. 204r; newsletter from London, 25 March 1653, Bod., Clar. 45, f. 205r; newsletter from Westminster, 26 March 1653, Worcester College, Clarke MSS 25, f. 1v; newsletter from Westminster, 29 March 1653, Worcester College Library, Clarke 25, f. 2; Paulucci to Sagredo, 2/12 April 1653, *CSPV*, p. 54; Nedham to [Whitelocke?], 22 March 1653, Longleat House, Whitelocke MSS XII, f. 50; Whitelocke, *Annals*, BL, Add 37345, f. 269v; Hyde to Nicholas, 18/28 March 1653, Bod., Clar. 45, f. 119v.

15 Paulucci to Sagredo, 12/22 March 1653, *CSPV*, p. 42; day's proceedings, 30 March 1653, *CSPD*, p. 242; newsletter from the Hague, 14/24 April 1653, Bod., Clar. 45, f. 284r; Aitzema, "Selections," Bod., Rawl. C734, f. 76r. For Bonnel's background and ideology see: Toby Bonnel's "Statement," 7 November 1653, Bod., Rawl. A8, p. 97; Toby Bonnel to John Johnson, 2 November 1659, CUL, Add. MSS 4, f. 39.

express its hope for "a good understanding and a firm union between the two States," the language of its letters made clear that peace at any cost was not desired. The English, the Rump felt compelled to remind the Dutch, had done everything to avoid war, "being deeply sensible of the effusion of so much Christian blood as would necessarily follow." But, the Dutch had recalled their ambassador Pauw "without giving any plain and clear answer" to the terms then offered by the Rump. Consequently all future negotiations must "proceed upon the same grounds, as formerly they offered" – grounds which assumed that the Dutch were in the wrong, and compelled them to offer compensation. The Dutch were being asked to "acquiesce in the issues of Providence, whereof they have had so gracious experience." Perhaps even more important than the language of the letters was their destination. One letter was sent as a response to the States of Holland and West Friesland; but a second letter was sent to the States General to initiate formal proceedings between the two sovereign bodies.[16]

Why had the English felt compelled to apply to the States General? Why was the advance from the States of Holland insufficient to begin negotiation? The answer to these questions lies in the perceived origins of the Dutch letter.

The English were concerned to establish whether the peace feelers only represented the inclinations of a small grouping within the Dutch polity. The Rump was well aware that most of the Dutch provinces were "very jealous" lest Holland "should hold any treaty apart (underhand) with England." A private letter from the provincial States of Holland, initially addressed to Lieutenant-Colonel Dolman, hardly served to allay these fears. It was common parlance in diplomatic circles that the letter was the scheme of the arch-republican Lord Nieupoort "who without any public order writ the letter into England." Though the Rump's scrutiny of the letter, and its interrogations of Dolman, were able to dispose of this apocryphal story, concern remained lest the feelers were "brought on with so much indirect proceedings, and so contrary to the foundation and constitution of that government." The States General did "in truth know nothing of the business." "It's said," reported a correspondent to the *Mercurius Politicus* from Holland, "that some of this very province were not consenting to it. But for certain the rest of the provinces appear no way satisfied with their sending, and it was for a while denied by those of Holland themselves." These circumstances seemed to mask some devious plotting. "The design of that letter is only to feel our pulses," opined one of Bulstrode Whitelocke's

16 Parliament to States of Holland and West Friesland, 1 April 1653, PRO, SP 105/98, ff. 4–5; Parliament to States General, 1 April 1653, PRO, SP 105/98, f. 5. I am not here implying that Dutch sovereignty did in fact lie in the States General, only that this was where the English perceived it to lie.

more skeptical acquaintances.[17] No wonder, then, that the Rump opted to make the most public of responses to the States of Holland's letter.

Why did the English believe that the States of Holland had made this covert approach to the Rump? How, in short, did they understand the workings of Dutch politics? The English political nation, in fact, knew quite a lot about the workings of Dutch politics. Most importantly, it knew that the United Provinces were torn by deep ideological divisions. "Our several interests, fashions, religions, and adversaries, are like so many cross winds and waves," explained one newsbook correspondent from the United Provinces, "this appears in the blue books and black mouths in every street and corner, which you must wonder the less at, if you remember your own scene in your late war." Just as support for the monarchy divided the English in the 1650s, so support for the Stadholderate delimited the parties in the Netherlands. "Still the thing called Stadholder and Captain General is the bone of contention that we are gnawing upon, and snarling about," wrote one observer. "The States themselves have had some hot contesting, whether they shall admit the young Prince of Orange, or not for their chief," reported the *Weekly Intelligencer*; "some are violent for it, and some as violent against it." These party divisions, the English were well aware, were reflected in the Dutch attitudes toward the war. "The Hollanders are in a great distraction, and exceedingly divided," ran one well-publicized report, "petitions upon petitions are presented to the States General for a compliance with England, yet those that were most forward in promoting the present war ... show themselves as high as ever."[18]

The English knew quite well that "those that were most forward in promoting the present war" were in fact the adherents of the House of Orange. "The Orange [party] are for a war," testified one political commentator, "they say it is impossible to make a good and lasting league with you, but that it is better for them to join with France to help the king." "If Orange shall ride us again, which is in no wise unlikely," warned the *Mercurius Politicus*, "look then for an endless war betwixt the Republics, and the espousing all quarrels, causes, and interests that shall crush yours." Orangist propagandists frequently accused "the States of Holland and good

17 *Mercurius Politicus*, 3–10 February 1653, pp. 2121–2122; Hyde to Rochester, 8/18 April 1653, Bod., Clar. 45, f. 276r; William Edgeman to Sir Richard Browne, 9/19 April 1653, Christ Church, Richard Browne Letters, Box D–L; William Edgeman to Richard Browne, 16/26 April 1653, Christ Church Browne MSS, Box D–L; Hyde to Nicholas, 15/25 April 1653, Bod., Clar. 45, f. 291r; Hyde to Taylor, 8/18 April 1653, Bod., Clar. 45, f. 271r; newsletter from The Hague, 21 April/1 May 1653, Bod., Clar. 45, f. 306v; *Mercurius Politicus*, 7–14 April 1653, pp. 2369–2370; letter of Dutch news addressed to Whitelocke, 25 March 1653, Longleat House, Whitelocke MSS XIII, f. 52r.

18 *Mercurius Politicus*, 1–8 July 1652, p. 1713; *Mercurius Politicus*, 9–16 September 1652, p. 1875; *Weekly Intelligencer*, 17–24 August 1652, pp. 567–568; newsletter from The Hague, 25 July 1652, PRO, SP 84/159, f. 127; *A Perfect Account*, 8–15 June 1653, p. 1014; *Moderate Publisher*, 10–17 June 1653, p. 1091.

Hollanders" of "correspondence with the Council of State," of "confederacy with the common enemy in obstructing the maritime and naval affairs," in short of "betraying our state to the Spaniard and English." The result was that "any who harbor thoughts or do but wish an accommodation with the English, are accounted enemies to the State of Holland."[19]

Not surprisingly, this belligerence of the Orangists grew out of their ideological predispositions to monarchy and absolutism. Orangist presses were spewing forth tracts, like *Clamor Regii Sanguinis ad Coelum,* defending divine right monarchy and others, like *Hollandts Vloeck*, "upbraiding England with Royal Murder." Orangist clerics were preaching up "absolute, arbitrary, sovereign" power, clothing the Princes of Orange "with kingly robes, and royal titles and prerogatives." The English knew quite well that William II had aspired "to a higher degree of sovereignty over those provinces than he or his predecessors [had] ever enjoyed." So it was hardly surprising that his son's followers, who denounced their republican opponents as "Arminians, traitors, no better than the meanest of the vulgar," aimed "to have an eminent head, qualified with full power, and this to be the young prince; that he be made general and Stadholder out of hand." Once a Prince of Orange regained control of the military he would be absolute "for he that hath the sword, plays Rex and doth what he will."[20]

Detestation of the English Commonwealth and support for an absolute monarchy at home, led the Orangists, naturally enough, to espouse the Stuart cause. "The ministers and people rail extremely against the present government in England," ran one report from the Netherlands, "saying they ought wholly to join with the king against his rebels."[21] There was every reason to believe that this pressure would soon take effect. From the moment the Dutch ambassadors left London in July 1652 there were persistent rumors that the Dutch would adopt the Royal cause. The Orangists "have long cried up the taking in of the Stuarts' interest," the *Mercurius Politicus* informed its readers, as "the only remedy for the distempers and misfortunes of these lands." After the battle off Portland, the Cavaliers were certain the Dutch would invite them to join forces. By the

19 Intelligence from Holland, September 1653, Bod., Rawl. A6, pp. 55–56; *Mercurius Politicus*, 26 August–2 September 1652, p. 1843; newsletter from United Provinces, 8/18 July 1653, Bod., Rawl. A4, p. 138; *The Declaration of the States of Holland, Concerning the King of Scots* (London, 1653), Thomason: 16 June 1653, pp. 7–8; *Mercurius Politicus*, 5–12 August 1652, pp. 1791–1792; *Weekly Intelligencer*, 2–9 November 1652, p. [658].

20 *The Moderate Publisher*, 18–25 March 1653, p. 768; *Mercurius Politicus*, 28 October–4 November 1652, p. 1986; *Mercurius Politicus*, 18–25 November 1652, pp. 2027–2028, 2031; *Britania Triumphalis* (London, 1654), Thomason: 28 April 1654, pp. 36–37, 42–43; *Dutch Intelligencer*, 15–22 September 1652, pp. 17–18.

21 Newsletter, 25 March 1653, Longleat House, Whitelocke MSS XIII, f. 52r; *Faithful Post*, 25 March–1 April 1653, p. 687; *Mercurius Politicus*, 24–31 March 1653, p. 2333; Whitelocke, *Annals*, BL, Add. 37345, f. 269r.

last battle, Hyde wrote to John Kent the Royalist resident in Venice, "the Dutch are instructed how necessary it is for them to join with the king, that they may carry on the war against the rebels prosperously."[22] While the Orangists were campaigning for the States General to support Charles II, they were themselves doing everything they could to aid British Royalists. The rebels in Ireland and Scotland, the Venetian Paulucci informed his colleague in Paris in March 1653, were "being aided by the Dutch as well as by a crowd of other malcontents."[23] In the spring of 1653, then, no one in England could doubt the close ties between Orange and Stuart.

While the strength of the States party, the good Hollanders, rested in the Province of Holland, Orangism was thought to be prevalent everywhere else. "Orange's arms are set up again by the Zeelanders," commented one newswriter in disbelief, "will any man pity these slaves, that will pin the badge of their vassalage upon their breasts and foreheads."[24] Friesland, which still had a member of the House of Orange–Nassau for Stadholder, was known to be firmly Orangist. Gelderland "stands much affected to the House of Orange." Indeed, when the States General mooted the possibility of making "our young tender Orange twig Stadholder" the only opposition came from Holland, "the other Provinces being most of them mean and mercenary, were for it tooth and nail." Not surprisingly it was these same Orangist provinces which were "hot for [war]" and threatened that any peace with England will "go nigh to cause a breach of the union."[25] Even the heart of Holland, Amsterdam, which had valiantly resisted William II's

22 Newsletter from The Hague, 25 July/4 August 1652, PRO, SP 84/159, f. 128r; *A Letter Sent from the States of Holland to the King of Scots*, (London, 1652), Thomason: 27 July 1652, pp. 3–4; *Mercurius Britannicus*, 9–16 August 1652, pp. 12–13; *A Perfect Account*, 18–25 August 1652, p. 686; *French Occurrences*, 16–25 August 1652, p. 90; Hyde to Sir George Carteret, 27 August/5 September 1652, Bod., Clar. 43, f. 292; *Weekly Intelligencer*, 19–26 October 1652, pp. 640–641; letter from The Hague, 4/14 November 1652, Bod., Clar. 44, f. 26; *Mercurius Politicus*, 4–11 November 1652, p. 2004 (quoted in text); *A Perfect Account*, 10–17 November 1652, p. 784; Edgeman to Browne, 21/31 December 1652, Christ Church, Browne MSS, Box D–L; Edward Massey to Charles II, 2 January 1653, Bod., Clar. 45, f. 4; Hyde to W. Curtius, 4/14 March 1653, Bod., Clar. 45, f. 154; Hyde to Joseph Kent, 11/21 March 1653, Bod., Clar. 45, f. 173r; Paulucci to Sagredo, 2/12 April 1653, *CSPV*, p. 54. Royalist optimism in March was duly reported in the London press. See *Mercurius Politicus*, 10–17 March 1653, p. 2306.

23 Paulucci to Sagredo, 19/29 March 1653, *CSPV*, p. 49; *French Occurrences*, 25 October–1 November 1652, p. [180]; *Weekly Intelligencer*, 9–16 November 1652, p. 661.

24 The literature for Zeeland's Orangism is too vast to be given full justice here. I provide only a sample: *Weekly Intelligencer*, 7–14 September 1652, p. 595; *Mercurius Politicus*, 26 August–2 September 1652, p. 1843; *Mercurius Politicus*, 2–9 September 1652, pp. [1858–1861]; *A Perfect Account*, 8–15 September 1652, p. 712; *French Occurrences*, 5–12 July 1652, p. [64]; *French Occurrences*, 7–14 September 1652, pp. 124–125; newsletter from the United Provinces, 19/29 August 1652, Bod., Clar. 43, f. 275.

25 *Mercurius Politicus*, 8–15 July 1652, p. 1731; *Weekly Intelligencer*, 7–14 September 1652, p. 594; *A Perfect Account*, 27 April–4 May 1653, p. 965; *A Perfect Account*, 20–27 July 1653, p. 1062; news from the Dutch Ambassador in Paris, 30 July/8 August 1652, Bod., Clar. 43, f. 229; Peterson to Coopman, 12 November 1653, Bod., Rawl. A8, p. 107.

assault in 1650, was rumored to be "most desirous" of a restoration of the Prince of Orange. "We have a very strong party in Holland," wrote that most cautious of Royalist observers Sir Edward Hyde, "who are so wise to discern that there can be no possibility for them to enjoy an equal and a lasting peace with the rebels of England."[26]

A mere assessment of Orangist political capital in the States General would, the English knew, vastly underestimate that party's power. Driven on by Orangist clerics, "the rabble," "the common sort," "the Boers" were overwhelmingly in favor of restoring to the young Prince of Orange to all of his father's powers. "The common sort here (as in all the world)," sneered the *Mercurius Politicus*, "are taken with the gaudiness and gaiety of a thing called a prince and a court" seemingly ignorant that through "knavery, treachery, and folly, the public interest goes to wreck." "Many of the Boers in every province are wheeled about," agreed the *French Occurrences*, "and cry [the Prince of Orange's] interest up so high, that they have entered into a protestation to live and die with him, and moreover have caused sundry papers to be fixed upon the city gates, wherein are these words NO PRINCE, NO STATE."[27]

What made Orangist Anglophobia so threatening, and any hopes of peace so tenuous, was the Orangist complexion of the Dutch fleet.[28] The Dutch Vice-Admiral and naval war hero Van Tromp was known to be "a devoted vassal to the Orange interest and family." In fact Van Tromp went into every battle flying an "Orange flag and bloody pendants." Van Tromp's Orangism translated directly into disdain for the English Commonwealth and support for the Stuart cause. The English press was quick to report that he had "declared for the Royal interest." In July Van Tromp was said to have protested "his innocency from having any design or intention to strike at the royal fort of monarchy" promising instead to "augment the splendor of the crown in its full orient brightness." After the Dutch defeat off Portland Van Tromp stormed into the States General furious at the half measures of his superiors. "If they did not think of another way of managing the war the English would be too hard for them," Van Tromp

26 *A Declaration of the Hollanders Touching the Late King, and the Commonwealth of England* (London, 1652), Thomason: 23 July 1652, p. 5; Hyde to Taylor, 30 October/9 November 1652, Bod., Clar. 44, f. 23.

27 *Weekly Intelligencer*, 9–16 November 1652, p. 668; *Mercurius Politicus*, 1–8 July 1652, p. 1713; *Mercurius Politicus*, 22–29 July 1652, p. 1767; *Mercurius Politicus*, 5–12 August 1652, p. 1792; *Mercurius Politicus*, 30 September–7 October 1652, p. 1923; *Mercurius Politicus*, 18–25 November 1652, p. 2035; *Mercurius Politicus*, 28 April–5 May 1653, p. 2411; *Dutch Intelligencer*, 1–8 September 1652, pp. 1–2; *French Occurrences*, 15–22 November 1652, p. 206; *A Perfect Account*, 6–13 October 1652, p. 736; newsletter from The Hague, 17/27 June 1653, Bod., Rawl. A3, pp. 284–285.

28 The politicization of the Dutch fleet has been previously noticed by Charles Wilson, pp. 65–66; Herbert H. Rowen, *John de Witt, Grand Pensionary of Holland, 1625–1672* (Princeton, 1978), p. 192.

declared; clearly the States General "ought to seek occasions by diversions, by sending relief to Scotland and to Ireland, and that if the king's flag had been up in his fleet, they had beaten the rebels' power." So fierce was Van Tromp's commitment that rumors circulated that he was "sacrificed to the English" at the Texel by the States of Holland, since he would "stand in their way" to prevent any peace which did "not stand with the interest of the Prince."[29]

Van Tromp's great antagonist in the Dutch fleet, opposing him on every issue of strategy and patronage, was Witte De Witt. De Witt was "zealous against the interest of the House of Nassau," having "declared for the Loevesteen Heeren, that is for them of Amsterdam and Holland against the Prince of Orange." The *Mercurius Politicus* went so far as to call the Vice-Admiral "a factor and brother" of the "best patriots, De Witt, Keysar, Bicker, Pauw, Stellingwerf and their adherents." Though De Witt had briefly taken over supreme command while Van Tromp was in disgrace – "screwed in much against the Zeelanders' minds" according to one purveyor of news – by the late autumn Van Tromp had become "the man of men again."[30]

De Witt's displacement no doubt reflected the sentiment of the Dutch fleet. The Dutch seamen, it was well known, "stand altogether inclined to Admiral Van Tromp, who is more a creature of the Orange party." Each rumor of De Witt's reinstatement in command was accompanied by threats that "many of the men and captains will not fight." This was not mere professional preference. Each naval riot – whether about strategy or material deficiencies – was accompanied with cries "for a governor and a prince." Entire Dutch naval squadrons were seen "to have set up the King of Scot's colors," expressing "great good will toward the Scottish king." When one Dutch man-of-war captured an English merchant ship in the Sound, its men taunted the English with cries of "king murderers and blood

29 *Faithful Scout*, 15–22 July 1653, p. 1091; *The Full Particulars of the Last Great and Terrible Sea-Fight Between the two Great Fleets of England and Holland ...* (London, 1653), Thomason: 4 August 1653, p. 7; *Several Proceedings*, 30 June–7 July 1653, p. 3119; *A Declaration of the L. Admiral Vantrump Concerning The King of Scots, and the Parliament of England ...* (London, 1652), Thomason: 25 June 1652, pp. 4–5; *French Occurrences*, 5–12 July 1652, p. 62; *French Occurrences*, 19–26 July 1652, p. 67; Hyde to Rochester, 11/21 March 1653, Bod., Clar. 45, ff. 169v–170r; Edgeman to Browne, 12/22 March 1653, Christ Church, Richard Browne Letters, Box D–L; Peterson to Coopman, 29 July/8 August 1653, Bod., Rawl. A4, p. 332; Peterson to Coopman, 4 August 1653, Bod., Rawl. A5, p. 44.

30 Peterson to Coopman, 4 July 1653, Bod., Rawl. A4, p. 92; Peterson to Coopman, 12/22 August 1653, Bod., Rawl. A5, p. 140; newsletter from the United Provinces, 19 June 1653, Bod., Rawl. A3, p. 307; *Mercurius Politicus*, 5–12 August 1652, p. 1791; *Several Proceedings*, 7–14 April 1653, p. 2923; newsletter from The Hague, Amsterdam and Middleburgh, 3/13 September 1652, Longleat House, Whitelocke MSS XII, f. 162r; *Mercurius Politicus*, 4–11 November 1652, pp. 1997–1998.

hounds."[31] The Dutch seamen were likely encouraged in these sentiments by the large numbers of British political exiles serving in the fleet.[32] In this situation, then, it was hardly surprising that in the early summer of 1653 reports were circulating that "part of the navy, if not all, that are in Zeeland will in a short time declare for the Prince." In early July, the *Faithful Post* was sure that the Dutch "navy hath declared for the Prince of Orange."[33]

The English were thus well aware of the power of Orange. They knew that the Orangist party in the Netherlands was committed to monarchy, to the House of Stuart, and to the evisceration of their Commonwealth. They also knew that Orangists were in control of the government of the majority of the United Provinces as well as the command of the fleet.[34] In the context of this political situation in the Netherlands, a political situation which had the greatest possible repercussions on Anglo-Dutch relations, it is hardly surprising that the Rump approached the letter from the States of Holland with a good deal of trepidation.

Fortunately for England, the good Patriots, the republican party in the United Provinces, were not about to succumb to the power of Orange without a struggle. Edward Hyde knew that there was a strong party in the Netherlands made up of those "who either upon old grudges, or upon new jealousies of the last Prince of Orange, improved by his design upon Amsterdam, are implacable enemies to that family, and consequently are apprehensive of anything which may contribute to the advancement of that House, which they conceive the restoration of the King of England would

31 *Mercurius Politicus*, 7–14 April 1653, p. 2369; newsletter from Amsterdam, 12/22 August 1653, Bod., Rawl. A5, p. 138; *Weekly Intelligencer*, 19–26 October 1652, p. 642; *Mercurius Politicus*, 2–9 September 1652, pp. 1860–1861; *Another Bloudy Fight at Sea Between the English and the Dutch* (London, 1652), Thomason: 30 July 1652, p. 6; *Mercurius Politicus*, 4–11 November 1652, p. 2003; *Faithful Post*, 8–15 April 1653, p. 705; John Tully to Richard Bradshaw, 27 April 1653, PRO, SP 82/9, f. 64r. *Moderate Intelligencer*, 27 June–4 July 1653, p. 72 provides an excellent iconographic description of one Dutch ensign, replete with ideological significance: "They have erected and set up the prince's standard at the Texel, being a black and bloody ensign, half checker'd, and the remaining part as white as snow, wherein is set forth the lively portraiture of the King of Scots and the Prince of Orange, with two helmets, three crowns, encompassed with a wreath of thorns, and the black rampant lion, and the white rose." The Dutch navy was said to seize only Parliamentarian merchants, while letting Royalists go free: newsletter from United Provinces, 19/29 August 1652, Bod., Clar. 43, f. 275.

32 Newsletter from United Provinces, 3/13 September 1652, Longleat House, Whitelocke MSS XII, ff. 162–163; *Mercurius Politicus*, 9–16 September 1652, pp. 1876–1877; *French Occurrences*, 20–27 September 1652, p. 138; *A Great and Terrible Fight in France* (London, 1652), Thomason: 12 November 1652, TT: E681(8), p. 6.

33 Newsletter from Amsterdam, 16/26 June 1653, Bod., Rawl. A3, p. 273; *Several Proceedings*, 23–30 June 1653, p. 3101; *Mercurius Politicus*, 23–30 June 1653, p. 2545; *Faithful Post*, 28 June–5 July 1653, p. 1076.

34 At least one Dutch commentator remarked on how "well informed" the English Council of State was. Its members knew "of all the circumstances to the very least which did happen ... and all the particulars we debated here, not without glosses." Beverning to De Witt, 17/27 June 1653, Bod., Rawl. A3, p. 279.

infallibly do." This opposition to the House of Orange, though entrenched, reflected ideological differences rather than desire for raw political power. "They of Holland," explained the *Mercurius Politicus*, "are at large against a Stadholder, and have thrown off all thoughts of admitting any new Lord, being so happily relieved by an unexpected divine hand from the former; for that they conceive such a course cannot stand with the good and safety of the provinces, and that it would prove a prejudice to the Union." Indeed the States party was so strongly committed to the republican cause that it "had rather fall to England than a Stadholder." When the Orangist provinces, led by Zeeland, led a desperate push to make the Prince of Orange Captain General in the autumn of 1652, Holland had steadfastly declared its commitment "to remain in the present constitution and order, as well as in relation to the civil government as military, without any alterations." It was this successful show of defiance which convinced at least one knowledgeable political observer that they would not easily be dislodged. "If Holland prevail in this particular against the inclination of all the rest," Edward Hyde complained to his friend Edward Nicholas, "it will be a measure for us to make a judgement of all the rest of their proceedings, and they will give the law as well in all other matters."[35]

Just as the Orangists blamed the States party for Dutch military defeats, so the republicans blamed their adversaries for the outbreak of the war. The States party was confident, wrote one of Thurloe's intelligence gatherers, "that they that have made this disjunction and breach with England, to get up the interest of the Prince of Orange, have been the causes of all this misery." In private debate, the States of Holland averred "how pernicious the English war was for this state, as ruining their commerce, and totally exhausting their treasures in such sort as they shall hereafter be able to find no possible means of redress." Consequently "the grave and sage people," "the good Patriots," "the moderate party," in short "the ruling and wiser part of Holland, which province you know hath most power and most credit, and I may add wisdom too," "do wish with all their hearts that there were a firm peace with England." Friendly observers gladly noted that the States party desired peace "with all their souls," while the Royalist Hyde glumly observed in the spring of 1653 that the republican party "was still ... obstinate for peace."[36] It was

35 Hyde to Taylor, 31 October/10 November 1652, Bod., Clar. 44, f. 23v; *Mercurius Politicus*, 21–28 October 1652, p. 1968; *Mercurius Politicus*, 11–18 November 1652, p. 2012; *Mercurius Politicus*, 18–25 November 1652, pp. 2035–2036; *Mercurius Politicus*, 9–16 December 1652, p. 2082; newsletter from United Provinces, 3/13 September 1652, Longleat House, Whitelocke MSS XII, f. 163r; letter from The Hague, 21/31 October 1652, Bod., Clar. 43, f. 351v; Hyde to Nicholas, 10/20 December 1652, Bod., Clar. 44, f. 146v.

36 Newsletter from United Provinces, 19 June 1653, Bod., Rawl. A3, p. 307; newsletter from The Hague, 7/17 April 1653, Bod., Clar. 45, f. 263v; *A Perfect Account*, 8–15 September 1652, p.709; *A Perfect Account*, 20–27 April 1653, p. 960; *Mercurius Politicus*, 1–8 July 1652, p. 1714; *Mercurius Politicus*, 26 August–2 September 1652, p. 1841; *Weekly*

the political power of the States party, then, which blocked any support for the Stuart cause. It knew that if Charles Stuart "were taken in, he and his young nephew, and his sister, would soon have an opportunity to wield the affairs of this state, and over-top them." "Nothing keeps us from all we desire," whined one Royalist, "but the disaffection of Holland."[37]

It was no doubt the political power of the States party which persuaded the States General to respond to the public letters from the Rump. "For their parts, they will yet contribute most willingly all that may make and serve for the advancement and accomplishment of so pious and Christian an union," the States General declared, and to that end "they are ready to enter into conference and negotiation."[38] Unfortunately, on the very day that John De Witt and his colleagues compelled their Orangist counterparts to approve this letter to initiate discussions with the English Commonwealth, Oliver Cromwell and the army dissolved the Rump.

Intelligencer, 29 March–5 April 1653, p. 798; letter to Dolman, 17/27 June 1653, Bod., Rawl. A3, p. 290; Hyde to L'Estrange, 27 May/6 June 1653, Bod., Clar. 45, f. 441r; Edgeman to Browne, 30 April/10 May 1653, Christ Church, Browne MSS, Box D–L; C. d'Aerssen de Sommelsdyck to Charles II, 16/26 December 1652, Bod., Clar. 44, f. 204; *Several Proceedings*, 7–14 April 1653, p. 2922; letter to Sir Alexander Hume, 30 January/9 February 1653, Bod., Clar. 45, f. 64v; *Moderate Occurrences*, 29 March–5 April 1653, p. 2; *Moderate Occurrences*, 26 April–3 May 1653, p. 40; *Several Proceedings*, 28 April–5 May 1653, p. 2964.

37 *Mercurius Politicus*, 27 January–3 February 1653, pp. 2206–2207; Aitzema, "Selections," Bod., Rawl. C734, f. 75v; newsletter, 25 March 1653, Longleat House, Whitelocke MSS XIII, f. 52v; Hyde to Nicholas, 8/18 January 1653, Bod., Clar. 45, f. 18r; Hyde to Rochester, 8/18 April 1653, Bod., Clar. 45, f. 276r; *A Perfect Account*, 30 March–6 April 1653, p. 935; *Mercurius Politicus*, 21–28 April 1653, p. 2394.

38 States General to Parliament, 20/30 April 1653, PRO, SP 105/98, f. 6.

8

Political upheavals and ideological divisions

How then did the dissolution of the Rump affect the delicate Anglo-Dutch negotiations? Did English foreign policy remain unchanged, existing in a truly separate sphere from domestic developments?

There could be no question that there was a noticeable change in the English political atmosphere in the spring of 1653. As early as January 1653 Ralph Josselin had complained that the world was "not minding the heir's interest and that he viz. Christ is not only ready to claim but to take his right in the world," adding for good measure "even so Lord Jesus come quickly." Indeed every indication seemed to support the claim of the French ambassador Bordeaux that the Anabaptist party was on the rise. The Monday gatherings at Blackfriars had "scandalized all the whole Parliament." In Somerset House a glazier was said to have preached "destruction to [the Rumpers] and all their adherents." The fiery radical Vavasor Powell's sermons were so popular that the Charterhouse could not hold the thousands who came to hear him. By April there could be no doubting the "great vein of preaching against the present Parliament, and much ranting among the soldiery to the same effect." Even an army newsletter-writer admitted that "our councils are private and high, something extraordinary is speedily expected." Significantly foreign policy was frequently discussed in these sermons and at these gatherings. The "zealous party in the army," observed one newsmonger, "are so gallant and resolute that they will as much scorn a peace of Holland, or any princes of the earth, as I heard them (three one after another in one day) affirm in the pulpit." "The reason the Independents lately appeared so hot against the Parliament," opined another commentator less than a week before Cromwell dissolved the Rump, "was upon a presumption that their clandestine treaty with the Hollanders should have taken effect."[1]

1 Josselin, *Diary*, 24 January 1653, p. 295; Bordeaux to de Brienne, January 1653, PRO, PRO 31/3/90, f. 576r; newsletter from London, 18 March 1653, Bod., Clar. 45, f. 204v; newsletter from London, 1/11 April 1653, Bod., Clar. 45, f. 223r; newsletter from London, 8 April 1653, Bod., Clar. 45, f. 269r; newsletter from London, 15 April 1653, Bod., Clar. 45, f. 292v; Edgeman to Browne, 16/26 April 1653, Christ Church, Browne MSS, Box D-L; newsletter from Westminster, 9 April 1653, Worcester College, Clarke MSS 25, f. 7v;

Not surprisingly the dissolution unleashed a new wave of apocalyptic excitement. Deeply felt and long-held beliefs in the corruption of the Rump were expressed with an enthusiastic fury. "It was no more than what I did apprehend the Lord would do and that suddenly," the radical naval administrator John Poortmans confided to his brother in the Lord, Robert Blackborne, "for that person, that people, or that power though never so strong, daring to wrest the staff out of his own hand shall feel that the weight of his finger is heavier than their loins." Consequently Poortmans could look upon the dissolution "as the dawning of the day of the redemption." Cromwell himself had expressed "a great deal of fear that [the Rump] will destroy again what the Lord hath done graciously for them and us. We all forget God and God will forget us and give us up to confusion and these men will help it on if they be suffered to proceed in their ways." The Rump, a group of officers stationed at Dalkeith proclaimed, endeavored "to perpetuate themselves and thereby to enslave the nation." "Nor shall we be led back again to stoop to any Egyptian yoke of bondage," they insisted, consequently welcoming the dissolution as "the great work of the Lord and his people." In a sermon delivered at Somerset House on 1 May Richard Coppin compared God's command to Cromwell with that which he had long ago given to David. "So the like command might come from the Lord to our general," Coppin explained, "to smite the late Parliament, and to slay them to their oppressive power, laws and actions, rules and private interests, and to spare none as to them." No wonder Bulstrode Whitelocke noted sourly that "diverse fierce men, pastors of churches, and their congregations were pleased at" the dissolution.[2]

But it was not just the hottest of men who greeted the dissolution with enthusiasm and expectation. All London "demonstrated great joy at the dissolution," averred the French ambassador. "We were at first like men in a dream, and could hardly believe for rejoicing, to see the wonderful goodness

newsletter from London, 8 April 1653, Bod., Clar. 45, f. 270v; newsletter from London, 15 April 1653, Bod., Clar. 45, f. 293r. Naturally I am uncomfortable relying so heavily on Royalist newsletters. But I have used only newsletters which display some internal evidence of reliability (e.g. claims to have been personally present at a sermon), and newsletters which Hyde did not reject as untrustworthy.

2 John Poortmans to Robert Blackborne, 23 April 1653, PRO, SP 18/35, f. 315r; Whitelocke, *Annals*, November 1652, BL, Add. 37345, ff. 241v–242r; *The Humble Remonstrance of the General Councel of Officers Met at Dalkeith the Fifth of May 1653* (London, 1653), Thomason: 14 May 1653, pp. 4–7; Richard Coppin, *Saul Smitten for not Smiting Amalek According to the Severity of the Command*, sermon delivered at Somerset House 1 May (London, 1653), Thomason: 20 August 1653, p. 9; Whitelocke, *Annals*, 20 April 1653, BL, Add. 37345, f. 271. For similar sentiments expressed at Blackfriars, see John Langley to Sir Richard Leveson, 3 May 1653, SRO, D593/P/8/2/2. See also John Spittlehouse, *A Warning-Piece Discharged* (London, 1653), Thomason: 19 May 1653, p. 11. Naturally Thomas Harrison and Vavasor Powell expressed similar sentiments. See *Mercurius Pragmaticus*, 16–25 May 1653, p. 2 (Harrison); newsletter from London, 6 May 1653, Bod., Clar. 45, f. 366 (Harrison); newsletter from London, April 1653, Bod., Clar. 45, f. 326v (Powell).

and kindness of God," gushed a petition from the people of Durham. "Great and marvellous are thy works Lord God Almighty," one group of army officers exclaimed to Colonel Robert Lilburne, "just and true are the ways thou King of Saints, who shall not fear thee, O Lord, and glorify thy name?" In Essex, Ralph Josselin compared the dissolution to the restoration of Israel. "This island hath afforded the greatest revolutions that I think any memory affords us, of any time or place," wrote the republican John Hall, "so I believe this to be the greatest of them." The dissolution was "acceptable amongst the generality," John Evelyn informed his friend Sir Richard Browne, so much so "that never men lost their honor with less pity."[3]

Significantly most of the fleet expressed "their delight at the dismissal of the late Parliament." "I trust the Lord will bring glory to himself and good to His people by all these revolutions," John Lawson wrote to his friend Robert Blackborne. Richard Deane was sure that "the end of all these terrible shakings" was "that Christ alone may be exalted." "Our fleet have sent hither their commissioners to approve of our late change of government," ran one report, "unless they should send them order not to fight the Dutch." While a large group of naval officers published their support for the dissolution, William Penn's men "severally declared abundance of affection to this good work."[4]

As soon as it became clear that the Council of Officers intended to assemble a new representative, that new government became the focus of apocalyptic expectations. Petitions poured into the Lord General and his officers beseeching him to fill the new representative "with able men of truth, fearing God, and hating covetousness" in hopes that "the scepter of the Lord may be advanced."[5] "Already the phanatique preachers in Black-

[3] Bordeaux to de Brienne, 22 April/1 May 1653, PRO, PRO 31/3/90, f. 654r; "Address from the People of Durham to Cromwell and the Council of Officers," 28 April 1653, Nickolls, pp. 90–91; letter from the army to Colonel Lilburne, 3 May 1653, Worcester College, Clarke MSS 25, f. 48; Josselin, *Diary*, 20, 23 April 1653, p. 302; [John Hall], *A Letter Written to a Gentleman in the Country Touching the Dissolution of the late Parliament and the Reasons Thereof* (London, 1653), Thomason: 16 May 1653, p. 1; Colonel Lilborne to Colonel Lambert, 17 May 1653, Worcester College, Clarke MSS 25, f. 53; Bradshaw to Cromwell, 19 May 1653, PRO, SP 82/9, f. 76r; John Evelyn to Sir Richard Browne, 2 May 1653, Christ Church, John Evelyn MSS Out-Letters 1433.

[4] Paulucci to Sagredo, 13/23 May 1653, *CSPV*, p. 75; John Lawson to Robert Blackborne, 25 April 1653, PRO, SP 18/35, f. 317r; Richard Deane to Richard Salwey, 22 April 1653, PRO, SP 18/35, f. 291; newsletter from London, 6 May 1653, Bod., Clar. 45, f. 365v; *A Declaration of the Generals at Sea* (London, 1653), Thomason: 27 April 1653; *Mercurius Politicus*, 28 April–5 May 1653, p. 2408; Whitelocke, *Annals*, 25 April 1653, BL, Add. 37345, f. 271v; Whitelocke, *Annals*, 2 May 1653, BL, Add. 37345, f. 272r. There is some circumstantial evidence to suggest that Robert Blake was less happy with the dissolution of the Rump. See: newsletter from London, 29 April 1653, Bod., Clar. 45, f. 335r; newsletter from London, 6 May 1653, Bod., Clar. 45, f. 366r; newsletter from London, 13 May 1653, Bod., Clar. 45, f. 382r.

[5] *Moderate Occurrences*, 26 April–3 May 1653, pp. 35–36. I am not, of course, claiming that the gathered churches selected the members to sit in the nominated Parliament, merely that the godly held special hopes for this Parliament. The best discussion of the formation

friars and their other mad assemblies take upon them to divine the necessity of a king," noted one Royalist purveyor of news, failing to note that the preachers meant King Jesus not King Charles II. Colonel John Jones expressed the hope that "the world may be convinced that our blessed, eternal, wise, powerful, and patient King Jesus can and now doth begin to govern the nations of the earth by his spirit in his saints." "I doubt not," agreed Robert Overton, "but religion and liberty shall again flourish, whilst tyranny and oppression like a desolate woman, shall die childless." After the English victory in the Three Days Battle, one of Thurloe's news gatherers marveled "that God in your infancy appears for you with wonders *in profundis*." John Milton was sure that God was now "finishing that great work, which by such visible signs, he hath made appear he hath in hand for the glory of his name, the felicity of these nations, and I believe for the blessed alteration of all Europe." "So now," John Canne wrote expectantly, "as the relics of monarchy which remain yet with us shall be moved, so will the remainders of the Antichristian Kingdom be removed with them. As Monarchy falls, so falls Antichristism."[6]

The enthusiasm with which Cromwell greeted the Nominated Parliament on 4 July 1653 is well known. Even Sir Harry Vane, who refused to sit in that Parliament, responded to his invitation with "an extract out of the apocalypse, where the reign of the saints is mentioned, which he says he believes will now begin." The initial meetings of the Nominated Parliament conformed to these expectations. Each morning as the members arrived "they joined in prayer ... one praying after another until there be a full number to make a house." One of their first declarations expressed confidence that "the records of no nation, not even the Jews, so show the actings of God as those of this nation and our enemies themselves see the finger of God. We trust he will not forsake us, but complete his work."[7] Although not every member of the Nominated Parliament was equally

of the nominated Parliament remains that of Austin Woolrych, *Commonwealth to Protectorate* (Oxford, 1982), pp. 103–143.

6 Newsletter from London, 20 May 1653, Bod., Clar. 45, f. 398r; John Jones to ?, 13 June 1653, Joseph Mayer (editor), "Inedited Letters of Cromwell, Colonel Jones, Bradshaw, and Other Legicides," in *Transactions of the Historic Society of Lancashire and Cheshire* new series, Vol. 1 (1861), p. 237; *More Hearts and Hands Appearing for the Work* (London, 1653), Thomason: 7 June 1653, pp. 1–2 (Robert Overton's letter); newsletter from Brussels, 11/21 June 1653, Bod., Rawl. A3, p. 238; [Hall], *A Letter*, p. 2; John Canne, *A Voice from the Temple to the Higher Powers* (London, 1653), Thomason: 13 June 1653, p. 20 (he places these developments in an international context on p. 14). Obviously there are differences in the nature of the enthusiasms of these commentators but in the heady Spring of 1653 these differences were not yet apparent.

7 Newsletter from London, 8 July 1653, Bod., Clar. 46, f. 70r; J. Robinson to Stoneham, 3 June 1653, Bod., Rawl. A3, p. 155; newsletter from London, 3 June 1653, Bod., Clar. 45, f. 452r; *Several Proceedings*, 14–21 July 1653, p. 3137; newsletter from London, 15 July 1653, Bod., Clar. 46, f. 109r; *Impartial Intelligencer*, 5–12 July 1653, p. 9; declaration of Parliament, 12 July 1653, *CSPD*, p. 21.

infused with the spirit of the saints, although the Gathered Churches did not select its membership, there can be no doubt that after the dissolution of the Rump the makers of policy thought they had a very special role to play indeed.[8]

It was in this context, in this confidence of their own special mission, then, that the Council of State received the letter which John De Witt had pushed through the States General in late April. At first glance, the Council of State did seem to continue the foreign policy of the Rump, informing the States General that "notwithstanding the late change and alteration of affairs ... they have the same good intentions towards the United Provinces, with sincere desires to put an end to the present war, and to establish a firm and lasting peace between the nations." But this statement masked very real differences within the Council as to how to proceed. There was a "long debate whether [the letter] were fit to be sent by our new Council." In the end the Council absolutely rejected the Dutch proposal to meet in a neutral place with a neutral Protestant arbitrator, insisting that all negotiations take place in Westminster. No doubt this in part reflected concern for the safety of the English commissioners after the murders of Ascham and Dorislaus on the continent. More significantly, however, this insistence probably resulted from the deep-felt English belief that they were in the right. The knowledge that Dutch ambassadors had sailed to England to beg for peace would certainly do much to convince European observers that God had sided with England.[9] In any case, the position taken by the Council does not reflect the views of Brenner's merchant-interlopers. Although the Council, as one might expect after so great a political change, was quite fluid and included both future servants of the Protectorate and future fifth monarchists, both Maurice Thompson and his brother Robert were specifically excluded from any role in the shaping of policy.[10]

This response almost certainly sparked a similar ideological struggle in the United Provinces. By late May it was common gossip that "in all likelihood" the States General would "resolve to send into England." Indeed the States of Holland had insisted that nothing should be included in their concurrent negotiations with France "which might in any wise hinder

8 John Patrick Laydon, "The Kingdom of Christ and the Powers of the Earth" (Cambridge, Ph.D. thesis, 1977), pp. 383–384.

9 Council of State to States General, 6 May 1653, PRO, SP 105/98, f. 7; newsletter from London, 13 May 1653, Bod., Clar. 45, f. 382v; newsletter from Westminster, 10 May 1653, Worcester College, Clarke MSS 25, f. 45; newsletter from London, 6 May 1653, Bod., Clar. 45, f. 365r.

10 Newsletter from Westminster, 26 April 1653, Worcester College, Clarke MSS 25, f. 13v (includes Salwey, Carew, Stapley, Pickering, Strickland, Lambert, and Harrison in Council); Thomas Harley to Sir Robert Harley, 21 May 1653, BL Loan 29/177, f. 8r (includes Moyer, Philip Jones, and Tomlinson); newsletter, 21 May 1653, Bod., Tanner MSS 52, f. 13r; newsletter from Westminster, 21 May 1653, Worcester College, Clarke MSS 25, f. 56v.

the treaty that was to be made with England."[11] That the States General did in fact decide to send ambassadors to England should not, however, serve to obscure the debate which this decision had provoked. Even after the results of the devastating Three Days Battle were revealed in The Hague, the proposal to send to England was known to be "much opposed by many."[12]

This uneasiness colored both the selection of ambassadors and their instructions. De Witt had wanted to send only two ambassadors to England, and those were to be "neither creatures of the House of Orange nor of the House of Nassau (as the Frisians are) but those who would be agreeable to the English."[13] Instead, the States General opted to send four envoys: two from Holland and one each from Zeeland and Friesland. The two representatives from Holland, Nieupoort and Beverning, were known adherents of De Witt and the States party. The committed republican Nieupoort had been instrumental in drawing up the initial letter to England, while one covert Orangist described Beverning as "neither a true friend of His Majesty nor of the House of Orange." In a letter to his fellow republican Peter De Groot, Beverning expressed his desire for peace because it was in "the true interest of our two commonwealths" and it would defend "the orthodox and reformed religion" against "the intentions of those, who on all sides underhand do persecute them." After several meetings with the Dutch diplomatic team, the French ambassador Bordeaux was convinced that they were deeply divided "touching the Prince of Orange."[14] Jongstall, the Frisian representative, was known to be "a great friend of Count William [of Friesland] and consequently of the House of Orange and Nassau," as well as being "well affected towards his Majesty of Great Britain." Reports were even current that Jongstall went "more to impede peace than to advance it." This is hardly surprising given that he was advised not to trust his "fellow commissioners of Holland, they are crafty knaves."[15] Van De Perre, from Zeeland, though less outspoken than

11 Extracts from secret affairs, 13/23 May 1653, Bod., Rawl. A3, p. 124; newsletter from Westminster, 28 May 1653, Worcester College, Clarke MSS 25, f. 60; newsletter from Amsterdam, 27 May/6 June 1653, Bod., Rawl. A3, pp. 117–118; Holland's advice concerning France, 24 May/3 June 1653, Bod., Rawl. A3, p. 68.

12 Letter to Lord Wentworth, 10/20 June 1653, Bod., Rawl. A3, pp. 213–214.

13 De Bacquoy/Van Ruyven to Hyde, 2/12 June 1653, Bod., Clar. 45, f. 449r (my translation); newsletter, 3/13 June 1653, Bod., Rawl. A3, pp. 156–157 (my translation).

14 De Bacquoy/Van Ruyven to Hyde, 16/26 June 1653, Bod., Clar. 45, f. 494v; De Witt to Beverning and Nieupoort, 22 July/1 August 1653, Bod., Rawl. A4, p. 279; Jongstall to William Frederick, 19/29 July 1653, Bod., Rawl. A4, p. 246; Beverning to De Groot, 2/12 September 1653, Bod., Rawl. A6, p. 24; Bordeaux to de Brienne, 25 July/4 August 1653, PRO, PRO 31/3/91, f. 62r.

15 Newsletter from The Hague, 17/27 June 1653, Bod., Rawl. A3, p. 284 (my translation); newsletter, 3/13 June 1653, Bod., Rawl. A3, pp. 156–157 (my translation); De Bacquoy/Van Ruyven to Hyde, 2/12 June 1653, Bod., Clar. 45, f. 449r (my translation); newsletter from the United Provinces, 24 June/4 July 1653, Bod., Rawl. A4, pp. 78–79 (my translation); Letter to Jongstall, 4 August 1653, Bod., Rawl. A5, p. 45; Beverning to Nieupoort, 3/13 February 1654, Bod., Rawl. A11, p. 112.

Jongstall, was no less of an Orangist. He advised a popular Orangist cleric in the autumn of 1653 that a republican tract should be "strongly set down." When rumors reached him in England that the Dutch commissioners would soon be recalled, and the peace treaty broken off, he claimed to be "well pleased as to my own particular."[16] This ideologically divided set of commissioners received a similarly ambivalent set of instructions. Though the Dutch were to treat for peace, they were to insist on "the omission of the preliminary satisfaction" demanded by England, and then "to treat on the 36 Articles that were left over from the previous year."[17] In other words, the Dutch were to pretend as if the war had never begun, as if the Lord had not expressed his will.

When Beverning arrived at Westminster on 20 June 1653, followed soon thereafter by his three colleagues, he did not find an English Council of State desperate for peace. The excitement generated by the dissolution of the Rump had only begun to die away when news reached England of the great victory in the Three Days Battle. "We are much animated by it," wrote one newsmonger. Even Hyde was forced to admit that "the rebels are full masters at sea." Naturally this victory followed so soon by the arrival of Beverning convinced many that it was this which had "reduced these boorish people to a little good manners, and wrought this good effect upon them." The Dutch were finally admitting that "God had laid a judgement upon them for their sins," thought one naval captain.[18]

This ideological context makes it difficult to believe that Cromwell wanted peace at any cost. All of the evidence indicating that Cromwell was in favor of peace before the autumn of 1653 comes from Royalist newsletters, the French ambassador, and the Venetian resident – hardly sources close to the Council. Bordeaux was notoriously badly informed. He was fed false information from the Council, apparently making them "merry to find by their French returns that the cheat passes so well with the Cardinal." Later Bordeaux himself complained that "no one of any condition desires to

16 Van de Perre to Teelinck, 13/23 September 1653, Bod., Rawl. A6, p. 109. For Teelinck's Orangism see G. Groenhuis, "Calvinism and National Consciousness: The Dutch Republic as the New Israel," in A. C. Duke and C. A. Tamse (editors), *Church and State Since the Reformation* (The Hague, 1981), Vol. VII (1981), p. 121.

17 Newsletter from United Provinces, 24 June/4 July 1653, Bod., Rawl. A4, p. 79 (my translation); newsletter from Amsterdam, 27 May/6 June 1653, Bod., Rawl. A3, p. 118; newsletter from The Hague, 10/20 July 1653, Bod., Rawl. A3, pp. 217–218; newsletter from Westminster, 11 June 1653, Worcester College, Clarke MSS 25, f. 69; Information from a merchant returned from the United Provinces, 28 May 1653, Worcester College, Clarke MSS 25, f. 59v.

18 Day's proceedings, 20 June 1653, *CSPD*, p. 426 (Beverning's arrival); newsletter from London, 17 June 1653, Bod., Clar. 45, ff. 498v–499r; Hyde to Father Wilford, 17/27 June 1653, Bod., Clar. 45, f. 500r; Edward Harley to Sir Robert Harley, 11 June 1653, BL, Loan 29/177, f. 22r; *Several Proceedings*, 23–30 June 1653, p. 3100; Theodorus to Lord Conway, 23 June 1653, *CSPD*, pp. 435–436; Captain Robert Clarke to Admiralty commissioners, 21 June 1653, *CSPD*, p. 433.

have any contact with me." Paulucci's Catholicism and friendship with the French ambassador prevented him from any intimate contact with the English political nation. Even Sagredo, the Venetian ambassador in Paris, concluded after reading Paulucci's despatches that "it is quite probable that Cromwell, whilst proclaiming a wish for peace, for the sake of popularity, may really desire the continuation of the war."[19]

In fact, most of the evidence suggests that though Cromwell was willing to accept peace if the Dutch displayed evidence of contrition, he was not ideologically opposed to the war. Colonel Robert Thompson described Cromwell as "hot and zealous against the Dutch" in May 1652. During the winter he offered a huge sum of money to help prosecute the war – hardly the action of a man anxious to see its conclusion at any cost. After Tromp had appeared in the Channel in early June, Cromwell was heard "to profess (in more than usual passion) that those insolent neighbors should not receive such good terms of peace from him, as he before intended them." Dutch observers, who met with Cromwell and his colleagues, listened to sermons, and had much greater access to English culture than their Royalist and Catholic counterparts, knew that Cromwell was not an advocate of peace at any cost. "There can be nothing expected but proud demands," opined one Dutch newswriter after the first batch of diplomatic correspondence had reached The Hague, "the Lord General and the army being made violent against" the Dutch. In private conversation with Beverning Cromwell "used many unhandsome expressions to the prejudice and dishonor of our state." As soon as it became clear that Cromwell had decided not to aid the Frondeurs in their last defense against the armies of the King of France, the Dutch ambassadors were convinced of Cromwell's bellicose intentions. "If the sad condition of Bourdeaux, whose relief Cromwell did affect, would not cause Cromwell to make a peace," they explained to their superiors, "he would more violently prosecute the war: and nothing could be devised that would take him off but the enslaving of them." No wonder one popular Dutch squib described Cromwell as "Holland's double pest." Nieupoort, who was on friendly terms with Cromwell, later told the States General that "Cromwell had dissolved the late Parliament because they were too much inclined to a peace with this State."[20] Cromwell might well have felt uneasy

19 For Bordeaux: newsletter from London, 27 May 1653, Bod., Clar. 45, f. 438v; Bordeaux to de Brienne, 13/23 October 1653, PRO, PRO 31/3/91, f. 111v; Bordeaux to de Brienne, 6/16 June 1653, PRO, PRO 31/3/91, f. 10r (where he attributes his information to Fleming – who later claimed that Cromwell would only agree to peace on the condition that the Orangists would be driven from power); Sagredo to Doge and Senate, 31 May/10 June 1653, *CSPV*, pp. 83–84.

20 Colonel Thompson, "Notes Upon the Dutch War," Bod., Clar. 47, f. 178r; Paulucci to Sagredo, 24 December/3 January 1652/3, *CSPV*, p. 2 (Cromwell's financial donation to the cause); newsletter from London, 3 June 1653, Bod., Clar. 45, f. 482r; newsletter from The Hague, 1/11 July 1653, Bod., Rawl. A4, pp. 54–55; Boreel to Dutch Ambassadors, 3/13 September 1653, Bod., Rawl. A6, pp. 58–59; newsletter from The Hague, 25 July/4 August

about fighting fellow Protestants, but until the Dutch had reformed he realized there was little choice.

The Council of State which governed England was no less irritated at the Dutch than the Lord General. Sir Oliver Fleming told the Venetian resident that though peace was a possibility the English "may even insist on the throwing over of the Prince of Orange." "Both Council and Commissioners of the Navy," noted the author of one intercepted Dutch despatch, "are for a prosecution" of the war. "Really all the intelligence I have out of England," concluded Edward Hyde, "persuades me that they are not there fond of an agreement." Since the power in England was now in "the hands of fortunate swordsmen puffed up with so many successes and victories, flushed in blood," agreed one Dutch intelligencer, "we fear that you will prosecute the war violently."[21]

One should not assume, however, that because there were no longer any voices clamoring for immediate peace with the Dutch at any cost, that there was consensus over war strategy much less over difficult domestic issues. There were still differences of opinion within the Council of State and the political nation, differences of opinion in areas of domestic policy which Woolrych has demonstrated led eventually to the resignation of Barebones. These differences emerged as soon as Barebones met. "Already they break palpably into factions," noted a newsletter-writer in the middle of July. Since Barebones was composed of men "who think themselves divinely inspired," noted Bordeaux with a touch of mockery, "one should not be surprised if they sometimes disagree." By the beginning of August he was sure that these spiritual differences were so great that they would be politically incapacitated. "Certainly they cannot be long in one house, that

1653, PRO, SP 84/159, f. 127r (reporting on one of the ambassadors' letters); "Upon the Nulling of the English Parliament," Dutch verses, 2 July 1653, Bod., Rawl. A4, p. 57; Letter from De Bacquoy/Van Ruyven, 1/11 September 1653, Bod., Clar. 46, f. 220r; see also Christopher Hill, *God's Englishman; Oliver Cromwell and the English Revolution* (New York, 1970), pp. 131–132. One need not believe that Cromwell was "captured" by the fifth monarchists to subscribe to this view. Cromwell merely agreed with many of his contemporaries that the Dutch had been corrupted by the pursuit of profit, and that they were in danger of being overwhelmed by a wave of Orangism. In fact, Laydon has argued persuasively that since the only distinguishing characteristic of fifth monarchists "was their repudiation of the Protectorate on the grounds that it represented an Antichristian usurpation of the proper role of Christ and his saints as ruler of the New Jerusalem." ("Kingdom of Christ," pp. 107–108). There were no fifth monarchists in the summer of 1653.

21 Paulucci to Sagredo, 1/11 July 1653, *CSPV*, pp. 95–96 (quoting Fleming); newsletter, 3/13 June 1653, Bod., Rawl. A3, pp. 159–160; intercepted Dutch letter, 16/26 June 1653, Bod., Rawl. A3, p. 271; newsletter, 17/27 June 1653, Bod., Rawl. A3, p. 291; Hyde to Nicholas, 10/20 June 1653, Bod., Clar. 45, f. 488v (this letter is especially valuable since Hyde had read the newsletters which claimed that Cromwell wanted peace at any cost); newsletter from The Hague, 29 April 1653, Bod., Rawl. A3, p. 24. I have not cited Venetian and French sources which make the same point; though they do exist. See: Gentillot to de Brienne, 2/12 July 1653, PRO, PRO 31/3/91, f. 38r; Paulucci to Sagredo, 13/23 May 1653, *CSPV*, p. 75.

are so furiously divided," noted one Royalist rather hopefully. It was with "exceeding great grief" that the radical John Jones heard "that there are contentions and divisions amongst you; the choicest and most singularly elected Parliament that ever was in England." It was his fear, Jones told Harrison, that "the hopes and expectations of the saints [would be] frustrated through your divisions." "Division, which is the murderess of councils, appeared very briskly in their very dawn," recalled one of the most eloquent of Cromwellian polemicists, "and there was a party headed, whom nothing could please, but the wildest and most extravagant devastation possible." Indeed, there could be no doubt that the most radical of millenarians did have a foothold in the Nominated Parliament. One newsletter-writer found many of the members of the Nominated Parliament "laboring in the Lord's harvest in the Monday congregation in Blackfriars."[22]

These ideological differences were manifest in debates about foreign policy. "Some very dear to the Lord [are] inclining much to our seeking after peace from Heb. 12,14., Rom. 12,18., James 3,17.," Harrison wrote to John Jones soon after the dissolution of the Rump, while "others humbly think Christ hath taken to himself his own power, begun to break here who will not bow, and is going on; whilst they are not free to own his dispensations, neither shall we own them, not because they are our enemies, but our Lord's." Few doubted on which side of the question Harrison and his supporters stood. In a detailed memorandum outlining the ideological divisions in the army and in Parliament, the Dutch ambassadors concluded that Harrison and his "anabaptists" "are men no ways inclined to an accommodation with this state." "The Anabaptists," agreed another Dutch observer, "were much more incensed against this state than the Independents were." So neatly poised were these two groups, that the Nominated Parliament found it necessary to appoint both the Independent John Owen and the very radical Richard Craddock to preach before them at the Thanksgiving service celebrating the English victory off the Texel.[23]

22 Newsletter from London, 21 July 1653, Bod., Rawl. A4, p. 270; newsletter from London, 22 July 1653, Bod., Clar. 46, f. 112; Bordeaux to de Brienne, 28 July/7 August 1653, PRO, PRO 31/3/91, f. 65r; Bordeaux to de Brienne, 1/11 August 1653, PRO, PRO 31/3/91, f. 67r; newsletter from London, 29 July 1653, Bod., Clar. 46, p. 133v; letter to Stoneham, 29 July 1653, Bod., Rawl. A4, p. 344; Letter from London, 1/11 August 1653, Bod., Rawl. A5, p. 6; newsletter from London, 5 August 1653, Bod., Clar. 46, f. 158v; John Jones to Thomas Harrison, 11 August 1653, Mayer, "Inedited Letters," pp. 238–239; *Confusion Confounded: Or, A Firm Way of Settlement Settled and Confirmed* (London, 1654), Thomason: 18 January 1654, p. 3; newsletter from London, 1 July 1653, Bod., Clar. 46, ff. 32–34. The final impressionistic claim is given substance by the thorough research of Woolrych (*Commonwealth to Protectorate*) presented in his appendices. Some observers were able to discern these ideological divisions well before the Nominated Parliament had assembled: newsletter from London, 7 May 1653, SRO, D593/P/8/2/2; newsletter from London, 17 May 1653, SRO, D593/P/8/2/2.

23 Thomas Harrison to John Jones, 30 April 1653, Mayer, "Inedited Letters," p. 226;

It was these two ideological groupings, then, which began negotiations with the Dutch in the early summer. What were their respective attitudes toward the Dutch? The more moderate group in the Council of State and in Barebones wanted to show the Dutch the rod of the Lord – wanted to make them aware that they had lost God's favor by seeking after profit rather than grace, by promoting Orangism rather than republicanism – in order to reform them.[24] It is "not that we desire their ruin," explained the *Several Proceedings of State Affairs*, "but would prevent their insolences and outrages against England." But those who would reform the Dutch knew their task was not facile. "They will not be reformed till they have sorely smarted," observed the *Mercurius Politicus*, "and it is their misery, that nothing but a miserable low condition will reduce them to a remembrance of their interest and reason." Because the Dutch had allowed their actions to be determined by their will – "by a will inflamed with ambition and covetousness" – "they will never think of doing you right, or of yielding to your right, till they be convinced that they have hitherto been in the wrong; such another argument as the last engagement was, may convince them." The Venetian resident, with unusual perspicacity, commented in the summer of 1653 that the English "observe that the United Provinces deserve punishment and correction for neglecting the friendship of this country."[25]

Nevertheless, once the Dutch had been stunned into realizing their crimes they were to be embraced, not incinerated. This had long been the message delivered from the pulpit to the English nation. When the Lord "deals against his own people, it is a great trouble to him, to make them suffer his corrections," preached George Newton to his Taunton congregation, "nor doth he aim a whit at satisfaction (for that he hath received from Christ to the extremity of justice) but only at their reformation: so that he gives correction to them, as physic to recover, and not as poison to destroy." This

"Memorandum of Dutch Ambassadors," 2/12 August 1653, Bod., Rawl. A5, pp. 21–22; Letter from De Bacquoy/Van Ruyven, 1/11 September 1653, Bod., Clar. 46, f. 220; *Several Proceedings*, 25 August–1 September 1653, p. 3233. For Craddock's radicalism see *Mercurius Cambro-Britannicus: Or, News from Wales, Touching the Glorious and Miraculous Propagation of the Gospel in Those Parts* (London, 1652), Thomason: 4 September 1652, *passim.*

24 Unfortunately the poor records kept by the Council and the attendance at the meetings of the commissioners with the Dutch make it difficult to identify with certainty those who held this position. But it is safe to suggest that Cromwell, Strickland, and Pickering all subscribed to this point of view. Anthony Ashley Cooper and Charles Wolsley, because they were both involved in the Protectorate's peace negotiations, also probably adopted this view. The widespread enunciation of this view in the press and in sermons suggests its broad purchase.

25 *Several Proceedings*, 16–23 June 1653, p. 3085; *Mercurius Politicus*, 2–9 June 1653, pp. 2494–2495; *Perfect Diurnall*, 25 July–1 August 1653, p. 2879; Letter to Whitelocke, 24 September 1652, Longleat House, Whitelocke MSS XII, f. 167v; Paulucci to Sagredo, 7/17 August 1653, *CSPV*, p. 111; *Mercurius Politicus*, 17–24 November 1653, p. 2887.

was also the message of Dr. John Owen, who was as popular with the Nominated Parliament as he had been with the Rump, in his sermon justifying the Dutch War. Godly reform, "the coming in of the kingdom of Christ, shall not be by the arm of flesh, nor shall it be the product of strifes and contests of men which are in the world," Owen insisted, "it is not to be done by might or power, but by the spirit of the Lord of Hosts." The Dutch needed to be prepared for conversion, not destroyed. Indeed, Owen concluded, "there is nothing more opposite to the spirit of the Gospel, than to suppose that Jesus Christ will take to himself a kingdom by the carnal sword and the bow of the sons of men." Hugh Peter, who appears to have eventually admitted that the Dutch needed some reformation, argued in the summer of 1653 that "God almighty had punished [the Dutch] long enough for their sins, and especially for their pride, covetousness, ambition, discord, ingratitude and unmercifulness, hardheartedness to the poor," consequently "pray[ing] and preach[ing] for peace."[26]

Laymen as well as clerics expressed these sentiments. The author of the *Seas Magazines Opened*, after berating the Dutch for their covetousness, ambition, and ingratitude, concluded by offering his support for a peace "when it shall please God to stir the same" for "I hold it a greater glory to obtain victory and safety by peace, than to gain victory and safety by victory." "What God in his secret hath determined we must submit unto," wrote one Londoner, but he hoped for a "firm peace" because "in human reason you should make Holland firmly yours, for your safety will more depend on it." Sir Oliver Fleming told the Venetian resident Paulucci in "strict confidence" that "even if they could knock out Holland with one arm, political expediency must prompt them to raise her with the other, for the honor and glory of republics in general." Oliver Cromwell himself was committed to these views. He was convinced of the possibility of godly reformation of the unregenenerate. "If they see you lay out your strength for God and his people," Cromwell told the Nominated Parliament of their less godly domestic brethren, "this is the way to fit them and bring them to their desired privileges." When the Dutch were "a little high upon it," he could assure William Penn that it "will return upon their own heads in the end." But he made it quite clear his own aim, in foreign as well as in domestic policy, was to encourage reformation rather than to eviscerate those who had deviated from the path of the Lord. "We desire from our hearts," he reportedly proclaimed after the Three Day Battle, an "establishment and union" not only with "all those that fear the Lord

[26] George Newton, *A Sermon Preached the 11. of May 1652 in Taunton* (London, 1652), Thomason: 16 July 1652, p. 10; John Owen, *A Sermon Preached to the Parliament, Octob. 13. 1652* (Oxford, 1652), Thomason: 30 October 1652, pp. 18–20; Dutch newsletter, 1/11 July 1653, Bod., Rawl. A4, p. 23 (mispaginated); newsletter from London, 5 August 1653, Bod., Clar. 46, p. 159r. The claim about Owen's relations with the Nominated Parliament is based on the frequency with which he was invited to preach to it.

amongst us" but also with the Dutch "nation (at least to all those that fear the Lord there)."[27]

At least some merchants agreed with the Lord General. "The Lord grant, that this bloody fight may be the last amongst Christians," prayed a group of Eastland merchants after the Three Days Battle, "and the means to a happy peace betwixt those two mighty commonwealths." "I am sorry there should be so much Christian blood spilt," agreed the Canary merchant John Paige, and "hope this may be a means to bring peace in the end." Although the London merchant Edward Barnard was concerned "that the Hollander is not yet low enough to help carry on the work that God hath cut out for them to do, they mind only the carrying on of their trade," he was "confident God in his due time will fit them for higher employment." That employment was to be high indeed. "In case these two mighty potentates should join together what would become of the kings of the earth?" Barnard asked Strickland rhetorically, "doubtless Babylon is upon his fall and that is likely to be the ... issue of this war with Holland."[28]

Fortunately many of the officers in the fleet also hoped that their victories would reform the Dutch and lead to peace. Generals Monk and Blake were glad that their victory in the Three Days Battle "had much abased and laid low" the enemy's spirits, but also prayed that "the issue thereof may be for good to them as also unto us." During the negotiations Blake and William Penn informed the Admiralty commissioners that they were "sorry the treaty with the Dutch has been delayed." Indeed Blake was said to be so sorry that he was unwilling to bring the war to the Dutch mainland. His conscience, it was said, "will not let him fight past Callice sands."[29] Rear Admiral Nehemiah Bourne also hoped that the Three Days Battle – "this late great achievement by God's blessing, and the English valor" – "may put a final end to the war betwixt both nations of England and Holland." Captain John Woolters expressed to Captain Andrew Ball his hopes "that God will make use of you as an instrument in his own hands to do something that may help promote the glory of God and the public good of our poor nation and purchase that peace which his own people have an

27 *The Seas Magazine Opened: Or, The Hollander Dispossessed* (London, 1653), Thomason: 15 August 1653, p. 4; J. R. to Richard Temple, 6/16 December 1652, Longleat House, Whitelocke MSS XII, f. 183r; Paulucci to Sagredo, 8/18 July 1653, *CSPV*, p. 99; notes on Cromwell's speech, 4 July 1653, Bod., Tanner MSS 52, f. 22v; Cromwell to William Penn, 9 July 1653, BL Loan 29/241, f. 190r; *Mercurius Politicus*, 9–16 June 1653, p. 2512.

28 *Mercurius Politicus*, 7–14 July 1653, p. 2567 (Eastland merchants' letter); Paige to Paynter and Clerke, 1 March 1653, Steckley, *John Paige*, p. 86; Edward Barnard to Walter Strickland, 4 June 1653, BL, Add. 4156, f. 6.

29 *Several Proceedings*, 7–14 July 1653, p. 3122 (Letter from Blake and Monk); Blake and Penn to Admiralty commissioners, 4 February 1654, *CSPD*, 6, p. 388; newsletter from The Hague, 14/24 June 1653, Bod., Rawl. A3, p. 261. For similar doubts about Blake's willingness to eviscerate the Dutch see: Letter to Whitelocke, 24 September 1652, Longleat House, Whitelocke MSS XII, f. 166v; Blake to Commissioners of the Navy, 1 December 1652, BL Loan 29/241, f. 169r.

interest in." "I pray that God will make this mercy a further blessing to us, in procuring a good peace between us, who were friends so long formerly, and so useful one to the other," exclaimed Captain Joseph Cubitt after the battle off the Texel, expressing concern that the English not be puffed up with the same pride which had "brought this evil upon [the Dutch]." When the naval commissioners Thomas Smith, Peter Pett, and Francis Willoughby heard news that the Dutch had desired to commence negotiations they prayed that "the little cloud which at present seems to be but as an hand, shall so increase that it shall cover the whole heavens over the two nations with the blessings of peace."[30]

Clearly, then, there was broad sentiment that England was fighting the Dutch to restore them to their original godly and republican ways. When that goal was reached, peace, even alliance and amalgamation, was possible. "O what is more wished or would be more welcome than peace?" asked one Englishman after the Three Days Battle had raised hopes of Dutch reform, "What is better or sweeter than peace? What is more splendid and beautiful than peace? Peace is that fair Astraea that linketh men together in the golden fetters of mutual amity, and maketh them to live as if their persons being many, their souls were but one." Indeed by the winter of 1653 many in England had reason to believe that the Dutch had returned to their pristine purity. "This English war doth put water of ten per one into the wines of covetousness of our merchants, traders and navigators," reported one of Thurloe's Dutch-based intelligencers. The Dutch knew that "the hand of the Lord hath been very much against them of late," Thurloe informed Bulstrode Whitelocke, so that "men are of opinion that the States of Holland will not neglect this opportunity of peace."[31]

Aligned against this view were those religious radicals who believed that the Dutch had permanently forsaken God's cause and that the Netherlands could only serve as the first stop on the road to Rome to destroy the Whore of Babylon. Although these men were willing to admit the ideological differences in the Dutch polity, they denied that the States party was any more virtuous than the Orangists. The Dutch people "begin to murmur at

30 *Weekly Intelligencer*, 31 May–7 June 1653, p. 861 (letter from N. Bourne); John Woolters to Captain Andrew Ball, 31 January 1653, PRO, SP 18/32, f. 156r; for Woolters see Bernard Capp, *Cromwell's Navy* (Oxford, 1989), p. 304; Captain Joseph Cubitt to Robert Blackborne, 2 August 1653, *CSPD*, p. 70 – I don't read this letter as expressing opposition to the war as Capp seems to do (*Cromwell's Navy*, p. 133); Tho. Smith, Peter Pett, Fra. Willoughby to Commissioners of the Navy, 26 March 1653, PRO, SP 18/34, f. 198r; John Poortmans to Robert Blackborne, 9 June 1653, *CSPD*, p. 397.

31 *A Declaration of the Further Proceedings of the English Fleet upon the Coast of Holland* (London, 1653), Thomason: 9 June 1653, p. 5; newsletter from United Provinces, 25 November/5 December 1653, Bod., Rawl. A8, p. 239; Thurloe to Whitelocke, 6 January 1654, in Sigismund Freiherrn von Bischoffshausen, *Die Politik des Protectors Oliver Cromwelll in der Auffassung und Thätigkeit seines Ministers des Staatssecretärs John Thurloe* (Innsbruck, 1899), p. 152.

their insolent and imperious yokemasters, and have declared that they are no longer able to undergo their monster-like burdens and taxes," reported the very radical *Moderate Occurrences*. "Now is the time for our high and mighty states-men to receive their just reward of a meritorious downfall," proclaimed the equally aggressive *Dutch Intelligencer*, "and why not here as well as in other republics where no conscience is made of heavy impositions and illegal taxes." These criticisms were ominously similar to those made of the disgraced and discredited Rump. William Lilly had predicted that it was the Rump's habit of "new and illegal assessment" which would lead the "commonalty joining with the soldier" into revolt. The author of *Vox Plebis* had complained of the Rump's "arbitrary and exorbitant practices," while the apocalyptic John Canne had castigated the Rumpers for "flying upon the spoil and giving countenance to the sins of Jeroboam." The moral was clear. "Nor do we hear anything of God to appear either in the one party or the other," testified one observer of the Dutch polity in the summer of 1653, "only God is dashing them one against another to confound their Babel towering against the power of God in England."[32]

The tyranny of the Dutch republican party grew naturally out of its Presbyterianism. Not surprisingly the Dutch hoped to "destroy your General Cromwell and his new government and set up the Presbyterian." For the radicals, Presbyterianism was not one of the many forms of godly Protestantism, but one of the more pernicious allies of the beast. This false religion led inevitably to "Antichristian rule and government." "What is it they either might or could do to advance monarchy," Spittlehouse asked of the Presbyterians, "which they have not attempted?" It was hardly surprising that the Presbyterian book-sellers in London had a "factor in Rome itself." Dutch insistence on their advocacy of the true religion was only a disguise for their Popery. "If in any age the devil hath transformed himself into an angel of light, or his apostles and ministers have transformed themselves into the apostles and ministers of Christ," warned Christopher Feak, John Simpson, George Cockayne, and Lawrence Wise, "they have done so in this apostatizing age in which we live." These "new and spiritual Antichristians," they warned, "are far worse than those gross and Popish Antichristians." No wonder that "the

32 *Moderate Occurrences*, 19–26 April 1653, p. 32; *Dutch Intelligencer*, 8–15 September 1652, p. 10; William Lilly, *Merlini Anglici Ephemeris* (London, 1653), Thomason: 16 November 1652, sig. B1r; *Vox Plebis: Or, The Voice of the Oppressed Commons of England Against their Oppressors* (London, 1653), Thomason: 18 April 1653, p. 5; Canne, *A Voice*, p. 15; *Several Proceedings*, 23–30 June 1653, pp. 3092–3093. The accusation of the Rump's corruption, after a virtuous and godly beginning, was a commonplace. See also *A Declaration of the Lord General and his Councel of Officers: Shewing the Grounds and Reasons for the Dissolution of the Late Parliament* (London, 1653), Thomason: 23 April 1653, pp. [3]–5; Milton, *A Defence*, p. 4; [John Hall], *Confusion-Confounded* (London, 1654), p. 2.

Jesuit hath no small foot" in the Dutch plans to aid the Scottish and Irish rebels.[33]

Why then had the Dutch sought peace? Certainly not because the Dutch had reformed, argued the radicals. That "viperous generation," argued the less than *Moderate Publisher*, still had "hopes to suck the Englishmen's blood, which is more sweet unto them than honey." "Mere necessity" had made the Dutch initiate negotiations, warned one radical; "be not deluded with fair promises or hopes of their plain and honest dealings for their intents are no such matter, but prosecute your business and in a short time you may have them in your power, then do what you will to them." "Although their flags and streams are for peace," thought many, "yet their hearts are for war." The arrival of the Dutch ambassadors was thought to be "either a blind to make us more secure or to gain time by cessation." Whatever the motive, the ostensible Dutch desire for peace was "but discourse."[34]

For the radicals, then, the Dutch could no longer be considered part of Israel. Some radicals evoked the image of Tyre, the great trading city which failed to aid its godly ally Jerusalem and was consequently laid waste. "Though the Dutch, like Tyre, join with the Kings of the Nations against us," predicted the *Moderate Publisher* with all the confidence of the Lord's chosen, "yet the righteous shall sing and rejoice."[35] Others compared the United Provinces to Egypt. "Were not the Hollanders puffed up in pride and hardness of heart like Pharaoh and the Egyptians," thought one naval man, "they would not go on in their obstinacy as they do." After the Three Days Battle the generals' chaplain was certain that God would make "a difference henceforward twixt Israel and Egyptians." "The Lord," thought the Parliamentary commissioners in Ireland after the battle off the Texel, had treated the Dutch as he had treated Pharaoh "gloriously throwing them that lifted up themselves into the Sea."[36]

33 Newsletter from The Hague, 10/20 June 1653, Bod., Rawl. A3, p. 238; John Spittlehouse, *The Army Vindicated In Their Late Dissolution of the Parliament* (London, 1653), Thomason: 24 April 1653, pp. 3–4; *The Beacons Quenched: Or The Humble Information of Divers Officers of the Army, and Other Wel-Affected Persons, to the Parliament and Commonwealth of England* (London, 1652) Thomason: 8 October 1652, pp. 6–7; *A Faithful Discovery of a Treacherous Design of Mystical Antichrist Displaying Christ's Banners* (London, 1653) Thomason: 12 June 1653, sig A2; newsletter from The Hague, 14/24 June 1653, Bod., Rawl. A3, p. 261.

34 *Moderate Publisher*, 1–8 April 1653, p. 782; newsletter from the Hague, 14/24 June 1653, pp. 260–262; *Mercurius Britannicus*, 13–20 June 1653, p. 47; newsletter from London, 24 June 1653, Bod., Clar. 46, f. 8v; *Faithful Scout*, 9–16 September 1653, p. 2053. Foreign ambassadors were aware of this line of argument in Westminster. See Gentillot to de Brienne, 28 June/8 July 1653, PRO, PRO 31/3/91, f. 25r; Paulucci to Sagredo, 30 July/9 August 1653, *CSPV*, pp. 107–108.

35 *Moderate Publisher*, 25 February–4 March 1653, p. 748. The *Mercurius Politicus*, 8–15 July 1652, pp. 1730–1731 also evoked this image, but it was almost certainly not a letter from a frequent contributor. The image is from Ezekiel 26–28.

36 *Good Newes from General Blakes Fleet* (London, 1652), Thomason: 20 September 1652,

It was inevitable, then, that "our English Hectors and sons of Mars" would "detest a confederacy with those impostors of the times, whose ingratitude against England cannot be paralleled." The radical prophetess Anna Trapnel warned against making "an ungodly and wicked peace with the Dutch, to the dishonor of God, and hindrance of carrying on God's work." "If they now made peace with these rogues and dogs the Dutch, after they had beaten and beaten and beaten the slaves, nay and almost quite conquered them," warned a preacher popular with the Nominated Parliament, "God's vengeance would follow upon such a heathenish peace; for where should they have a landing place when they went to do the great work of the Lord and tear the whore of Babylon out of her chair, if they gave back by making a peace with them a people and land, which the Lord had as good as given wholly up into their hands." These sentiments were typical of the radicals. "You Belgic provinces break forth / and weep most bitterly / A dire destruction is prepared / it draweth very nigh," ran one of the future fifth monarchist Christopher Feak's hymns. "The scope of their meeting is to preach down governments and to stir up the people against the United Netherlands," Beverning wrote to De Witt after visiting a Monday service at St. Anne's, Blackfriars, "good God what cruel and abominable and most horrible trumpets of fire, murder and flame." "The Dutch must be destroyed," Harrison, Cato-like, was said to have told a gathering of Londoners, "and we shall have heaven upon earth." No wonder the Dutch were anxious for Harrison and "the rest of that gang" to be turned out of office.[37]

Evisceration of the Dutch was to be the prelude for the great march on Rome. "Many temporal and spiritual patriots" opposed any peace with the United Provinces, insisting that "the work of the Lord is not yet done, that the sword must not be sheath'd until they have brought down the tyrants of the earth, and set up the cross of England, and the word of the Lord, even at the very gates and city of Rome." John Spittlehouse advised the Nominated Parliament, in a passage reprinted in the *Moderate Intelligencer*, that "the most facile way [to pull down the power of Rome] is by invading France and Holland, and so erect your standard before the Towers of Babylon." The *Faithful Scout* claimed – falsely – that Cromwell had promised Barebones that the Lord would lead them into the land of Canaan, "over the

p. 5; *Moderate Publisher*, 3–10 June 1653, p. 1087; C. H., E. L., M. C., J. J. to Christian friends, 18 August 1653, Mayer, "Inedited Letters,"p. 240.

37 *Faithful Post*, 3–10 June 1653, p. 1624; *Several Proceedings*, 12–19 January 1654, p. 3564 (Anna Trapnel's prophecy); newsletter from London, 10/20 October 1653, Bod., Rawl. A7, pp. 95–96; Christopher Feak, "Hymn," 11 August 1653, BL, Thomason MSS, TT: E710 (13); Beverning to De Witt, 26 August/5 September 1653, Bod., Rawl. A5, p. 258; Hugh Morrell to Cromwell, 20/30 December 1653, *CSPD*, p. 302; newsletter from London, 13 May 1653, Bod., Clar. 45, f. 380v; Peterson to Coopman, 8/18 July 1653, Bod., Rawl. A4, p. 164.

Narrow Seas into Holland, France, and so to Rome itself, to the end you may pluck up all Antichristian power." The Protectorate polemicist was not far wrong when he claimed that the radicals "condemned all as enemies to Reformation, who kept not an even pace with themselves in the House, or with the hot men at Blackfriars meeting, who pronounced all the Reformed Churches to be as the out-works to Babylon, and that they must be taken down before they could be a coming at the main fort."[38]

The dissolution of the Rump, then, significantly altered the outlook for Anglo-Dutch peace. No longer was there a politically powerful constituency pressing for immediate peace, and peace at any cost. Instead, the events of April 1653 left power in the hands of those convinced that war against the Dutch was necessary. Nevertheless the dissolution revealed that even those who supported the war could not agree on the aims of the war. Those, like Cromwell, who felt the war was fought to restore the United Provinces to godliness and republicanism were willing to entertain peace negotiations. However, the radicals, who knew that Holland would serve as the beachhead for the assault on Rome, violently opposed any peaceful settlement with the outwork of Babylon.

Prospects for peace were uncertain at best, then, when Beverning arrived at Whitehall on 20 June "in a rich barge and had audience of Cromwell and eleven more councillors of state." There were some observers who thought that this meeting could only be a prelude to a glorious peace. "The Hollander," speculated one newspaper rather optimistically, "will now be glad to embrace a peace on any terms." Dolman, who had the largest emotional investment in the negotiations, knew that "they will meet with many heats and disputes" but was sure that in the end "they will understand one another." Dolman and his compatriot and fellow officer in Dutch service Colonel Cromwell were heard to say "the Dutch will decline all their allies and relations of friendship that shall be thought obnoxious to our state, the family of Orange not excepted; so that many new conquests and fine chimeras are already prospected by our statesmen." The Dutch ambassadors themselves did not "despair of a good issue."[39]

38 *Moderate Intelligencer*, 20–27 June 1653, p. 64; John Spittlehouse, *The First Addresses* (London, 1653), Thomason: 5 July 1653, pp. 4–5 reprinted in *Moderate Intelligencer*, 4–11 July 1653, pp. 109–110; [Marchamont Nedham] *Faithful Scout*, 1–8 July 1653, p. 1073; *A True State of the Case of the Commonwealth* (London, 1654), Thomason: 8 February 1654, pp. 14–15. Ralph Josselin frequently dreamed about the great crusade against the Whore of Babylon; see Josselin, *Diary*, 12 September 1652, 14 November 1652, 21 November 1652, 28 March 1653, pp. 285, 289, 300–301.

39 Aitzema, "Selections," Bod., Rawl. C734, f. 79r; *Daily Proceedings*, 17 June 1653, p. 8; Dolman to Colonel Killegrew, 24 June 1653, Bod., Rawl. A3, p. 334; Dolman to his wife, 8 July 1653, Bod., Rawl. A4, p. 131; newsletter from London, 24 June 1653, Bod., Clar. 46, f. 8v; Letter from Van de Perre, 8/18 July 1653, Bod., Rawl. A4, p. 133; Ambassadors to Ruysch, 1/11 July 1653, Bod., Rawl. A4, p. 18.

There were others, however, who were less optimistic. Even the most moderate of the commonwealth's newspapers were skeptical of Dutch intentions. "The great hope is that the English will be kind and forget all the treachery of this people both in design and action," thought the *Mercurius Politicus* of the Dutch, "or else if this cannot be effected, the hope is, you will be so mild as not to follow up the victory, but give them time and leave to provide another fleet." "If they could have peace on their own terms they would be very glad of it," agreed the *Several Proceedings of State Affairs*, "but if not, then be sure they will endeavor to incense the people all they can against England."[40] Royalist observers, by contrast, were sure that English insolence would preclude the possibility of peace. "The rebels are so insolent upon their success," Edgeman explained to Sir Richard Browne, "that they contemn the Dutch in all their discourses as a people already at their mercy." The only peace to which the Council of State would agree, thought Edward Hyde, would be one which would "most absolutely destroy the liberty of that people and make them subordinate." "I do not think it will come to anything," concurred another Royalist observer.[41] The fairest assessment of the prospects for peace came from The Hague. The political pundits in the Dutch capital were sure "that the business is not so facile as some take it."[42]

This uncertain environment demanded delicate diplomacy. Beverning's performance in his first audience was masterfully crafted to assuage the fears of the Cromwellian moderates. Although the "just judgement of God is befallen us in these last times," Beverning averred in his opening speech, all history testifies to the close amity between England and the United Provinces. This friendship "established between both nations" was based on the "communion of faith and profession of the self same reformed religion, which they have from time to time so happily affirmed, and the liberty and freedom of the people." The Dutch consequently hoped for "a perfect amity and indissoluble union" based on aid against each other's rebels and free trade "in all jurisdictions of the one and the other." The end of such an alliance would be, he insisted, "to protect them of the household of faith." An Anglo-Dutch alliance would not only serve to guarantee the "security and preservation" of the reformed religion but would also "cause it more to prosper and flourish."[43] Beverning was conversing in the languages of a Protestant and a republican.

40 *Mercurius Politicus*, 23–30 June 1653, p. 2543; *Several Proceedings*, 16–23 June 1653, pp. 3086–3087.

41 Edgeman to Browne, 9/19 April 1653, Christ Church, Browne MSS, Box D–L; Edgeman to Browne, 19/29 June 1653, Christ Church, Browne MSS, Box D–L; Hyde to Nicholas, 17/27 June 1653, Bod., Clar. 45, f. 505r; newsletter from London, 6 May 1653, Bod., Clar. 45, f. 365.

42 Newsletter from The Hague, 3/13 June 1653, Bod., Rawl. A3, p. 175.

43 "Beverning's Speech," 20 June 1653, PRO, SP 105/98, ff. 9–11.

Beverning's speech yielded immediate results. The deputies soon "received visits from secret friends" assuring them that the English would not insist on the preliminary requirements of reparation, security towns and the suspension of Van Tromp. The English, Beverning wrote to his friend and political ally John De Witt, displayed "a perfect endeavor and disposition, wherewith to bind more closely the two nations with common privileges and benefits." "If we earnestly promote the point of religion," Beverning advised perceptively, "we shall yet come to right."[44] No longer did English observers claim that the Dutch deputies had merely come to spin out time. The Dutch waived all ceremonial forms, marveled an army intelligencer, "they press on for a speedy treaty." This sentiment was echoed even by the ever-suspicious Whitelocke. "They seem rather humble than high in their applications and deportment," agreed another observer.[45]

It was in this newly hopeful atmosphere, then, that the deputies had their first substantive meeting with the English Council of State. At this meeting the Dutch deputies took a much less conciliatory line than Beverning had taken the previous fortnight. They insisted that the three English preliminary demands be rescinded. It was unreasonable, they claimed, to demand that the Dutch recall and punish their greatest naval commander when the English fleet lay before their ports. Of course, if the Council of State would recall the English fleet and promise a cessation of arms "then they could give some hope of it." The English demand for satisfaction was simply unprecedented. No treaty of peace could be found with "the least mention of satisfaction of any damages or costs, done or sustained by the one or the other party," exclaimed the Dutch deputies, not in the treaties between "England, France and Spain, nor in any other treaty of any commonwealth or Prince of Europe in such an occurrence hath [the like] been insisted upon, much less agreed." After all, the Dutch deputies pointed out, "no wound can be closed up and healed by rubbing the sore again." As for security, the best hopes lay not in the cautionary towns proposed by the English, but in "a good peace and nearer union grounded upon the mutual interests of both commonwealths." Only such a peace, they suggested, would put the two commonwealths "in capacity to promote and protect the true reformed religion, in such places, at such times, and by such means and ways as shall be judged most suitable to that purpose."[46] Apparently buoyed by the encouraging hints from members of the Council of State, and now accompanied by the two Orangist ambassadors, Beverning had decided to follow

44 Newsletter from United Provinces, 2 July 1653, Bod., Rawl. A4, p. 75; Beverning to de Witt, 27 June 1653, Bod., Rawl. A3, pp. 279–280.

45 Newsletter from Westminster, 25 June 1653, Worcester College, Clarke MSS 25, f. 76; Whitelocke, *Annals*, BL, Add. 37345, f. 281r; newsletter from London, 24 June 1653, Bod., Clar. 46, f. 8v.

46 Memorandum of Dutch Ambassadors, 2/12 August 1653, Bod., Rawl. A5, pp. 12–13; Dutch deputies to Council of State, 1 July 1653, PRO, SP 105/98, ff. 13–15.

the letter of his brief from the States General.[47] The Dutch deputies were determined to recommence the negotiations where they had been before the clash between Blake and Tromp in the Downs. They refused to accept any responsibility for the war.

The English commissioners, however, were unable to pretend that the war had not happened. "The fleet of this commonwealth even in the midst of a treaty offered by themselves, was by way of surprise assaulted and attempted upon in their own roads," they reminded the Dutch deputies, a way of proceeding "very unsuitable to those constant demonstrations of affection and friendship received from this state." The English commissioners simply could not imagine leaving themselves vulnerable to another perfidious attack. "It cannot stand with reason or justice," they exclaimed, "that this commonwealth after so great a warning and preservation, and the expense of so much blood leave themselves naked, and exposed to the same surprise and danger, and without having obtained either reparation for the wrongs past, or security that the like be not attempted for the future."[48]

The English knew quite well that as long as there was a significant Orangist presence in the Dutch polity promises could never provide security. "We can expect no good effect by a treaty" because of the continued power of the Orangists "who have brought this business to so desperate an issue," argued a Council of State memorandum, "they having been the incendiaries and plotters of all the evils, besides they are not true to their own liberty, but would set up monarchy amongst you, and reduce their own countrymen to slavery." "If the present state of affairs in the United Provinces, and the spirit which of late hath been prevalent there be considered," insisted the English commissioners displaying their familiarity with Dutch domestic developments, "it is not easy to see by what other ways and means the liberty of the people and the profession of the true religion in that nation can be preserved and maintained there than by a real and substantial securing the intended peace and agreement against the attempts and artifices of those, who are enemies to the interest of God and his people, not only in this commonwealth but in that also." Clearly the English commissioners were ideologically committed to a peace which would simultaneously guarantee their own security and the reform of the United Provinces. Consequently there is no reason to doubt the contemporary rumor that the English would diminish their demands should the Dutch "make it appear to us that they mean honestly, and that it shall not lie in the power of the

47 Newsletter from The Hague, 3/13 June 1653, Bod., Rawl. A3, p. 157; newsletter from The Hague, 3/13 June 1653, Bod., Rawl. A3, pp. 166–167; orders of States General, 5 June 1653, Bod., Rawl. A3, pp. 97–98; newsletter from The Hague, 16/26 June 1653, Bod., Rawl. A3, pp. 276–277; newsletter from The Hague, 1/11 July 1653, Bod., Rawl. A4, p. 25; De Bacquoy/Van Ruyven to Hyde, 7/17 July 1653, Bod., Clar. 46, f. 59.

48 Council of State's answer, [29] June 1653, PRO, SP 105/98, f. 13; Council of State's answer, 13 July 1653, PRO, SP 105/98, ff. 16–17.

Prince of Orange to break the peace when that party finds it for their advantage so to do."[49]

The hard line taken by the English commissioners does not represent the victory of the radicals. Indeed it was Cromwell himself who, in a harangue reputed to have lasted three-quarters of an hour, insisted on "satisfaction and security." Cromwell pointed out that the "humors and spirits of many of the governors in the Netherlands were against this commonwealth," making it impossible for the English to rely on a treaty based solely on trust. Then he "brought all their miscarriages home to their own doors and insisted much on Tromp's beginning the war ... that upon that ground we might prosecute our revenge against him, for neither reparation for the past, nor safety for the future is so much desired by us as the death or banishment of that man, his ruin and the declension of the House of Nassau."[50] Although Thomas Harrison was among the commissioners present, he is unlikely to have had the influence to force Cromwell's hand. The other commissioners were Colonel John Desborough, Sir Gilbert Pickering and Walter Strickland – all of whom would be members of the first Protectorate Council and were religious moderates.[51] All of the evidence suggests that the commissioners had accurately expressed the sentiments of the more moderate segments of the Council of State. "It is not a bare peace that is to be insisted on, for that men may have when they please, if they will remit any part of their right or interest to their adversaries" argued the *Mercurius Politicus* which so often served as the mouthpiece of the moderate supporters of the commonwealth, "but it is a lasting peace that is principally to be desired; such a peace as follows a thorough prosecution of a just war, to a securing of those ends for which it was undertaken; such a peace, which though it make not the adverse party friends, yet shall deprive them of all opportunity to become enemies."[52]

This was hardly the response for which the Dutch deputies had hoped. Ostensibly the negotiations had reached an impasse. One of the Dutch deputies wrote "absolutely to a confidant that there is no hope of a peace between them." The States of Holland soon informed "all their public

49 "General Heads for a Narrative," 14 June 1653, Bod., Rawl. A3, p. 258; Council of State's answer, 13 July 1653, PRO, SP 105/98, f. 17; newsletter from London, 21 July 1653, Bod., Rawl. A4, p. 269.

50 Newsletter from London, 21 July 1653, Bod., Rawl. A4, p. 269; memorandum of Dutch Ambassadors, 2/12 August 1653, Bod., Rawl. A5, pp. 15–16; newsletter from United Provinces, 22 July/1 August 1653, Bod., Rawl. A4, p. 283; Bordeaux to de Brienne, 14/24 July 1653, PRO, PRO 31/3/91, f. 48.

51 Newsletter from London, 1 July 1653, Bod., Clar. 46, f. 31v; day's proceedings, 29 June 1653, *CSPD*, p. 445 (includes Colonel Sydenham among the commissioners, though no contemporary report records his presence at the negotiations); day's proceedings, 29 June 1653, *CSPD*, p. 451; Beverning to De Witt, July 1653, Bod., Rawl. A4, pp. 161–162.

52 Newsletter, 28 July 1653, Bod., Rawl. A5, p. 209; Bordeaux to de Brienne, 14/24 July 1653, PRO, PRO 31/3/91, f. 49v; *Mercurius Politicus*, 30 June–7 July 1653, p. 2560. Similar sentiments are expressed in *Mercurius Politicus*, 14–21 July 1653, p. 2582.

ministers" that "there is no good to be expected of the English treaty."[53] The Orangist deputy Jongstall complained to William Frederick that the English would "use us as they do the Scots." Dutch popular opinion felt that peace could only be achieved if they "will submit themselves under the yoke of the English," a demand which even "the good Hollanders did never dream of." No wonder rumors were spread throughout Europe that the Dutch deputies "had thoughts of going away."[54]

English sentiment was equally pessimistic. The Dutch "grumble much to think of the preliminary points touching satisfaction and security," scoffed the *Mercurius Politicus*, "and say they are not so low yet." The Dutch deputies had made it clear, insisted another pamphleteer, "that they had rather be all buried in the sea than submit."[55] "Though they were beaten," noted Bulstrode Whitelocke disapprovingly, "yet their spirits were up still against the English." The result, Walter Vane explained to Sir Robert Stone, was that "everybody fears" the negotiations "will come to nothing." After reviewing his newsletters from the United Provinces, France, and England Edward Hyde concluded that the Dutch embassy was not "like[ly] to produce any reconciliation."[56]

Clearly extraordinary measures were necessary to save the negotiations. In a meeting on 21 July the English commissioners reiterated their insistence on satisfaction. But, they made clear, this satisfaction was not aimed at devastating the Dutch economy. "This state doth not propound to themselves or aim at the obtaining great sums of money from the said United Provinces," explained the English deputies, emphasizing that they merely desired some public acknowledgment of Dutch guilt, "very much preferring a peace upon just and honorable grounds before any consideration of that nature." Security, then, was the major stumbling block. It was here that the English made a revolutionary proposal. "This state is willing to expect the said security by uniting both states in such manner as they may become one

53 Hyde to Lord Wentworth, 15/25 July 1653, Bod., Clar. 46, f. 86r; newsletter from The Hague, 18/28 July 1653, Bod., Rawl. A4, p. 244; newsletter from The Hague, 20/30 July 1653, Bod., Rawl. A4, pp. 254–255; Harlbers to Jongstall, 21/31 July 1653, Bod., Rawl. A4, p. 272.

54 Jongstall to William Frederick, 19/29 July 1653, Bod., Rawl. A4, p. 247; Peterson to Coopman, 8/18 July 1653, Bod., Rawl. A4, p. 164; newsletter from the United Provinces, 8/18 July 1653, Bod., Rawl. A4, pp. 150–151; newsletter from United Provinces, 8/18 July 1653, Bod., Rawl. A4, pp. 141–142; newsletter from London, 1 July 1653, Bod., Clar. 46, f. 31r; Bordeaux to de Brienne, 18/28 July 1653, PRO, PRO 31/3/91, f. 50; Gentillot to de Brienne, 20/30 July 1653, PRO, PRO 31/3/91, f. 55r; De Bacquoy/Van Ruyven to Hyde, 21/31 July 1653, Bod., Clar. 46, f. 99r.

55 *Mercurius Politicus*, 21–28 July 1653, pp. 2606–2608; *Perfect Diurnall*, 18–25 July 1653, p. 2862; *Mercurius Pragmaticus*, 6–13 July 1653, p. 61; *Weekly Intelligencer*, 5–12 July 1653, p. 914.

56 Whitelocke, *Annals*, 18 July 1653, BL, Add. 37345, f. 288r; Walter Vane to Robert Stone, 18/28 July 1653, Bod., Rawl. A4, p. 237; Hyde to Clement, 15/25 July 1653, Bod., Clar. 46, f. 83r; Hyde to Richard Browne, 11 July 1653, Christ Church, John Evelyn MSS 10, f. 24r; newsletter from London, 8 July 1653, Bod., Clar. 46, f. 71v.

people and commonwealth for the good of both," the English suggested to their astonished Dutch counterparts, "by which means not only the present breach will be made up, and the difficulties of adjusting each other's interests by articles of allegiance and confederation overcome, but all occasions of future difference removed, and the strength and riches of both nations, which are now employed one against another, will be united for the common defense and preservation of the whole."[57]

When the conference broke up that evening the Dutch were buzzing with excitement. Although Beverning could not be sure what the English had meant, he was certain that these were "significant words" suggesting that the English were willing to find a way round the diplomatic impasse. The Zeelander Van De Perre was impressed that the English "seemeth to take our business to heart before the rest," adding that in the last conference the English commissioners had offered "words and periods quite differing from the former" tenor.[58]

What then did the English mean by this "uniting both states"? Clearly, the Dutch had thought the English were proposing a sort of more intimate alliance. The English, however, were not disputing "words or expressions, but in things of greatest moment." They were not interested in "the establishing a league and union between two sovereign states and neighbors, but the making of two sovereign states one." They were interested in federation. Although the English did not intend to change "the municipal laws of either," they did envisage England and the United Provinces to be "so united [as] to be under one supreme power, to consist of persons of both nations according as shall be agreed upon and to have and enjoy the like privileges and freedoms in respect of habitations, possessions, trade, ports, fishing, and all other advantages whatsoever in each other's countries, as natives without any difference or distinction." The English had proposed, De Witt wrote to the Dutch ambassador in Paris, the creation of "a single and unified sovereign government, composed of representatives selected equally from the two nations." "Their meaning," Aitzema later averred, "was that as they had expelled the king, the States should do the like to the Prince of Orange and free themselves from that yoke as they had done from the King of Spain, for which they honored the States." The war had been fought because the forces of Orange had prevented the Dutch from accepting the proposals of St. John and Strickland. It would end by their acceptance and the permanent rejection of the House of Orange.[59]

57 Council of State to Dutch deputies, 21 July 1653, PRO, SP 105/98, f. 18v; Council of State to Dutch deputies, 22 July 1653, PRO, SP 105/98, f. 19v.

58 Van de Perre to Lord de Bruyn, 22 July/1 August 1653, Bod., Rawl. A4, p. 288; Van de Perre to De Vogelaer, 22 July/1 August 1653, Bod., Rawl. A4, p. 294; Beverning to De Witt, 22 July/1 August 1653, Bod., Rawl. A4, pp. 295–296; Beverning to Lord Ommersen, 22 July/1 August 1653, Bod., Rawl. A4, p. 285.

59 Van de Perre to Lord be Bruyn, 22 July/1 August 1653, Bod., Rawl. A4, p. 290; Dutch

The English proposed the creation of a single Anglo-Dutch state in all seriousness, convinced that it would best promote the interests of both nations. There is no evidence that this union was an attempt to conquer Dutch trade by peaceful means. Whatever the economic effects of the union might have been, the English would hardly have allowed the Dutch "all privileges and immunity both in purchasing lands ... and trade, as we ourselves enjoy" – a provision which would have nullified the Navigation Act – had the intent been to usurp Dutch trade. "The world was wide enough for both," Cromwell told the Dutch deputies in St. James's Park, "and if the two peoples could only thoroughly well understand each other, their countries would become the markets of the world; and they would dictate their will to Europe." This was not the language of a man who understood the Anglo-Dutch conflict as the ineluctable struggle between two mercantile nations, a struggle pitting two nations against one another in a mortal combat to monopolize very limited material benefits. Indeed Lieutenant-Colonel Dolman, who was concerned to protect both English and Dutch interests, wholeheartedly endorsed the proposal because the Dutch would not suffer "the least loss of [their] sovereignty or privileges." Instead all of the evidence suggests that the English were motivated by a particular ideological vision. Although they admitted the proposal was without precedent – "no age can produce a parallel" – the English insisted on the "real benefits which would accrue thereby." Not only would such a union be the best means for the English to achieve "security for the future," but, they were sure, it is the "most just and equal in itself, most honorable and profitable unto both, most easy and practicable in respect of the present difficulties, and lastly the most likely means by the blessing of God to obviate and prevent the designs of the enemies to the interest of Christ and his people in both nations." In fact, it was this last point, "the protection of the true confederates of the faith" which Beverning thought was "chiefly considered and taken to heart here by the present government."[60]

deputies to Council of State, 23 July 1653, PRO, SP 105/98, ff. 19v–20; Council of State to Dutch deputies, 25 July 1652, PRO, SP 105/98, ff. 20–21v; newsletter from The Hague, 18/28 August 1653, Bod., Clar. 46, f. 188r; De Witt to Boreel, 11/21 August 1653, *Lettres et Negociations de Mr. Jean De Witt*, Vol. I (Amsterdam, 1725), p. 7; Aitzema, "Selections," Bod., Rawl. C734, f. 79v. I have relied on this account of a sovereign imperial Parliament in preference to the alternative version which assigned each state a fixed number of seats in the other's sovereign assembly, because this version is found both in the diary notation of the negotiation and in the correspondence of De Witt. For the alternative see Sagredo to Doge and Senate, 23 August/2 September 1653, *CSPV*, pp. 120–121; "Memorandum of the Dutch Ambassadors," 2/12 August 1653, Bod., Rawl. A5, pp. 11–12. This latter document appears to refer to an earlier proposal.

60 Newsletter from London, 5 August 1653, Bod., Clar. 46, f. 160v; Cromwell, quoted in James Geddes, *History of the Administration of John De Witt*, Vol. I (London, 1879), p. 340; Dolman to Sir Robert Stone, 12 August 1653, Bod., Rawl. A5, p. 165; Council of State to Dutch deputies, 1 August 1653, PRO, SP 105/98, ff. 24–25; Beverning to States General, 4 July 1653, Bod., Rawl. A3, pp. 354–355. For similar conclusions that the union

Although the Dutch acknowledged English sincerity, indeed perhaps because they realized just how serious their English counterparts were, they were flabbergasted by the proposal. The Dutch deputies expostulated against these "impossible and unreasonable demands." "The unusual novelty of such a coalition and mixture," they told the English commissioners, would undoubtedly be "embroiled in all sorts of confusions and impossibilities." The republican Nieupoort thought it "an impossible and impracticable business." While Beverning was sure that the "exorbitant proceedings and the extravagant propositions" would "open the eyes of all the princes of Europe." John Thurloe, who was almost certainly present at the meetings, later recalled that "the Dutch wholly disliked" the proposed union.[61]

Why were the Dutch deputies so adamantly opposed to a national amalgamation? The answer lies in the Dutch conception of their own republicanism. The English proposition of union, they insisted, "was unexpected having never seen nor heard in any of the propositions and conferences of former times, the least coalition or mixture of the several sovereignties." The Dutch deputies were able to cite a lengthy pedigree of republican alliances to make their point – a pedigree which demonstrates conclusively that their own republicanism depended on neither the model of Rome nor that of Venice. They could think of no example of "coalition of nations and republics, and of mingling the sovereignties in such manner as is propounded," not "in any former ages, in any histories, or any treaty of any nation – the Amphictions in Greece; the associated cities in Italy in the first times of the Romans, who were so straightly and chastely confederated that they had the same friends and enemies – have yet mentioned every one of them, an absolute sovereignty. The same is and hath been observed by the Switzers, Grisons, and others in their confederations ..." It was against just such a threat to their sovereignty from Spain that the United Provinces had "employed their forces to the utmost hazards of their lives and fortunes." In order to organize their defense they had established the Union of Utrecht which was "the most complete and firm confederation that could possibly be made." Yet, even that union was made with "great precautions of their several sovereignties and privileges, which cannot admit of any mixture, and consequently no coalition so qualified as is here propounded." "How can it be conceived," they therefore asked of their English counter-

proposal had precious little to do with economic aggrandizement, see S. R. Gardiner, *History of the Commonwealth and Protectorate 1649–1656* (New York, 1965). Vol. III, p. 43; Herbert H. Rowen, p. 202; Woolrych, *Commonwealth to Protectorate*, p. 280.

61 Newsletter from The Hague, 4/14 August 1653, Bod., Clar. 46, f. 152v; Dutch Deputies to Council of State, 27 July 1653, PRO, SP 105/98, f. 22v; newsletter from The Hague, 12/22 August 1653, Bod., Rawl. A5, p. 161; Beverning to De Witt, 29 July/8 August 1653, Bod., Rawl. A4, pp. 324–326; "Thurloe's Review," PRO, SP 103/46, f. 236; "A Review of the Several Treaties with the Dutch," 26 March 1661, NMM, Clifford Papers Vol. I, Dw32.

parts, "for us to join ourselves more straightly to others than we are amongst ourselves?"[62] It was exactly in opposition to such a usurpation of sovereignty that the Dutch republican identity had been formed. No wonder Boreel was "enraged," insisting that such a coalition would be "submitting [the] state of the United Provinces to the English, with the loss of their dear bought liberties." "When we have lost all our fortunes, estates and country (as the Irish and Scots)," Nieupoort was said to have fumed, "then we are yet good enough to be admitted into this coalition." It was common gossip in The Hague that "the English do affect rather a predomination over Holland, than a coalition." The Dutch deputies informed the French ambassador that they had refused "the coalition or incorporation of the two republics" because it was "almost the same as that of England and Scotland."[63]

The choice offered the Dutch was quite clear: "either the incorporation of Dutch interests with those of England, or open hostilities."[64] The English knew that no peace could be secure unless the Dutch were reformed. The Dutch deputies, even the two republican Dutch deputies, however, could not imagine a united Anglo-Dutch state to be anything other than destructive to their liberties. Nevertheless the Dutch still hoped for peace. The English proposals, though unrealistic, had at least expressed a willingness to accept a peace; they had "come from so good a hand which we ourselves had endeavored to support from the beginning with all fair means." So, instead of departing from Westminster in disgust, which would have been "une rupture entière," they opted to send two of their number to The Hague to report on the English proposals and receive further instructions. When the deputies reached the Netherlands they explained plausibly enough that they had decided to leave their two colleagues in England because "there is some likelihood that Cromwell will dissolve and turn out once more this Parliament and that this change might bring moderation or change in the business." Nevertheless both parties were aware that the chances for peace were slender indeed. Cromwell and Nieupoort "wept at their parting," fully aware that neither side had lived up to the other's expectations.[65]

62 Dutch deputies to Council of State, 27 July 1653, PRO, SP 105/98, ff. 22–23; Dutch Ambassadors to States General, 29 July/8 August 1653, Bod., Rawl. A4, p. 327. I have quoted extensively from the diplomatic diary in the PRO, PRO both because it is a previously undiscovered source, and because of its value in elucidating the rich republican discourse.

63 Newsletter from The Hague, 26 August/5 September 1653, Bod., Rawl. A5, p. 283; Boreel to Dutch Ambassadors, 13/23 August 1653, Bod., Rawl. A5, p. 168; newsletter from The Hague, 12/22 August 1653, Bod., Rawl. A5, p. 152; Bordeaux to de Brienne, 1/11 August 1653, PRO, PRO 31/3/91, f. 66v.

64 Paulucci to Sagredo, 2/12 September 1653, *CSPV*, p. 125; Bordeaux to de Brienne, 4/14 August 1653, PRO, PRO 31/3/91, ff. 71v–72r.

65 Memorandum of Dutch Ambassadors, 2/12 August 1653, Bod., Rawl. A5, pp. 13–14; Bordeaux to de Brienne, 4/14 August 1653, PRO, PRO 31/3/91, f. 71v; Dutch deputies to Council of State, 2 August 1653, PRO, SP 105/98, f. 26; newsletter from London, 1/11

When Jongstall and Nieupoort returned to the United Provinces and reported the remarkable English proposals to their superiors, Dutch men and women of every political stripe erupted with rage. The States party, which had had such high hopes for peace, was now thoroughly disappointed. "I do not perceive that any good can be expected from thence," De Witt wrote to Beverning, "unless Providence shall please to dispose otherwise of the hearts of those with whom you have to do." Another "principal man of the States of Holland" openly claimed that such a mingling of sovereignties "would be infamous and impracticable." All of the Holland towns, previously the strongest supporters of peace with England, "unanimously rejected the proposed coalition," claiming that they "will rather fight to the last drop of their blood."[66] Not surprisingly the Orangists found even less to like in the proposed coalition. They universally followed Jongstall in arguing that the "strange and wonderful conditions" had put an end to any meaningful negotiations. They pointed out that such an alliance would involve them in endless wars because the English "do offend all the world." The Orangist clergy feared that the coalition would allow the English to "mingle the religions and introduce here Independency."[67] All sides insisted that they "have old Batavian hearts still." "The States General have been very high of late," Nieupoort wrote to Beverning who had remained in England, advising that the treaty should be immediately broken off and you "ought to come away with out delay." Rumors, based supposedly "on the votes which have passed in the several provinces, and in most of the towns of Holland, and even in Amsterdam itself," circulated that "the other two commissioners will be speedily recalled from London." "They would rather venture all to subdue England, than to be one with them," observed the *Moderate Intelligencer*, correctly capturing the flavor of Dutch popular opinion.[68]

Given the stiff opposition of all four Dutch deputies to the proposed

August 1653, PRO, SP 49/97, f. 45r; newsletter from London, 1/11 August 1653, Bod., Rawl. A5, p. 6; newsletter from The Hague, 12/22 August 1653, Bod., Rawl. A5, pp. 149, 154; newsletter from The Hague, 26 August/5 September 1653, Bod., Rawl. A5, p. 284.

66 De Witt to Beverning, 2/12 September 1653, Bod., Rawl. A6, p. 14; De Witt to Boreel, 11/21 August 1653, *Lettres et negotiations*, p. 8; letter, 20 August 1653, NMM, WYN/7/11; newsletter from The Hague, 26 August/5 September 1653, Bod., Rawl. A5, pp. 283–284; newsletter from The Hague, 18/28 August 1653, Bod., Clar. 46, f. 188v; newsletter from The Hague, 8/18 September 1653, Bod., Clar. 46, f. 258v; advice of Province of Holland, 8/18 September 1653, Bod., Clar. 46, f. 237r; newsletter from The Hague, 2/12 September 1653, Bod., Rawl. A6, p. 30.

67 Jongstall to William Frederick, 19/29 July 1653, Bod., Rawl. A4, p. 246; Newsletter from The Hague, 11/21 August 1653, Bod., Rawl. A5, p. 96; newsletter from The Hague, 12/22 August 1653, Bod., Rawl. A5, pp. 152–153.

68 Peterson to Coopman, 12/22 August 1653, Bod., Rawl. A5, p. 140; Nieupoort to Beverning, 2/12 September 1653, Bod., Rawl. A6, p. 33; Hyde to Clement, 2/12 September 1653, Bod., Clar. 46, f. 223r; Robert Stone to Sir Walter Vane, 9/19 September 1653, Bod., Rawl. A6, p. 175; *Moderate Intelligencer*, 22–29 August 1653, p. 184; *Several Proceedings*, 18–25 August 1653, p. 3227; newsletter from The Hague, 25 August/

sovereign union, why had the English refused to back down? Why had they risked destroying any hope for peace in their pursuit of an unprecedented and idealistic proposal? The answer lies in English perceptions of Dutch political developments.

Although the Cromwellian moderates hoped for peace with the Dutch, they desired peace only when the Dutch could demonstrate that they had reformed. Until that time they were determined to pursue the war with the same intensity as their more radical colleagues. Unfortunately news from the United Provinces in the summer of 1653 suggested that the Dutch had lapsed back into political corruption.

"There is a civil war amongst them about the young Prince of Orange," recounted news report after news report, "and all councils are in a maze." Throughout the United Provinces, "all along the sea coast, the Boors are up in arms, even from Gravesend to the ... Texel. Nothing but reinstating the prince in his royal honor and dignities will now serve the high exasperated Flemings." In every town there were demonstrations and counter-demonstrations. Orangist "boutefeus" were whispering insinuations too "easily swallowed by the credulous rabble" that "there is a necessity of having a head." "Those that are the assertors of liberty in Holland," by contrast, were seeking "not only to crush the prince but other provinces also."[69] The result, thought one observer, is that "the great union is in danger to be splitted." The Orangist activities, agreed Stellingwerf, a republican member of the States General, "will be a cause and means to confound and overturn and destroy the whole country."[70]

In Holland, the stronghold of Dutch republicanism, town after town raised the colors of the House of Orange in the summer of 1653. The popular celebration of the Kermesse in Enckhuysen, which was accompanied by the recruitment of men for the navy, was the occasion of the first great tumult. The townspeople first demanded "that the levy should be proclaimed in the name of the Prince of Orange, and when the drummer refused they maltreated and broke his drum, proceeding afterward to sack and demolish the burgomaster's house." Soon an Orangist mob, proclaiming that "there must be a head or Stadholder, *non esse Regem in*

4 September 1653, Bod., Rawl. A6, p. 9; Vryberge to Van de Perre, 18/28 September 1653, Bod., Rawl. A6, pp. 300–301.

69 *Faithful Post*, 6–13 May 1653, p. 1053; *Mercurius Politicus*, 5–12 May 1653, p. 2425; *Mercurius Politicus*, 23–30 June 1653, pp. 2544–2545; *Mercurius Politicus*, 14–21 July 1653, p. 2594; *Moderate Occurrences*, 10–17 May 1653, p. 54; *Faithful Scout*, 24 June–1 July 1653, p. [1068]; *Perfect Diurnall*, 8–15 August 1653, p. 2916; newsletter from The Hague, 25 July/4 August 1653, *CSPD*, p. 48; Paulucci to Sagredo, 16/26 July 1653, *CSPV*, p. 102; newsletter from United Provinces, 19 June 1653, Bod., Rawl. A3, p. 308; Peterson to Coopman, 4 July 1653, Bod., Rawl. A4, p. 92; newsletter from The Hague, 20/30 July 1653, Bod., Rawl. A4, p. 255.

70 Newsletter from The Hague, 15/25 December 1653, Bod., Rawl. A9, p. 71; newsletter from The Hague, 20/30 July 1653, Bod., Rawl. A4, pp. 257–258.

Israel," seized control of the town. The houses of known republicans were looted, and the prince's colors were placed on all the walls and turrets of the town. Within days an effective Orangist town government was established, a town government sufficiently well organized to repel an attempt by the States of Holland to reclaim the town for the republican party.[71]

Within weeks Orangist riots following the same pattern broke out in Hoorn, Aalkmaar, Haarlem, and Medemblick. "All the towns of North Holland have followed the example of Enckhuysen," reported the *Perfect Account* with dismay in mid-July, "openly declaring for the young Prince of Orange."[72] In Dordrecht, the home city of John De Witt, the regents were declaring themselves "more and more for the Prince of Orange."[73] Even in Amsterdam "the prince's vassals out-brave the others to their faces." One report went so far as to claim that "in Amsterdam itself now half the people declare for Orange." The result was that "the burgomasters do run daily a hazard of being swallowed up by the prince's party."[74] De Witt himself, who more than anyone else came to personify the republican party in the United Provinces, was often called "rogue" and "prince betrayer." Indeed, one story claimed that he would have been killed by an angry mob in The Hague "had not the Lord Brederode taken him into his coach and preserved him."[75]

71 Newsletter from The Hague, 16/26 June 1653, Bod., Rawl. A3, pp. 267, 277; newsletter from the United Provinces, 4 July 1653, Bod., Rawl. A4, p. 80 (my translation); newsletter from United Provinces, 2 July 1653, Bod., Rawl. A4, p. 75; Sagredo to Doge and Senate, 5/15 July 1653, *CSPV*, p. 98; *Mercurius Politicus*, 23–30 July 1653, p. 2545; Bisdonner to Dutch Ambassadors, 4/14 July 1653, Bod., Rawl. A3, pp. 335–336; De Witt to Beverning, 2/12 September 1653, Bod., Rawl. A6, p. 15; Aitzema, "Selections," Bod., Rawl. C734, f. 77v; De Bacquoy/Van Ruyven to Hyde, 30 June/10 July 1653, Bod., Clar. 46, f. 29r; newsletter from Westminster, 25 June 1653, Worcester College, Clarke MSS 25, f. 76v; newsletter from The Hague, 24 June/4 July 1653, Bod., Rawl. A3, p. 360; Letter to Beverning, 17/27 June 1653, Bod., Rawl. A3, p. 288; newsletter from United Provinces, 17/27 June 1653, Bod., Rawl. A3, p. 291; intelligence from Amsterdam, 16/26 June 1653, Nickolls, p. 97.

72 *A Perfect Account*, 13–20 July 1653, p. 1049; newsletter from United Provinces, 4 July 1653, Bod., Rawl. A4, p. 83; Whitelocke, *Annals*, 16 July 1653, BL, Add. 37345, f. 287v; *Perfect Diurnall*, 11–18 July 1653, p. 2859; *Weekly Intelligencer*, 19–26 July 1653, p. 930; De Bacquoy/Van Ruyven to Hyde, 16/26 June 1653, Bod., Clar. 45, f. 495r; newsletter from United Provinces, 19 June 1653, Bod., Rawl. A3, pp. 307–308; De Bacquoy/Van Ruyven to Hyde, 30 June/10 July 1653, Bod., Clar. 46, f. 29v; newsletter from United Provinces, 1/11 July 1653, Bod., Rawl. A4, pp. 34, 41.

73 Newsletter from United Provinces, 1/11 July 1653, Bod., Rawl. A4, p. 37; newsletter from The Hague, 20/30 July 1653, Bod., Rawl. A4, p. 254.

74 Newsletter from The Hague, 1/11 July 1653, Bod., Rawl. A4, p. 25; *A Perfect Account*, 29 June–6 July 1653, p. 1035; *Mercurius Politicus*, 23–30 June 1653, p. 2545. William Frederick appeared at Amsterdam in the hopes of provoking an Orangist revolution, but the burgomasters were able to thwart him. Newsletter from United Provinces, 1/11 July 1653, Bod., Rawl. A4, p. 33; Whitelocke, *Annals*, 2 July 1653, BL, Add. 37345, f. 281; *Weekly Intelligencer*, 28 June–5 July 1653, p. 911.

75 Newsletter from The Hague, 16/26 June 1653, Bod., Rawl. A3, p. 278; *Mercurius Politicus*, 7–14 July 1653, p. 2578; newsletter from The Hague, 29 October/8 November 1653, Bod., Rawl. A7, pp. 307–308.

Perhaps the best-reported Orangist rising took place in The Hague. When the Prince of Orange and his mother arrived at The Hague in early August, they were greeted by "a company of young boys riding upon sticks with Orange ribbons in their hats and prints of the Prince['s] arms on their breasts, calling themselves a troop of horse." This innocuous display of Orangist support turned ugly when the Fiscal ordered the boys to disperse. Instead they defied the order and with "a great many of the lower sort of the people" they marched on the Fiscal's house and "pelted his windows with stones as they did several other houses which were disaffected to the prince." The whole time the boys and their comrades were making their political point, chanting "God bless the Prince of Orange." Although the militia ultimately proved strong enough to subdue the Orangist boys' troop, to prevent a recurrence the States of Holland felt "bound to keep a guard of horse in several places, within and without the town, as if they were in ambuscado against an enemy."[76]

With such developments in the capital city, many observers thought it was only a matter of time before the States of Holland would succumb to the rising tide of Orangism. "The Orange party gathered heart in Holland, and carried on their design to make the young prince their captain general as his father was," noted Whitelocke. "Our States of Holland are now content to have a Captain General," agreed one Dutch merchant. "I must tell you our friends in all places are deceived if our condition be not upon the point of improving," exclaimed Edward Hyde with evident glee, citing "the disposition of the people generally in Holland" and their "brisk declarations on behalf of the Prince of Orange, and against that faction which opposes him." Most importantly, for Hyde, "in those disorders our Master is mentioned with kindness enough."[77]

Events in Zeeland, where two of the six voting towns were already Orangist in sympathy, followed a similar pattern. During Kermesse the townsmen of Middleburgh, "through the instigation of the Prince of Orange['s] party," insisted that the Orange colors should be flown from the town's tower. In Ziereckzee the daughters of the magistrates were soon obliged "to wear their knots and fancies upon their clothes of the prince's color." The Orangists in Ter Goes signified their victory by displaying on the town's highest turret a "white sarcenet flag with this motto engravened

[76] *Mercurius Politicus*, 28 July–4 August 1653, pp. 2622–2623; *Mercurius Politicus*, 4–11 August 1653, p. 2643; *Mercurius Politicus*, 11–18 August 1653, p. 2655; newsletter from The Hague, 4/14 August 1653, Bod., Clar. 46, f. 151r; Letter to Van de Perre, 29 July/8 August 1653, Bod., Rawl. A4, p. 329; De Witt to Beverning and Nieupoort, 29 July/8 August 1653, Bod., Rawl. A4, p. 231; newsletter from United Provinces, 18/28 July 1653, Bod., Rawl. A4, p. 240; newsletter from The Hague, 29 October/8 November 1653, Bod., Rawl. A7, pp. 305–307; Aitzema, "Selections," Bod., Rawl. C734, f. 77v.

[77] Whitelocke, *Annals*, 8 July 1653, BL, Add. 37345, f. 282r; Letter to Coopman, 1/11 July 1653, Bod., Rawl. A4, p. 44; Hyde to Rochester, 8/18 July 1653, Bod., Clar. 46, f. 66r; Aitzema, "Selections," Bod., Rawl. C734, f. 77v.

in letters of gold: God Preserve the Royal Family."[78] Not surprisingly Zeeland soon assumed the leadership of the movement to reestablish the House of Orange in its traditional offices. "The Zeelanders," reported the *Moderate Intelligencer*, "declare generally for a vice-king, and say they will no longer be without a head." The Zeelanders were said to be "much more disposed to the choosing of a captain general than the concluding of a peace with England." Indeed it was well known that the States of Zeeland were inclined to assist Royalist risings in Scotland.[79]

With Zeeland firmly in the Orangist camp, and Holland wavering, there appeared to be little that could prevent the restoration of the House of Orange.[80] "Tout est pour Orange" proclaimed one newsletter in early July. "The Prince of Orange party is like to prevail over all the Provinces," the *Weekly Intelligencer* warned its readers. One army newspaper calculated that "the burgomasters and states that dissent from the Royal party are not equal to them either in number or power." No one observing the dramatic and colorful events in the Dutch cities that summer could fail to draw the obvious conclusion. "Monsieur le Prince d'Orange will be Captain General and Admiral of these provinces within a few weeks," thought De Witt's secretary. Orangism "is taking doctrine in every town, and they catch men with it as fast as herrings," the *Mercurius Politicus* editorialized, "so that they are all mad for a change, and the wisest conceive it will be brought about, and that all interests will be taken in thereupon (not excepting the Stuarts) to carry on a desperate game against England."[81]

78 For Middleburgh: *Faithful Post*, 1–8 July 1653, p. 1645; Letter from Van De Perre, 8/18 July 1653, Bod., Rawl. A4, p. 133; *Impartial Intelligencer*, 5–12 July 1653, p. 16; newsletter from The Hague, 20/30 July 1653, Bod., Rawl. A4, p. 253. For Ziereckzee: Newsletter from The Hague, 20/30 July 1653, Bod., Rawl. A4, pp. 253–254. For Ter Goes: *Moderate Intelligencer*, 27 June–4 July 1653, p. 72; *Faithful Post*, 28 June–5 July 1653, p. 1072; Letter to Beverning, 17/27 June 1653, Bod., Rawl. A3, p. 289; newsletter from The Hague, 16/26 June 1653, Bod., Rawl. A3, pp. 277–278, 287; *Several Proceedings*, 23–30 June 1653, p. 3093; Aitzema, "Selections," Bod., Rawl. C734, f. 78r.

79 *Moderate Intelligencer*, 8–17 August 1653, p. 175; *Several Proceedings*, 4–11 August 1653, p. [3191]; newsletter from The Hague, 18/28 September 1653, Bod., Rawl. A6, pp. 313–314; Aitzema, "Selections," Bod., Rawl. C734, f. 73v; newsletter from The Hague, 2/12 September 1653, Bod., Rawl. A6, pp. 47–48; Letter to Whitelocke, 24 September 1653, Longleat House, Whitelocke MSS XII, f. 169r; newsletter from United Provinces, 18/28 July 1653, Bod., Rawl. A4, p. 240; Gentillot to de Brienne, 20/30 July 1653, PRO, PRO 31/3/91, f. 53r; Letter from De Bacquoy/Van Ruyven, 1/11 September 1653, Bod., Clar. 46, f. 220v; newsletter from The Hague, 2/12 September 1653, Bod., Rawl. A6, pp. 46–49; newsletter from The Hague, 9/19 September 1653, Bod., Rawl. A6, p. 104; Vrybergen to Van De Perre, 7/17 October 1653, Bod., Rawl. A7, p. 44.

80 Gelderland, Overijssel, and Groningen were firmly Orangist. Utrecht took no clear line, though it tended to follow Holland. Newsletter from United Provinces, August 1653, Bod., Rawl. A5, p. 175; Letter to Van De Perre, 17/27 September 1653, Bod., Rawl. A6, p. 279; newsletter from United Provinces, 17/27 September 1653, Bod., Rawl. A6, pp. 282–283; Royalist Newsletter, ca. 23 September 1653, Bod., Rawl. A6, p. 331; States of Groningen to States of Gelderland, 5/15 September 1653, Bod., Rawl. A6, pp. 67–68.

81 Newsletter from United Provinces, 1/11 July 1653, Bod., Rawl. A4, pp. 35, 41, 56; *Weekly Intelligencer*, 19–26 July 1653, p. 936; *Weekly Intelligencer*, 26 July–2 August 1653,

The English could hardly ignore the wave of Orangism sweeping the United Provinces. In fact, these developments united the Cromwellian moderates who wanted to reform the Dutch and the radicals who wished to eviscerate them. As much as the moderates hoped for an alliance with fellow republicans, they knew the Orangists to be allied with the House of Stuart.

Political commentators of every ideological predisposition knew that it was the Orangist risings which had obstructed the peace process. Although the more moderate members of the Nominated Parliament were certain that the Dutch "lovers of liberty" were in favor of peace, they "do hold suspect and do fear the domination of the Prince of Orange." "The differences, divisions and tumults that have lately happened in our countries, and are still threatening to break out again" Van De Perre wrote to a friend in Amsterdam, "may chance to cause that the negotiation ... may come to take no effect." "I do expect to hear by this post that the business is at a stand again," De Witt confided to Beverning, "by reason of the unreasonable resolution lately made by those of Zeeland concerning a captain general, which undoubtedly they will have heard of." If the English "did come to hear and understand" of the proposals to make the Prince of Orange captain general, warned one republican in the States General, the English "would break off all manner of treaty and would not suffer that the son of a daughter of the Stuarts should be captain general over these countries." Dolman's concern for the success of the treaty grew dramatically as reports of Orangist risings reached London, admitting that he feared "the Orange party will obstruct it." One observer knew that the events in the United Provinces "would change the inclinations of the English." The treaty might well "have swayed," noted one newsletter-writer after the two Dutch deputies had departed in August, "if the advance of the Orange party ... had not discovered other ends unto us."[82]

The end of the summer, then, seemed to bring with it the end of any

p. 944; *Faithful Post*, 8–15 July 1653, p. 1083; *Mercurius Politicus*, 7–14 July 1653, pp. 2570, 2578; *Mercurius Politicus*, 18–25 August 1653, p. 2683; newsletter from The Hague, 22 July/1 August 1653, Bod., Rawl. A4, p. 295; De Bacquoy/Van Ruyven to Hyde, 21/31 July 1653, Bod., Clar. 46, f. 99v (my translation); *A Perfect Account*, 13–20 July 1653, p. 1054; Theodorus to Viscount Conway, 25 July 1653, *CSPD*, p. 50; Hyde to Lord Wentworth, 29 July/8 August 1653, Bod., Clar. 46, f. 138r; intelligence from Amsterdam, 16/26 June 1653, Nickolls, *Original Letters*, p. 97.

82 Newsletter from London, 1 July 1653, Bod., Clar. 46, f. 34r; newsletter from The Hague, 12/22 August 1653, Bod., Rawl. A5, p. 151; Van De Perre to De Vogelaer (of Amsterdam), 22 July/1 August 1653, Bod., Rawl. A4, p. 293; Van De Perre to Vryberge (of Tholen), 22 July/1 August 1653, Bod., Rawl. A4, p. 286; Van De Perre to Lord De Bruyn, 22 July/ 1 August 1653, Bod., Rawl. A4, p. 290; De Witt to Beverning, 29 July/8 August 1653, Bod., Rawl. A4, p. 330; newsletter from The Hague, 20/30 July 1653, Bod., Rawl. A4, p. 261; newsletter from London, 15 July 1653, Bod., Clar. 46, f. 82r; newsletter from London, 15 July 1653, Bod., Clar. 46, f. 110r; newsletter from United Provinces, 18/28 July 1653, Bod., Rawl. A4, pp. 239–240 (my translation); newsletter from London, 22 July 1653, Bod., Clar. 46, f. 113v; newsletter from London, 5 August 1653, Bod., Clar. 46, f. 158v.

hopes for peace. Although the moderates within the Council of State had been anxious to join with a reformed Dutch polity in defense of Protestantism and liberty, Dutch reticence revealed the profound corruption of their state. Each new report of Orangist risings convinced the English of the absolute necessity of security. By the middle of July amalgamation appeared to provide the only guarantee that no future Van Tromp would assault the English in the Downs. When the Dutch rejected such an amalgamation as constitutionally impossible, the continuation of the war seemed inevitable.

9

The rejection of apocalyptic foreign policy

Contrary to all expert predictions, however, the States General decided to send Jongstall and Nieupoort back to England, armed with fresh instructions. Hopes and expectations for peace soared. "Is it any wonder that I am fallen from my confidence that there will be no peace," Edward Hyde whined to Edward Nicholas, "and can you ask me the reason, when you tell me your intelligence from England assures you that they will recede from all their extravagant propositions, and that that the people of Holland will grant anything [asked]?"[1] What had precipitated such a dramatic change in the course of events?

Traditionally historians have explained this change by highlighting the conciliatory effect of Cromwell's private meetings with the Dutch deputies.[2] Though there can be no doubt that Cromwell did meet with the Dutch deputies – especially with the republican Beverning – and that he spoke enthusiastically about what the Dutch and English could achieve together if allied, one should not overestimate his enthusiasm for peace without security before the autumn of 1653. In the much-discussed conferences with Beverning in St. James's Park, Cromwell expressed his "opinion that there must be one supreme authority to have the direction of all matters relating to the strict union for mutual defense of both states against all external enemies." To Beverning's protestations that such an alliance would invalidate all other Dutch treaties, Cromwell mockingly replied that the Dutch were willing to cast aside their French allies at Munster in 1648. Beverning concluded that Cromwell "hath no mind to

1 *Faithful Scout*, 21–28 October 1653, p. 1065; *Weekly Intelligencer*, 18–25 October 1653, p. 31; *Mercurius Politicus*, 13–20 October 1653, pp. 2806–2807; *The Perfect Diurnall*, 17–24 October 1653, p. 3082; Whitelocke, *Annals*, BL, Add. 4992, f. 44r; Bordeaux to de Brienne, 24 October/3 November 1653, PRO, PRO 31/3/92, f. 1v; Hyde to Clement, 20/30 October 1653, Bod., Clar. 46, f. 355r; Hyde to Nicholas, 11/21 November 1653, Bod., Clar. 47, f. 63v.

2 This explanation was originally advanced by S. R. Gardiner in *History of the Commonwealth and Protectorate 1649–1656* (New York, 1965), as discussed in Chapter 6. Recently Austin Woolrych has endorsed this view (*Soldiers and Statesmen* [Oxford, 1987]), p. 281.

moderate anything."[3] In this Beverning had surely gone too far. Cromwell did soften his position on the nature of the coalition. "I am informed underhand," Beverning admitted to Nieupoort, "that if we would agree to an union after the same form as we have in the United Provinces ourselves, that we should be soon agreed." Such a union, Hyde rightly explained to Lord Wentworth, required the Dutch to "consent to an utter suppression of the House of Orange, as well as to the renouncing of any compliance with our master."[4] Cromwell had not committed himself and his political allies to peace at any cost. Instead Cromwell had made it clear to the Dutch that he was ready to contemplate peace should there be evidence of significant change in the Dutch domestic political situation.

The improved prospects of peace derived rather from two parallel developments in the early autumn. In the United Provinces the return of the two deputies from England in August had provoked extensive discussions over the future of the Anglo-Dutch negotiations. Not surprisingly the debates divided along party lines. There is "hard tugging between the Prince's party and the Loevesteen Heeren," observed one Dutch merchant, if the Loevesteen "party get the better of it ... we may happily have peace with England, whereas the other will continue a war in maintenance of consanguinity with him." Peter De Groot, whose father had long suffered for his adherence to the States party, reported to Beverning that the Orangists "do apprehend that in the end some good treaty do not destroy the pernicious maxims which they do foment to the contrary." "The Royal and Orange party endeavor to infuse in [the States General] a diffidence of you," sneered one republican observer, "but the wiser sort laugh at it."[5] The peace "is carried on by them that would extirpate our royal family and the House of Orange," the Presbyterian Royalist James Bence wrote to his fellow Royalist the Marquis of Ormonde. More surprisingly, the republican party succeeded in persuading the States of Holland to vote for the return of the deputies, and the continuation of the treaty. Apparently the Holland regents based their optimism "chiefly" on the grounds "that the Parliament was now inclined to treat without a coalition." The Holland order, in fact,

3 Beverning to Nieupoort, 12/22 August 1653, Bod., Rawl. A5, pp. 123–124; Beverning to Jongstall, 12/22 August 1653, Bod., Rawl. A5, p. 102; Beverning to Lord of Amersongen, 12/22 August 1653, Bod., Rawl. A5, p. 101; newsletter from The Hague, 25 August/4 September 1653, Bod., Clar. 46, f. 205r; newsletter from The Hague, 26 August/5 September 1653, Bod., Rawl. A5, pp. 281–283.

4 Beverning to Nieupoort, 19/29 August 1653, Bod., Rawl. A5, p. 212; Beverning to Jongstall, 19/29 August 1653, Bod., Rawl. A5, p. 211; Hyde to Wentworth, 28 August/7 September 1653, Bod., Clar. 46, f. 215r; Paulucci to Sagredo, 14/24 August 1653, *CSPV*, pp. 115–116.

5 Peterson to Coopman, 9/19 September 1653, Bod., Rawl. A6, p. 183; De Groot to Beverning, 9/19 September 1653, Bod., Rawl. A6, p. 182; intelligence from Holland, September 1653, Bod., Rawl. A6, p. 53; newsletter from United Provinces, September 1653, Bod., Rawl. A6, p. 276. Loevesteen was the name ascribed to the republican party in the United Provinces.

emphasized "the inconveniences and the impossibilities which the project of coalition" offered by the English entailed. The objection, it is essential to note, was with the mingling of sovereignties, not with a close alliance. In place of the coalition the Dutch deputies were to offer "a near and strict alliance and confederacy between the two states with such uniting of both as hath ever been practiced between any two neighboring sovereign states."[6]

Once the States of Holland had established its position, the Hollanders made every effort to convince the other provinces. They soon despatched "some rhetoricians and logicians to persuade persons refractory out of their affection to the prince." In the States General the deputies of Holland drummed home the necessity of peace. Despite the other provinces' well-known detestation of the English, at least one observer was "confident the Province of Holland will carry the vote against all the rest."[7] Such confidence was not unmerited. Province after province brought in their votes in favor of continuing the treaty, invariably justifying their decision upon the claim that "there are several of the government there [that] are inclined to peace." "All the provinces (even they which had voted so directly for a war and the recalling the two ambassadors at London)," reported one enthusiastic witness with some exaggeration, "agreed that a new trial was to be made by new addresses to the Commonwealth." In fact, only Orangist Groningen stood out, powerless to prevent the return of the deputies.[8] Naturally the other provinces did not approach the renewal of the treaty with the same enthusiasm as that of the States of Holland – that could hardly be expected. Despite the States General's insistence that the deputies

6 Newsletter from United Provinces, 17/27 September 1653, Bod., Rawl. A6, pp. 281–282; Bordeaux to de Brienne, 29 August/8 September 1653, PRO, PRO 31/3/91, f. 88v; extract from secret resolutions of States of Holland, 8/18 September 1653, Bod., Rawl. A6, pp. 84–89; advice of Province of Holland, 8/18 September 1653, Bod., Clar. 46, f. 237r; newsletter from The Hague, 22 September/2 October 1653, Bod., Rawl. A6, p. 339; James Bence to Ormonde, 17/27 November 1653, Bod., Clar. 47, f. 80v.

7 Peterson to Coopman, 23 September 1653, Bod., Rawl. A6, p. 265; Letter from The Hague, 29 September/9 October 1653, Bod., Rawl. A6, p. 432.

8 Extract from Register of Overijssel, 24 September/4 October 1653, Bod., Rawl. A6, p. 398; Extract from Register of States of Gelderland, 24 September/4 October 1653, Bod., Rawl. A6, pp. 396–397; De Witt to Beverning, 30 September/10 October 1653, Bod., Rawl. A6, p. 461; newsletter from The Hague, 6/16 October 1653, Bod., Clar. 46, f. 314r; newsletter from The Hague, 6/16 October 1653, Bod., Clar. 46, f. 315r; Vryberge to Van De Perre, 7/17 October 1653, Bod., Rawl. A7, p. 43; newsletter from The Hague, 14/24 October 1653, Bod., Rawl. A7, pp. 129, 144–145; extract from notes of Zeeland, September 1653, Bod., Rawl. A6, p. 395; De Witt to Beverning, 7/17 October 1653, Bod., Rawl. A7, p. 40; newsletter from United Provinces, 14/24 October 1653, Bod., Rawl. A7, p. 137; newsletter from the United Provinces, 28 October/7 November 1653, Bod., Rawl. A7, pp. 262–263; De Bruyne to Van De Perre, 28 October/7 November 1653, Bod., Rawl. A7, p. 272; Peterson to Coopman, 4/14 November 1653, Bod., Rawl. A8, p. 26 newsletter from The Hague, 10/20 November 1653, Bod., Clar. 47, f. 61r; newsletter from The Hague, 13/23 October 1653, Bod., Clar. 46, f. 335v.

not conclude "anything beyond the 36 Articles," they had at least kept open the possibility of peace.[9]

There were parallel and reinforcing developments in England in the early autumn of 1653. From the beginning of September the Dutch deputies began sending reports that England "is inclined and well resolved to treat." From "their intimate friends," Beverning and Van De Perre had heard "that England now desires nothing more than an accommodation, and the friends advise them to make use of that opportunity." "I hope we shall not let slip this fair opportunity," Beverning hinted to De Witt, "now the humors here are so well disposed." "This state omits nothing to bring this war with Holland to a conclusion," agreed the French ambassador Bordeaux in the middle of October.[10] This new attitude was not manifest only in popular opinion. "Parliament, Council of State, and Lord General Cromwell, desire more than ever a peace with this state," reported one commentator. When the Venetian resident pressed the well-connected Sir Oliver Fleming on the possibilities of peace, he responded: "I fancy it will come." "The Lord General himself is more moderate," Beverning wrote to De Witt. "Those of the government were much inclined to treat and ... Cromwell had with great oaths protested that he desired nothing more and that he was willing that the word coalition should be no more named, by which he never understood to have any superiority over this state, but only thereby to live in the better correspondence with one another," Van De Perre's son reported on his return to The Hague in October.[11]

The English had not abandoned their war aims; they had not decided to "accept of a shitten peace" as one Royalist observer thought. Though "the general is hugely inclinable to [peace], if anything (that he calls reasonable) will serve the Dutch," it was well known that "otherwise he resolves to make a vast treasure (however he comes by it) to carry on the war with vigor." Rather, Cromwell and his political allies had become more enthusiastic about the possibilities of an Anglo-Dutch alliance. It was in this

9 Newsletter from The Hague, 11/21 October 1653, Bod., Rawl. A7, p. 100b; newsletter from The Hague, 12/22 October 1653, Bod., Rawl. A7, p. 100c.

10 Newsletter from United Provinces, 30 September/10 October 1653, Bod., Rawl. A6, p. 448; Van de Perre to de Bruyne, 30 September/10 October 1653, Bod., Rawl. A6, p. 471; intelligence from The Hague, 3 October 1653, Nickolls, *Original Letters*, p. 104; Beverning to Nieupoort, 7/17 October 1653, Bod., Rawl. A7, p. 46; Beverning to De Witt, 7/17 October 1653, Bod., Rawl. A7, p. 48; Bordeaux to de Brienne, 13/23 October 1653, PRO, PRO 31/3/91, ff. 110r, 112v; newsletter from The Hague, 14/24 October 1653, Bod., Rawl. A7, pp. 129–130; Bordeaux to de Brienne, 17/27 October 1653, PRO, PRO 31/3/91, f. 116r; newsletter from The Hague, 20/30 October 1653, Bod., Clar. 46, f. 359r.

11 Van De Perre to Max Teelinck, 9/19 September 1653, Bod., Rawl. A6, p. 184; intelligence from The Hague, 16 October 1653, Nickolls, *Original Letters*, p. 104; Paulucci to Sagredo, 20/30 October 1653, *CSPV*, p. 141; newsletter from United Provinces, 9/19 September 1653, Bod., Rawl. A6, p. 160; Bordeaux to de Brienne, 19/29 September 1653, PRO, PRO 31/3/91, f. 100r; newsletter from The Hague, 29 September/9 October 1653, Bod., Clar. 46, f. 300r; newsletter from The Hague, 13/23 October 1653, Bod., Clar. 46, f. 335r.

context that Beverning received the proposal for a vast Protestant alliance against all nations that "received the Council of Trent." In the proposed treaty each commonwealth would always "be governed by their own laws independent from one another." But there was to be a joint navy and a permanent Anglo-Dutch board of arbitrators.[12] At least some English politicians were looking forward to an Anglo-Dutch alliance with the same enthusiasm which lay behind the 1651 mission of St. John and Strickland.

The Dutch deputies attributed the altered English attitude to the political decline of the religious radicals. "The credit of Major General Harrison and of the Anabaptists doth lessen," Van De Perre wrote to his fellow Zeelander De Bruyn, "which may be held for one of the chiefest reasons of the ... change and melioration." "It is certain," Beverning agreed, "that the credit of Harrison and that faction of Anabaptists is now going down, who have been most against us."[13] No doubt, the reemergence of the ideological divisions between the radicals and their more moderate colleagues was a significant development. But why had that happened? Why had Cromwell suddenly become so optimistic about the possibility of putting an end to the war, and the conclusion of an Anglo-Dutch alliance? Indeed, how had the Holland republicans been able to persuade their compatriots to continue the peace negotiations? The answer to these questions lies in the sudden transformation of Dutch politics in the late summer and early autumn of 1653.

The death of the Orangist Vice-Admiral Van Tromp off the Texel in August 1653 proved a decisive setback for the Orangist cause. An ideological struggle immediately began over the appointment of Tromp's successor. "There is great canvassing at The Hague about the creation of a new Admiral," the *Mercurius Politicus* informed its readers, "touching which point they are not able to pitch yet upon any one person that might give content to all parties, but they are much divided." "The death of Admiral Tromp has somewhat upset matters in Holland," the Venetian ambassador Sagredo had learned from his Parisian vantage point, "and produced division among the provinces."[14]

After much dispute Jacob van Wassenaer, Lord of Opdam, accepted the

12 Newsletter from London, 10/20 October 1653, Bod., Rawl. A7, p. 534; newsletter from London, 14 October 1653, Bod., Clar. 46, f. 346r; newsletter from United Provinces, Bod., Rawl. A7, p. 140; newsletter from London, 7 October 1653, Bod., Clar. 46, f. 328r; newsletter from The Hague, 29 September/9 October 1653, Bod., Rawl. A6, p. 458; Bordeaux to de Brienne, 24 October/3 November 1653, PRO, PRO 31/3/92, f. 1v. This proposal has been linked by Gardiner to the undated proposal advanced by Vermuyden, *History of the Commonwealth*, Vol. III, pp. 48, 50. This identification has been accepted by Austin Woolrych, *Soldiers and Statesmen*, pp. 283–284. Although the two proposals are very similar, the emphasis on the fear of universal monarchy in the Vermuyden proposal suggests that it may date to December or early January.

13 Van De Perre to De Bruyne, 30 September/10 October 1653, Bod., Rawl. A6, p. 472; Beverning to De Witt, 30 September/10 October 1653, Bod., Rawl. A6, pp. 464–465.

14 *Mercurius Politicus*, 25–31 August 1653, p. 2701; Sagredo to Doge and Senate, 30 August/9 September 1653, *CSPV*, p. 124; newsletter from The Hague, 25 August/4 September

post of Lieutenant-Admiral of Holland, making him Tromp's heir as *de facto* leader of the Dutch naval war effort.[15] No greater victory for the republican cause could have been imagined. Early in the summer Opdam was heard to exclaim "the devil take all those who are for the Prince of Orange." He was well known to be "a complete Hollander, yea a head" and "an arch enemy of the Orange party and the King of Scots." This was no passing political fancy. In the 1660s Sir Henry Bennet's notorious spy Colonel Bampfield noted that Opdam "is very deeply engaged in the interests of Monsieur De Witt and that party."[16] Not surprisingly the Orangists had left no stone unturned to prevent Opdam's nomination. "The Prince's party do cross and endeavor all what they can to hinder the Lord of Opdam from accepting the charge of admiral," wrote one of Thurloe's many Dutch informants."[17]

Opdam immediately began to refashion the Dutch navy in his own image. The transformation of the Dutch fleet was as sudden as it was dramatic. Ship after ship was renamed after a suitable republican virtue in place of the traditional names of the Princes of the House of Orange. This newly republicanized fleet under Opdam's leadership did not seek to give battle at every opportunity as Van Tromp had done. In order "not to give any cause of a new provocation for a revenge by a new engagement," Opdam decided in October to deploy his fleet in the Sound. Later that month when some hotheads had proposed to blockade the Thames, the admiralty of the Province of Holland prevented the scheme on the grounds that it "might give offense to the English and hinder the treaty of peace whereof there was now so good appearance" – hardly a decision they would have taken had Tromp been admiral.[18] All of the hopes of the Royalists "are squashed,"

1653, Bod., Clar. 46, f. 205r; newsletter from United Provinces, 20 August 1653, NMM, WYN/7/11.

15 *Mercurius Politicus*, 22–29 September 1653, p. 2765; Letter to Van De Perre, 26 August/5 September 1653, Bod., Rawl. A5, p. 268; newsletter from The Hague, 8/18 September 1653, Bod., Clar. 46, f. 258r; extract from Register of States of Holland and West Friesland, 12/22 September 1653, Bod., Rawl. A6, p. 227; Herbert H. Rowen, *John De Witt, Grand Pensionary of Holland, 1625–1672* (Princeton, 1978), pp. 194–195.

16 Van Ruyven to Hyde, 16/26 June 1653, Bod., Clar. 45, f. 495r (my translation); newsletter from United Provinces, 9/19 September 1653, Bod., Rawl. A6, pp. 98–99, 143; Peterson to Coopman, 15 September 1653, Bod., Rawl. A6, p. 265; Royalist newsletter, 16/26 September 1653, Bod., Rawl. A6, p. 272; Letter from Van Ruyven, 1/11 September 1653, Bod., Clar. 46, f. 220v; Bampfield to Bennet, 7/17 July 1663, PRO, SP 84/167, f. 186. On Bampfield's fascinating career, see John Loftis and Paul H. Hardacre, *Colonel Joseph Bampfield's Apology* (Lewisburg, 1993).

17 Newsletter from United Provinces, 9/19 September 1653, Bod., Rawl. A6, pp. 161–162; V. Hoogh to Van De Perre, 9/19 September 1653, Bod., Rawl. A6, p. 178; newsletter from The Hague, 18/28 September 1653, Bod., Rawl. A6, p. 306; newsletter from The Hague, 2/12 September 1653, Bod., Rawl. A6, pp. 49–50.

18 Rowen, *John De Witt*, p. 197; newsletter from United Provinces, 14/24 October 1653, Bod., Rawl. A7, pp. 140–141; newsletter from The Hague, 27 October/6 November 1653, Bod., Clar. 47, f. 15r; newsletter from United Provinces, 28 October/7 November 1653,

wrote one very perceptive newsmonger. "As Tromp by his impudence or malice was the cause of the war," concurred another, "so likewise it is hoped that Opdam (a true Hollander) will be the cause of peace."[19]

Gaining control of the post of admiral was only the first of a whole series of political victories for the States party in the autumn of 1653. Enckhuysen, whose Orangist leaders hoped to "have given example to other towns and consequently to have cried up the Prince of Orange for captain," was the first target of the newly invigorated States party's political strategy. The republicans, after sneaking nine companies of foot soldiers into the city, proceeded to lead a counter-revolution against the newly seated Orangist magistrates, and retake the North Holland town.[20] Just as the Orangists had hoped the political revolution in Enckhuysen would spearhead an Orangist offensive throughout Holland and ultimately throughout the United Provinces, so the States party was certain that its success in Enckhuysen would set a powerful precedent. This "doth satisfy all men," asserted one observer, "that Holland will continue in the condition they are in at present and never submit themselves to the prince or the said count [William] as his lieutenant nor suffer themselves to be destroyed by tumults." The demise of Enckhuysen's Orangists "who were the ringleaders of the Orange faction," mourned one Royalist, "will prejudice our expectations and dash our hopes."[21]

The combination of the recapture of Enckhuysen and the establishment of a republican admiral consolidated the power of De Witt and the States party. "Since the reducing of Enckhuysen," the *Weekly Intelligencer* was able to inform its readers in early November, "the Orange party have much languished, and are now quite down." "The Holland faction against the noble House of Orange rule all the rest," whined one Orangist. "The Orange party is quite down, and they only in power who seek peace," ran one oft repeated report.[22]

Bod., Rawl. A7, pp. 258–260; Letter to Jongstall, 28 October/7 November 1653, Bod., Rawl. A7, pp. 269–270.

19 Newsletter from United Provinces, September 1653, Bod., Rawl. A6, p. 275; newsletter from United Provinces, 9/19 September 1653, Bod., Rawl. A6, p. 144.

20 *Several Proceedings*, 8–15 September 1653, pp. 3277–3278; *Mercurius Politicus*, 8–15 September 1653, p. 2731; Whitelocke, *Annals*, 20 September 1653, BL, Add. 4992, f. 36r; Robert Stone to Sir Walter Vane, 9/19 September 1653, Bod., Rawl. A6, p. 175; Bisdonner to Dutch Ambassadors, 9/19 September 1653, Bod., Rawl. A6, pp. 171–172; newsletter from United Provinces, 9/19 September 1653, Bod., Rawl. A6, p. 159; newsletter from The Hague, 9/19 September 1653, Bod., Rawl. A6, p. 97; newsletter from The Hague, 8/18 September 1653, Bod., Clar. 46, f. 258.

21 Newsletter from United Provinces, 9/19 September 1653, Bod., Rawl. A6, pp. 139–141; newsletter from The Hague, 9/19 September 1653, Bod., Rawl. A6, p. 98; Royalist Letter, 2/12 September 1653, Bod., Rawl. A6, p. 34.

22 *Weekly Intelligencer*, 1–8 November 1653, p. 47; Letter from United Provinces, 14/24 October 1653, Bod., Rawl. A7, p. 179; *Perfect Diurnall*, 31 October–7 November 1653, p. 3092; newsletter from Rotterdam, 28 October/7 November 1653, Bod., Rawl. A7, pp. 266–267; *A Perfect Account*, 2–9 November 1653, p. 1184; newsletter from Delft, 18/

All discussion of aiding Charles Stuart was quickly ended. In fact, the republican party prohibited the royal exile from entering the territory of the United Provinces. Middleton's plea for Dutch aid to the Scots Highlanders was "rejected upon this ground, because the two states are upon a treaty for peace, which peace the merchant and mechanic here groans after." So complete was the victory of the States party that in late December it was decided to tax the Prince of Orange like any other citizen, prompting his mother to weep "three hours together seeing her authority wholly annulled by that means."[23]

By reestablishing its political control in Holland, and ultimately in the entire United Provinces, then, the States party had once again made peace a real possibility. The Orangists no longer had the political clout to demand the recall of the deputies in London, or to insist that the States General provide support for British rebels; nor could they any longer count upon an Orangist navy to wreak havoc on the peace process by a daring military assault. The English moderates now could similarly be confident that a peace with the United Provinces would not immediately be nullified by an Orangist revolution. "England will now perceive," observed one newsletter-writer perceptively, "that they need not fear anything from the King's party or Prince of Orange who are and will be kept all under by the States of Holland and the naval strength being in the hands of Holland, England must believe that Holland will take care that they be not hereafter opposed in the peace which they will make."[24]

When Jongstall and Nieupoort returned to London from the United Provinces in October, they brought with them a newfound optimism, a belief that the altered political circumstance made peace a real possibility. In the first official conference between the Dutch deputies and the English commissioners since July, the Dutch emphasized the necessity of peace among God's people, among Europe's liberty-loving republics. "The merciful God we hope will preserve and keep us from the abomination of the Medianites killing by their own swords, and from the punishment of Israel," prayed the Dutch deputies, "when Ephraim did rise against

28 November 1653, Bod., Rawl. A8, p. 188; John Adams to ?, 18/28 November 1653, Bod., Rawl. A8, p. 193; *Mercurius Politicus*, 29 September–6 October 1653, p. 2780.

23 *Mercurius Politicus*, 8–15 September 1653, p. 2731; newsletter from Paris, 7/17 December 1653, Rawl. A9, p. 42; Letter from Rotterdam, 23 September/3 October 1653, Bod., Rawl. A6, p. 333; *Mercurius Politicus*, 29 September–6 October 1653, p. 2780; newsletter from United Provinces, 28 October/7 November 1653, Bod., Rawl. A7, p. 261; newsletter from The Hague, 29 October/8 November 1653, Bod., Rawl. A7, pp. 295–296; *A Perfect Account*, 2–9 November 1653, p. [1180]; Thurloe to Whitelocke, 21 January 1654, Sigismund Freiherrn von Bischoffshausen, *Die Politik des Protectors Oliver Cromwell in der Auffassung und Thätigkeit seines Ministers des Staatssecretürs John Thurloe* (Innsbruck, 1899), p. 157; newsletter from United Provinces, 30 December/9 January 1653, Bod., Rawl. A9, pp. 204–205; newsletter from Paris, 14/24 January 1654, Bod., Rawl. A10, p. 246.

24 Newsletter from United Provinces, 9/19 September 1653, Bod., Rawl. A6, p. 141.

Manasseh, Manasseh against Ephraim, and both together against Judah." Against the image of this fratricidal war, the Dutch offered a more optimistic vision, a vision of a great Protestant alliance. "Let us rather unite God's people, be as one body, and march as one man," they suggested, "that England as formerly be a nursing mother of brave men to maintain our good true liberties, and the United Provinces a bulwark to this Commonwealth against all who shall presume to disturb the constitution of your government, and the just interest of both nations. So that those that attack your liberty may be regarded as attacking our government, and those that shall provoke our state, as if provoking yours." The first article of the Anglo-Dutch alliance, the deputies thought, should be for "the propagation of the holy Gospel, with the protection of the profession of the same faith." Characteristically the security the Dutch offered was that of a great international Protestant alliance – which would include France "in regard of the free exercise of the reformed religion there."[25] The English commissioners must have been astounded with this new Dutch enthusiasm for the Protestant cause. "The Dutch pretend a great desire to agreement," reported the *Several Proceedings of State Affairs* enthusiastically, "they say in private, they will join with England offensive and defensive, if agreement be had."[26]

The return of the Dutch deputies, coupled with the enthusiastic reports from their first two conferences with the English commissioners after their return, convinced everyone that peace was imminent. "You may be confident," one newsletter-writer informed his audience, "unless the Dutch be bound up by other interests, they and we shall agree." "The Dutch negotiations seem to be progressing favorably," agreed the Venetian resident. Peter De Groot had already ordered the best Rhenish wine to celebrate the conclusion of peace. "Most men" in the United Provinces, reported the *Mercurius Politicus*, conclude "that a peace will be made between the two Commonwealths." The Dutch, Hyde glumly agreed, "promise themselves a peace with the rebels." "Charles Stuart and his

25 Dutch deputies to Council of State, 28 October 1653, PRO, SP 105/98, ff. 28v–29; Dutch deputies to Council of State, 2 November 1653, PRO, SP 105/98, ff. 29v–30. This evidence calls into question Simon Schama's assertion that "the superficial religious affinities between the Puritan Commonwealth and the Dutch Republic did nothing to palliate the bitter maritime disputes that produced the first Anglo-Dutch war in 1651. When Cromwell cited such affinities three years later [*sic*] to justify his startling proposal for a Godly union of the two republics, he was greeted with incredulous amazement in The Hague." Simon Schama, *Embarrassment of Riches* (Berkeley, 1988), p. 96. Obviously the amazement was with the proposal of republican fusion, not with the common Protestant cause. Indeed I hope to make clear elsewhere that it was precisely the emphasis on the rhetoric of Protestant internationalism in the first half of the seventeenth century which precluded the development of a true nationalism.

26 *Several Proceedings*, 27 October–3 November 1653, pp. 3390–3391.

[party]," ran one report from Paris, "had never more fear that a peace will be made between both Commonwealths than they have at present."[27]

Unfortunately, as soon as the English presented their proposals for peace, all of this optimism vanished almost as quickly as it had reappeared. The meeting of the Dutch deputies and English commissioners of 18 November opened with Cromwell delivering a long speech in which he explained that since the Dutch "had refused the coalition, and mingling of sovereignties," the two republics were now "to be considered as distinct in interest, and as having peculiar rights and privileges belonging to each other," the delimitations of which would be adjusted in the treaty.[28] When the English commissioners submitted their written draft of the treaty, it became clear just how broadly they conceived of the English "peculiar rights." The Orangist deputies may have bristled a bit at Articles 6, 8, 9, 10, and 12 which prevented either nation from aiding or harboring the other's rebels or exiles. But the real conflict lay elsewhere. The English insisted that in addition to the ships and goods seized during the war – which "shall be accounted, and be taken as part of satisfaction and reparation for the charges and damages" which England "had been put unto" – "the States General shall pay unto the Commonwealth such further sums" as shall be decided by arbitrators. The Dutch, then, were to be blamed for causing the war, and to pay accordingly. All Dutch ships were to "strike their flag, and lower their topsail" when passing any English man-of-war, paying their "respects due to the said Commonwealth of England to whom the dominion, and sovereignty of the British sea belongs." The two corollaries of this premise were stringent indeed. First, the English suggested that the Dutch "men of war not [exceed] such a number as shall be agreed upon in the treaty" – a number commonly rumored to be forty to the English sixty. Second, the Dutch were to lease for twenty-one years the right to fish in the British seas. The final, and most telling, English demand was that "neither the said States General of the United Provinces nor the particular states of any of the United Provinces shall at any time hereafter make, constitute, or appoint William Prince of Orange grandchild to the late King of England, nor any of his line, captain general, Stadholder, or commander of their armies or forces

27 Newsletter from London, 4 November 1653, Bod., Clar. 47, f. 43r; Paulucci to Sagredo, 10/20 November 1653, *CSPV*, p. 147; newsletter from The Hague, 3/13 November 1653, Bod., Clar. 47, f. 41r (Beverning); Van De Perre to Lord Bruin, 11/21 November 1653, Bod., Rawl. A8, p. 102; De Bruin to Van De Perre, 18/28 November 1653, Bod., Rawl. A8, p. 183; De Groot to Beverning, 18/28 November 1653, Bod., Rawl. A8, p. 167; *Mercurius Politicus*, 10–17 November 1653, p. 2873; Hyde to Kent, 11/21 November 1653, Bod., Clar. 47, f. 65r; newsletter from Paris, 2/12 November 1653, Bod., Rawl. A8, p. 5.

28 Council of State to Dutch deputies, November 1653, PRO, SP 105/98, f. 41; Jongstall to William Frederick, 18/28 November 1653, Bod., Rawl. A8, pp. 170–172 (identifies Cromwell as delivering the above cited speech).

at land."[29] The English, opined the French ambassador after reading a copy of the draft treaty, "continue to negotiate with a greater air of superiority than any prince had ever done with that state."[30]

Despite the obvious toughness of the terms which the English offered, they do not reveal an attempt to seize control of the vast Dutch trade network. "There hath not yet been anything spoken of in any of the conferences of the business of the Indies," Nieupoort revealed to a fellow Hollander – hardly what one would have expected had the war been about the control of trade. In fact, the Dutch were granted some mercantile advantages. Articles 13 and 20 specifically guaranteed free trade between the commonwealths for inhabitants of each state. While the twenty-third article provided that all Dutch citizens "being of the reformed religion" would have the complete rights of a British citizen when in British territory. Although the Navigation Act was not explicitly repealed, it is hard to see what force it could have retained with these provisions.[31]

The Dutch deputies, however, were more concerned with the haughty political claims implicit in the treaty than with the potential economic benefits they might reap. They objected to the clause demanding payment for fishing because it usurped their ancient right by putting the Dutch "out of an immemorial possession without cause, or reason, having always enjoyed the freedom of fishing." The English claim to be able to search any Dutch vessel in the British seas was "against the practice of our country, and subject to a thousand disorders and disputes, and injurious in the point of dominion and sovereignty." But, the two English demands which provoked the most indignation were those limiting the number of Dutch men-of-war and excluding the Prince of Orange. "We are so far from it," the Dutch deputies said of the proposed naval limitation, "that we should esteem ourselves unworthy of the goodness and favor of God, whereby his Divine Majesty hath blessed the endeavors of our superiors in the lawful preservation of their liberty, if we did but enter thereupon in a conference." The place of the Prince of Orange in the Dutch polity, all four Dutch deputies protested, "is a point absolutely appertaining to the disposition of the said states wherein with no more reason or equity the lords of this government are to meddle, than we in their elections in the like occurrences in this nation."[32] The Dutch deputies had certainly made it clear that they

29 Draft treaty, 18 November 1653, PRO, SP 105/98, ff. 32–36; newsletter from The Hague, 3/13 November 1653, Bod., Clar. 47, f. 41r; newsletter from London, 12 November 1653, Bod., Clar. 47, f. 72r. These newsletters confirm the 60 : 40 ratio of the respective navies.

30 Bordeaux to de Brienne, 26 November/6 December 1653, PRO, PRO 31/3/92, f. 46 (my translation).

31 Nieupoort to Lord Hans Van Loon, 2/12 December 1653, Bod., Rawl. A9, p. 5; draft treaty, 18 November 1653, PRO, SP 105/98, ff. 32–36.

32 Dutch deputies to Council of State, 22 November 1653, PRO, SP 105/98, ff. 38–39. These discussions were reported with varying degrees of accuracy by the French and Venetian representatives. See Bordeaux to de Brienne, 26 November/6 December 1653, PRO, PRO

were more concerned about protecting the sovereignty of the United Provinces than in expanding its trade.

The Dutch deputies were both amazed and furious at the "unreasonableness, extravagancy and unsufferableness" of the English propositions. Instead of advancing a compromise treaty, they fumed, "all is set down and propounded according to the inclination, and meaning of this government and to their greatest advantage." By this they did not mean, as historians have too often assumed, that the English had sought their own economic advantage. Rather the Dutch were concerned that the English had done everything possible to derogate from their status as a sovereign nation. "How many times hath his Excellency and the lords praised our ancestors who with so much zeal and vigor fought for the liberty of their country," they asked, "and how is it possible that they should now have the opinion that the posterity is grown so base that they should suffer themselves without reason, or necessity to be deprived, or frustrated of so notable a part thereof?" Though they had rejected the union because the "supreme power and constitution of our government only could not admit of such an unpracticable alteration," they still hoped for a coalition "for all other interests and advantages such as by the blessing of God, both nations do enjoy."[33] Instead the English had offered them virtual slavery. "We conceive it neither for the service nor the reputation of the state that we stay longer here," the Dutch deputies consequently explained to the Greffier, informing him that they would set sail for the United Provinces within five days.[34] The peace negotiations, it seemed, had reached their final impasse.

By late November the mood of informed political observers, which had been so optimistic only two months previously, was now dark indeed. "We are like to have a bloody summer and very dangerous," the Canary merchant John Paige informed his business partners. "Yesterday hopes of an adjustment were said to be on the wane and today the negotiations are reported as quite at an end," the Venetian resident in London explained to his compatriot in Paris in early December, "so the war will be resumed with greater bloodshed and animosity than ever, to the enormous inconvenience and detriment of all Europe." "There was never less probability of peace by this treaty than at present," observed a London-based newsletter-writer.[35]

31/3/92, ff. 46v–47r; Bordeaux to de Brienne, 1/11 December 1653, PRO, PRO 31/3/92, ff. 62v–64r; Bordeaux to Servien, 5/15 December 1653, PRO, PRO 31/3/92, f. 77r; Bordeaux to de Brienne, 5/15 December 1653, PRO, PRO 31/3/92, ff. 74r–75r; Paulucci to Sagredo, 2/12 December 1653, *CSPV*, p. 156.

33 Dutch deputies to Greffier, 25 November/5 December 1653, Bod., Clar. 47, f. 114r; Dutch deputies to Council of State, 22 November 1653, PRO, SP 105/98, ff. 38–39; Dutch deputies to Council of State, 25 November 1653, PRO, SP 105/98, ff. 39v-40.

34 Dutch commissioners to Greffier, 25 November/5 December 1653, Bod., Clar. 47, f. 114r.

35 Paige to Paynter and Clerke, 18 November 1653, Steckley, *John Paige*, p. 99; Paulucci to Sagredo, 9/19 December 1653, *CSPV*, pp. 157–158; newsletter from London, 3 December 1653, Bod., Clar. 47, f. 129r; newsletter from London, 9 December 1653, Bod., Clar. 47,

Political prognosticators had reached similar conclusions on the other side of the North Sea. De Witt told the States General in early December that the chances of peace were "no better than desperate." The "wiser sort" in Delft "expect no success of the treaty." The gossip in Rotterdam was that "all hopes of an accommodation are laid aside, and that our Ambassadors had desired leave of the Council of State to return home *re infecta*." Throughout the United Provinces, the *Perfect Account* confirmed, "many do now begin to despair."[36] Perhaps more importantly, Dutch political pessimism was accompanied by a new military build-up. The States General stepped up naval recruiting, placed orders for new men-of-war, and even began to contemplate providing aid to the Scots.[37] No wonder one Royalist was able to report triumphantly that "there is little hope of peace between the Hollander and the English rebels."[38]

Contemporaries marveled at the sudden change in the fortunes of the Anglo-Dutch peace. "The treaty between the two republics is subject to many revolutions," admitted the French ambassador. "This peace which all England and all Holland did not doubt would be concluded," he confided to another Parisian correspondent, "is now blocked by some unknown motives."[39] What, in fact, had happened to the negotiations? Why had the English, who had promised to moderate their position in the early autumn, insisted on such hard terms?

It was certainly not because the radicals had captured the committee conducting the negotiations with the Dutch. In fact, that committee changed too frequently and too dramatically to have established any continuity or coherent sense of policy. Even if it had, the members who are known to have taken an active role were predominantly Cromwellian moderates.[40]

f. 150r; *Weekly Intelligencer*, 6–13 December 1653, p. 84; *Faithful Scout*, 2–9 December 1653, p. 1240; *Several Proceedings*, 1–8 December 1653, p. 3467.

36 Newsletter from The Hague, 8/18 December 1653, Bod., Clar. 47, f. 135r; Jongstall to his wife, 25 November/5 December 1653, Bod., Rawl. A8, p. 238; newsletter from Delft, 18/28 November 1653, Bod., Rawl. A8, pp. 186–187; *A Perfect Account*, 30 November–7 December 1653, pp. 1210, 1216; *Mercurius Politicus*, 9–16 December 1653, pp. 3136–3137 (Rotterdam); *Mercurius Politicus*, 22–29 December 1653, p. 3150 (Rotterdam), p. 3149 (Hamburg); *Perfect Diurnall*, 19–26 December 1653 (hopelessly mispaginated) (Hamburg); Beuningen to Dutch Deputies, 30 December/9 January 1653/54, Bod., Rawl. A9, pp. 214–215.

37 The evidence for this new build-up is vast. I only provide a sample here. Newsletter from The Hague, 17/27 November 1653, Bod., Clar. 47, f. 78r; newsletter from United Provinces, 18/28 November 1653, Bod., Rawl. A8, p. 150; Whitelocke, *Annals*, 30 November 1653, BL, Add. 4992, f. 59r; newsletter from The Hague, 1/11 December 1653, Bod., Clar. 47, f. 121r; Whitelocke, *Annals*, 8 December 1653, BL, Add. 4992, f. 59v; Whitelocke, *Annals*, 14 December 1653, BL, Add. 4992, f. 60v.

38 Luke Whittington to Ralph Parker, 11 December 1653, *CSPD*, p. 297.

39 Bordeaux to Servien, 5/15 December 1653, PRO, PRO 31/3/92, f. 77r (my translation); Bordeaux to de Brienne, 26 November/6 December 1653, PRO, PRO 31/3/92, f. 47v (my translation).

40 The committee at various times included Norton, Wolsley, Ashley Cooper, Lawrence, Tichborn, Cromwell, Strickland, Moyer, Montague, Carew, Jones, Pickering, Howard,

Nor does the evidence suggest that Cromwell had again veered back into agreement with the radicals about the conduct of the war. Observers of every ideological predisposition were in agreement that Cromwell continued in his support of the peace throughout the autumn. The Dutch commissioners reported that Cromwell's most trusted friends repeatedly assured them of his good inclinations. Edward Hyde was certain in early December that Cromwell "hath a good mind to compose that difference which hath cost them so much money and blood." Indeed so obvious was Cromwell's desire for peace, that rumors abounded that he had signed a private treaty with the Dutch deputies.[41]

"Having gained Cromwell, they conclude the matter done," one newsletter sagaciously said of the Dutch, "notwithstanding the multitude that is against it. I doubt me they are in the right, for if we mistake him not he is *dominus factotum.*" It is this observation that Cromwell was only the leader of a faction which holds the key to understanding the perplexing developments of November and December 1653.[42]

Party animosity dominated the activities of the Nominated Parliament in the autumn. "The two cabals or factions in the Parliament do struggle very much for the upper hand of one another," commented one observer of the Nominated Parliament, "the general and his cabal or faction receiving so much opposition from his adverse party that he cannot do what he would. Harrison and his party do rail and preach every day against the general and the peace with Holland. So that it is thought and believed that they are both embroiled and their cabals or factions ready to make a separation in the House of Parliament." "I find Cromwell gives Harrison leave to make a party against him," marveled Robert Harley. "O England, how great are thy divisions in thy own bowels," lamented one sympathetic to the Nominated Parliament.[43]

Cromwell's profound disappointment in the Nominated Parliament was

Bennet, and Viscount Lisle. Of these men, Woolrych *Commonwealth to Protectorate*, has classified only three – Moyer, Carew, and Bennet – as radicals. Day's proceedings, 14 July 1653, *CSPD*, p. 26; day's proceedings, 29 October 1653, *CSPD*, p. 223; *Several Proceedings*, 17–24 November 1653, p. 3432; newsletter from The Hague, 24 November/4 December 1653, Bod., Clar. 47, f. 109v; Beverning to De Witt, 18/28 November 1653, Bod., Rawl. A8, p. 175.

41 Richards to Stoneham, 23 September 1653, Bod., Rawl. A6, p. 334; Bordeaux to de Brienne, 5/15 December 1653, PRO, PRO 31/3/92, f. 74v; Hyde to Rochester, 11/21 November 1653, Bod., Clar. 47, f. 68r; Jongstall to William Frederick, 11/21 November 1653, Bod., Rawl. A8, p. 105; Jongstall to William Frederick, 18/28 November 1653, Bod., Rawl. A8, p. 168; Hyde to Nicholas, 2/12 December 1653, Bod., Clar. 47, f. 128r; Hyde to Rochester, 25 November/5 December 1653, Bod., Clar. 47, f. 115r; Hyde to Clement, 2/12 December 1653, Bod., Clar. 47, f. 120r; Hyde to Rochester, 2/12 December 1653, Bod., Clar. 47, f. 123r.

42 Newsletter from The Hague, 28 October/7 November 1653, Bod., Rawl. A7, p. 284.

43 Sir Walter Vane to Mons. Chantillot, 25 November 1653, Bod., Rawl. A8, p. 265; Robert Harley to Sir Robert Harley, 2 November 1653, BL Loan 29/177, f. 37r; William Parker to Mr. Fielder, 4 November 1653, Bod., Rawl. A8, p. 76; newsletter from London, 24

well known. "He is more troubled now with the fool, than before with the knave," sneered one Royalist newsletter-writer.[44] Indeed so concerned had Cromwell become with the Harrisonian radicals, and with their obvious ties to the hot preachers at Blackfriars, that he despatched Peter Sterry with several other ministers in early December "to oppose spirit to spirit, and to advise Feak and the rest to obedience as the most necessary way to bring in the Kingdom of Christ." Predictably enough, the radicals scoffed, insisting that they were "unable to reject the inspiration of the Holy Spirit."[45]

Despite, or perhaps because of, their overwhelming defeat in the elections for a new Council of State in early November, the radical members of the Nominated Parliament dominated the debates and votes of the House in November and early December. "The faction of Harrison and the Blackfriars men growing very high," lamented Sir Walter Vane, the other party was not "able to do in the Parliament what they please." "The Anabaptistical party," agreed another observer, "are very prevalent in the House." Every indication, then, seems to support Woolrych's claim that in the face of newfound radical organization and assertiveness "the moderates were leaving the field to their antagonists." It was almost certainly this radical presence which exerted influence on the Council of State, and the commissioners negotiating with the Dutch. "How can distractions be avoided," asked one purveyor of news, "for the Parliament voting one way and the Council directing another." In the end, at least in the Dutch negotiations, Parliament prevailed. "The Anabaptists in Parliament were the hindrance of the peace," remarked one political pundit, "and the faction appeared the most prevalent in the House so it was found necessary to dissolve the Parliament to bring that faction under." "That body rather favored the continuance of the war," agreed the Venetian resident Paulucci. "The confusion and distraction in England is so great," concluded Edward Hyde, "that Cromwell could not bring his people to those condescensions which were necessary towards a peace, but insisted on all their old insolent demands."[46] The English negotiators had gotten tough with the Dutch because the newly dominant radical party had forced them to do so.

November 1653, Bod., Clar. 47, f. 113r; Bordeaux to de Brienne, 17/27 November 1653, PRO, PRO 31/3/92, f. 36v.

44 Newsletter from London, 2 September 1653, Bod., Clar. 46, f. 230v. This sort of assessment had become a commonplace of Royalist political analysis. See Hyde to Rochester, 29 September/9 October 1653, Bod., Clar. 46, f. 303r; Hyde to Wentworth, 16/26 September 1653, Bod., Clar. 46, f. 279v; newsletter from London, 16 September 1653, Bod., Clar. 46, f. 274v.

45 Newsletter, 2 December 1653, Bod., Rawl. A9, p. 9; Bordeaux to de Brienne, 1/11 December 1653, PRO, PRO 31/3/92, f. 65r (my translation); for the ties between the radical preachers and the Harrisonians see Woolrych, *Commonwealth to Protectorate*, pp. 287–288, 325.

46 Bordeaux to Mazarin, 7/17 November 1653, PRO, PRO 31/3/92, f. 11; Sir Walter Vane to Sir John Sayers, 25 November 1653, Bod., Rawl. A8, p. 237; Royalist Letter, 2 December 1653, Bod., Rawl. A9, pp. 9–10; Woolrych, *Commonwealth to Protectorate*, pp. 314–315;

These developments in Parliament and at the negotiation table need to be placed within the wider context of a radical offensive in the late autumn of 1653. Pamphlets, broadsides, and sermons created a spirited if not always unified attack upon the Cromwellian moderates. The tithe-supported clergy, fumed the radical William Dell, "have made themselves, contrary to God's command, lords and masters in the Church of God," thereby setting "wide open the floodgates to Antichrist and his kingdom to break in upon the world and to overflow it." John Rogers demanded that the Parliament throw "down the standing of lawyers and priests." "It is not enough to change some of the laws, and so to reform them (as is intended by most of you) according to the rule of the fourth monarchy, which must all to pieces," Rogers told members of the Nominated Parliament in his immense but widely disseminated *Sagrir*, "O no! that will be to poor purpose, and is not your work now, which is to provide for the fifth [monarchy]." This could only happen, he explained if the laws of the nation became one with the "Word of God." "The expectation of our present governors was at first very great but some think their proceedings are very little answerable," wrote one radical expressing a common sentiment, but "the Lord whom we seek, whom we desire shall suddenly come to his temple."[47] The religious radicals soon tapped into the anti-Cromwellian rhetoric developed the previous summer during Lilburne's famous show trial. By September "barbarous libels" and "infamous pictures" defaming "our noble General" were "thrown about in great quantities." In one of these libels Cromwell was accused of "not having the fear of God before his eyes" and endeavoring "to make us his lord and masters his perpetual slaves and vassals." By December Cromwell had become in the eyes of the Blackfriars men "the man of sin, the red dragon, and many other Scripture ill names."[48]

Naturally the religious radicals did not ignore the Dutch War. "Now those that so passionately desire a peace with this country may see their error in the work of the Lord," argued one radical after a North Sea storm had severely damaged the Dutch fleet, demanding that the English "continue their good resolution to extirpate the whore of Babylon and idolatry." The

newsletter, 9/19 December 1653, Bod., Rawl. A9, p. 53; newsletter from The Hague, 13/23 January 1654, Bod., Clar. 47, f. 303r; Paulucci to Sagredo, 15/25 December 1653, *CSPV*, p. 161; Hyde to Clement, 9/19 December 1653, Bod., Clar. 47, f. 154r.

47 Paulucci to Sagredo, 20/30 October 1653, *CSPV*, p. 141; William Dell, *The Tryal of Spirits* (London, 1653), Thomason: December 1653, pp. 8–9; John Rogers, *Sagrir Or Doomes-Day Drawing Nigh* (London, 1653), Thomason: 7 November 1653, sig. A4, pp. 2, 122, 137; Mary Cary, *The Resurrection of the Witnesses and England's Fall from (The Mystical Babylon) Rome* (London, 1653), Thomason: 14 November 1653, *passim*; Letter to Lieutenant Hickermight, 17 October 1653, Bod., Rawl. A7, pp. 185–186.

48 Newsletter, 9/19 September 1653, Bod., Rawl. A6, pp. 185–186; Richards to Stoneham, 23 September 1653, Bod., Rawl. A6, p. 334; newsletter from London, 16 September 1653, Bod., Clar. 46, f. 274r; "Proclamation by the Supreme Lord the free born People of England," BL, Thomason MSS: late September 1653, TT: E714 (7); newsletter, 2 December 1653, Bod., Rawl. A9, p. 9.

time had come to begin the crusade against Antichrist. "His Excellency the Lord Jesus hath sent out his summons to other nations also," insisted John Rogers, "and the blade of that sword (whose handle is held in England) will reach to the very gates of Rome ere long." The United Provinces were to be the first stop on the glorious march. "Woe! woe then be to thee O Flanders full of blood! and Zeeland and Holland full of treacheries! (as if this were the way of the war to Rome)," warned Rogers, "Alas ! Alas! weep thou unhappy Babylon!" Mary Cary agreed that God favored England because "now in England there are a more considerable number of the faithful servants, and witnesses of Jesus Christ, than in any kingdom in the world." Since the time had now come "to begin that great work of overcoming the Beast, and of destroying (the great Babylon) Rome," Cary offered "a word of caution to the Dutch, Danes, French and all other nations of Europe, to caution them to beware how they do ever henceforward make war against ... the commonwealth of England." Indeed the "Anabaptist faction" was widely known to "have decried all peace with the Princes and states of the world." No wonder one of Thurloe's intelligence gatherers thought that the radicals "will make us stink in the nostrils of all the godly abroad."[49]

The Cromwellian moderates did, belatedly, defend themselves against this radical assault. The clamor of the radicals for liberty of conscience, the moderates claimed, was really a covert plot "to establish their several parties, and exclude all others from power and interest in the nation." "Their common hate and detestation to the persons of all men of other beliefs" was quite ironic, maintained the Cromwellian polemicist John Hall, "since nothing in the world can be more Antichristian than to force the consciences and beings of other men under their own sway and domination." Even worse, the religious logic of the radicals led inevitably to anarchy. Their "chief work is to preach and advance Christ's personal reign here on earth, being the ancient error and foppery of the chiliasts or millinaries, huffed and exploded out of the Church of Christ in the very infancy thereof," pointed out one moderate; such doctrines could now only lead "to the destruction of the magistracy of England." "Such a tenet," agreed Hall, "cannot consist with the very being of a civil magistrate." The author of *Sedition Scourg'd* thought such "an irregular and dangerous liberty" would either cause a return to civil war or reduce England "under its former tyranny." In short these "ill made brains, and disturbed fancies, strongly tinctured with an hypochondriac melancholy"

[49] Letter from The Hague, 4/14 November 1653, Bod., Rawl. A8, pp. 45–46; Rogers, *Sagrir*, sig. A2r, pp. 15–18, 133–134; Cary, *Resurrection*, pp. 49–50, 132–133; Richards to Stoneham, 23 September 1653, Bod., Rawl. A6, p. 334; intelligence to Thurloe and Cromwell, 16 November 1653, Bod., Rawl. A8, p. 129.

were asking Englishmen "to quit our discourse, our natural reason, our experiences drawn even from common sense."[50]

This confrontational language made peaceful resolution of the ideological struggle impossible. Not surprisingly, then, the conflict was not confined to pamphlet wars. In July a woman preaching at Somerset House "was like to be stoned by the multitude, had not a guard fetched her away." This led the noted conservative Independent William Strong to preach "boldly at Westminster against the liberty of the times which opened the way to Popery." Those were fighting words. The battle ultimately broke out at St. Paul's in October when "an anabaptistical soldier was preaching." A group of apprentices began throwing stones at the soldiers who responded with their pistols. Ultimately Colonel Whalley and Alderman Tichborn were able to quell the riot, but not until "some heads were broken." Subsequently such attacks occurred with increasing regularity. So threatening had the situation become that in early November Cromwell called a conference – attended by leaders of various religious groupings, such as John Owen, Stephen Marshall, Philip Nye, Henry Jessey, and Thomas Harrison – to "persuade them that hold Christ the Head, and to the same in fundamentals, to agree in love." Cromwell had pleaded in vain; less than a month later *A Perfect Account* reported several congregations "have not only been disturbed, but several mutinies have been raised to breach of the peace of this Commonwealth."[51]

Not surprisingly this situation led many observers to conclude that the Nominated Parliament, a Parliament now torn apart with divisions, could not continue much longer. "Here is a general change foreseen," the Dutch deputies optimistically informed the States General in November. "Certain it is, without some quick remedy of prevention, the frame of government must needs fail, when the main pins are drawn out of the hearts of the people, by those harangues of sedition," thought one of Thurloe's intelligencers. "If the Parliament sits out its appointed

50 Intelligence to Thurloe and Cromwell, 16 November 1653, Bod., Rawl. A8, pp. 130–131; [John Hall], *Confusion-Confounded* (London, 1654), pp. 3–8; *Strena Vavasoriensis: A New-Years Gift for the Welch Itinerants* (London, 1654), Thomason: 30 January 1654, p. 5; *Sedition Scourg'd* (London, 1653), Thomason: 20 October 1653, p. 8.

51 Newsletter from London, 22 July 1653, Bod., Clar. 46, f. 113r; newsletter from London, 29 July 1653, Bod., Clar. 46, f. 130r; for Strong see Tai Liu, *Puritan London* (Newark, 1986), p. 114; A. N. to Lord Inchiquin, 16 October 1653, Bod., Rawl. A7, p. 182; *Weekly Intelligencer*, 11–18 October 1653, p. 24; Paulucci to Sagredo, 20/30 October 1653, *CSPV*, p. 142; newsletter from London, 21 October 1653, Bod., Clar. 46, f. 363r; *Mercurius Politicus*, 13–20 October 1653, p. 2795; *Weekly Intelligencer*, 25 October–1 November 1653, pp. 37–38; *Several Proceedings*, 27 October–3 November 1653, p. 3391; *A Perfect Account*, 16–23 November 1653, p. 1193.

term," concurred the Venetian resident Paulucci, "it will be a wonder."[52]

It was not a great surprise, then, when a group of moderate members of Parliament resigned the sovereign power of the Nominated Parliament on the morning of 12 December. This should not, however, minimize the magnitude of the event. This resignation marked the final failure of the Parliament of Saints. The religious radicals were irrevocably stripped of their political power. "Major Harrison and his pulpit beaters are all eclipsed," attested one witness to these exciting developments. Though Christopher Feak and Vavasor Powell "cannot forbear their excesses," Thurloe was sure by late December that "to think they have a party or can make one, is vain."[53] The possibility of forging a millenarian consensus had been "rudely shattered."[54] Never again would a powerful group of men within the political nation advocate the establishment of a government which would prepare for the rule of Christ on earth. It was a measure of just how close these men had come to power in the late autumn that they were able effectively to obstruct the Anglo-Dutch peace process, paving the way for their preferred policy of a millenarian crusade, a crusade for which the United Provinces were to be the beachhead. Although the foreign policy of the Protectorate, and subsequently of the Restored Monarchy, would at times be quite aggressive, it was always couched in the language of national interest. The Harrisonian radicals, by contrast, had wanted take the eschatological struggle to the very gates of Rome, had wanted to wage and win the war for universal and eternal truth.

52 Dutch Ambassadors to States General, [15] November 1653, Bod., Rawl. A8, p. 126; intelligence to Thurloe and Cromwell, 16 November 1653, Bod., Rawl. A8, pp. 129–130; Paulucci to Sagredo, 2/12 December 1653, *CSPV*, p. 155; Bordeaux to de Brienne, 8/18 December 1653, PRO, PRO 31/3/92, ff. 83v-84r (my translation); Bordeaux to Servien, 5/15 December 1653, PRO, PRO 31/3/92, f. 78; Hyde to Nicholas, 18/28 November 1653, Bod., Clar. 47, f. 93; Hyde to Richard Browne, 6 December 1653, Christ Church, John Evelyn MSS 10, f. 34r; John Langley to Sir Richard Leveson, 3 December 1653, SRO, D593/P/8/2/2.

53 Henry Hart to Mr. Wilkey, 27 December 1653, Bod., Rawl. A9, p. 165; Thurloe to Whitelocke, 29 December 1653, Bischoffshausen, *Politik*, p. 150; Letter to Mr. Rider, 14 December 1653, Bod., Rawl. A9, pp. 66–67; Paulucci to Sagredo, 15/25 December 1653, *CSPV*, p. 160.

54 John Patrick Laydon, "The Kingdom of Christ and the Powers of the Earth" (Cambridge, Ph.D. thesis, 1977), p. 432.

10

The Protectorate's new foreign policy

In early December 1653, the Nominated Parliament granted the Dutch deputies their passports in recognition that their negotiation had failed. Cromwell and his more moderate colleagues, however, hinted to the Dutch that they should hold out a bit longer, that a change of government was imminent.[1] The Dutch knew that it was the radical members of the Nominated Parliament and their fiery preachers who had obstructed the negotiations. Cromwell, Hugh Peter, and many of the commissioners had made it clear to the Dutch deputies that their hands were tied by the temporary ascendancy of the radical millenarians. However, the Dutch were convinced, as were most political observers, that the situation could not last for long, that Cromwell would put an end to this Parliament just as he had dissolved the Rump. A new regime, especially a new regime which was not so deeply influenced by Thomas Harrison and the hot men of St. Anne's Blackfriars, would certainly be more amenable to peace.

Sure enough, as soon as the Nominated Parliament submitted its resignation and the Protectorate was proclaimed, the prospects for peace were dramatically transformed. Cromwell immediately sent word to the Dutch deputies "that now he is advanced to a quality fit to treat with them" assuring them "of his desires of peace." "There is probability of peace with the Dutch," trumpeted the *Several Proceedings of State Affairs*. The bookstalls in London were filled with copies of *The Peace-Maker* which outlined the benefits of an Anglo-Dutch alliance. "Most men" believed that "the peace will be concluded, if not done already." The formerly belligerent *Moderate Publisher* christened Cromwell "Beati Pacifici." "This day we may, I hope, without offense say the peace with the Dutch is concluded in matter, though not in form or ceremony," bragged one newspaper, "Blessed be God! Though some be for war, our David is for peace." These were not

1 *Mercurius Politicus*, 22–29 December 1653, p. 3145 (based on a letter from Amsterdam dated 7 December); Bordeaux to Servien, 5/15 December 1653, PRO, PRO 31/3/92, ff. 77–78; Bordeaux to de Brienne, 8/18 December 1653, PRO, PRO 31/3/92, f. 82v; Hyde to Rochester, 9/19 December 1653, Bod., Clar. 47, f. 147r; Hyde to Nicholas, 9/19 December 1653, BL, Egerton MSS 2534, f. 144.

idle rumors. John Desborough and Robert Blake reported to the Lord Protector that "all is agreed unto" by Nieupoort and Beverning. By the middle of January the news had reached as far as Rotterdam and Paris where it was "taken for granted."[2]

These tidings soon struck a popular chord. "Every street in this city and the Exchange itself is full of the news of peace with Holland," reported the *Weekly Intelligencer* from London. When the Dutch ambassadors returned to London in March to put the finishing touches to the treaty, they found "all the streets on both sides full of people" crying "God bless the Lord's Ambassadors" and "God send us peace." The official publication of the treaty "excited universal acclamation" in the English capital. "Since the publication of the peace," the Venetian resident noted almost a full month after the event, "they have spent most of the time here in celebrating it."[3]

The peace elicited a similar response in the United Provinces. "Our country here is full of joy for the peace," wrote one correspondent from Rotterdam. "Great is their joy that the peace with England doth go so happily on," agreed another observer, "it was almost beyond their expectations, their joys therefore no doubt are doubled." Indeed so universal were the celebrations that the *Mercurius Politicus* doubted if there would be sufficient wine in all the United Provinces. In Paris, English and Dutch merchants were spotted together "drinking merrily toward that peace."[4] Conversely, the news demoralized the English Royalists. It "hath struck us dead," Hyde admitted to Nicholas, "so that we know not what to say, nor can I tell you what the king is to do." Although Hyde had hoped that "left to my books I should outlive this storm," a month later he was forced to acknowledge that the certainty of

2 Newsletter from London, 23 December 1653, Bod., Clar. 47, f. 223r; Sagredo to Doge and Senate, 27 December/6 January 1653/54, *CSPV*, pp. 166–167; *Several Proceedings*, 8–15 December 1653 (unpaginated); *The Peace-Maker* (London, 1653), Thomason: 16 December 1650; Letter to Monsr. Paten, 19/29 December 1653, Bod., Rawl. A9, p. 52; *Moderate Publisher*, 23–30 December 1653, p. 88; *Several Proceedings*, 22–29 December 1653, pp. [3519–3520, 3488]; John Desborough and Robert Blake to Cromwell, 5 January 1654, Bod., Rawl. A10, p. 92 (of course, no formal agreement was made – this might refer in fact to the Exclusion clause); newsletter from Paris, 7/17 January 1654, Bod., Rawl. A10, pp. 120–121; *Mercurius Politicus*, 13–19 January 1654, pp. 3196, 3199–3200; Robert Rawlins to John Buxton, 22 December 1653, HMC. *Various Collections*, Vol. II, p. 270.

3 *Weekly Intelligencer*, 17–24 January 1654, f. 138; Dutch Ambassadors to States General, 3/13 March 1654, Bod., Rawl. A12, p. 30; Jongstall to States of Friesland, 3/13 March 1654, Bod., Rawl. A12, p. 54; *Weekly Intelligencer*, 28 February–7 March 1654, pp. 184–185; Paulucci to Sagredo, 28 April/8 May 1654, *CSPV*, p. 209; Paulucci to Sagredo, 6/16 May 1654, *CSPV*, p. 11; Whitelocke, *Annals*, BL Add. 4992, f. 86v.

4 *The Perfect Diurnall*, 30 January–6 February 1654, p. 3318; *Weekly Intelligencer*, 28 February–7 March 1654, p. 184; *Mercurius Politicus*, 23 February–2 March 1654, p. 3308; Whitelocke, *Annals*, BL Add. 4992, f. 86v; newsletter from Paris, 21/31 January 1654, Bod., Rawl. A10, p. 395.

the peace "breaks my mind, and wastes my spirit so much, that I cannot hold out longer."[5]

Despite the widespread contemporary enthusiasm for the peace in England and Holland, it was subsequently harshly criticized. Even before it was concluded, Cromwell was accused of losing the peace. "It is a great blame to the reputation of our arms," argued one radical critic, "that a nation so often beaten and that cannot six months hence find money to keep five ships at sea, should have peace at their own rate." The Dutch deputies brag "how prudently, politically, and stoutly they carried on their negotiation in England," claimed another opponent of the peace, "by which means they obtained their desires and granted not the tenth part of what they might by their instructions." Edmund Ludlow later recalled that England had been "cheated into an unjust and disadvantageous agreement" by "the treachery" of Cromwell and his supporters. The resulting treaty, Ludlow claimed, gave the Dutch free license "to interrupt our trade."[6]

Not surprisingly both Anglican Royalists and republicans after the Restoration were quick to resuscitate this aspect of the radical critique of the Protectorate. The peace with the Dutch, argued that violent Anglican Royalist and hammer of the Dutch Edward Cliffe, redounded "to the perpetual infamy of that usurper Cromwell." Cromwell "more esteemed his own ambition than the welfare of his country," Cliffe maintained, "for had he not had more envy to the royal family in relation to his own safety, than he had affection to promote the commonwealth ... he would not at such a time as that have made peace with Holland, when all England was for war, being their indisputable victors." The Dutch "had been so humbled by several great losses, their trade so spoiled, and their subjects so impoverished" that they would have accepted any terms, argued Cromwell's Anglican Royalist biographer James Heath. But "this puny and unfledged prince came to a treaty with them upon most mean and inconsiderable terms." Although their emphases were different, the criticism of the radicals were no less caustic. "The original cause of the low condition that we are now (in relation to trade) reduced unto," argued the commercial radical Slingsby Bethel, "had its beginning in Oliver's time." Although the English "had brought the proud Hollanders upon their knees to beg peace of us," Cromwell failed to procure "those advantages for trade, as they who beat [the Dutch] did intend to have had." Cromwell, in short, had acted "as if the Lord had infatuated, and deprived him of common sense and reason; he neglected all our golden opportunities, misimproved the victory, God had

5 Hyde to Nicholas, 10/20 January 1654, Bod., Clar. 47, f. 321r; Hyde to Nicholas, 6 February 1654, Bod., Clar. 47, f. 362r.

6 Newsletter from The Hague, 28 October/7 November 1653, Bod., Rawl. A7, pp. 284–285; newsletter from The Hague, 18/28 January 1654, Bod., Rawl. A10, pp. 340–341; C. H. Firth (editor), *The Memoirs of Edmund Ludlow* (Oxford, 1894), pp. 355, 364. It is not coincidental that all of these criticisms come from Cromwell's political opponents.

given us over the United Netherlands, making peace (without ever striking a stroke) so soon as ever things came into his hands, upon equal terms with them." "The villainous ambition and folly of Cromwell," another radical Henry Stubbe informed his fellow Englishmen during the third Dutch War, "did subject you to these abuses."[7]

Had Cromwell, in fact, abandoned the professed war aims of the Rump and the Nominated Parliament? Had he surrendered potential national economic benefits in order to pursue personal aggrandizement? Did England win the war, only to have the Lord Protector forfeit the peace?

Certainly the nature of the proclaimed and widely publicized war aims makes it difficult to accept these criticisms. Indeed there is no evidence that even those who would have pursued the war, did so in the hopes of procuring economic benefits. A close examination of the economic consequences of the war itself and of the Protectorate's actual negotiations with the Dutch makes it even more difficult to condemn Cromwell for having lost the peace.

Although everyone agreed that the English had won the war, that they had established themselves as "Masters and Lords of the Narrow Seas," the English navy had done little to improve the economic condition of the merchant community.[8] The English strategy had been to humble the Dutch people, not to seize their trade. The consequences of the war, in fact, proved to be nothing short of a disaster for the English merchant community. There is precious little evidence to support Charles Wilson's

7 Edward Cliffe, *An Abbreviate of Holland's Deliverance By, and Ingratitude to the Crown of England and House of Nassau* (London, 1665) p. 15; James Heath, *Flagellum: or The Life and Death, Birth and Burial of Oliver Cromwell The Late Usurper* (London, 1663), pp. 151–152; Slingsby Bethel, "The World's Mistake in Oliver Cromwell," in *The Harleian Miscellany* (London, 1810), Vol. 7, pp. 348–349, 353; Henry Stubbe, *A Further Iustification of the Present War Against the United Netherlands* (London, 1673), sig. B1. These sentiments have been echoed by more recent historians. See Charles Wilson, *Profit and Power* (London, 1957), p. 77; G. M. D. Howat, *Stuart and Cromwellian Foreign Policy* (New York, 1974), p. 76; Menna Prestwich, "Diplomacy and Trade in the Protectorate," in *Journal of Modern History* Vol. 22 No. 2 (June 1950), p. 105. "The negotiations that ended in the peace of 1654," argues Prestwich, " illustrate to what lengths Cromwell would go in his neglect of English economic interests for the sake of the Protestant chimera." For a different conclusion see Herbert H. Rowen, *John de Witt, Grand Pensionary of Orange, 1625–1672* (Princeton, 1978), pp. 212–213. For another, later but similar, Anglican Royalist criticism see Sir Philip Warwicke, "Memoirs," HL, HM 41956, f. 105.

8 Thurloe to Whitelocke, 21 January 1654, Sigismund Freihern von Bischoffshausen, *Die Politik des Protectors Oliver Cromwell in der Auffassung und Thätigkeit Seines Ministers des Staatssecretärs John Thurbe* (Innsbruck, 1899), p. 156; Thurloe to Whitelocke, 10 March 1654, Bischoffshausen, *Politik*, p. 172; Thurloe to Whitelocke, 31 March 1654, Bischoffshausen, *Politik*, p. 176; Hyde to Kent, 2/12 December 1653, Bod., Clar. 47, f. 127r; newsletter from The Hague, 16/26 February 1654, Bod., Clar. 47, f. 400v; Paige to Clerke, 22 January 1654, Steckley, *John Paige*, p. 100; Paulucci to Sagredo, 21/31 January 1654, *CSPV*, p. 178.

claim that "English merchants could look back on the Dutch War with some satisfaction."[9]

The great trading companies all suffered economic setbacks. Immediately after the war broke out the English East India Company began to express concern for its assets in India and the safety of the ships then at sea.[10] Predictably enough, news soon arrived that the Dutch East India Company "have received order from the States General to take all the English, and do all the harm they can to them in the East Indies." By contrast, there is no evidence that the English Council of State made the least effort to protect or advance the English cause in the Indian Ocean.[11] Rumors soon proliferated that the Dutch had in fact sent a fleet to the Indies to drive the English out. By the summer of 1653 reports confirmed that the Dutch had successfully wreaked havoc in the Indies while seizing English East Indiamen as they returned to home waters. One Dutch East India Captain reported upon his return from the Indies that the Dutch "shall in a short time have turned the English out of the Indies."[12] That autumn the East India Company gave over all pretence of maintaining a trade with the Indies, declaring that it would send no more ships eastward "until there be an agreement between us and the Dutch."[13] In reviewing the effects of "the late differences in India" Sir Jeremy Sambrooke concluded that "the English have been enforced to forbear buying any India commodities" while "the Hollander hath bought at his own prices." Once the war was ended, he surmised, the English company would again be able to purchase Indian goods at "the ancient prices," allowing it the privilege of "buying cheap in India and selling dear in

9 Wilson, *Profit and Power*, p. 77.

10 Court of Committees, 13 July 1652, *Cal. EIC*, pp. 178–179; Court of Committees, 29 July 1652, *Cal. EIC*, p. 181; court of committees, 27 August 1652, *Cal. EIC*, p. 186.

11 *Terrible and Bloudy Newes From Sea* (London, 1652), Thomason: 6 August 1652, p. 7; *French Occurrences*, 2–9 August 1652, p. 75; Court of Committees, 27 August 1652, *Cal. EIC*, p. 186; Court of Committees, 26 August 1653, *Cal. EIC*, p. 254.

12 *Mercurius Politicus*, 9–16 September 1652, p. 1878; *Weekly Intelligencer*, 14–21 September 1652, p. 599; *Mercurius Politicus*, 16–23 September 1652, p. 1891; *Mercurius Politicus*, 11–18 November 1652, pp. 2012–2013; newsletter from United Provinces, 3/13 September 1652, Longleat House, Whitelocke MSS XII, f. 164r; Letter to Whitelocke, 24 September 1652, Longleat House, Whitelocke MSS XII, f. 165v; George Strelly (of Plymouth) to Robert Blackborne, 26 August 1653, *Cal. EIC*, pp. 254–255; Captain Thomas Sparling to Admiralty Committee, 15 July 1653, *Cal. EIC*, p. 245; newsletter from The Hague, 11/21 August 1653, Bod., Clar. 46, f. 170r; Whitelocke, *Annals*, 11 August 1653, BL, Add. 4992, f. 25v; Letter to Jongstall, 4/14 November 1653, Bod., Rawl. A8, p. 74; newsletter from The Hague, 10/20 November 1653, Bod., Clar. 47, f. 61r.

13 General Court of Adventurers, 11 November 1653, *Cal. EIC*, p. 274. One can trace the growing pessimism in the Company's correspondence with its factories in the East: East India Company to president and Council at Surat, 1 April 1653, IOL, E/3/84, f. 113v; East India Company to president and Council at Fort St. George, 1 April 1653, IOL, E/3/84, f. 115v; East India Company to president and Council at Surat, 12 September 1653, IOL, E/3/84, f. 123r.

England."[14] The Company had clearly learned its lesson, for five years later it abandoned a design to expand its trade into China and Japan "upon fears of war with Holland."[15]

The Levant Company fared little better during the war. The outbreak of hostilities in European waters immediately placed the Company's assets in the Mediterranean in "extreme danger" because of "the Hollander's strength in those seas." Reports soon began pouring in of Dutch seizures and English impotence. With the force of the English navy deployed in the Channel, the Turkey traders were easy prey not only for the Dutch but for Royalist privateers and French pickaroons (small pirating vessels). The consequence was that "all merchants" coming from the Streights "are looked upon in a lost condition."[16] Although the Company did eventually succeed in compelling the Council of State to send a meager convoy to the Streights, it was a case of too little too late. The Dutch had already despatched a large military force to the Mediterranean, which subsequently engaged and annihilated the English squadron under Henry Appleton. When the news reached London it produced "the saddest exchange that ever was seen." The Dutch said, George Downing reported a decade later, "that the defeat with Appleton in the Streights during the war with Cromwell was a great cause of the increase of their Smyrna and other Streights' trade." The Council of State then gave over any pretence of protecting the English merchants, leading one merchant to comment that "it seems very hard that we have no guard there for so great a trade."[17] The prospects for the Levant Company were bleak indeed. By January 1653 it complained that its trade "is now of late totally obstructed by the Hollanders." The Court of Assistants began to embark on a program of complete retrenchment, dismissing its ambassador in Constantinople, relieving chaplains of their duties, and refusing to send out any ships "in respect of the wars and great obstructions at sea." The English "are in

14 Sir Jeremy Sambrooke, "Report on the East India Trade," 1654, IOL, H/40, f. 35r.

15 Thomas Pengelly to Thomas Davis, 24 January 1659, Pengelly Letterbook, Bod., Add. MSS C267, f. 23v.

16 Court minutes of Levant Company, 24 September 1652, PRO, SP 105/151, f. 85r; governor of Levant Company to Council of State, 4 October 1652, PRO, SP 105/144, f. 49v; *A Perfect Account*, 27 October–3 November 1652, p. 765; Whitelocke, *Annals*, November 1652, BL, Add. 37345, f. 239v; *Faithful Scout*, 4–11 November 1653, p. 1083 (French deprivations); Levant Company to Lord Protector, 13 March 1654, PRO, SP 105/144, f. 64r (French deprivations); newsletter, 3 November 1652, Worcester College, Clarke MSS 24, f. 44; Paige to Clerke, 4 January 1653, Steckley, *John Paige*, p. 83. Significantly, the Dutch differentiated between English Royalist and Parliamentarian traders, only seizing the latter. See Henry Appleton to Commissioners of the Navy, 17/27 September 1652, PRO, SP 18/24/Pt. II, f. 89.

17 Court Minutes of Levant Company, 31 January 1653, PRO, SP 105/151, f. 94r; *Mercurius Politicus*, 30 September–7 October 1652, p. 1922; *Mercurius Politicus*, 7–14 October 1652, p. 1930; newsletter from London, 1 April 1653, Bod., Clar. 45, f. 221r; Downing to Henry Bennet, 31 January 1665, PRO, SP 84/174, f. 73r; Bernard Capp, *Cromwell's Navy* (Oxford, 1989), p. 80; Whitelocke, *Annals*, 8 September 1653, BL Add. 4992, f. 35v; *Perfect Diurnall*, 28 November–5 December 1653, p. 3164.

hazard of a total loss of that trade, which hath so much conduced to the honor and benefit of this nation," agreed the Levant Company, "unless some speedy and effectual means be used for the prevention thereof."[18] It is eloquent testimony to the ideological rather than purely economic concerns of the English Commonwealth that such "effectual means" were never sent.

Less-glamorous trades were also devastated by the Dutch War. The Eastland trade soon came to a grinding halt. Already in the autumn of 1652, Dutch merchants could claim that the Eastland trade was "most entirely in our hands." When the King of Denmark opted to side with the Dutch and seize all English merchant ships in his ports, the situation of the English went from bad to worse. Nor could the English hope to circumvent the problem by trading with Hanseatic middlemen. "Our Hamburg trade is blocked up since these wars with Holland," mourned the Canary merchant John Paige who had been seeking to diversify his portfolio. "The common security for the trade of merchants at sea [was] disturbed," complained one group of Eastland merchants, with the result that trade to the Baltic was "in a great measure broken off." Hinton's thorough study of the Eastland trade provides statistical substantiation of the merchants' laments.[19] The merchants trading to Newfoundland, Greenland, and Iceland also suffered depredations because of the war. By one account the combined effect of Royalist pirates and Dutch attacks meant that those merchants "have not gotten the tenth of what was formerly gained there by whales and other commodities."[20] The Dutch navy had sufficiently disrupted English trade

18 Court minutes of Levant Company, 18 November 1652, PRO, SP 105/151, f. 86v; Court minutes of Levant Company, 7 December 1652, PRO, SP 105/151, f. 87v; Court minutes of Levant Company, 7 January 1653, PRO, SP 105/151, f. 91v; Levant Company to Council of State, 13 January 1653, PRO, SP 105/144, f. 50r; Court minutes of Levant Company, 21 January 1653, PRO, SP 105/151, f. 93; Court minutes of Levant Company, 29 July 1653, PRO, SP 105/151, f. 98r; Levant Company to Thomas Bendish, 31 August 1653, PRO, SP 105/144, f. 54v; Charles Longland to Admiralty committee, 5 September 1653, *CSPD*, p. 130; Court minutes of Levant Company, 13 December 1653, PRO, SP 105/151, f. 102v; Levant Company to Lord Protector, 29 December 1653, PRO, SP 105/144, f. 61v; Charles Longland to Admiralty commissioners, 6 February 1654, *CSPD*, p. 390.

19 *Mercurius Politicus*, 9–16 September 1652, p. 1878; petition of Thomas Corbitt, Robert Whitelocke, Francis Asty, for Merchant Adventurers and Eastland Company, 16 July 1653, *CSPD*, p. 31; Whitelocke, *Annals*, 18 October 1652, BL Add. 37345, f. 237v; petition of Slingsby Bethel, Alexander Baron, Daniel Farrington, William Johnson, for Merchant Adventurers, 24 March 1653, PRO, SP 18/34, f. 147r; Paige to Clerke, 1 February 1653, Steckley, *John Paige*, p. 85; Richard Bradshaw to John Thurloe, 10 September 1653, PRO, SP 82/9, f. 110v; *Several Proceedings*, 8–15 September 1653, p. 3266; R. W. K. Hinton, *The Eastland Trade and the Common Weal* (Cambridge, 1959), p. 229. "The Dutch war," Maurice Ashley points out, "had a disastrous effect on the fortunes of the [Eastland] Company." Maurice Ashley, *Financial and Commercial Policy under the Cromwellian Protectorate* (London, 1962), p. 126.

20 *French Occurrences*, 24–31 August 1652, p. 101; *A Perfect Account*, 8–15 September 1652, p. 711; *Dutch Intelligencer*, 15–22 September 1652, p. 18; Whitelocke, *Annals*, 24 September 1652, BL Add. 37345, f. 223v; Whitelocke, *Annals*, 20 October 1653, BL Add. 4992, f. 44r; newsletter from Westminster, 26 November 1653, Worcester College, Clarke MSS 25, f. 161v; Whitelocke, *Annals*, 28 November 1653, BL Add. 4992, f. 59r.

with the Iberian peninsula that that the Spanish merchants were "at a stand."[21] Even the shipbuilders of Trinity House were compelled to admit that "by reason of the present decay of trade, their incomes are exceedingly decayed, as the wars have increased, so that the revenues are so small they will not discharge their necessary occasions."[22]

The maritime infrastructure of the domestic economy was also dealt a severe blow by the war. The Dutch navy was perfectly poised to sever the trade in salt, fish, and coal on the east coast of Great Britain. In the first summer of the war Van Tromp had succeeded in "cutting off all trading of coals and salt." Hundreds of small ships were seized, and their men impressed, by the Dutch navy. Even the colliers that arrived safely told "stories of the dangers they were in, and how they escaped from small men-of-war." "We are fearful," wrote one Yarmouth merchant, that "we shall lose our whole fishing trade for this year." As far north as Leith "our coasts are full of Dutch private men-of-war, so that a merchant man does not stir." Meanwhile on the coast of Sussex the Dutch fleet "do possess themselves of all the vessels that pass that way, which doth amaze the inhabitants in those parts."[23]

The economic dislocations were manifest nationwide. Fear of the Dutch caused many "timorous gentlemen" to "remove themselves and their families higher into the country." The once active trading towns were quickly becoming quiet backwaters. "This populous place being at present in a very sinking condition," moaned the bailiffs of Yarmouth, "will be inevitably ruined, our misery being so apparent that not three boats are now preparing to go forth upon fishing employment, where above one hundred and fifty sail in former years have been making ready at this season for those voyages."[24] But it was the metropolis which suffered most grievously.

21 *A Perfect Account*, 13–20 October 1652, p. [750]; newsletter from Westminster, 25 June 1653, Worcester College, Clarke MSS 25, f. 76v; petition of Rowland Wilson and eighteen other merchants trading to Spain and Portugal, 9 August 1653, *CSPD*, p. 81; *Mercurius Politicus*, 18–25 August 1653, p. 2681.

22 Committee of Trinity House to Council of State, 20 August 1653, *CSPD*, p. 97.

23 Newsletter from London, 27 July 1652, Worcester College, Clarke MSS 22, f. 118v; *A Perfect Account*, 15–22 September 1652, p. 714; *The Declaration of the Cardinal Mazarini* (London, 1652), Thomason: 24 August 1652, p. 8 (letter from Yarmouth); *Mercurius Politicus*, 26 August–2 September 1652, p. 1839 (from Leith); *Weekly Intelligencer*, 30 November–7 December 1652, p. 719 (Sussex). Accounts of seized ships fill the pages of all the Commonwealth's newspapers throughout the Dutch War. I provide only a sample here: *Mercurius Britannicus*, 26 July–2 August 1652, pp. 25, 29; *French Occurrences*, 26 July–2 August 1652, p. 79; *Weekly Intelligencer*, 17–24 August 1652, p. 571; *Weekly Intelligencer*, 14–21 September 1652, p. 602; bailiffs of Ipswich to Richard Bradshaw, 12 July 1652, PRO, SP 18/24/ Pt. I, f. 108r; newsletter from Yarmouth, 22 July 1652, PRO, SP 84/159, f. 125; newsletter from Berwick, 20 October 1652, Worcester College, Clarke MSS 24, f. 39; Edgeman to Richard Browne, 16/26 April 1653, Christ Church, Browne MSS, Box D–L.

24 *Weekly Intelligencer*, 14–21 September 1652, p. 603; John Arnold and Robert Horner (bailiffs of Yarmouth) to General Monk, 6 January 1653, PRO, SP 18/32, f. 42r.

Coal was after all the fuel which kept London warm during the winter. Consequently each time the Dutch intercepted a fleet of colliers it had an immediate effect on the London economy. "Coals that were sold on Monday last for 40 shillings are now at £4," reported one Londoner after the Dutch had seized one particularly large fleet. "If the Dutch have taken our colliers as it's reported," the same man noted the following week, "we must pray for fair weather, for coals are already at £5 the cauldron." The Venetian resident thought that the price of coal in London had trebled since the outbreak of the war. Although the Rump, the Lord Mayor of London, and the Court of Aldermen devised many ingenious methods of coal rationing and price regulation, they were unable to prevent widespread misery. "Several brewers have left off brewing for want of firing, and most of our cooks have not wherewith to dress their meat," reported one newsletter-writer, adding that "the cries of the poor are very lamentable for want of fuel." "Our dearth of coals exasperates," wrote another, "and I assure you, if the Dutch keep them from us, we shall shortly cut one another's throats." So bad had the crisis become, that by late April wealthy Londoners were traveling as far as Ipswich to get fuel.[25] Admittedly when a great fleet of colliers evaded the Dutch and arrived safely in London in late April the severest crisis was over, but coal supplies were periodically threatened thereafter.[26]

The maritime chaos which inevitably accompanied a war between the two great naval powers also placed the West Country trade at risk. Dutchmen-of-war, supported by French pirates and Royalist privateers, were so numerous on the western coasts that "not a small vessel escapes them." The Irish Sea, reported the *Weekly Intelligencer*, "is so infested with pirates, that it hinders all traffic." Not only did these scoundrels feast upon the rich trading vessels returning to English waters, but they were so bold to "come even to the shore, and seize upon our fishermen." Although the materials do not exist to conduct a statistical survey of the hardship engendered on England's western coast as a result of the war, the incessant and numerous petitions and letters of complaint give an impression of the scale of the misery. In Barnstaple, which was probably not atypical, the "incursions of

25 Newsletter from London, 25 March 1653, Bod., Clar. 45, f. 205v; newsletter from London, 1 April 1653, Bod., Clar. 45, f. 222r; Paulucci to Sagredo, 2/12 April 1653, *CSPV*, p. 55; newsletter from Westminster, 19 January 1653, Worcester College, Clarke MSS, f. 105; *A Perfect Account*, 15–22 December 1652, p. 822; *French Occurrences*, 27 September–4 October 1652, p. 649; *CJ*, 10 December 1652, p. 227; newsletter from London, 8 April 1653, Bod., Clar. 45, f. 269v; newsletter from London, 15 April 1653, Bod., Clar. 45, f. 292r; George Radcliffe to Sir Richard Browne, 19 April 1653, Christ Church, Browne MSS, Box R–W; Nathaniel Bacon to Sir Henry Vane Jr., 13 April 1653, *CSPD*, p. 277 (Ipswich).

26 Paulucci to Sagredo, 22 April/2 May 1653, *CSPV*, p. 63; Whitelocke, *Annals*, 27 July 1653, BL Add. 37345, f. 289r; Whitelocke, *Annals*, 20 March 1654, BL, Add. 4992, f. 76v.

the Brest and Dutch pirates" reduced "many poor families ... to beg their bread."[27]

The English, of course, were able to capture many Dutch prize ships to offset partially their own losses. However, these benefits were hardly sufficient to sustain the claim that the English benefitted economically by the war. The great merchant traders, the men and women who could provide long-term benefits to the livelihood of the nation, were unlikely to be the same people who sent out private men-of-war to prey on Dutch shipping. In fact, the evidence suggests that the instant riches of prize ships lured men away from mercantile enterprises. One London trader complained that "finding much plunder and the like stories," ship masters and seamen "care not for merchant voyages."[28] After the naval reforms of Winter 1652–1653, the English government made every effort to limit the number of private men-of-war capable of capturing prize ships on the grounds that they diverted men from enlisting in the navy. Nor did English naval strategy, geared to defeating the Dutch in set-piece battles and blockading the Dutch coast, facilitate the capture of valuable merchant ships. The prizes that did come in did little to invigorate the English domestic economy. Much of the money was initially earmarked to pay seamen's salaries. The notorious corruption and ineptitude of the prize office, unfortunately, meant that the pickings were small indeed – so small that on at least one occasion the seamen rioted to procure their fair share of the prize goods. So hard were prize ships to come by that toward the end of the war Nehemiah Bourne, who as a prominent naval officer should have been well placed to reap the benefits of naval booty, was compelled to grovel in order to procure one prize ship to replace three merchant ships he had lost in the state's service.[29]

For the vast majority of the English population the economic effects of the Dutch War were hardly such as to convince them that they had won a trade war. The Essex clergyman Ralph Josselin, after the first few months of the war, expressed "great fear as if we should no way employ our poor by reason of decay of trade through our breach with Holland." The following

27 Whitelocke, *Annals*, 6 August 1652, BL Add. 37345, f. 216v; *Weekly Intelligencer*, 21–28 September 1652, p. 610; *Weekly Intelligencer*, 5–12 October 1652, p. 627; petition of Thomas Horwood and merchants and inhabitants of Barnstaple, 3 September 1653, *CSPD*, p. 126. The petitions and complaining letters were often reprinted in newsbooks. Bulstrode Whitelocke assiduously recorded them in the relevant volumes of his *Annals*.

28 This assertion is supported in substance, by the complaints registered by the East India Company and the Levant Company of the deadness of trade. Paige to Paynter and Clerke, 12 March 1653, Steckley, *John Paige*, p. 89.

29 Day's proceedings, 16 March 1653, *CSPD*, p. 217 (order limiting private men of war); Sagredo to Doge and Senate, 16/26 August 1653, *CSPV*, p. 117 (comment on few prizes taken in battle); Nehemiah Bourne to Navy Commissioners, 24 February 1653, PRO, SP 18/33, f. 208r; *A Perfect Account*, 26 October–2 November 1653, pp. 1169–1170; Bordeaux to de Brienne, 30 October/9 November 1653, PRO, PRO 31/3/92, ff. 6v–7r; Charles Longland to Admiralty committee, 15 July 1653, *CSPD*, p. 30; Petition of Nehemiah Bourne to the Lord Protector, 31 January 1654, *CSPD*, pp. 375–376.

spring he abstained from the purchase of books "in regard of the trouble of the times." "Such times were never known in England," the York merchant Edward Parker confided to Ralph Parker, "trade being so much decayed that there is scarce one in twenty knows how to live." "Trade now visibly hangs its head," reported one London-based newsmonger in the summer of 1653.[30] As a consequence, inflation and scarcity were rampant. Naturally the merchants were hardest hit. "Trading is dead here," wrote one merchant to his Parisian partner, "it is impossible to furnish you with any commodities as are vendable in your shops." The morale of the merchant community was miserable. The merchants, reported one observer, "hang the head and talk of nothing but the losses and how they shall recover their trade again, which is absolutely decayed both in city and country." The result was that merchants "break daily and also many other tradesmen throughout the kingdom." One linen draper reported that "in his street there is no less than six of his profession and two merchants broke already."[31] Contemporaries were certainly less convinced of the economic benefits of the war than more recent commentators.

Not surprisingly the merchants greeted the first signs of peace with gushing enthusiasm. They immediately welcomed the resignation of the Nominated Parliament, Thurloe wrote to Whitelocke, because that Parliament wanted "to make war with all the world which would have broken all the merchants." The conclusion of a peace, thought the London merchant Israel Bernhard, "will be welcome to all merchants." "You cannot imagine what great satisfaction [the very discourse of peace] gives generally to the country," the religious moderate Anthony Nicholls wrote to his more enthusiastic friend Colonel Robert Bennet, "an absolute settlement with that nation will be of great advantage to this commonwealth; for a unity with that people would make those two commonwealths entire masters of the whole ocean; and you might so dispose of the trade of the whole world

30 Josselin, *Diary*, 19 September 1652, p. 285; Josselin, *Diary*, 4 May 1653, p. 303; Edward Parker to Ralph Parker, 27 June 1653, *CSPD 5*, p. 443; newsletter from London, 3 June 1653, Bod., Clar. 45, f. 484; Letter to Mr. Rider, 14 December 1653, Bod., Rawl. A9, p. 67.

31 Paige to William Clerke, 4 January 1653, Steckley, *John Paige*, p. 83; Letter from London to D'Esmond in Paris, 4 June 1653, Bod., Rawl. A3, p. 84; Bordeaux to Servien, 16/26 December 1652, PRO, PRO 31/3/90, f. 534r; Bordeaux to de Brienne, 16/26 December 1652, PRO, PRO 31/3/90, f. 530v; Paulucci to Sagredo, 31 December/10 January 1652/1653, *CSPV*, pp. 5–6; Paulucci to Sagredo, 22 January/1 February 1653, *CSPV*, p. 16; Paulucci to Sagredo, 17/27 April 1653, *CSPV*, p. 60; Paulucci to Sagredo, 7/17 August 1653, *CSPV*, pp. 111–112; Paulucci to Sagredo, 8/18 January 1654, *CSPV*, p. 172; newsletter from Rotterdam, 15/25 December 1652, Bod., Tanner MSS 53, f. 172r; newsletter from London, 16/26 July 1652, Bod., Clar. 43, f. 215; newsletter, 4 December 1652, Worcester College, Clarke MSS 24, f. 66v; newsletter from Westminster, 29 March 1653, Worcester College, Clarke MSS 25, f. 2; newsletter from London, 25 March 1653, Bod., Clar. 45, ff. 205v–206r; newsletter from London, 8 April 1653, Bod., Clar. 45, f. 269v; newsletter from London, 26 August 1653, Bod., Clar. 46, f. 208r.

as you please, and where you please: there [are] advantages enough for all." As soon as news began to seep out that the treaty had been concluded it "became a source of great satisfaction to the entire population and especially to the merchants." "The merchants on both sides have great cause to rejoice," explained the *Loyal Messenger*, "for the pirates begin already to seek out for shelter, and to strike off from the Narrow Seas a fair riddance. And the navigable affairs seem somewhat clear, the cloud of pickaroons being gallantly expelled."[32]

The ink on the treaty was hardly dry when the merchants began to stumble over each other in a mad rush to make up for lost time. The Levant Company immediately appointed a new minister to send out to the East to go along with the new ambassador they were finally able to finance. In the same letter that the East India Company informed two of their factors in India that a peace had been concluded they noted that the Company was once again "fitting out some ships for India." Thurloe thought the revival of trade was the surest sign that the war had ended. "The peace with England being concluded," reported the *Perfect Account*, "our merchants are lading of goods on shipboard as fast as lighters can be gotten to carry them where the ships ride at anchor."[33]

The merchant community's universal enthusiasm for the peace certainly casts doubt upon claims that Cromwell had forfeited the nation's economic future in order to gratify his self-seeking ambition. The Treaty of Westminster did not confirm England's economic gains from the war because there were no economic gains to be confirmed. "My Lord Protector hath made a peace with the Dutch and an honorable one," the Spanish merchant William Meredith informed his son, reiterating what for the merchant community was the central result – "the seas will be open."[34] The merchants, it must be emphasized, were not ecstatic because Cromwell had signed a peace which would cripple the Dutch economy, but because he had ended a war which had proved to be an unmitigated economic disaster. Nevertheless the economic futility of the war should not surprise us. After all, the war had been fought because the Dutch had appeared to the Rump

32 Thurloe to Whitelocke, 23 December 1653, Bischoffshausen, *Politik*, p. 148; Letter from Israel Bernhard, 5/15 November 1653, Bod., Rawl. A8, p. 83; Anthony Nicholls to Colonel Robert Bennet, 9 November 1653, Folger, Xd483 (112); Paulucci to Sagredo, 8/18 April 1654, *CSPV*, p. 202; *Loyal Messenger*, 3–10 April 1654, p. 32. See also *A Perfect Account*, 18–25 January 1654, p. 1272; East India Company to president and Council of Surat, 20 February 1654, IOL, E/3/84, f. 130.

33 Court minutes of Levant Company, 8 May 1654, PRO, SP 105/151, f. 107; William Cockayne, Thomas Andrew, and Nathan Wyche (London) to William Watson and Richard Bridgeman, 7 April 1654, IOL, E/3/84, f. 134v; Thurloe to Whitelocke, 5 May 1654, Bischoffshausen, *Politik*, p. 182; *A Perfect Account*, 5–12 April 1654, p. 1360.

34 William Meredith Sr. to William Meredith Jr., 19 December 1654, Society of Antiquaries, 203, f. 84r.

as fallen Protestants and bad republicans. It is against these ideological aims of the war that the peace must be measured.

Although the establishment of the Protectorate did make peace with the Dutch a possibility, it did not make it inevitable. Cromwell and his negotiating team were not so desperate for peace that they were willing to end the war at any cost. Within days of the resignation of the Nominated Parliament the Dutch deputies returned to the negotiating table. So tough were the Protector's demands that after a fortnight of haggling the Dutch again demanded their passports. This time the Dutch deputies and their train got as far as Gravesend before a saving expedient was found. Far from conceding every Dutch demand Cromwell had merely clarified his position: the Dutch were to guarantee that the King of Denmark would restore the English merchant goods which he had seized or the war would continue. The Dutch deputies agreed, and the draft treaty "was there agreed on, concluded and signed, God Almighty be praised."[35] The Dutch departed from Gravesend for The Hague as planned on 4 January, carrying with them a treaty to be ratified rather than the certainty of another season of human misery.

The Treaty of Westminster legally encodified the war aims of the Cromwellian moderates. "You cannot I presume think that [the Dutch] have cause to brave it," James Waynright wrote to his trading partner Richard Bradshaw after the articles of the treaty were published, "but plead necessity that they made those articles." John Thurloe later recalled that the Dutch were not able in this treaty to obtain all "the advantages in trade which they had insisted upon in all their former treaties."[36] The English, it must be admitted, did retreat from some of the more extreme demands advanced by the Nominated Parliament. The Dutch were no longer required to limit their navy to forty men-of-war, nor was it insisted that they pay for the right to fish in the British seas. But these concessions were only made

35 Dutch deputies to Lord Protector, 28 December 1653, PRO, SP 105/98, f. 55 (demand for passport); Whitelocke, *Annals*, BL, Add. 4992, f. 65r; newsletter from The Hague, 15/25 December 1653, Bod., Clar. 47, f. 166r; *Several Proceedings*, 19–26 January 1654, pp. 3580–3581; Thomas Lade to ?, 13/23 January 1654, Bod., Rawl. A10, p. 228; Thurloe to Whitelocke, 6 January 1654, Bischoffshausen, *Politik*, p. 151; Thurloe to Whitelocke, 27 January 1654, Bischoffshausen, *Politik*, p. 158; Paulucci to Sagredo, 14/24 January 1654, *CSPV*, p. 174; newsletter from The Hague, 13/23 January 1654, Bod., Rawl. A10, pp. 219–220; newsletter from The Hague, 13/23 January 1654, Bod., Clar. 47, f. 302; Hyde to Nicholas, 13/23 January 1654, Bod., Clar. 47, f. 296v; *Moderate Publisher*, 6–13 January 1654, p. 97; *True and Perfect Dutch Diurnall*, 3–10 January 1654, p. 24. There is much contemporary dispute about who was sent to Gravesend and what was said. The majority of commentators indicates that Viscount Lisle was the emissary, a claim made all the more probable by the close friendship between Beverning and Nieupoort and the Sidney family. Thurloe's claim that Cromwell merely clarified his position on Denmark seems most reliable given that he was a participant in the negotiations.

36 "Thurloe's Review," PRO, SP 103/46, f. 237; James Waynright to Richard Bradshaw, 5 May 1654, in Susan Maria Ffarrington (editor), *The Farington Papers* (Manchester, 1856), p. 175.

because the Dutch had admitted the central issue of principle: they agreed that their ships would strike the flag and lower the topsail "in such a manner as ever under any former government in times past." In 1654 the Dutch were willing to acknowledge that the Protectorate was the legitimate sovereign power in England, retaining all of the international rights previously claimed by the monarchy.[37]

The English, by contrast, were able to realize most of their goals. The Dutch agreed that each commonwealth should refrain from aiding or even providing shelter for the other's enemies. In Article 27 the Dutch guaranteed that "justice be done upon those who were authors of the murder committed upon the English in Amboyna." Both sides hoped to advance "the glory of God, the propagation of the Gospel of Jesus Christ, and the protection of the professors of the same." Consequently "the reformed Helvetian Cantons, the Protestant cities and Princes of Germany, and all other states, and Protestants professing the reformed religion" were to be "invited and comprehended in this confederacy as also the crowns of Sweden and Denmark." Cromwell had succeeded in firmly reattaching the Dutch to the Protestant cause. Finally, all economic disputes were to be referred to a board of arbitrators who would act after the treaty had been ratified – a decision which hardly would have been acceptable to either side had the war really been about seizing each other's trade routes.[38] When it came to specific criticisms, even the radical critic of the Protectorate Edmund Ludlow could only quibble that "there was no provision made by this treaty for the coalescence so much insisted upon during the administration of affairs by the Parliament." The Treaty of Westminster conceded "most of the English claims made to Pauw in 1652," concludes

37 "Thurloe's Review," PRO, SP 103/46, f. 236v; Thurloe to Whitelocke, 6 January 1654, Bischoffshausen, *Politik*, p. 152; Dutch account of differences, 23 December 1653, PRO, SP 105/98, f. 43; answer of Council of State, 26 December 1653, PRO, SP 105/98, f. 45; Dutch deputies' paper, 28 December 1653, PRO, SP 105/98, ff. 53–54; Council of State to Dutch deputies, 28 December 1653, PRO, SP 105/98, f. 55v; Dutch deputies to Council of State, 29 December 1653, PRO, SP 105/98, f. 56v; Dutch deputies' comments on proposed treaty, 12/22 January 1654, Bod., Rawl. A10, p. 187; newsletter from The Hague, 13/23 January 1654, Bod., Clar. 47, f. 302v; Whitelocke, *Annals*, 23 May 1654, BL Add. 4992, f. 87v. The English insisted, Paulucci revealingly noted, "that the Dutch should strike to the English colors as in the time of Queen Elizabeth." Paulucci to Sagredo, 8/18 January 1654, *CSPV*, pp. 171–172. This and the following paragraphs make reference to *Articles of Peace, Union and Confederation Concluded and Agreed Between his Highness Oliver Lord Protector ... and the Lords the States General of the United Provinces of the Netherlands* (London, 1654).

38 "Thurloe's Review," PRO, SP 103/46, ff. 236–237; Dutch account of differences, 23 December 1653, PRO, SP 105/98, f. 42v; answer of Council of State, 26 December 1653, PRO, SP 105/98, f. 46; Dutch deputies' paper, 28 December 1653, PRO, SP 105/98, f. 54r; Council of State to Dutch deputies, 28 December 1653, PRO, SP 105/98, f. 55v; Thurloe to Whitelocke, 12 May 1654, Bischoffshausen, *Politik*, p. 184; *Articles of Peace, Union and Confedertion Concluded and Agreed Betweem his Highness Oliver Lord Protector ... and the Lords the States General of the United Provinces of the Netherlands* (London, 1654), Articles 27, 30.

Rowen in his encyclopedic study of the career of John De Witt, and gave "the Dutch almost nothing more than mere peace."[39]

The issue which provoked the hottest discussions, which required the greatest diplomacy to overcome – for the English the central issue – was that of the political exclusion of the Prince of Orange. "It's most certainly said," Edward Nicholas explained to his friend Edward Hyde, "that Cromwell will not agree to any peace with these countries unless this state shall by some act (public or private) consent to exclude that prince and his family." The Dutch deputies, even the Holland deputies, knew quite well that such an exclusion would provoke widespread public rage in the United Provinces. To return to the United Provinces with a treaty which publicly prevented the young prince from assuming his traditional role in the Dutch polity was not only unconstitutional, it was unthinkable. So, after much haggling a compromise was worked out. The English demand was "put in a secret article," acceded to only by the two representatives of the Province of Holland. Although this Act of Seclusion did eventually become known, and provoke the anticipated popular unrest in the United Provinces, De Witt was able to present it as a *fait accompli*.[40] The Protectorate had secured the minimum political aims of the war.

The argument can certainly be made, as Bethel and Edward Cliffe have done, that the exclusion of the House of Orange and the articles against aiding and abetting rebels demonstrate Cromwell's fanatical concern for his own political safety at the expense of the welfare of the nation. Nevertheless this would be to misunderstand the political context of the treaty. Cromwell hated the House of Orange not only because it was so closely allied with the House of Stuart, but because it wished to establish an absolute monarchy in the United Provinces. In the conferences with the Dutch deputies Cromwell inveighed against the House of Orange because "the late Prince was a great tyrant over the provinces." It was precisely because such arbitrary power was incompatible with the Word of God, natural law, and gothic liberty

39 C. H. Firth (editor), *The Memoirs of Edmund Ludlow* (Oxford, 1894), p. 378; Rowen, *John De Witt*, pp. 212–213.

40 Nicholas to Hyde, 26 January/5 February 1654, Bod., Clar. 47, f. 335; J. North to Dudley North, 6 July 1654, Bod. North MSS C4, f. 74r; Dutch account of differences, 23 December 1653, PRO, SP 105/95, f. 43; answer of Council of State, 26 December 1653, PRO, SP 105/98, f. 45r; Dutch deputies' paper, 28 December 1653, PRO, SP 105/98, f. 53v; Council of State to Dutch deputies, 28 December 1653, PRO, SP 105/98, f. 55v; Aitzema, "Selections," Bod., Rawl. C734, f. 80; "Thurloe's Review," PRO, SP 103/46, f. 237r; Sagredo to Doge and Senate, 10/20 January 1654, *CSPV*, p. 173; East India Company to president and Council at Fort St. George, 20 February 1654, IOL, E/3/84, f. 132; Paulucci to Sagredo, 19/29 May 1654, *CSPV*, p. 217; Thurloe to Whitelocke, 12 May 1654, Bischoffshausen, *Politik*, pp. 183–184; Thurloe to Whitelocke, 18 May 1654, Bischoffshausen, *Politik*, pp. 185–186. Many of the provinces, when ratifying the proposed treaty in the winter of 1654, specifically required that the Prince of Orange not be excluded in the treaty. That De Witt and the republicans were able to push through this secret clause is a testimony to the Grand Pensionary's political acumen.

that the English had fought a war against their king. "The true foundation and ground of this great war on the Parliament's part," John Thurloe wrote to Bulstrode Whitelocke who needed no persuading, was that "sober Christians were afraid of imposing upon their consciences, and everybody of having arbitrary power set up over their estates to the distraction of all their liberties." "We never fought, nor was it ever declared by the Parliament or army, that we took up arms for or against any particular form of government whatsoever," argued one Cromwellian polemicist, "but we took up arms against the king because he demeaned himself as a tyrant, and had projected a wicked design of introducing his own will and power above law."[41]

It was not mere convenience which led the Protectorate to pursue the Protestant and republican foreign policy of its predecessor regimes. Although it is undeniable that some saw in the Protectorate the trappings of monarchy – that the regime implicitly rejected the more apocalyptic republicanism of the Rump and the Nominated Parliament – the Protectorate was a mixed government, in conscious opposition to the absolute form of monarchy of the Stuarts. This was a distinction Protectorate apologists were at pains to make. "It is not a single person, but a sole power which makes a monarchy so called," argued the author of *The Grand Catastrophe*. The Protector would not be hereditary, he would be below the law, and his power rested upon "the general consent of the people." "This person is not to exercise his power by a claim of inheritance, or by virtue of any personal right over and above the people," argued Marchamont Nedham in his classic *A True State of the Case of the Commonwealth*, "the power he is invested with, is not to make him great and glorious, otherwise than in order to the peace and advantage of those that are governed by him; whereas the kings of this nation pretended always, and maintained and interest of their own, as they were kings, distinct and superior to that of the people." The moment Charles II assumed the throne, by contrast, "he becomes at the very instant as absolute as the Grand Seignor, and will then be fully enabled to accomplish what his family had long projected, viz. the enthroning himself upon an interest of mere will and power, against the common interest of the people."[42] The proper Biblical analogy – and for

41 Newsletter from The Hague, 13/23 January 1654, Bod., Clar. 47, ff. 302v–303r; Thurloe to Whitelocke, 23 December 1653, Bischoffshausen, *Politik*, p. 148; Marchamont Nedham, *A True State of the Case of the Commonwealth* (London, 1654), Thomason: 8 February 1654, p. 5. John Lisle had also thought the war was fought in defense of "the rights and liberties of the nation." Ludlow, "A Voyce," Bod., English History MSS C487, p. 1083.

42 *The Grand Catastrophe, Or the Change of Government* (London, 1654), Thomason: 18 January 1654, p. 13; *Weekly Intelligencer*, 20–27 December 1653, p. 98; J. P., *Tyrants and Protectors Set Forth in their Colours* (London, 1654), Thomason: 9 June 1654, pp. 2, 6–7, 34–35; Bulstrode Whitelocke to John Thurloe, 20 January 1654, Bod., Rawl. A10, p. 312; Nedham, *A True State of the Case of the Commonwealth*, pp. 28–29, 48–50. It

Protectorate theorists the Bible served only as analogy not as model – was not the rule of the Hebrew kings but the rule of the Israelite judges.[43] "Through the blessing of God," prayed John Thurloe, "the breaches will be repaired, and the people be governed by the good old laws, and all arbitrariness in government laid aside." The Protectorate, hoped the *Moderate Publisher* in a revealing comparison, would "come near to the government that was in Queen Elizabeth's days."[44]

The Protectorate, then, had procured the peace which the moderates had hoped for all along. That the peace did not provide England with the wealth of the Indies was only because that was not the aim of the war. Nor was it in the Indies, in the Levant, or in the Baltic that the English had been militarily successful. Cromwell made sure that in the future the Dutch Republic would recognize the English government as a legitimate sovereign power, while doing all he could to ensure that the United Provinces remained a republic. To accuse Cromwell of wishing to keep Orange and Stuart from power in the Netherlands and in England is merely to accuse him of defending the Good Old Cause.

Nevertheless the Protector's peace did not provide for an offensive alliance, or much physical security for the future of peaceful relations between the two regimes. The Anglo-Dutch amalgamation which St. John and Strickland had proposed in 1651 was not even hinted at in the Treaty of Westminster. Why had the Protector abandoned these proposals?

The answer to these questions lies in the Protectorate government's understanding of European politics. Just as Cromwell conceived of his regime in terms of the Elizabethan domestic polity, so he and his supporters

should be noted that this reading of the theoretical basis of the Protectorate was being widely disseminated and eagerly read in early 1654: Sir Thomas Gower to Sir Richard Leveson, 18 February 1654, SRO, D868/8/7. For the ways in which the Protectorate looked like a monarchy see Roy Sherwood, *The Court of Oliver Cromwell* (London: Croom Helm, 1977). In two elegant articles Derek Hirst has done much to elucidate the Protectorate's self-perception, showing that it was not a monarchy: " 'That Sober Liberty': Marvell's Cromwell in 1654," in John M. Wallace (editor) *The Golden and The Brazen World* (Berkeley, 1985), pp. 17–55; and "The Lord Protector, 1653–1658," in John Morrill (editor), *Oliver Cromwell and the English Revolution* (London, 1990), especially pp. 121–122.

43 *The Grand Catastrophe*, p. 11; *Strena Vavasoriensis: A New-Years Gift for the Welch Itinerants* (London, 1654), Thomason: 30 January 1654, pp. 16–17. For the claim that God did not prescribe a single form of government see John Jones to Colonel Philip Jones, 13 January 1654, in Joseph Mayer (editor), "Inedited Letters of Cromwell, Colonel Jones, Bradshaw, and Other Regicides," in *Transactions of the Historic Society of Lancashire and Cheshire*, new series Vol. 1 (1861), pp. 219–220; *Perfect Diurnall*, 6–13 February 1654, p. [3329].

44 Thurloe to Whitelocke, 21 January 1654, Bischoffshausen, *Politik*, p. 155; *Moderate Publisher*, [30 December–6 January 1654], p. 94. Peter Gaunt has highlighted both the theoretical limitations on the Protector's powers, and the actual role which his Council played in achieving that aim in his " 'The Single Person's Confidants and Dependants'? Oliver Cromwell and his Protectoral Councillors," in *Historical Journal* Vol. 32 No. 3 (1989), pp. 537–560.

understood the international situation in Elizabethan terms.[45] The Cromwellian moderates still believed that the greatest threat to England and Protestantism lay in the unholy alliance between the Pope and the King of Spain. In late November 1653, just as the debate over Anglo-Dutch relations was reaching its most critical phase, the London printer Philamon Stephens brought out the first English translation of Tommaso Campanella's classic *Spanish Monarchy*. The translator had felt compelled, he said, to publish an English edition of Campanella's work because he "found a kind of an accomplishment of some counsels of his, that were given long ago, as namely touching a war with the Dutch." Campanella had written his treatise as a form of advice from afar to Philip III. The aim, the destiny, of the Spanish king, Campanella claimed, was to establish a universal monarchy to extirpate Protestantism within Europe and to drive back the Turk from her borders.[46] However powerful Spain had become on land, Campanella argued, the two great Protestant maritime powers, England and the United Provinces, would always be poised to prevent any attempts to establish a universal monarchy. "It is most certain," he averred, "that if the King of Spain could but once make himself master of England and the Low Countries, he would quickly get to be sole monarch of all Europe, and of the greatest part of the New World." Campanella offered a two-fold plan to humble these potential enemies. "As concerning the weakening of the English," he suggested, "there can no better way possibly be found out, then by causing divisions and dissensions among themselves." To prevent England and the United Provinces from conducting a united campaign against him, the King of Spain need only "craftily underhand sow new seeds of dissension amongst them."[47]

Every effort was made to disseminate and popularize this new understanding of the Anglo-Dutch conflict in the waning months of 1653. The *Perfect Diurnall*, *Several Proceedings of State Affairs*, and *A Perfect Account* all ran advertisements for the new English translation of Campanella's treatise. The *Mercurius Politicus* elucidated Campanella's arguments

45 Cromwellian neo-Elizabethanism was, of course, an ideological construct. So the Protectorate's foreign policy should not be seen as duplicating that pursued in the later sixteenth century. For the differences see my essay "Britain and the World in the 1650s," in John Morrill (editor), *Regicide to Restoration: The Consequences of the English Revolution* (London, 1992).

46 Tho[mas] Campanella, *A Discourse Touching the Spanish Monarchy* (London, 1653), Thomason: 29 November 1653, sig. A2v. The best analysis of Campanella, and one from which I have profited greatly, is that of Anthony Pagden, *Spanish Imperialism and the Political Imagination* (New Haven, 1990), pp. 37–63.

47 I have used Edmund Chilmead's 1660 edition: *Thomas Campanella An Italian Friar and Second Machiavel His Advice to the King of Spain for Attaining the Universal Monarchy of the World* (London, 1660), preface by William Prynne, pp. 120, 155, 157, 165. It should be emphasized that, unlike the Restoration understanding of of universal monarchy, Campanella's version does not argue that control of trade routes was essential to establish a universal monarchy.

and applied them to the war at hand. One printer even brought out a bowdlerized version which naturally emphasized the centrality of an Anglo-Dutch war to Spain's aspirations.[48]

The war between England and the United Provinces, the Cromwellian moderates agreed, was "meat and drink and music for Spain." "The great Popish design is to keep the balance even betwixt both commonwealths," commented the *Mercurius Politicus*, "that they may spin out and spend one another." The differences between the English and the Dutch, any reader of Fulke Greville, Lord Brooke's celebrated *Life of Sidney* knew, were "not as sprung from any difference of religious faith, but misty opinion; and accordingly molded first upon the desks of busy idle lecturers, then blown abroad, to our disadvantage by a swarm of Popish instruments, rather Jesuits than Christians." The King of Spain's ambition, Thomas Scot argued in a pamphlet reprinted in the 1650s, was "the whole Empire of Christendom." All of this created an imperative for the two great Protestant powers to end their conflict. It is essential "for these two states to remember," argued Sir Cornelius Vermuyden in his famous "Paper concerning the Dutch," "how the Spaniard hath been very busy this hundred years and more, to settle him into a fifth monarchy; and to bring his designs to pass, he did massacre, murder, bring to martyrdom, them of the reformed religion throughout all Europe ... and will so still, so soon as he can find an opportunity, if not prevented." "It no sooner pleased God to raise my master" to the Protectorate, George Downing later recalled, than he concluded a peace to provide a "common bulwark against the designs and strengths of their common enemies." Since it was well known that England and the United Provinces "are now alone left in a capacity of relief and succor to others now in distress and misery," Downing asked, if the two Protestant maritime powers were at war "what would then hinder an Universal Empire over our estates, liberties, religion, friends and allies so long contended for?"[49]

48 *Perfect Diurnall*, 21–28 November 1653, p. 3160; *Several Proceedings*, 24 November–1 December 1653, p. [3456]; *A Perfect Account*, 30 November–7 December 1653, p. 1216; *The Plot of the Jesuites* (London, 1653), Thomason: 1 November 1653, p. 9. The *Mercurius Politicus* material is discussed below.

49 *Mercurius Politicus*, 18–25 November 1652, p. 2030; *Mercurius Politicus*, 26 May–2 June 1653, p. 2485; *Mercurius Politicus*, 10–17 November 1653, pp. 2861–2862; Fulke Greville, Lord Brooke, *The Life of the Renowned Sir Philip Sidney* (London, 1652), pp. 52–53; *Peace-Maker*, p. 14; [Thomas Scott], *The Spaniards Cruelty and Treachery to the English in the Time of Peace and War, Discovered* (London, 1656), p. 54; Sir Cornelius Vermuyden, "Paper Concerning the Dutch," 1653–1654, Bod., Rawl. A12, p. 113; "The Medley of Nations," Bod., Rawl. Poet. 37, f. 111 (section on "the Spaniard" probably datable to 1650s); Downing to States General, 28 January 1658, Downing Letterbook, Downing College, ff. 4–9. This was also Mazarin's interpretation of the Anglo-Dutch conflict. See Sagredo to Doge and Senate, 13/23 September 1653, *CSPV*, p. 128; Bordeaux to de Brienne, 3/13 February 1653, PRO, PRO 31/3/90, f. 600. Bernard Capp long ago noticed the persistence of a rhetoric of universal monarchy in mid-seventeenth century

In order to spark this conflict the Spanish and their Jesuit allies had gained control of a party both in England and in the United Provinces. In England, not surprisingly, it was those who were hottest for war against the Dutch, the Anabaptists, who were revealed as the agents of Spain and the Society of Jesus. It was well known "that a priest or Jesuit may be found among all ranks of men," pointed out the author of *The Establishment*, "yea, in the pulpit also, and perhaps there especially; and with such pretense of zeal, affection and devotion too, that the Devil himself scarce can act his part more cunningly, while he transforms himself into an angel of light." William Sclater warned the Southampton grand jury to beware of "Jesuitical impostors, those who carry Jesus in their names, but Abaddon and Apollyon in their hearts; those wolves in sheep's clothing, those serpents, that creep unawares into secret chambers, beguiling unsettled and unstable souls." These men were, he insisted, "most pernicious incendiaries, not only in a church, but in a state."[50] The religious radicals bore all the marks of agents of the King of Spain. They endeavored "to twist the spiritual and civil interest both in one" which was the "very Papal and Prelatic principle." They attacked Protestant universities, they denounced godly Protestant ministers, and above all they preached rebellion against a godly magistrate. "Are not all divisions and differences both spread and fomented by their artifices," William Spurstowe asked of Popish emissaries in a sermon preached before the Lord Mayor of London, "that they may thereby scandalize our religion and ensnare such as are weak in the faith, by pleading the unity of their Church?"[51]

The evidence for the infiltration of the gathered churches by the Jesuits was simply too substantial for the moderates to ignore. Their researches revealed that there were at least twelve Jesuit priests in London "preaching in gathered churches" – the same churches which spewed out the most violent Hollandophobic sermons. Only the establishment of the Protectorate had foiled their designs. "I confess I am glad of the news" of the establish-

England, but he placed this rhetoric exclusively in the context of millenarian enthusiasm rather than as an explanatory force in the formation of English foreign policy. See B. S Capp, *Fifth Monarchy Men* (Oxford, 1989), pp. 20–22.

50 *The Establishment: Or, A Discourse Tending to the Settling of the Minds of Men, about some of the Chief Controversies of our Times* (London, 1653), Thomason: 20 November 1653, p. 76; William Sclater, *Civil Magistracy by Divine Authority*, preached at Southampton Assizes 4 March 1652 (London, 1653), Thomason: 30 October 1652, p. 37.

51 *A True State of the Case of the Commonwealth* (London, 1654), Thomason: 8 February 1654, p. 27; William Spurstowe, *The Magistrates Dignity and Duty: Being a Sermon Preached on October 30 1653 at Paul's Church* (London, 1654), Thomason: 24 January 1654, pp. 38–39; *A Beacon Set on Fire* (London, 1652), Thomason: 21 September 1652, pp. 5–6; [Dr. Francis Chenell], *The Beacon Flaming with a Non-Obstante* (London, 1652), Thomason: 15 December 1652, p. 10; John Philip to John Gunter, February 1654, Bod., Rawl. A11, p. 342; Job Herbert to Thurloe, 24 February 1654, Bod., Rawl. A11, p. 337; Charles Roberts to John Gunter, February 1654, Bod., Rawl. A11, p. 343; information of N. N. of Spain now of London, 9 August 1653, Bod., Rawl. A5, p. 71.

ment of the Protectorate, wrote one of Lady Hatton's correspondents, " which defeats those busy sectaries that obstructed all proceedings by their opposition to the Lord General; the English Papists are no less his enemies, and have had a great hand I perceive here in fomenting those." Naturally the new government, unlike a government of the religious radicals, had no desire to compel tender consciences but only "to suppress the ill disposed of them ... who were guided by a Jesuitique party who had the power of them." No wonder the Popish princes "who had a design in confederacy from the Pope against all Protestants" were deeply "troubled at the settlement of England under the Lord Protector."[52] The Jesuits in London, predictably enough, were to be found "glorying and rejoicing in nothing more than in the present war between the two commonwealths, openly expressing they will claw and destroy each other and so become a prey to the King of Spain and that this will be a just reward for their heresy and rebellion."[53]

In the United Provinces it was the Orangist party which had become the dupes of the Jesuits. "The holy conclave of priests and Jesuits," reported the *Mercurius Politicus* with horror, "are not without a party and influence among the men in power." It was the Jesuits "who have blown the coals in The Hague and Zeeland against the Parliament of England." "The Jesuit hath veiled himself in the habit of a Zeelander," revealed one neo-Elizabethan, "and had influence by cunning upon their counsels, and by that means been the only instrument of embroiling the two republics, and of hindering an happy accommodation." The sole aim of the "Jesuitish spirit of Zeeland" was "to set up again the old monarchic form, and shipwreck our dear and dear-bought liberty." Naturally after an entire packet of Jesuit letters was intercepted by the States of Zeeland – an event given full play in the press and the army newsletters – there could be no doubting that "the hand of Spain is much in this war."[54] When peace became a real possibility with the establishment of the Protectorate, the King of Spain and his Jesuit allies did all they could to prevent an agreement. "It's no wonder," commented the *Mercurius Politicus*, "if all the Jesuits in Europe (who are said to have a notable influence in the Dutch Council) employ all their wits

[52] Newsletter from The Hague, 25 July/4 August 1652, PRO, SP 84/159, f. 128r; Letter to Lady Hatton, 24 December/3 January 1653/1654, Bod., Rawl. A9, p. 159; Letter to Mr. Ryder, 14 December 1653, Bod., Rawl. A9, pp. 66–67; *Several Proceedings*, 26 January–2 February 1654, pp. 3599–3600.

[53] Information of N. N. of Spain now of London, 9 August 1653, Bod., Rawl. A5, p. 71.

[54] *Mercurius Politicus*, 9–16 September 1652, p. 1877; *Mercurius Politicus*, 18–25 November 1652, pp. 2028–2031; *Mercurius Politicus*, 3–10 February 1653, pp. 2116–2117; *Mercurius Politicus*, 19–26 May 1653, p. 2466; *Mercurius Politicus*, 25–31 August 1653, p. 2688; newsletter from Westminster, 21 May 1653, Worcester College, Clarke MSS 25, f. 57; *Several Proceedings*, 12–19 January 1654, pp. 3555–3556; *Peace-Maker*, p. 16. The prevalence of this line of argument in the *Mercurius Politicus* is no coincidence; it was, after all, the mouthpiece of the Cromwellian moderates.

and insinuations to hinder it." The Pope was using all of his artifices "to obstruct the treaty, and advance Popery." On the Exchange it was rumored that the King of Spain tried to bribe the Protector with promises of Dunkirk and Mardyke in order to prevent a peace. When the peace was finally announced in the United Provinces, a correspondent to the *Faithful Scout* found that "the Jesuitical party seem to be very much offended; but the generality of the people do exceedingly rejoice."[55]

Since he believed the Anglo-Dutch War had been engineered by Jesuits in the employment of the King of Spain, Cromwell was necessarily less concerned about the creation of a single Anglo-Dutch state, or with the maintenance of security towns in the United Provinces. The mere conclusion of peace was enough to deal a mortal blow to the Spanish monarch's universal aspirations. By excluding the Prince of Orange from control of the Dutch army and navy, the Protectorate in conjunction with the true Dutch patriots had gone a long way toward preventing the accession to power of the King of Spain's agent in the Netherlands. In England, the establishment of the Protectorate had barred the religious fanatics, notoriously corrupted with Jesuitical opinions, from achieving the ascendancy they had so long desired.

The inevitable corollary of this analysis of international politics was that the true enemy of all the nations of Europe, and especially of all the Protestant nations, was the King of Spain. Consequently many hoped that "when God shall in his mercy make [the English and the Dutch] friends, they will have an equal and perfect hatred of those that set themselves together by the ears." Cromwell had long hoped for an international Protestant alliance "against the House of Austria whose power was becoming too great." "These two nations," thought the Venetian ambassador in Spain when peace between England and the Netherlands was all but signed, "united and armed, hang like a cloud or tempest over the dominions of the Catholic king." In fact, the Cromwellians hoped to imitate Elizabethan policy by depriving the Habsburgs of the source of their wealth: the West Indies. The notorious Spanish cruelties, coupled with the immense wealth which Spain garnered from the West Indies, convinced Cornelius Vermuyden "what an infinite good would arise to the honor of God, by the increasing of the Kingdom of Christ, to make a conquest upon the Spaniard there." "Having lost America," Vermuyden concluded, the Spaniard's "sword as it were is taken out of his hand, and so consequently all Europe will be discharged of the cruel wars, and perpetual attempts and plots, either by himself or by the Emperor in Germany, where there of late was

[55] *Mercurius Politicus*, 16–22 December 1653, p. 3051; *Mercurius Aulicus*, 27 March–3 April 1654, p. 24; *Mercurius Politicus*, 9–16 March 1654, p. 3340; *Politique Informer*, 23–30 January 1654, p. 2; *Perfect Diurnall*, 19–26 December 1653, p. 3221; *Faithful Scout*, 13–20 January 1654, pp. 1273–1274.

near to have extirpated the true religion, and did set up instead thereof Popery and idolatry, and this by the help of the Spaniard's money." "But for his Indies," Thomas Scot had noticed long before, the King of Spain "were the poorest prince in Christendom." This would be no difficult task. "It were easily demonstrated," Colonel Robert Bennet's moderate friend Anthony Nicholls explained, "how that the whole profits of the King of Spain's West Indies might be brought to England and Holland." By the spring of 1654 this strategy had captured the English popular imagination. "Since the peace with Holland," the Canary merchant John Paige reported, "most men cry up war with Spain, saying the fleet and army must be kept in employment and no place worth their attempting like unto the Indies."[56] Cromwell and his colleagues, then, hoped to prevent the corruption of England and the United Provinces by the Hispanified Jesuits by striking them at the heart of their power.

The first Anglo-Dutch War was not, in fact, the first great trade war, but arose out of a deeply felt ideological conflict, a conflict predicated on a sophisticated English understanding of the Dutch polity. The Dutch, English men and women felt, had forsaken the virtues of republicanism and Protestantism for absolute monarchy and the associated sins of pride and covetousness. For those in England who were convinced that the millennium was imminent, and that God had selected the English to initiate the final phase of the eschatological struggle, this apostasy at such a critical time could only mean that the Lord meant the United Provinces to be the first stage on the march to Rome. These religious radicals were committed to the evisceration of the United Provinces. Aligned against such men were those who, though convinced and committed Protestants, did not believe that they were living in the last days. Since they felt less urgency in their pursuit of the eschatological struggle, these Cromwellian moderates were willing to forgive the Dutch their temporary corruption. Nevertheless as long as the Orange party, the party of Jesuitism and absolute monarchy, threatened to gain control of the Dutch polity both groups of English politicians

[56] *The Moderate Publisher*, 22–27 July 1653, p. 1141; *A Cat May Look Upon a King* (London, 1625), pp. 30–31; Bordeaux to de Brienne, 12/22 September 1653, PRO, PRO 31/3/91, f. 96v; *A Christian and Brotherly Exhortation to Peace* (London, 1653), Thomason: 30 December 1653, pp. 2–3; Giacomo Quirini to Doge and Senate, 22 February/4 March 1654, *CSPV*, p. 188; Cornelius Vermuyden, "Paper Concerning the Dutch," 1653/1654, Bod., Rawl. A12, p. 113; Charles Longland to W. Black, 12 March 1655, NMM, AGC/L/2; Anthony Nicholls to Colonel Robert Bennet, 9 November 1653, Folger, Xd483 (112); Paige to Clerke, 27 May 1653, Steckley, *John Paige*, p. 107. The belief was widespread that the result of an Anglo-Dutch peace would be an attack on the Spanish Indies; see Edward Hyde to Earl of Rochester, 12/22 August 1653, Bod., Clar. 46, f. 174r; James Waynwright (London) to Richard Bradshaw, 12 May 1654, HMC, *6th Report*, p. 437. A plan similar to Vermuyden's survives among the Clifford Papers. See "The Proposal," 1654?, NMM, Clifford Papers, Vol. I, Dw21, f. 1.

supported the war. It was when the States party regained control of Dutch politics that the two English ideological groupings came into irreconcilable conflict. Had the Harrisonian radicals proved victorious, there can be no doubt that the English would have pursued an apocalyptic foreign policy, a foreign policy of world conquest.

The victory of the Cromwellians with the resignation of the Nominated Parliament, then, represents the final defeat of one very powerful strand of Interregnum political argument. In its place, the Cromwellians hoped to revive their understanding of the Elizabethan ideals of domestic unity and opposition to the foreign policy aspirations of the Spanish monarchy. By blaming the corruption of the Dutch nation on a Spanish/Jesuit plot, Protectorate politicians were able to conclude a peace with the Dutch in the full confidence that an attack on Spain would prevent any Dutch relapse. Rather than limit the size of the Dutch navy or demand cautionary towns to keep the Dutch committed to republicanism and Protestantism, the new English regime was certain that those aims were best achieved by threatening the Escorial rather than the Binnenhof. The Protectorate, under the guise of neo-Elizabethanism, had initiated a new phase in English foreign policy – a phase in which religion would form but one part of the national interest. It was a measure of this dramatic transformation that the French ambassador Bordeaux could report that Cromwell and his supporters had "given over all their ideas of war and conquest."[57] The war against Spain was to be a defensive war to prevent the establishment of a universal monarchy, not an offensive crusade to eviscerate all the allies of the Whore of Babylon.

[57] Whitelocke, *Annals*, 25 June 1654, BL Add. 4992, f. 91r (the reference is to Deuteronomy 33.19); Bordeaux to de Brienne, 3/13 November 1653, PRO, PRO 31/3/92, f. 8v. For an interesting discussion of the western design in terms of traditional English foreign policy, see Karen Ordahl Kupperman, "Errand to the Indies: Puritan Colonization from Providence Island through the Western Design," in *William and Mary Quarterly*, Vol. 45 No. 1 (January 1988), pp. 88–99.

Part III

POPERY, TRADE AND UNIVERSAL MONARCHY: IDEOLOGY AND THE OUTBREAK OF THE SECOND ANGLO-DUTCH WAR

11

Historiographical overview

In May 1660, after almost a decade in the political wilderness, Charles II entered the United Provinces, the last stop on his triumphal return to the British Isles. The treatment which the States General and the States of Holland afforded their royal guest "was incredibly splendid and noble," recalled the Earl of Clarendon, "and the universal joy so visible and real, that it could only be exceeded by that of [the king's] own subjects."[1] Samuel Pepys, who had come with his fellow former Cromwellian the Earl of Sandwich to The Hague to bring Charles II back to England, could not "speak enough of the gallantry of the town."[2] Charles II himself declared "his meaning of keeping a true and firm friendship and alliance with [the Dutch], nay that he should be jealous if any other king or prince should have a more near and stricter friendship and alliance with them than himself." On 23 May after almost interminable festivities Charles finally boarded his ships at Scheveling. The shore, wrote one observer, was "covered black with people ... come from several towns far and near to see the king's departure and were forced for want of lodgings to walk all night or lie in the open fields." The salutes and countersalutes from the English and Dutch ships were so tremendous that "the air was set on fire and the smoke like a cloud had made the fleet invisible."[3] Charles II's first act in foreign policy as the undisputed king of Great Britain could hardly have been more satisfying, the prospects for Anglo-Dutch friendships could hardly have been better.

Yet the promised friendship and alliance never materialized. After four years of heated diplomatic exchanges, Dutch and English ships were again setting the air on fire. This time the smoke could not obscure their clashes on the coasts of Africa and India, in the New Netherlands, or eventually in the Channel itself. Ostensibly the Restored Monarchy, which had done so

1 W. Dunn Macray (editor), *Clarendon's History of the Rebellion* (Oxford, 1888), Vol. VI, p. 228.

2 Pepys, *Diary*, Vol. I, 15 May 1660, p. 139.

3 Aitzema, "Selections," Bod., Rawl. C734, ff. 259r–260v.

much to obliterate any memory of the Commonwealth, had adopted its foreign policy. What had happened?

Many historians argue that the continuities in foreign policy were quite real. The Restoration had not changed the national interest of England. "English policy," Sir Keith Feiling claims, "could not fail to be continuous, guided as it must be by continuous geographic law." Charles II "could no more cancel Puritan foreign policy than he could their Church settlement, and for war and peace, as for the management of Parliament, he must depend on their experience, their co-operation, and their wealth." Although Feiling is alive to the Anglo-Dutch disputes over the place of the Prince of Orange in the Dutch polity, he dismisses this dispute as "the effect, not the cause of the ill relations between Holland and England."

In the view of Feiling, then, Anglo-Dutch conflict was all but inevitable. "Trade was the life-blood of both countries," he argues, "and economic causes extinguished the wide hopes and good intentions with which both had entered on the peace conferences of December 1660."[4] More recently, Charles Wilson in his classic account of Anglo-Dutch relations in the mid seventeenth century, reached similar conclusions. Despite the valiant efforts of John De Witt and the Earl of Clarendon "to divert the currents of [their] time from the channels in which they were now running strongly," war was unavoidable. "The balance of economic influence," argues Wilson, had shifted "away from the industrialists who urged caution to the more ambitious merchants who urged risk and change." In this context, then, it is not surprising to discover that in "matters of national policy" the otherwise antagonistic "cavaliers and Roundheads were not far apart."[5] In his magisterial account of Dutch economic development in the seventeenth century, Jonathan Israel substantially supports this view. "The second and hardest-fought of the three seventeenth-century Anglo-Dutch wars," he points out, "grew out of the unresolved legacy of the first, aggravated by England's accelerating colonial expansion after 1654 and Dutch efforts to obstruct it."[6]

Historians of Dutch politics draw a picture which largely corroborates this interpretation of the outbreak of the second Anglo-Dutch War. The Dutch nationalist historian Pieter Geyl acknowledges Charles II's ostensible concern for the welfare of William III, but concludes that the English king

4 Sir Keith Feiling, *British Foreign Policy, 1660–1672* (London, 1930), pp. 3–4, 91–93.

5 Charles Wilson, *Profit and Power* (London, 1957), pp. 9, 110, 120–121. In this scenario, Bennet's rise to power in England represents the unleashing of the natural developments in foreign policy. Dutch opposition to English attempts to reestablish the Princes of Orange are dismissed as opposition to an economically centralized state, p. 105.

6 Jonathan Israel, *Dutch Primacy in World Trade 1585–1740* (Oxford, 1989), p. 271. It should be noted that Israel gives by far the best account of the economic devastation wreaked by the first Dutch War, and unlike Wilson explains why the economic conflict did not begin prior to the 1650s.

only wanted the restoration of the power of Orange because it "might prove a useful instrument in vitiating the hated commercial policy of Holland." "In contrast to the first English war," Geyl posits that "the causes of the second were purely economic."[7] Herbert Rowen, in his exhaustive study of the political career of John De Witt, finds little reason to disagree with this conclusion. "Charles remembered his nephew's cause," he asserts, "because he was outraged by De Witt's success in outwitting him by sending De Ruyter to Guinea undetected."[8]

Against this chorus of agreement, there have been only a few dissenting voices. These revisionist historians emphasize political accident and the role of English political faction in the outbreak of the war. J. R. Jones has often described the factional and often seedy world of English Restoration politics. Not surprisingly he finds that the second Anglo-Dutch War "was pushed without scruple by a combination of Court factions, composed of ruthlessly ambitious politicians who planned to use the war to climb into high offices, ruining Charles's leading minister, Clarendon, and replacing his system of administration by one that gave ministers more power." These politicians only used a rhetoric of national interest as a cover for their real aims of career advancement and sheer plunder.[9] Ronald Hutton, while pointing to the economic competition which led to the first Anglo-Dutch conflict, locates the origins of the second war in "a surplus of energy at Charles's court among men grown used to excitement during the turbulence of the past two decades, and the new confidence of his government in 1664." The economic aggression initiated by the Restoration court, after Clarendon had ceased to serve as an effective restraining influence, was not meant to lead to war "as Charles and James both expected the Dutch to concede the claims of English merchants to compensation and to a greater share of the tropical trade." Nevertheless when the Dutch put up some resistance the Stuart brothers, egged on by popular enthusiasm, were quite happy to carry on with this new and exciting adventure.[10] For J. L. Price the war was the result of poor intelligence and shoddy economic thinking. "Far from being the logical conclusion to long years of economic and colonial rivalry," he maintained, "it was rather an ill conceived attempt to compensate for the continued inability of the English economy to compete effectively with the Dutch." Ultimately English insularity, resulting in "poor

7 Pieter Geyl (translated by Arnold Pomerans), *Orange and Stuart 1641–1672* (London, 1969), pp. 179, 190.

8 Herbert Rowen, *John De Witt, Grand Pensionary of Holland, 1625–1672* (Princeton, 1978), pp. 544–545. There is narrative discussion of the events preceding the outbreak of the war in an earlier chapter.

9 J. R. Jones, *Britain and the World 1649–1815* (Glasgow, 1980), pp. 53, 71–75. It should be said that Jones gives by far the best account of the ideological issues at stake, but ultimately dismisses them as secondary to factional politics. He also gives the best account of Sir George Downing's political ideas.

10 Ronald Hutton, *The Restoration.* (Oxford, 1985), pp. 215–216.

and misleading intelligence," deserves the blame for English involvement in the ignominious conflict.[11]

In order to reassess the outbreak of the second Anglo-Dutch War it is necessary to place the political and economic developments in their intellectual, cultural, and religious contexts. Too often historians have been content to accept the propagandistic and *post-facto* explanations of contemporaries at face value, underestimating the potential of early modern governments and polemicists to present images which served their own ideological predispositions.

Charles II's glorious departure from Scheveling in May 1660, for example, was perhaps not all that it seemed. After fulminating on the lavishness of Charles's reception and treatment by the Dutch States General, Clarendon could not but muse "that no man would have imagined, by the treatment he now received, that he had been so lately forbid to come into that place." John Dryden thought it ironic indeed that Holland seemed "to regret a king." Certainly the Orange tinge of the crowds which blackened the Dutch coast upon Charles's departure left room for contemplation. The Dutch people, thought Clarendon, "had always passion for [the king's] prosperity" it was only "the rudeness of their superiors, whom they were always bound to obey" which had prevented Charles from visiting The Hague.[12]

Ideological divisions in both the United Provinces and in England, not the cold logic of commercial competition or factional politics, I claim, drove the English and Dutch to war again in the 1660s. The newly restored English monarchy and its most enthusiastic supporters, the Anglican Royalists, perceived the Dutch republican party to be the natural allies of its own domestic enemies. Anglican Royalists merchants, it is true, did fear and loathe the Dutch commercial success. But the way in which these merchants understood economic competition was colored by their ideological presuppositions. Anglican Royalists were concerned not only about secular declines in their own profit margins, but in the perceived designs of the republican Dutch on universal dominion. I maintain that Anglican Royalist ministers, courtiers, and merchants all believed that the only means to prevent the Dutch from pursuing universal dominion and from bringing their fanatical and republican friends to power in England was to compel the Dutch to restore rational government in the United Provinces, to compel them to restore the Prince of Orange.

11 J. L. Price, "Restoration England and Europe," in J. R. Jones (editor) *The Restored Monarchy 1660–1688* (London, 1979), pp. 122–126. This discussion intentionally omits the important works of Michael McKeon and Paul Seaward which receive full treatment later in this Part.

12 Edward Hyde, *History of the Rebellion and Civil Wars in England* (Oxford, 1843), Vol. VI, p. 227; Aitzema, "Selections," Bod., Rawl. C734, f. 259r; John Dryden, *Astraea Redux: A Poem on the Happy Restoration and Return of His Sacred Majesty Charles the Second* (London, 1660), Thomason: 19 June 1660, p. 12.

12

The establishment of an Orangist foreign policy

On 1 November the promised embassy from the United Provinces disembarked on English soil, hoping to achieve a triple alliance among France, England and the United Provinces to guarantee commerce and mutual defense.[1] Despite "the demonstration of honor and kindness" to which they were treated, little progress was made in their negotiation by the following spring. It is true, of course, that the Dutch were irritated with the renewal of the Navigation Act and the discussion of a nationalist fishing measure in the House of Commons. But this was hardly the cause of the delay. It was soon clear to everyone that the Navigation Act was not being enforced.[2] Instead the difficulties were ideological. "The treaty here with the Dutch is not at all advanced," Charles's chief minister, the Earl of Clarendon, complained to his French correspondent Bastide, because of "sharp expostulations between us upon the affair of the Prince of Orange." Given the ideological outlook of the three Dutch ambassadors this was hardly surprising. Simon Van Horn, a burgomaster of Amsterdam, was said to be "one of the chiefest" of the republican faction. Louis of Nassau, the Heer of Beeverweert, "shows himself outwardly as if he were neutral for that he being descended from the House of Orange, which he inwardly hated by reason of a reproach of his birth objected to him by the late Prince of Orange's mother." The third ambassador, Rippenda Van Farnsum, was "well affected to the interest of Orange, but is overvoted by the two others." "Beeverweert and Horn being wholly of De Witt's faction," opined George Downing, "would . . . never do any good to the Prince of Orange."[3]

1 Aitzema, "Selections," Bod., Rawl. C734, ff. 90v–92v.

2 Downing to Clarendon, 8 August 1662, Bod., Clar. 77, ff. 171v–172r.

3 Clarendon to Bastide, 1 April 1661, Bod., Clar. 74, f. 301r; Clarendon to Bastide, 8 April 1661, Bod., Clar. 74, f. 313v; "Considerations Regarding the Dutch," 1662, Bod., Clar. 78, f. 144v – this is a manuscript pamphlet ostensibly circulated at court outlining an interpretation of Dutch politics. That it survives among Clarendon's papers, and echoes the view of Dutch politics frequently voiced by Clarendon during the Interregnum, is certainly significant. Downing to Clarendon, 12/22 July 1661, Bod., Clar. 104, f. 182v; Downing to Clarendon, 18/28 October 1661, Bod., Clar. 105, f. 81v. Rowen and Feiling have emphasized Beeverweert's lineage and his marital connection with the Duke of Ormonde's family to argue for his Orangism (Herbert H. Rowen, John De Witt, *Great Pensionary of*

It was in this context that Charles II decided to send Sir George Downing, Cromwell's former ambassador to the States General, back to the Netherlands. "I am of opinion that nothing is of more importance," wrote Clarendon in a note which he slipped across the Council table to Charles II in December, "than to send away Sir George Downing or, somebody else into Holland, both in respect of your nephew, and your own affairs, to watch De Witt and Beverning who play the Devil at present."[4] Although Downing's full instructions don't survive, the only extant note outlines the same policy. Downing was ordered to make sure that "the Province of Holland ... be disposed by the example of the other provinces to give to the Prince of Orange some assurance that at his coming to his age of discretion he shall be provided with those charges, which his ancestors have been provided withal."[5] It was thus concern for Orange, and presumably fear of the pernicious designs of the Holland republicans, rather than commercial greed, which set the tone for George Downing's embassy to the United Provinces.

As soon as he arrived in The Hague Downing set about establishing a new coterie of diplomatic contacts. Instead of the Zeeland and Holland republicans, who had been frequent guests at his dinner parties in the 1650s, Downing's new connections were Orangists from Friesland, Groningen, and Gelderland. All this was "in order to making a party in the States General," a party which was necessary according to Downing "in regard De Witt and the king do not draw the same weight and consequently that the king must expect that De Witt will be doing him all the mischief he can."[6]

How, then, did Restoration politicians understand the workings of Dutch politics? The experience of the Interregnum – waiting in vain for the States General to adopt the Stuart cause during the first Anglo-Dutch War – had taught them to appreciate the bitter ideological divisions which were

Holland, 1627–1672 (Princeton, 1978), p. 448; Keith Feiling, *British Foreign Policy, 1660–1672* (London, 1930), p. 85), but I find almost universal agreement among contemporary commentators that at this point in time he was acting upon the instructions, and in the interest of John De Witt.

4 W. Dunn Macray (editor), *Notes Which Passed at Meetings of the Privy Council* (London, 1896), 20 December 1660, p. 48. Macray has dated this note to December 1661, but this must be a mistake for 1660 since Downing was already in the United Provinces in December 1661.

5 "Instructions for George Downing," 1661, in N. Japikse, *De Verwikkelingen Tusschen De Republiek en Engeland Van 1660–1665* (Leiden, 1900), p. xix.

6 Macray, *Notes*, November 1661, p. 46; Downing to Clarendon, 21 June 1661, Bod., Clar. 104, f. 143v; Downing to Clarendon, 12/22 July 1661, Bod., Clar. 104, f. 185v; Downing to Clarendon, 23 August/2 September 1661, Bod., Clar. 105, ff. 16v–17r; Downing to Clarendon, 18/28 October 1661, Bod., Clar. 105, f. 80; Downing to Clarendon, 20 May 1664, Bod., Clar. 108, ff.4v–5r; Pieter Geyl (translated by Arnold Pomerans), *Orange and Stuart 1641–1672* (London, 1969), pp. 169–171; Rowen, *John De Witt*, pp. 514, 538; Scott, *Algernon Sidney*, p. 176. For Downing's 1650s connections, see the Downing "Diary" for 1658 at Downing College, Cambridge.

endemic in the United Provinces. Restoration historians elucidated the antecedents of these ideological rifts. "There is amongst the magistrates of the Dutch of late years risen a faction, called the Loevesteen faction," observed the author of one court memorandum, who are "deadly and irreconcilable enemies against the interest" of the House of Orange "and if it were in their power they very likely would destroy the prince and his interest." "The House of Nassau, and the indulgence of the crown of England," argued Edward Cliffe, "with their own blood and treasure, in tender of the Netherlands calamity, preserved, nurs't, and bred up the seven United States from less than nothing, to such a vast bulk" only to have the republican Province of Holland repay it "with ingratitude, encroachments, deceits, and manifold absurdities." The States party of Holland was committed to gaining "a sovereignty over the other six provinces, by undermining their equality and blowing up the prince's birthright, to their more facile entrance at the breach."[7] The States General, agreed the Earl of Clarendon, "at this time were made a property by the States of Holland."[8]

The States party had not, however, been swept into power on the crest of a wave of popular enthusiasm. Instead, its strength, in this view, came from clever political manipulation and graft. Republican politics took place not in the open assembly of the States General, but behind closed doors in cabals and juntos. "I never did nor do apprehend De Witt's power," Downing told Clarendon, "but only his cunning and dissimulation at which he is as good as I ever knew any." In fact, Downing was "certain that nine parts in ten of [the Dutch people] are for the prince." Although the birth of William III was greeted with "the exceeding joy of six and three quarters of the seventh province, the other overswaying quarter" used the prince's minority to effect "by power, what they could not insensibly bereave his father by craft."[9] If Charles II could only explain to the Orangist multitude that "his good intents are interrupted by them of the Loevesteen faction for their own ends out of an inveterate hatred they have to suppress the House of Orange," thought the author of the court pamphlet "Considerations Regarding the Dutch," they would "very likely take a course to rout and quash that faction out of the magistracy and government."[10]

7 "Considerations Regarding the Dutch," 1662, Bod., Clar. 78, f. 144; Edward Cliffe, *An Abbreviate of Holland's Deliverance By, and Ingratitude to the Crown of England and House of Nassau* (London, 1665), preface, pp. 9–10; the same argument is outlined in W. W., *The English and Dutch Affairs Displayed to the Life* (London, 1664), pp. 50–54.

8 Edward Hyde, *The Life of Edward Earl of Clarendon* (Dublin, 1760), p. 108.

9 Cliffe, *An Abbreviate*, pp. 12–13; "Memorial Concerning De Witt and His Cabal," 1660s, Bod., Clar. 92, ff. 32v–33r; Downing to Clarendon, 15 August 1662, Bod., Clar. 104, f.99r; Downing to Clarendon, 29 August 1662, Bod., Clar. 77, f. 313r; Downing to Clarendon, 6 January 1662, Bod., Clar. 106, f. 27v; Downing to Clarendon, 23 August/2 September 1662, Bod., Clar. 105, f. 13v.

10 "Considerations Regarding the Dutch," 1662, Bod., Clar. 78, f. 144v. The accuracy with which this and other anti-republican pamphlets described the potential fury of the Orangist

Unfortunately for Charles II, the republican faction now in power in the Netherlands was historically committed to an anti-Stuart policy. Cognizant of the Dutch ingratitude for the heroic role which Queen Elizabeth had played in their emancipation from Spanish rule, and well aware that the time would come that England would demand reparations for the atrocities of Amboyna, the Netherlanders were always on the look out to keep the Stuarts busy at home. "There being (anno 1639) some distempers in Scotland," recalled William De Britaine, " they did greatly promote them, and contribute their assistance to them, in all manner of military provisions."[11] "When the flames burst out in England betwixt the king and Parliament in 1642," noted Edward Cliffe, the Dutch "stirr'd up, and blow'd the coals on both sides." Indeed the very idea of rebellion was Dutch. In 1641 the States party had "sent over their rabbles of sedition here into England, and infus'd their antimonarchical principles and dangerous doctrines into some giddy heads of the English nation, who thereby became so intoxicated, that they were never at rest till (like men infected with the plague) they infected others; and thereby a great party of the people became disobservant to the laws of the nation, and rebels to their king." "Ambition and treason can never find a better cloak for their wearing," insisted Edward Bellamy in a pamphlet which temporarily enjoyed much favor at court in 1662, "than that which is made of the Holland fashion."[12] After the death of the Royal Martyr, the States party continued its perfidy. In 1653, for example, "Opdam, De Witt, Berkel, Stellingwerf, and others of their cabal" were heard to say "that they had rather see the[ir] country lost than the king restored."[13] Nor were the Dutch republicans less active in their campaign against the Stuarts' allies, the House of Orange. In 1654 Cromwell and De Witt joined in an unholy alliance to exclude both Stuart and Orange from their rightful possessions. Far from being a clause which Cromwell forced on the defeated Dutch, the Act of Seclusion carried with it "a vehement suspicion of Holland's proposing it themselves." "De Witt and Beverning advised and pressed Cromwell to make that demand, and to insist upon it," wrote Clarendon to Downing, "when otherwise he intended

mob – it predicted that the republican junto would "be torn to pieces by them" – leads me to question J. L. Price's image of an insular and poorly informed English government, "Restoration England and Europe," in J. R. Jones (editor), *The Resotred Monarchy* (London, 1979).

11 William De Britaine, *The Dutch Usurpation* (London, 1672), p. 24; W. W., *English and Dutch Affairs*, p. 41. It should be noted that I have been willing to cite pamphlets from a later period in establishing the ideological context of the 1660s court. This is because all evidence indicates that in the 1670s the arguments from the 1660s were rehabilitated and employed for the same ends. Almost every element of the argument appears in abbreviated form in the manuscript material.

12 Cliffe, *An Abbreviate*, p. 50; De Britaine, *Dutch Usurpation*, pp. 25–26; Edward Bellamy, *Philanax Anglicus* (London, 1662), pp. 34–35.

13 "Memorial Concerning the Practices of the Pensioner De Witt and those of his Caball": Bod., Clar. 92, f. 31. There are many more examples included in this pamphlet.

no such matter, and offered to him that Holland would join if he would assist them to compel the other provinces to submit."[14]

The States party, knowing that it would never be able to be reconciled to Orange and Stuart, had now raised its hatred of monarchy to an ideology. "Tell them of monarchy but in jest, and they will cut your throat in earnest," warned the author of *The Dutch Drawn to the Life*, "the very name they think bears tyranny in its forehead; they hate it more than a Jew doth images, a woman old age, or a Non-Conformist a surplice." "Now being rich and proud," exclaimed Arise Evans, "they disdain all kings, and call themselves the High and Mighty States of Holland." "The Dutch," John Finch wrote to Henry Bennet who hardly needed convincing, "are sworn enemies to all princes and monarchs."[15]

No sooner had Charles II departed from Scheveling than De Witt and his cabal began plotting the overthrow of the English monarchy. De Witt "and his complices held commonly no other discourse than the little consideration or esteem they ought to have of the king," reported one commentator, "saying that the king was not capable of doing what Cromwell had done." De Witt was predicting "some revolution in England, which he most passionately desired, saying that his Majesty would not be three years King of England." Thus it was ideological fervor, not economic competition, which made the Dutch republicans desire the overthrow of English monarchy. Downing was confident that no "kindness or compliment" would moderate De Witt and his cabal. "It's a plain case," he wrote to Clarendon, "that the king can have no firm friendship in this country without the Prince of Orange and his restitution." Almost every diplomatic despatch reaffirmed that "unless the Prince of Orange be restored the King can have nothing but trouble from hence." "It is confidently believed in Holland," wrote the author of "A Memorial Concerning De Witt and His Cabal," "that De Witt and those of his party will never be friends to the king, and that they will always stir up his Majesty's enemies to raise rebellions and seditions in England."[16]

14 Cliffe, *An Abbreviate*, p. 16; Clarendon to Downing, 11 October 1661, Bod., Clar. 104, f. 15r; Clarendon to Downing, 25 October 1661, Bod., Clar. 104, f. 17r. Clarendon was convinced of the veracity of the story. "We know all that I writ to you concerning De Witt to be very true and therefore shall make no scruple of charging him with it," he informed Downing. Naturally there was no written evidence since De Witt "advised to Beverning, and Beverning by word of mouth advising Cromwell and Thurloe."

15 *The Dutch Drawn to the Life* (London, 1664), pp. 39–40; Arise Evans, *Light for the Jews* (London, 1664), pp. 53–54; John Finch to Lord Arlington, 27 June/7 July 1665, PRO, SP 98/5 (unfoliated); Cooper to Nicholas, 3/13 February 1662, PRO, SP 84/165, f. 80r; "Passages of the Books Printed at Amsterdam," January 1662, PRO, SP 84/165, f. 35r.

16 "Memorial Concerning De Witt and His Cabal," 1660s, Bod., Clar. 92, f. 32; Downing to Clarendon, 21 June 1661, Bod., Clar. 104, f. 142v; Downing to Clarendon, 9/19 August 1661, Bod., Clar. 104, f. 238; Downing to Clarendon, 16/26 August 1661, Bod., Clar. 104, f. 249; Downing to Clarendon, 23 August/2 September 1661, Bod., Clar. 105, ff. 13r–15v.

Not surprisingly the Dutch republicans, like their English allies and co-conspirators, were poor Protestants. Although nominally Presbyterian, hardly a recommendation in Restoration England, the Dutch were more concerned to promote "that which suited with their interest and constitution, than as what corresponded with truth." "Their trade is their God," thought the Duke of York's secretary William Coventry. "Beware of Amsterdam," warned the Royalist apocalyptic Arise Evans, "that damned rebellious city of Holland that provokes God to his face, in which atheists and Devils have their abode." The pagan Africans, thought the author of the African Company pamphlet *The Golden Coast*, "keep their fetishes day" "more solemnly and strictly than the Hollanders do their Sunday." Indeed, Anglican Royalist polemicists often cited Amsterdam as an example of the irreligion which religious toleration would beget. "You may be what Devil you will there," concluded the author of *The Dutch Drawn to the Life*.[17]

In this ideological context, Charles II could not help but be committed to the restoration of the Prince of Orange. Indeed one need not see Charles II as ideologically committed to the evisceration of republicanism or altruistically concerned for the welfare of his nephew to believe that he was interested in the cause of Orange. Given his understanding of Dutch politics, Charles II must have seen the reestablishment of the Stadholder as being in his own self-interest. Should the States General restore William III to his "ancestors' commands," wrote the principal secretary of state Edward Nicholas to Downing, "I am confident they cannot reasonably desire anything of his Majesty that he will not condescend unto." Clarendon promised "that the king our master will use all the intercession he can in his nephew's behalf." When Sir George Downing assured the Princess Dowager that Charles II was committed to "countenance and follow the advice of such as are the down right friends of the Prince of Orange," he thought "there never was a greater truth than this." The experienced international diplomat Abraham De Wicquefort was convinced that the English wanted "no less than the reestablishment of the Prince of Orange." In fact, when Charles II first exploded in anger at the Dutch ambassadors, it was not over some point of commercial dispute but over the guardianship of the Prince of Orange.[18] The Earl of Clarendon, for all of his caution in foreign affairs,

17 *Dutch Drawn to the Life*, pp. 43, 48–49; William Coventry, "Discourse on the Dutch War," Longleat House, Cov. MSS, CII, f. 7; Evans, *Light for the Jews*, p. 53; *The Golden Coast, or a Description of Guinney* (London, 1665), p. 80; Roger L'Estrange, *Toleration Discussed* (London, 1663), p. 102.

18 Nicholas to Downing, 21 June 1661, PRO, SP 44/1, p. 3; Nicholas to Downing, 6 December 1661, PRO, SP 44/1, p. 26; Clarendon to Downing, 22 November 1661, Bod., Clar. 104, f. 21; Downing to Clarendon, 6 January 1662, Bod., Clar. 106, f. 27v; Wicquefort to ?, 4/14 May 1662, PRO, SP 84/165, f. 229r (my translation); Charles II to Amalia Van Solms (Princess Dowager), May 1662, PRO, SP 84/165, f. 267; Geyl, *Orange and Stuart*, p. 165.

was adamantly insistent upon the restoration of the House of Orange. He told Downing that the Orangists "can never wish anything that may be any real advantage and benefit to the prince, which the king will not concur with them in." "I am heartily sorry to find De Witt and his cabal not at all abated in their malice [to the Prince of Orange]," wrote Clarendon after De Witt had refused voluntarily to restore William III to all of his father's offices, "but if they could not be gotten, we must take the other way with them, for which we have very good materials." Clarendon soon explained that "the other way" was to build up an Orangist coalition to attack De Witt.[19]

It is in this ideological context that one must place the Anglo-Dutch negotiations of 1661–1662.[20] The Holland pensionary John De Witt, it soon became clear, was not so much interested in retaining political power as in preventing a new Orangist monarchy. He told Downing that "if there were not one man more in the country of his mind, yet that he must oppose the restitution of the Prince of Orange." "He and his friends," Downing wrote to Clarendon in June 1661, "are resolved to bring things to any point with the king rather than yield to this particular."[21] Indeed, the Holland republican theorist Pieter de la Court published a pamphlet in 1662 emphasizing just this point. The Dutch, de la Court argued, should always try to avoid war with England, emphasizing that "we ought never to undertake a war by reason of any imposition or toll whatsoever upon goods; for those remedies will always be worse for Holland than the disease." However, "above all, we are to observe, that in order to shun or avoid war with England, we must not suffer ourselves to be seduced to alter the commonwealth for a monarchical government." "We must defend our free government, though it should be a war with England," de la Court vehemently concluded, "for 'tis better and more commendable to fight for our lives, though with the utmost hazard of perishing, than to hang

19 Clarendon to Downing, 16 July 1661, Bod., Clar. 104, f. 4v; Clarendon to Downing, 8 November 1661, Bod., Clar. 104, f. 19; Downing to Clarendon, 2/12 August 1661, Bod., Clar. 104, f. 226v; Clarendon to Downing, 27 June 1662, Bod., Clar. 104, f. 75v; Cornbury to Downing, 21 June 1661, BL, Add. 22919, f. 151v.

20 I have deemphasized the negotiations in England in favor of those in the United Provinces, because all significant developments occurred between De Witt and Downing at The Hague. Clarendon was instructing Downing, while Downing was constantly advising Clarendon on the finer points of economic detail. It was painfully obvious to the Dutch ambassadors that the English commissioners did nothing without precise instruction from Clarendon and Charles II. Consequently they too began to depend on letters from The Hague for new developments.

21 Downing to Clarendon, 21 June 1661, Bod., Clar. 104, ff. 141–143; Downing to Clarendon, 13/23 September 1661, Bod., Clar. 105, f. 48r. I have concentrated on De Witt, but his allies held similar views. For Nordwick see Downing to Clarendon, 19/29 July 1661, Bod., Clar. 104, f. 200r; for Van Hoorn see Downing to Clarendon, 15 August 1662, Bod., Clar. 104, f. 101v and above; for De Graeff see Downing to Clarendon, 24 June 1661, Bod., Clar. 104, f. 160v.

ourselves like Judas, for fear of receiving some smarting wounds in the battle, and to murder ourselves by a double death of soul and body without hopes of a resurrection."[22]

Downing's predictions proved to be right on the mark. The Dutch republicans were soon conducting a prolific and effective Anglophobic propaganda campaign. They circulated newsletters with "malignant stories" of rebellions in England, which blinded the people "against their true interest." By mid 1662, the Friesland Orangist Van Ruyven (alias De Bacquoy) informed Joseph Williamson that "people are certain in Holland that things are not going well for the King in England."[23] Not only were the Dutch in "this present Hollands' age" trying to bury "the deserts with the bodies of the House of Nassau," but they were claiming that Charles was not supporting his nephew's cause. "De Witt and his cabal," complained Downing, "do industriously scatter reports that the king cares not for ... the business of the Prince of Orange."[24] This claim made it easy for the republicans to assert that "the king had no friendship for them and intended nothing but the ruin of their trade." "In Holland people speak impertinently of the English economic pretensions," wrote Van Ruyven, "and the publishers of gazettes are beginning to publish them with great effrontery."[25] It was soon common for anti-Orangist squibs to attack Charles II and the institution of monarchy along with William III and his progenitors. The streets of Amsterdam swarm "with scurrilous squibs, such crackers as takes the vulgar there like wildfire, who being strangers to intelligence, easily suffers reason to be racked in print." "De Witt and the rest of his party" were using "all means possible to render his Majesty's person odious to the people of the United Provinces, saying that his Majesty has an inveterate hatred against them." "De Witt and his Cabal," agreed Downing, "do make it their business by all imaginable devices to incense the people against the King of England."[26]

22 [Pieter De la Court], *The True Interest and Political Maxims of the Republick of Holland and West-Friesland* (London, 1702), pp. 239, 287–288.

23 Downing to Clarendon, 21 June 1661, Bod., Clar. 104, f. 142; Downing to Clarendon, 3 February 1662, Bod., Clar. 106, f. 75r; De Bacquoy/Van Ruyven to Williamson, 31 May/10 June 1662, PRO, SP 84/165, f. 296r. On De Bacquoy's complicated identity, see William Temple to Arlington, 6/16 November 1666, PRO, SP 77/35, ff. 246–247; information of Theodore Van Ruyven, May 1667, PRO, SP 29/202/123 I.

24 Cliffe, *An Abbreviate*, pp. 8–9; Downing to Clarendon, 21 June 1661, Bod., Clar. 104, f. 142v; Downing to Clarendon, 9/19 August 1661, Bod., Clar. 104, f. 238r; Downing to Clarendon, 30 December 1661, Bod., Clar. 106, f. 9r.

25 Downing to Clarendon, 23 August/2 September 1661, Bod., Clar. 105, f. 14v; De Bacquoy/Van Ruyven to Williamson, 3 February 1662, PRO, SP 84/165, f. 71 (my translation).

26 Cliffe, *An Abbreviate*, preface; "Memorial Concerning De Witt and his Cabal," Bod., Clar. 92, f. 33r; Downing to Clarendon, 19/29 July 1661, Bod., Clar. 104, f. 199v; Downing to Clarendon, 26 July/5 August 1661, Bod., Clar. 104, f. 220; Downing to Clarendon, 13 January 1662, Bod., Clar. 106, f. 43r; Downing to Clarendon, 20 June 1662, Bod., Clar. 76, f. 380r.

De Witt was not content to conduct merely a printed war against the alliance of Orange and Stuart. He constantly raced across his home province of Holland lobbying in the *vroedschepen* of the great cities against the appointment of Orangist deputies, or the adoption of Orangist resolutions. Through contacts in Zeeland, De Witt was said to be "blowing the fire which was already alight against the Prince of Orange." Should De Witt and those of his party succeed in gaining Zeeland, Van Ruyven warned, the States party would no longer "listen to the other five provinces or even the King of England."[27] Indeed the situation was becoming increasingly desperate. "From one day to the next," Van Ruyven informed Williamson in June 1662, De Witt's party gains more power "while that of His Majesty and the Prince of Orange begins to decline." Each new vacancy in the *vroedschepen* of the Dutch towns was being filled by "none but such as are enemies to the Prince Orange," observed the Elector of Brandenburg's specialist on the House of Orange. The Elector himself, who along with Charles II was one of William's guardians, told Downing that "De Witt did daily get ground." Not only were the towns beginning to enjoy "the sweet in this their present sovereignty," not only was the ministry being purged, but De Witt was filling the militia – "the chief support of the authority of the Prince of Orange" – with "persons who are against the Prince of Orange." "I am sure," Downing concluded, "it is now high time to think of the business of the Prince of Orange."[28]

At the same time that he was pursuing a domestic policy aimed at extirpating the power of the House of Orange, De Witt was also looking abroad for allies in his struggle. "Holland is completely resolved" on a French alliance, wrote Wicquefort to Williamson, "because she has no other enemy than England and the moment this state concludes an offensive and defensive alliance with France, England can no more trouble them." "If that treaty be ended before the king's with France and before the business of the Prince of Orange be done," warned Downing in October 1661, "I do plainly foresee that it will make De Witt and his party very bold and upon this account it is that De Witt doth his utmost to advance that treaty." By February 1662 Downing was sure that the imminent Franco-Dutch treaty could be explained solely in terms of De Witt's "zeal against the King of

27 Downing to Clarendon, 2/12 August 1661, Bod., Clar. 104, f. 226r; Downing to Clarendon, 16/26 August 1661, Bod., Clar. 104, f. 248r; De Bacquoy/Van Ruyven to ?, 10/20 January 1662, PRO, SP 84/165, f. 29v; De Bacquoy/Van Ruyven to Williamson, 2/12 May 1662, PRO, SP 84/165, f. 211 (my translation).

28 De Bacquoy/Van Ruyven to Williamson, 14/24 June 1662, PRO, SP 84/165, f. 324r (my translation); Downing to Clarendon, 24 June 1661, Bod., Clar. 104, f. 157r; Downing to Clarendon, 19/29 July 1661, Bod., Clar. 104, f. 200r; Downing to Clarendon, 16/26 August 1661, Bod., Clar. 104, f. 248; Downing to Clarendon, 23 August/2 September 1661, Bod., Clar. 105, ff. 17v–18r; Downing to Clarendon, 30 August/9 September 1661, Bod., Clar. 105, f. 23v; Downing to Clarendon, 6/16 September 1661, Bod., Clar. 105, ff. 37v–38r.

England upon the account of the Prince of Orange."[29] In any event, English politicians were convinced that despite all of the fearful rumors, no Franco-Dutch treaty would ever be signed. Clarendon was sure that France "will enter into no obligations to the prejudice of our master." Downing and other observers of the Dutch political scene felt that France represented too much of a military threat to the United Province for the States General to accede to an offensive and defensive alliance.[30] Consequently, when the alliance was in fact signed in March 1662, it provoked a flood of English recriminations. The key to the treaty had been Louis XIV's guarantee of Dutch fishing rights in the North Sea, fishing rights of which Charles II felt were his alone to dispose. "Certainly never any King of France since the wars with France gave any King of England so just and real occasion of offense," fumed Downing. "There is but one thing that can hinder or obstruct a very near alliance between our Master and France," wrote Clarendon to the Earl of St. Albans in Paris before the treaty was completely settled, "that is, if France enter into such a treaty with Holland as the Dutch brag of." Charles II received the news of the treaty with "scant satisfaction." "We do now begin to see," wrote William Morrice describing court opinion, "how ill laid our confidence was in the French." As late as August, Downing predicted that with every future mention of France "I shall always remember the word *pêche*."[31] De Witt had found an ally in his struggle against Stuart and Orange in what must have seemed, from the perspective of Whitehall, like the unlikeliest of places.

It is against this background of Anglo-Dutch confrontation over the future of the House of Orange and of the republican cause that one must place the negotiations taking place simultaneously in Westminster and The Hague. Some of the issues in dispute do, at first glance, appear to have an economic basis, but closer examination reveals that the kernel of the disagreement was over sovereignty, honor, and the House of Orange. In short, the celebrated bitterness between Downing and De Witt reflected conflicting ideologies, not conflicting desires for private profit.

The dispute over fishing rights, which became a *cause célèbre* with the Franco-Dutch treaty of March 1662, was not about English encroachment

29 Wicquefort to Williamson, 25 January/3 February 1662, PRO, SP 84/165, f. 43r (my translation, somewhat less than elegant); Downing to Clarendon, 18/28 October 1661, Bod., Clar. 105, f. 79v; Downing to Clarendon, 3 February 1662, Bod., Clar. 106, f. 78v.

30 Clarendon to Downing, 13 December 1661, Bod., Clar. 104, f. 26r; Wicquefort to Williamson, 12/22 March 1662, PRO, SP 84/165, f. 137r; Downing to Clarendon, 21 March 1662, Bod., Clar. 106, f. 151; Downing to Clarendon, 30 May 1662, Bod., Clar. 76, f. 353; Downing to Clarendon, 22 August 1662, Bod., Clar. 77, f. 268r.

31 Wicquefort to Williamson, 19/29 March 1662, PRO, SP 84/165, f. 134r; Downing to Clarendon, 21 March 1662, Bod., Clar. 106, f. 150; Clarendon to St. Albans, 17 June 1661, Bod., Clar. 74, f. 466; Alvise Grimani to Doge and Senate, 20/30 May 1662, *CSPV*, p. 145; William Morrice to Downing, BL, Add. 22919, f. 203r; Downing to Clarendon, 1 August 1662, Bod., Clar. 77, f. 133v.

on Dutch economic life blood. There is no evidence of English seizures of Dutch herring busses. "The Kings of England have suffered them to fish," expostulated Downing, "and that seeing his Majesty did suffer them the same grace why they should needlessly provoke him who was so gracious that I understood not." Of course, what Downing refused to understand was that the Dutch viewed their fishing as a natural right, not a "grace" to be enjoyed at the king's whim.[32]

A much more central concern, and one which dogged the negotiations throughout, was that of reparations for ships seized by the Dutch. The English insisted that all claims from ships seized after 1654 be considered, while the Dutch refused to consider anything prior to 1659. It soon became clear that Clarendon, Downing, and Charles himself were little concerned as to whether the merchants involved actually received financial compensation. "I confess this referring to the year 54 when we were so little concerned in any damage the English did sustain, and would have done what mischief we could our selves, would have been of little importance to me," admitted Clarendon, "if it were not for the honor of it that the king should not seem less careful of the people than Cromwell was." "The difference is so small and so ridiculous," concurred Downing, "that it is not worth the looking after." Indeed Downing was sure that the Dutch were just as indifferent to the economic implications of the treaty. "I know the humor of these people," Downing reminded Clarendon, and "that neither the terms of 1654 or 1659 is of so great value to them, as the letting it be seen that they can bring his Majesty to their beck."[33] There were, of course, certain ships for which the English very much wanted to ensure that reparations were granted, but, these ships were invariably owned by Royalists whom Charles II wanted to reward for their loyalty.[34] The issue then was that "De Witt [and his party] do not love the king and make it their study to make him little esteemed and accounted of." The Restoration regime was exceedingly conscious that Englishmen and women were constantly comparing it to its predecessors. One English minister of state told the Dutch ambassadors that they "could expect no more favorable terms from the king than such as you were content with in the usurpation of Cromwell." "I will not suffer the king and true sovereign to be worse dealt withal than the usurper," proclaimed Downing.[35]

32 Downing to Clarendon, 3 February 1662, Bod., Clar. 106, f. 79.

33 Clarendon to Downing, 16 May 1662, Bod., Clar. 104, f. 65r; Clarendon to Downing, 23 May 1662, Bod., Clar. 104, f. 67r; Downing to Clarendon, 8 August 1662, Bod., Clar. 77, f. 173r; Downing to Clarendon, 30 May 1662, Bod., Clar. 76, f. 352.

34 Downing to Clarendon, 30 December 1661, Bod., Clar. 106, ff. 6v–8r. These were the "particular cases" mentioned in Newsletter addressed to Ormonde, 26 August 1662, Carte 222, f. 1r.

35 Downing to Clarendon, 30 December 1661, Bod., Clar. 106, f. 8v; Dutch Ambassadors to States General, 28 June/8 July 1661, Bod., Clar. 104, f. 165v; Downing to Clarendon, 30 December 1661, Bod., Clar. 106, f. 9v; Clarendon to Downing, 25 October 1661, Bod.,

The second major issue preventing completion of the Anglo-Dutch treaty in the summer of 1662, Beeverweert reported to the States General, was that regarding aid to each other's rebels. Initially it was the Dutch who raised objections, claiming that a complete prohibition of trade to enemies or rebels would bring "the total ruin of each other's traffic and navigation." But, in February 1662, the States General instructed their ambassadors to accede to English demands.[36] It was now the turn of the English, fully aware that the Orangists were quickly losing strength, to attempt to find a loophole. They claimed that subjects of the English monarch could serve in the forces of foreign princes engaged in a war against the United Provinces. The implications were potentially subversive, both because it provided a means for England to aid any enemy of the States General and because the Prince of Orange was a sovereign in his own right.[37]

Given that there were precious few economic issues in dispute, it is not surprising that contemporaries thought the Anglo-Dutch tension had little to do with trade and commerce. "The city of Amsterdam which is more economically interested than the others will acquiesce to the treaty and Holland will consent as well," wrote the Orangist De Chauran to Williamson, "if it weren't for the fact that the English wanted to include the interests of the Prince of Orange." De Witt was loath to grant any concessions to the English "fearing that when other matters are adjusted some thing concerning the Prince of Orange should be started and upon this single account all this ado." A burgomaster of Holland told one of Downing's informants that "they would yield" if "they were sure no new matter would be proposed." "It is most certain," Downing informed Clarendon in June 1662, that "De Witt hath searched most industriously and doth still for how to break off the treaty with the King of England and all this singly upon the score of the Prince of Orange least at the conclusion thereof the King of England should speak something for the Prince of Orange."[38]

Clar. 104, f. 17r; Downing to Clarendon, 29 August 1662, Bod., Clar. 77, f. 314r; Pepys, *Diary*, Vol. III, 12 March 1662, p. 45. I have not discussed separately the claims of the East India Company. But it is clear that in 1662 the Company was not interested in a war. They were concerned that a means of fair arbitration be found, that Pulo Run be restored, and that a treaty be settled to divide the Indies. See "East India Company Proposals," 1662, Bod., Clar. 92, f. 59r; East India Company petition, 2 April 1662, IOL, Home Miscellanies M42, p. 39; Clarendon to Downing, 11 April 1662, Bod., Clar. 104, f. 55.

36 Sir Edward Nicholas's notes of treaty negotiations, 16 January 1662, PRO, SP 84/165, f. 182v; Dutch Ambassadors to States General, 20/30 December 1661, Bod., Clar. 106, ff. 17v–18r; Dutch Ambassadors to States General, 17/27 January 1662, Bod., Clar. 106, ff. 72v–73r; Downing to Clarendon, 27 January 1662, Bod., Clar. 106, f. 66; project of instructions for Dutch Ambassadors, 16 February 1662, Bod., Clar. 106, f. 101r. It is unclear why the Dutch conceded this point, though perhaps it was because it was included in the peace treaty of 1654.

37 De Bacquoy/Van Ruyven to Williamson, 14/24 June 1662, PRO, SP 84/165, f. 323v.

38 M. De Chauran to Williamson, 22 January/1 February 1662, PRO, SP 84/165, f. 38v (my translation); De Bacquoy/Van Ruyven to Nicholas, 15/25 August 1662, PRO, SP 84/166, f. 103v; Downing to Clarendon, 7 March 1662, Bod., Clar. 106, f. 125; Downing to

Dutch republican discussions of trade were but a part of their anti-Orangist position. The republicans abhorred "a peace with England out of fear that the Orange interest should thereby go up," opined the author of one court memorandum, "so in consideration of their own subsistence they will always under the one or the other pretext hinder the peace with England all what they can." "It is not these matters [of trade] that De Witt values," Downing told Clarendon, "but his eye is upon greater matters, especially that of the Prince of Orange." "It is the cunning of De Witt by any means possible to make a breach" – a breach which the States party saw as inevitable – "upon the account of trade in which they have all one interest."[39]

De Witt did, in fact, attempt to break off the treaty in the summer of 1662. Claiming that there was no hope of resolving the interminable disputes between England and the United Provinces, Holland, Zeeland, and Utrecht pressed for the recall of the Dutch ambassadors in late May.[40] However, Friesland, Groningen, Gelderland, and Overijssel – the predominantly Orangist provinces – refused to vote for the abrogation of the treaty. Indeed, the Orangists cities of Ter Veer and Flushing in Zeeland, which had been so active in lobbying for war in 1652, were now spearheading the campaign to conclude an Anglo-Dutch alliance. Jongstall of Friesland, the member of the Dutch embassy in 1653–1654 who had attempted to block acceptance of Cromwell's peace terms, was now warning Hollanders that Friesland would not support this Anglo-Dutch war.[41] "It is strange to see that the temper here [of] the generality of all sorts will not endure to hear of a breach with England," wrote Downing drawing the obvious conclusion, "but those who are the prime men engaged against the Prince of Orange

Clarendon, 24 May 1662, Bod., Clar. 76, f. 320r; Downing to Clarendon, 13 June 1662, Bod., Clar. 76, f. 365r; Downing to Clarendon, 20 June 1662, Bod., Clar. 76, f. 381v; Downing to Clarendon, 22 August 1662, Bod., Clar. 77, ff. 266r, 269r; Downing to Clarendon, 29 August 1662, Bod., Clar. 77, f. 314v.

39 "Considerations Regarding the Dutch," 1662, Bod., Clar. 78, f. 144; Downing to Clarendon, 20/30 September 1661, Bod., Clar. 105, f. 60v; Downing to Clarendon, 16/26 August 1661, Bod., Clar. 104, f. 249v; Downing to Clarendon, 30 December 1661, Bod., Clar. 106, f. 10r.

40 De Bacquoy/Van Ruyven to Williamson, 23 May/2 June 1662, PRO, SP 84/165, f. 275v; Wicquefort to Williamson, 15/25 May 1662, PRO, SP 84/165, f. 234r; Downing to Clarendon, 13 June 1662, Bod., Clar. 76, f. 365r. De Bacquoy/Van Ruyven to Williamson, 31 May/10 June 1662, PRO, SP 84/165, f. 297r describes the lobbying tactics which De Witt used in the Orangist provinces.

41 De Bacquoy/Van Ruyven to Williamson, 10/20 June 1662, PRO, SP 84/165, f. 319; De Bacquoy/Van Ruyven to Williamson, 14/24 June 1662, PRO, SP 84/165, f. 322r; De Bacquoy/Van Ruyven to Williamson, 28 June/8 July, PRO, SP 84/166, f. 31v; Wicquefort to Williamson, 27 June/7 July 1662, PRO, SP 84/166, f. 19r; extract from secret resolution of States General, 26 August/5 September 1662, PRO, SP 84/166, f. 104v; Downing to Clarendon, 22 August 1662, Bod., Clar. 77, f. 267r; Downing to Clarendon, 29 August 1662, Bod., Clar. 77, f. 316r. For Ter Veere and Flushing: De Bacquoy/Van Ruyven to Williamson, 26 January 1662, PRO, SP 84/165, ff. 45v–46r; Downing to Clarendon, 21 March 1662, Bod., Clar. 106, f. 153r. For Jongstall see Geyl, *Orange and Stuart*, p. 181.

cause all those jarrings and at bottom the reason is, because they fear least at last something of the Prince of Orange should be started."[42]

George Downing's spectacular capture of the regicides Corbet, Okey, and Barkstead convinced many observers that the English and Dutch were about to conclude a treaty. "I think this will advance the treaty," the experienced diplomat de Wicquefort informed Joseph Williamson. Henry Appleton, the former Rump naval captain and current political exile, feared "that in all probability it may be a means to incline the king ... to embrace a treaty of peace with them." Clarendon even told the Dutch ambassadors that the news of the capture was "so exceedingly well received by the king" that he was sure "all things would be consented to."[43] But all of this was quite premature. Far from aiding Downing in his quest to capture the regicides, the Dutch had done all they could to make his task difficult. The *vroedschap* of Amsterdam advised that the gatekeeper of Delft open the gates to let the regicides escape. In the end the States of Holland took "pains" "to satisfy malcontents ... that the rendition of those three persons was a singular case."[44]

This reality soon damped any hopes of a quick treaty. Wicquefort quickly heard that the English were making new difficulties in the treaty. "From one day to the next we are put in greater despair of being able to bring the treaty to a conclusion," wrote the Dutch ambassadors in early June. More ominously rumors began to circulate that Dunkirk pirates were acting on English orders in attacking Dutch ships. And by the end of June Charles II had armed twenty men-of-war.[45] On both sides of the North Sea, things began to look like war. "There are so many things between the crown and the states to cause friction," wrote the Venetian ambassador Giavarina to the Doge and Senate, "that in the end they will come to a rupture." Clarendon reported in June that in England there were "stronger inclinations to a war with them than in reason there ought to be." "The business

42 Downing to Clarendon, 29 August 1662, Bod., Clar. 77, f. 315.

43 Wicquefort to Williamson, 23 February/5 March 1662, PRO, SP 84/165, f. 105; Henry Appleton to Mr. Green at Leiden, July 1662, Bod., Rawl. Letters 61 (Appleton Letterbook), f. 9r; Clarendon to Downing, 28 March 1662, Bod., Clar. 104, f. 52r; Grimani to Doge and Senate, 15/25 April 1662, *CSPV*, p. 134; Dutch Ambassadors to States General, 24 March 1662, Bod., Clar. 106, f. 161r; Dutch Ambassadors to Greffier, 7/17 April 1662, PRO, SP 84/165, f. 165v; Wicquefort to Williamson, 2/12 April 1662, PRO, SP 84/165, f. 179r.

44 Downing to Clarendon, 13 March 1662, Bod., Clar. 106, f. 133r; Downing to Clarendon, 14 March 1662, Bod., Clar. 106, ff. 137v–138r; Downing to Clarendon, 21 March 1662, Bod., Clar. 106, ff. 152v–153r; Letter to Edward Nicholas, 21 March 1662, BL, Egerton MSS 2538, f. 41r.

45 Wicquefort to Williamson, 26 April 1662, PRO, SP 84/165, f. 192r; Dutch Ambassadors to States General, 5/15 May 1662, PRO, SP 84/165, f. 209r; Dutch Ambassadors to States General, 12/22 June 1662, PRO, SP 84/165, f. 325v (my translation); Dutch Ambassadors to States General, 5/15 May 1662, PRO, SP 84/165, f. 209v; Clarendon to Downing, 27 June 1662, Bod., Clar. 104, f. 75; Grimani to Doge and Senate, 18/28 July 1662, *CSPV*, p. 167.

between us and the States of Holland are variously reported," the Anglican Royalist merchant Sir George Smith informed his friend Sir George Oxenden; "wise men are of opinion that it rather savors tending to war than peace." "It is supposed that after all this time spent," the East India Company warned Oxenden in his official capacity as President of Surat, "it may break off without a settlement." The East India Company was in fact quite well informed. "I was warmer with [the Dutch ambassadors] than ever I was before in my life," Clarendon bragged to Downing in August 1662. Aitzema recorded that the ambassadors "were like to depart *re infecta*."[46]

The Anglo-Dutch war which was about to break out in the summer of 1662 was to be fought primarily over the position of the Prince of Orange within the Dutch polity, an issue which represented the English Restoration regime's hatred of republicanism. It was Downing's insistence on promoting the Orangist cause, rather than his determined defense of English economic interests, which made progress in the treaty so difficult. A Dutch proverb held "that if the devil reigned in England, they must keep fair." Yet now, an Orangist member of the States General told Downing, "every little difference is so great that they must rather break than come to any temperament about it." The reason, he said, "is plain, to wit the business of the Prince of Orange."[47]

46 Giavarina to Doge and Senate, 25 April/5 May 1662, *CSPV*, pp. 137–138; Giavarina to Doge and Senate, 20/30 June 1662, *CSPV*, p. 158; Clarendon to Downing, 6 June 1662, Bod., Clar. 104, f. 69v; Sir Henry Bennet, "Navigation of the United Provinces," 1662, PRO, SP 84/166, ff. 217–225; Sir George Smith to Sir George Oxenden, 25 August 1662, BL, Add. 40711, f. 1r; East India Company to president and Council of Surat, 25 August 1662, IOL, E/3/86, f. 81r; Clarendon to Downing, 8 August 1662, Bod., Clar. 104, f. 89; Aitzema, "Selections," Bod., Rawl. C734, f. 96r.

47 Downing to Clarendon, 26 July/5August 1661, Bod., Clar. 104, f. 222.

13

The Anglo-Dutch treaty of 1662

Despite the predictions of all the international pundits, no Anglo-Dutch war did break out in the summer of 1662. What explains this tremendous change of events? In order to answer that question it is necessary to examine English domestic politics.

The Restoration, even if it was not a complete return to the pre-Civil War polity, was a victory for the Anglican Royalists. Republicans, religious radicals, and even some Cromwellians were quite dissatisfied with the new regime. But the discussion and ultimate passage in May 1662 of the Act of Uniformity deeply offended the sensibilities of the Presbyterians who considered themselves responsible for the triumphant return of Charles II.[1] The strict requirements of the Act of Uniformity made it impossible for even the more moderate of Presbyterian clergymen to remain within the Established Church. For many it must have seemed as if the ideological and religious divisions of the late 1630s and 1640s had been recreated.

Not surprisingly the movement of the Bill for Uniformity through the Houses of Parliament began to rekindle old fears. The Essex minister Ralph Josselin "heard many strange passages visional and prophetical of alterations in England." The passage of the Act forced Independents, Presbyterians, and sectaries to shelve the differences which had dominated the politics of the 1640s and 1650s. "Three or four societies that for this 12 years or more could scarcely give each other a good word now upon publishing of the Act of Uniformity are all united," warned the government informant William Williamson, "there will be some villainy designed or else they lost their old orders." Secretary Nicholas was warned "that the people will fall into a grand mutiny." By July rumors had reached Dunkirk "of a late design in England of 7,000 malcontents listed and ready to take arms." "Our discourse of the discontents that are abroad and by reason of the

1 The best discussion of the ideological context of the passage of the Act of Uniformity is that provided by Paul Seaward, *The Cavalier Parliament and the Reconstruction of the Old Regime 1661–1667* (Cambridge, 1989), pp. 56–70, 171–182.

Presbyters," Samuel Pepys confided in his diary, "God preserve us, for all these things bode very ill."[2]

Reports poured in from all over the country of discontents, murmurings and plots. Lord Fauconberg claimed that in Lancashire "not one man in the whole county intends to conform." The situation was similar in Yorkshire and in the West Country. Naturally fears were greatest in London where fanatics were said to have infiltrated the magistracy, and a variety of Dissenting congregations were known to have prayed for Vane and Lambert during their trial. When the celebrated Presbyterian divine Zachary Crofton preached after being freed from prison, "his hearers crowded so hard that they could scarcely fetch their breaths at the doors they were so numerous."[3] Broadsheets, pamphlets, and ballads were distributed in London and elsewhere proclaiming the revival of the Good Old Cause. "The time's but short, for he that lives to see / This Babel fall, shall find in Sixty Three / A Curtain drawn, by which he soon shall know, / It's near the ending of this Poppet-show," predicted one popular poem. The Earl of Northampton, after having a few leaflets dropped on his doorstep, was convinced that the Presbyterian party was committed to"monarchy's eternal destruction and the Church's fall."[4] "The disconcerted and fanatic party speak broad treason and say with much boldness that their deliverance is at hand," Dean Guy Carleton warned Joseph Williamson; "doubtless (if some course be not taken to disarm them) they will be up in rebellion very suddenly." Sir Hugh Smith could not but conclude "that there is a general design of the disturbing the peace of the nation." Significantly secretary Nicholas, after sifting through the variety of reports, submitted a memorandum which concluded that there were "dangerous designs for a rising to kill the king, seize the Tower and Windsor Castle."[5]

Naturally many of the fears focused around the ejection of the ministers

2 Josselin, *Diary*, 11 May 1662, p. 489; William Williamson to Sir William Compton, 1 June 1662, PRO, SP 29/56/1; Mr. Baskerville to Nicholas, 3 June 1662, PRO, SP 29/56/17; Lord Rutherford to Nicholas, 8 July 1662, PRO, SP 29/57/33; Pepys, *Diary*, Vol. III, 31 August 1662, p. 183.

3 Lord Fauconberg to Nicholas, 16 July 1662, PRO, SP 29/57/70; John Mascall to Archbishop of York, 16 April 1662, Bod., Clar. 76, f. 148r; examination of John Hugill (Yorkshire), 14 July 1662, PRO, SP 29/57/70 I; C. P. to Nicholas, 16 July 1662, PRO, SP 29/57/72; T. Rugge, July 1662, "Mercurius Politicus Redivivus," BL, Add. MSS 10117, f. 38v; Osbert Peck to Mr. Garrett, 2 June 1662, PRO, SP 29/56/8; William Williamson to Nicholas, 27 March 1662, BL, Egerton MSS 2537, f. 335r.

4 *The Wheel of Time Turning Round to the Good Old Way; Or The Good Old Cause Vindicated* [24 March 1662]. This broadside proclaimed that those "who did defend the Good Old Cause" would soon herald a new "day of Liberty." Northampton to Charles II, 18 August 1662, Bod., Clar. 77, f. 236v. For distribution of the pamphlets in London see T. Rugge, "Mercurius Politicus Redivivus," October 1662, BL, Add. MSS 10117, f. 50v; Giavarina to Doge and Senate, 12/22 September 1662, *CSPV*, pp. 190–191.

5 Dean Guy Carleton of Carlisle to Williamson, 27 August 1662, PRO, SP 29/58/83; Sir Hugh Smith to Nicholas, 12 July 1662, PRO, SP 29/57/42; memorandum of Sir Edward Nicholas, 21 August 1662, *CSPD*, pp. 464–465 (original in shorthand).

who refused to conform to the Act of Uniformity. Despite official claims that Londoners showed little affection for their ejected ministers, many observers found grounds for concern. "Sunday last there was great tumults in several churches in London by reason of the Episcopal ministers bringing in of the liturgy," wrote the sympathetic Dutch ambassadors. The Venetian ambassador described an instance "when the congregation mutinied, dragged the minister from the pulpit, tore his priest's robes, and pulled to pieces the books of common prayer, singing indecent and derisory songs instead." Even an Anglican Royalist newsletter sent to the Duke of Ormonde admitted that the "factious inveterate incendiaries" succeeded in provoking "some disturbance."[6] It was commonly believed that all of this activity was merely the prelude to a horrible plot. "For certain, some plot there hath been," reflected Samuel Pepys in October, "though not brought to a head." Thomas Rugge also thought there had been "a plot intended against the person of the king's Majesty and the Duke of York and the Duke of Albemarle and some other person of quality."[7]

Many people made ominous comparisons to 1642. "There have been some heats this week in the Lords House as great as ever were in 41, 42 or 43," wrote William Morrice describing the passage of the Uniformity Bill. Developments were not more reassuring outside Parliament. "The Presbyterian party sets up meetings, appointeth days of fasting and possesseth the people that now persecution is approaching and profaneness and idolatry is coming in like a flood," William Williamson told Edward Nicholas, "they walk in the very same way as they did in the first war against his Sacred Majesty of Blessed Memory." The Venetian ambassador thought that those "who caused the past disorders" desired "nothing more eagerly than to see them again." Clarendon, who had warned against the "danger to which this country has recently been exposed of relapsing into past infirmities" in January, could only be reassured by military calculations in the summer of 62. The Presbyterians could not now "begin a war with any great assurance," George Morley Bishop of Winchester told his fearful friend Clarendon, because they don't have "now the advantages they had formerly, when they had a Parliament, the navy, all the magazines of arms, and the strongest garrisons in the kingdom, together with the unanimous assistance of all Scotland, and the militia of London." Edward Phelips reported from the West Country "how pregnant the ill humors that lately disturbed this kingdom do still abound amongst us." The Dutch ambas-

6 Dutch Ambassadors to States General, 29 August/8 September 1662, Bod., Clar. 77, f. 310v; Giavarina to Doge and Senate, 29 August/8 September 1662, *CSPV*, p. 185; newsletter from London, 26 August 1662, Carte 222, f. 2r; John Stanyon to George Oxenden, 25 August 1662, BL, Add. MSS 40711, f. 1v; T. Rugge, "Mercurius Politicus Redivivus," 24 August 1662 BL, Add.. MSS 10117, f. 43v.

7 Pepys, *Diary*, Vol. III, 31 October 1662, p. 245; T. Rugge, "Mercurius Politicus Redivivus," October 1662, BL, Add. MSS 10117, f. 54v.

sador Beeverweert told his republican friends in Holland that he thought "the people would soon chase his Majesty of Great Britain out of England."[8]

Did the makers of policy feel there was a real threat to the regime? Although it is certainly true that Restoration politicians were not averse to employing agents provacateurs or to deploying fears of plots for political ends, there can be no doubt that the rumors of the summer of 1662 were taken very seriously indeed. William Coventry, the Duke of York's secretary, told Samuel Pepys on 3 September "how the fanatics and the Presbyters that did intend to rise about this time did choose this day as the most auspicious to them in their endeavors against monarchy – it being fatal twice to the king." "Without all doubt," wrote the well-connected Daniel O'Neill to Ormonde, "there is a great and considerable part of this kingdom that retain their malice and watch only their opportunity." "We are now again alarmed with intelligence of risings intended betwixt this and Christmas," Sir Henry Bennet averred, "against which I hope all fitting provisions are made." It was with relief that Charles II informed his sister in November that "I believe for this time their designs are broken." Common gossip was full of the court's fears. The Act of Uniformity, thought the Venetian ambassador, causes "the court to fear fresh insurrections and that they may originate in London." The Earl of Sandwich informed Pepys of "the jealousies that the court hath of people's rising." "There is a real design," opined secretary Nicholas in his shorthand summary of the information flowing into his office.[9]

The seriousness with which the government took the reports of plottings deeply affected domestic policies. "There being too much reason to believe that there is at present a design amongst persons of desperate principles to make some sudden insurrections," the lieutenants and deputy lieutenants of the counties were told in July that they "cannot be too vigilant and watchful upon all those who are publicly taken notice of and known to be of the Republic party." Town walls were dismantled in Northampton, Gloucester,

8 William Morrice to Downing, 21 March 1662, BL, Add. MSS 22919, f. 203r; William Williamson to Nicholas, 19 March 1662, BL, Egerton MSS 2537, f. 331r; William Williamson to Nicholas, 27 March 1662, BL, Egerton MSS 2537, f. 335r; Giavarina to Doge and Senate, 27 December 1661/6 January 1662, *CSPV*, p. 91; Giavarina to Doge and Senate, 11/21 April 1662, *CSPV*, p. 133; Morley to Clarendon, 3 September 1662, Bod., Clar. 77, f. 340r; Nicholas Buckeridge to George Oxenden, 13 January 1663, BL, Add. 40711, f. 5r; E. Phelips to Nicholas, 7 July 1662, PRO, SP 29/57/25; De Bacquoy/Van Ruyven to Williamson, 5/15 July 1662, PRO, SP 84/166, f. 41r (my translation).

9 Pepys, *Diary*, Vol. III, 3 September 1662, p. 186; Pepys, *Diary*, Vol. III, 27 October 1662, p. 237; O'Neill to Ormonde, 13 September 1662, Carte 32, f. 25r; Bennet to Ormonde, 11 October 1662, Carte 46, f. 8r; Charles II to Henriette-Anne, 4 November 1662, in Cyril H. Hartmann, *Charles II and Madame* (London, 1934), p. 60; Giavarina to Doge and Senate, 4/14 July 1662, *CSPV*, p. 161; De Bacquoy/Van Ruyven to Williamson, 19/29 October 1662, PRO, SP 84/166, f. 180v; shorthand notes by Secretary Nicholas, 11 June 1662, *CSPD*, p. 404.

and Coventry and corporations were purged throughout England to make sure that any dissenting insurrection would not begin from a position of strength. Indeed John Miller has pointed out that "the purges of corporations in 1662–3 were far more systematic and extensive than the more piecemeal changes of the 1640s and 1650s."[10]

It was in this political context – a context in which Clarendon and other Royalists must have felt their first priority was to ensure the safety of the regime – that Clarendon and Downing were negotiating with the Dutch in the summer of 1662.[11] "His Majesty thinks that it is best to put a conclusion to [the treaty] without delay," Clarendon wrote to Downing in early August. The reasons for Charles's insistence were not hard to find. "If an open rupture results," the Venetian ambassador observed, "there is good reason to fear that they will get the worst of it here, because the malcontents at home are constantly increasing, especially the Presbyterians who are only waiting for a suitable opportunity to give vent to their evil intentions." A Middleburgh burgomaster told the double agent Joseph Bampfield that "he believed the king's want of money and the disorders in England would keep him in peace with those countries." Clarendon thought that mere rumor of war "encourages all seditious humors here and discourages all trade." Downing also felt that a war at this juncture would benefit "all unsettled and discontented humors at home." Even the Orangist Van Ruyven admitted that "the present times are not favorable" for a war to include the Prince of Orange.[12] By contrast, an Anglo-Dutch peace would very much

10 "Instructions to Lieutenants and Deputy Lieutenants of Counties," 17 July 1662, PRO, SP 29/57/74; News from London, 10 August 1662, PRO, SP 84/166, f. 214r; Giavarina to Doge and Senate, 25 July/4 August 1662, *CSPV*, pp. 169–170; Giavarina to Doge and Senate, 15/25 August 1662, *CSPV*, p. 180; T. Rugge, "Mercurius Politicus Redivivus," 8 August 1662, BL, Add. 10117, f. 42v; Northampton to Charles II, 18 August 1662, Bod., Clar. 77, f. 236r; Lord Brereton to Lord Norwich, 9 September 1662, Bod., Clar. 77, f. 380; Dutch Ambassadors to States General, 5/15 September 1662, Bod., Clar. 77, f. 345r; Downing to Clarendon, 22 August 1662, Bod., Clar. 77, f. 267v; John Miller, "The Crown and the Borough Charters in the Reign of Charles II," in *English Historical Review* Vol. 100 (1985), pp. 62–63.

11 It is always difficult to determine who was making policy at the Restoration court. But in this case it seems likely that Albemarle, York, Clarendon, and Southampton were the advisors consulted by Charles II. York is known to have advised war. Albemarle, though no friend to the Dutch, was very conscious of the need to put down rebellion at home. He was said to have been instrumental in promoting the sale of Dunkirk "because the king promised that the money which was to be taken for it should not be touched by him, but should be kept in the Tower for an extraordinary occasion that might fall in." Burnet's "History," BL, Add. 63057A, f. 90r. Southampton later opposed the war, and knew better than anyone the poverty of the king's finances. Clarendon was clearly the most influential politician in 1662, and it is his advice which appears to have been listened to. W. D. Macray (editor) *Notes Which passed at Meetings of the Privy Council* (London, 1896), August 1662, p. 71 reveals that Clarendon, York, Southampton, and Albemarle were those let in on the Dunkirk negotiations. Given the proximity in time, I think it is a safe guess that they advised on Dutch affairs as well. William Morrice to Downing, 4 July 1662, BL, Add. 22919, f. 234r reveals differences in the Privy Council.

12 Clarendon to Downing, 8 August 1662, Bod., Clar. 104, f. 88; Giavarina to Doge and

increase the strength of the regime at home. If England "were without a foreign enemy," Clarendon told Charles II in the summer of 1662, "[the king] would be able to preserve himself against the factions and distempers in his own kingdom." In July, just at the time when Clarendon's fears of a rebellion were reaching a peak, the Lord Chancellor told George Downing that a peace "will give the great blow to all the seditious purposes now on foot, and give a new life to trade which is very dead." Several months later, upon hearing that the treaty was finally signed, Downing claimed that "a breathing [was] given to his [Majesty's] revenue and quashing to discontented turbulent humors."[13] The hope, clearly, was that peace with the Dutch would improve customs revenues and free up money to be used against the rebels at home.

It was also a desire to strengthen the government's hand at home which lay behind the decision to sell Dunkirk to France. Clarendon was well aware that the sale "would be as ungracious and unpopular an act to the whole world, as can be put in practice."[14] The Venetian ambassador thought that only the poverty of the crown would prompt the English to consider "a course to which in other circumstances they would not descend." The huge sum spent to maintain Dunkirk "would be far better spent at home," argued James Howell in his officially sponsored pamphlet *A Discourse of Dunkirk*, "to maintain a military actual strength for security of prince and people against any civil insurrection." "The little revenue his Majesty hath kept out of the sale of Dunkirk," Bennet later informed Ormonde, "being not to be touched for a less occasion than an insurrection here at home." When Louis XIV complained that Charles II did not use the money from the sale to aid the Portuguese against Spain, the English responded that the money had always been intended "for the suppression of any sudden insurrection in England, which was at that time apprehended."[15]

Senate, 15/25 August 1662, *CSPV*, p. 189; Giavarina to Doge and Senate, 8/18 August 1662, *CSPV*, p. 174; Bampfield to Williamson, 4/14 December 1662, PRO, SP 84/168, f. 166v; Clarendon to Downing, 20 June 1662, Bod., Clar. 104, f. 73r; Downing to Clarendon, 27 June 1662, Bod., Clar. 106, f. 175v; De Bacquoy/Van Ruyven to Williamson, 28 June/8 July 1662, PRO, SP 84/166, f. 31v.

13 Edward Hyde, *The Life of Edward Earl of Clarendon* (Dublin, 1760), pp. 95–96; Clarendon to Downing, 29 August 1662, Bod., Clar. 104, f. 90; Clarendon to Downing, 25 July 1662, Bod., Clar. 104, f. 84v; Downing to Clarendon, 5 September 1662, Bod., Clar. 77, f. 351v.

14 Clarendon to D'Estrades, 9 August 1662, Bod., Clar. 80, f. 147r. It should be noted that Downing was violently opposed to the sale of Dunkirk: Downing to Nicholas, 26 September/6 October 1662, PRO, SP 84/166, f. 154; Downing to Clarendon, 26 September 1662, Bod., Clar. 78, f. 9. This should put to rest claims that he was a mere timeserver. In fact, from the moment that Louis XIV deserted the cause of the Prince of Orange, Downing was violently anti-French – he seemed to begin to fear French pretensions to universal monarchy.

15 Giavarina to the Doge and Senate, 3/13 October 1662, *CSPV*, p. 195; T. Rugge, "Mercurius Politicus Redivivus," 18 November 1662, BL, Add. 10117, f. 56r; [James

On 4 September, then, fearing rebellion at home and desiring peace abroad, the English agreed to sign a treaty of alliance with the Dutch. Although an Anglican Royalist newsletter claimed that "the Dutch ambassadors have struck sail and yielded," the terms of the treaty reflect compromise rather than diplomatic victory. Most importantly nothing was done for the Prince of Orange, nothing was done about the one issue that had for so long prevented agreement. It is true, of course, that the two ships *Bona Esperanza* and *Bon Aventura* were left to be adjudicated separately, but the balance of the treaty did resolve all outstanding economic differences. English claims were to be considered by an international board of commissioners, but the claims to be considered were to go back only to 1659 – not 1654 as the English had demanded. Dutch fishing rights were guaranteed, while the Dutch agreed to recognize Charles II's sovereignty over the British seas.[16] Significantly there is little evidence that the merchant community was unhappy with the terms of the treaty. We can "now hope our affairs in India will be carried on by you," wrote the governor of the East India Company governor of the East India Company Thomas Chamberlain to his factory at Surat, "without receiving any disturbance from the Dutch."[17]

It is true, as historians have pointed out, that many contemporaries felt "that in spite of this accommodation it will not be long before there is an open rupture." This peace was, after all, a peace of convenience. But the outstanding issue was not economic but ideological. It was the issue of the Prince of Orange not means of economic arbitration which was left out of the treaty. Since De Witt knew that Charles II neglected to act in the interests of his nephew only out of fear, "still retaining a jealousy that one time or another he will do it," Downing correctly predicted, the republicans "will continue to do the king all imaginable mischief." "There is nothing the seditious and discontented people do so much fear as a peace with Holland, to the country from which they promised themselves infinite advantages,"

Howell], *A Discourse of Dunkirk* (London, 1664), p. 7; Bennet to Ormonde, 23 December 1662, Carte 46, f. 23v; "Memorial to Louis XIV," January 1663, Bod., Clar. 79, ff. 33v–34r; Edmund Ludlow, "A Voyce from the Watchtower," Bod. English History MSS 387, pp. 936–937; "Notes Concerning Dunkirk," 1662, Bod., Clar. 78, f. 216r; "The Dunkirk Money How Dispensed," Bod., Clar. 78, f. 215.

16 Newsletter to Ormonde, 2 September 1662, Carte 32, f. 3v; Giavarina to the Doge and Senate, 5/15 September 1662, *CSPV*, p. 187; Clarendon to Downing, 5 September 1662, Bod., Clar. 104, f. 92r; Dutch Ambassadors to States General, 5/15 September 1662, PRO, SP 84/166, f. 113; Aitzema "Selections," Bod., Rawl. C734, f. 96v; Charles H. Wilson, *Profit and Power* (London, 1957), p. 109.

17 Thomas Chamberlain to President and Council of Surat, 25 September 1662, IOL E/3/86, f. 82v; George Smith to George Oxenden, 26 March 1663, BL, Add. 40711, f. 28v; John Stanion to George Oxenden, 6 April 1663, BL, Add. 40711, f. 9v. This is not to say that there was no anti-Dutch feeling in the merchant community, but rather that little of it stemmed from dissatisfaction with the treaty. I argue below that a segment of the merchant community was anti-Dutch for ideological reasons.

Clarendon proclaimed, "and we may after 2 or 3 years settling at home, be in the better position to do what we find fit." Charles and James left no doubt what it was they wished to do. As the Dutch ambassadors took their formal leave they were told that "there could be nothing more agreeable to his Majesty" than to restore the Prince of Orange.[18]

[18] Keith Feiling, p. 97; Herbert H. Rowen, *John De Witt, Grand Pensionary of Holland, 1625–1675* (Princeton, 1978) p. 542; Giavarina to Doge and Senate, 12/22 September 1662, *CSPV*, p. 193; Downing to Clarendon, 6/16 September 1661, Bod., Clar. 105, f. 36v; Clarendon to Downing, 16 August 1661, Bod., Clar. 104, ff. 230v–231r; Clarendon to Downing, 30 August 1661, Bod., Clar. 104, f. 81; De Bacquoy/Van Ruyven to Williamson, 19/29 September 1662, PRO, SP 84/166, ff. 147v–148r (my translation).

14

The Northern Rebellion and the reestablishment of Anglican Royalist consensus

Despite the uneasy peace of 1662, less than three years later English and Dutch navies would be fighting on the coast of Africa, the Mediterranean, and ultimately in the Channel. Why did this happen? Why had a government which in 1662 feared for its very existence, opted so quickly to test itself in the field of international conflict? Much of the answer lies in the changing domestic political scene.

Although no great rising had materialized in 1662, the government did not emerge unscathed from the political maneuvers of 1662. The government, including the Earl of Clarendon as Charles's chief minister, was attacked for corruption. Clarendon was accused of having sold Dunkirk for personal profit, of having married Charles to a barren Portuguese princess to ensure the succession of his daughter Anne's children by the Duke of York, and having taken bribes variously from France, the United Provinces, and Portugal.

Parliament, in the session of 1663, demonstrated a temper far different from that of the previous year. Factional strife rather than the ordered implementation of government legislation was the business of both houses. Sir Philip Warwick observed to Pepys "how obedient this Parliament was for a while; and the last sitting, how they begun to differ and to carp at the king's officers." "Most of my time is taken up with the business of the Parliament in getting them to do what is best for us all," Charles complained to his sister, "and keeping them from doing what they ought not to do." "We are following into the courses of the old Long Parliament with a much swifter pace than that did," O'Neill wrote to Ormonde; "our purest Cavaliers are more troublesome and malicious inspectors into the king's and his ministers behavior than ever Hampden or Pym were." "The people who not long since roasted the Rump and burnt the arms of the Commonwealth in the bonfires which they made for joy of Charles Steward's return," Ludlow declared triumphantly, "would now willingly learn Hebrew and ring the bells backward."[1]

1 Pepys, *Diary*, Vol. V, 22 November 1664, pp. 327–328; Charles II to Henriette-Anne, 11 May 1663, Cyril H. Hartmann, *Charles II and Madame* (London, 1934), p. 74; O'Neill to

The failure of a Presbyterian plot to materialize in 1662 made the government's claims seem incredible and the threat from Dissent less significant. Consequently some members of Parliament began to explain the country's malaise with the revival of Popery. Sir Richard Everard acquainted a committee of the House of Commons "with the confidence the Popish party were grown to in that they caused the mass book to be printed in England and exposed their Popish trumperies." One newsletter reported that "the principal debate of the House was concerning the prevention of the growth of Popery." My French sources "tell me," the Catholic Sir Richard Bellings wrote to Clarendon's son Cornbury, "your fellow commoners fall so severely upon Catholics that I must expect to be persecuted when I come to England."[2] Indeed it is possible that the celebrated Parliamentary confrontation between Bristol and Clarendon in the summer of 1663 was over conflicting definitions of Popery. "I am of the Church of Rome, not of its court," Bristol claimed, and "should be the first to draw my sword to oppose the Pope's reducing England to his See." He implied that Clarendon was a Papist of the other sort. Significantly, when the Clarendonians began their counterattack, they tried to reassert the Popery of rebellion. One of Bristol's supporters, Sir Richard Temple, for example, was "taxed for a Protectorian."[3] Perhaps the passage of the Irish Cattle Bill in the same session was an attempt to find an anti-Papist remedy to the country's economic woes. In any case, there can be no doubt that the temper of Parliament and nation in 1663 was less enthusiastic about the Restored Monarchy than it had been the previous two years.

The revelation of the attempt on Dublin Castle in the summer of 1663 caused many magistrates to inquire more closely into the depth of discontent in their own areas. The results were hardly encouraging. "I may say we are here rather in a great silence than peaceable," John Trelawney wrote from the West Country, "many words drop full of discontent." Similar nervous reports poured into the offices of the secretaries of state from all

Ormonde, 20 June 1663, Carte 32, f. 597; O'Neill to Ormonde, 15 May 1663, Carte 32, f. 405v; Ludlow, "A Voyce," Bod., English History MSS C487, f. 976. "I have heard from knowing persons," Ludlow also claimed, "that the three nations are now so sick of that which they so earnestly longed for; that the court cannot trust any other parliament, and that 'tis more than probable if it should be put to a new election, there would be none chosen but Commonwealth men for their representatives." (f. 962).

2 Ludlow, "A Voyce," Bod., English History MSS C487, pp. 955–956; newsletter to Ormonde, 22 May 1663, Carte 222, f. 12r; Sir Richard Bellings to Cornbury, 22 April/2 May 1663, Bod., Clar. 79, f. 172; O'Neill to Ormonde, 11 July 1663, Carte 32, f. 709r.

3 Earl of Salisbury to Earl of Huntingdon, 13 July 1663, Carte 77, f. 524r; Sir Roger Burgoyne to Sir Ralph Verney, 22 June 1663, BL, Microfilm M636/19; newsletter to Ormonde, 1 July 1663, Carte 72, ff. 20v–21r; Ludlow, "A Voyce," Bod., English History MSS C487, pp. 963, 969; "Articles of Treason against Clarendon," 10 July 1663, Carte 72, f. 22. Significantly, the Countess of Castlemaine, who had already converted to Catholicism, was also well known to be a patroness of Dissenting ministers. Cf. newsletter to Ormonde, 2 September 1662, Carte 32, f. 3.

over the country. Indeed so confident was Algernon Sidney of "the approaching of our deliverance," he thought "it seasonable to draw towards his native country."[4]

In early October pamphlets were distributed, ballads sung, and sermons preached criticizing the Restoration regime. "There was seized in the press a libel" which claimed "that the people may put their king to death and that the law of God excepts the king no more than any other person." Ralph Josselin confided to his diary that "strange libels [are] cast about in London against the king." Ludlow knew of many books "published to show the evil government of Charles Steward, yea even of monarchy itself as Antichristian." "The old king deserved to be beheaded," proclaimed Bulstrode Whitelocke's former housemate George Cockayne, and "why should [Charles II] not be beheaded as well as another." "They begin afresh to lurk and creep in the night into corners to preach up rebellion as they did at the first rebellion under a pretence of religion," wrote the ever-vigilant John Carlisle from Dover of the Dissenting ministers. Dissenting letters compared the reign of Charles II to that of Tiberius. "The Fanatiques" sneered Roger L'Estrange in his *Intelligencer*, "are observ'd of late to be very busy with their prodigies and prophecies ... of a most pernicious and dangerous influence upon the common people." All of this "doth not a little contribute to confirm the jealousies of an insurrection," commented one newsletter-writer, for the "usual method is to go accompanied with a treasonable libel."[5]

All of these dire predictions were soon borne out. In early October, upon reception of reports of "an intended general rebellion," magistrates from several northern counties began rounding up suspects. The plot, Thomas Gower explained to Sir Henry Bennet, "appears to have been deeply laid, secretly carried out and mischievously intended." The examinations of the plotters soon made clear, as one newsletter-writer explained, "that there were men of great estate concerned with it and a bank of money about London and that their numbers much increased in the south." Although the pretence of the rebellion "was to force his Majesty to perform his promise at

4 For Ireland: Edward Harley to Lady Harley, 2 June 1663, BL, Loan MSS 29/180, f. 19r; Angelsey to Clarendon, 24 May 1663, Bod., Clar. 79, f. 251r. Trelawney to Williamson, 2 October 1663, PRO, SP 29/81/8; Alan Lloyd to Ormonde, 2 October 1663, Carte 33, f. 168r; Thomas Bridges to Bennet, 5 October 1663, PRO, SP 29/81/16; Ludlow, "A Voyce," Bod., English History MSS C487, p. 977.

5 T. Rugge, "Mercurius Politicus Redivivus," October 1663, BL Add. 10117, f. 79r; Josselin, *Diary*, 11 October 1663, p. 501; Ludlow, "A Voyce," Bod., English History MSS C487, p. 1013; "Information of Matthew Morgan of Carrington," 23 January 1664, PRO, SP 29/91/22; "An Account of Conventicles in London," August 1664, PRO, SP 29/101/102; anonymous letter, 2 December 1663, PRO, SP 29/85/15; Walter Slingsby to Henry Muddiman, 8 November 1663, PRO, SP 29/83/53; Bennet to Ormonde, 17 October 1663, Carte 46, f. 98v; , 12 October 1663, p. 54; John Carlisle to Williamson, 28 December 1663, PRO, SP 29/86/71; newsletter, 17 October 1663, Carte 72, f. 38v.

Breda," Captain Robert Atkinson testified that "the true intent [was] to destroy the government, to restore a Gospel magistracy and ministry according to their interpretation."[6]

The secretaries were soon inundated with reports from all over England of a planned rising. In Chichester a group of dissenters "took out the surplice in derision, put it on a bay whom they called Pope, whilst others kicked the common prayer book about the church." Rumors reached Richmond on 12 October that "there would be a general rising of the Fanatiques." The fanatics are "grown higher than ever since his Majesty came into England," wrote Walter Slingsby from the Isle of Wight, "and the Presbyterians more troublesome." In the Midlands there were said to be 5,000 men "in readiness," made up of "Presbytery, Independency and Anabaptism all leavened with the destructive and rebellious spirit of fifth monarchy." In London, one Anglican wrote "we are all in a sad condition ... expecting every night to have our throats cut by the Presbyterians."[7] The conclusion was plain to Anglican Royalists: a general rebellion had been planned. "Few places have been free from the symptoms of rebellion," reported one newsletter. One of the Northern plotters who escaped told Bennet's spy Edward Riggs that "had they not been betrayed [they] had fully accomplished and brought to pass their old cause: a design all over England." The plot "having been so universal throughout the whole kingdom," Thomas Dolman told Henry Coventry, that "were they prosperous [they] would confound all laws Divine and human, in short would destroy king, government, nobility and gentry." Sir Richard Ford, at once the hammer of dissent and the Dutch, heard from an informant "that we should very suddenly see very great alterations in all the three

6 T. T. to Henry Muddiman, 5 October 1663, PRO, SP 29/81/17; Colonel John Frescheville to Richard Frescheville, 12 October 1663, PRO, SP 29/81/66; "Duke of Buckingham's Intelligence from York," 6 October 1663, PRO, SP 29/81/29; Thomas Gower to Bennet, 23 October 1663, PRO, SP 29/82/47; Josselin, *Diary*, 1 November 1663, p. 502; Josselin, *Diary*, 12 November 1663, p. 502; newsletter to Ormonde, 14 November 1663, Carte 222, f. 43; "Information of Captain Robert Atkinson," 26 November 1663, PRO, SP 29/84/64. The best discussion of the Northern Rebellion currently available is in Robert L. Greaves, *Deliver Us From Evil* (Oxford, 1986).

7 John Hetherington to Williamson, 10 October 1663, PRO, SP 29/81/56; newsletter to Ormonde, received 13 October 1663, Carte 222, f. 34r; *Intelligencer*, 19 October 1663, p. 61 (Preston and Richmond); Walter Slingsby to Muddiman, 8 November 1663, PRO, SP 29/83/53 (Isle of Wight); Sir Philip Musgrave to Williamson, 19 November 1663, PRO, SP 29/84/13 (Hartley Castle); Nathaniel Cole to Williamson, 12 February 1664, PRO, SP 29/92/77 (Bristol); Letter to Nicholas Mosely, 6 February 1664, PRO, SP 29/94/64 (Midlands); Sir Thomas Penyston to Cornbury, 3 January 1664, Bod., Clar. 81, f. 32r (Oxford); Jo. Hetherington to Williamson, 31 December 1663, PRO, SP 29/86/87 (Lewes); Guy Carleton to Sir William Blakestone, 19 December 1663, PRO, SP 29/86/18 (Carlisle); M. Clapham to Mrs. Philipps, 12 October 1663, PRO, SP 29/81/69 (London); Charles II to Commission of Lieutenancy of London Militia, 24 November 1663, PRO, SP 29/84/38 (London).

kingdoms." "That many treasons have been plotted since the king's return into England, how near to a birth a late intended rebellion was, how bloody the design, how generally laid, aiming as well at the sacred person of our gracious sovereign, as a massacre of persons of all qualities whom they knew to be loyal," Dean Guy Carleton eloquently exclaimed, "is a thing so plain, that he that runs may read it even yet in the peremptory carriage and proud language of that party."[8]

After the false alarms of 1662, the government and a large part of the political nation was at first predisposed to be quite skeptical of the revelations. Soon, however, they were persuaded that there had been a real threat to the existence of the regime. When Sir Henry Bennet first received intelligence of the plot, he told Ormonde that "all circumstances make us conclude it a false alarm." But he soon admitted his error, telling Ormonde that "the plot was a real one" and "that it had a conjunction with the disaffected parties of all his Majesty's dominions."[9] "The continual discourse of plots and insurrections had so wearied the king, that he even resolved to give no more countenance to any such informations, nor to trouble himself with inquiry into them," admitted Clarendon, "but when the intelligence was continued from several parts and so particular for the time and place of the rendezvous ... his Majesty thought it time to provide against it." The Duke of York, always alert to any threat of rebellion, knew that "the restless party of the republicans were secretly working to destroy the government." The Duke of Buckingham, acting for the moment as the great magnate of the north, needed little convincing that the Nonconformists "will make some attempt, since the same intelligence is brought to us from so many several hands." Both the Dutch secretary Cuneus and Louis XIV himself concluded that it "was not possible to doubt the veracity of the reports of a great conspiracy." Indeed Pepys had heard that the court was so shaken "that care is taken to lay up a hidden treasure of money by the king against a bad day." So when Charles II told Parliament in March 1664 that the fanatics "are now even in those parts, and at this time, when they see

8 Newsletter, October 1663, Carte 222, f. 4r; Edward Riggs to Bennet, 29 January 1664, PRO, SP 29/91/79; Letter to Lord Wharton, 18 January 1664, Carte 81, f. 197r; De Bacquoy to Williamson, 27 December/6 January 1663/4, PRO, SP 84/169, f. 10v; Thomas Dolman to Henry Coventry, 21 December 1663, Longleat House, Cov. MSS IV, f. 1v; Sir Richard Ford to Clarendon, July 1663, Bod., Clar. 80, f. 43r; Dean Guy Carleton to Sir William Blakestone, 19 December 1663, PRO, SP 29/86/18; Oliver Foulis, *Cabala: Or, The Mystery of Conventicles Unveil'd* (London, 1664), p. 63. Significantly, Ludlow who often castigated the government for manufacturing plots, accepted that the "honest party" expected a rising in the autumn of 1663; Ludlow, "A Voyce," Bod., English History MSS C487, p. 997.

9 Bennet to Ormonde, 6 October 1663, Carte 46, f. 95r; Bennet to Ormonde, 17 October 1663, Carte 46, f. 98; Bennet to Ormonde, 24 October 1663, Carte 46, f. 102r; Bennet to Ormonde, 3 November 1663, Carte 46, f. 108r; Bennet to Ormonde, 24 November 1663, Carte 46, f. 116; Bennet to Ormonde, 12 December 1663, Carte 46, f. 128v; Bennet to Ormonde, 23 January 1664, Carte 46, f. 146v.

their friends under trial and execution still pursuing the same consultations," he was speaking with conviction.[10]

Unlike most historians, contemporaries recognized the Dutch component in the Northern Rebellion.[11] "We meet with too many of that sullen tribe abroad," wrote Joseph Kent from Italy of the Dissenting exodus, "who have still a smack of their ancient rancor against his Majesty." But, it was above all to the United Provinces that the political and religious exiles had fled. "Upon the passing of the Act of Uniformity," Gilbert Burnet recalled, many Dissenters began "talking of going over to Holland." One Scottish minister explained the exodus in Foxeian terms. "Since the king's coming into England," he told Joseph Bampfield, "there has more died in prisons for Non-conformity than were put to death in all Queen Mary's reign."[12] By July 1661 Downing could already marvel at the vast "numbers of people" that "flock out of England into this country." In 1663 Joseph Bampfield reported that "many Presbyterians and Independents, both ministers and others, are come into Holland and into these parts [Zeeland], and daily more expected." Indeed there were several entire congregations which left England for the United Provinces. Even Samuel Pepys's brother-in-law felt that he could live better in Holland.[13]

Those migrating to the United Provinces were not the dregs of society, not men who were unable to find work in England and hence sought employment elsewhere. "All those numbers of people which come daily from England into this country," commented George Downing who had every reason to minimize the significance of the exodus, "are generally handicraft people and merchants who come hither *singly* upon the point of liberty of conscience or upon the account of being against oaths and for the murderers." The skills and resources which these religious and political exiles brought with them were not inconsequential. Downing worried that

10 Edward Hyde, *The Life of Edward Earl of Clarendon* (Dublin, 1760), p. 104; J. S. Clarke (editor), *The Life of James the Second* Vol. I. (London, 1816), p. 396; Duke of Buckingham to Duke of Albemarle, 11 October 1663, PRO, SP 29/81/61; De Bacquoy to Williamson, 1/11 November 1663, PRO, SP 84/168, f. 98r; Louis XIV to Comminges, 10/20 February 1664, PRO, PRO 31/3/113, f. 38; Pepys, *Diary*, Vol. V, 20 January 1664, p. 21; *His Majesties Most Gracious Speech to Both Houses of Parliament on Monday the One and Twentieth of March, 1663/4* (London, 1664), p. 5; Ormonde to Charles II, 2 November 1663, Bod., Clar. 80, f. 245r; Nicholas Buckeridge to George Oxenden, 1 July 1664, BL, Add. 40709, f. 44r (evidence that Anglican Royalist merchants took the plot seriously).

11 Though Greaves has acknowledged the importance of the United Provinces "as a base of operations and refuge." Greaves, *Deliver Us From Evil*, pp. 203–204.

12 Joseph Kent to Joseph Williamson, 26 October 1663, PRO, SP 98/4, f. 265r; Burnet's "History," BL, Add. MSS 63057A, f. 87v; Bampfield to Bennet, 4/14 December 1663, PRO, SP 84/168, f. 168v.

13 Downing to Clarendon, 12/22 July 1661, Bod., Clar. 104, f. 184v; Bampfield to Williamson, 24 July/3 August 1663, PRO, SP 84/167, f. 221r; Bampfield to John Taylor, 7/17 August 1663, PRO, SP 84/167, f. 255r; T. Rugge, "Mercurius Politicus Redivivus," June 1664, BL, Add. MSS 10117, f. 111r; *Newes*, 20 June 1664, p. 394; Pepys, *Diary*, Vol. V, 3 February 1664, p. 37; Pepys, *Diary*, Vol. V, 10 February 1664, p. 44.

some were bringing the secrets of the English woolen trade to Amsterdam, others had managed to buy up the better part of Delft haven, while at least one brought the designs for English men-of-war.[14] Naturally the government found cause for concern. Holland, Clarendon thought, had become "a receptacle for all the seditious and discontented persons." "I find that this country is full of the worst of his Majesty's enemies," Downing concurred, "who daily flock hither out of England." "Prithee tell me truly," sneered Oliver Foulis in his officially sanctioned pamphlet, "is the conventicle broke in England, and must it be made up in Amsterdam!"[15]

George Downing's bombastic letters might have exaggerated the quantity, but certainly not the quality, of the émigrés to the United Provinces. Desborough, Bourne, Joyce, White, and Oliver St. John were all known to have spent time in the Netherlands. Several celebrated ministers of the 1650s had moved themselves and their congregations to Dutch territory, while others like John Lawrence were "employed by the church at Yarmouth into Holland frequently." Rotterdam was a particular haven for the disaffected. It was there that "several of the Old Army live," and enjoyed the services of "an Independent, Anabaptist, and Quaker church, and do hire the best houses." Indeed almost one out of four dangerous persons listed in Joseph Williamson's famous "Spy Book" lived in the United Provinces.[16]

14 Downing to Clarendon, 23 August/2 September 1661, Bod., Clar. 105, f. 18v; Downing to Clarendon, 6/16 September 1661, Bod., Clar. 105, f. 37r; Downing to Clarendon, 1 August 1662, Bod., Clar. 77, f. 134v; Downing to Clarendon, 15 August 1662, Bod., Clar. 104, f. 100r; Downing to Clarendon, 11 December 1663, Bod., Clar. 107, ff. 34v–36r. Naturally some like Henry Appleton felt that they could have "neither liberty nor safety" in the United Provinces while they were officially on good terms with England, but the evidence suggests that this was a minority view. Henry Appleton to daughter and wife, 7 November 1661, Bodl., Rawl. Letters 61, f. 3v.

15 Clarendon to Downing, 8 August 1662, Bod., Clar. 104, f. 88v; Downing to Clarendon, 6 June 1661, Bod., Clar. 104, f. 131v; Cornbury to Downing, BL, Add. MSS 22919, f. 151v; Foulis, *Cabala*, 1664, p. 2.

16 Private correspondence, November 1663, PRO, SP 29/85/71; Muddiman's newsletter, 5 March 1664, Bod., Tanner MSS 47, f. 85r; Edward Riggs to Bennet, 12 February 1664, PRO, SP 29/92/74; William Morrice to Downing, 30 December 1661, BL, Add. 22919, f. 180r; Edward Riggs to Bennet, 1 January 1664, PRO, SP 29/90/1; examination of Richard Tyler, 12 May 1664, PRO, SP 29/98/56; Downing to Clarendon, 14 June 1661, Bod., Clar. 104, f. 138v; Bampfield to Bennet, 17/27 June 1663, PRO, SP 84/167, f. 211r; William Davidson to Nicholas, 5 November 1660, BL, Egerton MSS 2537, f. 252r; Joseph Williamson's "Spy Book," PRO, SP 9/26, *passim* (25 out of 111 names in the book – others might well have passed through the United Provinces.). Edward Riggs to Williamson, 17 February 1664, PRO, SP 29/93/88 provides a list of names. In Rotterdam: Colonel Fitz; Colonel Kelsey; Major Burton; Mr. Steeret's son; Lieutenant-Colonel Joyce; Captain Grimes; Captain White; Lieutenant Codness; Mr. Goodaile; Mr. Tyler; Captain Vivian; Captain Wright; Captain Stringer; Captain Spurway; Captain Browne; Mr. Richardson (minister of Ripon); Mr. Jacus; Mr. Heilin; Lieutenant Fairellis; Mr. Raven; Mr. Madder (minister); Mr. Thorne (minister); Mr. Downing; Mr. Smith (minister); Mr. White; Mr. Twiselton; Mr. Tyllin (minister). In Arnhem: Colonel Desborough; Colonel White; Major Groves; Captain Nicholson; Sir Michael Lewesey; Colonel Walton. Oliver St. John at the Spa; Captain Johnson at Leiden.

In the context of the Northern Rebellion, this expatriate community began to take on additional significance. Almost from the moment of the Restoration, the Netherlands had provided a pipeline of arms and supplies to opponents of the Charles II's government.[17] But in the autumn of 1663 the Dutch connection was particularly active. "Here are more fanatics and arming men in Rotterdam than in anywhere else," wrote Bennet's informant Edward Riggs. In mid October the London customs authorities seized a ship in the Port of London "with sundry arms" from "beyond seas" for which ominously "no proprietors appear." Subsequent investigations into the Northern Rebellion revealed the meaning of these mysterious movements. The plotters believed confidently that "forces from Holland should assist them." According to Ludlow, the plotters had desperately searched for a port "to receive succors from Holland."[18]

More significant than the actual flow of arms was the role which the United Provinces played in the planning and implementation of the Northern Rebellion. Captain Robert Atkinson revealed that the plotters had "agents and friends beyond seas." One Dissenting minister told Sir William Blakestone that the plotters "were encouraged from beyond sea, by those ministers there," and "that many silenced ministers did now profess and had obtained licenses for physic, and those having more liberty of going abroad, did still keep up that party." "There is no resolution among these people, until they receive advice from their agents ... in Holland," insisted Sir Thomas Gower. In the United Provinces "they can consult," explained Joseph Bampfield who had every reason to know, "with more safety than in England or Scotland."[19] It was no coincidence that after the failure of the rebellion the most celebrated of the plotters, Dr. Edward Richardson, turned up at Delft.[20]

The Restored Monarchy was especially concerned by the obvious connivance of the Dutch republicans. Sir Robert Walsh claimed openly that "he knew of ten thousand arms that are lately bought and that with the

17 W. D. Macray (editor), *Notes Which Passed at Meetings of the Privy Council* (London, 1896), December [1661], p. 17; Downing to Clarendon, 11/21 October 1661, Bod., Clar. 105, f. 68r; Downing to Clarendon, 22 August 1662, Bod., Clar. 77, ff. 268v–269r; *Intelligencer*, 31 August 1663, p. 6.

18 Edward Riggs to Bennet, 9 October 1663, PRO, SP 29/81/46; Edward Riggs to Bennet, 1 January 1664, PRO, SP 29/90/1; Privy Council Register, 21 October 1663, PRO, PC 2/56, f. 297r; Sir Thomas Gower's "Particulars of Charges," October 1663, Bod., Clar. 80, f. 77r; Ludlow, "A Voyce," Bod., English History MSS C487, pp. 1005–1006.

19 "Information of Captain Robert Atkinson," 26 November 1663, PRO, SP 29/84/64; Sir William Blakestone to Williamson, 23 April 1664, PRO, SP 29/97/19; Sir Thomas Gower to Bennet, 14 October 1664, PRO, SP 29/103/59; Bampfield to Williamson, August 1663, PRO, SP 84/167, f. 241r; Bampfield to Bennet, 17/27 July 1663, PRO, SP 84/167, f. 211v.

20 Charles Gringand to Williamson, 29 January 1664, PRO, SP 84/169, f. 57r; Thomas Gower to Bennet, 7 November 1663, PRO, SP 29/83/47; Downing to Clarendon, 6 November 1663, Bod., Clar. 107, f. 11r. Other plotters were spotted planning in Rotterdam, Riggs to Bennet, 30 November 1663, PRO, SP 29/84/90.

connivance of some of the principal of the States sent to England." "I am fully persuaded," wrote Bampfield, that "Holland will underhand countenance [the] Presbyterians and Independents." Two separate interrogations in the north revealed that the plotters had "a correspondency with the Dutch" and that there were "preparations in Holland to assist them." When the English government pressed the States General to deliver up those dissidents who had fled abroad, one Dutch magistrate exclaimed "that as long as his head stood upon his shoulders, none should be delivered." De Witt himself declared "it [to be] a thing wholly impossible."[21] These activities and connections only served to confirm the image of the Dutch republicans as inveterate enemies of the English monarchy. "The false, envious, perfidious Hollander," wrote Arise Evans in 1664, "takes all occasion and advantage to do what mischief they can to the king and his subjects." " 'Tis feared that those who in another sense have for so many years been a plague to our nation," commented the London Common Council after passing legislation to prevent the disease entering London from the United Provinces, "will not be wanting to pour in the disease upon us at this time."[22]

More significant, perhaps, than the revelations that a few dissidents had in fact planned to take up arms against the king and his government, was their effect on the popular imagination. This activity confirmed a particular Anglican Royalist understanding of English politics and recent English history. Anglican Royalists claimed that Presbyterianism was intrinsically inimitable to stable government. "Neither Scotland nor England had an hour's peace or quiet," argued Oliver Foulis, "since Knox set footing in the one, or they that had conferred notes with him in the other." The reason for this, claimed Roger L'Estrange, was "their erecting an ecclesiastical supremacy to overtop the prerogative royal." Since Presbyterians "are bound to do the utmost of their power for reformation and preservation of religion," asked the author of *Presbytery Displayed*, "what sacred person of any king can be preserved?" "Presbytery," the Duke of Newcastle warned Charles II before his coronation, "is as destructive to monarchy as uncomely in it." Indeed, all Presbyterian theorists stripped magistracy of its coercive power. "Show me," L'Estrange demanded of his Nonconformist opponents, "where ever your opinions yet gain'd footing in the world without violence, and blood: Show me again any one sermon or discourse (authoriz'd by a

21 Downing to Clarendon, 12/22 July 1661, Bod., Clar. 104, ff. 184v–185r; Bampfield to Taylor, 30 October/9 November 1663, PRO, SP 84/168, f. 70v; Bampfield to Bennet, 2 February 1664, PRO, SP 84/169, f. 63v; John Kilby to Earl of Bridgewater, 24 March 1664, Bod., Clar. 81, f. 142r; "Particulars of the Proceedings of John Atkinson," April 1664, PRO, SP 29/97/98; Bampfield to Taylor, 7/17 December 1663, PRO, SP 84/168, f. 174v; Downing to Bennet, 27 November/7 December 1663, PRO, SP 84/168, f. 148v; "Expedients to Prevent the Disturbance of Government," 1664, PRO, SP 29/109/93.

22 Arise Evans, *Light for the Jews* (London, 1664), pp. 9–10; London Common Council to Morrice, 22 October 1663, CLRO, Remembrancia 9, f. 34r.

Non-conformist) from 1640 to this instant, that presses obedience to the magistrate, unless where the faction was uppermost." By collecting "the sayings and doctrines of the great leaders and abettors of the Presbyterian reformation," the author of *Evangelium Armatum* revealed "their pious and peaceable maxims, which like razors set with oil, cut the throat of Majesty with so keen a smoothness." These "tender and soft conscienc'd men," the Bishop of Chichester told his listeners, "made no scruple to preach up the highest rebellion in the state and foulest disorder in the Church." All of this took on an increased edge in the wake of the Northern Rebellion. Nonconformists may "differ in their shapes and species," Sir Edward Turner told the House of Commons in May 1664, "but in this they all agree, they are no friends to the established government either in Church or state." That the Nonconformists had failed in rebellion so far reflected a lack of means not conviction. "If God would trust them with the sword once more," warned Oliver Foulis, "what gallant things they would do in the fear of God!" Their hatred of the regime went so deep that "if the Turk should foot in England set / Jack Presbyter will be his Mahomet." Small wonder that Charles II blamed the last rising on "Our old enemies."[23]

Dissenters were, according to the Anglican Royalists, pursuing the same course they had followed twenty years earlier. Gadding to puritan lectures, celebrating false prodigies, tumultuous petitioning, production of seditious pamphlets, claiming traitors to be martyrs and patriots – all this seemed like 1642 all over again.[24] "That spirit of hypocrisy, scandal, malice, error, and illusion that actuated the late rebellion," insisted L'Estrange, is "reigning still, and working not only by the same means, but in very many of the same persons, and to the same ends." The Nonconformists, by insinuating "a blind and furious opinion of the extraordinary piety of those teachers, who

23 Oliver Foulis, *Cabala: Or the Mystery of Conventicles Unveil'd* (London, 1664), pp. 3, 64; Roger L'Estrange, *Toleration Discussed* (London, 1663), pp 31, 34–35, 72; *A Rod for the Fools Back: Or, An Answer to a Scurrilous Libel, Called the Changeling.* (1663); *Presbytery Displayed* (London, 1663), pp. 7, 23–24; Duke of Newcastle's "Treatise," 1660–1661, Bod., Clar. 109, pp. 13–14; *Evangelium Armatum* (London, 1663), sig. A3v; Henry [King], *A Sermon Preached at the Funeral of the Right Reverend Father in God Bryan Lord Bishop of Winchester ... April 24 1662* (London, 1662), pp. 20–21; *His Majesties Gracious Speech to Both Houses of Parliament Together with the Speech of Sir Edward Turnor Kt Speaker of the Honourable House of Common, On Tuesday May 17 1664 at their Prorogation* (London, 1664), p. 9; Samuel Sorbiere, *A Voyage to England* (London, 1709), originally published in French in early 1664, p. 24; [Lawrence Womock], *Pulpit Conceptions, Popular Deceptions* (London, 1662), pp. 1–2; Thomas Bellamy, *Philanax Anglicus* (London, 1662), sig. (a)r; *His Majesties Most Gracious Speech on Monday the One and Twentieth of March, 1663/4*, p. 4.

24 Foulis, *Cabala*, pp. 48–62; [Sir John Birkenhead], *Cabala: Or an Impartial Account of the Noncomformists Private Designs, Actings and Wayes* (London, 1663), May 1663, p. 18; Roger L'Estrange, *Considerations and Proposals In Order to the Regulation of the Press*, (London, 1663), 3 June 1663, sig. A3; *Newes*, 25 February 1664, pp. 129–130; Benjamin Laney, *Five Sermons Preached Before His Majesty at Whitehall* (London, 1669), sermon preached 27 March 1664, p. 43.

pretending more intimate acquaintance with God, and immediate possession by his Spirit ... animated the people to the late Rebellion," recalled the author of *Evangelium*, "and still they endeavor to captivate their pity, by a bold and impudent insinuation of these two things, that they are the people of God, and that they are persecuted." "Nothing can be more certain," proclaimed the officially sanctioned *Intelligencer*, than that the Nonconformists "want only power and opportunity to revive the quarrel, and to embroil the nation in a new rebellion."[25]

It was true, of course, that the Nonconformist "rants much against the Pope of Rome, and the Whore of Babylon," but in fact "none so much resemble the beast as himself." The Nonconformists, by attacking the clergy as Antichristian, were in fact making it easier for Popery to triumph. "Truly these men are much beholden of the beast," sneered Lawrence Womock, for "by Antichrist they understand not only the Pope of Rome, or the great Turk, but the very hierarchy of the Church, with the solemn service of God, which is performed and upheld by it." Consequently the Anglican Royalist merchant Charles Porter was hardly surprised to find "our fanatics and Papists" fighting "under the same terms viz. liberty of conscience."[26]

Almanacs drummed home the same points for a more popular audience. "The giddy brains of fanatics," advised Richard Saunders, "run into extremes out of rash zeal, in opposition to Antichrist and humane traditions." In the end they "will quite demolish all that tends to order and decency." The ultimate goal of the Nonconformist, Richard Saunders concluded, was to "ruin the weal public for every small private interest." "Under pretense of religion," William Lilly prognosticated, the Nonconformists "endeavor subversion of government." "Ever since Cromwell brewed religions together, the sectaries are drunk with gallimaufry," *Poor Robin* explained to his audience, "they still cry out for liberty of conscience, and freedom for the exercise of arms." The moral in the popular press, then, was the same as in the learned sermons of Anglican divines and in the caustic pamphlets of the Anglican Royalist polemicists: "The Body-politic's nor safe nor free / Whilst but one member dares rebellious be."[27]

25 L'Estrange, *Press*, sig. A2v; *Evangelium Armatum*, sig. A1v; *Intelligencer*, 19 October 1663, p. 59.

26 *The Character of a Phanatique* (London, 1661), Thomason: 26 March 1660, broadside; *Aron-bimnucha: Or An Antidote to Cure the Calamities of their Trembling For Fear of the Ark* (London, 1663), pp. 88–90; Charles Porter to George Oxenden, 5 March 1663, BL, Add. 40711, f. 6v.

27 Richard Saunders, *Apollo Anglicanus* (London, 1664), sig. A5r–A6r; William Lilly, *Merlini Anglici Ephemeris* (London, 1664) 16 September 1663, sig. B6v–B7v; *Poor Robin 1664: An Almanack After a New Fashion* (London, 1664), sig. B1r; George Wharton, *Calendrium Carolinum: Or, A New Almanack After the Old Fashion For the Year of Christ 1664* (London, 1664), sig. D1r. Lilly was particularly concerned to demonstrate his loyalty in the 1664 edition because he himself had been implicated in the Northern Rebellion. See Sir Brian Broughton to Williamson, 8 December 1663, PRO, SP 29/85/48.

The intrinsic perfidy of Nonconformity convinced Anglican Royalists to pursue rather drastic measures to remedy this domestic cancer. Clearly the solution was not indulgence. "Certainly the humor of these people is not to be rooted out by gentle persuasions," the judge Robert Hyde informed his cousin the Lord Chancellor in the wake of the Northern Rebellion, "nor are they to be taken off by mildness, no more than thieves and robbers are lessened by pardons." Instead it was necessary to eliminate the Nonconformists. "There is an absolute necessity we should take up these seditious principles by the roots," Sir Thomas Dolman advised Lord Lovelace. "Gag, crush and geld them," urged the Anglican Royalist East India merchant Humphrey Gyfford, so "that in our generation they shall not be suffered to foment, scratch or bite and in good time that there may be no more of their breed, which God of his mercy grant." The Royal chaplain Dr. Creighton thought Charles II should "do as the Emperor Severus did, to hang up a Presbyter John ... in all the courts of England." There were good precedents for this action, pointed out the Anglican clergyman Lawrence Womock, for in David's church there was "not a Non-conformist amongst them." "Uniformity," insisted L'Estrange, "is the cement of both Christian, and civil societies; take that away, and the parts drop from the body; and one piece falls from another." After two decades of observation, the Anglican Royalists were sure that the safety of the polity could be ensured by only one means. "Raise such an addition of standing troops as may secure [the] government against these treasonable plots and attempts for the future," advised the Duke of York's friend and future governor of Tangier Lord Belasys, "without which I am confident we shall be perpetually alarmed." "Without an army in your own hands," the Duke of Newcastle had advised Charles at his accession, "you are but a king upon a courtesy of others, and cannot be lasting." "I am in deliberation of raising two regiments of horse more, of five hundred men a piece, the one to lie in the north the other in the west," Charles II belatedly proclaimed to his sister, "which will I doubt not for the future prevent all plotting." In short absolutism was the only answer. In early 1664 Samuel Pepys knew that those around the king were advising him "how neither privileges of Parliament nor city is anything; but his will is all and ought to be so." "These old notions of mixed governments, privileges, and conditions have by several accidents of state been put out of the issue of things," argued another of York's friends the Earl of Peterborough, "they are not to be practiced any longer, and the consequence of all undertakings, can no more be, but monarchy or a commonwealth."[28]

28 Robert Hyde to Clarendon, 30 July 1664, Bod., Clar. 82, f. 44r; Thomas Dolman to Lord Lovelace, 15 April 1664, PRO, SP 29/96/110; Humphrey Gyfford to George Oxenden, 25 March 1664, BL, Add. 40711, f. 24v; Pepys, *Diary*, Vol. V, 25 March 1664, pp. 96–97 (Creighton); *Aron-Bimuncha*, pp. 10–11, 15; L'Estrange, *Toleration*, pp. 39–40, 86; Lord Belasys to Bennet, 22 October 1663, PRO, SP 29/82/26; Duke of Newcastle's "Treatise," Bod., Clar. 109, p.1; Charles II to Henriette-Anne, 10 December 1663, Hartmann, *Charles*

This time, unlike in 1662, the Anglican Royalists were determined to let the nation know just how serious the Northern Rebellion was, just how serious was the threat from Nonconformity. Accounts of the rebellion and the subsequent trials of the plotters dominated the pages of the official newsbooks. The Anglican Royalist almanac writer, George Wharton, immediately proclaimed 11 October 1663 as a red-letter day when "a general commotion [was] designed by the Fanatics." Sensational trials and executions were used to reinforce the reality of the rebellion. "It would very much conduce to the settlement of the public peace if more of those heinous offenders were made examples to deter others from the like mischievous practices," advised Charles II. "The judges," Bennet assured Ormonde, knew that their duty was to make "many such examples as this age hath much need of." And examples were made. York, Leeds, Doncaster, and North Allerton were soon decorated with the heads of the conspirators.[29] Charles was aware of the critical role which propaganda had played in the rebellion. He was furious at pamphleteers "who not only seek to overthrow him, but all government whatsoever." Consequently it was thought fit "some example should be made."[30] To make sure that the political nation drew the correct moral from all this, the newsbooks began advertising and the publishers producing a whole variety of pamphlets and sermons reinforcing the necessity of obedience and the sin inherent in rebellion.[31]

There can be no doubt that the Anglican Royalist argument had captured the popular imagination. Taking its lead from the court – Bennet enjoined "severity" for " 'tis no more than what the government needs" – the political nation began its severest crackdown on Dissent. All over England conventicles were broken up and the usual suspects were arrested. Former Cromwellian officers were enjoined to leave London. "The whole kingdom have generally received such satisfaction by the late trial of the traitors," bragged Joseph Williamson in his newsletter, "that at their several Quarter Sessions they have seemed to be more severe than formerly against the Quakers and other loose principled people as men that under a pretext of conscience do endeavor to cover their wicked conspiracies." In 1664, remembered

II and Madame, p. 89; Pepys, *Diary*, Vol. V, 22 February 1664, p. 60 (he was probably referring to Charles Berkeley and Henry Bennet among others); Earl of Peterborough to Williamson, 14 October 1663, PRO, SP 29/81/94.

29 Wharton, *Calendrium Carolinum*, 1664, p. 44; Charles II to Sir Godfrey Copley, 24 February 1664, PRO, SP 44/17, p. 11; Bennet to Ormonde, 2 January 1664, Carte 46, f. 136r; Williamson's newsletter, 23 January 1664, Carte 222, f. 48r; T. Rugge, "Mercurius Politicus Redivivus," January 1664, BL, Add. 10117, f. 84r.

30 Robert Southwell to Ormonde, 23 February 1664, Carte 33, f. 324r; Muddiman's newsletter, 27 February 1664, Bod., Tanner MSS 47, f. 79v. The example was John Twynne T. Rugge, "Mercurius Politicus Redivivus," February 1664, BL, Add.10117, f. 86v; *Newes*, 25 February 1664, pp. 135–136; Cuneus to States General, 26 February/7 March 1664, Bod., Clar. 107, f. 119v.

31 For the advertisements: *Newes*, 28 January 1664, p. 67; *Newes*, 31 March 1664, p. 211; *Newes*, 28 April 1664, p. 275; *Newes*, 5 May 1664, p. 292.

Ludlow, "he who talks of liberty, civil or spiritual and of such trifles as laws and privileges of Parliament is laughed at, the Convention itself seeming to effect no other names than loyal and obedient." The Nonconformist pogrom had become so severe that even Samuel Pepys prayed in August that "I would to God they would either conform, or be more wise and not be ketched."[32]

The revelations of the Northern Rebellion and the subsequent propaganda campaign had a profound effect on the Cavalier Parliament which reassembled in March 1664. The factious session of 1663 was followed by one of the most loyal sessions on record. "The truth is," Charles informed his sister, "both Houses are in so good humor as I do not doubt but to end this session very well." "The House," Sir Henry Bennet wrote to Ormonde, is "really in a better temper towards his Majesty's service than ever I yet saw them." The Venetian ambassador in Paris heard that the Parliament gives "an impression of the most steadfast devotion of those realms to the king." The English members of Parliament "are in a mood to accede to the most difficult things," wrote the French ambassador Comminges, "just as in other times they objected to the most just and reasonable demands." Even Ludlow was forced to admit that "the leading party of [the Parliament] are gained to the king."[33]

The legislation of the spring 1664 session of Parliament, as Greaves and Seaward have shown, was a response to the Northern Rebellion. Parliament repealed the Triennial Act because it was perceived to have been the

32 Bennet to Ormonde, 22 December 1663, Carte 46, f. 132v; Robert Southwell to George Lane, 23 February 1664, Carte 33, f. 324r (Charles II's desire to punish rebels); Williamson's newsletter, 30 January 1664, Carte 222, f. 46r; Ludlow, "A Voyce," Bod., English History MSS C485, ff. 998, 1021; Pepys, *Diary*, Vol. V, 7 August 1664, p. 235. For evidence of the prosecution and persecution of Dissenters see for example: Robert Hyde to Clarendon, 30 July 1664, Bod., Clar. 82, f. 44r; T. Rugge, "Mercurius Politicus Redivivus," BL, Add. 10117, ff. 85v–121v; newsletter, 12 December 1663, Carte 222, f. 6v; Muddiman's newsletter, 26 March 1664, Bod., Tanner MSS 47, f. 105r; Josselin, *Diary*, 3 January 1664, p. 504. There were in fact lists of "usual suspects." See diary of Isaac Archer, CUL, Add. 8499, pp. 52–53; Josselin, *Diary*, 2 December 1660, p. 472. For the expulsion of Cromwellians from London: "Intelligence from London," 11/21 April 1664, *CSPV*, p. 13; Muddiman's newsletter, 14 April 1664, Bod., Tanner MSS 47, f. 119; newsletter, 16 April 1664, Carte 222, f. 66r.

33 Charles II to Henriette-Anne, 24 March 1664, Hartmann, *Charles II and Madame*, pp. 97–98; Charles II to Henriette-Anne, 28 March 1664, Hartmann, *Charles II and Madame*, p. 99; Charles II to Henriette-Anne, 19 May 1664, Hartmann, *Charles II and Madame*, p. 101; Bennet to Ormonde, 26 March 1664, Carte 46, f. 178; Bennet to Sir Richard Fanshawe, 7 April 1664 *Original Letters of his Excellency Sir Richard Fanshawe* (London, 1701), p. 57; Bennet to Ormonde, 7 April 1664, Carte 46, f. 181v; Sagredo to Doge and Senate, 19/29 April 1664, *CSPV*, p. 11; Sagredo to Doge and Senate, 26 April/6 May 1664, *CSPV*, p. 13; Sagredo to Doge and Senate, 7/17 June 1664, *CSPV*, p. 24; Comminges to De Lionne, 24 March/3 April 1664, PRO, PRO 31/3/113, ff. 108–109; Comminges to De Lionne, 7/17 April 1664, PRO, PRO 31/3/113, ff. 132–125 (misfoliation, my translation); Comminges to De Lionne, 9/19 May 1664, PRO, PRO 31/3/113, f. 166; Ludlow, "A Voyce," Bod., English History MSS C487, p. 1002.

ideological basis of the rebellion. Parliament passed the Conventicle Act in part because it was from conventicles that much of the support for the rebellion had come.[34] Only the Dutch connection of the Northern Rebellion remained to be dealt with – by what was now – a committed Anglican Royalist Parliament.

[34] Greaves, *Deliver Us From Evil*, p. 204; Paul Seaward, *The Cavalier Parliaments and the Reconstruction of the Old Regime* (Cambridge, 1989), pp. 137–140, 189–192. The divisions over those two bills saw Anglican Royalists facing off against dissenters and former Cromwellians: *CJ*, 28 March 1664, p. 538 (Triennial bill); 14 May 1664, p. 565 (Conventicle bill). The Conventicle bill was proposed by Job Charlton and Lord Fanshawe.

15

The April 1664 trade resolution

On 21 April 1664 the House of Commons passed a resolution declaring "that the several, and respective wrongs , dishonors and indignities done to his Majesty by the subjects of the United Provinces, by invading his rights in India, Africa, and elsewhere; and the damages, affronts and injuries done by them to our merchants are the greatest obstructions of foreign trade," adding "for the prevention of the like in future; and in prosecution thereof, this House doth resolve, they will with their lives, and fortunes assist his Majesty against all opposition whatsoever." Though Samuel Pepys thought it "a very high vote," Joseph Williamson waxed enthusiastic: "Great zeal is in the Parliament to get themselves justice by the only argument that moves Holland, arms."[1]

Historians have explained the passage of the April trade resolution either as the result of pressure from the London mercantile community, or as an attempt to reassert English national honor. However, that the resolution was passed by a Parliament convinced of the urgency of eradicating sectarianism and sedition, makes one wonder whether it was the straightforward piece of economic confrontationalism or national self-aggrandizement which historians have claimed it to be. Indeed at least one important member of Charles's Privy Council saw the resolution as part and parcel of the Anglican Royalist reaction.[2] It will "be a point of infinite reputation to his Majesty's government," wrote Sir Henry Bennet to the Duke of Ormonde, that "in so short a session the world shall see the Triennial Bill repealed, and such a vote as this, after they had been prepared to expect nothing but contests and disputes with the crown in the most jealous points

1 The argument of this and the following chapter was originally advanced in my "Popery, Trade and Universal Monarchy: The Ideological Context of the Outbreak of the Second Anglo-Dutch War," *English Historical Review* Vol. 107 (January 1992), pp. 1–29; *Newes*, 5 May 1664, pp. 289–290; Pepys, *Diary*, Vol. V, 21 April 1664, p. 129; Joseph Williamson to Richard Fanshawe, 21 April 1664, *Original Letters of his Excellency Sir Richard Fanshaw*, (London, 1701), p. 86.

2 My use of the term Anglican Royalist is based on the definition established by Mark Goldie in "John Locke and Anglican Royalism," *Political Studies* Vol. 31 (1983), pp. 86–102.

belonging to it."[3] Charles Davenant, whose father Sir William was one of the Restoration court's favorite playwrights, recalled that "the good Cavaliers who were then very strong in the House" demanded war against the Dutch "out of their old hatred to a Commonwealth."[4] Closer examination of the context of the passage of the resolution makes it even more difficult to accept the claims traditionally made for it by historians.

The legislative history of the April trade resolution is well known. On 23 March, in response to a petition from the clothiers of the old and new draperies, the House of Commons established a committee to investigate problems in the woolen industry. Three days later the brief was expanded to include "the general decay of trade" and the membership was doubled. At this point Sir Thomas Clifford, a close ally of Sir Henry Bennet, became chairman of the committee. Although the committee itself was too large to have any specific ideological outlook, Paul Seaward has indicated its close connections to court. The surviving minutes of the committee also demonstrate the overwhelming dominance of Anglican Royalists at the committee meetings – men like Clifford, Sir Richard Ford, Sir Thomas Bludworth, Sir Theophilus Biddolph, Sir Thomas Strickland, Sir Thomas Littleton, and Sir John Shaw. Immediately the committee shifted its focus from investigation of domestic obstructions to the success of the woolen industry, to foreign obstructions in foreign trade. "The several companies of merchants of London both incorporate and not corporate" were asked to "bring in a narrative of their present condition of their respective foreign trades and what obstructions they find and from whom."[5]

Despite the ostensibly neutral wording of the instructions to the companies, it was made quite clear what sort of grievances were wanted. Before Parliament convened the political nation was already "devoting attention to the decisions which will be taken by agreement with the claims against the Dutch." The Africa merchant and naval supplier Captain George Cocke told Samuel Pepys that "the king's design is, by getting under-hand the

3 Bennet to Ormonde, 23 April 1664, Carte 46, f. 187; Bennet to Ormonde, 19 April 1664, Carte 46, f. 185v.

4 Charles Davenant, *Essays Upon I. The Ballance of Power II. The Right of Making War, Peace, and Alliances III. Universal Monarchy* (London, 1701), p. 18.

5 The best account of the legislative history is Paul Seaward, "The House of Commons Committee of Trade and the Origins of the Second Anglo-Dutch War, 1664," in *The Historical Journal* Vol. 30, No. 2 (1987), pp. 444–446. *CJ*, 23 March 1664, pp. 535–536; CJ, 26 March 1664, p. 537; "Order in the House of Commons," 23 March 1664, SP 29/95/21; minute of the Committee of Trade, 26 March 1664, SP 29/95/54; minute of the Committee of Trade, 1 April 1664, SP 29/96/7; minute of the Committee of Trade, 28 April 1664, SP 29/97/70. For the request for merchant grievances see minute of the Committee of Trade, 26 March 1664, SP 29/95/55; Richard Ford to Mr. Marsh (Clerk of the House of Commons), March 1664, SP 84/219, f. 339r; a copy of the memorandum sent out survives in IOL, 26 March 1664, Home Miscellanies H/42, f. 109. For the Anglican Royalism of Thomas Strickland see "Roger Morrice's 'Eminent Worthies,'" Pt. III, 1651, Doctor Williams' Library MSS 31J (unfoliated).

merchants to bring in their complaints to the Parliament, to make them in honor begin a war." The French ambassador Comminges knew that the merchants had been "impelled by the cabals of servants of the king." They were, he wrote to Louis XIV, "excited for the King of England in order to make it seem as if the whole nation was in concert with him, and in order to scare the Hollanders." "The merchants," wrote Ludlow, "are encouraged by the court instruments to make their complaints against the Hollanders." "The king endeavors the ruin of the United Provinces by establishing the power of the Prince of Orange," Algernon Sidney determined, so "that the merchants and Parliament are both stirred up by him to move for a war, and the steps made toward it, are marks of the obedient Parliament's compliance with his commands." Not surprisingly, Pepys found merchants at the Exchange, on 1 April, hard at work preparing their claims "against the Dutch." Naturally Sir George Downing was blamed at the time, as he has been ever since, for inciting the merchant community to bring in the complaints against the Dutch. But, William Coventry, who as a member of the committee for trade, the secretary of the Duke of York, and an important courtier in his own right, was in a good position to know, thought it "not improbable" that Downing "received his lesson from hence." Downing's reaction to the news of Parliament's trade resolution tends to confirm this impression. Although he was ecstatic about the political benefits that it might confer, he was very skeptical about the economic grounds of the resolution. "I do not believe," he told Clarendon, "that any new pretences were offered to the committee of Parliament that I have not already" presented.[6]

There was no mistaking the intention of those who promoted the trade resolution. "The conspiracy for promoting the war with Holland grows stronger," William Morrice wrote to Downing on 1 April, though "I find most sober men antipodes to it." The Earl of Clarendon later reflected that the trade resolution was put on by "they who were very solicitous to

[6] Sagredo to Doge and Senate, 22 March/1 April 1664, *CSPV*, p. 2; Pepys, *Diary*, Vol. V, 30 March 1664, p. 105; Pepys, *Diary*, Vol. V, 1 April 1664, p. 107; Pepys, *Diary*, Vol. V, 5 April 1664, p. 113; Comminges to Louis XIV, 25 April/5 May 1664, PRO, PRO 31/3/113, ff. 153–154; Ludlow, "A Voyce," English History MSS 487, ff. 1016–1017; Algernon Sidney, "Court Maxims," Warwickshire Record Office, ff. 163–164, 176–177; William Coventry, "Discourse on the Dutch War," Longleat House, Cov. MSS CII, f. 5; Downing to Clarendon, 20 May 1664, Bod., Clar. 108, f. 6r. While Charles II is sometimes portrayed as an uncommitted bystander in the events leading up to the outbreak of the war, contemporaries did not see him that way: Edward Conway to George Rawdon, 10 September 1664, HL, Hastings MSS HA 14405; Edward Conway to George Rawdon, 27 September 1664, HL, Hastings MSS HA 14406; News from The Hague, 23 March/2 April 1665, *CSPV*, p. 99. Charles II had in fact personally given the orders to take the New Netherlands, orders delivered before the trade resolution: William Morrice to Henry Coventry, 10 February 1665, Longleat House, Cov. MSS LXIV, f. 105. Given the king's known passion for naval affairs, these reports seem all too plausible: "A Short Character of Charles II," NRO, WKC 7/66, p. 2.

promote a war with Holland" so that they "might make a further advance much more easy."[7]

Despite the committee's intention for the merchants to bring in claims against the Dutch, both Michael McKeon and Paul Seaward have demonstrated that only "one-third of the testimony relates to Dutch obstructions and two-third relates to other causes."[8] This has led both scholars to dismiss the economic rhetoric surrounding the Anglo-Dutch War. For Seaward the war was in fact fought for honor and national pride, while McKeon has claimed the war was an attempt to advance the economic self-interest of courtiers rather than the nation as a whole. Though they are right to emphasize that the trade resolution was a rhetorical stance, both scholars overlook the fact that a significant part of the economic community did want a war with the Dutch. A closer investigation of the complaints presented to the committee of trade reveals that the Anglican Royalist merchants, a segment of the merchant community now riding the crest of the Anglican Royalist reaction, enthusiastically desired a second Anglo-Dutch war.

Only three groups of merchants actually brought in complaints against the Dutch. The first of these was the Levant Company. It complained that the Dutch furnish "Turkey with manufactures of wool privately gotten from England and Ireland" and that they procured "commissions and letters of mart from our enemies on purpose to weaken our shipping and destroy our trade."[9] In the context of the affairs of the Levant Company this was a strange complaint indeed. The court minutes of the Company since the Restoration, though they are full of economic grievances, do not include a single complaint against the Dutch prior to the outbreak of the war in 1665. In November 1660, when they were asked by the Council of Trade to list the chief obstructions to their trade, the Company complained of the high cost of English manufactures, the coining of false money, and the unfair trading practices of the Venetians – nothing about the Dutch.[10] Not a single letter from Livorno or Florence prior to the passage of the trade resolution so much as hinted a desire for a new Dutch war. Indeed the prevailing impression is one of Anglo-Dutch cooperation. In the winter of 1664, for

7 William Morrice to Downing, 1 April 1664, BL, Add. 22920, f. 33v; Edward Hyde, *The Life of the Earl of Clarendon* (Dublin, 1760), p. 106. The Privy Council was known to have plumped for war two days before the trade resolution was passed: Thomas Salusbury to Earl of Huntingdon, 19 April 1664, HL, HA 10659. James Ralph later concluded that "the resolution was taken before the pretense was thought of. " [James Ralph], *The History of England* (London, 1744), Vol. I. p. 103.

8 Michael McKeon, *Politics and Poetry in Restoration England: The Case of Dryden's Annus Mirabilis* (Cambridge MA, 1975), pp. 117–118; Seaward, "Committee of Trade," pp. 446–448.

9 "Notes of the Reports to the Council for Trade," 1 April 1664, SP 29/96/6; "Proceedings of the Committee for Trade," 18 April 1664, SP 29/98/35.

10 Court minutes of Levant Company, 28 November 1660, SP 105/152, f. 4r and *passim*.

example, Van Tromp freed English ships held captive by the Algerian pirates. From Florence, where many Levant merchants traded, John Finch admitted that much English business in Italy was in "Italian or Dutch hands," certainly making it unlikely that the Levant merchants would want a war against the Dutch. When there was a scuffle between English and Dutch factors in the Levant September 1663, the Earl of Winchilsea made it quite clear the Dutch had acted "in contempt of their resident here, and their consul at Smyrna," who guaranteed immediate satisfaction.[11]

The main foreign antagonists of the Levant merchants were the Algerian pirates. In January 1662, before Sir John Lawson signed the peace treaty with the Algerians, Pepys reported that because "the Turks do take more and more of our ships in the Straights ... our merchants here in London do daily break, and are still likely to do so." After a year's grudging acceptance of the terms of the peace, the Algerians were back at it by the spring of 1663. Because of them, there was "but small encouragement to drive the Levant trade" thought one merchant. Another was sure "the City of London will also feel the smart of this great blow." By January 1664, this time without being urged on from court, the Levant Company twice complained to the Privy Council "of their great losses sustained by the Algiers men of war." At the end of the month the Company wrote to Winchilsea that the Algerian violations of the peace treaty "have been of late so notorious and so many, as (we must believe) puts the king's Majesty upon a necessity of vindicating his own honor."[12] In addition to the Algerians, the Levant Company thought it necessary to complain about the Venetians whose "ill treatment of our merchants" threatened the Turkey traders "in all their voyages." In 1663, French economic harassment also

11 Cuneus to States General, 14 March 1664, SP 84/169, f. 258r; Joseph Kent to Williamson, 23 February 1664, SP 98/5 (unfoliated); John Finch to Lord Arlington, 3/13 June 1665, SP 98/5, (unfoliated); Winchilsea to Bennet, 15/25 September 1663, SP 97/18, f. 45r. When informed that some in England feared a Dutch design to "engross the whole trade of cloth in these dominions," Winchilsea could only respond that Dutch power "in these parts is very weak when it comes to stand in competition with the English interest." Winchilsea to Earl of Southampton, 26 April 1664, LRO, DG7/Box 4984, Winchilsea Letterbook, f. 110.

12 The complaints against the Algerians are numerous: T. Mundy, "Some Occurrences," January 1662, Bod. Rawl. A315, p. 246r; Pepys, *Diary*, Vol. III, 19 January 1662, p. 13; Mun Browne to George Oxenden, 13 May 1663, BL, Add. 40711, f. 54r; Joseph Kent to Williamson, 26 October 1663, SP 98/4, f. 265; Downing to Clarendon, 20 November 1663, Bod., Clar. 107, f. 21r; Morgan Read to Bennet, 23 November 1663, SP 98/4, f. 272r; Joseph Kent to Williamson, 23 November 1663, SP 98/4, f. 274v; Downing to Clarendon, 27 November 1663, Bod., Clar. 107, f. 26v; De Bacquoy/Van Ruyven to Williamson, 3/13 January 1664, SP 84/169, f. 23r; Privy Council Register, 8 January 1664, PRO, PC 2/56, f. 342v; Privy Council Register, 15 January 1664, PRO, PC 2/56, ff. 345v–346r; Josselin, *Diary*, 24 January 1664, p. 504; Thomas Maynard to Clarendon, 1/11 February 1664, Bod., Clar. 81, f. 68av; Pepys, *Diary*, Vol. V, 9 February 1664, pp. 41–42; 7 April 1664, pp. 225–226 (claims Turks are actually Presbyterians); W. Boreel to States General, 8/18 April 1664, SP 101/122/196; Duke to Williamson, 22 April 1664, SP 84/170, f. 81r; Levant Company to Winchilsea, 22 January 1664, SP 105/113, ff. 38v–39r.

began to be a problem. Significantly, other than the lists of grievances presented to the committee of trade, there is no mention of the Dutch.[13]

Indeed the Levant Company had very good reason to fear an Anglo-Dutch war. Jonathan Israel has demonstrated that the first Dutch War was devastating to the English trade in the Mediterranean. There was no reason to believe that a new war would be any better. Already in the autumn of 1664, while Anglo-Dutch tension was high but war had not yet broken out, Morgan Read reported that the Genoese were taking over English trade in the Mediterranean. "It is most probable that whilst we are contesting" with the Dutch, William Coventry correctly predicted, "others will step into the trade, as Hamburgers, Danes, Swedes, French, Genoeses ... so that for the Turkey and European trade there is very little advantage to be obtained by war."[14]

Why then did the Levant Company decide in March 1664 to submit a list of grievances against the Dutch, to supply ammunition for what was well known to be a campaign to begin a new Dutch war? The Company itself appears to have had a slight slant to Dissent, but in the aftermath of the Northern Rebellion that apparently counted for little.[15] On 30 March 1664 the Levant Company appointed a committee to report the conditions of their trade to the Commons committee. This committee was dominated by Anglican Royalists – men like Sir George Smith, John Buckworth, Nicholas Penning, Alderman John Langley, Sir Thomas Bludworth, Thomas Vernon, and Francis Clarke.[16] It is certainly significant that one of the two known

13 For the Venetians: court minutes of Levant Company, 8 March 1664, SP 105/152, f. 101v; Winchilsea to Bennet, 11 June 1664, SP 97/18, f. 91. For the French: court minutes of Levant Company, 15 May 1663, SP 105/152, f. 70; court minutes of Levant Company, 19 June 1663, SP 105/152, f. 74r. At least one Levant merchant blamed the Company itself for the loss of English trade in the region: Arnold White (Smyrna) to Winchilsea, 26 November 1661, LRO, DG7/Box 4962, Bundle VI.

14 Israel, *Dutch Primacy in World Trade 1585–1740* p. 211; Morgan Read to Bennet, 26 August/5 September 1664, SP 98/5, unfoliated; William Coventry, "Paper on Dutch Wars," 1665, BL, Add. 32094, ff. 50v–51r. Indeed once the war seemed imminent, the government showed little interest in protecting Levant Company assets: court minutes of Levant Company, 17 January 1665, SP 105/152, f. 123r.

15 My claim that the Levant Company leaned slightly to Dissent is based on an, admittedly impressionistic, analysis of the lists of the court of assistants in the court minute book and the selection of John Bradgate (a Presbyterian) as minister of Smyrna against the wishes of Sir Thomas Bludworth and the violent complaints of the Earl of Winchilsea. court minutes of Levant Company, 20 August 1662, SP 105/152, f. 37r; court minutes of Levant Company, 30 October 1662, SP 105/152, f. 45v; court minutes of Levant Company, 28 January 1664, SP 105/152, f. 97r; Winchilsea to Duchess of Somerset, 23 March 1665, HMC, *Finch MSS*, p. 364. Also Winchilsea claimed that "the companies of merchants in England ... commonly are for the major part composed of factious members." His closest contacts were naturally with the Levant Company. Winchilsea to Southampton, 13 August 1664, HMC, *Finch*, pp. 326–327; Winchilsea to Humphrey Henchman, 29 June 1664, LRO, DG7/Box 4984, Winchilsea Letterbook, f. 141. See the discussion in Sonia Anderson, *An English Consul in Turkey: Paul Rycaut at Smyrna, 1667–1678* (Oxford, 1989), p. 102.

16 Court minutes of Levant Company, 30 March 1664, SP 105/152, f. 105v. The full committee was: John Joliffe, Sir George Smith, Buckworth, Penning, Richard Holworthy,

Nonconformists on the committee to draw up the Levant Company's petition, John Joliffe, submitted another petition as governor of the Muscovy Company – a trading area in which Jonathan Israel has shown was very much dominated by the Dutch – with not a single mention of the Dutch. In the 1670s John Joliffe was in fact known to be an opponent of the third Dutch War.[17] In this context, then, the Levant Company resolution appears as the ideological vision of its Anglican Royalist members, not as an accurate depiction of the Levant Company's trade.

The second group of merchants to bring an anti-Dutch petition was the East India Company.[18] The Dutch had, of course, been making spectacular gains in the East Indies, but the East India Company had good reason to resent the actions of other nations as well. The Portuguese had refused to relinquish Bombay, which was granted to England as part of Catherine of Braganza's dowry, and the Spanish had refused to allow the English East India Company to sell its goods in Spanish ports. Charles II had done little to help the Company, exempting East India goods from the purview of the Navigation Act.[19] More recently, and more ominously for the East India

Alderman Gregory, Langley, John Gould, John Prestwood, Bludwoth, Vernon, Clarke, Benjamin Albyn, Alderman Love. The only known Dissenters of the group are Joliffe and Love, who because of their prestige and seniority in the Company, could hardly be kept off. George Smith was a close friend of the Anglican Royalist George Oxenden, and was known to harbor suspected Royalists during the 1650s; see "List of Suspected Persons," BL, Add. 34014, ff. 7v, 43r. I am indebted to Henry Roseveare for pointing me in the direction of this valuable source. Smith was knighted immediately after the Restoration, and was "a chief officer" in the London militia aimed at putting down Dissenting tumults. J. R. Woodhead, *The Rulers of London 1660–1689*. (London, 1965), p. 151. John Buckworth is listed as a Tory by Woodhead (*Rulers of London*, p. 41) and among the Anglican Royalist Paul Rycaut's friends by Sonia Anderson (*Paul Rycaut*, p. 93). Nicholas Penning only became active in London politics in 1659, but remained active as a common councilman until 1669, which suggests a Royalist background. He was also a friend of Rycaut (Anderson, *Paul Rycaut*, p. 93). Langley also "knew Rycaut well" and was probably an Anglican Royalist (Anderson, *Paul Rycaut*, p. 93). Thomas Bludworth was "a staunch Tory," active in the London militia, fined off (paid to avoid becoming) for alderman in the 1650s and was picked for sheriff "by the king" in 1662. He was another of Rycaut's friends. (Woodhead, *Rulers of London*, p. 33; Pepys, Vol. III, 10 August 1662, p. 162, Anderson, *Paul Rycaut*, p. 93). Thomas Vernon was a Tory and friend of Rycaut. (Woodhead, *Rulers of London*, p. 167; Anderson, *Paul Rycaut*, p. 93). Francis Clarke was a Tory (Woodhead, *Rulers of London*, p. 47). For defense of my claim for the Anglican Royalism of the City Militia, see Bishop of Winchester to Clarendon, 3 September 1662, Bod., Clar. 77, f. 340r.

17 Notes of the Committee for Trade, 1 April 1664, SP 29/96/6, SP 29/96/7; Israel, *Dutch Primacy* pp. 43–48. For Joliffe see Woodhead, *Rulers of London*, p. 99; B. D. Henning (editor), *The House of Commons 1660–1690* (London, 1983), Vol.II, pp. 657–658.

18 For the petition, see Clifford's notes, 5 April 1664, PRO, Kew, CO 77/9, f. 83; East India Company petition to Committee of the House, April 1664, IOL, I/2/6, ff. 113–114. Significantly the petitioners couched their complaint in the idiom of universal monarchy. If the Dutch gained control of the East Indies, they warned, they would "accrue such a treasure as to enable them to give laws to all Europe."

19 Oxenden, Goodier, and Aungier to East India Company, 6 April 1663, IOL, E/3/28, f. 6; "Royal Proclamation Touching the Free Importation of Nutmeg, Cinnamon, Cloves and Mace," 20 December 1662, Journal of London Common Council, CLRO, J45,

Company, the French had established an East India Company which meant to break into the trade by attacking English and Dutch ships. Louis XIV hoped to aid his company by establishing a colony on Madagascar because it would be "a fit place for him to pirate in."[20]

In fact, the Company showed little sign of actually supporting the campaign to start a new Dutch war. "We are endeavoring a restitution for past wrongs and a settlement of trade for the future," the East India Company explained to its factors in India in March 1664. The goal was not war but "that a fair correspondency may be continued between us and [the Dutch] in the future." When it was clear that the committee of trade was soliciting complaints against the Dutch, the Nonconformist governor of the East India Company intentionally delayed submitting the East India Company list "because they would not be said to be the first and only cause of a war with Holland." When the complaints were finally brought in, they did not prove to be terribly significant. "As to the wrongs we pretend they have done us," William Coventry informed Pepys "that of the East Indies for their not delivering of Poleron, it is not yet known whether they have failed or no. That of their hindering the *Leopard* cannot amount to above £3,000, if true." After both Houses of Parliament had enthusiastically supported the trade resolution, the East India Company made every effort to impress upon the government how disastrous a Dutch war would be. "For the public concernment," the East India Company wrote to the sympathetic Earl of Southampton, "the Company hopes it is in the interest of the kingdom, for as to their concerns as merchants, they must needs say that the worst of peace is better than the best war, by which they cannot expect but to be present sufferers in one kind or other." "There is a great rumor flies up and down the world, that in this present conjuncture of affairs, the merchants are great incendiaries to a war with the Dutch, and if there happen one, 'twill be called the Merchants War, which I suppose is a great mistake," complained the East India merchant Edward Adams who had brought one of the private complaints against the Dutch in April, "for to me it seems not rational for any intelligent merchants to be forward to that war, the main dispute and decision whereof must be argued at sea, the place where he is most concerned." "If any such merchants there be, that are so warlike, and promise to themselves great gain by trading in troubled

ff. 266v–267r; Privy Council Register, 7 October 1663, PRO, PC 2/56, f. 290v; Privy Council Register, 25 October 1663, PRO, PC 2/56, f. 297v.

20 Downing to Clarendon, 20 November 1663, Bod., Clar. 107, ff. 21v–22r; W. Boreel to States General, 19/29 February 1664, SP 84/169, f. 155v; East India Company to president and Council of Surat, 9 March 1664, IOL, E/3/86, f. 194v; W. Boreel to States General, SP 101/122/3; Duke to Williamson, 22 April 1664, SP 84/170, f. 81r; Downing to Clarendon, 22 April 1664, Bod., Clar. 107, f. 211v; Holles to Bennet, 22 May 1664, SP 78/118, f. 188v; *Newes*, 9 June 1664, p. 371; Boreel to States General, 19/29 August 1664, SP 84/172, f. 159r; Boreel to States General, 16/26 September 1664, SP 101/122/264; Winchilsea to Bennet, 12/22 July 1664, SP 97/18, f. 128r.

waters," Adams concluded, "I do declare myself to be none of them." In October 1664 the East India Company "pointed out to the King of England" that a new war "will be the cause of the complete ruin of the trade in the East Indies, because it is very easy for the Dutch to drive out the English from thence."[21]

The East India Company had good reason to fear a second Anglo-Dutch war. Both Israel and Loughead have shown that the first Anglo-Dutch War was "nearly disastrous for the company."[22] This memory was in fact ever present on the minds of the East Indian merchants. "The last wars that broke out in Oliver's time," wrote George Oxenden, "hath made us the burnt children that now fly from the fire." When rumors began to reach the East of Anglo-Dutch hostilities, the merchants in India were at a loss. One merchant was so startled that he knew "not what to resolve on," and decided to hope that "the next news from Bussara will be peace." "I hope in God we shall hear better news," wrote another to George Oxenden. Oxenden himself felt that if the rumors were true, they must give Bombay "over for lost." William Coventry, in his paper analyzing the possible economic advantages of an Anglo-Dutch war, thought that in theory the English might gain in the East Indies, but the reality of Dutch strength convinced him "how impossible it is." So, when the Anglican Royalist George Oxenden wrote to his friend Nicholas Buckeridge to explain that an Anglo-Dutch war was inevitable, he thought it was because of "state policy and the nation's right" not because of the economic advantages it would bring.[23]

The most sensational claims against the Dutch were brought in by the Royal Adventurers for trade in Africa. The Dutch, they testified, claimed "to

21 East India Company to president and Council of Surat, 9 March 1664, IOL, E/3/86, f. 192v; Pepys, *Diary*, Vol. V, 2 April 1664, pp. 108–109; Pepys, *Diary*, Vol. V, 29 May 1664, pp. 159–160; East India Company memorandum to Earl of Southampton, 25 May 1664, IOL, Home Miscellanies, H/42, p. 110; Edward Adams, *A Brief Relation of the Surprizing Several English Merchants Goods, by Dutch Men of War* (London, 1664) [May], pp. [12–13]; "Proceedings of the Committee for Trade," 19 April 1664, SP 29/98/35 (Adams's complaint); newsletter from The Hague, 20/30 October 1664, *CSPV*, pp. 49–50. Adams was probably a Dissenter – based on his activities in his London vestry. His trading partner was the Nonconformist merchant John Pollixfen. Petition of Edward Adams, undated, SP 84/219, f. 234r.

22 Peter Loughead, 'The East India Company in English Domestic Politics, 1657–1688' (Oxford, D.Phil. thesis, 1980), p. 63; Israel, *Dutch Primacy* p. 212.

23 George Oxenden to William Jearsey, 28 September 1664, BL, Add. 40698, f. 98r; William Jearsey to George Oxenden, 25 November 1664, BL, Add. 40698, f. 155v; John Willett to George Oxenden, 18 August 1664, BL, Add. 40698, f. 59r; George Oxenden to Humphrey Cooke, 3 November 1664, BL, Add. 40698, f. 146r; William Coventry, "Paper on Dutch War," BL, Add. 32094, f. 50v; George Oxenden to Nicholas Buckeridge, August 1664, BL, Add. 40698, f. 80v. Dutch strategy in the war immediately justified the concerns of the East India merchants. The Dutch chose to devote most of their resources to fighting the colonial war. Downing to Bennet, 31 January 1665, SP 84/174, f. 72r; Downing to Clarendon, 27 January 1665, Bod., Clar. 108, f. 193r; Downing to Bennet, 24 January 1665, SP 84/174, f. 43r.

have right to the African Coast by conquest from Portugal." In defense of that pretension, the Dutch "have set natives upon us" and "shot at our flag." The result was that the Company was "like to lose all their footing." These claims were supported by a whole range of individual claims against ships seized on the coast of Africa by the Dutch.[24]

Although William Coventry was right to tell Pepys that "truly" the concrete claims brought in by the Africa Company "did not amount to above £2 or 300," that company did appear to have the greatest reason to fear the Dutch. But closer examination suggests that it might not have been the Company's pursuit of profit which determined its Hollandophobic outlook. The original aim of the Company, the Duke of York himself stated in his memoirs, was to hinder "the Dutch from being absolute masters of the whole Guinea trade." Instead of seeking unoccupied territory on which to build their bases for trade, which the French did, the Africa Company chose "to traffic from Cape Verde to Cape Bon Esperance which hath long since been performed by the Portugals and after them by the Dutch." In order to pursue this policy, the Company had to oust the English East India Company from its possessions, since that company was trading in harmony with the Dutch. Clearly, then, from the outset hatred of the Dutch as much as pursuit of profit influenced the policies of the Africa Company. Indeed the actions of the Africa Company suggest that it was more interested in attacking Dutch merchants and seamen than in bringing gold back to England. In an early anonymous court memorandum considering the possibility of a new Dutch war, it was suggested that the Africa Company "favor and countenance the trade of the Swede in Guinea" in order to procure another ally against the Dutch. In late 1663 George Downing, who was always more interested in out-competing the Dutch than in eviscerating them, was furious that the Company had declined an offer to buy Fredericksburg which would "have given the occasion to vie with the Dutch and have let them into that trade" in favor of sending Robert Holmes on a military mission to the coast of Guinea.[25]

In fact, it must have been quite clear that an Anglo-Dutch war would have proved disastrous to the economic livelihood of the Africa Company. The account books of the Company reveal that the early voyages which

24 "Notes of the Reports to the Committee for Trade," 1 April 1664, SP 29/96/6; "Proceedings of the Committee for Trade," 1 April 1664, SP 29/98/35; petition to Committee for the Advance of Trade, 1664, SP 84/170, f. 26r.

25 Pepys, *Diary*, Vol. V, 29 May 1664, pp. 159–160; James S. Clarke, *The Life of James the Second* Vol. I (London, 1816), p. 399; petition of Royal Africa Company, 2 January 1665, SP 29/110/13; T. Mundy, "Some Occurrences," July 1662, Bod. Rawl A315, f. 240v; East India Company petition to Duke of York, May 1662, IOL, Home Miscellanies H/42, f. 45; East India Company to agents and factors at Fort Cormantine, 11 July 1662, IOL, E/3/86, f. 74r; "An Essay in Case of War," SP 84/163, f. 179v; Downing to Clarendon, 27 November 1663, Bod., Clar. 107, f. 25v; Downing to Bennet, 18/28 December 1663, SP 84/168, f. 207v.

"brought home such store of gold that administered the first occasion of the coinage of those pieces that had the denomination of guineas," were successful because they had exchanged Dutch manufactured goods for native gold.[26] Africa Company proponents argued that "the very being of the plantations depend upon the welfare of it, for they must be utterly ruined if they either want supply of negro servants for their work, or be forced to receive them at excessive rates." Yet it was well known that fragile supply lines, like those between the coast of Africa and the West Indies, would be first to go in an Anglo-Dutch conflict. "Our plantation trade will be in worse condition than before the war," William Coventry pointed out, "because they will not be supplied with loose people or commodities so freely or so cheap, and their own commodities will not be taken off them at so good rates as in peace." It must have come as no surprise then when the shares of the Royal Company plummeted from 100 to 55 when it became certain there would be another Anglo-Dutch War.[27]

Nevertheless it is quite clear that the Africa Company did want to provoke a war with the Dutch. On 8 March 1664, a full three weeks before the committee of trade began investigating the causes of England's economic malaise, the Africa Company petitioned Charles II about the "abuses offered by the Dutch to our nation." Within a week Joseph Williamson, an assistant of the Company and very much an Anglican Royalist, complained in his newsletter that "the Dutch use all their endeavors to obstruct" the Africa trade. On 23 March Sir Nicholas Crispe, Sir Richard Ford and Mr. [Edward] Seymour brought in a petition to the House of Commons. Indeed it might well have been this petition which provoked the alteration of the trade committee's brief. "The Royal Company of merchants for Guinea have brought complaints to the king and Parliament against the Dutch, for having impeded the trade of the English on the coasts of Guinea, and for having ill-treated them," reported the Venetian ambassador; "accordingly the king and Parliament have appointed commissioners to examine this matter." When the lists of complaints began coming in from the various trading companies both Muddiman and Williamson wrote in their newsletters that "the Dutch were much complained of, especially by the Guinea Company." No wonder that Sir George Carteret told Pepys in December that the Guinea "trade brought all these troubles upon us between the Dutch and us." No wonder indeed that Sir Orlando Bridgeman was later

26 Edward Hyde, *The Life of Edward Earl of Clarendon* (Dublin, 1760), p. 94; "Account Books," PRO, Kew Gardens, T 70/309, *passim*; Privy Council Register, PRO, PC 2/56, f. 332r (request for permission to ship Dutch goods for Africa).

27 "Memorial of the Royal Company," 1663, PRO, Kew, CO 1/17, f. 264r; W. Coventry, "Paper on Dutch War," BL, Add. 32094, f. 50v; De Bacquoy/Van Ruyven to Bennet, 10 January 1665, SP 84/174, ff. 14v–15r. The nightmares about the plantations were already becoming a reality by January 1665: Downing to Clarendon, 27 January 1665, Bod., Clar. 108, f. 195r.

convinced that the Africa Company was "the principal cause of the Dutch war."[28]

Why was the Africa Company so interested in an Anglo-Dutch war? The Marxist literary critic Michael McKeon has explained the Company's outlook by "the special relationship" which it enjoyed with the court, implying that rather than seeking to advance the national interest the Company was trying to line the pockets of the courtiers and their select merchant allies.[29] Not only do the economic policies pursued by the Company make it unlikely that many of its members hoped to reap short-term profits, but a closer inspection of the minute books reveals that defining the membership as courtiers and noblemen is much too imprecise.

In fact the Company by 1664 was solidly Anglican Royalist. Unlike the East India Company and the Levant Company, which both retained sizeable numbers of Dissenters after the Restoration, the meetings of the Africa Company were dominated by men who had impeccable Royalist credentials from the 1650s, and were prominent in attacks on Nonconformists in the 1660s. Naturally the Company would not decline to accept money from those with whom it differed ideologically, but such men were not allowed to participate in making Company policy. So while the Nonconformist and apocalyptic Earl of Pembroke had, along with the Duke of York, proposed the foundation of an African company in 1660, the minute books reveal that he played a minimal role in Company affairs. Indeed it might well have been this Anglican Royalist exclusiveness which prompted him to sell his shares to Lord Belasys in 1664.[30] Lord Ashley Cooper only attended two of the twenty-one meetings of the court of assistants between 1664 and 1667, and was never elected to the policy-making committee of seven. His experience contrasts remarkably with that of the Duke of York who "was constantly present himself at all councils, which were held once a week in his own lodgings at Whitehall." The most active men in the Company, besides the Duke of York, were Lord John Berkeley, the sub-governor; Thomas Grey, the deputy governor; Sir Ellis Leighton, the company's secretary; Sir Richard Ford, a former deputy governor; Sir William Ryder;

28 Minute book of Royal Adventurers, 8 March 1664, PRO, Kew, T. 70/75, f. 6r; Williamson's newsletter, 12 March 1664, Carte 222, f. 59r; minute book of Royal Adventurers, 23 March 1664, PRO, Kew T.70/75, f. 8r; minute book of Royal Adventurers, 29 March 1664, PRO, Kew, T.70/75, f. 9r; Williamson's newsletter, 2 April 1664, Carte 72, f. 49r; Muddiman's newsletter, 2 April 1664, Bod., Tanner MSS 47, f. 111v; Sagredo to Doge and Senate, 19/29 April 1664, *CSPV*, p. 11; Comminges to Louis XIV, 25 April/5 May 1664, PRO, PRO 31/3/113, ff. 154–155; Pepys, *Diary*, Vol. V, 22 December 1664, p. 353; Sir Orlando Bridgeman to Arlington, 11 July 1668, SRO, D1287/18/3/1.

29 McKeon, *Politics and Poetry*, pp. 112–116.

30 Pepys, *Diary*, Vol. I, 3 October 1660, p. 258. Minute book of Royal Adventurers, 8 March 1664, PRO, Kew, T.70/75, f. 6v; Joseph Williamson's "Spy Book," SP 9/26, f. 139r. Given the dating of the sale of his shares, Pembroke may well have been indicating opposition to the Hollandophobic policy being pursued by the company.

Captain George Cock; Alderman John Bence; Sir Nicholas Crispe; John Buckworth; Henry Brouncker; Sir John Shaw; Sir John Wolstenholme; John Cutler; and Colonel William Ashburnham.[31]

All of these men had a similar outlook and a history of devotion to the Stuart cause. Lord John Berkeley's tirade against the former Cromwellian Earl of Angelsey prompted Pepys to call him "the most hot, fiery man in discourse without any cause, that ever I saw." In 1663 Lord Berkeley blamed the lack of "harmony" in politics on "the artifice of those that heretofore differed from us."[32] Thomas Grey, whom William Coventry thought the most important of the court party in the Africa Company, was almost certainly a Roman Catholic follower of the Duke of York. His economic ideas, however, were impeccably Anglican Royalist. He told Samuel Pepys that "it is not the greatest wits but the steady man that is a good merchant: he instanced in Ford and Cocke, the last of whom he values above all men as his oracle." Consequently it is not surprising to find him predicting that the Dutch would rather surrender than fight a war against England.[33] Despite his Presbyterian upbringing Sir Ellis Leighton was a Roman Catholic convert and a member of the Duke of York's entourage. In 1672 he advised the Dublin Corporation that "if any body could find out a shape of government, or devise any rules that would make you more subject to the will and personal power of the prince, you [should] petition the king for that model and for those rules."[34]

In the year prior to the Dutch War, William Coventry claimed that the Africa Company was "much steered by Sir Richard Ford, Captain George Cocke, Sir William Ryder of the merchants." Richard Ford was perhaps the single most powerful merchant in Restoration London. He was at one time governor of the Merchant Adventurers and an important assistant of the East India Company as well as being deputy governor of the Africa Company. His record in the 1640s and 1650s was impeccable. In 1642 "to preserve my loyalty and that I might contribute to the Rebellion" he fled to Rotterdam, where he immediately made high-level contacts with Orangists

31 Hyde, *Life*, p. 95. The selection of significant members is based on an analysis of PRO, Kew, T.70/75 and PRO, Kew T.70/309. Because the minute book covers 1664–1667 I have given additional weight to attendance at its meetings in 1664 and 1665, because it is the Company's policies in those years which interest me here. Nevertheless the ideological composition of the Company did not change until after the conclusion of the Anglo-Dutch War when the Earl of Angelsey took over the company.

32 Pepys, *Diary*, Vol. V, 3 December 1664, p. 336; John Berkeley to Ormonde, 2 June 1663, Carte 32, f. 519v.

33 William Coventry, "Discourse on the Dutch War," Longleat House, Cov. MSS CII, ff. 5–6 (includes the comment that Grey wanted war "to make his court to his R. H."); Pepys, *Diary*, Vol. V, 18 October 1664, p. 300; Pepys, *Diary*, Vol. V, 7 November 1664, p. 315; Pepys, *Diary*, Vol. V, 17 December 1664, pp. 348–349; Henning, *House of Commons* Vol. II, p. 444.

34 Pepys, *Diary*, Vol. V, 18 October 1664, p. 300 (and note); *The Speech of Sir Ellis Leighton Kt At the Tholsell of Dublin April the 4th* 1672 (Dublin, 1672), p. 6.

in order to supply Charles I's army. He returned to London in the late 1650s and "was among the most active of those that contrived and actuated the City's interest to be instrumental to his Majesty's blessed Restoration." His loyalty was soon rewarded with a post at court. Ford then used his prestige in the City to round up Dissenters, and was among the first to provide the government with news of the 1663 rebellion. He was a persistent hammer of the Dutch republicans, arguing as early as 1660 that it is "the interest of this kingdom to have a peace with Spain and a war with France and Holland." In the summer of 1664 he was active in heating up anti-Dutch sentiment by translating Dutch Anglophobic broadsides into English.[35] Although Sir William Ryder's pre-Restoration record is difficult to discern, his will reveals his close friendship with the Anglican Royalist Mayor of London and fellow Africa Company assistant Sir John Robinson and with Sir Richard Ford. The Dutch he described as "that insulting nation" noted especially for their bribery and their perfidy.[36] George Cock(e) had been granted a reversion to the office of the keeper of the Council Chamber by Charles I. "In the service of the Royal faction of most honored memory" he was apparently "twice shot and twice taken prisoner and when after some years' imprisonment released, in pursuant of his loyalty he left this kingdom and hath for eleven years remained abroad." At the Restoration he became a captain in the company of Lord Rutherford's regiment at Dunkirk, a regiment known for its intolerance of Nonconformity and its leanings to Catholicism. In February 1664, predictably enough, he was lecturing the customers of a London coffee house "of the good effects of some kind of a Dutch war and conquest."[37]

35 William Coventry, "Discourse on the Dutch War," Longleat House, Cov. MSS CII, ff. 5–6; petition of the Company of Royal Adventurers, 20 November 1663, PRO, Kew, CO 1/17, f. 235r; Merchant Adventurers petition, undated, SP 82/10, f. 12r; Sir Richard Ford to Clarendon, 29 April 1662, Bod., Clar. 76, f. 185; Sir Richard Ford to Clarendon, 5 May 1662, Bod., Clar. 74, f. 201r; Sir Richard Ford to Clarendon, July 1663, Bod., Clar. 80, f. 43; Pepys, *Diary*, Vol. I, 25 September 1660, p. 253; Pepys, *Diary*, Vol. V, 8 August 1664, p. 235; Pepys, *Diary*, Vol. V, 22 November 1664, p. 328; Pepys, *Diary*, Vol. V, 24 December 1664, p. 355; Richard Ford to Downing, 11 July 1662, BL, Add. 22919, f. 236r; Richard Ford to Williamson, 14 November 1664, SP 29/104/109 (recommending Oxenden's friend Humphrey Gyfford); Henning, *House of Commons*, Vol. II, pp. 344–346. He was also evidently a close friend of Joseph Williamson's: Richard Ford to Williamson, 17 July 1665, SP 29/127/9.

36 William Ryder to George Oxenden, 26 March 1662, BL, Add. 40711, ff. 26v–27r. I owe the information on Ryder's will to the kindness of Henry Horwitz. Ryder's "fearing the issue of a Dutch war" almost certainly reflects his economic fears rather than his political opposition: Pepys, *Diary*, Vol. V, 28 May 1664, p. 159. Ryder was closely associated with the Anglican Royalist merchants George Smith and George Oxenden: George Smith to Oxenden, 8 March 1666, BL, Add. 40710, f. 32r; George Smith to Oxenden, 14 March 1666, Add. 40712, f. 25r; Sir William Ryder to Oxenden, 22 August 1667, BL, Add. 40713, f. 15r. For the intolerance of Sir John Robinson see Ludlow, "A Voyce," Bod., English History MSS C487, p. 996.

37 Privy Council Register, 9 October 1663, PC 2/56, f. 291v; petition of Gorge Cock, 25 June 1660, SP 29/5/7; the humble petition of Gorge Cock, April 1661, SP 29/34/107; Charles

The other important members of the Company had similar ideological predispositions. John Bence had supported Charles II in the 1650s, and was counted a court supporter at the Restoration. He was sufficiently well trusted in 1664 to be elected alderman during a period of royal intervention in city politics.[38] Sir Nicholas Crispe had been one of the original investors in the African trade in the early seventeenth century. "After the Rebellion began he betook himself to serve the king," raised a regiment in the king's service and expended a large portion of his fortune in financing the Royalist cause. After the defeat of Charles I he fled to the Spanish Netherlands. He returned sometime before the Restoration and signed the *Declaration of the Nobility and Gentry That Adhered to the Late King, Now Residing In and About the City of London* in April 1660. After the Restoration he maintained Anglican Royalist connections, and was employed by Joseph Williamson to round up Nonconformists.[39] Henry Brouncker, who replaced William Coventry as one of the Company's committee of seven in June 1664, was the son of one of the gentlemen of Charles I's Privy Chamber. He had joined the exiled Stuart court in the 1650s and was known to be no enemy to Roman Catholicism. At the Restoration he was a member of the Duke of York's household, holding the position of groom of the bed-chamber.[40] Sir John Shaw had financed the Royalist war cause, and subsequently sent money to Charles II from his base in Antwerp. At the Restoration he was rewarded by being named a commissioner of the customs. In the early 1660s he provided Joseph Williamson with the names of Nonconformists who traveled to and from the United Provinces. It should certainly come as no surprise that he was counted "doubly vile" by Shaftesbury during the Exclusion Crisis.[41] Sir John Wolstenholme "suffered

Dalton (editor), *English Army Lists and Commission Registers 1661–1714* Vol. I *1661–1685* (London, 1892), p. 18; Pepys, *Diary*, Vol. III, 15 December 1662, pp. 282–283; Lord Rutherford to Nicholas, 16 August 1662, SP 29/58/53; Alsop, Bridge, and Lillington to Nicholas, 5 August 1660, BL, Egerton MSS 2537, f. 136r; Pepys, *Diary*, Vol. V, 2 February 1664, p. 35; Pepys, *Diary*, Vol. V, 22 November 1664, p. 329; Pepys, *Diary*, Vol. V, 2 December 1664, p. 335.

38 Woodhead, *Rulers of London*, p. 29; Rep. Book of the London Court of Aldermen, 15 November 1664, CLRO, Rep. 70, f. 7.

39 Hyde, *Life*, p. 94; Nicholas Crispe to Sir Richard Browne, 6 November 1647, Christ Church, Browne MSS, Box D–L; Nicholas Crispe to Williamson, 19 March 1664, SP 29/94/115; *A Declaration of the Nobility and Gentry That Adhered to the Late King, Now Residing in and about the City of London* (London, 1660), Thomason: 20 April 1660, broadside; will of Sir Nicholas Crispe, in *Collections Relating to the Family of Crispe* (privately published, 1882–1897), pp. 32–34; *Certain Considerations Relating to the Royal African Company of England* (1680), p. 3; Henning, *House of Commons*, Vol. II, pp. 169–170.

40 Clarke, *Life of James the Second*, p. 415; minutes of Royal Adventurers, 20 June 1664, PRO, Kew T.70/75, f. 16r; Henning, *House of Commons*, Vol. I, pp. 728–729. Other members of the households of Charles and James were active in the Company, including Allan Apsley, Henry Progers, and Thomas Povey.

41 Henning, *House of Commons*, Vol. III, pp. 429–430; Sir John Shaw to Williamson,

infinitely" for his Royalism after the surrender of York, and was accordingly awarded the post of customs commissioner at the Restoration.[42] Sir John Cutler was a good friend of Sir William Ryder and Sir Richard Ford, sharing their anti-Dutch sentiments. It is likely that his knighthood granted at the Restoration was a reward for some noble service during the Interregnum. Cutler's active involvement, both financial and administrative, in the rebuilding of St. Paul's suggests the depth of his Anglican sentiment. His Anglican Royalism is confirmed by his support of the king during the Exclusion Crisis.[43] William Ashburnham's Anglican Royalist credentials couldn't have been better. Implicated in the Army Plot, imprisoned by the Protectorate, and a petitioner for the Restoration of the monarchy in 1660, he emerged naturally enough as a court supporter at the Restoration and an enemy of Exclusion twenty years later.[44]

The committee of trade resolution, then, was not the result of a unanimous calculation by English merchants that the Dutch were their sole economic rivals and that those rivals could only be dealt with by a mercantilist war of aggression. Instead the resolution represented the views of the Anglican Royalist segment of the political nation, a segment which included politicians as much as merchants.

Naturally there were other interpretations of England's economic situation. One group of people, which included William Coventry and the Earl of Clarendon, claimed that there was in fact no economic malaise. The Earl of Clarendon recalled that in 1663 many people complained of a "great decay of trade," but he dismissed these claims as being "but pretenses, and resulted from combinations rather than reason. For it appeared by the

29 February 1664, SP 29/93/71; "Commissioners of the Customs," 24 October 1660, BL, Egerton MSS 2537, f. 217r.

42 John Wolstenholme to Phineas Andrewes, 20 April 1645, Bod., Tanner MSS 60, f. 122r; "Commissioners of the Customs," 24 October 1660, BL, Egerton MSS 2537, f. 217r. Significantly Sir John's second son appears in the Anglican Royalist Henry Oxenden's "Oxideni Amici" Folger, Va300, f. 51. His daughter married into the Anglican Royalist circle in Yorkshire: Elizabeth Clifford to Earl of Burlington, 29 August 1665, BL, Althorp Papers B4. Linda Popofsky has identified Wolstenholme as a member of the Customs Syndicate against which the Levant Company aligned itself in the 1629 attack on tonnage and poundage. Linda S. Popofsky, "Tonnage and Poundage in 1629," in *Past and Present* No. 126 (February 1990), p. 52.

43 Pepys, *Diary*, Vol. V, 19 February 1664, p. 52; Pepys, *Diary*, Vol. V, 17 February 1664, p. 51; Pepys, *Diary*, Vol. V, 29 September 1664, pp. 282–283 (evidence that George Carteret lived in his house); Guildhall, 25200/31, 32, 33, 34; Woodhead, *Rulers of London*, p. 55; Henning, *House of Commons*, Vol. II, pp. 183–184. Toby Barnard has included Cutler in another grouping of Anglican Royalist merchants. Toby Barnard, "An Anglo-Irish Industrial Enterprise: Iron-Making at Enniscorthy, Co. Wexford, 1657–92," in *Proceedings of the Royal Irish Academy* Vol. 85, C, No. 4, pp. 105–107. At the outset of the war Cutler donated a thousand pounds towards the rebuilding of the Loyal London: Richard Browne to John Evelyn, 11 March 1665, Christ Church, John Evelyn-In-Letters, 401.

44 *A Declaration of the Nobility and Gentry*, broadside; Henning, *House of Commons*, Vol. I, p. 554. His brother John was also an assistant of the Africa Company.

customs, that the trade was greater than it had ever been." Throughout 1663 this was the view taken by the official newsletters. "I can not but acquaint you in contradiction of some who endeavor to raise a discontent in the people by daily complaints of the deadness of trade," wrote Williamson in his newsletter, "that by an equal computation it is adjudged that the Port of London only will pay off the whole account for customs and defray the full charges of farmers this year." The corollary of this position was that England "could only become rich by peace." Even if the English gained all "the advantage aimed at by a war with the Dutch," argued William Coventry, it would "never bring to the king's coffers the profit of one shilling." If Charles II "engaged in a war with Holland," Clarendon reasoned, it "would interrupt and disturb all the trade of the kingdom upon which the greatest part of his revenue did rise." "It is not a popular discourse," admitted Coventry, "but it is a true one, that the crown may pay too dear for some present advantages to the people ... the enriching the people by beggaring the crown is no good policy." Coventry, whose economic guru was the Nonconformist John Joliffe, was willing to admit that the Dutch were England's great economic rivals, but the key to defeating them was not to conquer their trade but to remedy the "pride and the laziness of the merchant."[45]

Nonconformists naturally blamed much of the decay of trade, a decay which they very much knew existed, on the intolerance of the Restoration regime. In September 1662 pamphlets were distributed throughout London praising "the quick trading and civil days and plenty of money in the days of Oliver Cromwell" as compared to "the restraint that was upon the people separated from the worship used by the Lords Spiritual, and want of trading among the citizens of London and other cities of trade and commerce." It "can scarce be imagined how trading is decayed since the Act of Restraint [of conventicles] came out," observed one correspondent of Viscount Conway, " 'tis feared shortly the poor will cause tumults for want of bread."[46]

[45] Hyde, *Life*, pp. 92, 94, 96; Williamson's newsletter, 21 August 1663, Carte 222, f. 28; Williamson to Ormonde, 22 August 1663, Carte 33, f. 83r; newsletter, 23 December 1663, Carte 222, f. 9r; William Coventry, "Paper on Dutch Wars," BL, Add. 32094, ff. 51–52; Pepys, *Diary*, Vol. V, 18 October 1664, p. 300; Pepys, *Diary*, Vol. V, 29 May 1664, p. 160. For Coventry's political outlook see D. T. Witcombe, "The Parliamentary Career of Sir William and Mr. Henry Coventry 1661–1681" (Oxford, B. Litt. thesis, 1934), pp. 14–15. Like Clarendon he was less inclined to persecute dissent at all cost than his Anglican Royalist brother, for example. See William Coventry to Bennet, 14 November 1664, SP 29/104/104, where he defends one Taylor, who though a fanatic, is a good administrator. It is, of course, true that Clarendon despised William Coventry. I think that this hatred probably dates from Coventry's support of his impeachment. In any case, it is not impossible for two men with similar ideological outlooks to find each other personally unpleasant. It should be noted that William Coventry went out of his way to distance himself from the second Dutch War, and wrote a pamphlet in opposition to the third war.

[46] T. Rugge, "Mercurius Politicus Redivivus," September 1662, BL, Add. 10117, f. 46v; T. Bromley to Viscount Conway, 2 June 1664, SP 29/99/9.

The Nonconformists were far from united in identifying the foreign enemy. One man implicated in the Northern Rebellion thought that the French and the Irish "spoil the trade of the nation." Indeed the wealth of petitions from Huguenot merchants complaining against the French, the well-known Francophobia of Londoners in the early 1660s, and Thomas Papillon's complaint to the committee of trade in April 1664, suggest that the Nonconformist and Francophobic merchant grouping which Margaret Priestley has described for the 1670s might already have been coming into existence.[47] But not all merchants, not even all Nonconformist merchants, were yet ready to identify France as the principal trade rival. In the West Indies, an area still populated by former Cromwellians, the Spanish remained the great enemies of English merchants.[48] Of course, neither of these variants of Nonconformist economic argument found much favor in the context of an Anglican Royalist reaction. Charles II ordered the Governor of Jamaica, Sir Thomas Modyford, to prevent all attacks on Spanish shipping in June 1664. Meanwhile the pro-French outlook of the court prevented any attack on Colbert's expansionist economic policies until France entered the war against England in 1665.[49]

There were then several ways of understanding England's economic circumstances in 1664. That these different interpretations were closely allied to different ideological perspectives should hardly surprise us. Indeed contemporaries were well aware that the ideological divisions which so

47 Witcombe, "Sir William and Mr. Henry Coventry,", p. 31; 4 merchant petitions, 1664, SP 78/119, ff. 21–28; Petition of Several Masters of Ships and Mariners, 29 April 1664, SP 29/97/66; Bennet to Hollis, 22 February 1664, SP 78/118, f. 75r; notes of reports of the Council of Trade, 1 April 1664, SP 29/96/6, SP 29/96/7; "Testimony of Dobson," 1 February 1664, SP 29/92/3; Margaret Priestley, "London Merchants and Opposition Politics in Charles II's Reign," in *Bulletin of the Institute of Historical Research* Vol. 29 (1956), pp. 205–219.

48 Extract from a Letter from Jamaica, 1663, PRO, Kew CO 1/18, f. 262r; De Bacquoy/Van Ruyven to Williamson, 14/24 June 1663, SP 84/167, ff. 162v–163r; Letter from Sir Charles Littleton, 1 February 1664, PRO, Kew CO 1/18, f. 30r; Sagredo to Doge and Senate, 28 June/8 July 1664, *CSPV*, p. 28. For non-West Indies complaints against the Spanish see: Morgan Read to Henry Bennet, 6/16 April 1663, SP 98/4, f. 189r; Privy Council Register, 23 October 1663, PRO, PC 2/56, f. 301r; Privy Council Register, 11 December 1663, PRO, PC 2/56, f. 334v.

49 For the restraint on anti-Spanish economic activity see: Cuneus to States General, 29 April/9 May 1664, SP 101/122/26; Charles II to Sir Thomas Modyford, 15 June 1664, SP 44/17, p. 41; Muddiman's newsletter, 16 June 1664, Bod., Tanner MSS 47, f. 169r; Joseph Martyn to Bennet, 26 June 1664, PRO, Kew CO 1/18, f. 173r; T. Rugge, "Mercurius Politicus Redivivus" September 1664, BL, Add. 10117, f. 117v. For restraint on anti-French activity: O'Neill to Ormonde, 5 May 1663, Carte 32, f. 391r; O'Neill to Ormonde, 27 June 1663, Carte 32, f. 625r; O'Neill to Ormonde, 19 September 1663, Carte 33, f. 132; Chauran to Williamson, 2/12 February 1662, SP 84/165, f. 68r. I am tempted to guess that former Cromwellians tended to have anti-Spanish sentiments, in accord with the anti-Spanish rhetoric of the Protectorate; while opponents of the Protectorate, in line with those who claimed that Cromwell's alliance with France was a disaster for England, were anti-French. But it should be emphasized that given the dearth of pamphlet material, this must remain only a guess.

dominated the debates in the Houses of Parliament were just as prevalent in the merchant community. "Very many merchants are become such sectaries," lamented Sir Edward Nicholas, "as they think they do not err in breaking their word and faith with any man that is not of their faith and principle." "Commonly the captains and masters of merchants ships being men ill affected and of different principles from the Church of England," the Earl of Winchilsea wrote to the sympathetic Bishop of London, "make choice of mates, pursers and surgeons of the like temper." "A Presbyterian forfeits his charter that keeps touch with a son of the Church," hyperbolized Roger L'Estrange.[50] One should not, of course, assume that no Nonconformist did business with an Anglican. Nevertheless it is very likely that Anglican Royalists and Nonconformists understood England's economic situation in very different ways.

The trade resolution of 21 April 1664 should be understood, then, neither as the necessary result of Anglo-Dutch economic competition, nor as an attempt by politicians to create an economic argument where there was none to be made. Instead the trade resolution should be understood as the victory in the economic sphere of an Anglican Royalist reaction which, during the same session of Parliament, succeeded in repealing the Triennial Act and in passing the Conventicle Act.

[50] Nicholas to Thomas Maynard, 16 November 1661, SP 44/1, f. 17; Winchilsea to Bishop of London, 24 June 1664, HMC, *Finch*, p. 321; Roger L'Estrange, *Toleration Discussed* (London, 1663), p. 1. See also Elizabeth Dallyson to George Oxenden, 16 April 1662, BL, Add. 40696, f. 206r for some personal attacks by an Anglican Royalist merchantess against Dissenting merchants, including Thomas Papillon.

16

Popery, trade, and universal monarchy

Why did Anglican Royalists feel that the Dutch were the economic enemy? Why, in short, should the battle against republicanism and irreligion be conducted in economic terms? The answer to these questions lies in the way Restoration Englishmen understood the workings of European politics, an understanding conceived in terms of the idiom of universal monarchy.

The English in the late sixteenth and early seventeenth centuries had feared and loathed the King of Spain and the House of Habsburg not just because they were the current enemies, but because they pretended to a universal monarchy of all the known world. The vast territories inherited by Charles V made it possible for the first time since Charlemagne for a secular prince to reclaim the *imperium* of Rome. In English and Protestant eyes the foreign, indeed the imperial, policy of Charles V and his son Philip II was a necessary adjunct to their alliance with the Antichristian Church of Rome. "Popish and Spanish invisible arts and counsels," argued Fulke Greville in his famous *Life of Sidney*, aimed "to undermine the greatness and freedom both of secular and ecclesiastical princes ... and by their insensible fall, a raising up of the House of Austria many steps toward her long-affected Monarchy over the West." Spain's goal, opined Lord Burghley in 1590, was "to be lord and commander of all Christendom, jointly with the Pope and with no other associate." "By fraud, policy, treason, intestine divisions and wars," recalled the author of *Philanax Protestant*, "the Pope and Spaniard too" tried to reduce all Protestant princes and realms to "their long prosecuted universal monarchy." "It hath been hitherto the only business of the Spaniards," concurred one Cromwellian propagandist, "to be always in wars, that so they may be ready upon all occasions to produce that monarchy of the whole Christian world, which they have long since conceived."[1] The King of Spain was dangerous precisely because he sought universal monarchy with the ecclesiastical support of the Church of Rome.

1 Fulke Greville, Lord Brooke, *Life of the Renowned Sir Philip Sidney* (London, 1652), pp. 29–30 – I am grateful to Wallace MacCaffrey for pointing out Greville's discussion of universal monarchy to me; BL, Lansdowne MSS 103/63/182–186 (I owe this reference to the kindness of Wallace MacCaffrey); *Philanax Protestant* (London, 1663), p. 22; *The*

In the middle of the seventeenth century, an economic element was added to the concept of universal monarchy. The long and exhausting conflicts of the Eighty Years War and the Thirty Years War convinced most Europeans that the key to military victory was no longer martial prowess, but economic resources. "Since the wealth of the Indies came to be discovered and dispersed more and more," commented one very keen observer, "wars are managed by much treasure and little fighting, and therefore with little hazard to the richer nation." "Since the discovery of the Indies, and increase of trade," agreed Sir William Coventry, the "foundations of a vaster Empire" were "navigation and commerce." It was for this reason that the King of Spain had struggled for so long to retain control of the Low Countries, for by "conjoining their dominion, and forces by sea to his large empires, and armies upon the main, [he] would probably enforce all absolute princes to acknowledge subjection to him before their time." In the spring of 1664 Sir Henry Bennet published Thomas Mun's famous treatise, *England's Treasure by Foreign Trade*. This treatise, which Sir Richard Ford called "the most rational and demonstrative discourse on that subject which I ever yet heard or read," did complain of Dutch encroachment on English trade. More significantly, Mun explained the importance of trade in the context of the struggle for universal monarchy. By the wealth he had garnered in the Indies – "the very sinews of his strength" – Mun claimed, the King of Spain "is enabled not only to keep in subjection many goodly states and provinces in Italy and elsewhere, (which otherwise would soon fall from his obeisance) but also by a continual war taking his advantages doth still enlarge his dominions, ambitiously aiming at a Monarchy."[2] No longer, then, would the aspiring universal monarch express his power in terms of territorial control. The universal monarchy of the later seventeenth century would be established through control of trade.

Restoration Englishmen and women understood very well the key role that control of the sea would play in the establishment and prevention of universal monarchy. "To pretend to universal monarchy without fleets was

King of Spain's Cabinet Counsel Divulged; Or, A Discovery of the Prevarications of the Spaniards With All the Princes and States of Europe, for Obtaining the Universal Monarchy (London, 1658) Thomason: 1 October 1657, p. 88.

2 [William Petyt], *Britannia Languens: Or, A Discourse of Trade* (London, 1680), p. 11; *Englands Appeal From the Private Caballe at Whitehall to the Great Council of the Nation* (1673), pp. 6–7; Greville, *Life of Sidny*, pp. 55–56; Paul Seaward, "The House of Commons Committee of Trade and the Origins of the Second Anglo-Dutch War, 1664," in *The Historical Journal* Vol. 30 No. 2 (1987), pp. 443–444 (for Bennet's role in the publication of Mun); Sir Richard Ford to Williamson, 22 March 1664, PRO, SP 29/95/15; license granted to Sir Richard Ford to print Mun, 24 March 1664, *CSPD*, p. 527; Thomas Mun, *England's Treasure by Forraign Trade* (London, 1664), p. 56. For the composition of Mun's pamphlet see B. E. Supple, "Thomas Mun and the Commercial Crisis, 1623," in *Bulletin of the Institute of Historical Research* Vol. 27 (1954), pp. 91–94. Mun's response to the economic depression of 1623 represented an Anglican court analysis as against the puritan analysis offered by [Thomas Scott], *The Belgick Pismire* (London, 1622).

long since looked on, as a politick chimaera," argued the Anglican Royalist John Evelyn in a tract originally meant as his introduction to a projected history of the second Anglo-Dutch War, for "whoever commands the ocean, commands the trade of the world, and whoever commands the trade of the world, commands the riches of the world, and whoever is master of that, commands the world itself." Only when Rome had established a powerful fleet, and surpassed Carthage and Agrigentum as naval powers, could they "be said to speed conquerors of the world." "It is the sea that terrifies and masters the land," the Marquis of Newcastle explained to Charles II, it "makes great kings if not your subjects, yet subjects to you, and must subject themselves to your will." Although less learned than Evelyn, Newcastle also knew that "all story tells us, that they that have been ever strongest by sea, hath given the law to their land neighbors." "That Prince, whose flags are bow'd to on the seas, / Of all kings shores keeps in his hands the keys," argued the King in the Earl of Orrery's play *Henry V*, first performed in the summer of 1664. "No king can him, he may all kings invade; / and on his will depends their peace and trade." It was in this context that the minister Simon Ford could tell his congregation that "the engrossers [of trade], or obstructors thereof have been in all ages accounted the common enemies of mankind."[3]

Spain, however, had been forced in 1659 to sign the ignominious Treaty of the Pyrenees. As a result Englishmen no longer feared Spain's pretensions to a universal monarchy, but instead commented on her weakness. When the Spanish ambassador in Paris openly told the King of France "that the ambassador of his master shall no more contend for precedency," it prompted George Downing to remark "on the extreme weakness and lowness of the affairs of that crown." The failure of the Spanish monarchy to subdue the Portuguese campaign for independence only served to confirm its demise. After Don John of Austria's devastating defeat at the hands of the Conde De Villaflore, most Englishmen thought that "the Spanish grandeur did so sink in the fatal carnage of that field" that "it will not buoy up again (at least for some years) from that important ruin."[4] Sir Richard Fanshawe's instructions as English ambassador to Spain informed him "that the monarchy of Spain, is fallen to a great declination, more especially in all maritime strength, not only by having the whole kingdom of Portugal

[3] John Evelyn, *Navigation and Commerce, Their Original and Progress* (London, 1674), pp. 15–17, 32–33; Marquis of Newcastle, "Treatise," 1660–1661, Bod., Clar. 109, pp. 6–7, 41–42; Roger Boyle, *The History of Henry the Fifth: And the Tragedy of Mustapha, Son of Solyman the Magnificent* (London, 1668), p. 40 (I owe this reference to the kindness of Ingrid H. Tague); Simon Ford, *The Lords Wonders in the Deep*, preached in Northampton 4 July 1665 (Oxford, 1665), p. 8. For the dating of the performance of *Henry V* see Pepys, *Diary*, Vol. V, 13 August 1664, pp. 240–241.

[4] Thomas Philipot, *The Original and Growth of the Spanish Monarchy* (London, 1664), preface.

dismembered and separated from it, with all its dependencies, but into such a decay of shipping, mariners, and indeed all means of entertaining their navigation and commerce with the West Indies." "We look on Spain as decaying" and "fear it not," commented the courtier in Algernon Sidney's "Court Maxims." "The more I see of Spain in these times," Fanshawe wrote after his arrival, "the more strongly I am of opinion it will be very hard for their monarchy to subsist long without England and against it, impossible." This reality had already forced the King of Spain to allow others to trade in the Caribbean, in short to abandon "his sole dominion in the Indies." "The vast increase in power by land and sea which other nations have made upon them since Queen Elizabeth's time," Fanshawe pointed out to Clarendon, "hath so altered the balance that Spain must no more pretend to the universal monarchy."[5]

In the absence of the old pretender to universal monarchy, the English began to ponder who would be the next aspirant. Many Europeans already feared the growing power of the young Louis XIV. In Italy, where the French military had flexed its muscle in the early 1660s, he was looked upon "as aspiring to the universal land monarchy." Despite their recent triumphant treaty with the French, the Dutch were already skeptical of Louis XIV's intentions. "It is generally talked here," reported George Downing from The Hague, "that the King of France designs to have the affairs of the Empire brought to such a condition [by the Turk] as that they may at last be forced to declare him King of the Romans and that then he will undertake their defense." In England, many Nonconformists began to comment that the King of France "has rendered himself absolute arbiter even over other kings and that everybody ought to submit blindly to his wishes in everything." Nonconformists in London were circulating copies of Comenius' prophecy that Louis XIV would become "Emperor of the whole world," much to the delight of the French ambassador.[6] Indeed public debate about the third Anglo-Dutch War centered on whether England should identify France or the United Provinces as the real claimant to the throne of the universal monarchy.[7] In the ideological context of the early

5 Downing to Clarendon, 28 March 1662, Bod., Clar. 106, f. 168v; "Instructions for Sir Richard Fanshawe," 14 January 1664, in Nickolls, *Original Letters*, p. 5; Algernon Sidney, "Court Maxims," Warwickshire Record Office, f. 179; Fanshawe to Bennet, 3/13 August 1664, PRO, SP 94/46, f. 176r; newsletter, 21 November 1663, Carte 222, f. 44; Muddiman's newsletter, 14 June 1664, Bod., Tanner MSS 47, f. 167r; Richard Fanshawe to Clarendon, 30 July 1662, Bod., Clar. 77, f. 164r.

6 John Finch to Lord Arlington, 15/25 August 1665, PRO, SP 98/6 (unfoliated); Joseph Kent to Williamson, 29 December 1663, PRO, SP 98/4, ff. 285v–286r; Downing to Clarendon, 30 October 1663, Bod., Clar. 106, f. 225v; Grimani to Doge and Senate, 1/11 April 1662, *CSPV*, p. 130; Comminges to De Lionne, 21/31 March 1664, PRO, PRO 31/3/113, ff. 105–102 (misfoliated); Downing to Clarendon, 12 February 1664, Bod., Clar. 107, f. 84; Thomas Clarges to Ormonde, 17 November 1663, Carte 33, f. 221v.

7 "From Butterboxes to Wooden Shoes: The Shift in English Popular Sentiment From Anti-Dutch to Anti-French in the 1670s," in *The Historical Journal* (1995).

1660s it was very difficult for politicians to voice their concerns about France, which was after all a true monarchy and a monarchy with which Charles II was thought to be on good terms.

The obvious heir to Spain's universal pretensions in Anglican Royalist eyes was the United Provinces. The Dutch, it seemed, like the Spanish before them, were seeking to use a trade monopoly as the foundation of a universal monarchy. The danger which the Dutch represented was not, as historians have often assumed, that they would outcompete their English rivals, but that using unfair means they would exclude everyone else from trading in the Indies. The Dutch, as Thomas Mun put it, "do hinder and destroy us in our lawful course of living, thereby taking the bread out of our mouths."[8] The English feared the political program which was perceived to motivate Dutch economic expansion, not the economic expansion itself.

Recent developments in Africa and the East Indies confirmed Dutch pretensions to universal monarchy. In early 1663 the East India trader Richard Craddock had warned George Oxenden that "the Dutches wicked intentions, [their] main drift, and utmost endeavors are to over run this coast and quite banish the English off the whole Indian trade." By that summer the worst fears of the English had been realized. The Dutch had conquered the whole of the Malabar coast. "They have proclaimed themselves lords of all the South Seas," complained three English East India merchants, "prohibiting all nations whatsoever to trade on the [Malabar] coast." When the news reached England it provoked an immediate outcry. "Great talk of the Dutch proclaiming themselves in India lords of the Southern Seas and deny traffic there to all ships but their own, upon pain of confiscation," Samuel Pepys reported from the Exchange. The newsletter-writers soon disseminated the news that the Dutch "call themselves masters of the South Sea coast of Malabar" to their Anglican Royalist readers. The Dutch in the East Indies had made clear "that whatever their masters do or say at home, they will do what they list and will be masters of all the world there, and have so proclaimed themselves sovereign of all the South Seas," Sir Thomas Chamberlain told Pepys. Not any nation "under heaven," agreed the East India merchant John Darrell, "durst then look or fall into their foresaid South Seas (as they term and challenge them) but all the nations must be subject to seizure and confiscation of men, ships, and goods, to that insolent and arbitrary government, notwithstanding any treaty or contract made here with the States of Holland to the contrary, which are but nets and snares to delude the English." The English fury was not directed at Dutch economic success, but the unfair and tyrannical means which they had used to gain control of the trade. The Dutch were "not contented with the ordinary course of a fair trade," claimed the author of

8 Mun, *England's Treasure*, p. 29. For similar Spanish pretensions see Greville, *Life of Sidney*, pp. 127–128.

The Dutch Drawn to the Life, but had taken "diverse islands, built several forts, and endeavored a new dominion over us." It was this pretended sovereignty, argued the Anglican Royalist merchant Richard Craddock, that occasioned "a national business ... so that in a year or two more we shall not only have a tug with the Hollanders, but I hope to see their butter boxes fly."[9]

At almost the same time in West Africa, the Dutch West India Company's director of the North Coast of Africa, John Valkenburg, proclaimed the Dutch to be "masters of the whole coast of Guinea." The Dutch, as they had done in the East Indies, were using unfair trading practices. At "every port or place on that coast where the English had any factory or trade," reported Robert Holmes, the Dutch "endeavored to engage the natives against the English and their interest with design to turn them out of all their trade there." "They still retain their old principle to use all base means whatever to hinder us," newsletter-writer Henry Muddiman told his readers. The plan, Downing thought, was for the Dutch to become "absolute sole masters of the gold and also of the negro trade and thereby also to be able to overthrow all his Majesty's plantations in the West Indies for want of slaves." The Africa Company was quick to place these developments in a worldwide context. They "discourse evidently with all," wrote one newsletter-writer, "that the Dutch will leave no stone unturned to discourage and at length ruin [the Guinea trade] as they have well near done our Turkey and East Indy trade."[10]

9 "Remonstrance of the East India Merchants," 13 December 1660, Longleat House, Cov. MSS CV, ff. 18v–19r; Richard Craddock to George Oxenden, 23 April 1663, BL, Add. 40697, f. 14v; John Hunter, Henry Boye, Peter Cooke, to East India Company, 25 August 1663, IOL, E/3/28, f. 36r; De Bacquoy/Van Ruyen to Williamson, 4/14 October 1663, PRO, SP 84/168, f. 25; Privy Council Register, 25 October 1663, PRO, PC 2/56, f. 297v; George Oxenden and Henry Gary to East India Company, 28 January 1664, IOL, E/3/28, f. 99r; Pepys, *Diary*, Vol. V, 29 January 1664, p. 30; Pepys, *Diary*, Vol. V, 9 February 1664, p. 41; newsletter, 9 February 1664, Carte 222, f. 51; newsletter to Sancroft, 13 February 1664, Bod., Tanner MSS 47, f. 60r; Consul Lannoy to Winchilsea, 29 August 1664, HMC, *Finch*, p. 329; Pepys, *Diary* Vol. V, 15 February 1664, pp. 49–50; John Darrell, *A True and Compendious Narration: Or (Second Part of Amboyna)* (London, 1665), pp. 8–9; *The Dutch Drawn to the Life* (London, 1664), p. 143; Richard Craddock to George Oxenden, 10 June 1663, BL, Add. 40697, f. 24r; Ed. Winter, Will. Gyfford, and Edmund Reade to East India Company, 10 December 1663, IOL, E/3/28, f. 23r. See also "Review of the Several Treaties with the Dutch," 20 March 1661, NMM, Clifford Papers, Vol. I, Dw32; Benjamin Lannoy (Aleppo) to Winchilsea, 7 September 1661, LRO, DG7/Box 4962, Bundle V; Henry Coventry to Ormonde, 13 February 1664, Carte 47, f. 420v. Interestingly a letter from East India merchants in Bantam warning that the Dutch "call themselves Masters of all the South Sea Coast of Malabar to Cape Cammaroon" was copied verbatim in one of Joseph Williamson's newsletters: Letter from Bantam, 25 August 1663, PRO, Kew CO 77/9, f. 19r; Williamson's newsletter, 14 March 1664, Houghton Library, Gay 15.25F.

10 Downing's Memorial, 4 August 1664, Bod., Clar. 108, f. 54r; Aitzema, "Selections," Bod., Rawl. C734, ff. 101v–102r; extract of Letter from Cormantine, 26 June 1663, PRO, Kew CO 1/17, f. 158r; Captain Stokes to Duke of York, 29 June 1663, Longleat House, Cov. MSS XCV, f. 1; Downing to Clarendon, 25 September 1663, Bod., Clar. 106, f. 206r;

The English understood the recent success of the Dutch overseas trading companies not in the context of twentieth-century supply-and-demand curves, but in terms of the seventeenth-century idiom of universal monarchy. The English political nation invariably complained about the Dutch insatiable desire to control all of the trade, not about slight improvements in Dutch economic indicators. "They think no monarchs are friends to republics," wrote one Englishman from the United Provinces, but seek "a monopoly of trade which they make their interest." The Dutch, the Earl of Clarendon told Parliament, have "an immoderate desire to engross the whole traffic of the universe." Although the East India Company hoped the English and the Dutch could "be neighbors in situation and yet continue friends," its directors told Sir John Webster, the Dutch had "an unlimited avarice to engross all the trade of the whole world unto themselves." In a conference with the Dutch ambassador Van Goch, Charles himself fumed "that it seemed they wanted to possess all the Indies to the exclusion of all others." "The true quarrel," thought Denzil Hollis, was not about petty economic trifles, "not what is past, but what to come, the apprehension of our co-partnership in their Guinea and East India trade." "If they can vanquish his Majesty or reduce him to terms," William Morrice explained to Henry Coventry, "they think they shall easily be masters of the commerce of the universe." The Dutch, thought John Darrell, "will never be satisfied until they have subjected the trade and treasure of all countries and nations upon earth to their unlimited East-India arbitrary government." The English had to act immediately, for now the two "Dutch Companies of East and West Indies are met together, in hopes also to command from North to South, and so to cross all the subjects of emperors, kings, princes and potentates of the whole universe, save only the Narrow Seas of England which is the chief stumbling block."[11]

Letter from the ship *Charles*, 28 January 1664, BL, Add. 22920, f. 21r; Hollis to Winchilsea, 7 April 1664, HMC, *Finch*, p. 305; Holles to Downing, 7 April 1664, BL, Add. 22920, f. 35; Journal of Robert Holmes, Magdalen College Cambridge, Pepys Library, 2698, ff. 87r, 103; newsletter, 8 March 1664, Carte 222, f. 61v; Muddiman's newsletter, 21 April 1664, Bod., Tanner MSS 47, f. 127; Africa Company petition, 15 June 1664, PRO, SP 29/99/83; Downing to Clarendon, 6 November 1663, Bod., Clar. 107, f. 9v; Downing to Bennet, 3/13 January 1665, PRO, SP 84/174, f. 1r; Edward Hyde, *The Life of Edward Earl of Clarendon* (Dublin, 1760), pp. 107–108; Clarendon, "A Brief Narrative of the Late Passages," [November 1664], Bod., Clar. 83, f. 397.

11 W. Cooper to Nicholas, 16/26 February 1662, PRO, SP 84/166, f. 103r; *His Majesties Most Gracious Speech, Together with the Lord Chancellors, To the Two Houses of Parliament, At their Prorogation On Monday the Nineteenth of May, 1662* (London, 1662), pp. 12–13; East India Company to Sir John Webster, 3 July 1662, IOL, Home Miscellanies H/42, f. 56; Downing to Clarendon, 12 February 1664, Bod., Clar. 107, f. 86r; Van Goch to States General, 17/27 June 1664, PRO, SP 84/171, f. 208v (my translation); Hollis to Bennet, 10/20 September 1664, PRO, SP 78/119, f. 74r; Hollis to Fanshawe, 16 October 1664, *Original Letters of his Excellency Sir Richard Fanshaw* (London, 1701), p. 274; William Morrice to Henry Coventry, Longleat House, Cov. MSS LXIV, f. 5r; William De Britaine, *The Dutch Usurpation* (London, 1672), p. 18; Darrell, *A True and Compendious Narration: Or*

Just as the Dutch were imitating the commercial policies of the Spanish, so they were seen to be following in their inhumanity. Newspapers, pamphlets, and popular poems all reminded the English political nation of the atrocities committed by the Dutch at Amboyna. The tense atmosphere of 1664 soon provided new evidence confirming the perfidy of the Dutch. The governor of the Dutch West India Company was reported to have "offered a bendy of gold apiece for so many heads of Englishmen as should be brought him by any persons whatsoever." In Newfoundland De Ruyter's fleet, after having retaken most of the Guinea Coast, committed "outrages and villanies, ravishing women and maids even before their husbands, parents, and friends' faces." Even in the Channel, the Dutch were known to be seizing English ships and throwing the crews overboard. Those that survived fared little better. "What measures they take of barbarity in Holland," John Evelyn exclaimed in a letter to Roger L'Estrange, they "have lately dragg'd some of our men fallen into their hands through their towns in chains, more like slaves than Christians."[12]

Naturally the United Provinces, as a republic, would not attempt to build up the massive standing armies normally associated with monarchies; but this would in no way hinder the Dutch in their drive for universal dominion. Religion and dynastic ties, Roger Coke pointed out, were as nothing against the interest of trade. The Dutch could keep potential enemies at peace by threatening to cut off their vital economic supplies. Indeed in case of necessity the Dutch could simply hire a mercenary army. "It is rooted in these people to strain to the utmost to get the mastery of his Majesty at sea," explained George Downing, for once they "out power his Majesty at sea then all is their own." The Dutch could achieve universal monarchy by usurping "the universal dominion of the seas." The potential consequences of such a development were already becoming clear. The result of Dutch pretensions in Africa and in the East Indies, thought Edward Adams, was "that the King of Great Britain, France, and Ireland, must not treat of or conclude peace with a foreign prince, or provide for the increase of trade and privileges of his own subjects without asking the States of Holland

(Second Part of Amboyna) (London, 1665), pp. 9–10. For similar French views see De Thou to Brienne, 22 November/2 December 1660, in N. Japikse, *De Verwikkelingen Tusschen De Republiek en Engeland Van 1660–1665* (Leiden, 1900) p. iv.

12 For Spanish cruelty: *The Coppie of the Anti-Spaniard Made at Paris by a French Man, a Catholique* (London, 1590), p. 9; Greville, *Life of Sidney*, pp. 124–125; *The King of Spain's Cabinet Council Divided* (London, 1658), Thomason: 1 October 1657, pp. 89, 103–104, 133–135. For Amboyna see for example: *Dutch Drawn to the Life*, pp. 144–145; W. W, pp. 17–19, 22–23, 25; "East India Company Proposals," 1662, Bod., Clar. 92, f. 59r; Poem on the Second Dutch War, BL, Egerton MSS 2560, f. 80v; journal of Robert Holmes, Pepys Library, 2698, ff. 121r, 137r (the journal is filled with atrocity stories); Robert Holmes to William Coventry, 8 February 1664, Longleat House, Cov. MSS XCV, ff. 11r, 13v; T. Mundy, "Some Occurrences," summer 1664, Bod., Rawl. A315, p. 244r; newsletter, 18 November 1664, PRO, SP 29/105/12; Evelyn to L'Estrange, 24 February 1665, Christ Church, John Evelyn MSS Out-Letters.

leave." England needed to defend herself, preached Simon Ford, "except ... we can be content to change our merchant ships into sculls and oars to ply betwixt London and Amsterdam and no farther, to export our English treasure, and import what they please to allow us for it: which will (in effect) be no other, than to make them the upper and ourselves the Netherlands." The result of the "overswelling greatness of the Dutch," argued one foreign-policy memorandum almost certainly written by Sir Nicholas Crispe, was that they would soon be not only "our corrivals in trade, but if increasing as they have done this last age, in the next they will swallow us up wholly." Already, Downing thought, the King of Denmark was being brought "into an esclavage" and his subjects reduced "to mere tributaries to their merchants." "By reason of their maritime forces," he warned, the Dutch would soon be "able upon all occasions to cast the balance of Europe." "You think the narrow seas for us too much / Yet the whole globe too little for the Dutch," rhymed the Anglican Royalist publisher and poet John Crouch, "Thus, while fair liberty you give and crave / You would be free to make the world a slave."[13] One needed only look to Dutch claims in the East Indies to understand the logic of the Dutch strategy. There, William De Britaine pointed out, the Dutch styled themselves "The States General of the United Provinces of Batavia, Amboyna, T[ai]wan, and c., commanders of all the seas of the world; protectors of all the kings and princes in Europe; and supreme moderators of all the affairs of Christendom." "The Dutch now having made an absolute conquest of all the South-East Seas of Africa, half of the whole universe from Japan and China to Cape Bon-Esperanza," warned John Darrell, they now "endeavor to carry on and propagate the said old war and design into Europe and America (the other half of the whole universe)." Consequently the Dutch had to be considered "universal enemies (especially of England) ... who may compare their conquests by sea with the Great Turk by land, and allow him ten foot for one." No wonder Sir Henry Bennet thought the Anglo-Dutch war would be fought "for the dominion of the seas and the trade that belongs to it."[14]

13 John Crouch, *Belgica Caracteristica. Or The Dutch Character* (London, 1665), p. 7.

14 Roger Coke, *A Treatise Wherein is Demonstrated That the Church and State of England Are in Equal Danger With the Trade of It* (London, 1671), pp. 130, 135; "Paper on the Spanish Trade," 1664, PRO, SP 94/46, f. 106r; Downing to Clarendon, 12 August 1664, Bod., Clar. 108, f. 64v; Downing to Clarendon, 2 September 1664, Bod., Clar. 108, f. 173r; Downing to Clarendon, 22 September 1664, Bod., Clar. 108, f. 84r; Downing to Clarendon, 16/26 August 1661, Bod., Clar. 104, f. 252r; Downing to Clarendon, 12 February 1664, Bod., Clar. 107, f. 84r; *A Justification of the Present War against the United Netherlands* (London, 1672), sig. A3r; Edward Adams, *A Brief Relation of the Surprizing Severaly English Merchants Goods, by Dutch Men of War* (London, 1664) [May] pp. 11–12; Ford, *Lords Wonders*, pp. 12–13; De Britaine, *Dutch Usurpation*, p. 20; Darrell, *True and Compendious Narration*, pp. 34–36 (a similar comparison to the Turk is made in De Britaine, *Dutch Usurpation*, pp. 33–34); Bennet to Fanshawe, 29 September 1664, Nickolls, *Original Letters*, p. 279; Crouch, *Belgica Caracteristica*, p. 7. Even those who did not think the Dutch were seeking universal monarchy thought control of the

Surely the identification of the Dutch as aspiring to universal monarchy must have caused some discomfort to English Protestants. Spain's insatiable desire for power seemed perfectly plausible in light of its close alliance with the Antichristian papacy. How did the English reconcile the Protestantism of the Dutch with their claims to a Papist-style universal monarchy?

For Anglican Royalists, the Dutch were simply not good Protestants. The very origin of the United Provinces lay in an ungodly rebellion. Even Grotius "confesseth" that the Dutch state was begun "by a revolt from their lawful sovereign," commented the translator of Grotius's *De Rebus*, "and the Sacred Scripture parallels rebellion to the sin of witchcraft." This touched Anglican Royalist sensibilities at their most tender point. "Those that are true Protestants abhor that disobedience to magistrates," proclaimed the Lord Chief Justice of Ireland in 1663. "The difference between the faults of the Pope and those of the Protestants about the point of obedience, is this," wrote Peter Du Moulin, "that disobedience with us is a crime, but with him it is a law." "He that rebels against his king, rebels against his God," agreed Richard Carpenter. Those Protestants who had adopted the Papal theory of resistance, thought the author of *Philanax Protestant*, were a "loose, giddy, turbulent and discontented sort of Protestants that have nothing indeed of Protestants but the name." Any government which was not a monarchy, and there could be no doubt that the United Provinces had little of monarchy in it, was not divinely approved. In the days when there was no king in Israel, argued William Goodman, "every man did that which was right in his own eyes; but that which was neither right in itself, nor in the sight of God." Any state which was not governed by a monarch, preached Simon Ford on the eve of the war, was a "state heresy."[15]

The Presbyterianism of the United Provinces was in fact no better than

United Provinces was key to that aim. "Even whilst it was nothing near so considerable as it is now," wrote William Coventry, "all Europe hath looked upon [the United Provinces], not only as a fair step, but as the best part of the way to the Universal Monarchy." *An Appeal*, p. 29. See also James Howell, *Dodona's Grove, or the Vocall Forrest*. 3rd edition (Cambridge, 1645), p. 22; Arlington to Fanshawe, 29 September 1664, Thomas Bebington (editor), *The Right Honoourable the Earl of Arlington's Letters* ... (London, 1701), Vol. II, p. 48; Henry Coventry to Clarendon, 1/11 October 1664, Bod., Clar. 83, f. 239v; Clarendon, "A Brief Narration of the Late Passages," November 1664, Bod., Clar. 83, f. 377r.

15 Hugo Grotius, *De Rebus Belgicus: Or, The Annals, and History of the Low-Countrey Warrs* (translated by T. Manley) (London, 1665), Manley's preface, sig. A4r; Lord Chief Justice of Ireland's judgement against Alex. Jephson, Richard Thompson, and Edmund Warren, 7 July 1663, Carte 32, f. 693v; Peter Du Moulin, *A Vindication of the Sincerity of the Protestant Religion in the Point of Obedience to Sovereigns* (London, 1664), pp. 109–110; Richard Carpenter, *Rome in her Fruits*, preached 5 November 1662 (London, 1663), p. 13; *Philanax Protestant*, p. 3; *Philolaus: Or, Popery Discovered to the People* (London, 1663), p. 25; William Goodman *Filius Heroum, The Son of Nobles Set Forth in a Sermon Preached at St. Mary's in Cambridge before the University, on Thursday the 24th of May 1660* (London, 1660), pp. 4–5; Ford, *Lords Wonders*, p. 13.

disguised Popery. "Popery and Presbytery, though they look diverse ways with their heads," commented the Duke of Newcastle, "are tied together like Samson's foxes by their tails, carrying the same firebrands of covetousness and ambition, to put all into a combustion wherever they come." Indeed Presbyterianism and Jesuitism had the same ideological roots. "There have been two new sects broached within this 120 years, both the same year, both to the same end," averred Oliver Foulis, "I mean the Jesuits and the Presbyterians, the one set up by John Calvin, the other by Ignatius Loyola, the one is confessed to be the Boutefeu of Christendom, the other is known to be the incendiary of the Protestant part of it." "The Puritan-Church policy and Jesuitical society began together," agreed Bishop Owen in a tract reprinted in 1663, "they are so fast linked behind, and tail tied together with firebrands between them, that if they be not quenched by the power of Majesty, they cannot choose (when the means are fitted to their plot) but set the Church on fire, and the state in an uproar." Toleration, the chief characteristic of the religious culture of the United Provinces, was but a ploy to bring in Popery. "Universal toleration," thought the author of *Fair Warning*, was "the greatest design that [the] conclave of Rome manageth." Rutherford, Sir John Birkenhead exclaimed, even admitted that "they indeed of Rome are well affected to our cause, we are for liberty of conscience, so are they, we would restrain the overgreat power of kings, so would they; they would have the kings accountable for their actions, so would we." In the context of Anglican Royalist claims that all English Nonconformists were Papists in disguise, Dutch Presbyterianism must have been suspect indeed.[16]

Naturally the Dutch, like the English Nonconformists, had long ago lost any real religiosity. "All those true Netherland zealots who contended for religion, were either destroyed by the Spanish Inquisition or fled their

16 Duke of Newcastle, "Treatise," 1660–1661, Bod., Clar. 109, pp. 10–11; Oliver Foulis, *Cabala*, p. 4; David Owen, *Herod and Pilate Reconciled: Or the Concord of Papists, Anabaptists, and Sectaries against Scripture, Fathers, Councils, and Other Orthodoxal Writers, for the Coercion, Deposition, and Killing of Kings* (London, 1663), sig. A3r; *Fair Warning: Or, XXV Reasons Against Toleration and Indulgence of Popery* (London, 1663), pp. 18–19; *Fair-Warning: The Second Part. Or XX Prophecies Concerning the Return of Popery* (London, 1663), p. 47; [Sir John Birkenhead], *Cabala: Or an Impartial Account of the Nonconformists Private Designs, Actings and Ways* (London, 1663), p. 24. On Dutch Presbyterianism see: Downing to Bennet, 6/16 November 1663, PRO, SP 84/168, f. 87v; Coke, *Treatise* p. 134; H. P. to John Knowles, 19 March 1664, PRO, SP 29/94/117. The literature on nonconformists as agents of Popery between 1640 and 1660 is vast. I give only a sample here: Du Moulin, *Vindication*, pp. 53, 58–61, 64; *Fair Warning*, pp. 8–9, 12; *Fair-Warning*, Vol. II, pp. 5–7, 13, 47, 51, 55, 60; Carpenter, *Rome in Her Fruits*; Thomas Pierce, *The Primitive Rule of Reformation: Delivered in a Sermon Before His Majesty at Whitehall Feb. 1 1662 [1663]* (London, 1663), sig. A4v, pp. 16, 19–20; *Poor Robin 1664: An Almanack After a New Fashion* (London, 1664), sig. B7r; *Philanax Protestant*, pp. 5–7; [Birkenhead], *Cabala*, pp. 20, 23; Foulis, *Cabala*, p. 56; *Aronbimnucha: Or An Antidote to Cure the Clalamities of their Trembling or fear of the Ark* (London, 1663), p. 67.

country," thought Edward Cliffe, "of which a good honest stock yet remains in England, but all the rest proved mere pretenders." "No, no," complained another pamphleteer, "I should injure Christendom to reckon the United Netherlands a part thereof; such are their practices, that 'tis a crime in them to profess that religion, and a great mistake in those that entitle them thereunto." The Dutch now were simply "perfidious, self-ended neighbors." This was a necessary consequence of seeking universal monarchy. From the Dutch "we may learn, that those which study to be great by any means, must by all means forget to be good: they must dismiss that puny thing called conscience." The Dutch, Sir Edward Nicholas agreed, were only concerned with interest to which they "would readily have sacrificed all other considerations to that their idol."[17]

In the early 1660s, then, it was clear to most members of the English political nation that the United Provinces were in fact following the now decayed Spanish monarchy in seeking to establish a universal dominion. "Just as the King of Spain had claimed the dominion of Asia and of Africa," commented the Orangist Van Ruyven, "so their High Mightinesses claim the same right by succession." John Evelyn, marveling at the fantastic growth of Dutch power, commented that "if it prove as solid, and permanent, as it has been speedy, Rome must herself, submit to the comparison." Already "they think themselves in the same condition as the ancient Romans were with the Carthaginians," wrote the directors of the East India Company, "when they told them they would treat of peace when they had removed their city ten miles further into the country." "They are of the former King of Spain's mind," noted Downing making a significant comparison, "*Il faut passer par l'Angleterre* first bring down his Majesty and then they shall do well enough with the French." The Dutch had succeeded in applying the principles of Popery and universal monarchy to trade. "By these steps they have climb'd up to the immense pyramids of dominion and power in the Indies, that they are become formidable to the greatest emperors and princes there," noted William De Britaine, "ever making good in their practice that Lemma of Loyola (the apostle of their state) *Cavete vobis Principes*." "These people do arrogate to themselves St. Peter's power on the Seas," wrote George Downing who had been well trained in identifying Popery at Harvard College, "it is mare liberum in the

17 E[dward] Cliffe, *An Abbreviate of Holland's Deliverance By, and Ingratitude to the Crown of England and House of Nassau* (London, 1665), pp. 52–55; *A Justification*, pp. 2, 4; William Andrews, *Newes from the Starrs: Or an Ephemeris for the Year of Man's Redemption by Jesus Christ, 1665* (London, 1665), 29 August 1664, sig. C3v; De Britaine, *Dutch Usurpation*, p. 19; Edward Nicholas to Downing, 23 May 1662, BL, Add. 22919, f. 217r; Downing to Clarendon, 16 October 1663, Bod., Clar. 106, f. 215v. See also James Howell, *The Parly of Beasts* (London, 1660), pp. 10–11. For similar claims about English Presbyterians see: *Satyr on the Adulterate Coyn Inscribed The Common-Wealth* (London, 1661), broadside; *Presbytery Displayed* (London, 1663), p. 9.

British Seas, but mare clausum on the coast of Africa and in the East Indies." "Being now in the exorbitant greatness of their power," the Anglican Royalist merchant Walter Travers drew the obvious conclusion, the Dutch are "grown as dogmatical in point of trade, as ... the Jesuits are in tenet and opinion." According to Richard Fanshawe the Hollanders, "with the sole commerce with the West-Indies, from the East by the Philippines, and from Guinea for Negroes ... exclusive to the whole world besides, and even to Spain it self," could now make good their "title derived to them from the King of Spain, and to his Catholic Majesty from the Pope."[18]

English concern about Dutch economic aggrandizement in the spring of 1664, then, was not a purely secular concern about profits and losses. Indeed most merchants realized quite well that the war would prove to be a short-term economic disaster. Instead the economic complaints against the Dutch were placed in the context of the rhetoric of universal monarchy. Anglican Royalists knew that English economic problems stemmed not from intolerance of Nonconformity, but from the international activities of the natural allies of the Nonconformists. War against the Dutch was necessary to prevent them from achieving what had evaded the Kings of Spain: universal monarchy. It was no doubt these "airy notions and rhetorical discourse" which William Coventry, who was already having his doubts about the wisdom of the war, thought had provoked the Anglo-Dutch conflict.[19]

18 De Bacquoy/Van Ruyen to Bennet, 1/11 October 1664, PRO, SP 84/172, f. 115r (my translation); Evelyn, *Navigation and Commerce*, p. 62; East India Company to Sir John Webster, IOL, Home Miscellanies H42, f. 56; Downing to Bennet, 9/19 September 1664, PRO, SP 84/172, ff. 13v–14r; De Britaine, *Dutch Usurpation*, p. 23; Downing to Clarendon, 20 November 1663, Bod., Clar. 107, f. 22r; Walter Travers to George Oxenden, 5 July 1663, IOL, E/3/28, f. 17r; Fanshawe to Bennet, 23 November 1664, Nickolls, *Original Letters*, pp. 357–358 (Fanshawe concludes by suggesting the Dutch ambassador may get a Cardinal's cap). Another copy of this letter is in PRO, SP 94/47, ff. 170v–171r.

19 William Coventry, "Paper about the Dutch Wars," 1665, BL, Add. 32094, f. 50r.

Part IV

THE MEDWAY, BREDA, AND THE TRIPLE ALLIANCE: THE COLLAPSE OF ANGLICAN ROYALIST FOREIGN POLICY

17

Historiographical overview

Excitement and anticipation spread throughout Europe on the eve of the first international conflict to be fought by Britain's newly restored king. "All the world and the Pope himself is big with expectation of what issue his Majesty's grand engagement with Holland will have," gushed Charles II's envoy in Italy Joseph Kent.[1] The English themselves were brimming with confidence and enthusiasm. The Earl of Arlington informed the English ambassador in Spain, Sir Richard Fanshawe, that "the whole people of what opinion or interest soever are greatly fond of this war."[2] A Venetian observer noted "the great inclination of the people here to the rupture and war against the Dutch."[3] Even the exceedingly cautious William Coventry marveled at the unanimity of the fleet. "I have not heard one rodomontade from any of them," Coventry wrote to Arlington, instead all of the seaman displayed "an assurance of beating [the Dutch]."[4]

English confidence was matched by the government's naval preparations. The Irish Viscount Conway wrote to his countryman Sir George Rawdon that Charles II had prepared "the powerfullest fleet that ever went out of England."[5] "I believe the English fleet the most considerable that any one monarch has ever put to sea," Samuel Tuke informed his friend Sir John Evelyn.[6] The English Admiral James Duke of York proudly recorded in his memoirs that the nation "never hitherto had seen [a fleet] so glorious and formidable."[7] Nor was the fleet poorly provisioned. Sir Thomas Clarges presumed it to be "better mann'd and [to] consist of better ships than any

1 Joseph Kent to Joseph Williamson, 17/27 June 1665, SP 85/8, f. 3r.

2 Arlington to Fanshawe, 6 April 1665, BL, Harleian MSS 7010, f. 231v.

3 News from London, 6/16 April 1665, *CSPV*, p. 106.

4 William Coventry to Arlington, 18 April 1665, SP 29/118/75. Arlington passed on this assessment to Fanshawe. See Arlington to Fanshawe, 30 March 1665, Thomas Bebington (editor), *The Right Honourable the Earl of Arlington's Letters ...* (London, 1701), Vol. II, p. 74.

5 Edward Conway to Rawdon, 28 March 1665, HL, HA14419.

6 Samuel Tuke to John Evelyn, 12 August 1665, Christ Church, Evelyn In-Letters 1298; see also John Evelyn, *Diary*, 8 May 1666, p. 436.

7 James S. Clarke (editor), *The Life of James the Second*, Vol. I (London, 1816), p. 405.

has yet been seen in England."[8] The Duke of Buckingham's chaplain Thomas Sprat proclaimed "our sea-provisions [to be] far stronger than ever they were in any age or country before ... Never was there a greater abundance of materials in readiness! Never more skillful builders! Never more formidable preparations! Never more expert seamen! Never more valiant commanders!"[9]

A little more than two years after the opening battle of the second Anglo-Dutch War, however, the enthusiastic accolations had turned into bitter recriminations, the expectant cheers had been transformed into tears of shame. In early June 1667 the Dutch battle fleet sailed unopposed up the Medway, easily breaking through the chain across the river which alone protected the English great ships at Chatham. Led by Cornelius De Witt, with the English republican Colonel Dolman at his side, the Dutch burned and captured what remained of the glorious English navy. "Since the affront we have received here at Chatham," Sir William Coventry admitted to the Duke of Ormonde, the enemy "hath ... left such marks of our weakness and his power and made such impressions on the minds of men as that I am not sure I shall ever see the consequences of it overcome."[10] Arlington lamented that "we have received a great affront which we shall not quickly be able to wash off."[11] "By God!" screamed Sir William Batten at the Navy Board, "I think the devil shits Dutchmen."[12]

The effects of the Dutch exploit were soon apparent throughout England. "People are ready to tear their hairs off their heads," John Rushworth exclaimed to Lady Ranelagh.[13] Samuel Pepys recorded that "hardly anybody at court but doth look as if they cried."[14] "The ill news comes so thick," wrote Sir John Bramston from Chelmsford, "that we are not able to keep up the spirits of the people. Indeed we ourselves are so dejected that we cannot communicate it."[15] John Evelyn recalled that "this alarm was so great, as put both county and city into a panic fear and consternation, such as I hope I shall never see more; for everybody were flying, none knew why or whither."[16]

The Dutch had dealt a crushing blow. While many thought that "a peace

8 Sir Thomas Clarges to George Rawdon, 5 May 1666, HL, HA 14202; see also William Coventry to Arlington, 18 April 1665, SP 29/118/75.

9 Thomas Sprat, *Observations on Monsieur de Sorbier's Voyage into England* (London, 1665), pp. 169–171.

10 Sir William Coventry to Ormonde, 22 June 1667, Carte 47, f. 488r.

11 Arlington to Ormonde, 15 June 1667, Carte 46, f. 490r.

12 Pepys *Diary*, Vol. VIII, 19 July 1667, p. 345.

13 John Rushworth to Lady Ranelagh, 15 June 1667, SP 29/205/76. On the same day Lady Ranelagh wrote in slightly more muted tones to her brother. See Lady Ranelagh to Earl of Burlington, 15 June 1667, BL, Althorp Papers B4 (unfoliated).

14 Samuel Pepys, *Diary*, Vol. VIII, 12 June 1667, p. 261.

15 Sir John Bramston (Chelmsford) to Will Harris, 13 June 1667, SP 29/205/2.

16 Evelyn, *Diary*, 11 June 1667, p. 484.

may be bought too dear," there could be no serious objections to the Earl of Clarendon's conclusion that "a peace in this conjuncture would be very seasonable, and it is not in our part to refuse it."[17] Joseph Williamson's assistant James Hickes knew that the English "must now bow and buckle to their enemies."[18]

Historians have offered remarkably similar explanations for the causes and consequences of the English defeat in the second Anglo-Dutch War. While scholars have disagreed whether the war was fought as a consequence of commercial conflict or as the result of faction-fighting at the English court, none have thought that either side posed an ideological threat to the other. If the English lost the war, the proponents of this view naturally claimed, it was the result of structural failure rather than loss of ideological commitment. There was simply nothing at stake politically. The Dutch, Charles Wilson has insisted, "offered no threat to either England or France." From an English perspective, then, the wars had an "essentially offensive character."[19] Nor could there have been any thought of advancing an ideological program within Dutch political culture. There was no political opposition in the United Provinces. Sir Keith Feiling, who was more aware of Dutch party politics than most, has argued that while the English might have dallied with the Dutch Orangist opposition they knew very well of "the patent weakness of the Orange cause."[20]

English perceptions of the international situation, public concern with the conduct of the war, had little to do with the ignominious defeat at Chatham. In the accounts of most historians this was because the conduct of foreign policy remained very much a royal prerogative. "Our foreign policy," Feiling reminds his readers, "was still in a real sense personal to the King."[21] J. R. Jones has seen little reason to revise Feiling's classic assessment. "Public opinion," he contends, "whether spontaneous or in the shape of pressure groups seems to have had very little effect on those who made the major decisions. It was not just a constitutional fiction that foreign affairs were reserved, as exclusively a matter for the government, or (under the monarchy) for the royal prerogative."[22] Jonathan Israel, however, has

17 Clarendon to Hollis and Henry Coventry, 14 June 1667, Bod., Clar. 159, f. 33r.

18 James Hickes to Williamson, 14 June 1667, SP 29/205/64.

19 Charles H. Wilson, *Profit and Power* (London, 1957), pp. 145–146.

20 Keith Feiling, *British Foreign Policy 1660–1672* (London, 1930), p. 198.

21 Feiling, *British Foreign Policy*, p. 20. Feiling denies that public opinion had anything to do with the diplomatic revolution of 1667–1668. See p. 232.

22 J. R. Jones, *Britain and the World 1649–1815* (Glasgow, 1980), p. 53. It is perhaps appropriate at this point to note that I am uncertain as to Ronald Hutton's position on the relationship between public opinion and the conduct of the war. At one point he suggests that with the licensing act of 1662 all "hope that governments might be converted by force of argument" came to an end, that the government had successfully promoted a "lack of interest in public affairs" (*The Restoration* (Oxford, 1985). p. 157) Then he seems to maintain that public Hollandophobia "had been the decisive factor in the outbreak of full-scale conflict" and prevented the English government from pursuing any peace initiative in

noticed that "at the heart of England's difficulties was the country's complete loss of appetite for the struggle." This diminution of English popular support was the result not of an altered perception of the ideological stakes in the conflict with the Dutch but rather the consequence of the "crushing losses" sustained by the English mercantile sector.[23]

In almost every historical explanation for the Medway disaster, then, the English lost the economic means rather than the ideological will to continue the war.[24] The English failed to send out a fleet in 1667, Jones has argued, because "financial and material resources neared exhaustion by the end of 1666."[25] "With the navy debt growing and little sign of adequate credit forthcoming," Charles Wilson maintains, "the king listened readily to those of his advisers who preached a doctrine of limited strategic liability."[26] Ronald Hutton, while blaming Parliament for failing to vote supply quickly enough in 1666, has exonerated Charles II for failing to set out a fleet, claiming that "had the government sent forth the fleet for a third year, bankruptcy would probably have resulted." "Unequivocally the Dutch had won," Hutton concludes, "by sheer financial stamina."[27]

Unsurprisingly, with its navy devastated and its political morale at a nadir, Charles II's government quickly acceded to the peace terms offered by the Dutch at Breda. Nevertheless the Dutch were remarkably lenient, demanding very few economic concessions given that they had been victorious in a trade war. The English, Wilson comments, "obtained reasonable terms." "The Treaty of Breda," he concludes, "was glorious as the Revolution of 1688 was glorious – not as an act of conquest and humiliation but of moderation and good sense."[28] Feiling also feels that England's enemies "as a whole gave England much better terms than her administration deserved."[29]

This conclusion of the second Anglo-Dutch War, a war which had been described in such epic terms, seems inexplicably anti-climactic. Why were

1665 or 1666 (pp. 223, 275). But Hutton also insists that, as a result of the plague, "most English people had lost all interest in the war" "long before" the Parliamentary session of 1665 (p. 225).

23 J. Israel, *Dutch Primacy in World Trade 1585–1740* (Oxford, 1989), pp. 277–278.

24 The exception is Paul Seaward's subtle and perceptive study of the Cavalier Parliament (*The Cavalier Parliament and the Reconstruction of the Old Regime 1661–1667* [Cambridge, 1989]). His account, however, discusses exclusively the shift in perceptions of domestic threats to the regime. He does not analyze their European dimensions.

25 Jones, *Britain and the World*, pp. 80–81, 91.

26 Wilson, *Profit and Power*, p. 138. Israel makes a similar argument, p. 278.

27 Hutton, *Restoration*, pp. 257, 261, 275. Feiling also blames the failure to set out a fleet on the delay in voting supply Feiling, *British Foreign Policy*, pp. 205–206. Seaward contests this claim, arguing that the navy's books balanced. The real problem was that the government had precious little credit. Seaward, *The Cavalier Parliament*, pp. 238–239, 303.

28 Wilson, *Profit and Power*, pp. 141–142.

29 Feiling, *British Foreign Policy*, p. 226.

the Dutch so lenient? I claim that this was because the English and the Dutch conceived of the conflict in terms other than those in which it is usually described. Indeed many of the English voices heard after the descent on Chatham suggest that many new questions should be asked about the conflict. Samuel Pepys, for example, remarked in his diary immediately after the Dutch had destroyed the English ships in dry-dock at Chatham, that the people "do think verily that the French [king], being come down with his army to Dunkirk, it is to invade us – and that we shall be invaded."[30] "It is more than suspected that the French has betrayed us abroad with the conjuncture of those that help them at home," opined Thomas St. Serfe the same day in his newsletter .[31] Full of trepidation Waldine Lagoe wrote from Manchester to his friend Roger Kenyon, exclaiming that "it is feared the French are also coming over from Dunkirk to land in England. 'The Lord in mercy appear for us.' "[32] This popular fear of France in the wake of a Dutch assault on the English navy demands an explanation. This Francophobia, unaccounted for in the traditional accounts of the Anglo-Dutch conflict, reflects a profound shift in English public attitudes toward the war, and necessarily toward their own government. The French entry into the war on the side of the Dutch, coupled with the manifest incompetence of the war effort conducted by an increasingly authoritarian government, convinced a wide spectrum of the English population that French-style absolutism posed at least as great a threat as Dutch-style republicanism to the English way of life. In addition, I suggest, the ostentatious loyalty of the English Nonconformist community in the face of the plague, the Great Fire, and ultimately the Dutch raid on the Medway, marginalized the identification of Nonconformity with rebellious principles. In this new ideological context, a context radically transformed by the English experience during the war, many in England became convinced that Louis XIV desperately wanted to sit atop the throne of the universal monarch.

30 Pepys, *Diary*, Vol. VIII, 13 June 1667, p. 265.
31 St. Serfe's Newsletter, 13 June 1667, LOC, 18124, Vol. I, f. 210r.
32 Waldine Lagoe (Manchester) to Roger Kenyon, 15 June 1667, HMC, *Kenyon*, p. 79.

18

The circulation of news and the course of the war

Far from being a period in which public issues were deemed uninteresting or unimportant, the Restoration was an age mad for news and political information. "You cannot imagine to what a disease the itch of news is grown," John Cooper informed the appreciative government newsletter-writer Joseph Williamson.[1] Sir George Fletcher confessed that he was "infected" with "the love of news," while George Davenport begged his friend William Sancroft, the Dean of St. Paul's, to send "a lick of news" to Durham.[2] "You could not come into a tavern, alehouse, tippling or coffee-house, or sit at dinner" without being entertained with political gossip, "men, women and children of every rank to the very lowest, raving out their ill-digested humor which they call'd opinion, sparing neither law nor gospel, as if they would have as many governors as people."[3]

News – especially news about the war with the Dutch – was widely desired and ubiquitously available throughout the three kingdoms, and amongst a wide variety of social strata. In both London and Dublin, the Earl of Arlington thought, "the licentious discourses of the people" had "grown too big to be mastered."[4] Samuel Pepys gossiped about the merits of the Dutch War with his friends at the Royal Society and with his cheesemonger.[5] "We are all very much concerned in this war," Robert Mein reported from Edinburgh, "so that thousands of people attend the post

1 John Cooper (Thugacton) to Williamson, 24 August 1667, PRO, SP 29/214/125. See also Sir Roger Burgoyne (Wroxall) to Sir Ralph Verney, 19 June 1665, Firestone Library, Verney MSS, Reel 20 (unfoliated); Edward Cooke to Ormonde, 22 June 1667, Carte 35, f. 490r; Seth Ward (Exeter) to Sheldon, 22 July 1665, in J. Simmons (editor), "Some Letters from Bishop Ward of Exeter, 1663–1667," in *Devon and Cornwall Notes and Queries* Vol. 21 (1940–41), p. 329.

2 Sir George Fletcher to Williamson, 1 July 1667, PRO, SP 29/208/4; George Davenport (Durham) to Sancroft, November 1667, Bod., Tanner MSS 45, f. 232r.

3 *The Mercury*, 1–5 August 1667 (unpaginated newspaper).

4 Arlington to Ormonde, 18 January 1668, Carte 46, f. 585v. The physician James Yonge retells in his journal the remarkable story of how he and his cell-mates continued to keep abreast of the military developments by having English newspapers smuggled into their Dutch prison. F. N. L. Poynter (editor) *The Journal of James Yonge* (Hamden CT, 1963), p. 95.

5 Pepys, *Diary*, 4 June 1666, Vol. VII, p. 148; 4 March 1667, pp. 95–96.

office for good news."[6] "For me to send you news to Norwich," Thomas Bradford chastised one Norfolk clerical correspondent, "is to throw water into the sea."[7] Coventry and Warwick were so full of political gossip, much of it apparently "ill news," that the Earl of Northampton attempted – albeit unsuccessfully – to trace its source.[8] So much information about the war was readily available that country gentlemen in Lancashire and Lincolnshire had little difficulty in keeping extremely accurate lists of English naval commanders, squadron formations, and ships taken and lost.[9] The Earl of Clarendon told Parliament in 1665 that he was sure that "your own observations and the general communication of all that hath fallen out" in England's relations with the Dutch "hath left few men ignorant of anything who have had any curiosity to inform themselves."[10]

Parliamentary discussions were almost as widely known as battle results. "The country's ears are all for Parliament news," Richard Watts attested from Deal.[11] Those ears were rarely disappointed. Colonel Sandys complained in the Commons that "their debates were published abroad, yea and into Holland also, as appears by the Dutch gazettes, and by our own also."[12] Sir Heneage Finch also warned his fellow members of Parliament that "experience hath taught us that we are not here like a Privy Council, our discourses in this place will be sure to take air, and where the town is full of honorable spies let no man doubt that which every man whispers to his private friend may at last come to their knowledge."[13]

A wide range of media provided news and information about the conflict with the Dutch. Church bells rang and bonfires burned throughout the country after each English victory.[14] Feast Days provided opportunities for clergymen throughout the country to explain to their flocks the broader meaning and importance of the war with the Dutch.[15] The official government newspaper, the *Gazette*, was widely read. Copies of the *Gazette* came to Ipswich, for example, "every post and are

6 Robert Mein (Edinburgh) to Williamson, 7 July 1666, PRO, SP 29/161/125; see also Robert Mein (Edinburgh) to Williamson, 3 June 1666, PRO, SP 29/158/22.

7 Thomas Bradford to Dr. Browne, 9 June 1665, Bod., Tanner MSS 45, f. 12r.

8 Ra. Hope (Coventry) to Williamson, 29 September 1666, PRO, SP 29/173/83.

9 Sir Antony Oldfield Letterbook (Lincolnshire), 1665–1667, CUL, Dd943, pp. 73–75, 86–92, 255–260; Roger Kenyon, June 1666, HMC, *Kenyon*, pp. 77–78.

10 *His Majesties Gracious Speech to both Houses of Parliament Together with the Lord Chancellor's*, 10 October 1665 (Oxford, 1665), p. 4. Both Clarendon and Charles emphasized that they thought it important to keep Parliament informed about the war so that they could have "the continuance of your cheerful supply for the carrying it on." Charles II's *Speech*, 10 October 1665, p. 2.

11 Richard Watts (Deal) to Williamson, 1 November 1667, PRO, SP 29/222/3.

12 Caroline Robbins (editor), *The Diary of John Milward* (Cambridge, 1938), 22 October 1666, p. 29.

13 Speech of Sir Heneage Finch at Oxford, 1665, LRO, DG7/Box 4956.

14 R. Hutton, *The Restoration* (Oxford, 1985), p. 222 for one example.

15 For example see Pepys, *Diary*, Vol. VI, 5 April 1665, p. 73; Josselin, *Diary*, 5 April 1665, p. 517.

communicated."[16] Sir George Downing informed Williamson that its compactness meant that the newspaper was being sent "everywhere."[17] In addition, Dutch newspapers were apparently eagerly sought after and readily obtainable by those who sought a broader perspective on the war.[18]

Manuscript newsletter-writers supplemented the printed newspapers, providing their readers with slightly more gossip and a broader range of political interpretations. Joseph Williamson,[19] Thomas St. Serfe,[20] Henry Oldenburg,[21] and Henry Muddiman[22] all produced newsletters throughout the period of the Dutch War. Williamson's newsletter, dispatched from secretary Arlington's office, invariably enunciated an Anglican and pro-government position.[23] St. Serfe provided his readers with similar views. Henry Muddiman, by contrast, was more critical of governmental and especially high Anglican policy. Sir George Downing, for example, complained Muddiman published things "that might lie asleep very well."[24] Muddiman himself had a Presbyterian background, and – after his break with Arlington – wrote from the office of the Presbyterian secretary of state Sir William Morrice.[25] Very few of Oldenburg's newsletters survive, but he

16 John Knight (Ipswich) to Muddiman, 20 July 1665, PRO, SP 29/127/45.

17 Sir George Downing (East Hatley) to Williamson, 25 November 1665, PRO, SP 29/137/99; Downing to Williamson, 6 January 1666, PRO, SP 29/144/55. See also Pepys, *Diary*, Vol. VI, 22 November 1665, p. 305. Readership of the *Gazette* appears to have gone up substantially during the early years of the Restoration. The newsbook became even more popular after Williamson replaced L'Estrange as its editor. L'Estrange to Arlington, 17 October 1665, PRO, SP 29/134/117; L'Estrange to Arlington, 19 October 1665, PRO, SP 29/135/8; Cominges to de Lionne, 11 February 1664, PRO, PRO 31/3/113, f. 37; Dr. Thomas Smith (Rydal) to Williamson, 7 December 1665, PRO, SP 29/138/54. The episode is discussed in George Kitchin, *Sir Roger L'Estrange* (London, 1913), pp. 148–156.

18 Henry Muddiman to Williamson, 17 August 1665, PRO, SP 29/129/46; Richard Forster (Newcastle) To James Hickes, 20 June 1665, PRO, SP 29/124/137.

19 These newsletters were compiled from the letters which now make up the majority of pieces in the State Papers Domestic (PRO). The State Papers also include various volumes of Joseph Williamson's journal which appears to be the basic text from which the newsletters were copied.

20 Sir Robert Moray to Henry Oldenburg, 27 November 1665, in A. Rupert Hall and Marie Boas Hall (editors), *The Correspondence of Henry Oldenburg*, Vols. II–IV (Madison, 1966–1967), Vol. II, p. 625. An entire run of the newsletters is preserved in LOC, 18124.

21 Oldenburg to Boyle, 25 August 1664, *Oldenburg Correspondence*, Vol. II, pp. 209–210.

22 J. G. Muddiman, *The King's Journalist 1659–1689* (London, 1923), pp. 165–166 and *passim*.

23 This is based on a thorough reading of Williamson's newsletters, journals, and correspondence. By February 1666 Williamson and his subordinate James Hickes were making it clear that Williamson and not Muddiman had the exclusive support of Arlington. See Jo. Sudbury to William Sancroft, 24 February 1666, BL, Harleian MSS 3785, f. 118r; James Hickes to Williamson, 14 February 1666, PRO, SP 29/148/7.

24 Downing to Williamson, 20 January 1666, PRO, SP 29/145/89. In fact, Muddiman's greater willingness to publish a wide variety of news, even if it did not reflect well on the government, seems to have won him a wider readership. James Hickes to Williamson, 27 December 1667, PRO, SP 29/225/177.

25 Muddiman, *King's Journalist*, pp. 151, 194–195; Dr. T. Lamplugh (Albin Hall) to Williamson, 8 April 1666, PRO, SP 29/153/55; Richard Watts (Deal) to Williamson, 1 March 1666, PRO, SP 29/150/3; Jo. Mascall (York) to Williamson, 24 February 1666,

was sufficiently critical of government activity in 1667 to land himself in gaol.[26] While newsletters were substantially more expensive than printed newspapers, they still enjoyed a remarkably wide readership. In Norwich, for example, copies of Muddiman's newsletters were circulated on market day, leading one observer to comment that "the poor countrymen" went home with "sacks full of news."[27] Newsletters were freely circulated among the country gentry, used by local clergymen to inform their flocks, and were eagerly read by seamen "who have little else to do but read."[28]

For those with more leisure, and more money to spare, there was a wide variety of pamphlet material available, much of it commenting on European affairs. "Never age was so pregnant [with books]" commented one pamphleteer.[29] In London, at least, one could also "find great variety of French and foreign books."[30] But there is no reason to believe that country gentlemen were unable to place the Anglo-Dutch conflict within a European context. Country-house libraries were apparently well stocked with polemical works about European affairs.[31] For the less learned, of course, ballads – many of which offered commentary on contemporary events – were hawked in market towns and along major thoroughfares throughout the country.[32]

Developments in the Dutch War were eagerly discussed and hotly debated in a variety of places throughout the country. Londoners rushed to the Exchange to gather the gossip about the latest news. "News 'twixt us and the Dutch" was "constantly debated in and about the old Exchange and other places pro and contra" observed Thomas St. Serfe, who was himself not above listening in on merchants' conversations in order to gather material for his newsletter.[33] Restoration coffee houses had quickly become places to discuss "state news," the locales where "the best statesmen sit," the public spaces where one could receive "fresh news from all

PRO, SP 29/149/22; Henry Muddiman to Richard Watts, 20 February 1666, PRO, SP 29/148/99.

26 Pepys, *Diary*, Vol. VIII, 25 June 1667, p. 292.

27 T. Corie (Norwich) to Williamson, 28 November 1666, PRO, SP 29/179/110.

28 John Bower (Bridlington) to Williamson, 23 June 1666, PRO, SP 29/159/81; Sir Ralph Verney (Ditchley) to Edmund Verney, 4 September 1665, Firestone Library, Verney MSS, Reel 20 (unfoliated); Dr. Richard Rawlinson (Petworth) to Williamson, 16 October 1665, PRO, SP 29/134/113; William Coventry to Williamson, 1 April 1665, PRO, SP 29/117/1.

29 [Hugh Peters], *A Dying Fathers Last Legacy to an Only Child* (London, [1665]), p. 2.

30 Pepys, *Diary*, 6 November 1667, p. 521.

31 See for example the list of books in Sir Anthony Oldfield's library at Spalding from the 1660s. Sir Anthony Oldfield's Letterbook, 1660s, CUL, Dd943, ff. 224–225.

32 See the illuminating comments in Heneage to Sir John Finch, 17/27 August 1666, LRO, DG7/Box 4984, Letters folder. On ballads and the Dutch War, see the *Euing Collection* ballads discussed below (note 66). On circulation of ballads see, among others, Tessa Watt, *Cheap Print and Popular Piety, 1550–1640* (Cambridge, 1991), pp. 12–13, 76–77.

33 Thomas St. Serfe, Newsletter, 22 March 1666, LOC, 18124, Vol. I, f. 44r. Samuel Pepys often gadded to the Exchange to garner the latest news, and to observe popular political sentiment. See for example, Pepys, *Diary*, Vol. VI, 16 October 1665, p. 268.

parts."[34] Coffee houses were not exclusively London phenomena. Places as diverse as Bristol, Dublin, Nottingham, Oxford, Yarmouth, and Harwich had their own coffeemen and women.[35] There is also some suggestion that information and political analysis was circulated through Nonconformist networks, passing from conventicle to conventicle possibly through migrating preachers.[36]

Newsbooks, newsletters, pamphlets, and ballads all reported and commented upon international affairs. Coffeewits, Anglican preachers, Dissenting ministers, and merchants on the Exchange each offered their own glosses on the war.[37] News of each significant development in the conflict was eagerly anticipated and quickly circulated throughout the three kingdoms. The rhythm of bells and bonfires, of gossip alternating between deliriousness and dejection, made it easy for Britons everywhere to follow the narrative of this naval conflict.

34 Oldenburg to Boyle, 6 October 1664, *Oldenburg Correspondence*, Vol. II, p. 249; Dr. Peter Mews to Williamson, 19/29 July 1667, PRO, SP 84/183, f. 35r; Thomas St. Serfe, *Tarugo's Wiles: Or, The Coffee-House*, dedicated to George Marquesse of Huntley (London, 1668), p. 24. St. Serfe's play was performed in October 1667. William Van Lennep (editor), *The London Stage*, Pt. I 1660–1700 (Carbondale, Illinois, 1965), pp. 119–120. One historian of the coffee house has highlighted its importance for circulating news about the war. Edward Forbe Robinson, *The Early History of Coffee Houses in England* (London, 1893), pp. 143–144. Many contemporaries identified the coffee houses as significant locales for the dissemination of information. Edward Hyde, *The Life of Edward Earl of Clarendon* (Dublin, 1760), pp. 357–358; Pepys, *Diary*, Vol. VI, 3 January 1665, p. 3; Vol. VI, 24 May 1665, p. 108; Vol. VII, 16 February 1666, p. 45; information to Secretary Bennet, 9 March 1665, PRO, SP 29/114/90; Dr. Peter Mews to Williamson, 24 May/3 June 1667, PRO, SP 84/182, f. 139r; St. Serfe's Newsletter, 5 December 1665, LOC, 18124, Vol. I, f. 10r. The vast contemporary literature on coffee houses attests to their political importance. See, for example, *Knavery in all Trades: Or, The Coffee-House* (London, 1664); *A Character of Coffee and Coffee-Houses* (London, 1661); *The Vertues of Coffee* (London, 1663); *The Coffee Scuffle, Occasioned By a Contest Between a Learned Knight and a Pitiful Pedagogue* (London, 1662); *The Maidens Complaint against Coffee: Or, the Coffee-House Discovered* (London, 1663); *A Cup of Coffee: Or, Coffee in its Colours* (London, 1663); *The Character of a Coffee-House* (London, 1665). I have commented at length on the ideological and social significance of coffee houses in my "'Coffee Politicians Does Create': Coffee Houses and Restoration Political Culture," *Journal of Modern History* (December 1995).

35 J. Cooper (Newark) to Williamson, 27 July 1667, PRO, SP 29/211/28; Richard Bower (Yarmouth) to Williamson, 21 October 1667, PRO, SP 29/220/93 (coffeehouse run by Bower's wife); Sir William Batten (Harwich) to Samuel Pepys, 14 May 1665, PRO, SP 29/121/49; Anthony Wood's diary, 1663, Bod., Wood's Diaries MSS 7, f. 4r; Jonathan Barry, "The Cultural Life of Bristol 1640–1775" (Oxford, D. Phil. thesis, 1985), p. 117; Peter Borsay, *The English Urban Renaissance* (Oxford, 1989), pp. 145–146.

36 John Ironmonger to Sir Thomas Gower, 8 March 1665, PRO, SP 29/114/89; Elizabeth Finch (Bath) to Sir Heneage Finch, 6 July 1667, LRO, DG7/Box 4984, Letters Folder. Much of the evidence for this is indistinguishable from government informants reporting on radical plotting.

37 This and the following paragraphs are not meant to be a comprehensive narrative account of the naval conflict. The best such account is now J. D. Davies, *Gentlemen and Tarpaulins: The Officers and Men of the Restoration Navy* (Oxford, 1991), pp. 133–158.

All England eagerly anticipated the naval campaign of 1665.[38] After nearly fourteen months of build-up, everyone listened anxiously for the low thundering booms which would give the signal that the Restoration regime's first foray into European warfare had begun. "Every good English heart" was necessarily concerned, Denzil Hollis reminded Arlington, "when the honor and glory of his sovereign, the life of his sovereign's brother, and of so many of his good subjects, the flower and strength of the nation, and I may say the fortune of England is laid at stake, and playing at one cast ... my heart bleeds to think of it, my eyes water, and my hand shakes. I can neither see nor hold my pen to write."[39] But write many pens did as soon as the first good news of the English victory off Lowestoft (3 June 1665) began to trickle in along the English coast. "I believe [this] will prove the greatest defeat that ever the Dutch received at one time," an exhausted William Coventry wrote to Arlington from the fleet.[40] "This is a mighty victory," agreed Downing, "they never received such a blow before."[41]

Knowledge about and enthusiasm for the victory at Lowestoft was not limited to a select few well-informed courtiers. Many soon took up William Coventry's recommendation that a published "account" of the battle should be prepared because "it is but reasonable the people should have a leaf of news for their money."[42] Poets provided rhyming glosses on the event.[43] The news of the victory quickly spread along the streets of London. Within hours the exploits at Lowestoft were current at the Exchange.[44] By the time secretary William Morrice recommended to London's Lord Mayor "that the emblems and testimonies of joy and triumph may be seen and heard through the City by blaze of fire and sound of bells for this great and most important victory," his advice was already superfluous.[45] The City was already ablaze with celebratory fire. The Dutch ambassador Van Goch informed his superiors of the joy among the nobility "as well as among the

38 There had been a national day of humiliation in preparation for the war. William L. Sachse (editor), *The Diary of Roger Lowe* (New Haven, 1938), 5 April 1665, p. 82.

39 Hollis to Arlington, 7/17 June 1665, PRO, SP 78/120, f. 188r; see also Hollis to Arlington, 3/13 June 1665, PRO, SP 78/120, f. 175r.

40 William Coventry to Arlington, 4 June 1665, PRO, SP 29/123/41.

41 Downing to Fanshawe, 8 June 1665, BL, Harleian MSS 7010, f. 286r. See also Henry Coventry to Charles II, June 1665, Longleat House, Cov. MSS LXIV, f. 181r; Thomas Rugge, "Mercurius Politicus Redivivus," 13 June 1665, BL, Add. 10117, f. 140r; Henry Sturges to Sir James Thynne, 10 June 1665, Longleat House, Thynne MSS X, f. 182r.

42 William Coventry to Arlington, 4 June 1665, PRO, SP 29/123/41. The printed accounts and celebrations of the victory include: *A Summary Narration of the Signal Victory ... 3d of June 1665* (London, 1665); *A Second Narrative of the Signal Victory*. 3 June 1665 (London, 1665); *One Broad-Side More for the Dutch: Or, The Belgick Lion Couchant* (London, 1665); *Upon His Royal Highness His Late Victory Against the Dutch* [1665]; Edmund Waller, *Instructions to a Painter* (London, 1665).

43 See for example W. Smith, *Ingratitude Reveng'd: Or, A Poem Upon the Happy Victory of his Majesties Naval Forces Against the Dutch; June 3 and 4 1665* (London, 1665).

44 Pepys, *Diary*, Vol. VI, 5 June 1665, pp. 117–118.

45 William Morrice to Lord Mayor of London, 8 June 1665, Bod., Tanner 45, f. 11r.

commonalty which they expressed by bonfires and ringing of bells."[46] When England's naval heroes paraded through London a fortnight after the event they were greeted with "the formalities of joy of guns, bells and bonfires."[47] It would have been difficult indeed to have missed London's celebrations for England's great naval victory in June 1665.

The news quickly spread throughout the three kingdoms. Thomas Rugge observed that "as soon as ever the news came" into a particular locality "they all strove who should outdo one another in the demonstrations of joy."[48] As soon as the battle had ended, Richard Bower informed Williamson from Yarmouth, the victory "set our bells at work and colors flying."[49] The news that "we have entirely defeated the Hollanders" quickly reached Buckinghamshire.[50] In Dartmouth there was "a day of great rejoicing."[51] Anthony Wood observed the "great rejoicing for the overthrow of the Dutch at Oxford: bonfires, bells ringing, drinkings."[52] Similar celebrations occurred in Plymouth, Chester, Norwich, Knighton, Newcastle, and Berwick.[53] More slowly, but no less ineluctably, the news reached English merchants and envoys in the Mediterranean and the East.[54] Those who missed the first wave of enthusiastic celebrations could hardly have missed the lectures, sermons, and thanksgivings celebrating the victory in every parish throughout England.[55]

The highly publicized victory at Lowestoft raised expectations that the Restored Monarchy would defeat the Dutch even more quickly than the English Commonwealth had done. All hoped that the Earl of Sandwich

46 Van Goch to States General, 9/19 June 1665, PRO, SP 86/176, f. 159v. See also Pepys, *Diary*, Vol. VI, 8 June 1665, p. 123; Thomas Rugge, "Mercurius Politicus Redivivus," June 1665, BL, Add. 10117, f. 140v; Evelyn, *Diary*, 8 June 1665, p. 410.

47 Thomas Rugge, "Mercurius Politicus Redivivus," 16 June 1665, BL, Add. 10117, f. 141r.

48 Rugge, "Mercurius Politicus Redivivus," 16 June 1665, BL, Add. 10117, f. 141r.

49 Richard Bower (Yarmouth) to Williamson, 5 June 1665, PRO, SP 29/123/44.

50 Edmund Verney (East Claydon) to Sir Ralph Verney, 5 June 1667, Firestone Library, Verney MSS, Reel 120 (my translation).

51 G. S (Dartmouth) to Williamson, 13 June 1665, PRO, SP 29/124/50.

52 Anthony Wood, *Diary*, 9 June 1665, Bod., Wood's Diaries MSS 9, f. 19v.

53 David Gross (Plymouth) to Williamson, 8 June 1665, PRO, SP 29/123/94; T. T (Chester) to Muddiman, 12 June 1665, PRO, SP 29/124/42; William Nowell (Norwich) to Muddiman, 12 June 1665, PRO, SP 29/124/38; Richard Dillington (Knighton) to Williamson, 10 June 1665, PRO, SP 29/124/21; Richard Forster (Newcastle) to James Hickes, 9 June 1665, PRO, SP 29/123/96; Richard Forster (Newcastle) to James Hickes, 10 June 1665, PRO, SP 29/124/18; Robert Mein (Edinburgh) to Muddiman, 10 June 1665, PRO, SP 29/124/14.

54 George Legat to Williamson, 4/14 July 1665, PRO, SP 79/1, f. 193r; John Willett (Bussara) to George Oxenden, 7 October 1665, BL, Add. 40710, f. 6r; John Stevens (Mazagon) to George Oxenden, 25 May 1666, BL, Add. 40710, f. 57r.

55 John Hacket to Gilbert Sheldon, 17 June 1665, Bod., Tanner 45, f. 13r; Josselin, *Diary*, 4 July 1665, p. 519; *His Majesties Gracious Speech*, 10 October 1665, p. 12; John Dolben, *A Sermon Preached before the King On Tuesday 20th June 1665* (London, 1665); Andrew Clark (editor), *The Life and Times of Anthony Wood* (Oxford, 1892), Vol. II, 4 July 1665, p. 40.

would triumphantly conclude the war that the Duke of York had so successfully begun. The entire country anxiously followed Sandwich's movements into the Danish Sound, confidently expecting that the next news from the Baltic would yet again set all England's bells ringing and spark off bonfires throughout the realm. Unfortunately when the news finally arrived, it came via Amsterdam, where the Dutch had already begun a raucous celebration for their defeat of Sandwich and his fleet at Bergen (July–August 1665).[56] "The whole news of the town is that from Bergen," Henry Muddiman soon reported.[57] It was not long before many throughout the three kingdoms knew of Sandwich's failure to capture the huge Dutch merchant fleet trapped in the Danish harbor of Bergen. While Arlington could blame the English failure on Danish perfidy, the Bishop of Limerick was sure that "all considering honest men" stood "amazed" as "the wealth of Holland was at Teddyman's mercy."[58] Gilbert Talbot thought that now the Dutch "will lie in their harbors and laugh at us."[59] When Sandwich managed to capture a few Dutch ships on his return voyage from the Sound, the secretary of state hoped the news of "this moderate good fortune" would be sufficient to "check the petulancy of the Dutch and animate our men which were a little dispirited."[60]

The ambiguous conclusion to the first year of the war raised both hopes and fears to a fever pitch prior to the outset of the 1666 campaign. It was not until the first week of June that the Dutch fleet, now ostensibly working in concert with the French, was sighted by the Duke of Albemarle – one of the two English admirals – off the English coast. Although the English fleet had divided, Prince Rupert having led his squadron off to the south in search of the French, Albemarle opted to engage the Dutch on his own. The ensuing Four Days Fight (1–4 June 1666) proved to be one of the most violent battles in the war. "Never was so desperate nor so bloody a fight at sea since the world began," thought William Temple.[61] One official narrator

56 Newsletter from Rotterdam, 10/20 August 1665, PRO, SP 101/47, f. 216r; newsletter from Rotterdam, 11/21 August 1665, PRO, SP 101/47, f. 213r; newsletter from Rotterdam, 18/28 August 1665, PRO, SP 101/47, f. 216r; Downing to Arlington, 15 August 1665, PRO, SP 84/177, f. 76r.

57 Henry Muddiman to Williamson, 21 August 1665, PRO, SP 29/129/80; see also Pepys, *Diary*, Vol. VI, 19 August 1665, pp. 195–196.

58 Arlington to William Temple, 24 August 1665, Thomas Bebington (editor), *The Right Honourable the Earl of Arlington's Letters* (London, 1701), Vol. I, pp. 17–18; William Bishop of Limerick to Ormonde, 29 November 1665, Carte 34, f. 516r (reporting on discussions in Oxford).

59 Gilbert Talbot to Henry Coventry, 28 August 1665, Longleat House, Cov. MSS XXV, f. 105r.

60 William Morrice to Henry Coventry, 14 September 1665, Longleat House, Cov. MSS LXIV, f. 226r.

61 William Temple to Carlingford, 7/17 June 1666, in Karl Taaffe (editor), *Memoirs of the Family of Taaffe* (Vienna, 1856), p. 116; see also Giustinian to Doge and Senate, 12/22 June 1666, *CSPV*, p. 15.

opined that the Four Days Fight was "the sharpest conflict that ever was fought."[62]

Before the smoke had cleared, and well before all of the blood, gore, and body parts had washed ashore, Charles II "made a sudden stop" while at prayer in his chapel "to hear the relation, which being with much advantage on our side, his Majesty commanded that public thanks should immediately be given as for a victory."[63] The news spread like wildfire. Samuel Pepys went to "spread this good news a little" on the Exchange but found "it had broken out before." In church reports of the battle were "handed from pew to pew."[64] An "Official Account of the Battle" was swiftly produced proclaiming that the English had won "a happy and seasonable victory."[65] "Great Britain now may take it's ease," enthused one balladeer, "King Charles is sovereign of the seas."[66] Correspondents throughout the kingdom enthused over the "great deliverance," this victory that "England may have occasion for many ages hereafter to rejoice in," this "happiest news that hath come to England in some years."[67] The early news of victory soon provoked widespread celebrations. Sir Robert Paston gushed to his wife that "the bells and bonfires the last night proclaimed our signal victory over the Dutch."[68] In East Claydon, Buckinghamshire, and undoubtedly in a great many places besides, there were "fires of joy" and thanksgivings to "the God of arms who gave us such a great victory over our enemies."[69]

Of course, the government was soon well aware that there had been no such great victory.[70] This did not stop them from ordering victory celebrations. "There was however order given for bonfires and bells," complained Sir John Evelyn, "but God knows it was rather a deliverance than a triumph."[71] The Dutch seethed at the thanksgiving celebration "saying that England will not care to mock God if so be it can calm the common people,

[62] Narrative of engagement, 8 June 1666, Carte 72, f. 76r. There is another copy of this narrative at PRO, PRO SP 29/158/61.

[63] Evelyn, *Diary*, 6 June 1666, p. 439.

[64] Pepys, *Diary*, Vol. VII, 6 June 1666, p. 151.

[65] "Official Account of the Battle," 7 June 1666, PRO, SP 29/158/48.

[66] "Englands Triumph and Hollands Downfall," 1–4 June 1666, in John Holloway (editor), *The Euing Collection of English Broadside Ballads* (Glasgow, 1971), p. 138.

[67] Henry Oldenburg to Robert Boyle, 8 June 1666, *Oldenburg Correspondence* Vol. III, p. 155; Silas Taylor to William Coventry, 5 June 1666, BL, Add. MSS 32094, f. 135r; Sir Ralph Verney (London) to Edmund Verney, 6 June 1666, Firestone Library, Verney MSS Reel 21 (unfoliated).

[68] Sir Robert Paston to his wife, 7 June 1666, NRO, Bradfer-Lawrence MSS. IC/1; see also Pepys, *Diary*, Vol. VII, 6 June 1666, p. 152.

[69] Edmund Verney (East Claydon) to Sir Ralph Verney, 11 June 1666, Firestone Library, Verney MSS, Reel 21 (unfoliated, my translation). There were celebrations in Hull as well: see *Current Intelligence*, 11–14 June 1666.

[70] Sir Thomas Clifford to Arlington, 6 June 1666, PRO, SP 29/158/46I; Pepys, *Diary*, Vol. VII, 7 June 1666, pp. 152–153; Arlington to Ormonde, 9 June 1666, Carte 46, f. 315r; Arlington to Temple, 11 June 1666, Bebington, *Arlington's Letters*, Vol. I, p. 84.

[71] Evelyn, *Diary*, 6 June 1666, p. 440.

for they conclude if the common people were not persuaded by you so to believe, they would revolt and thrust king and parliament out."[72] One angry poet later denounced "the lying bells" which had announced an English victory after the Four Days Fight.[73] That the English were well informed about the actual outcome of the Four Days fight well before the Fire of London demonstrated divine vengeance, is a testimony to the wide availability of information about the war. Less than a week after the battle Samuel Pepys surveyed London "to see how people do take this late fight at sea" and, to his surprise, he found that "all give over the thought of it as a victory, and do reckon it a great overthrow."[74]

England's defeat in the Four Days Fight vastly increased the stakes for the next naval encounter. Sir William Coventry, who was both the best-informed naval administrator and a political moderate, expressed what soon became the common view. "By the next fight," he informed his naval office colleague Pepys, "if we beat, the Dutch will certainly be content to take eggs for money . . . or if we be beaten, we must be contented to make peace, and glad if we can have it without paying too dear for it."[75] Correspondents throughout the country echoed Sir William Coventry's assessment of the political situation. "We have all at stake," Sir Nathaniel Hobart explained to his friend Ralph Verney.[76] "God bless us with the encounter for we throw for a great stake," Arlington prayed to Ormonde.[77] Even the Archbishop of Canterbury Gilbert Sheldon later confessed that "being deeply apprehensive of our great concernment in the success of the last action, I could not meet with my usual cheerfulness in the day nor rest quietly in the night."[78]

Sheldon and all England could soon sleep much more easily. On St. James's Day (25 July 1666) the English soundly defeated the Dutch navy in what "ought to [be] accounted the greatest victory that ever was yet acquired."[79] An official account of the battle immediately published the news of the victory.[80] Lady Palmer was sure that it was "such a victory as

72 Letter from Rotterdam to Henry Smith (London), 15/25 June 1666, PRO, SP 29/159/4. See also Giustinian to Doge and Senate, 12/22 June 1666, *CSPV*, p. 17; Giustinian to Doge and Senate, 19/29 June 1666, *CSPV*, pp. 22–23; Ludlow, "A Voyce," Bod. English History MSS C487, f. 1120.

73 Sir John Denham, *Directions to a Painter* (London, 1667), p. 19.

74 Pepys, *Diary*, Vol. VII, 9 June 1667, p. 156.

75 Pepys, *Diary*, Vol. VIII, 27 June 1666, p. 184.

76 Sir Nathaniel Hobart (London) to Sir Ralph Verney, 26 July 1666, Firestone Library, Verney MSS, Reel 21 (unfoliated).

77 Arlington to Ormonde, 17 July 1666, Carte 46, f. 335r; see also William Temple to Arlington, 23 July/2 August 1666, PRO, SP 77/34, f. 398r; William Temple to Ormonde, 13/23 July 1666, Carte 47, f. 288v; Sir Roger Burgoyne to Sir Ralph Verney, 9 July 1666, Firestone Library, Verney MSS, Reel 21 (unfoliated).

78 Gilbert Sheldon to Williamson, 31 July 1666, PRO, SP 29/165/100.

79 St. Serfe's Newsletter, 31 July 1666, LOC, 18124, Vol. I, f. 93r.

80 *The Victory over the Fleet of the States General*, 27 July 1666 (London, 1666), p. 8.

may produce a lasting peace."[81] Samuel Pepys enthused that it was an outcome "just such as I could have wished, and as the kingdom was fit to bear – enough to give us the name of conquerors and leave us masters of the sea."[82]

By the early afternoon of 29 July all London was "full of a victory," a victory which was "accompanied with bells and bonfires."[83] "The cannons from the Tower did roar, / When the good news did come to shore," recalled one balladeer, "The bells did ring and bonfires shine, / And healths carrous'd in beer and wine."[84] All three kingdoms soon followed London's lead. "We no sooner had the joyful news of his Majesty's most glorious victory," gushed Robert Mein to Williamson from Edinburgh, "but it was proclaimed by the great guns from the castle to all the country ... and at night all the streets were filled with bonfires."[85] In Dublin "printed relations of our victory at sea" were circulated, while the celebrations were punctuated with the usual "bells and bonfires."[86] "The people" in Berwick rejoiced "greatly for our fleet's last happy success against the Dutch."[87] George Sitwell quickly received the "happy tidings of a great victory over our enemies the Dutch" at his Derbyshire home.[88] Popular celebrations of the victory were held in places as geographically and socially diverse as Hull, Launceston, Plymouth, Newcastle, Pembroke, and Swansea.[89]

The bonfires had barely burnt out, the sound of bells had just faded away

81 Lady Palmer to Sir Edward Dering, 31 July 1666, CKS, U1007/C39; see also Newsletter from Dover, 29 July 1666, Carte 72, f. 81r.

82 Pepys, *Diary*, Vol. VII, 31 July 1666, p. 230.

83 Pepys, *Diary*, Vol. VII, 29 July 1666, p. 225; Arlington to Sandwich, 2 August 1666, Bebington, *Arlington's Letters*, Vol. II, p. 182; Arlington to Ormonde, 31 July 1666, Carte 46, f. 343r; Evelyn, *Diary*, 29 July 1666, p. 446.

84 "England's Royall Conquest," 25–26 July 1666, *Euing Collection*, p. 153.

85 Robert Mein (Edinburgh) to Williamson, 7 August 1666, PRO, SP 29/166/116.

86 Edward Conway (Dublin) to George Rawdon, 11 August 1666, HL, HA 14441.

87 Mark Scott (Berwick) to Williamson, 5 August 1666, PRO, SP 29/166/82.

88 George Sitwell (Derbyshire) to Francis Sitwell, 4 August 1666, in Philip Riden (editor), *George Sitwell's Letterbook 1662–1666* (Derbyshire Record Society, 1985), Vol. X, p. 226.

89 John Bower (Hull) to James Hickes, 10 August 1666, PRO, SP 29/167/30; Francis Bellott (Launceston) to Williamson, 4 August 1666, PRO, SP 29/166/81; David Grosse (Plymouth) to Williamson, 3 August 1666, PRO, SP 29/166/56; John Clarke (Plymouth) to James Hickes, 3 August 1666, PRO, SP 29/166/48; Jo. Carlisle (Dover) to Williamson, 1 August 1666, PRO, SP 29/166/11; John Knight (Ipswich) to Williamson, 31 July 1666, PRO, SP 29/165/107; Richard Forster (Newcastle) to Williamson, 3 August 1666, PRO, SP 29/166/42; Richard Forster (Newcastle) to Williamson, 4 August 1666, PRO, SP 29/166/67; Richard Forster (Newcastle) to Williamson, 7 August 1666, PRO, SP 29/166/117; Dr. John Fell (Oxford) to Williamson, 7 August 1666, PRO, SP 29/166/113; Heneage Finch to Sir John Finch, 3/13 August 1666, LRO, DG7/Box 4984, Letters Folder; Dr. James Alban Gibbes (Rome) to Arlington, 1 August 1666, PRO, SP 29/166/6; Francis Mallory (Pembroke) to Williamson, 6 August 1666, PRO, SP 29/166/107; John Man (Swansea) to Williamson, 5 August 1666, PRO, SP 29/166/85.

when the news of another great English naval triumph began to circulate throughout Britain. While the Romans had always claimed that Hannibal had lost his chance by failing to follow up his great triumph at Cannae, one historically minded intelligencer noted, "modern historians and all posterity could not say the same about England."[90] Guided by Captain Van Hemskerke, a "disobliged" Orangist, the English fleet led by Robert Holmes sailed up the Vlie and destroyed over one hundred richly laden Dutch merchant vessels with hardly any resistance. "So great a loss or shame never befell them since they were a state," William Temple wrote of the Dutch after Holmes's exploit.[91] In the Netherlands Dutch trade and credit was dealt a devastating blow. "The tears and lamentations of those poor wretches are indescribable," the Venetian Giustinian informed the Doge and Senate, so much so that "the universal desperation of the people is something to be feared."[92]

England's naval success had an even greater impact at home than it did on the continent. As soon as the faintest rumors reached Harwich "our carpenters hearing the news shouted and hallowed and betook some to ringing of bells."[93] Less than a day later Samuel Pepys found London "full of this good news."[94] A narrative account of the attack on the Vlie was soon in print, while a ballad entitled "The Dutch Damnified or the Butter-Boxes Bob'd" made the event accessible to an even wider audience.[95] The usual wave of celebrations soon followed. In Edinburgh the news of the fleet's success was immediately greeted with "the great guns from the castle and the ringing out of all the bells in and about the town," and subsequently solemnized by "sermons in every church."[96] In Coventry "'tis almost incredible with what general resentments of joy we have received the welcome tiding of the late happy success of our fleet, which we failed not by all imaginable emblems and expressions to manifest."[97] In places as far afield as Chester, Bideford, Dover, Bath, Lyme, Newcastle,

90 News from Antwerp, 18/28 August 1666, PRO, SP 77/35, f. 64r (my translation).

91 Rupert and Albemarle to Charles II, 11 August 1666, PRO, SP 29/167/75; William Temple to Ormonde, 18/28 August 1666, Carte 47, f. 291; Arlington to Ormonde, 18 August 1666, Carte 46, f. 355v; William Coventry to Ormonde, 18 August 1666, Carte 47, ff. 460–461; Pepys, *Diary*, Vol. VII, 15 August 1666, p. 247; William Temple to Carlingford, 11/21 August 1666, *Memoirs of Taafe*, p. 160.

92 Giustinian to Doge and Senate, 21/31 August 1666, *CSPV*, p. 60. See also Temple's similar reports: Temple to Arlington, 18/28 August 1666, PRO, SP 77/35, f. 62v; Temple to Arlington, 24 August/3 September 1666, PRO, SP 77/35, f. 93v.

93 Silas Taylor (Harwich) to Williamson, 14 August 1666, PRO, SP 29/167/118.

94 Pepys, *Diary*, Vol. VII, 15 August 1666, p. 248. See also Josselin, *Diary*, 19 August 1666, p. 529.

95 Pepys, *Diary*, Vol. VII, 17 August 1666, p. 252; "The Dutch Damnified or The Butter-Boxes Bob'd," 1666, in the *Euing Collection*, pp. 84–85; *Current Intelligence*, 13–16 August 1666.

96 Robert Meine (Edinburgh) to Williamson, 21 August 1666, PRO, SP 29/168/73; Meine to Williamson, 23 August 1666, PRO, SP 29/168/117.

97 Ralph Hope (Coventry) to Williamson, 20 August 1666, PRO, SP 29/168/57.

Truro, and Lynn 23 August was celebrated as a national thanksgiving for the great victory over the Dutch. In each place the local clergyman's sermon was soon followed by "ringing of bells, bonfires, and other demonstrations of joy."[98]

98 M. Anderton (Chester) to Williamson, 25 August 1666, PRO, SP 29/168/167; P. Manaton (Bideford) to Williamson, 24 August 1666, PRO, SP 29/168/137; John Carlisle (Dover) to Williamson, 24 August 1666, PRO, SP 29/168/138; Sir Christopher Gyse (Bath) to Williamson, 23 August 1666, PRO, SP 29/168/118; Anthony Thorold (Lyme) to Williamson, 25 August 1666, PRO, SP 29/168/159; Richard Forster (Newcastle) to Williamson, 24 August 1666, 24 August 1666, PRO, SP 29/168/146; Hugh Acland (Truro) to Williamson, 27 August 1666, PRO, SP 29/169/15; Edward Bodham (Lynn) to Williamson, 24 August 1666, PRO, SP 29/168/136; Andrew Clark (editor), *The Life and Times of Anthony Wood* (Oxford, 1891), Vol. II, 23 August 1666, p. 84.

19

The popular understanding of the war

For many, Holmes's attack on the Dutch ships in the Vlie took on additional significance: it was widely felt that the final blow of the war had been struck. When the Dutch "hear what Sir Robert Holmes hath done," thought Hull resident Luke Whittington, "they will be much more humble."[1] The Oxford scientist John Wallis hoped that "the issue of it may be a good peace; which well established would be much more acceptable than the news of desolations, though this, as the case stands, be good news too."[2] "I hope this may somewhat allay their insolency," Hugh Acland wrote of the Dutch from Cornwall, "and make them to sue for to have peace with us."[3]

Hopes for peace, of course, necessitated a clear conception of acceptable concessions. Peace required well-defined war aims. Why, then, did the English people think they were fighting the Dutch? Why did they celebrate each victory so enthusiastically? Why were they so anxious to hear the latest rumors about Dutch morale and martial preparedness?

There can be no doubt that there was initial enthusiasm for the war.[4] Mariners were "freely coming in and cheerfully offering themselves in the service and in some counties above their proportion."[5] The city merchant

1 Luke Whittington (Hull) to James Hickes, 20 August 1666, PRO, SP 29/168/65.

2 John Wallis (Oxford) to Oldenburg, 18 August 1666, A. Rupert Hall and Maria Boas Hall (editors), *The Correspondence of Henry Oldenburg*, Vols. II–IV (Madison, 1966–1967), Vol. III, p. 213.

3 Hugh Acland (Truro) to Williamson, 23 August 1666, PRO, SP 29/168/116.

4 This was already quite clear in 1664: William Morrice to Fanshawe, 6 June 1664, in Nickolls, *Original Letters*, p. 137; Charles II to his sister, 19 September 1664, in Cyril H. Hartmann, *Charles II and Madame* (London, 1934), p. 113; Van Goch to States General, 23 September/3 October 1664, PRO, SP 84/172, f. 247r; *The Dutch Drawn to the Life* (London, 1664), pp. 4–5. This was made manifest in the enthusiastic support which London gave to two loans to fight the war. Muddiman's Newsletter, 9 June 1664, Bod., Tanner MSS, 47, f. 163v; journal of London Common Council, 9 June 1664, CLRO, 54J, f. 389v; Thomas Rugge, "Mercurius Politicus Redivivus," 15 June 1664, BL, Add. 10117, f. 110v; Pepys, *Diary*, Vol. V, 26 October 1664, p. 307; William Morrice to Henry Coventry, 28 October 1664, Longleat House, Cov. MSS LXIV, f. 19v; Thomas Rugge, "Mercurius Politicus Redivivus," October 1664, BL. Add. 10117, f. 120r; Downing to Henry Coventry, 4 November 1664, Longleat House, Cov. MSS XLI, f. 3r.

5 William Morrice to Henry Coventry, 27 January 1665, Longleat House, Cov. MSS LXIV, f. 93r. See also Morrice to Coventry, 24 February 1665, Longleat House, Cov. MSS LXIV,

Sir Richard Ford enthused that "the number of seamen [was] greater than ever, and the most part of them full of animosity against the Hollander."[6] "From the city of Oxford a hundred volunteers have been sent to London for the service of the fleet, and the governors of other towns have done the same," observed one Venetian commentator, "this shows the general disposition of the country to take up the quarrel, everyone exerting himself according to his capacity to make his contribution, either with his purse or his person."[7]

Early recruitment efforts were buoyed when a disaffected Dutch mariner, posing as a Swede, circulated "the most horrid and astonishing news that ever was yet told in my memory – that De Ruyter, with his fleet in Guinea, hath proceeded to the taking of whatever we have – forts, goods, ships, and men – and tied our men back to back and thrown them all into the sea – even women and children also."[8] The news spread like wildfire, inciting people all England over into a frenzy of agitation. It "had such an effect on the people," Edmund Ludlow learned from his extremely well-informed sources, "that the Dutch ambassador could not pass without affronts, and was in danger for his life."[9] Commissioner Middleton, who heard the "Dutch news" in Portsmouth, was "easily persuaded" by the tale because "I knew their mercies are but cruelties."[10] James Scudamore was confident that the English would soon repay "that barbarism which none but such a barbarous nation as the Dutch could have acted ... with honor and interest."[11] Although the atrocities in Guinea were soon revealed to be wild

f. 121r. This was the continuation of a pattern which had begun to manifest itself almost as soon as the trade resolution had passed in late April 1664: Cuneus to Greffier, 27 May/6 June 1664, PRO, SP 84/171, f. 186r; Muddiman's Newsletter, 23 June 1664, Bod., Tanner 47, f. 175r; Thomas Rugge, "Mercurius Politicus Redivivus," September 1664, BL, Add. 10117, f. 118v.

6 Sir Richard Ford, "Grounds for War," 1664, Bod., Clar. 83, f. 374r.

7 News from London, 30 March/9 April 1665, *CSPV*, p. 103. For Newcastle see Richard Forster to James Hickes, 14 March 1665, PRO, SP 29/114/132. For Scottish and Irish volunteers see Thomas Rugge, "Mercurius Politicus Redivivus," 15 March 1665, BL, Add. 10117, f. 135r. I am well aware that there were many reasons why men might volunteer to serve, not least of which was to avoid impressment. For this see Richard Forster (Newcastle) to James Hickes, 7 March 1665, PRO, SP 29/114/70. However the extraordinarily high level of volunteers at the outset of the war, when England's economy was in much better shape than in later years, compared with the decline thereafter suggests a great deal about popular attitudes to the conflict. For the subsequent difficulties of recruitment see J. D. Davies *Gentlemen and Tarpaulins: The Officers and Men of the Restoration Navy* (Oxford, 1991), p. 138.

8 Pepys, *Diary*, Vol. VI, 23 February 1665, p. 42.

9 Ludlow, "A Voyce," Bod., English History MSS C487, p. 1062. A Venetian observer told almost the same story. News from London, 2/12 March 1665, *CSPV*, pp. 89–90.

10 Commissioner Thomas Middleton (Portsmouth) to Samuel Pepys, 1 March 1665, PRO, SP 29/114/3; see also Richard Forster (Newcastle) to James Hickes, 28 February 1665, PRO, SP 29/113/101.

11 James Scudamore (Craddock) to Williamson, 27 Februatry 1665, PRO, SP 29/113/79. See also Antony Trevor to Williamson, 27 February 1665, PRO, SP 29/113/84.

exaggerations,[12] Samuel Pepys quickly discovered that "the generality of the people [do] fear that there is something of truth in it – and I do fear it too."[13] Indeed at frequent intervals throughout the spring and summer of 1665 new examples of the "savage and inhumane" behavior of the Dutch were widely disseminated, and generally believed.[14]

English anti-Dutch sentiment, then, was reaching a feverish pitch in the spring of 1665. Parliament-men, the Earl of Arlington was sure, "have no jealousy in or out of the House but of our making a peace, so fond they are of the war."[15] "Never was men so ready to go to dinner or a bride's bed as those country men were in their thoughts to have satisfaction of the Dutch," the Londoner Thomas Rugge recorded in his diary, "and they in several countries was ready to rise to kill, slay and destroy all Dutchmen in their ways."[16] "The anger and indignity of the English nation was so provok'd," recalled the high church cleric and future Bishop of Oxford Samuel Parker, "that they never before concurr'd with so general and unanimous spirit, as now, to revenge [the Dutch] treachery."[17] Indeed when war was finally proclaimed in March 1665 foreign observers remarked on "the great shoutings and rejoicings amongst the people," on the people's "joy at this rupture."[18]

Was this joy economically motivated? Did the English people believe they were finally about to begin the long-desired trade war against their primary commercial rival? Did they believe this conflict would immediately and significantly improve their standard of living?

In fact, very few thought that war with the Dutch would be in their short-term economic self-interest. Most were convinced, as was Sir George Downing, that "this war ... must necessarily for the present stop and hinder a great deal of trade and draw away a great deal of money extraordinary for ship provisions and the like."[19] In the event, Downing's fears proved to

12 Alvise Sagredo to Doge and Senate, 3/13 March 1665, *CSPV*, pp. 85–86; R. Mein to Henry Muddiman, 1 March 1665, PRO, SP 29/114/1; Thomas Osborne to Lady Osborne, 25 February 1665, in Andrew Browning, *Thomas Osborne Earl of Danby and Duke of Leeds 1632–1712*. (Glasgow, 1944), Vol. II (Letters), p. 11; Pepys, *Diary*, Vol. VI, 25 February 1665, pp. 43–44.

13 Pepys, *Diary*, Vol. VI, 27 February 1665, p. 46.

14 Francis Nelthorp to George Oxenden, 12 August 1665, BL, Add. 40710, f. 1r; narrative by Major Robert Holmes, 6 March 1665, PRO, SP 29/114/68; William Morrice to Henry Coventry, 7 July 1665, Longleat House, Cov. MSS LXIV, f. 186r; Downing to Clarendon, 23 June 1665, Bod., Clar. 108, ff. 239v-240r.

15 Arlington to Henry Coventry, 13 January 1665, Longleat House, Cov. MSS LXV, f. 86v.

16 Thomas Rugge, "Mercurius Politicus Redivivus," February 1665, BL, Add. 10117, f. 132v; see also Samuel Tuke to John Evelyn, 14 March 1665, Christ Church, Evelyn In-Letters 1295.

17 Thomas Newlin (translator), *Bishop Parker's History of his Own Time* (London, 1727), p. 86.

18 M. Van Gogh to States General, 16 March 1665, PRO, SP 84/175, f. 188r; news from London, 23 March/2 April 1665, *CSPV*, p. 98.

19 Downing to Clarendon, 3 March 1665, Bod., Clar. 108, f. 276r.

be greatly understated. Trade, wrote one East India merchant, "was never more interrupted from the beginning of the world by those unnatural wars now in Europe, where the several princes seem to play at nine pins to tip down one another."[20]

Before the first cannon volley was fired, even before war was declared, it was well known that Dutch military strategy would be to eviscerate English long-distance trade. The Dutch "discourse very publicly," Downing reported in despatch after despatch, that "we shall wholly destroy the English in the East Indies, we are masters of Guinea, we shall ruin the English trade in the Caribee islands and western parts, and we doubt not but now by the orders sent to Cadiz and the Streights, to be masters of those seas and to take and ruin all the English shipping there."[21] By late December 1664 it was already coffee-house gossip "that the Dutch will avoid fighting with us at home but do all the hurt they can to us abroad."[22]

Given the vast maritime resources of the Dutch – and the Dutch were well known to be more powerful outside Europe than within it – English trading companies were more than a little concerned about the war's implications for their mercantile endeavors. The English East India Company, which had always been ambivalent about the government's aggressive Hollandophobia, understood full well the dangers that the conflict held for them. The governors of the Company desperately hoped for "some composure of the differences between our king's Majesty and the Dutch."[23] The Company's factors in India also understood the dangers all too well. "If the war continue," George Foxcroft informed his superiors from Fort St. George, the Dutch "will use their utmost endeavors to root us out of the trade of the Indies."[24] William Blake, who had an extensive trade with Persia, hoped "a war with the Dutch would not break out," fearing that as the Dutch "are so powerful in India at present" the English there might be overwhelmed.[25] When war was declared, the historian James Ralph later recalled, "the East

20 George Oxenden (Surat) to John Stanian, 24 November 1666, IOL, E/3/29, ff. 276v-277r.

21 Downing to Arlington, 27 January 1665, PRO, SP 84/174, f. 50r; Downing to Arlington, 31 January 1665, PRO, SP 84/174, f. 72r. See also Downing to Clarendon, 14 October 1664, Bod., Clar. 108, f. 101; Downing to Bennet, 18 October 1664, All Souls College, 309 (unfoliated). Others provided similar reports of Dutch strategy: De Bacquoy/Van Ruyven to Bennet, 31 January 1665, PRO, SP 84/174, f. 60; Gilbert Talbot to Henry Coventry, 14 February 1665, Longleat House, Cov. MSS XXV, f. 37r; Robert Southwell to Sir Paul Davys, 20 June 1665, Carte 34, f. 294r; Ludlow, "A Voyce," Bod., English History MSS C487, p. 1076.

22 Pepys, *Diary*, Vol. V., 26 December 1664, pp. 356–357.

23 East India Company to president and Council in Surat, 17 March 1665, IOL, E/3/86, f. 238v.

24 George Foxcroft (Fort St. George) to East India Company, 26 September 1665, IOL, E/3/29, f. 83v. The Council in Surat expressed similar concerns before they knew war had broken out. George Oxenden, John Goodier *et al.* (Surat) to Lieutenant-Colonel Cooke, 9 September 1665, IOL, E/3/29, f. 39r.

25 William Blake (Hugly) to George Oxenden, 21 October 1665, BL, Add. 40710, f. 7r.

India Company of England was struck with terrible apprehensions and made no scruple to give out that it was a court war, which was set on foot solely for the interest of the Duke of York, and some other great persons, who were engag'd with him."[26]

The progress of the war did not make the East India traders more enamored of the conflict with the Dutch. In letter after letter East India merchants bemoaned "this unhappy war," this war which continued "to your worships' and your servants' exceeding hindrance and prejudice," all hoping "this last summer may period our wars with the Dutch."[27] The maritime war, the East India merchants knew, had made it far too dangerous to risk richly laden ships in the long passages between Britain and the Indies. "The dangers at sea are inexpressible," Francis Clarke warned George Oxenden.[28] "During the wars," the East India Company in London informed some of their factors in India, "nothing less than a miracle can preserve ships from ruin and destruction."[29] The overall impact on the East India trade was devastating. "The Company," lamented John Mascall, "do not adventure 1/3 part of what they would have done had it been times of peace."[30]

War against the Dutch was no more desirable, at least in the short term, for other English long-distance traders. The Levant Company, which had had little reason to complain of the Dutch prior to April 1664, knew that the war would jeopardize the entirety of its trade. "There is also great fear among the Turkey traders of their ships," the Dutch ambassador Van Goch informed his superiors prior to the first naval battle, "by reason of the Netherlands ships of war and privateers which are crossing up and down in those parts."[31] Throughout the war, in letter after letter, the Levant Company complained of "the great danger of surprisal," "the dangers at sea" which "are so great," "these troubles abroad" which "threatened a destruction to our trade."[32] In the event, the Company was compelled to

26 James Ralph, *The History of England* Vol. I (London, 1744), p. 99.

27 William Blake to Sir George Oxenden, October 1666, BL, Add. 40710, f. 37v; East India Company to president and Council of Surat, 7 March 1666, IOL, E/3/87, f. 1r; E. Swinglehurst (Gombroone) to East India Company, 18 May 1666, IOL, E/3/29, f. 219r.

28 Francis Clarke to George Oxenden, 13 March 1666, BL, Add. 40712, f. 29v.

29 East India Company to president and Council in Surat, 16 April 1667, IOL, E/3/87, f. 32v. Similar sentiments are plentiful: Henry Oxenden to George Oxenden, 24 March 1666, BL, Add. 40712, f. 6r; Stephen Flower (Spahawne) to George Oxenden, 28 August 1666, BL, Add. 40710, f. 35v; Cesar Chamberlain (Corvar) to George Oxenden, 23 April 1666, BL, Add. 40710, f. 46v; Henry Chowne to George Oxenden, 10 March 1666, BL, Add. 40712, f. 20v; George Oxenden *et al.* to East India Company, 1 January 1666, IOL, E/3/29, f. 158r; James Oxenden to George Oxenden, 8 January 1667, BL, Add. 40713, f. 28v.

30 John Mascall to George Oxenden, 6 March 1666, BL, Add. 40712, f. 22r.

31 M. Van Goch to States General, 2/12 June 1665, PRO, SP 84/176, f. 136v.

32 Levant Company to Winchilsea, 26 June 1665, PRO, SP 105/113, f. 57v; Levant Company to Consul Cave, 15 February 1666, PRO, SP 105/113, f. 65r; Levant Company to Captain Sam Chamblet, 16 March 1666, PRO, SP 105/113, f. 68v.

adopt severe austerity measures, measures not dissimilar from those it followed during the first Anglo-Dutch War. The Company was unable to present the government's ambassador in Constantinople, the Earl of Winchilsea, his annual gift because "the state of our trade [does not] go on so freely as before the war."[33] More seriously the Levant merchant Thomas Pearle reported that "by reason of the war with the French and Dutch we are not like to have any general shipping this year, so the expense of the Company will be the heavier."[34] War with the Dutch, England's Levant merchants knew before the first shots were fired, would be an unmitigated short-term economic disaster. Nothing that happened during the war compelled those merchants to revise their assessment.

Even the members of the Royal Africa Company, that company which had played such a significant role in promoting the April 1664 trade resolution, knew before the outbreak of the war that their economic survival would be put in jeopardy. "They find their credit totally extinct," the Royal Company's general court complained to the Privy Council, "so that they are not in any degree capable to still the clamors of their creditors much less to preserve and maintain their trade without some speedy and extraordinary supply from his Majesty."[35] The Dutch admiral De Ruyter's spectacular successes on the coast of Africa in the autumn of 1664, and the Company's failure subsequently to reestablish its foothold, convinced even the hawkish Africa Company investor the Earl of Peterborough to pray for "a good peace."[36] By 1666, the Company's directors claimed that "their stock hath been so much exhausted by (almost insupportable) losses of their goods and seats of trade on the coast of Africa that they are not capable to proceed farther."[37]

More traditional overseas merchants, those trading with other European countries, could be sure that war with the Dutch boded ill for their particular trades. Merchants trading to Italy so greatly feared the Dutch Mediterranean fleet that by the summer of 1665 there were no English ships to be found in Italian waters.[38] Indeed those Levant ships which were lucky

33 John Langley (London) to Winchilsea, 1 October 1666, LRO, DG7/Box 4984, Letters Folder.

34 Thomas Pearle (London) to Winchilsea, 19 February 1666, LRO, DG7/Box 4962, Bundle V. It appears that the Company also suffered badly from raised insurance rates: see Allan Broderick to Ormonde, 18 November 1665, Carte 34, f. 489r.

35 Royal Africa Company, "A Brief Narrative," January 1665, PRO, SP 29/110/14. It was almost certainly for this reason that the Royal Africa Company voluntarily surrendered many of their merchant ships to the Navy Board: minutes of the Royal Africa Company, 13 February 1665, PRO, Kew, T70/75, f. 35r.

36 Peterborough to Williamson, 18 August 1665, PRO, SP 29/129/59. This sentiment might have been partly motivated by the rumors circulating in the merchant community that the Dutch merchants were pressing for further military action in Africa. See George Oxenden to Henry Gary, 20 March 1665, BL, Add. 40699, f. 91v.

37 Petition of the Royal Adventurers Trading to Africa, 1666, PRO, SP 29/186/1.

38 Joseph Kent to Williamson, 17/27 June 1665, PRO, SP 85/8, ff. 2–3.

enough to reach Livorno were forced to remain in port because the remainder of the voyage back to England was fraught with too much danger.[39] The Merchant Adventurers thought "it is a madness to adventure" to trade with the Hanseatic cities.[40] So many Dutch men-of-war and privateers patrolled the seas between England and the Hanseatic towns that "at present no insurance will pass between Hamburg" and London.[41] Even before the French entered the war on the Dutch side in 1666, English trade with France had slowed to a virtual standstill. Without a convoy, Denzil Hollis complained to Arlington, "all trading must stop."[42] English merchants in Bordeaux – a port of central importance in the claret trade – reported that "their ships and goods [were] snapped up by Dutch capers if they stir out of the harbor and [were] even troubled by them in the very river."[43] Spanish merchants, Baltic merchants, and even Virginia merchants all voiced the same laments.[44] Surely very few overseas merchants could have felt that war with the Dutch would have been in their immediate economic interest.

Most who cared to contemplate the matter must have known that the war would have been no more advantageous to the domestic economies of the three kingdoms. High taxes, blockage of the naval arteries, and the uncertain business climate which is the necessary concomitant of war wreaked havoc in all economic sectors. "Our nation is so embroiled with wars," reported one merchant, "that all trade is in a manner stopped."[45] Later in the war Samuel Pepys observed that "the merchants do give themselves over for lost, no man knowing what to do, whether to sell or buy, not knowing whether peace or war to expect."[46] The Venetian ambassador was certainly right to conclude that the "hostilities which are still proceeding are more hurtful to merchants than to princes."[47]

The English prince, in this case, was badly hurt as well. "This war grows very burdensome," Arlington wearily admitted to Ormonde after the

39 William Temple to Arlington, 9/19 October 1666, PRO, SP 77/35, f. 191.

40 William Atwood to Thomas Scott, 24 February 1665, PRO, C109/23, Pt. II (unfoliated letterbook). I am grateful to Henry Roseveare for pointing me in the direction of this very suggestive chancery master's exhibit.

41 Atwood to Thomas Scott, 13 January 1665, PRO, C109/23, Pt. II (unfoliated letterbook); Sir Ralph Verney (London) to Edmund Verney, 1 June 1665, Firestone Library, Verney MSS Reel 20 (unfoliated). For Dutch sea patrols see Newsletter from Amsterdam, 1/11 December 1665, PRO, SP 101/47, f. 318r.

42 Hollis to Arlington, 4/14 March 1665, PRO, SP 78/120, f. 64v.

43 Hollis to Bennet, 8/18 February 1665, PRO, SP 78/120, f. 41v. See also Richard Colston to Joseph Williamson, 7/17 March 1665, PRO, SP 78/120, f. 62r.

44 Anthony Carew to Ormonde, 18 February 1665, Carte 34, f. 38r; Arlington to Henry Coventry, 26 May 1665, Longleat House, Cov. MSS LXIV, f. 167v (Baltic merchants); Oldenburg to Moray, 28 September 1665, *Oldenburg Correspondence*, Vol. II, p. 527 (Virginia merchants).

45 Richard Craddock to George Oxenden, 5 March 1666, BL, Add. 40712, f. 41r.

46 Samuel Pepys, *Diary*, Vol. VIII, 15 March 1667, p. 113.

47 Giustinian to Doge and Senate, 26 February/8 March 1667, *CSPV*, p. 140.

second campaigning season, as "the money for it as well as the means of spending it, fit with strange qualms."[48] This was hardly surprising since the customs returns – an important source of governmental revenue as well as an excellent indicator of economic activity – already showed a 10 percent decline in the year between the passage of the April trade resolution and the outbreak of hostilities.[49] Business uncertainty and the zealous efforts of privateers had already begun to take their toll.

Agricultural as well as commercial sectors were bound to suffer in war. Farmers could have predicted that "the greatness of taxes" necessary to finance an expensive naval war would cause the misery that they in fact did by the conflict's end. It was with sadness, but not with surprise, that Samuel Pepys entered in his diary that "the farmers do break every day almost."[50] The uncertainty which accompanied early modern warfare hurt the farmers as well as merchants. "I doubt the noise of [the French] invading us hath made tenants the more backward in paying rents and taking land," opined Sir Ralph Verney at the height of one of the many invasion scares during the war years.[51]

The economic dislocation which was to be expected, and which in fact did occur, was not localized but affected the entire country. Before war was declared the Essex clergyman Ralph Josselin lamented that there was "no trade by reason of the Dutch troubles."[52] The Dutch had so devastated the bustling trade of the Cinque Ports that before the first campaigning season was over Yarmouth had "become like a country village."[53] "The trade of this town and the neighboring ports of Wells, Burnham, Cley, Boston etc. being now wholly laid aside by reason of the great hazard and difficulties of the sea pirates and foreign men of war," the mayor of King's Lynn wrote to Horatio Lord Townshend, that it "makes us sensible not only of our want of trade for livelihood, but of supplies for our subsistence."[54] In Hull, Sir Anthony Gilby reported, "our fears ... are so great by reason of the Dutch fleet being upon our coast that not a ship dares stir out."[55] Dutch naval activity was not limited to the Channel. By July 1665, the Bristol merchant Isaac Morgan complained that "there's few ships going out or coming into this port that miss the rogues."[56] Sir John Knight measured the city's loss of commerce in the first few months of the war alone in thousands of

48 Arlington to Ormonde, 16 October 1666, Carte 46, f. 388r.
49 "Account of His Majesty's Customs," 25 March 1665, PRO, SP 29/116/20.
50 Pepys, *Diary*, Vol. VIII, 27 February 1667, p, 84.
51 Sir Ralph Verney (London) to Edmund Verney, 10 January 1667, Firestone Library, Verney MSS Reel 21 (unfoliated).
52 Josselin, *Diary*, 12 February 1665, p. 515.
53 Richard Bower (Yarmouth) to Williamson, 16 June 1665, PRO, SP 29/124/96.
54 Thomas King (King's Lynn) to Horatio Lord Townshend, 26 April 1665, BL, Add. 63081, f. 164r.
55 Sir Antony Gilby (Hull) to Williamson, 5 May 1667, PRO, SP 29/199/73.
56 Isaac Morgan (Bristol) to ?, 1 July 1665, Carte 34, f. 309r.

pounds.[57] By the last year of the war Sir John concluded that "all navigation between Bristol and London is for the most part cut off."[58] "The merchandise of Kersies" upon which most Devon families depended, lamented Seth Ward Bishop of Exeter, was "by reason of the war ... very much hindered."[59]

Ireland and Scotland also had much to lose economically. "This poor land will be utterly undone for want of trade," exclaimed Robert Mein from Edinburgh before battle was joined, "we are always losers" during maritime conflicts in the North Sea.[60] The Dutch were no less able to disrupt Irish trade. By the spring of 1665 Dutch privateers "hath so affrighted the merchants [in Dublin] that they are afraid to trade to Chester water."[61] In the west of Ireland it was said "the enemy are so busy here that people are running into the hills."[62] "Trade is absolutely dead," moaned the Earl of Orrery to his brother the Duke of Burlington the following year, "all seamen, nay the very fishermen perish, for that we have none to sail our own ships nor will English ships come hither."[63]

The most profound, the most widely felt, and surely the most predictable, economic ramification of the war was the massive increase in the price of coal, the primary source of fuel for a majority of the English people. From the outset of hostilities the Dutch targeted the Newcastle coal fleets, as they had done in the previous war.[64] The price of coal immediately skyrocketed in London, so much so that "most of the cooks was fain to use wood instead of coals."[65] "At the first rumor of war with Holland," observed a Venetian intelligencer, the price of coal "at first doubled and then tripled, to the great distress of the poor people here, many of whom died for lack of fuel in this severe season."[66] By March the Lord Mayor of London and the justices of the peace for Middlesex, Kent, and Surrey had opted to regulate

57 Sir John Knight (Bristol) to Navy Commissioners, 1 July 1665, PRO, SP 29/126/8. See the similar complaint by the mayor John Willoughby, September 1665, PRO, SP 29/133/66.

58 Sir John Knight (Bristol) to Navy Commisioners, 15 March 1667, PRO, SP 29/194/12.

59 Seth Ward to Sheldon, 3 July 1665, in J. Simmons (editor), "Some Letters from Bishop Ward of Exeter, 1663–1667," in *Devon and Cornwall Notes and Queries* Vol. 21 (1940–1941), p. 288.

60 Robert Mein (Edinburgh) to Henry Mudiman, 11 March 1665, PRO, SP 29/114/107.

61 Thomas Jones (Dublin) to Ormonde, 22 April 1665, Carte 34, f. 154r.

62 Intelligence from the west of Ireland, 30 April 1665, Carte 34, f. 198r. Similar compaints were registered throughout Ireland. See Irish Merchants' petition, 21 April 1665, Carte 34, f. 162r; George Rawdon to Ormonde, 10 June 1665, Carte 34, f. 251r.

63 Roger Boyle Earl of Orrery to Burlington, 10 April 1666, BL, Althorp Papers B4 (unfoliated).

64 William Morrice to Henry Coventry, 13 January 1665, Longleat House, Cov. MSS LXIV, f. 88r; William Say to Ludlow, in "A Voyce," Bod., English History MSS C487, p. 1059.

65 The price of coal in London can be traced in the pages of Thomas Rugge's "Mercurius Politicus Redivivus." For February–April 1665, see BL, Add. 10117, ff. 131–138; see also Sir Ralph Verney (London) to Edmund Verney, 18 May 1665, Firestone Library, Verney MSS Reel 20 (unfoliated).

66 News from London, 9/19 March 1665, *CSPV*, p. 92.

the price of coal.[67] But this was hardly a solution. Regulating the price could not guarantee a constant supply of coal, indeed it lowered the incentive for the colliers to risk facing the Dutch fleet along the English coast. Moreover, in Newcastle it was thought that "my Lord Mayor's proceeding" will "cause many thousands of people [to] go a begging."[68] Naturally the fluctuation in the price of coal did not affect all England equally; not all places depended on coal for fuel, while others could procure coal overland instead of by sea. However, there is every reason to believe that the hardship was quite general.[69]

Some have speculated that the obvious economic disadvantages of war with the Dutch were overlooked by contemporaries because they were seduced by hopes of the huge potential riches which could be procured by seizing Dutch shipping.[70] Capturing Dutch prizes, however, was never an economic goal, Arlington explained to Sir Richard Fanshawe, "our business being rather to damnify our enemies than to enrich ourselves."[71] While the wealth of Dutch East Indiamen might line the pockets of a few lucky merchant seamen, no one thought they could offset the massive economic losses caused by the war. Noting that "the prizes taken are poor barks of small value, and do not repair our loss at Guinea," Thomas Salusbury explained to the Earl of Huntingdon that "this is not the way to reimburse the poor merchants which have and do lose their ships to the Dutch."[72] George Downing reminded Clarendon that "it's true you have taken a great many ships in the Channel but for the future you shall take few more there, and what you have there not of great value; two or three English ships in the Streights if fall into the hands of the Dutch more worth than them all."[73] In fact, the first few months of the war represented the high point of prize intake. William Coventry, who knew that the Dutch would cease sending

67 Order at Meeting of Lord Mayor and justices of the peace for London, Middlesex, Kent, and Surrey, 20 March 1665, PRO, SP 29/115/54; M. Van Gogh to States General, 3 April 1665, PRO, SP 84/175, f. 227v.

68 Richard Forster (Newcastle) to James Hickes, 25 April 1665, PRO, SP 29/119/67 I.

69 Luke Whittington (Hull) to Williamson, 28 February 1665, PRO, SP 29/113/103; Richard Bower (Yarmouth) to Williamson, 24 June 1665, PRO, SP 29/125/40; Richard Forster (Newcastle) to James Hickes, 22 June 1666, PRO, SP 29/159/71.

70 There is, of course, some warrant for this belief. "A war with Holland is that which will most probably pay for the powder and shot that will be spent on them; as it did in the last when the prize office brought into the Exchequer 960 thousand pounds clear money beyond all plunders and sharkings, on sea and land," argued Sir Richard Ford. See Sir Richard Ford, "Grounds For War," 1664, Bod., Clar. 83, f. 374r. Ford's memorandum, it must be emphasized was intended to convince the government that the war would not be overwhelmingly costly. It did not deny that in the commercial sector the war could be devastating in the short term. Ford thought merchants would support the war because it was in their long-term interest.

71 Arlington to Fanshawe, 20 April 1665, BL, Harleian MSS 7010, ff. 243v–244r.

72 Thomas Salusbury to Earl of Huntingdon, 9 January 1665, HL, HA 10663.

73 Downing to Clarendon, 17 February 1665, Bod., Clar. 108, f. 274v. See a similar assessment by Robert Meine (Edinburgh) to Williamson, 16 August 1666, PRO, SP 29/167/166.

their ships through the Channel once the battle fleets had engaged, was quite right to doubt whether "the remainder of the prizes to be taken henceforward is like to be so considerable."[74] From Dover John Carlisle lamented that there was "little doings as to prizes,"[75] while Arlington was astounded that the Irish prizes amounted "to a much less sum than we imagined."[76] Much of the profits from the few prize ships which the English did seize were embezzled by seamen, providing little compensation to the commercial sectors which were so badly damaged by the war. Embezzlement, Francis Mallory wearily speculated after the wealth of yet another prize ship vanished before his very eyes, "I fear is all the nation over."[77]

There were very few, then, in any of the three kingdoms who were fighting the war for their short-term economic self-interest.[78] For England, Scotland, and Ireland the sea represented an economic lifeline. It made no sense to sever it. Nevertheless many Britons did see the war against the Dutch as a conflict "against those grand enemies of our commerce."[79] This was so because the English, Scots, and Irish were not fighting to increase short-term profits, but to defend their long-term economic viability. When Henry Coventry lectured Charles II that he was now "engaging in a foreign war of greater concernment to yourself and nation than ever any of your royal predecessors were and through success in it will bring greater hopes of wealth and security to both than any age could boast of," he did so in the knowledge that England was fighting a war against a nation which sought control of all the world's trade, which lusted after universal dominion.[80]

Their quarrel with the Dutch, the English insisted with great frequency, was not over the incremental commercial gains of the Netherlanders, but rather the Dutch political strategy to engross all the world's trade. "The Dutch of late Lord it more than ever," complained Stephen Flower from Persia, "and are now painting a ship to place on the top of their house to the view of all, bragging to the Persians they are masters of the sea and command the whole world."[81] English merchants in Bantam were convinced that the Dutch "do endeavor to get to themselves the whole Indies."[82]

74 William Coventry to Earl of Falmouth, 1 April 1665, BL, Add. 32094, f. 48v.
75 Joseph Carlisle (Dover) to Williamson, 4 August 1665, PRO, SP 29/128/32.
76 Arlington to Ormonde, 10 July 1666, Carte 46, f. 331r.
77 Francis Mallory (Pembroke) to Williamson, 22 October 1666, PRO, SP 29/175/151. See also Robert Southwell to Ormonde, 16 October 1665, Carte 34, f. 440r; Joseph Carlisle (Dover) to Williamson, 14 March 1665, PRO, SP 29/114/133.
78 The Earl of Winchilsea ridiculed this notion. See Winchilsea to Bennet, 14/24 March 1665, PRO, SP 97/18, f. 120r.
79 John Man (Swansea) to Williamson, 27 August 1666, PRO, SP 29/169/22.
80 Henry Coventry to Charles II, 6 March 1665, Longleat House, Cov. MSS LXIV, f. 126v.
81 Stephen Flower (Gombroone) to Sir George Oxenden, 16 February 1665, BL, Add. 40710, f. 27r. See also William Thomson to Sir George Downing, 3 March 1665, IOL, E/3/86, f. 235v.
82 William Turner, James Brown, Robert Hoppers, Harmon Gibbon (Bantam) to East India Company, 8 May 1666, IOL, E/3/29, f. 218r.

Netherlandish proceedings were not dissimilar in Africa. Sir Richard Ford decried the Dutch for claiming "the whole sovereignty of it by right of war as their entire conquest from the Portugal, who used the title of Lord of Guinea."[83] The Dutch also pursued "an universal sovereignty ... in the Baltic Sea, and the trade about the Northern cape to Russia," according to the author of *Europae Modernae Speculum*, so that "in a few years if uninterrupted they will gain all the wealth in the world into their hands."[84] The goal, according to the author of one court memorandum, was clear: the Dutch intend "to make themselves monarchs of the sole trade of the whole East and West Indies."[85] Henry Coventry was instructed to explain to the Swedes that the Dutch "meant to engross the whole trade [of Africa and the East Indies] to themselves by assuming what dominion they please ... which is a presumption no other prince must endure."[86] While the blunt Duke of Albemarle complained of Dutch "grasping of trade," the more poetic John Crouch could ask "did the communicative sun create / all spices to make incense for one state?"[87] Edmund Waller eloquently summarized contemporary English opinion in describing the Dutch as "those greedy mariners, out of whose way / diffusive nature could no region lay."[88]

Broadsides, poems, pamphlets, and diplomatic correspondence all insisted that it was not merely trade routes that were at stake. The English and the Dutch, Thomas St. Serfe proclaimed uncontroversially in his newsletter, were fighting "for the empire of the sea."[89] "Scarce had poor Holland baffled potent Spain," recalled one historically minded poet, "when she usurps upon the spacious main."[90] The Dutch had long sought "this pretended Empire of the sea and traffic," agreed another polemicist.[91] The scholarly John Evelyn was able to be more precise, claiming that " 'tis since the year 1622 that the Hollanders have taken a resolution to have the monarchy of trade of the whole world."[92] "You dare attempt to make the seas your own," wrote the wildly popular poet Abraham Cowley accusingly

83 Sir Richard Ford, "Grounds for War," 1664, Bod., Clar. 83, f. 393v.

84 *Europae Modernae Speculum: Or, A View of the Empires, Kingdoms, Principalities and Common-Wealths of Europe* (London, 1665), pp. 62, 67.

85 "Narrative of the Late Passages Between His Majesty and the Dutch," 1665, PRO, SP 84/178, f. 62r.

86 Instructions for Henry Coventry (in Clarendon's Hand), May 1664, Bod., Clar. 159, f. 77v.

87 Oldenburg to Boyle, 30 December 1665, *Oldenburg Correspondence*, Vol. II, p. 654; John Crouch, *The Dutch Embargo* (London, 1665), p. 7.

88 Edmund Waller, "Instructions to a Painter," 1665, *POAS*, p. 25.

88 St. Serfe's Newsletter, 5 December 1665, LOC, 18124, Vol. I, 10v.

90 William Smith, *Ingratitude Rveng'd: Or, A Poem Upon the Happy Victory of his Majesties Naval Forces Against the Dutch; June 3 and 4 1665* (London, 1665), p. 1.

91 Untitled MSS pamphlet, 1665, NMM, Clifford Papers Vol. III, Dw100, f. 15.

92 John Evelyn's notes for his "History of the Second Dutch War," Christ Church, John Evelyn MSS 134, f. 63.

of the Dutch, "O'er the vast ocean, which no limit knows, / The narrow law of fens and ponds impose."[93] Edmund Waller instructed his painter to "draw the whole world expecting who shall reign, / after this combat, o'er the conquer'd main."[94] After the battle of Lowestoft, the Duke of York was praised for having fought so valiantly in a struggle for "the empire of the sea."[95] This was no poetic hyperbole, for James himself described the battle in his memoirs as a dispute for "the mastery of the sea."[96] The following year Sir John Birkenhead lambasted the Dutch for boasting that they "were Lords of the Seas."[97] "The event of this last great battle," Carlingford informed his friend Winchilsea rather optimistically, "must decide the Hollanders or our right of being masters of the sea."[98]

While the Dutch and the English certainly inflated the significance of their conflict, other Europeans also accorded this maritime struggle worldwide significance. "The two maritime and warlike nations," thought one Venetian, were deciding to whom "the empire of these seas shall belong."[99] The crafty Dutch, wrote an incensed diplomat to the Chancellor of Sweden, hope "to play the only masters of all trade and commerce belonging naturally unto other princes and states in the whole world ... to the ruin and slavery of other nations."[100] From an English as well as a European perspective, then, war was necessary to prevent the Dutch from achieving an empire of the sea.[101]

Unsurprisingly for a culture steeped in classical history, the English accorded this struggle for naval supremacy epic significance. The Dutch admiral De Ruyter, one balladeer claimed, hoped for "Alexander's portion."[102] More commonly, the Anglo-Dutch War was compared to two pivotal struggles in Roman history, struggles which indeed determined the universal empire. John Dryden compared the Dutch to Carthage, and thought the Anglo-Dutch struggle "may prove our second

93 Abraham Cowley, "Of Plants," Book VI, 1665, in *The Second and Third Parts of the Works* 6th edition (London, 1689), p. 163. On Cowley's contemporary popularity see Allan Broderick to Ormonde, 17 August 1667, Carte 35, f. 644r; Pepys, *Diary*, 12 August 1667, p. 383; Evelyn, *Diary*, Vol. VII, 1 August 1667, pp. 489–90.

94 Waller, "Instructions to a Painter," 1665, *POAS*, p. 22. The 1667 response to this poem, falsely attributed to Sir John Denham on the title page, agreed on this point if on nothing else: "Draw pensive Neptune biting of his thumbs, / To think himself a slave, who'er o'recomes." Sir John Denham, *Directions to a Painter*. (London, 1667), p. 6.

95 *To His Royal Highness the Duke of Yorke. On our Late Sea-Fight.* (Oxford, 1665), p. 3.

96 James S. Clarke (editor), *The Life of James the Second* (London, 1816), Vol. I, p. 410.

97 Sir John Birkenhead, *A New Ballad* (1666), broadside.

98 Earl of Carlingford to Winchilsea, 6 July 1666, LRO, DG7/Box 4984, Letters Folder.

99 Giustinian to Doge and Senate, 31 July/10 August 1666, *CSPV*, p. 49.

100 M. Appelbome to Chancellor of Sweden, 6/16 October 1665, Bod., Clar. 83, f. 251.

101 Naturally after English victories many Europeans feared that Charles II would become the monarch of the sea. But in all cases the struggle was understood in terms of the idiom of universal monarchy.

102 *The Routing of De Ruyter: Or the Barbadoes Bravery* (London, 1665), broadside.

Punic War."[103] "Ambitious thoughts the Dutchmen still possess, / they will contest although without success," predicted the author of an extended poem on the Punic War analogy, "so mutinous Carthage oftentimes rebell'd, / So Rome her insolence as often quell'd."[104] In that great battle between Scipio and Hannibal, Restoration historians knew, "the reward of the victory was Africa, whose example, the universe, soon after, followed."[105] The Anglo-Dutch conflict reminded the poet Edmund Waller of the battle of Actium. "For a less prize, with less concern and rage, / The Roman fleets at Actium did engage," he wrote of the struggle between Mark Anthony/John De Witt and Octavian/Charles II, "They, for the empire of the world they knew, / These for the old contend and the new."[106]

The English knew that – just as in these classical struggles – universal dominion was at stake in their war with the Dutch. "For if England should succumb in this war," Thomas Thynne was instructed by secretary Morrice to ask his Swedish hosts, "who are they that shall then make a stop of the universal monarchy of the sea to Holland, or of the land to France when joined with Holland?"[107] "The sole rule of the vast ocean lies / at stake, and must be the victors prize," rhymed one poet, "English and Dutch struggling at once to be / Lords of the World, if Conquerors at Sea."[108] "If they can beat the English," warned George Downing drawing on all his diplomatic and economic expertise, "all the world is their own."[109] "You think the Narrow Seas for us too much," sneered the Anglican Royalist poet John Crouch, "yet the whole globe too little for the Dutch."[110] The English consul in Aleppo was appalled to hear his Dutch counterpart proudly proclaiming "that the Kings of England and France in respect of their riches and power were no more in comparison with the High and Mighty States than were a couple of boys to an

103 Dryden, "Annus Mirabilis," in Edward Niles Hooker and H. T. Swedenberg, Jr. (editors), *The Works of John Dryden*, Vol. I Poems 1649–1689 (Berkeley, 1956) p. 60, lines 16–20. This was, of course, the same analogy which Andrew Marvell drew in his "Character of Holland," written in support of a very different Anglo-Dutch War in 1653. Marvell made every effort to distance himself from the Restoration Anglo-Dutch struggles, which he saw as part and parcel of French strategy to gain a universal monarchy.

104 *Bellum Belgicum Secundum* (London, 1665), p. 1.

105 *The Roman History of Lucius J. Florus* (London, 1669), pp. 53, 60, 71–72. This analogy was commonplace among Anglican Royalists. See Roger Palmer, Earl of Castlemaine, *An Account of the Present War Between the Venetians and the Turk* (London, 1666), pp. 103, 108–109. Prior to the Restoration William Coventry had also compared the Dutch to Carthaginians. See W[illiam] C[oventry], *Trades Destruction is Englands Ruine, or Excise Decryed* (London, 1659), 28 May 1659, p. 4.

106 Waller, "Instructions to a Painter," *POAS*, p. 26; see also "To His Royal Highness," 1665, p. 3.

107 William Morrice's Instructions to Thomas Thynne, November 1666, PRO, SP 95/6, f. 106v.

108 *An Essay: Or, a Narrative of the Two Great Fights at Sea* (London, 1666), p. 1.

109 Downing to Arlington, 16 May 1665, PRO, SP 84/176, f. 32.

110 Crouch, *Dutch Embargo*, p. 7.

elephant."[111] In Persia, too, Dutch agents were purportedly confidently assuring local magnates that "England and the whole world was at their command."[112] John Dryden eloquently summed up the commonplace view of the war, a view which claimed that the English and Dutch fleets "disputed the command of the greater half of the globe, the commerce of nations, and the riches of the universe."[113]

Naturally the Dutch had not risen to these lofty political heights merely through economic virtue. English pamphleteers, politicians, and merchants were all convinced that Dutch economic prosperity was the result not of their skill but of their unfair trading practices. Clarendon complained to Parliament of the "depredations by the Dutch upon our merchants in all parts."[114] His sovereign excoriated the "violences, usurpations and depredations of the Estates General and their subjects."[115] Charles's Lord Chamberlain, the Earl of Manchester, reminded the Lord Mayor and aldermen of London, who needed no convincing, that war was necessary against those "insulting and injurious neighbors."[116] "The Dutchman is the Tartar of the seas," opined Christopher Wase, "and no less cruel if his gain command, / To sack a fleet or to unplant a land; / old friendship slights, now rich and potent grown, / nor bless'd enough till he be bless'd alone."[117] "How durst you all countries rights invade, / and call your thefts and usurpations trade," asked one popular scribbler.[118] The Dutch, averred Sir Richard Ford, "by most unjust practices both at home and abroad in most parts of the world, have by fraud and force destroyed our commerce and reduced our trade to be no other than a mere consumption of our stock."[119] "Shall our merchants labor still in vain," asked one poet rhetorically, "when Dutchmen's fraud dare intercept their gain?"[120] In Africa, wrote John Evelyn in his capacity as official historian of the

111 Benjamin Lannoy to Sir John Finch, 1 November 1666, PRO, SP 97/18, f. 215v. He told the same story to another member of the Finch family. See Lannoy to Winchilsea, 15 October 1666, LRO, DG7/Box 4984, Letters Folder.

112 Stephen Flower to George Oxenden, 22 April 1665, BL, Add. 40710, ff. 14v–15r.

113 John Dryden, "An Essay of Dramatic Poesy," 1668, in John L. Mahoney (editor), *An Essay of Dramatic Poesy and Other Critical Writings by John Dryden* (New York, 1965), p. 3. Dryden made the same point in "Annus Mirabilis": "Our Fathers bent their baneful industry / To check a monarchy that slowly grew: / But did not France or Holland's fate foresee, / Whose rising pow'r to swift dominion flew." In *Works*, Vol. I, p. 89.

114 *His Majesties Gracious Speech*, 10 October 1665, p. 8.

115 Charles II to Duke of York, 22 March 1665, PRO, SP 29/115/76.

116 Van Goch to Greffier, 9/19 December 1664, PRO, SP 84/173, f. 238v.

117 Christopher Wase, "The Divination," 1666, *POAS*, p. 64; see also "Narrative of the Late Passages Between his Majesty and the Dutch," 1665, PRO, SP 84/178, f. 62r.

118 *To His Royal Highness*, pp. 6–7. See the similar language in Joseph Hatcher to Williamson, 10 June 1665, PRO, SP 29/124/22.

119 Sir Richard Ford, "Grounds for War," 1664, Bod., Clar. 83, f. 373r.

120 *Bellum Belgicum Secundum*, p. 2. Another poet claimed the English "fought with those who broke all nations laws." *To His Royal Highness*, p. 6.

Anglo-Dutch War, the Dutch achieved dominion "by no other title than of force and fraud."[121]

The tales of Dutch barbarity, tales which revived memories of Spanish actions in the previous century, were oft retold in the London press. In reminding his readers of that most barbarous of Dutch actions, the massacre at Amboyna, one author emphasized that this was hardly an exceptional action. "The Dutch (who would be no better neighbors to us in the Indies than in Europe)," this author fumed, "have razed and demolished the English forts, and laying violent hands on the English themselves, who made not the least resistance; they have tied them to stakes with ropes about their necks; they have seized upon their goods, they have imprisoned their persons, they have whipped them at the post in the open market place, and having washed their torn and wounded bodies with vinegar and salt they have again doubled their scourges to multiply their torments."[122] It was these "robberies at Guinny and Bantam / with all the villainies of Amsterdam" which provoked a demand that the Dutch "restore what ye have gained by fraud and stealth / pirates and robbers of both India's wealth."[123]

The English wanted to put an end to perfidious Dutch trading practices, to halt the States General's inexorable drive toward the universal monarchy, not seize upon Dutch trading routes. "And as for the engrossing the trade of the world to ourselves, it is what we intend to punish not to practice," William Morrice bluntly emphasized.[124] Clarendon derided those "very foolish discourses of many of getting the dominion of the whole seas," insisting that the English only wanted to bring the Dutch "within the limits of good neighborhood."[125] This was not merely rhetoric. A series of rough notes of war aims in the Lord Chancellor's hand suggests that his economic aims were limited to "such a regulation of trade, especially in the East Indies and in Africa, as his Majesty's subjects may be secure from the affronts and oppressions they have undergone in those parts."[126] Even the extremely Hollandophobic Duke of York urged his relation and successor as admiral Prince Rupert to give the Dutch "a sound bang [that] will teach them better

121 Notes for John Evelyn's "History of the Second Dutch War," Christ Church, John Evelyn MSS 134, f. 2.

122 [Robert Clavell], *His Majesties Propriety and Dominion on the British Seas Asserted* (London, 1665), sig. B6. The author of *A True Relation of the Unjust, Cruel, and Barbarous Proceedings Against the English at Amboyna*, 3rd edition (London, 1665) also argued that the events of Amboyna were typical of Dutch activity (sig. A4v). Robert Holmes described similar Dutch activities on the West Coast of Africa: "Examination of Sir Robert Holmes," 14 January 1665, PRO, SP 29/110/87.

123 *To His Royal Highness*, pp. 5–6; Crouch, *Belgica Caracteristica*. p. 5.

124 William Morrice's instructions for Thomas Thynne, November 1666, PRO, SP 95/6, f. 107.

125 Clarendon to Henry Coventry, December 1665, Bod., Clar. 83, f. 388v.

126 Notes in Clarendon's Hand, 1666, PRO, SP 84/179, f. 13r. These views were repeated in his instructions to St. Albans, 1666, Bod., Clar. 84, f. 43r.

manners."[127] This point was made repeatedly in mercantile correspondence. The East India trader Henry Chowne informed Sir George Oxenden that Charles II was fighting so that he would not "be bound up by the Dutch."[128] For the East India Company a successful conclusion of the war would "be to bring the Dutch to a more fair correspondency for the time to come in all places."[129] "We may hope to see their pride abated," the factors at Hugly wrote of the Dutch, "and that the commerce may be prosecuted by more conscientious and less cruel men than they in all their actions have demonstrated themselves to be."[130] The naval supplier Sir William Ryder hoped that after "we have chastised them here" the Dutch could be "brought to some regulation of trade."[131] A successful war would bring the Dutch to a "superlative degree of humility," chimed in John Stevens from Bombay, "and then they must perforce permit their neighbors to share with them in trade."[132]

Why, in the English view, did the Dutch set out to pursue the empire of the sea? What provoked them to aspire after universal dominion? What aspects of their political culture had provoked them to mimic their historical nemesis the King of Spain?

English observers thought that two separate, though for some interrelated, factors served to corrupt the Dutch polity, to transform it from a virtuous Protestant commonwealth into an irreligious and ambitious republic. First, the very republicanism of the United Provinces – a republicanism now firmly entrenched under the leadership of the Grand Pensionary of Holland, John De Witt – had deprived the Dutch of virtue. For the supporters of England's Restored Monarchy, Dutch republicanism was all too reminiscent of the political ideology of the Stuarts' political enemies. Sir John Birkenhead warned that dark days would soon come to "De Witt's new Holland Rump" as the Duke of Albemarle "once before / hath fir'd one Rump, and will do more."[133] Another penny poet assured his readers that the "States / with our Rump have quite worn out their dates."[134] While the States General appeared to act like the Rump Parlia-

127 James Duke of York to Prince Rupert, 17 July 1666, Victoria and Albert Museum, Forster and Dyce Collection, F48G24/10.

128 Henry Chowne to George Oxenden, 10 March 1666, BL, Add. 40712, f. 20v.

129 East India Company to agent and Council in Bantam, 7 March 1666, IOL, E/3/87, f. 6v. The Company used almost identical language the previous year. See East India Company to president and Council of Surat, 15 June 1665, IOL, E/3/86, f. 243v.

130 Will Blake, Shem Bridges, and Robert Elmes (Hugly) to Surat, 12 April 1666, IOL, E/3/29, f. 207r.

131 Sir William Ryder to George Oxenden, 1 March 1666, BL, Add. 40712, f. 45r; see also Ryder to Oxenden, 3 January 1666, BL, Add. 40712, f. 43v.

132 John Stevens (Bombay) to George Oxenden, 10 February 1666, BL, Add. 40710, f. 12r. Similar views are expressed by other East India merchants. See Thomas Kendal to Oxenden, March 1666, BL, Add. 40712, f. 30r; Richard Craddock to Oxenden, 5 March 1666, BL, Add. 40712, f. 41r.

133 Birkenhead, *A New Ballad*.

134 *Two Royal Acrosticks on the Dutch in the Ditch* [1666], broadside.

ment, many thought its leader, John De Witt, was governed by the same principles as the Lord Protector Oliver Cromwell. "The truth is," Dr. Peter Mews wrote of De Witt, "he is insolent beyond a parallel, save only his type Cromwell, and will prove as pernicious to [the Dutch] as Cromwell was to the English nation."[135] De Witt "sways that Commonwealth in the same kind of usurping tyranny that Cromwell did formerly in England," agreed the newsletter-writer and playwright Thomas St. Serfe.[136]

The pernicious consequences of republican rule were no different in the contemporary United Provinces than they had been in Interregnum England. "Commonwealths regard not fame," commented Roger Boyle Earl of Orrery in his successful play *Mustapha*, "disdaining honor they can feel no shame."[137] No wonder that the lawyer Charles Molloy thought "a right Dutchman can never be a true friend, a loyal subject, or a good neighbor; for his trade carries away his heart; riches his allegiance, and thriving his soul."[138] George Oxenden understood well the implications of republicanism on commercial relations, for "although princes stand upon punctilios of honor, we never observed that the States of Holland did, or could be tied up by any articles made with them any longer than they apprehended it to be advantageous to them."[139] It was this absence of honor, this lack of political virtue which was the necessary accompaniment of a well-ordered society, that induced the Dutch to grasp after universal dominion. "When slaves are turn'd princes, no tyrants so evil / when beggars are mounted, they ride to the devil," was one balladeer's gloss on Dutch political culture.[140] Another broadside described an imperialistic Dutch cow – an allegorical image of the Netherlandish people – whose "sides with fat ambitiously do swell; / 'tis only seeming fat, she is not well; / She's out of time, her looks declare her sick / of tumult and disorder, lunatic."[141]

Not only did Dutch republicanism, much like that of classical Rome,

135 Dr. Peter Mews to Williamson, 14/24 June 1667, PRO, SP 84/182, f. 149r.

136 St. Serfe's Newsletter, 25 August 1666, LOC, 18124, Vol. I, f. 103r.

137 Roger Boyle, Earl of Orrery, *The Tragedy of Mustapha* (London, 1668), p. 56. The play was first performed in April 1665. See William Van Lennep (editor), *The London Stage*, Pt. I 1600–1700 (Carbondale, Illinois, 1965), p. 87; see also Cowley, "Of Plants," 1665, in *Works*, Book VI, p. 144; John Beale to John Evelyn, 23 July 1666, Christ Church, Evelyn In-Letters 53. The poem included in the letter is entitled "The Hollanders"; Orrery to Ormonde, 2 July 1667, in *Orrery State Letters*, Vol. II, p. 190; Sir Richard Ford, "Grounds for War," 1664, Bod., Clar. 83, f. 373r. For Ford's Orangism see Pepys, *Diary*, 4 July 1665, pp. 146–147.

138 Charles Molloy (Lincoln's Inn), *Holland's Ingratitude: Or, A Serious Expostulation with the Dutch* (London, 1666), p. 44.

139 George Oxenden *et al.* (Surat) to East India Company, 10 September 1666, IOL, E/3/29, f. 238v.

140 "Holland Turn'd to Tinder," 25–26 July 1666, in John Holloway (editor), *The Euing Collection of English Broadside Ballads* (Glasgow, 1971), p. 208.

141 *Hollands Representation: Or, The Dutch-mans Looking-Glass* (London, 1665), broadside.

bring with it unlimited political ambition, but it was also necessarily incompatible with monarchy. The Dutch people had become "vermin antimonarchical."[142] "Methinks," one polemicist sneered at the Dutch, "that since the establishment of your republic you have always been of a religion that has commended you a mortal hatred against all kings."[143] Dutch political ideology, concurred Charles Molloy, sought to "dismantle the royal fort of monarchy, by teaching subjects to depose their princes, and be no losers by the bargain, which (by the way) would have rendered you unacceptable to all neighbor monarchs, for thereby you'd furnish their subjects with a pretense upon all occasions of advantage to do the like."[144] It was "the manners of a commonwealth," Clarendon informed Parliament, which had given rise to the Dutch "dialect of rudeness, so peculiar to their language, and their people, that it is high time for all kings and princes to oblige them to some reformation."[145]

The English had already experienced the bitter consequences of Dutch political principles. The Dutch, proclaimed one pamphleteer, were "a precedent for the shedding of that royal blood which to this day calls to heaven for vengeance."[146] "From the beginning of this rebellion in England," Charles II's Lord Chancellor and the future historian of the Great Rebellion had long before concluded, the Dutch republicans "kept close correspondence with those rebels and have always advanced their interest."[147] Ominously, many English men and women thought, the Dutch were up to their old tricks. "Every day" Dutch republican presses spewed forth "villainous pamphlets" which were ingeniously disseminated not only in the United Provinces but "have flown abroad and fill'd each part of Christendom."[148] The intended consequence of letting "ribald pen vomit out floods of reproaches" was all too familiar. Charles Molloy was not alone in the belief that the Dutch hoped "to involve us in a civil war again."[149]

142 *The Glorious and Living Cinque-Ports of our Fortunate Islands* (Oxford, 1666), p. 1.
143 MSS pamphlet, 1665, NMM, Clifford Papers Vol. III, Dw100.
144 Molloy, *Holland's Ingratitude*, p. 4.
145 Clarendon's Speech, in *His Majesties Gracious Speech to both Houses of Parliament Together with the Lord Chancellor's*, 10 October 1665 (Oxford, 1665), pp. 9, 15–16.
146 *The Dutch Nebuchadnezzar: Or, a Strange Dream of the States General* (London, 1666), pp. 2–3.
147 Edward Hyde to Taylor, 30 October/9 November 1652, Bod., Clar. 44, f. 23v. His contempt for republics was motivated by far more than a particular historically conditioned antipathy for the Dutch. "God bless me from living under the laws and customs of a Commonwealth," Hyde prayed to his close friend Edward Nicholas. Hyde to Nicholas, 1/11 January 1653, Bod., Clar. 45, f. 10v; see also "The Loyal Subject's Resolution," 1665, *Euing Collection*, p. 257.
148 Downing to Arlington, 23 May 1665, PRO, SP 84/176, f. 45r; N. R., *The Belgick Lyon Discovered* (London, 1665), broadside; William Davidson (Antwerp) to Earl of Lauderdale, 14/24 December 1666, in W. Del Court (editor), "Sir William Davidson in Nederland," in *Bijdragen voor Vaderlandsche Geschiedenis en Oudheidkunde* 4th series, Vol. V (1906), p. 392.
149 Molloy, *Holland's Ingratitude*, 166, p. 7.

Recruitment ballad after recruitment ballad disseminated this theme to the broadest possible audience. "Good princes are great examples / for loyal hearts to follow," one imaginary young sailor informed his lover before marching off to sea, "he that on authority tramples, / I wish the sea may swallow. / The Dutch-man was ever a traitor / against their sovereign."[150] "Although they be rebellious, yet we shall pull them down," promised another balladeer.[151] "Plainly demonstrating the justness of his cause, / encouraging his friends to daunt his foes," another imaginary valiant mariner explained that he was fighting "for king and country, in the seas he'll perish, / to tame the rebels and make England flourish."[152]

Constantly bombarded with such sentiments in a wide variety of media, it is hardly surprising that most in England knew what was at stake in their struggle with the Dutch. "If I am not mistaken the stake on our side is greater than we generally imagine," one naval volunteer wrote to a friend just before the battle of Lowestoft, "for if we have ill fortune here I expect worse at land; these vile people [the Dutch] having most of them the same rebellious thoughts they had and want no industry to put their wickedness in execution when they shall find a good occasion."[153] John De Witt "alone was the author of all the [Dutch] wars with England," argued the high church cleric Samuel Parker, explaining he was "a man of the meanest birth, but proud, insolent and morose, and there fore an inexorable enemy to kings because he could not bear their greatness."[154] Charles Davenant, whose opinions were much more moderate than Parker's, later recalled that "the good Cavaliers" had supported war against the Dutch "out of their old hatred to a common-wealth."[155] Fear and loathing of republicanism in any of its manifestations convinced many that the English Restored Monarchy would never be secure until the United Provinces were reduced to a more rational form of government. The author of one broadside aptly summarized English popular opinion when he insisted that "the States must bow unto the States state-holder."[156] One poetic mariner knew full well that he was fighting against a "rebel-state," fighting "to cure rebellion in the

150 "The Faithful Lovers Farewell," 1665 or 1666, *Euing Collection*, p. 180.

151 "Englands Valour and Hollands Terrour: Being an Encouragement for Seamen and Soldiers to Serve his Majesty in his Wars Against the Dutch," 1665, *Euing Collection*, p. 157.

152 "The English Seaman's resolution," 1665 or 1666, *Euing Collection*, p. 160.

153 Benjamin Bathurst (with the fleet) to ?, 30 May 1665, BL. Loan 57/1, f. 27r.

154 Parker's, *History of his Own Time*, pp. 127–128.

155 [Charles Davenant], *Essays Upon I. The Ballance of Power II. The Right of Making War, Peace, and Alliances III. Universal Monarchy* (London, 1701), p. 18.

156 *Two Royal Acrosticks on the Dutch in the Ditch*. It was no doubt with such an eventuality in mind that English almanacs predicted popular tumults in the United Provices. See William Lilly, *Merlini Anglici Ephemeris: Or Astrological Judgements for the Year 1665* (London, 1665), sig. A8v; William Andrews, *Newes from the Starrs: Or an Ephemeris for the Year of Man's Redemption by Jesus Christ, 1665* (London, 1665), sig. B3r.

breast," and that his and his nation's struggle would not end until his compatriots could "make the Prince Van Orange King."[157]

A second and, for some, complementary explanation for Dutch political corruption lay in their religious culture. Just as Dutch republicanism resurrected unpleasant memories of the Interregnum, so the religious liberty of the United Provinces reminded Anglican Royalists of their old antagonists, the puritans. The Netherlands, warned one contemporary poet, was a place where "all factions crowd, and yet are free, / the largest conscience here hath liberty. / One prays by 's beads, another (which alas / is but the same) prays by the hour-glass, / a third is sainted from his ghastly face, / yet brimstone hell's known fuel gives that grace, / dippers in every corner do appear, / 't may be because there is more water here. / The land with spiders and sects doth swarm, / only those poisonous creatures do less harm; / Nor is 't to schismatics unfitly given, / it being the farthest in the world from heaven."[158] Dutch liberty of conscience, good Anglicans knew, was not only unsightly, it was also profoundly dangerous. In "our late times," the Bishop of Lincoln Benjamin Laney explained to Charles II in a sermon preached just after the Declaration of War with the Dutch, when there was liberty of conscience "one would think all Hell had broke loose." "All the discord and divisions of the Church grow from hence," he advised his sovereign, and "it's no quieter in the Commonwealth, where it destroys the very foundation of government, and frustrate the ordinance of God for it in princes and magistrates, for what is left for them to do, if everyone must follow the dictate of his own conscience, that is, in plain terms to be bound only to obey himself."[159]

That the Dutch should be guilty of irreligion, of moral laxity, came as no surprise to the English. The Dutch state, they well knew, had been founded in rebellion against King Philip II of Spain. And Anglican minister after

157 *Folly in Print, or a Book of Rymes* (London, 1667), pp. 66–67, 114. See also John Crouch, *Belgica Caracteristica: Or The Dutch Character* (London, 1665), 1665, p. 8. Ludlow similarly thought the Anglo-Dutch struggle, at bottom, was over forms of government: Ludlow, "A Voyce," Bod., English History MSS C487, p. 1071. Algernon Sidney's courtier in his "Court Maxims" thought that the primary aim of the war was "to make the Prince of Orange master [of the United Provinces] so shall we kill two birds with one stone: destroy them we hate and fear in Holland, and set up the title and power of the Orange family, that may help us to destroy our more hated and feared enemies at home." "Court Maxims," Warwickshire Record Office, f. 159.

158 *Bellum Belgicum Secundum*, p. 6; see also [Thomas Tomkins], *The Modern Pleas* (London, 1675), pp. 221–222. I am grateful to Nicholas Von Maltzahn for pointing this pamphlet out to me.

159 [Benjamin Laney], *A Sermon Preached Before his Majesty at Whitehall, March 12 1664/5* (London, 1665), pp. 25–27.

160 Theophilus Earl of Huntingdon, sermon notes, 30 January 1664, HL, HAP Box 21 (5); Evelyn, *Diary*, 4 October 1665, p. 421; Thomas Sprat, *Observations on Monsieur de Sorbier's Voyage into England* (London, 1665), p. 114; John Evelyn (translator), *The Pernicious Consequences of the New Heresy of the Jesuits Against the King and the State* (London, 1666), sig. a4. This point and the entire argument of this paragraph has been

Anglican minister informed his flock, "he that resisteth the [supreme civil] power resisteth God" – no matter what the pretext.[160] It was Jesuitical, indeed anti-Christian, to depose kings. "The whole Council of Trent freed subjects from their obedience, so did the Rump Parliament," exclaimed John Evelyn in a powerfully evocative comparison; "there were never any two doctrines more conformable, than that of the Fathers (as they will be called forsooth) and that of their novelists, who have so improved the zeal of their predecessors, as if the aphorisms of Emmanuel Sa, Bellarmine and Mariana, were not the suggestions of a diabolical, but the dictates of the sacred spirit."[161] Not only did Anglicans associate these pernicious political principles with the radical sects, they accused all non-episcopal denominations of disseminating leveling anti-monarchical ideas. The lay Anglican, Sir Geoffrey Shakerley, was "confident" that Presbyterians were "the source from whence all other sects and our disturbances do rise."[162] "The very form of [the Dutch] Church," concurred one courtier, "showeth the spleen they bear to a monarchy, preferring so much popular government as they will presume to deny God a monarchy in his Church."[163] It was this affinity between Dutch Calvinists and English Presbyterians, the identity between the resistance theories of the predikanten and the Jesuits, which convinced many English men and women of the corruption of Dutch religious culture. No wonder John De Witt was popularly vilified in England as "that Jesuit and proud and politic Machiavel."[164]

It was hardly surprising that this religious culture, "whose reason is flat rebellion, and their truth is treason," should aspire after universal dominion.[165] The Dutch, charged one pamphleteer, had made religion "itself a gross piece of hypocrisy, all thy devotions being as a masque to conceal the pharisaism of thy heart, thy ambition, covetousness or some such impious design."[166] Another was sure they had turned "religion out of doors to let in policy."[167] Charles Molloy agreed that religion, and necessarily "all marks of honor almost blended amongst them in those of profit."[168] No wonder that the English resident in Venice described the Dutch as "those most infidelian Christians."[169] No wonder, indeed, that one penny poet

discussed more thoroughly in Pt. III. All I intend to show here is that the claim that the Dutch were bad Protestants did not end with the outbreak of the war.

161 Evelyn, *Pernicious Consequences*, sig. a4. See also John Dolben, *A Sermon Preached before His Majesty on Good Friday*, 24 March 1665 (London, 1665), pp. 23–24.

162 Sir Geoffrey Shakerley (Chester) to Williamson, 8 December 1666, PRO, SP 29/181/14.

163 Mr. Covert's memorandum, 1665 or 1666, PRO, SP 84/219, f. 126v.

164 *The Glorious and Living Cinque Ports*, p. 10.

165 *A Hue and Cry after the Dutch Fleet* (London, 1666), broadside.

166 *Dutch Nebuchadnazzar*, pp. 4–5.

167 *Quaeries: Or, a Dish of Pickled-Herring Shread, Cut and Prepared according to the Dutch Fashion* (London, 1665), p. 3.

168 Molloy, *Hollands Ingratitude*, p. 2.

169 Giles Jones to Williamson, 6/16 July 1666, PRO, SP 99/46, f. 133r.

asserted that Charles II was fighting the Dutch to make sure that "false sects and schisms, with all vain opinions, / shall not take root or bide in his dominions."[170]

Dutch religious corruption, in Anglican eyes, was not merely a future danger, a disease which was slowly impelling the Dutch people towards ever more ambitious and covetous acts. Instead the affinity between the Dutch and Britain's religious minorities presented an immediate threat. "All our banished for their or their Father's crimes, all that cannot live under a government where justice and the laws have drove out rebellion, disorder and unbound ambition," all these, fumed one pamphleteer, were given protection by John De Witt, who "uses them kindly, he assists them, gives them [hearing] at his counsels, aye and takes their advices, and trusts to their fine intelligence."[171] "The horrid murderers of our late Royal master, have been received into the most secret councils in Holland," Clarendon proclaimed in open Parliament; they "and other prostituted persons of our nation are admitted to a share in the conduct of their affairs, and maintain their correspondence here upon liberal allowances and pensions."[172]

Far from being fearful "of a revival of English republicanism," as Jonathan Scott has claimed, all of the evidence suggests that De Witt and his cohort were actively supporting and praying for just such a development.[173] George Downing was sure that De Witt "very diligently" supported "any that can make any stirs either in England or Scotland."[174] The English religious exiles "have great business in hand with the great men here," wrote William Davidson, who was an experienced commentator on Dutch political affairs, business tending toward "a rising in the west and north."[175] "There was an assembly of rebels that sat in Holland," Samuel Parker recalled with anger, "who joined counsels with the very States themselves, although to that time there had been a very Carthaginian war with the States."[176] This was not only the view of hostile English commentators. "Those in Holland of the honest party" – a party which very much included De Witt – offered "a firm league" to the English exiles, Ludlow recalled.[177] The regicide William Say was convinced "that the heart of those

170 George Eliot, *An English Duel* (1666), broadside.

171 MSS Pamphlet, 1665, NMM, Clifford Papers Vol. III, Dw100, f. 9. See also Molloy, *Hollands Ingratitude*, 1666, pp. 5–6.

172 Clarendon's Speech in *His Majesties Gracious Speech*, 10 October 1665, p. 17.

173 Scott, *Algernon Sidney*, p. 176. Scott's claim that De Witt rejected Sidney's proposals seems to be based largely on Gilbert Burnet's account. James Ralph, an historian whom Scott elsewhere relies upon, argues that Burnet's claim "that De Witt rejected [Sidney's] proposals . . . is wide of the truth." [Ralph], *History*, Vol. I, p. 116.

174 Downing to Clarendon, 10 March 1665, Bod., Clar. 108, f. 284.

175 William Davison, to Thomas Taylor, 23 June/3 July 1665, PRO, SP 84/176 (unfoliated). William Morrice expressed similar opinions. See Morrice to Henry Coventry, 2 February 1666, Longleat House, Cov. MSS LIII, f. 310r.

176 Parker, *History of his own Time*, pp. 92–93.

177 Ludlow, "A Voyce," Bod., English History MSS C487, pp. 1065, 1109, 1122–1125.

who now governed in Holland [hoped] to endeavor a relief to the honest party in England."[178] Algernon Sidney, whom Aphra Behn thought was "in great esteem with De Witt," was convinced that "the Hollander and Fanatic ... know their interests [are] as inseparable as that of the Houses of the Stuarts and Orange."[179] Merchant correspondence, diplomatic despatches, and spy reports are filled with information about the large numbers of English and Scots religious exiles meeting and plotting, at the connivance of the Dutch, in the United Provinces.[180]

In addition to plotting insurrection, many English and Scots – one enthusiastic spy claimed there were "fifteen thousand expert fighting Englishmen on their side" – enlisted to serve in the States General's navy, providing the Dutch with expert information on English geography and naval tactics.[181] Indeed Sir William Davidson was certain that the fanatics had helped plan the assault on Chatham, an assault which was to have

178 William Say to Ludlow, in Ludlow, "A Voyce," Bod., English History MSS C487, f. 1058.

179 Aphra Behn to ?, 12/22 September 1666, PRO, SP 29/171/65; Sidney, "Court Maxims," Warwickshire Record Office, ff. 171–172. The "Court Maxims" were almost certainly written while Sidney was in the United Provinces where, if the double agent William Scott can be trusted, it was designed "sooner or later for the press." William Scott's answer to Aphra Behn, 21 September 1666, PRO, SP 29/172/81 I. For Sidney's movements see: Downing to Arlington, 26 May 1665, PRO, SP 84/176, f. 51r; Downing to Clarendon, 26 May 1665, Bod., Clar. 108, f. 247r; Downing to Arlington, 30 May 1665, PRO, SP 84/176, f. 53v; Downing to Arlington, 9 June 1665, PRO, SP 84/176, f. 68v; Letter from Rotterdam, 29 May 1665, PRO, SP 29/122/74; William Scott (Rotterdam) to Aphra Behn, 25 September/5 October 1666, PRO, SP 29/173/4.

180 Information, 1665, PRO, SP 29/143/143; fugitives in Holland, PRO, SP 29/143/135; Hollis to Bennet, 4/14 February 1665, PRO, SP 78/120, f. 39v; Nicholas Oudart to Williamson, 10/20 February 1665, PRO, SP 84/174, f. 109r; Williamson's notes, March 1665, PRO, SP 29/116/127; Letter from Rotterdam to Bennet, 10 March 1665, PRO, SP 29/114/104; William Davidson (Amsterdam) to Lauderdale, 24 March/3 April 1665, in Del Court, "Sir William Davidson," p. 381; Davidson to Arlington, 18/28 May 1665, PRO, SP 84/176, f. 35r; newsletter from Rotterdam, 9/19 June 1665, PRO, SP 101/47, f. 206r; Davidson (Amsterdam) to Arlington, 15 June 1665, PRO, SP 29/124/71; Davidson to Arlington, 18 June 1665, PRO, SP 84/176, f. 81r; Downing to Clarendon, 30 June 1665, Bod., Clar. 108, f. 310v; Downing to Arlington, 18 July 1665, PRO, SP 84/177, f. 26v; Downing to Clarendon, 21 July 1665, Bod., Clar. 108, ff. 336–337; Dr. William Denton to Sir Ralph Verney, 24 July 1665, Firestone Library, Verney MSS Reel 20 (unfoliated); William Temple to Arlington, 19/29 December 1665, PRO, SP 77/33, f. 367v (specifically mentions support for Sidney); newsletter from Middleburgh, 27 March/6 April 1666, PRO, SP 101/48, f. 199r; Ed. Custis to Williamson, 14/24 July 1666, PRO, SP 77/34, f. 389r; W. Swann (Nieuport) to Williamson, 18 July 1666, PRO, SP 82/11, f. 27r; William Scott's answer to Aphra Behn, 21 September 1666, PRO, SP 29/172/81 I; William Scott (Rotterdam) to Aphra Behn, 25 September/5 October 1666, PRO, SP 29/173/4; John Merryman to Williamson, 12/22 April 1667, PRO, SP 77/36, f. 195r.

181 Information to Ormonde, 20 February 1665, Carte 34, f. 62r. See also John Ironmonger to Sir Thomas Gower, 21 February 1665, PRO, SP 29/113/19; information, 12 January 1665, PRO, SP 29/110/77; newsletter from Flushing, 15/25 March 1665, PRO, SP 101/47, f. 184; Downing to Arlington, 21 July 1665, PRO, SP 84/177, f. 33r; St. Serfe's Newsletter, 21 November 1665, LOC, 18124 Vol. I, f. 5r; Ed. Custis to Williamson, 4/14 July 1666, PRO, SP 77/34, f. 392r; Aphra Behn (Rotterdam) to ?, 12/22 September 1666, PRO, SP 29/171/65.

included a Dutch landing so that "all the discontented party might draw up in arms together."[182] There was very good reason for Charles II's government to believe that the morally debased Dutch were making common cause with the English regime's radical religious opponents.

The government in Whitehall did not keep their fears and suspicions of religious plotting secret. Circulating everywhere were rumors, gossip, and news of plots germinated in the United Provinces so that they might hatch in Britain. One northern justice of the peace received a letter "pointing much at the Presbyterians," claiming that "the Dutch do make the [war] wholly upon the account of the old English rebels."[183] It was also widely reported that letters from the Netherlands "to be spread with the saints in England" carefully explained that the Dutch "meant no wrong to the good people of England nor to the liberty of any Christian, but against papists and such lewd persons as seek to destroy Christian liberty."[184] "Wicked anti-monarchical" pamphlets and broadsides were "sent into this country as we suppose from our banished ministers in Holland" which were said to speak a language "which is very consonant both with the practice and profession of many considerable persons in this country."[185]

Anglicans, hardly surprised by Dutch sympathy and support for their coreligionists, were convinced that a Dutch victory would unleash a chain of events reminiscent of 1638–1642.[186] "The soberer fanatics," thought one government correspondent, were waiting anxiously to "see what advantages they might have by the war with Holland."[187] One former Cromwellian officer was so confident of Dutch support that he urged a government informant to "be of good cheer for once again we shall eat roast meat."[188] After the English victory at Lowestoft Sir Thomas Osborne suggested to

182 Testimony of Sir William Davidson, November 1667, PRO, SP 29/223/189.

183 Letter to Sir Edward Bagot, March 1665, PRO, SP 29/116/112. See also Clarendon to Lancashire justices of the peace, 25 March 1665, HMC, *Kenyon*, p. 75.

184 Letter from the United Provinces, 3 August 1665, PRO, SP 29/128/115. It was also rumored that "the Dutch had a ship with the Covenant on the stern and under it was written 'if the king take me, he will not keep me'" – a sneering reference to Charles II's insincere support of the Covenant in the 1650s. Robert Clark to John Sicklemore, 6 May 1665, PRO, SP 29/120/92.

185 Alexander Archbishop of Glasgow to Arlington, 10 February 1666, PRO, SP 29/147/82. One such pamphlet which was certainly printed in Rotterdam and distributed in Britain was Loeophilus Misotyrannus's *Mene Tekel: Or, the Downfall of Tyranny* (London, 1663), printed on 30 January 1663. See Downing to Bennet, 27 January 1665, PRO, SP 84/174, ff. 50–51; Downing to Clarendon, 3 February 1665, Bod., Clar. 108, f. 201v.

186 This fear was made explicit by an anonymous correspondent from Carlisle who warned that one Colonel Gibb Ker, commissioned by "the Hollanders," could well spark off "the same spirit of rebellion as ... was in the [year 1638] when they entered that wicked covenant which was the bane of these three nations." Letter from Carlisle to Williamson, 3 May 1665, PRO, SP 29/120/25.

187 Information of A. W., March 1665, PRO, SP 29/114/11; see also Leonard Williams to Bennet, 9 February 1665, PRO, SP 29/112/61.

188 The Examination of Edward James by Henry Wroth, 22 February 1665, PRO, SP 29/113/40; see also Pepys, *Diary*, Vol. VI, 13 June 1665, p. 126.

Arlington that "the nation was never in more danger of the Fanatic party than it would have been at this present if his Highness had received the least defeat."[189] "If the king's fleet had been beaten," the Anglican cleric Samuel Parker agreed, "[the schismatics] had presently joined in open war."[190]

While the victory at Lowestoft might have thwarted plans for a Nonconformist rising supported by the Dutch fleet, it did not put an end to fears of a joint Dutch/fanatic assault on the English government.[191] Reports of their joint activities caused concern throughout the three kingdoms. In Lincolnshire a justice was sure he had uncovered evidence that the Dutch admiral was in deep consultation with a former Cromwellian governor of Lynn.[192] In Durham the religious radicals were "placing great confidence still on their Dutch friends," having been "assured that the Dutch have engaged to land all the English and Scotch and some assistance somewhere in the northern parts, which is relied on and expected by all that party."[193] The Dissenters in Leeds were "very high in their expectations from the Dutch."[194] Elsewhere in Yorkshire "the party" placed "all their hopes ... upon the good success of the Dutch."[195] In fact, stories of radical sympathy for the Dutch poured in from all corners of Britain.[196] When one newsletter-writer publicized a plot to assassinate Charles II and much of his government, he could confidently report that "the foundation of it was from a Rump party in Holland who had a subcommittee in London to whom they transmitted money and counsel."[197]

Of course, it was not only in England that the Dutch and their religiously committed allies intended to do damage to Charles II's government. "In case the king and the Dutch did not agree, it was expected that there would be a rising in arms in England and that in case there should be a rising in arms in England, it was expected there would be a like rising in Ireland," confessed

189 Sir Thomas Osborne to Arlington, 13 June 1665, BL. Egerton MSS 3328, f. 20r.

190 Parker, *History of his own Time*, p. 92. See also Edward Hyde, *The Life of Edward Earl of Clarendon* (Dublin, 1760), p. 290.

191 Richard Greaves, *Enemies Under His Feet: Radicals and Nonconformists in Britain, 1664–1677* (Stanford, 1990), pp. 15–48.

192 Anthony Oldfield to Edward Christian, 5 February 1665, PRO, SP 29/112/23.

193 Dean Guy Carleton to Williamson, 30 January 1666, PRO, SP 29/146/66; Durham intelligence, 1666, PRO, SP 29/187/157; John Dobson to Sir William Clarke, 14 March 1665, Bod., Clar. 83, f. 80r.

194 John Bettson (Leeds) to Robert Lye, 26 May 1665, PRO, SP 29/122/50.

195 Christopher Sanderson to Arlington, 24 October 1665, PRO, SP 29/135/61. See also Sanderson to Sir Philip Musgrave, 3 March 1665, PRO, SP 29/114/22; John Ironmonger to Sir Thomas Gower, 8 March 1665, PRO, SP 29/114/89; Sir Thomas Gower to Arlington, 21 October 1665, PRO, SP 29/135/25.

196 Albemarle to Arlington, 19 December 1665, PRO, SP 29/139/64; Captain Andrew Newport (Portsmouth) to Williamson, 22 August 1665, PRO, SP 29/129/98; Benjamin Harrison (Dover) to Sir Thomas Peyton, 9 February 1666, PRO, SP 29/147/86I; William Coventry to Arlington, 12 August 1665, PRO, SP 29/129/11.

197 St. Serfe's Newsletter, 28 April 1666, LOC, 18124 Vol. I, f. 58r; see also "The Valiant-hearted Seaman," 1665, *Euing Collection*, p. 609.

the radical Dublin shoemaker Thomas Rawkins.[198] Reports poured into the government of contacts with the radical cells in the United Provinces, of gun-running, of preparations for a rebellion. In Ulster "the Presbyterians ... generally wish a good and speedy success to the Dutch," assuring themselves that "if the Dutch do get one battle at sea they will all raise in arms."[199] No wonder the Earl of Orrery was sure that "if God should not prosper his Majesty's navy, we should neither want foreigners, nor some at home to disturb us."[200] Dissident Scots were also known to be caballing with the Dutch, convincing many that "the Dutch have a design in Scotland."[201] In short, thought the Archbishop of Glasgow, the situation in Scotland was no different than in England or Ireland, "if his Majesty's dangers and difficulties grow (which is the ground of [the] hope and confidence [of the disaffected persons]) you will certainly find them ready to receive what impressions Dutch or French shall make upon them and as forward to engage in a new rebellion as ever."[202]

It was these ubiquitous fears, coupled with the reports from their spies and ambassadors abroad, which convinced Charles II and his government to warn all English men and women of the dangers implicit in the collusion between the Dutch and the Nonconformists. In Parliament Clarendon denounced "those unquiet and restless spirits in your own bowels, upon whose infidelity, I doubt, your enemies abroad have more dependence on than upon their own fleets."[203] This was a theme oft-repeated and endlessly discussed in the early phases of the war. The Speaker of the House of Commons persuaded Sir Robert Paston, whose ideological predilections and known adamant support of the war must have made him an easy target, that "many wicked spirits were now at work contriving and hoping for some issue in the Dutch War that might promote their interests."[204] In a circular to all of the nation's justices of the peace Clarendon reiterated that "many seditious persons ... under the title of a Council, hold correspondence with the foreign enemies to this kingdom and distribute their order to some signal men of their party in the several counties, who have provided

198 Examination of Thomas Rawkins, 2 January 1665, Carte 47, f. 229r; see also Michael Boyle to Ormonde, 6 March 1665, Carte 34, f. 84r.

199 Intelligence to Ormonde, 21 June 1665, Carte 34, f. 153r. See also Intelligence to Ormonde, received 1 May 1665, Carte 34, f. 181r; Sir John Birkenhead to Ormonde, 14 August 1666, Carte 35, f. 28r; Orrery to Ormonde, 18 May 1666, in *Orrery State Letters*, Vol. I, p. 274.

200 Orrery to Ormonde, 3 July 1666, *Orrery State Letters*, Vol. II, p. 44.

201 Downing to Clarendon, 10 March 1665, Bod., Clar. 108, ff. 282v–284r; John Ironmonger to Sir Thomas Gower, 19 March 1665, PRO, SP 29/115/43; Earl of Falmouth to Arlington, 20 April 1665, PRO, SP 29/118/99; Williamson's Newsletter, 11 May 1665, Houghton Library, Gay 15.25F.

202 Archbishop of Glasgow to Arlington, 2 December 1665, PRO, SP 29/138/16. See also Archbishop of Glasgow to Williamson, 20 August 1666, PRO, SP 29/168/72.

203 Clarendon's speech, 10 October 1665, in *His Majesties Gracious Speech*, p. 17.

204 Sir Robert Paston to his wife, 2 March 1665, NRO, Bradfer-Lawrence MSS IC/1.

arms and listed men, to be ready upon any short warning to draw together to a body, by which with the help they promise themselves from abroad, they presume to be able to do much mischief."[205]

The investigations of Charles II's agents abroad, the reports of zealous Anglican justices and lords lieutenant, as well as official government pronouncements, all tended to confirm an image of the Dutch republic as a religiously corrupt state devoid of honor and any sense of justice. The religious pluralism and nominal Calvinism of the United Provinces unleashed an unlimited ambition, an ambition which had manifested itself in the Dutch drive for universal dominion. Anglicans were also convinced that the Dutch were making common cause with their natural allies, the English Nonconformists, to overturn the newly restored monarchy. In this conception, then, war against the Dutch was not only desirable but essential for self-preservation. It was in this sense – as a war against the foreign allies of the enemies of the Church of England – that it was claimed in England's "victory God's will is done."[206] Undoubtedly the Anglican Royalist merchant George Oxenden was expressing the same sentiment when he confidently asserted of the Dutch that "God being on our side were they as sand on the sea shore we shall trample on them."[207]

The English believed, then, that they were fighting the Dutch in order to thwart their enemies' drive toward universal dominion, a drive for which every Dutch economic advance seemed to provide proof positive. That the Protestant maritime republic should seek to dominate the world was immediately comprehensible to the English because its causes were so familiar. All supporters of the Restored Monarchy were convinced from their own painful experience during the Interregnum that republics unleashed all human vices, freeing the passions from the rules of order and honor which normally brought them under control. The more convinced Anglican supporters of the regime also believed that Dutch religious culture – a culture corrupted by the same Calvinism and religious liberty which had proved so devastating to the Church of England – inevitably deprived the Dutch people of any morality. Both those who feared

205 Clarendon to Lords Lieutenant, Deputy Lieutenants and justices of the peace of Surrey, 31 March 1665, in Sir William Haward's Collection, Bod., Don MSS b8, f. 298; another copy is in Clarendon to Viscount Townshend, 25 March 1665, Raynham Hall MSS, Townshend Personal Papers, Townshend Lieutenancy Book, on deposit at the NRO. For the persistence of Charles II's fears, see Sagredo to Doge and Senate, 17/27 October 1665, *CSPV*, p. 216; Charles II to Lords Lieutenant, 15 July 1666, PRO, SP 29/163/13; another copy is in Arlington to Townshend, 13 July 1666, Raynham Hall MSS, Townshend Lieutenancy Book on deposit at NRO. See similar sentiments in Arlington to Ormonde, 3 July 1666, Carte 46, f. 329v; Arlington to Lord Townshend, 15 August 1665, Raynham Hall MSS, Townshend Lieutenancy Book on deposit at NRO.

206 "The Royal Victory," 2–3 June 1665, *Euing Collection*, p. 513.

207 George Oxenden (Surat) to John Stanion, 24 November 1666, IOL, E/3/89, f. 277r. See also [Laney], *A Sermon Preached Before His Majesty*, p. 8.

republicanism and those who loathed religious heterodoxy agreed in their support of a war against the republican and religiously tolerant Dutch. It was to protect the very integrity of the Restored Monarchy, and the principles to which it was committed, that most English men and women volunteered their financial resources and in many cases their lives during the second Anglo-Dutch War.

20

The government's war aims

What, then, were the government's war aims? Did Charles II and his government intend to achieve the same goals through their war with the Dutch as did his subjects? Was the government indeed fighting a war to achieve some short-term economic advantage while those who were fighting the war hoped to prevent the Dutch from achieving universal dominion?

In fact, the available evidence suggests that those running the war knew well that there was no hope of garnering any immediate economic returns, that it would be militarily counterproductive to pursue immediate economic rewards. Overseas trade, it was soon concluded, needed to be curtailed in order to man his Majesty's ships. "When the seamen find it will be a war," reasoned William Coventry who was the Duke of York's primary advisor on naval affairs, "you must not expect many volunteers to man the ships however big they may talk before, for when a war comes the merchants' wages rise high, and then some for profit, and some for fear of broken bones all decline the service, so then you must resolve to press."[1] This was why he advised secretary of state Bennet "that nothing will conduce more to the manning the fleet than the observation of the embargo."[2] Within a fortnight the Council of War agreed upon "a general embargo through the whole kingdom" in order that "his Majesty's fleet be manned."[3] Naturally many merchants lobbied against an embargo which effectively put an end to their commercial endeavors, but they appear to have had little success. When Sir William Coventry heard rumors that the embargo would be lifted, he fumed that it "will have a very ill consequence, not only in the recruiting this fleet ... but also in keeping those we have."[4] He need not have been so fearful. The Duke of Albemarle, who along with Prince Rupert replaced the

1 William Coventry, "Discourse on the Dutch War," 1666, Longleat House, Cov. MSS CII, pff 10–11. Coventry provided the economic data to buttress his conclusions in a letter the previous year. Coventry to Earl of Falmouth, 24 May 1665, Carte 34, ff. 228v–229r.

2 William Coventry to Bennet, 11 October 1664, PRO, SP 29/103/41. See also his "Paper on the Navy" addressed to the Duke of Albemarle, 1665, BL, Add. 32094, f. 38v.

3 Minutes of Council of War, 23 October 1664, Longleat House, Cov. MSS XCV, f. 65r. See also Van Gogh to States General, 4/14 November 1664, PRO, SP 84/173, f. 176v.

4 Sir William Coventry to Arlington, 5 May 1665, PRO, SP 29/120/68.

Duke of York as Lord Admiral for the campaign of 1666, ordered that seamen be impressed "out of the merchant ships inward or outward bound."[5] By the following summer the press had "extended to all sorts of trades men ... servants and others."[6] Clearly Charles II's government realized that naval recruitment and normal mercantile activity could not coexist, and that short-term profits needed to be sacrificed for long-term economic survival.

Not only did the English pursue a naval recruitment policy which was inimical to mercantile interests, England's naval strategists refused to divert resources to protect the rich cargoes of its long-distance traders. In a meeting hosted by Clarendon in January 1665, England's naval experts unanimously agreed that the navy could not spare men-of-war to convoy Levant Company ships, establishing the principle that commercial interests needed to be sacrificed to military ones. The former Cromwellian naval officer Sir George Ayscue, aptly summarizing the sentiments of the Navy Board, proclaimed that "the war and trade could not be supported together – and therefore, that trade must stand still to give way to that."[7] "No trade should be suffered in English shipping," Sir George Downing similarly advised, for "if the merchants shall be let alone they will adventure till they be ruined and withal besides the loss of their stocks, the kingdom is weakened by the loss of so many good ships as will be lost and of their guns and men." Although this policy might prove deleterious to particular interests, Downing reasoned, "without doubt England can hold out much better without trade than [the Dutch]."[8] In his notes relative to a future Dutch war William Coventry insisted that the king's fleet not "be distracted or divided for convoying" merchant ships. "Nothing but the king's fleet being superior to the Dutch", he was confident, "can ever give" the merchants security.[9] Naturally many merchants had high hopes that the government would protect their trade against the Dutch privateers and men-of-war. But by the second year of the war even colliers, who received more government attention than most, were "troubled no more care is taken for preservation of trade."[10] The English pursued a war policy which paid scant

5 Sir William Clarke to Samuel Pepys, 15 December 1665, PRO, SP 29/139/36.

6 Thomas Rugge, "Mercurius Politicus Redivivus," 30 June 1666, BL, Add. 10117, f. 167r.

7 Pepys, *Diary*, Vol. VI, 15 January 1665, pp. 10–12. Sir William Penn, Sir John Lawson, and William Coventry all expressed similar opinions at this conference. Indeed instead of providing convoys, the Navy Board in some instances decided to seize commercial ships and employ them in their battle fleets. See Pepys's notes of merchant men seized in Magdelen College, Pepysian Library, MS 2265, f. 19(ii).

8 Downing to Clarendon, 3 March 1665, Bod., Clar. 108, f. 277r. Downing, perhaps because of his American upbringing, did make an exception for the plantation trade: Downing to Arlington, 11 July 1665, PRO, SP 84/177, f. 11v.

9 William Coventry, "Discourse on the Dutch War," 1666, Longleat House, Cov. MSS CII, f. 11; Sir William Coventry to Arlington, 5 May 1665, PRO, SP 29/120/68.

10 Richard Forster (Newcastle) to Williamson, 17 November 1666, PRO, SP 29/178/94.

attention to trade, the historian of the Restoration navy has concluded, "with a general abandoning of commitments overseas in favor of a main fleet strategy."[11]

England's diplomatic maneuvers also suggest that the government was not fighting a war for short-term economic advantage. Before war was declared William Coventry proposed suspending the Navigation Act in favor of the French, seemingly in an effort to convince Louis XIV to join the war on the English side.[12] Apparently English diplomats followed up this gambit with a more radical proposition, a suggestion that should Louis XIV ally with England, Charles II would then be willing to allow the new French East India Company all of the possessions taken from the Dutch in Africa and the Indies.[13] A similar preoccupation with breaking the Dutch trade monopoly rather than advancing English trade at all costs is manifest in the English proposal to the Duke of Courland to pool their mercantile resources on the river Gambia.[14] Henry Coventry's refusal to jeopardize a proposed defensive alliance with Sweden over "[one] or two points of trade" reflects a similar set of priorities.[15] Clearly the English government was far more concerned with breaking up the Dutch commercial monopoly, with putting a halt to the Dutch drive toward universal dominion, than in procuring short-term economic advantages.

Close reading of the Anglo-Dutch diplomatic exchanges just prior to the outbreak of the war also reveals that the conflict could not have been about short-term economic grievances. By the summer of 1664 the major outstanding grievance, the primary bone of contention between the States General and the English, was Dutch non-payment of restitution for two ships – the *Henry Bonaventura* and the *Bona Esperanza* – seized in the 1650s.[16] "Upon this a war cannot be," Denzil Hollis correctly observed to Downing, "I see not *causam belli* only *litigandi*."[17] Indeed Downing himself, who understood more than anyone else the significance of minute economic grievances, noted that he only pressed those claims because of "a letter from the king to me," a letter presumably written because "the persons concerned in them were such as had suffered very much for the king

11 J. D. Davies, *Gentlemen and Tarpaulins: The Officers and Men of the Restoration Navy* (Oxford, 1991), p. 134.

12 William Coventry, "Essay on France," 1664, Longleat House, Cov. MSS CI, f. 25v.

13 Sagredo to Doge and Senate, 13/23 September 1664, *CSPV*, p. 42. Although I have found no trace of such a proposal in the surviving state papers, the emphasis on the Guinny trade and the similarity of the priorities to those present in Coventry's "Essay" give the story a certain plausibility.

14 Van Goch to States General, 16/26 August 1664, PRO, SP 84/172, f. 168r.

15 Henry Coventry to Charles II, 6 March 1665, Longleat House, Cov. MSS LXIV, f. 126. William Morrice's reply suggests that Henry Coventry assessed the situation correctly. Morrice to H. Coventry, 5 May 1665, Longleat House, Cov. MSS LXIV, f. 161r.

16 De Bacquoy/Van Ruyven to Williamson, 21/31 May 1664, PRO, SP 84/170, f. 198; Downing to Bennet, 29 July 1664, PRO, SP 84/171, f. 96.

17 Hollis to Downing, 2 September 1664, BL, Add. 22920, f. 46.

and his father."[18] So little did these ships actually matter to Charles II and his government once the war had begun, that in a list of English demands sent to Downing after the English victory at Lowestoft, the ships in question were entirely omitted – an omission which the perceptive and horrified Downing realized would "make a strange outcry."[19]

Not only were there few outstanding economic grievances between the English and the Dutch, in the autumn of 1664 John De Witt announced he was willing to accede to the long-term economic settlement for which George Downing had long been pressing. In the late summer rumors began to circulate that the Anglo-Dutch squabble "will come to an amicable conclusion."[20] De Witt's ideological ally and close friend Peter De Groot informed Downing that "if his Majesty did not seek pretexts of difference as desiring a war that he did not doubt but that things would be composed."[21] The Dutch "have set themselves on the road to an accommodation," reported a Venetian intelligencer in the early autumn.[22] The Dutch "begin to boggle in the business," the treasurer of the navy Sir George Carteret informed Samuel Pepys, they "may offer terms of peace for all this."[23] Sir George Downing, who was always quick to note Dutch intransigence, now claimed that "their hearts go pit a pat" and that "they do begin a little to put a little water into their wine" so that their was now hope that the English would achieve "reasonable satisfaction."[24] A month later he triumphantly confirmed his own suspicions. The Dutch, he informed Clarendon, had advanced a remarkable proposal, one which "must be kept under greatest secrecy and seriously considered." "This is quite of another nature than anything before," he enthused, "and thus all the year's conferences, and the business of commissioners, and an umpire, and all those stories will be out of doors, and quietness settled, and all the present measures in Europe changed, and what gained will be clear and present and sure gain" while "many things may happen ere an end the

18 Downing to Clarendon, 15 August 1662, Bod., Clar. 104, f. 97r. Downing's assessment of Charles II's motives was undoubtedly correct. See petition to Charles II, 12 July 1664, PRO, SP 84/171, f. 72r; Josselin, *Diary*, 18 August 1664, p. 511 (Royalism of Sir John Jacob); Downing to Clarendon, 24 May 1662, Bod., Clar. 76, f. 322r; De Bacquoy/Van Ruyven to Nichols, 15/25 August 1662, PRO, SP 84/166, f. 102v.

19 Downing to Arlington, August 1665, All Souls, Codrington Library, 309 (unfoliated).

20 *Newes*, 7 July 1664, p. 435.

21 Downing to Clarendon, 16 September 1664, Bod., Clar. 108, f. 81. He might well have been referring to the decision to restore Pula Run which was taken about this time. See Downing to Clarendon, 26 August 1664, Bod., Clar. 108, f. 76v; Peter Loughead, "The East India Company in English Domestic Politics, 1657–1688" (Oxford, D. Phil. thesis, 1980), p. 72; Keith Feiling, *British Foreign Policy, 1660–1672* (London, 1930), p. 105.

22 Intelligence from London, 26 September/6 October 1664, *CSPV*, p. 46.

23 Pepys, *Diary*, Vol. V, 19 September 1664, p. 275. By November Pepys heard Charles II say "that the Dutch do begin to comply with him." Pepys, *Diary*, Vol. V, 29 November 1664, p. 333.

24 Downing to Clarendon, 16 September 1664, Bod., Clar. 108, ff. 79–80.

other way."[25] Downing urged secretary Bennet to "strike while the iron is hot."[26]

Inexplicably the English Privy Council failed to respond. Downing could only "wonder" at his superiors' silence.[27] William Morrice claimed that Dutch demands for the restitution of the New Netherlands quashed the "overtures."[28] But the New Netherlands had been seized after the passage of the April trade resolution, and was hardly a major trading entrepot. No wonder De Witt could offer the States General no explanation for the rejection of his offer other than some "exorbitant pretenses" of the English crown.[29] No wonder Gilbert Burnet later concluded that "the grounds [of war] were so slight, that it was visible there was somewhat more at bottom than was openly owned."[30]

There was indeed "somewhat more at bottom" in the government's actions than was officially proclaimed in the April 1664 trade resolution. Charles II and his closest advisors were convinced that there could be no lasting peace with the United Provinces without the restoration of the Prince of Orange. All of the English diplomatic correspondence throughout the war had a decidedly Orangist tinge. The Earl of Arlington married Mademoiselle de Beverweert a daughter of an illegitimate branch of the House of Orange – "a bastard Orange for pimp Arlington" in Andrew Marvell's colorful language – during the war.[31] This marriage, to a woman he had never met, almost certainly reflected an already highly developed political outlook. Arlington's office had long been employing

25 Downing to Clarendon, 21 October 1664, Bod., Clar. 108, f. 191r. The plea for secrecy was apparently kept. The text of the proposal has not survived, nor is it discussed in the standard historical accounts of the outbreak of the war.

26 Downing to Bennet, 21 October 1664, PRO, SP 84/172, f. 139r. This mangled document appears to contain the text of a proposed treaty from De Witt, with Downing's handwritten advice on it.

27 Downing to Bennet, 4/14 November 1664, PRO, SP 84/173, f. 8r.

28 William Morrice to Henry Coventry, 28 October 1664, Longleat House, Cov. MSS LXIV, f. 19r.

29 De Bacquoy/Van Ruyven to Bennet, 13 December 1664, PRO, SP 84/173, f. 93v. This was a position he constantly reiterated throughout the war. See, for example, Sylvius (Antwerp) to Arlington, 9/19 December 1665, in R. R. Goodison (editor), "Further Correspondence Relating to the Buat Affair," in *Bijdragen en Medeelingen van het Historisch Genootschap* Vol. 57 (1936), p. 28.

30 Gilbert Burnet, *History of My Own Time*, Vol. I (Oxford, 1823), p. 375. This was the view of a large part of Charles II's diplomatic corps. Downing to Clarendon, 16 September 1664, Bod., Clar. 108, ff. 80–81; Gilbert Talbot to Henry Coventry, 8 October 1664, Longleat House, Cov. MSS XXV, f. 2r; Hollis to Bennet, 17/27 September 1664, PRO, SP 78/119, f. 80r. The Earl of Sandwich was no doubt right to comment that "my master's honour ... is far engaged not to accommodate." Sandwich to Bennet, 31 October 1664, PRO, SP 29/103/159. Given the image of the Dutch as necessarily ambitious and untrustworthy, it would have been very difficult indeed for Charles II to explain to Parliament his acceptance of yet another treaty from such duplicitous negotiators.

31 Andrew Marvell (?), "Second Advice to a Painter," April 1666, *POAS*, p. 51; newsletter from the Hague, 2/12 January 1666, Carte 222, f. 81r.

Orangist spies.[32] More significantly, English diplomats overseas all thought that one of the principal war aims was to restore the Prince of Orange. Denzil Hollis claimed to wish "with all my heart" to see "the Prince of Orange restored."[33] George Downing was sure that except for "De Witt and those that are influenced by him and that party there's not a man [in the United Provinces] but whose outcry is for peace."[34] In elegantly phrased letter after elegantly phrased letter William Temple insisted that "we shall no way have reason from Holland without the breaking of De Witt's party which must be done by the endeavors of raising the prince."[35] Arlington himself made it clear that he felt De Witt would "make no rare advances" toward peace until the Orangist "party by [its] prevalency force him to it."[36] "If the Prince of Orange could be restored before the peace," Arlington had Sir Gabriel Sylvius write to the Orangist confidant Henri Fleury de Coulan, Sieur de Buat, "there would be little difficulty in procuring a good peace, because that would give the king assurance of their intentions of making and (which is more) of keeping the peace with the king."[37]

Unsurprisingly English overseas representatives were instructed to emphasize that the restoration of the Prince of Orange to his rightful place in the Dutch polity was a central – perhaps the central – English war aim. "When the prince shall be reestablished," Sir Walter Vane was told to assure the Elector of Brandenburg, "we will harken to very moderate terms of accommodation, and that it would not only be very dishonorable to us to make a peace without his inclusion, whose Exclusion was a main part and inducement to the treaty with Cromwell, but that then De Witt and his party would then so root themselves in the government, that there would remain very little hope of the prince's ever obtaining any thing after-

32 The evidence for this permeates the State Papers Foreign for the period. See for example: William Temple to Arlington, 24 August/3 September 1666, PRO, SP 77/35, f. 93r; Letter from Antwerp, 1/11 December 1666, PRO, SP 77/35, f. 306v.

33 Hollis to Arlington, 24 February/6 March 1666, PRO, SP 78/122, f. 96v; Hollis to Arlington, 19/29 August 1665, PRO, SP 78/121, f. 47r.

34 Downing to Arlington, 2 May 1665, PRO, SP 84/176, f. 2r.

35 Temple to Arlington, 21/31 March 1666, PRO, SP 77/34, f. 128v. This was Temple's position until late 1666. It is significant in analyzing the decision to support the Triple Alliance in 1667–1668 that while Temple's attitude towards De Witt and the republicans underwent a sea change, there is little to suggest that Arlington's did. See Temple to Arlington, 19/29 December 1665, PRO, SP 77/33, ff. 366–367; Temple to Arlington, 26 January/5 February 1666, PRO, SP 77/34, f. 35r; Temple to Arlington, 29 May/8 June 1666, PRO, SP 77/34, f. 275v; Temple to Arlington, 28 June/8 July 1666, PRO, SP 77/34, f. 342v.

36 Arlington to Temple, 9 February 1666, Thomas Bebington (editor), *The Right Honourable the Earl of Arlington's Letters* ... (London, 1701), Vol. I p. 58. See also Arlington to Ormonde, 24 February 1666, Carte 46, f. 259; Arlington to Temple, 5 November 1666, Bebington, Vol. I, p. 105.

37 Sylvius (with Arlington's advice) to Buat, 25 February 1666, Longleat House, Cov. MSS CI, f. 46v. Edmund Ludlow appears to have had knowledge of Arlington's connections with Sylvius, Buat, and the Orangists: Ludlow, "A Voyce," Bod., English History MS C487, pp. 1128–1129.

wards."[38] When England was in a much weaker military position in late 1666, Clarendon still instructed the Earl of St. Albans to "move the French king to take the interest of the Prince of Orange to heart in this conjuncture."[39]

All of the available evidence suggests that Charles II's advisors and diplomats very much shared his own sentiments. "His Majesty is so far incensed against that insolent people," one merchant thought, "that he is resolved, with God's persuasion, before he makes peace, to bring them upon their knees."[40] The Venetian ambassador in Paris knew that "every week" Charles wrote letters to his sister "in which biting remarks against the Dutch may be read."[41] Indeed he once told his sister, the Duchess of Orleans, that he did "not care a turd for anything a Dutch man says of me."[42] Charles, like most English men and women, directed his deprecations not against the Dutch people as a whole, but against the republican party. Orangists he treated with the utmost respect. When the English captured the Dutch sea captain Cornelius Evertson early in the war, Charles II personally granted him his liberty based on his and his family's Orangism.[43] When John Kievet "of the Prince of Orange's party, now not welcome in Holland" fled to England, Charles II quickly knighted him "for some merit on the prince's behalf."[44] Given these outward manifestations of the king's sympathies it was predictable that upon the rejection of De Witt's generous terms in the autumn of 1664, the Earl of Huntingdon's friend Salusbury concluded that Charles II "visibly intends greatness to the Prince of Orange."[45] "The Dutch must not expect peace from his Sacred Majesty," opined the English resident in Venice Giles Jones, until they "prepare their stomachs for the receiving of their prince."[46] Clearly, for both Charles II

38 Instructions for Sir Walter Vane, October 1665, Goodison, "Buat Affair," pp. 44–46. See also the pre-war addendum to Sir Richard Fanshawe's instructions: Henry Bennet to Fanshawe, 17 March 1664, *Original Letters of his Excellency Sir Richard Fanshaw*, (London, 1701), pp. 49–50.

39 Instructions to St. Albans (in Clarendon's hand), 1666 (probably autumn), Bod., Clar. 84, f. 43r.

40 Stephen Flower to George Oxenden, 24 April 1665, BL, Add. 40710, f. 17r.

41 Giustinian to Doge and Paris, 26 June/6 July 1666, *CSPV*, p. 27.

42 Charles II to Duchess of Orleans, 27 February 1665, Cyril H. Hartmann,*Charles II and Madame* (London, 1934), p. 149. This was apparently in response to a Dutch merchant's claim that the Dutch would "only pay his Majesty reparations with shit." Hollis to Arlington, 8/18 March 1665, PRO, SP 78/120, f. 71r (my translation).

43 Gervase Jacques to Earl of Huntingdon, 25 April 1665, HL, HA 7649; Evelyn, *Diary*, 24 April 1665, p. 407; William Morrice to Henry Coventry, 21 April 1665, Longleat House, Cov. MSS LXIV, f. 157v.

44 Evelyn, *Diary*, 2 December 1666, pp. 470–471.

45 Thomas Salusbury to Earl of Huntingdon, 8 December 1664, HL, HA 10662.

46 Giles Jones to Williamson, 14/24 July 1665, PRO, SP 99/46, f. 71r; see also [James Ralph], *The History of England*, Vol. I, (London, 1744) p. 49; Sagredo to Doge and Senate, 6/16 October 1665, *CSPV*, pp. 211–212. The Orangist agent Gabriel Sylvius was convinced of Charles II's commitment to his master's cause: Edward Hyde, *The Life of Edward Earl of Clarendon* (Dublin, 1760), pp. 331–334. Sylvius tells the same story: Sylvius to Arlington,

and his ministers, the restoration of the Prince of Orange represented the best hope for a reasonable and lasting peace with the Dutch. It is this context which explains why when John Evelyn planned his officially sponsored history of the second Dutch War he proposed to begin with the seclusion of the Prince of Orange.[47]

For Anglican Royalists, for those in the government who were most committed to the Church of England, the war was also necessary to reform Dutch religious culture and to break asunder the ties between the Dutch and the English Nonconformists. In the Anglican Royalist construction the English regime could never be stable as long as the pipeline – both military and ideological – between the United Provinces and England's conventicles remained freely flowing. Naturally this meant that Anglican Royalists were the most fiercely committed to the war, were those who were confident that England could never be safe until the Dutch were brought to their knees. Daniel Fleming, Joseph Williamson's Cumberland friend and ideological fellow traveler, hoped the English fleets would "reduce the Dutch from their late Hogen Mogen, to their (not long since) poor and distressed states."[48] English "confidence was then grown so high," the Presbyterian Richard Baxter unsympathetically recalled of his Anglican neighbors, "that [they] talked of nothing but bringing down the Dutch to our mercy, and bringing them to contempt and ruin."[49]

More importantly, committed Anglicans within the government believed that winning the war and suppressing Nonconformity at home were intimately interrelated projects. After the victory at Lowestoft Sir Thomas Osborne, Yorkshire justice and future Lord Treasurer, remarked to Arlington upon "how good the effects of it will be in [Charles II's] own kingdoms."[50] At the same time William Morrice was confident the victory will make the king "more safe at home."[51]

Equally, many Anglicans thought the suppressing of domestic Dissent would make victory over the foreign enemy all that much easier. "If you carefully provide for the suppressing [of] your enemies at home," Clarendon informed the assembled Houses of Parliament, "you will find your enemies abroad less exalted, and in a short time more inclined to live in amity with

6/16 January 1666, PRO, SP 77/34, f. 5v; Sylvius (with Arlington's advice) to Buat, 25 February 1666, Longleat House, Cov. MSS CI, f. 46. See also Sylvius to Arlington, 9/19 December 1665, PRO, SP 77/35, f. 353r.

47 John Evelyn, notes for history of the second Dutch War, Christ Church, Evelyn MSS 134, (unfoliated section). For early discussions about the book see John Evelyn, Queries for Mr. Williamson, 1667?, PRO, SP 84/183, f. 114r.

48 Daniel Fleming (Rydal) to Williamson, 3 August 1666, PRO, SP 29/166/39.

49 Matthew Sylvester, *Reliquiae Baxterianae* (London, 1696), Pt. III, p. 16.

50 Osborne to Arlington, 13 June 1665, BL, Egerton MSS 3328, f. 20r.

51 William Morrice to Henry Coventry, 9 June 1665, Longleat House, Cov. MSS LXIV, f. 175v.

you, than to make war upon you."[52] It was for this reason that he was "most solicitous to free the country from seditious persons and seditious and unlawful meetings and conventicles, the principal end of which meetings is ... to confirm each other in their malice against the government and in making collections for the support of their party who are listed to appear in any dangerous undertaking."[53] It was this fear of the domestic allies of the Dutch, this perceived danger from the Nonconformists, which led Parliament in October 1665 to pass the Five Mile Act "to prevent the seeds of sedition sown by the Non-conformist preachers."[54]

The Five Mile Act – though admittedly few were prosecuted under its provisions – was typical of governmental attitudes in the early months of the war. Every effort was made to silence, disperse, and emasculate the Church's domestic enemies. The official journalist Roger L'Estrange took every opportunity "to tear and present the whole rabble of the faction."[55] Many lords lieutenant, like the Earl of Orrery who was hardly a rabid Anglican, hoped to "settle the militia in the cities and towns and those only to consist of such as receive the communion according to the Church of England and take the oaths of allegiance and supremacy, for since the Dutch and French are enemies, I shall equally fear fanatics and Papists."[56] Gilbert Sheldon, Archbishop of Canterbury and increasingly influential in the House of Lords and on the Privy Council, advocated a purge of the merchant community to complement his purge of the London vestries.[57] Sheldon advised that Nonconformist merchants "have a good sum of money given them" in order to induce them to "sit still and withdraw their stocks," predicting that "the trade should not at all be abated but carried on by those that are loyal and conformable without any abatement of his Majesty's customs."[58]

52 Clarendon's speech, 10 October 1665, in *His Majesties Gracious Speech to both Houses of Parliament Together with the Lord Chancellor's* (Oxford, 1665), p. 19.

53 Clarendon to Viscount Townshend, 25 March 1665, Raynham Hall MSS, Townshend Lieutenancy Book, on deposit at NRO.

54 Peter Barwick to William Sancroft, 4 November 1665, Bod., Tanner MSS 45, f. 32r; Ralph, *History*, Vol. I, p. 125; Ludlow, "A Voyce," Bod. English History MSS. c487, ff. 1098–1099; Nathaniel Hobart (Oxford) to Sir Ralph Verney, 1 November 1665, Firestone Library, Verney MSS, Reel 120 (unfoliated). For the legislative history of the act see D. T. Witcombe, "The Parliamentary Career of Sir William and Mr. Henry Coventry 1661–1681" (Oxford, B. Litt. thesis, 1934), pp. 36–37; Ronald Hutton, *The Restoration* (Oxford, 1985), pp. 235–236; Paul Seaward, *The Cavalier Parliament and the Reconstruction of the Old Regime 1661–1667* (Cambridge, 1989), pp. 192–193; John Spurr, *The Restoration Church of England 1646–1689* (New Haven, 1991), p. 52.

55 L'Estrange to Arlington, 19 October 1665, PRO, SP 29/135/8.

56 Orrery to Ormonde, 18 May 1666, Bod., Clar. 84, f. 169v.

57 On the purge of the London vestries see Paul Seaward, "Gilbert Sheldon, the London Vestries, and the Defence of the Church," in Tim Harris, Paul Seaward, and Mark Goldie (editors), *The Politics of Religion in Restoration England* (Oxford, 1990), pp. 49–73.

58 Gilbert Sheldon (?), Paper Concerning Trade, 1660s, Bod. Add. MSS C304A, f. 187. I am grateful to John Spurr for calling my attention to this important document.

Apparently Sheldon, and his Anglican Royalist allies, made a number of attempts during the Anglo-Dutch War to rid the merchant community of its Nonconformist elements. William Swann, England's Anglican resident in Hamburg, complained vociferously of the "disobedience" of many of the English merchants in northern Germany. He therefore insisted that "none be suffered to bear any office or sit in Council of the Company [of Merchant Adventurers], but those that come constantly to divine prayer according to the act of uniformity, and that receive the Sacrament three times in the year."[59] A similar attempt was made to achieve conformity among the English merchants in India. The committed Anglican Royalist George Oxenden was known to insist upon "conformist" chaplains and regular religious observance at Surat.[60] Upon the conclusion of his agency at Fort St. George, Edward Winter – who was such a committed Anglican Royalist that in 1651 he publicly "upon his knees" drank a health "to the prosperity of King Charles the Second and to the confusion of his enemies"[61] – protested vehemently to his friend Gilbert Sheldon that his replacement was ideologically unsound. George Foxcroft, Winter, and his friends claimed, was "of most rotten and unsound principles who had he loved the Church half so well as he did the lands thereof, could never [have] had so little allegiance for his king."[62] In a flamboyant gesture Winter seized Foxcroft, his son, and his closest associates at Fort St. George, refusing to surrender his charge to such dangerous men. After a long struggle Winter gave way, upon a promise of pardon from Charles II, probably because the London-based government of the East India Company was dominated by the "Presbyterian faction."[63]

Anglican Royalists also attempted to achieve religious conformity within

59 Memorial from William Swann, July 1664, PRO, SP 82/10, f. 92r.

60 Henry Oxenden to George Oxenden, 7 October 1667, BL, Add. 40713, f. 21r. Oxenden's distaste for Presbyterianism and Nonconformists in general is omnipresent throughout his correspondence both in the BL and the IOL.

61 Deposition of W. Fairfax, 13 October 1651, PRO, Kew, CO 77/7, f. 87r.

62 Edward Winter to Gilbert Sheldon, 28 September 1665, IOL, E/3/29, f. 89r; Joseph Farley's deposition against George Foxcroft, 16 September 1665, IOL, E/3/29, f. 41r. Interestingly, while Foxcroft insisted that he was loyal to the king, he never denied the charge of religious Nonconformity. Foxcroft to East India Company, 26 September 1665, IOL, E/3/29, f. 76r.

63 For the surrender of Fort St. George see Williamson's newsletter, 29 January 1667, Bod., Don MSS C.37, f. 9r. For the Presbyterianism of the East India Company see Elizabeth Dallyson to George Oxenden, March 1666 (?), BL, Add. 40712, f. 8v; John Stanian to George Oxenden, March 1666, BL, Add. 40712, ff. 27v–28r (significantly Stanian claims that the Presbyterians wanted to bring the trade "as fast as it can be wrought ... into the order of the Dutch"); Henry Oxenden to George Oxenden, 1 April 1666, BL, Add. 40712, f. 8r (he claims Barnardiston, Sir William Thomson, Boone, Mascall, Papillon, Clarke, and Sir Andrew Riccard – all Presbyterians – dominate the Company). Andrew Riccard acknowledged that by 1666 "the genius of the new committee is a little altered from that of their predecessors" but insisted that "it's for the advantage." Riccard to George Oxenden, 28 February 1666, BL, Add. 40712, f. 26v. See Levant Company to Consul Cave, 1 February 1667, PRO, SP 105/113, f. 78r for more evidence of Riccard's Presbyterian sympathies.

the Levant Company at the outset of the war. In this case Heneage Finch, Earl of Winchilsea, led the Anglican crusade. Winchilsea, in his capacity as ambassador in Constantinople, complained to anyone who would listen about the Levant Company's appointment of a "factious Presbyterian minister" to Smyrna.[64] Naturally he blamed this activity on "the malice of some Presbyterians amongst" the Levant merchants – later singling out "Mr. William Love, one eminent for disturbance who thinks the Company's order more powerful than his Majesty's commission."[65] The Anglican Winchilsea made the inevitable ideological association between the company's Presbyterianism and its "democratic principles, as if they had forgot to whom they owe their allegiance."[66] Winchilsea's attempt to remove the Presbyterian minister, which appears to have been a first step toward easing the Presbyterians out of positions of influence within the Levant Company, ultimately failed. Just as the coordinated effort of Sheldon and Winter had foundered upon the rock of the East India Company's powerful Nonconformist leaders, so Winchilsea's effort was thwarted by the powerful Presbyterians in the Levant Company. Indeed John Joliffe, who was also very influential in the East India Company, probably advanced the same argument in both cases. "The Company are not judges of the laws of conformity," he insisted, and he learned from "the opinion of good council that his Majesty's public ministers abroad are not legally founded in jurisdiction in that point."[67] No wonder Henry Oxenden concluded that Joliffe who was everywhere "powerful" "still adheres to Love."[68]

Whatever the ultimate success of the attempts by Anglican Royalists, almost certainly led by Sheldon, to purge the merchant community in the early months of the war, there can be no doubting their attempt. Similarly in the early months of the war Anglican justices and lords lieutenant throughout the country made every effort to clamp down and stamp out gatherings of Dissenters. "If the government here and there can be supported," Clarendon advised his friend Ormonde, "it must be done by great severity, no other expedient can do it."[69] Everywhere Clarendon's injunction was taken to heart. "The conventicles are now hotly pursued,"

64 Winchilsea to Duchess of Somerset, 23 March 1665, LRO, DG9/Box 4984, Winchilsea Letterbook, f. 235; Winchilsea to Bennet, 24 March 1665, PRO, SP 97/18, f. 120r.

65 Winchilsea to Duchess of Somerset, 23 March 1665, LRO, DG 9/Box 4984, Winchilsea Letterbook, f. 235; Winchilsea to Bennet, 24 June 1665, PRO, SP 97/18, f. 125r.

66 Winchilsea to Sir Heneage Finch, 25 June 1665, LRO, DG9/Box 4984, Winchilsea Letterbook, ff. 261–262.

67 John Joliffe (London) to Winchilsea, 16 January 1666, LRO, DG7/Box 4984, Letters Folder. Joliffe said this was for two reasons: first "these laws are by his Majesty limited to England and extend not to his other dominions" and, second, that though there were "many recusants in all princes dominions but I never find that his Majesty's ambassadors or agents did meddle with them."

68 Henry Oxenden to George Oxenden, 7 October 1667, BL, Add. 40713, f. 20v.

69 Clarendon to Ormonde, 7 July 1666, Carte 47, f. 118v.

the journalist Henry Muddiman informed his future competitor Joseph Williamson, "no meeting but presently snapped and the brethren presented according to the strictness of the law."[70] "Though the war grows hot abroad, yet the zeal for episcopacy cools not at home," lamented the unsympathetic Ludlow. "The profane" he learned from his myriad informants were "persecuting the professors of religion with cruel hatred, interrupting their meetings and dragging them to prisons for serving the Lord according to their consciences."[71] "The king and Parliament having now sufficiently experienced the impudence and spirit of their faction," the high churchman Samuel Parker later recalled, "resolved to check and curb their insolence by stricter laws; lest being engaged in a foreign war, they might be disturbed by intestine tumults."[72]

Throughout England Anglicans pursued the Nonconformists, whom they perceived to be the domestic allies of the Dutch, with ferocity and determination. The Duke of Albemarle "daily" rounded up Dissenters and "dispose[d] of them to the Tower or other restraints."[73] Lord Brouncker apprehended "some Presbyter-people" who were attending "a private meeting in Covent Garden."[74] In less-fashionable districts of the metropolis "many Quakers and other sorts of people that met in private" were arrested.[75] Indeed so many were taken that barges could be seen "daily" on the Thames transporting Nonconformists to the foreign plantations.[76]

This was not merely a metropolitan phenomenon. In "Guildford and other places" Quakers were regularly "clapped into prison."[77] The governor of Hull apprehended "fanatics of several persuasions" attending a conventicle.[78] "Having notice of a conventicle" the Mayor of Lyme immediately broke it up and "executed the law" upon those he could catch.[79] After surrendering his command of the fleet the Duke of York went into Yorkshire where he "secured" those "most likely [and] most capable of making disorder."[80] Justices in Lancashire "took a very severe course" with a group of Presbyterians who resisted apprehension at a Christmas Day

70 Muddiman to Williamson, 22 August 1665, PRO, SP 29/129/99.
71 Ludlow, "A Voyce," Bod., English History MSS C487, pp. 1063, 1101.
72 Thomas Newlin (translator), *Bishop Parker, History of his Own Time* (London, 1727), p. 87.
73 Muddiman to Williamson, 5 September 1665, PRO, SP 29/132/28; Ludlow, "A Voyce," Bod., English History MSS C487, pp. 1093–1094.
74 Pepys, *Diary*, Vol. VI, 21 August 1665, p. 199.
75 Thomas Rugge, "Mercurius Politicus Redivivus," August 1665, BL, Add. 10117, f. 143v.
76 Gervase Jacques (London) to Earl of Huntingdon, 25 April 1665, HL, HA 7649.
77 Thomas Rugge, "Mercurius Politicus Redivivus," 8 February 1665, BL, Add. 10117, f. 131r.
78 Luke Whitington (Hull) to James Hickes, 19 March 1665, PRO, SP 29/115/40.
79 Antony Thorold (Lyme) to Williamson, 22 July 1666, PRO, SP 29/164/53.
80 William Coventry to Ormonde, 26 August 1665, Carte 47, f. 425r; William Coventry to Williamson, 14 August 1665, PRO, SP 29/129/29.

conventicle.[81] Ronald Hutton is certainly right to conclude that "initially" the outbreak of the Anglo-Dutch War intensified "the campaign of orthodoxy against religious and political dissent."[82]

Charles II's government, then, adopted two separate and possibly complementary strategies to put a halt to the Dutch drive toward universal monarchy. One strategy which received support from Royalists of all religious persuasions, was to overturn the intrinsically anti-monarchical and morally corrupt political regime of the Dutch republican leader John De Witt. The United Provinces once again governed by a Prince of Orange, the English reasoned, could not but be a virtuous regime. A second strategy was proposed by the more committed Anglicans, men and women who were convinced that England would never be safe from the ideological and political threat posed by the Dutch until the ties between the English fanatics and their Dutch brethren were permanently severed. Such a severance required not only a complete and devastating victory over the Dutch military forces, but also the evisceration of the political power of English Nonconformity. Anglican Royalists wanted not only to reverse the exclusionary terms of Cromwell's treaty of Westminster, but also to eliminate the ideological sources that had created Cromwell's England. Significantly, at the outset of the war, both of these prongs of the English government's strategy reflected the desires and fears of a majority of the English political nation.

81 Roger Bradshaigh (Haigh) to Williamson, 30 January 1666, PRO, SP 29/146/68.
82 Hutton, *Restoration*, p. 230.

21

An Orangist revolution?

How successful were the English at achieving their war aims? Was there any evidence that English pressure, either external or internal, succeeded in destabilizing the Dutch republican regime? While Dutch political culture was fluid, its ebbs and flows frequently responding to the most recent battle news from the North Sea, there can be no doubting the ubiquity of popular political criticism throughout the United Provinces in the first two years of the war.

Almost as soon as Parliament resoundingly signaled its support of the war, the usually booming Dutch economy began to wilt. The United Provinces "is in an uproar for want of trade," Gilbert Talbot informed his fellow ambassador Henry Coventry during the war's first spring, the Dutch navy "must be forced to fight us or their leaders will be torn in pieces."[1] In letter after letter George Downing reported that "the people here are weary of the war" not so much for what they had already lost "but because they see no probability of an end thereof, and (say they) how is it possible for us to hold out and have no trade."[2] So discontented were the people that "many poor artists daily quit this country for want of employment, and many merchants speak of removing this spring if the peace be not made before."[3]

Not only had the war severed Dutch trade routes, but the astronomically high taxes necessitated by the war were crushing the domestic economy. Contributions toward the war effort consumed all the profits from the richest East India Company voyages.[4] According to William Temple, in the

1 Gilbert Talbot to Henry Coventry, 30 May 1665, Longleat House, Cov. MSS XXV, f. 73r.

2 Downing to Arlington, 28 April 1665, PRO, SP 84/175, f. 117v; Downing to Arlington, 11 July 1665, PRO, SP 84/177, f. 12v; see also Sylvius to Arlington, 28 November/8 December 1665, PRO, SP 77/33, f. 337v (my translation); Sylvius to Arlington, 25 November/5 December 1665, Goodison, "Buat Affairs," p. 18; John Evelyn, notes for "History of Second Dutch War," Christ Church, Evelyn MSS 134, p. 88; newsletter from The Hague, 19/29 January 1666, PRO, SP 101/48, f. 49r; newsletter from Rotterdam, 26 January/5 February 1666, PRO, SP 101/48, f. 68r.

3 Downing to Arlington, 15 June 1665, PRO, SP 84/176, f. 79r. See also Downing to Clarendon, 13 January 1665, Bod., Clar. 108, f. 255v; Downing to Clarendon, 23 June 1665, Bod., Clar. 108, f. 239.

4 Downing to Clarendon, 13 January 1665, Bod., Clar. 108, f. 256v.

erstwhile prosperous Dutch towns "discontents" were "ripening into tumults" because the tax rates were becoming "insufferable."[5] "The charges wherewith the people are taxed" combined with "no trade," George Downing was sure, "are two extremities that cannot live long together."[6]

Given the economic situation, then, it was hardly surprising that "all generally wish for nothing more than a peace."[7] After surveying the voluminous correspondence crossing his desk, Arlington reported to Ormonde that "all the letters from Holland say confidently the party for peace grows very strong."[8] The Dutch "cannot well subsist much longer" without a peace, opined the Duke of Albemarle's secretary Sir William Clarke, "their trade being absolutely at a stand and their seamen not to be prevailed with to serve aboard their men-of-war."[9]

Dutch popular opposition to the war, the popular outcries for peace, were not unpoliticized manifestations of despair. Instead the Dutch enunciated their criticism of the war in sharp, and politically volatile, language. "The people of Holland will have peace with the king on any terms," reported the somewhat optimistic Earl of Castlemaine, "they are in a kind of tumult."[10] The States General, thought another observer, lived in "fear of the communality."[11] The popular political rage was expressed throughout the United Provinces with all of the rich symbols and traditional political celebrations associated with the House of Orange. The "chief misfortune" of the Dutch republican government, thought a Venetian observer, was that "in the very heart of the provinces" – presumably both metaphorically and physically – "are the Prince of Orange and his party."[12] By the first autumn of the war it was known that "the Prince of Orange is publicly prayed for in the churches, and much talk of having him restored to all his dignities."[13] Significantly the young prince's birthday was "now more solemnly kept in the Netherlands than ever heretofore."[14]

Fending off the growing Orangist opposition to the war required all of

5 Temple to Arlington, 3/13 October 1665, PRO, SP 77/33, f. 298v. This letter is transcribed slightly differently in *The Works of Sir William Temple* (London, 1814), Vol. I, p. 218.

6 Downing to Clarendon, 3 March 1665, Bod., Clar. 108, f. 276v. See also William Morrice to Henry Coventry, 5 May 1665, Longleat House, Cov. MSS LXIV, f. 161v.

7 Roquil (United Provinces) to Sir Philip Froude, 1 July 1666, PRO, SP 29/161/1.

8 Arlington to Ormonde, 20 February 1666, Carte 46, f. 257v. The Venetian Giustinian used almost identical language in describing the Dutch political situation six months later. Giustinian to Doge and Senate, 24 July/3 August 1666, *CSPV*, p. 47.

9 Sir William Clarke, Diary, 7/17 May 1666, BL, Add. 14286, f. 21v. See also Thomas Rugge, "Mercurius Politicus Redivivus," 27 May 1666, BL, Add. 10117, f. 161r.

10 Castlemaine to Williamson, 15/25 January 1665, PRO, SP 77/33. f. 191r.

11 Newsletter from Amsterdam, 25 May 1665, PRO, SP 101/47, f. 193r.

12 Sagredo to Doge and Senate, 4/14 August 1665, *CSPV*, p. 176.

13 Robert Southwell to Ormonde, 24 October 1665, Carte 34, f. 452v.

14 St. Serfe's newsletter, 26 November 1665, LOC 18124, Vol. I, f. 7r.

the vast political acumen of John De Witt and his republican supporters.[15] De Witt committed himself ideologically, physically, and emotionally to the war effort, proclaiming that the Dutch "must rather perish than yield an ace to the king."[16] De Witt set a superhuman example, volunteering to serve on the Dutch fleet like "a Roman dictator," investing his own money in Dutch privateers to harass English trade, offering diplomatic alternatives to capitulation to England.[17] So successful was De Witt in promoting his cause, so skillful was he at negotiating the tricky waters of Dutch politics, that William Temple concluded that the Grand Pensionary of Holland "has far greater power in the government than ever any Prince of Orange had."[18] While people marveled at his "great zeal, industry and diligence" they also muttered that De Witt was "the principal cause of embroiling the state in this war," and that it was his "stratagems" which had "embroiled and engaged this state."[19]

Orangist whispering and murmurings, the subtle reminders of the century-long ideological struggle which gripped the Dutch polity, soon developed into political demonstrations and demands for political action. The economic stress of the war combined with the general perception – a perception encouraged at every turn by Charles II and his ministers at home and abroad – that England was fighting on behalf of the Prince of Orange led ineluctably to Orangist agitation throughout the United Provinces.

Even in Holland, De Witt's own province and the center of republican power, the outbreak of war with England brought with it a revival of Orangist agitation. "The clergy generally throughout Holland," remarked Edmund Ludlow with incredulity, prayed for Charles II "dignifying him in their expressions and prayers with the title of Sacred Majesty, and are for the setting up of his nephew the Prince of Orange."[20] These sentiments were not the ravings of a few renegade predikanten. Rumors spread that "many towns of Holland have proposed placing the prince on the Council of State."[21] All of the evidence did indeed support William Temple's assertion

15 This story is told in far greater detail than it can be here in Herbert Rowen, *John De Witt, Grand Pensionary of Holland, 1625–1672* (Princeton, 1978), pp. 574–682.

16 Downing to Arlington, 11 July 1665, PRO, SP 84/177, f.12v.

17 Downing to Arlington, 18 July 1665, PRO, SP 84/177, f. 26v; Downing to Clarendon, 20 January 1665, Bod., Clar. 108, f. 260v. The alliance with France is discussed more extensively below. De Witt always claimed, with some justice, that he was willing to negotiate but that Charles II was uninterested. See, for example, Sylvius to Arlington, 9/19 December 1665, PRO, SP 77/33, f. 353v.

18 Temple to Arlington, 28 December/7 January 1665/66, PRO, SP 77/35, f. 357v.

19 Newsletter from The Hague, 29 May/8 June 1666, BL, Add. 32094, f. 87v; Mons. Nypho to Arlington, 10/20 October 1666, PRO, SP 77/35, f. 198r.

20 Ludlow, "A Voyce," Bod., English History MSS C487, p. 1102.

21 Letter from The Hague, 29 November 1665, PRO, SP 84/178, f. 39r; see also Downing to Fanshawe, 22 June 1665, BL, Harleian MSS 7010, f. 305; newsletter from Rotterdam, 1/11 December 1665, PRO, SP 101/47, f. 319r; newsletter from The Hague, 13/23 February 1666, PRO, SP 101/48, f. 114r; Sylvius to Temple, 9/19 December 1665, PRO, SP 77/33, f. 371r.

that "the Prince of Orange's faction grows certainly in Holland more considerable."[22] In Amsterdam, where William III's father had received his most devastating political reversal, there was open discussion of "the change of the state and some move that the Prince of Orange be restored."[23] In Rotterdam a popular minister was exiled just before the war began for accusing the States General "of great ingratitude in forgetting the family of Orange, and comparing them to Nebuchadnezzar who was turned a grazing, and justifying the putting to death of Barnevelt."[24] Orangist sentiment soon resurfaced in Rotterdam, where by the summer it was "generally reported" among the populous that "the States' rejecting [of the Prince of Orange] is the main cause of the war."[25] When William visited Rotterdam the following spring he was "so thronged with people that they broke his coach and then took the coach up and him in it and carried it upon their shoulders."[26] In The Hague "all the popular preachers cry up the Prince of Orange as much as the Jews presently in expectation of their messiah."[27] At Leiden, a town with a much stronger Orangist tradition than Amsterdam, Rotterdam, or The Hague, when the drums began beating "for more men in the name of the States General, the women got about the drums and cut them in pieces crying out, the devil take the States, beat for the prince."[28] The citizens of the north Holland towns, towns which were also traditional centers of Orangism, "were entirely for peace and much inclined toward the Prince of Orange."[29]

Throughout Zeeland Orangist agitation began almost as quickly, as rumors of war with England spread from island to island. The Grand Pensionary of Holland and others of "the pure republican interest" quickly became suspicious of the Anglophilia of their Zeeland neighbors and "their

22 Temple to Carlingford, 3/13 March 1666, Beinecke Library, Osborn Collection, Carlingford Papers Box II (unfoliated); Temple to Ormonde, 2/12 March 1666, Carte 47, f. 273r.

23 Newsletter from Amsterdam, 11/21 October 1665, PRO, SP 101/47, f. 300r; Ludlow, "A Voyce," Bod., English History MSS C487, pp. 1088–1089.

24 Downing to Clarendon, 20 January 1665, Bod., Clar. 108, f. 260v.

25 Newsletter from Rotterdam, 16/26 June 1665, PRO, SP 101/47, f. 208r.

26 Hollis to William Coventry, 7/17 March 1666, BL, Althorp Papers C13 (unfoliated). See also Williamson's newsletter, 13 March 1666, Carte 222, f. 92; newsletter from The Hague, 6/16 March 1666, PRO, SP 101/48, f. 148v; newsletter from The Hague, 2/12 March 1666, PRO, SP 101/48, f. 142r.

27 Newsletter from The Hague, 9/19 March 1666, PRO, SP 101/48, f. 157r. For more about Orangism in The Hague, see also Downing to Clarendon, 13 January 1665, Bod., Clar. 108, f. 255r; newsletter from The Hague, 2/12 January 1666, Carte 222, f. 80r; newsletter from The Hague, 22 January/1 February 1666, PRO, SP 101/48, f. 51r.

28 Downing to Arlington, 9 June 1665, PRO, SP 84/176, f. 67r. See also newsletter from Rotterdam, 16/26 June 1665, PRO, SP 101/47, f. 208r; Thomas Corney (Amsterdam) to Thomas Kempe, 9/19 June 1665, PRO, SP 29/124/72I.

29 Sylvius to Arlington, 9/19 December 1665, PRO, SP 77/33, f. 354v. See also P. A. Rompf to his father, 29 November/9 December 1665, Goodison, "Buat Affair," p. 21; De Bacquoy/Van Ruyven to Bennet, 14/24 January 1666, PRO, SP 84/174, f. 37v; Downing to Clarendon, 20 January 1666, Bod., Clar. 108, f. 261v.

forwardness to set on foot the Prince of Orange's interest."[30] Every week brought news to Holland of Zeelanders insisting upon the "re-establishment of the Prince of Orange in the offices of his ancestors."[31] Almost every report claimed that in Zeeland the Prince of Orange's party "grows stronger every day."[32] Purveyors of gossip maintained that, upon assurances from Charles II "of freedom of commerce in all his Majesty's dominions," the magistrates of Zeeland were contemplating dividing "from Holland upon the Prince of Orange's interest."[33]

The Bishop of Munster's invasion of the United Provinces in the autumn of 1665, an invasion financed in part by and planned in consultation with England, raised the political temperature in the inland provinces as well.[34] As the bishop's troops advanced effortlessly across the inland provinces, the local inhabitants grew increasingly bitter at the inability of their government to protect them. The "swarms of women and children" who fled Friesland initiated "a great cry among the people for peace."[35] So successful was the Bishop of Munster's invasion "that most considering persons" concluded "that the Dutch are so far lost that they must betake themselves either to the French protection or to a truckling peace with England."[36] For many, especially for those in the traditionally Orangist inland provinces of Friesland, Groningen, Utrecht, and Overijssel, negotiation with England necessarily implied elevation of the Prince of Orange, the traditional leader of the Dutch land armies. Indeed Denzil Hollis, almost certainly relying upon French sources, learned that in the inland provinces "the Prince of Orange's party [was] beginning to stir." At Breda, for example, "the people cried openly in the streets 'Vivat the Prince of Orange and the Bishop of Munster,'" a conjunction which seemed perfectly natural since the Bishop of Munster's troops ostentatiously played Orangist tunes as they marched

30 Captain Honeywood to Bennet, 30 January 1665, PRO, SP 84/174, f. 58r.

31 Newsletter from The Hague, 14/24 December 1665, PRO, SP 101/47, f. 329v. See also Downing to Clarendon, 13 January 1666, Bod., Clar. 108, f. 256v; Downing to Bennet, 31 January 1666, PRO, SP 84/174, f. 73r; newsletter from The Hague, 22 September/2 October 1665, PRO, SP 101/47, f. 273r; St. Serfe's newsletter, 17 January 1666, LOC 18124 Vol. I, f. 21r; newsletter from The Hague, 20 February/2 March 1666, PRO, SP 101/48, f. 126r; newsletter from The Hague, 13/23 March 1666, PRO, SP 101/48, f. 166; newsletter from The Hague, 13/23 March 1666, PRO, SP 101/48, ff. 168–169; newsletter from The Hague, 20/30 March 1666, PRO, SP 101/48, f. 182v; St. Serfe's newsletter, 9 June 1666, LOC 18124, Vol. I, f. 76r.

32 Sylvius to Arlington, 28 November/8 December 1665, PRO, SP 77/33, f. 337v.

33 Letter from Rotterdam, 29 May 1665, PRO, SP 29/122/74. Although no evidence survives that an actual offer of a separate peace was made at this time to Zeeland, such ideas were frequently floated in the Privy Council. Coming so soon after the king's personal emancipation of Captain Evertson this story seems all too plausible.

34 For Bishop Von Galen of Munster's invasion in September 1665 and the negotiations which led up to it see Rowen, *John De Witt*, pp. 598–610; K. H. D. Haley, *An English Diplomat in the Low Countries* (Oxford, 1986), pp. 53-91.

35 Robert Southwell to Ormonde, 21 October 1665, Carte 34, f. 452v.

36 Temple to Arlington, 29 September/9 October 1665, PRO, SP 77/33, f. 294v; Temple to Arlington, 20/30 October 1665, PRO, SP 77/33, f. 307r.

by Deventer and Zwoll.[37] In Gelderland the English-bankrolled troops of the Bishop of Munster were playing their songs to committed Orangists. There had been an Orangist riot at Tiel when naval recruiters had sought able-bodied seamen in the name of the States General.[38] The following spring the Gelderland provincial assembly voted to make the young Prince of Orange captain general of their armed forces.[39] Groningen, Deventer, and Overijssel "seeing themselves reduced to misery" by the Bishop of Munster's forces had acted more quickly than their neighbor province. Not only did they propose that the States General name the Prince of Orange captain general and admiral but they also proposed that he lead an ambassadorial mission to his uncle Charles II asking for peace and political alliance.[40]

The economic devastation of the war in the maritime provinces combined with the military destruction in the inland provinces brought on by the Bishop of Munster's invasion revitalized the Orangist movement throughout the United Provinces. By the winter of 1665–1666 events seemed about to prove George Downing – who had predicted long before that any military setback would provoke "strange doings" in the United Provinces – a prophet.[41] "If the war continues," enthused the Orangist Gabriel Sylvius, "it will be a miracle if there is not an insurrection for the people murmur loudly against the government and speak openly of the restoration of the Prince of Orange."[42] Upon traversing the United Provinces on his diplomatic mission to Germany Sir Walter Vane concluded that "all the provinces are inclined to the re-establishment of the Prince of Orange."[43] "Impartial letters of men of known discretion" concurred with "the general opinion of the people" in the Netherlands that "the Prince of Orange's faction will carry it against De Witt."[44]

37 Hollis to Arlington, 18/28 October 1665, PRO, SP 78/121, f. 123.

38 Downing to Arlington, 20 June 1665, PRO, SP 84/176, f. 84r.

39 Newsletter from The Hague, 6/16 April 1666, PRO, SP 101/48, f. 228v.

40 John Evelyn, notes for history of the second Dutch War, Christ Church, Evelyn Letters 134, f. 2; Propositions of the States of Overijssel, 24 October 1665, PRO, SP 84/178, f. 198r. See also newsletter from United Provinces, 10/20 October 1665, PRO, SP 101/47, f. 298r; Allen Broderick to Ormonde, 22 October 1665, Carte 34, f. 448v; Temple to Ormonde, 27 October/6 November 1665, Carte 47, f. 264; William Coventry to Ormonde, 29 October 1665, Carte 47, f. 429r; Arlington to Ormonde, 1 November 1665, Carte 46, f. 220r; Temple to Arlington, 24 October/3 November 1665, PRO, SP 77/33, ff. 312-313; Thomas Rugge, "Mercurius Politicus Redivivus," October 1665, BL, Add. 10117, f. 148r. Apparently the proposal was seconded by Friesland in the States General. See Ludlow, "A Voyce," Bod., English History MSS C487, p. 1100.

41 Downing to Arlington, 19 May 1665, PRO, SP 84/176, f. 38r.

42 Sylvius to Temple, 9/19 December 1665, PRO, SP 77/33, f. 371r. See also Sylvius to Arlington, 28 November/8 December 1665, Goodison, "Buat Affair," pp. 19–20; Sylvius to Williamson, 9/19 December 1665, Goodison, "Buat Affair," pp. 24–25; Sylvius to Arlington, 9/19 Deecember 1665, Goodison, "Buat Affair," p. 29.

43 Sir Walter Vane to Arlington, 29 December/8 January 1665, BL, Add. 16272, f. 25r.

44 St. Serfe's newsletter, 12 December 1665, 22 February 1666, LOC, 18124 Vol. I, ff. 12r, 32r; see also [James Ralph], *The History of England* (London, 1744), Vol. I, p. 111.

Charles II and his privy councilors, indeed all England, were fully cognizant that an Orangist revolution would necessarily, indeed was intended to, bring an end to the war. "One victory more," William Temple predicted, would give Charles II a peace with the Dutch "upon his own terms."[45] "If it please God to give us the blessing to beat them once more soundly," chimed in Sir Robert Moray, then nothing could "hinder us from being *les maîstres*."[46] After reviewing the news of the Dutch economic plight, of the successes of Munster's armies, of English-supported Orangist activity, Arlington gleefully reported in letter after letter that "when the Hollanders shall make up their accounts of this year's losses and expenses I believe they will not go with any heart to the undertaking of another."[47]

Nevertheless the Dutch did not capitulate that winter. No Orangist revolution took place. The English had always known that the Dutch republican regime had a choice – they could accept "a sudden and submissive peace" with England or they could take the "desperate measures of falling under the French king's protection."[48] The English simply could not bring themselves to believe that a Dutch regime, even one so corrupt as that of De Witt, would sacrifice its political independence to so powerful a neighbor. But this was exactly the option John De Witt and his political allies selected in the face of the Bishop of Munster's invasion. "That faction which ever opposed the House of Orange seeing themselves on the brink of destruction," the East India merchant Peter Vandeputt informed George Oxenden, "have now brought in the French amongst them for their private ends, which in the end might prove worse than an open enemy to the country."[49] De Witt turned to France despite his fear of "their greatness," the diplomat Sir Walter Vane concurred, because in the face of "the great inclination everybody had for the restoring the House of Orange" he thought that was "his last refuge."[50]

The French troops which arrived to defend the United Provinces against Munster's invasion, and the subsequent French declaration of war against England, completely altered the political situation in the United Provinces.

45 William Temple to Arlington, 18/28 August 1665, PRO, SP 77/33, f. 267v.

46 Sir Robert Moray to Oldenburg, 9 September 1665, in Rupert A. Hall and Marie Boas Hall (editors), *The Correspondence of Henry Oldenburg*, Vol. II–VI (Madison, 1966–1967), Vol. III, pp. 504–505.

47 Arlington to Carlingford, 23 September 1665, in Karl Taaffe (editor), *Memoirs of the Family of Taaffe* (Vienna, 1856), p. 65; Arlington to Fanshawe, 23 September 1665, BL, Harleian MSS 7010, f. 404v; Arlington to Temple, 23 September 1665, in Thomas Bebington (editor), *The Right Honourable the Earl of Arlington 's Letters ...* (London, 1701), Vol. I, p. 31.

48 William Temple to Thomas Clifford, 20/30 September 1665, NMM, Clifford Papers Vol. II, Dw87.

49 Peter Vandeputt to George Oxenden, 16 March 1666, BL, Add. 40712, f. 53r.

50 Sir Walter Vane to Arlington, 8/18 December 1665, BL, Add. 16272, f. 11r. Some claimed that De Witt did not fear the French because they did not represent an economic threat. Newsletter from The Hague, 13/23 March 1666, PRO, SP 101/48, f. 169v.

"Ever since France declared itself so openly for Holland," reported one of Williamson's informants from the continent, "the face of affairs here has radically changed."[51] "The King of France's declaration hath put new life into the governing party there," thought Arlington.[52] New life indeed. The pivotal magistracy elections in Amsterdam, which had previously appeared to be delicately poised between the Loevesteen and Orangist parties, now swung in the direction of De Witt and his political allies.[53] The language of Dutch political discourse was now spoken with a French accent. The French ambassador d'Estrades and the Holland Grand Pensionary were always to be found in tandem, William Temple related to Arlington, so that De Witt "is by all there thought to be too firmly linked with the French ever to be removed."[54] The Dutch republicans were now said to be thoroughly "influenced by France," to have become "the French party" or a "French faction."[55] There now seemed to be little hope that an Orangist popular rebellion, even one with the implicit support of the King of England, could succeed in overthrowing John De Witt and in ending the Anglo-Dutch conflict.

It was not long before French political and military support for the Dutch republican regime had its effect. The Prince of Orange, who only months before had seemed likely to become captain general of the Dutch armed forces,[56] was made by John De Witt and his Holland supporters "a child of the States."[57] This political maneuver entailed placing the young prince's education in the hands of a predominantly republican commission headed by De Witt himself. The Orangists and Anglophiles who had previously made up the prince's little court were summarily dismissed, in some cases with pensions, leaving observers to conclude that the Prince of

51 Nypho to Williamson, 14/24 February 1666, PRO, SP 77/34, f. 76r.

52 Arlington to Ormonde, 6 February 1666, Carte 46, f. 250. See also William Morrice to Henry Coventry, 23 February 1666, Longleat House, Cov. MSS LXIV, f. 313v.

53 Sir Walter Vane to Arlington, 15/25 December 1665, BL, Add. 16272, f. 14r; Vane to Arlington, 30 January/9 February 1666, BL, Add. 16272, f. 49r.

54 Temple to Arlington, 6/16 March 1666, PRO, SP 77/34, f. 114r.

55 Arlington to Ormonde, 19 December 1665, Carte 46, f. 231; Arlington to Temple, 9 February 1666, Bebington, *Arlington's Letters*, Vol. I, p. 59; St. Serfe's newsletter, 28 April 1666, LOC, 18124 Vol. I, f. 58r.

56 On the Captain General dispute see Rowen, *John De Witt*, pp. 668–671; newsletter from The Hague, 12/22 January 1666, PRO, SP 101/48, ff. 28r, 35r; newsletter from The Hague, 22 January/1 February 1666, PRO, SP 101/48, ff. 50–51; newsletter from The Hague, 25 January/4 February 1666, PRO, SP 101/48, f. 57; newsletter from The Hague, 30 January/9 February 1666, PRO, SP 101/48, ff. 72–73; newsletter from The Hague, 9/19 February 1666, PRO, SP 101/48, f. 102Ar; newsletter from The Hague, 13/23 February 1666, PRO, SP 101/48, ff. 111r, 114r; St. Serfe's newsletter, 15 February 1666, LOC, 18124 Vol. I, f. 30r; Arlington to Ormonde, 17 February 1666, Carte 46, f. 256r; newsletter from The Hague, 18/28 February 1666, PRO, SP 101/48, f. 121r; newsletter from The Hague, 20 February/2 March 1666, PRO, SP 101/48, f. 122r; newsletter from The Hague, 20/30 March 1666, PRO, SP 101/48, f. 187r.

57 Letter to Philip Froude, 6 April 1666, National Library of Scotland, Adv. MSS 19–1–26, f. 61r.

Orange's "party will find themselves frustrated of their expectations and designs."[58] "They have not so much as left him a footman that he had, but changed all," exclaimed Denzil Hollis.[59] There could be no doubting that with this triumph over the Orangists "Monsieur De Witt is become master of that party."[60]

Purging the prince's household confirmed for all who cared to comment that the political balance in the United Provinces had shifted back in favor of the republican party. That it had done so was largely because the French intervention had not only vastly increased De Witt's prestige, it had compelled the Bishop of Munster to accept a peace and withdraw from the war.[61] The implications of the bishop's surrender, leaving England without an ally in the war, were immediately apparent. While the prospects for the House of Orange recently had appeared to be quite rosy, the normally optimistic Arlington informed Ormonde that "the delivery from the bishop may perhaps change the face of things again and leave us with no other hope than what we can gain by our swords."[62] "Those of the prince's party had hoped to gain a great deal by this land war," noted one particularly lucid intelligencer, however they "now see themselves trumped by this peace and the prince forced to undergo a second childhood."[63]

While the republican resurgence was initially buoyed by the Dutch naval victory in the Four Days Battle, the English victory in the St. James's Day Fight (25 July 1666) followed quickly by Sir Robert Holmes's spectacular raid on the Vlie breathed new life into the Orangist cause. Convinced that his defeat at the hands of the English navy on St. James's day had been the result of treachery, De Ruyter vowed that "several of my captains and particularly Tromp shall answer for it."[64] Within days the Dutch seaman Cornelius Van Tromp, who "the previous month had been liberator and defender of their country," was publicly denounced as a traitor on the streets of Rotterdam, Amsterdam, and The Hague.[65] When the States of Holland relieved him of his command it was widely perceived to have been because Van Tromp "was of entire devotion to the Prince of Orange, as his father had always been, and all his children continued to be."[66] Immediately

58 Newsletter from The Hague, 3/13 April 1666, PRO, SP 101/48, f. 225r. See also newsletter from The Hague, 3/13 April 1666, PRO, SP 101/48, f. 221r; newsletter from The Hague, 6/16 April 1666, PRO, SP 101/48, ff. 232–233.

59 Hollis to Arlington, 11/21 April 1666, PRO, SP 78/122, f. 140v; see also St. Serfe's newsletter, 7 April 1666, LOC, 18124 Vol. I, f. 50r.

60 Letter from The Hague, 7/17 April 1666, PRO, SP 101/48, f. 239r.

61 Haley, *English Diplomat*, pp. 82–87.

62 Arlington to Ormonde, 21 April 1666, Carte 46, f. 288.

63 Newsletter from The Hague, 17/27 April 1666, PRO, SP 101/48, f. 272v (my translation).

64 William Temple to Ormonde, 7/17 August 1666, Carte 72, f. 86r.

65 Newsletter from Antwerp, 4/14 August 1666, PRO, SP 77/35, f. 15v (my translation).

66 Edward Hyde, *The Life of Edward Earl of Clarendon* (Dublin, 1760), p. 275. See also Ludlow, "A Voyce," Bod., English History MSS C487, p. 1071.

the fleet, and the entire United Provinces, entered "into the quarrel of their chiefs."[67] "They are in a great confusion there," Dr. William Denton informed his friend Sir Ralph Verney, "peaching one another of cowardice."[68] In Holland republican mariners openly proclaimed that "if a Zeelander [were to be] in danger next fight they will not relieve [him]."[69] Elsewhere "the seamen and soldiers [were] much dejected and ... extremely passionate for Van Tromp."[70] "Whenever Tromp shows himself in [The Hague]," reported the Venetian Giustinian, "he is always received with great acclamations, exalting his name and the House of Orange."[71] So passionate had party feeling among the sailors become that in Flushing and elsewhere "in the streets of Zeeland" the mariners "kill and stab one another daily."[72] All of this made Thomas St. Serfe seem prescient for having predicted that "the laying aside of Tromp may be of dangerous consequence both because he was a popular man among the mariners and is likewise beloved of the Prince of Orange's faction."[73]

The English victories which gave rise to party violence in the fleet had no less of an impact on the rest of Dutch society. "There had never been seen so great an uproar" as was witnessed at The Hague after news began to filter in of the defeat of the Dutch fleet on St. James's Day.[74] After the burning of the Dutch ships in the Vlie, Amsterdam was the site of unprecedented "desolation and mourning."[75] "Mothers cry and mourn for their children, wives for their husbands, sisters for their brothers, and poor orphans for their fathers, such is the desolation that there is among them," noted one sympathetic observer; "they say one to another that the English are too powerful for us, and it would be much better if we concluded a peace."[76] Clarendon pithily observed that the English victories "hath put them all out of their wits."[77]

Just as defeat had politicized the Dutch seamen, so it reinvigorated the ideological struggle between Orangists and Loevesteeners in the Dutch towns. In Amsterdam, Rotterdam, and The Hague "the Orange party is

67 [Ralph], *History*, Vol. I, pp. 133–134.
68 Dr. William Denton to Sir Ralph Verney, 2 August 1666, Firestone Library, Verney MSS Reel 21 (unfoliated).
69 Ed. Custis to Arlington, 26 August/5 September 1666, PRO, SP 77/35, f. 96.
70 ? to Sir Philip Froude, 29 August/8 September 1666, PRO, SP 77/35, f. 101r.
71 Giustinian to Doge and Senate, 28 August/7 September 1666, *CSPV*, p. 65.
72 Ed. Custis to Arlington, 26 August/5 September 1666, PRO, SP 77/35, f. 96r; William Scott's answers to Aphra Behn, 21 September 1666, PRO, SP 29/172/81I; see also News from Antwerp, 22 August/1 September 1666, PRO, SP 77/35, f. 81.
73 St. Serfe's newsletter, 23 August 1666, LO, 18124 Vol. I, f. 102v.
74 William Temple to Ormonde, 7/17 August 1666, Carte 72, f. 87r.
75 Aphra Behn to Mr. Halsall, 27 August 1666, PRO, SP 29/169/38; Temple to Ormonde, 18/28 August 1666, Carte 47, f. 291v.
76 Newsletter from Antwerp, 4/14 August 1666, PRO, SP 77/35, f. 15.
77 Clarendon to Ormonde, 18 August 1666, Carte 47, f. 125v.

increasing and many adherents are disclosing themselves."[78] "At night from the cabarets and crossroads of Amsterdam, The Hague and elsewhere," reported one intelligencer, "one hears cries of 'Long Live the Prince of Orange' while the sailors cry 'Long Live Tromp.' "[79] The North Holland towns of Haarlem, Enckhuysen, and Hoorn soon "declared for the Prince of Orange," following the lead of much of Zeeland.[80] Throughout the United Provinces there was "great animosity of one against another, and faction against faction."[81]

It was clear to all that the Dutch Republic was again ripe for revolution in the autumn of 1666. "Things are in so universal a disorder," reported the government spy and future dramatist extraordinaire Aphra Behn, "that if God give our fleet good success at sea we shall see strange things."[82] Indeed many knowledgeable observers of Dutch politics were convinced that "upon the least misfortune a revolution in the States was to be apprehended," that "if they should have a defeat, [it] will undo De Witt."[83] The Dutch "distempers" were "much about the same height as was that of the English nation in the year 1659 when the Rump first began their fatal end," commented the Scots newsletter-writer Thomas St. Serfe.[84] An English newsletter predicted the following week that if the Dutch "receive a blow this next engagement, De Witt will be lost and the Prince of Orange will up."[85]

78 Arlington to Ormonde, 23 August 1666, Carte 46, f. 358r; Giustinian to Doge and Senate, 4/14 September 1666, *CSPV*, p. 67.

79 News from Antwerp, 8/18 September 1666, PRO, SP 77/35, f. 125r.

80 William Temple to Arlington, 6/16 September 1666, PRO, SP 77/35, f. 119r; newsletter from Holland, 27 August/6 September 1666, PRO, SP 101/50, f. 53.

81 News from Antwerp, 5/15 September 1666, PRO, SP 77/35, f. 116; see also Thomas Corney to Nicholas Oudart, 25 August/4 September 1666, PRO, SP 77/35, f. 92r.

82 Aphra Behn to Halsall, 14 September 1666, PRO, SP 29/171/120. This was common gossip in Italy as well: Joseph Kent to Williamson, 8/18 September 1666, PRO, SP 85/8, f. 128r. English merchants heard similar tales from their Dutch counterparts: see John and Charles Banks to Thomas Clifford, 21 August 1666, PRO, SP 82/11, f. 31r.

83 ? to Sir Philip Froude, 28 July/7 August 1666, PRO, SP 77/34, f. 414v; Pepys, *Diary*, Vol. VII, 23 July 1666, p. 216 (reporting the opinions of William Coventry and George Downing). See also Benjamin Glanville to Williamson, 19/29 August 1666, PRO, SP 77/35, f. 70r.

84 St. Serfe's newsletter, 25 August 1666, LOC, 18124 Vol. I, f. 103r.

85 Williamson's newsletter, 3 September 1666, PRO, SP 29/170/57. See also Arlington to Ormonde, 23 August 1666, Carte 46, f. 358v; Arlington to Ormonde, 28 August 1666, Carte 46, f. 359v; William Temple to Lord Lisle, August 1666, in *The Works of Sir William Temple* (London, 1814), Vol. I, p. 254; Temple to Arlington, 2 July 1666, Carte 35, f. 5r; Temple to Ormonde, 3/13 July 1666, Carte 47, f. 287r; Temple to Carlingford, [18/28 August 1666], *Memoirs of Taaffe*, p. 162; Temple to Arlington, 18/28 August 1666, PRO, SP 77/35, f. 62v; Temple to Carlingford, 25 August/4 September 1666, *Memoirs of Taaffe*, p. 163; Temple to Carlingford, 1/11 September 1666, *Memoirs of Taaffe*, pp. 163–164. So confident were the English that revolution was imminent that in late August all London thought De Witt had fled the country: William Coventry to Ormonde, 18 August 1666, Carte 47, f. 461v; Pepys, *Diary*, Vol. VII, 16 August 1666, p. 250; St. Serfe's newsletter, 21 August 1666, LOC,18124 Vol. I, f. 101r.

Despite the unpredictable vicissitudes of early modern warfare and the domestic devastation wrought by the plague,[86] then, in the autumn of 1666 the restored English monarchy was on the threshold of achieving its war aims. Dissenters had been politically cowed – the pipeline of arms and ideas which ran from the religiously tolerant Holland towns to the underground conventicles in England's metropolis and throughout the countryside had failed to mount a single serious threat to the government's stability. Instead it was the republican regime in the United Provinces, that source of seditious principles and fount of unbridled ambition, which tottered on the precipice of destruction. By the late summer and early autumn English men and women throughout the country were confident that they were about to win the war with the Dutch. Certain that he and his navy "shall give them another blow" the Duke of Albemarle bragged that the Dutch "will be easily persuaded to give his Majesty satisfaction."[87] "Holmes' exploit puts us almost into a transport," rejoiced Sir Roger Burgoyne, "it may prove a means to procure us an honorable and lasting peace."[88] With "a happy issue of the next engagement," Joseph Williamson confidently predicted in his widely disseminated newsletter, "in all probability the war will be at an end, so near are [the Dutch] to total confusion at home."[89]

86 For the effects of the plague see Paul Slack, *The Impact of Plague in Tudor and Stuart England* (Oxford, 1985), *passim*; Ronald Hutton, *The Restoration* (Oxford, 1985), pp. 225–233.

87 Albemarle to Arlington, 8 August 1666, PRO, SP 29/166/146. It is true, of course, that Albemarle had long predicted an easy victory over the Dutch, but this letter reflects a political rather than a military assessment. For his earlier brags see: William Sancroft to Thomas Sancroft, 1 January 1666, Bod., Tanner MSS 45, f. 53r; Arlington to Temple, 9 February 1666, Bebington, *Arlington's Letters*, Vol. I, p. 61.

88 Sir Roger Burgoyne to Sir Ralph Verney, 19 August 1666, Firestone Library, Verney MSS Reel 21 (unfoliated). For others who believed the victory would lead to peace see John Maurice (Minehead) to James Hickes, 7 August 1666, PRO, SP 29/166/119. This view was, of course, consonant with official assessments: Sir Thomas Clifford to Arlington, 11 July 1666, PRO, SP 29/162/73; Arlington to Ormonde, 31 July 1666, Carte 46, f. 343r. For a merchant's view see William Atwood (London) to Richard Wickstead, 4 August 1666, PRO, C109/23 Pt. II (unfoliated) and a similar view from Amsterdam: H. O. to Williamson, 14/24 August 1666, PRO, SP 101/50, f. 168.

89 Williamson's Newsletter, 3 September 1666, PRO, SP 29/170/57; see also John Lysle (West Cowes) to Williamson, 3 September 1666, PRO, SP 29/170/46.

22

Victory denied and wartime consensus shattered

The clinching English victory never came. Instead of bonfires lighting English celebrations, and great guns informing the countryside of English victories the following summer brought with it the flames of English men-of-war fired in the Medway by the Dutch navy and the sounds of Dutch guns bombarding the English coast. What had happened? Why did the English, who had seemed to be on the threshold of a total victory over the Dutch and their allies in the autumn of 1666, suffer such an ignominious defeat at the hands of the Dutch republican leader John De Witt the following summer?

At the exact moment in which English hopes for victory were being widely expressed, they received a damaging blow in the Netherlands. In early August 1666 the English government's chief Orangist agent, the Sieur de Buat, mistakenly delivered to John De Witt a letter from Arlington which "enlightened" De Witt as to "the design of promoting the sovereignty of the Prince of Orange, and of the constraining of the States to conclude a peace to the betraying of their liberties."[1] Buat was quickly incarcerated, brought to trial and ultimately beheaded for his treason.[2] At his trial, Buat claimed – and the States General did everything to publicize Buat's statements in his own defense – that "what he did was with a good intention," an intention to "make the King of England the greatest monarch in the world."[3]

The charges against Buat were not trumped up. He had long been working in close concert with Arlington, Clarendon, and Charles himself. Buat passionately believed that his actions were all intended "only to settle a good peace and promote the interest of his master the Prince of Orange," an interest which he perceived to be indifferentiable from that of the United

1 Ludlow, "A Voyce," Bod., English History MSS C487, p. 1129. This episode is discussed from the Dutch perspective most fully by Rowen, *John De Witt, Grand Pensionary of Holland, 1625–1672* (Princeton, 1978), 613–622.

2 Nypho to Arlington, 11/21 August 1666, PRO, SP 77/35, f. 38r; *Current Intelligence*, 16–20 August 1666 (unpaginated); Thomas Corney to Williamson, 6/16 October 1666, PRO, SP 77/35, f. 135r.

3 John Evelyn, notes for history of second Dutch War, Christ Church, Evelyn MSS 134, p. 35; Ludlow, "A Voyce," Bod., English History MSS C487, p. 1134.

Provinces as a whole.[4] Passionate, extremist, and blundering Buat might have been, but he was not politically inept. By the late summer Buat had drawn "many of the greatest amongst the burgomasters to delight in his conversation and to trust him much."[5] He had, thought a Venetian observer, tapped into a party "numerous and powerful in the Provinces."[6] Arlington's assessment after the St. James's Day battle that "this was the time ... to promote the Orange faction in council, city and country" was merited by Buat's political achievement.[7]

Buat's arrest meant much more to the English than simply the demise of a sympathetic politician.[8] It signaled the collapse of the Orangist cause. The States General left no stone unturned in "the discovery and pursuit of the accomplices of Buat."[9] Upon pressure and threats of torture, and perhaps because of his own conviction that his actions had been perfectly justified, Buat revealed the names of more than sixty political allies – many of them highly placed in the Dutch government – who were all committed to the Orangist cause and to peace with England.[10]

These revelations initiated a mass exodus of Orangists, stumbling over one another to reach the borders of the United Provinces before De Witt and the States General were able to have them imprisoned. Most spectacularly John Kievet, Van Tromp's brother-in-law, burgomaster of Rotterdam and "next to De Witt the most considerable man" in Holland, fled to England.[11] One deputy of the States of Holland was dismissed for visiting

4 Muddiman's newsletter, 30 August 1666, PRO, SP 29/169/96; Sylvius to Arlington, 9/19 December 1665, in R. R. Goodison (editor), "Further Correspondence Relating to the Buat Affair," in *Bijdragen en Medeelingin van het Historisch Genootschap* Vol. 38, p. 27.

5 Edward Hyde, *The Life of Edward Earl of Clarendon* (Dublin, 1760), pp. 331–332.

6 Giustinian to Doge and Senate, 28 August/7 September 1666, *CSPV*, p. 63. For evidence of his earlier activity and attempts to convert Beverning to the Orangist cause see Sylvius to Arlington, 25 November/5 December 1665, PRO, SP 77/33, f. 335r; P. A. Rompf (The Hague) to his father, 29 November/9 December 1665, Goodison, "Buat Affair," p. 21; Sir Walter Vane to Arlington, 8/18 December 1665, BL, Add. 16272, f. 11r; Sylvius to Arlington, 9/19 December 1665, PRO, SP 77/33, f. 353r; Sir Walter Vane to Arlington, 29 December/8 January 1665/6, BL, Add. 16272, f. 24r.

7 Ludlow, "A Voyce," Bod., English History MSS C487, pp. 1128–1129 (based on Arlington's letter seized from Buat).

8 For evidence of English popular discussions of the event see Oldenburg to Boyle, 16 October 1666, Rupert A. Hall and Marie Boas Hall (editors), *The Corespondence of Henry Oldenburg*, Vols. II–VI (Madison, 1966–1967), Vol. III, p. 245; J. J. (Newcastle) to Richard Forster, 5 November 1666, PRO, SP 29/177/86I; newsletter from Antwerp, 29 September/9 October 1666, PRO, SP 77/35, f. 169r.

9 Temple to Ormonde, 12/22 October 1666, Carte 47, f. 300; Giustinian to Doge and Senate, 11/21 September 1666, *CSPV*, p. 74; Ludlow, "A Voyce," Bod., English History MSS C487, p. 1134.

10 Arlington to Ormonde, 23 August 1666, Carte 46, f. 358.

11 Temple to Carlingford, 1/11 September 1666, in Karl Taaffe (editor), *Memoirs of the Family of Taaffe* (Vienna, 1856), p. 164; Hyde, *Life*, p. 337; newsletter from The Hague, 20/30 August 1666, PRO, SP 101/50, f. 277; James Banckes to Thomas Banckes, 26 August/5 September 1666, PRO, SP 77/35, f. 95r; Ludlow, "A Voyce," Bod., English History MSS C487, p. 1129; entry to Ormonde, 26 August 1666, Carte 47, f. 462r.

Buat in prison.[12] Another had his cushion removed for admitting that his father had been an Orangist.[13] The honor guard of the States General was summarily purged not only of its Orangist officers but also of all Orangist symbols and insignia.[14] The supporters of De Ruyter and the republican party decisively won the ideological struggle in the Dutch navy.[15] Although it no doubt took longer for the republican triumph to reach the local governments, by the following spring it was clear that "the magistrates of the towns [are] almost all creatures of the Pensionary."[16] There could be no doubting the extent of the republican victory. "The friends and good servants of the Prince of Orange are oppressed and persecuted," was the unanimous conclusion of the observers of the Dutch political scene.[17]

The effect of the republican political triumph upon Anglo-Dutch relations was immediately apparent.[18] The result of Buat's demise, Clarendon recalled from his French exile, was that "the Prince was much lower than before, and all hopes of reviving almost extinguished or expired; De Witt stood firmer upon his own feet than ever, and directed all preparations for the war without control; and all the present expectations in England vanished."[19] All of the contemporary evidence supports the Lord Chancellor's assessment. There could be little hope for an immediate peace, opined one of Arlington's political informants, "because De Witt and all his faction are as powerful as ever and the entire party of the Prince of Orange is oppressed and persecuted."[20] Arlington himself concluded that "the cutting off [of] poor Buat's head is likely to terrify all that party which so earnestly desires [peace]."[21] The Dublin merchant and former unofficial contact

12 Aphra Behn (Antwerp) to Halsall, 14 September 1666, PRO, SP 29/171/120.

13 Newsletter from The Hague, 6/16 September 1666, Carte 47, f. 298r.

14 Hyde, *Life*, p. 337.

15 Giustinian to Doge and Senate, 21/31 August 1666, *CSPV*, p. 61; Jo. Carlisle (Dover) to Williamson, 24 August 1666, PRO, SP 29/168/138; Jo. Carlisle (Dover) to Williamson, 26 August 1666, PRO, SP 29/169/9; Aphra Behn to Halsall, 27 August 1666, PRO, SP 29/169/38; Ludlow, "A Voyce," Bod., English History MSS C487, p. 1143.

16 Newsletter from Flanders, 9/19 March 1667, PRO, SP 77/36, f. 125r (my translation).

17 Letter to Arlington, 18/28 August 1666, PRO, SP 77/35, f. 64v (my translation). See also Nypho to Arlington, 1/11 September 1666, PRO, SP 77/35, f. 108; Temple to Ormonde, 18/28 August 1666, Carte 47, f. 291v; Temple to Arlington, 24 August/3 September 1666, PRO, SP 77/35, f. 93r.

18 K. H. D. Haley, *An English Diplomat in the Low Countries* (Oxford, 1968), p. 97.

19 Hyde, *Life*, p. 337.

20 Letter to Arlington, 13/23 October 1666, PRO, SP 77/35, f. 203v; see also Temple to Arlington, 5/15 October 1666, PRO, SP 77/35, f. 181v; Temple to Arlington, 18/28 September 1666, PRO, SP 77/35, ff. 142–143; Temple to Arlington, 23 November/3 December 1666, PRO, SP 77/35, f. 287.

21 Arlington to Ormonde, 13 October 1666, Carte 46, f. 385v. See also Pepys, *Diary*, Vol. VII, 8 October 1666, p. 315. From the perspective of republican sympathizers De Witt's revival was a natural revulsion against foreign intervention. "The more our enemies exclaim upon De Witt and the other patriots of our country," argued one newsletter-writer, "the more sensibly we find them to be the support of the nation." newsletter from Holland, 9/19 November 1666, PRO, SP 101/50, f. 90. This was the general consensus: St.

between the Rump and the States General, Toby Bonnel, knew that "the Dutch are generally for keeping up this war hoping yet to make their gains by it," pointing out that however popular the Orangist seaman Cornelius Van Tromp might once have been now "the children spit at him for a false hearted traitor."[22] The political implications of the failed Orangist revolution were not hard to discern. "It seems in short," Temple advised Arlington who almost certainly understood the situation all too well, "if his Majesty desires only a general peace, and to end where he began, it is in his hands, if an advantageous peace he must expect another conjuncture."[23]

The collapse of the Orangist party, then, explains the failure of the English to achieve their war aims in the autumn of 1666. A second development in September 1666, this time within England, shattered the popular mood of enthusiasm and confidence. On 2 September, in Pudding Lane, a fire began in a baker's shop which soon engulfed the entire city of London, and many of its suburbs. When the flames finally subsided, they were revealed to have transformed the economically thriving metropolis into a city of ashes. "We have undergone the highest calamity this nation hath ever felt by a terrible fire which hath destroyed three parts of four of the whole city of London," a still shocked Clarendon informed the Earl of Winchilsea.[24] "I believe there never was any such desolation by fire since the destruction of Jerusalem," scribbled a thoroughly shaken Sir Heneage Finch to his friend Viscount Conway, "nor will be till the last and general conflagration."[25] Naturally since London was very much the economic fulcrum around which England's commerce turned, the devastating effects of the Fire were felt throughout the country.[26] "The money, the furnishings, the precious capital lost," led a Venetian observer and many subsequent historians to conclude that the Fire "will constrain the English to abandon

Serfe's newsletter, 18 October 1666, LOC, 18124, Vol. I, f. 122r; Muddiman's newsletter, 1 November 1666, PRO, SP 29/177/6. See also Temple to Arlington, 26 October/5 November 1666, PRO, SP 77/35, f. 277r; Temple to Arlington, 30 October/9 November 1666, PRO, SP 77/35, f. 231; Temple to Arlington, 23 November/3 December 1666, PRO, SP 77/35, f. 287r; Allan Broderick to Ormonde, 10 November 1666, Carte 35, f. 122r; Thomas Corney to Nicholas Oudart, 7/17 December 1666, PRO, SP 77/35, f. 324r.

22 Toby Bonnel (Dublin) to John Johnson, 23 October 1666, CUL, Add. 4, f. 4v.

23 Temple to Arlington, 5/15 October 1666, PRO, SP 77/35, f. 181v.

24 Clarendon to Winchilsea, 20 September 1666, LRO, DG7/Box 4984, Letters Folder. For other reactions to the Fire, see James Oxenden to George Oxenden, 8 January 1667, BL, Add. 40713, f. 29r; Humphrey Bishop of London to Sancroft, 10 September 1666, Bod., Tanner MSS 45, f. 101r.

25 Sir Heneage Finch to Lord Conway, 8 September 1666, HL, HA 14724. The number of people shocked and devastated by the Fire of London could be multiplied endlessly. The most thorough discussion of the Fire remains Walter George Bell, *The Great Fire of London in 1666* (London, 1920).

26 See for, example, Ralph Hope (Coventry) to Williamson, 9 September 1666, PRO, SP 29/171/12; Thomas Waade (Whitby) to Williamson, 10 September 1666, PRO, SP 29/171/41.

their high pretensions and to humble themselves before" the King of France.[27]

The Fire triggered a sea-change in national sentiment. While Sir Robert Holmes's dramatic raid on the Vlie had prompted national celebrations and prophecies of a victorious peace, the Great Fire prompted national lamentations and predictions of impending doom. "Everybody," thought Samuel Pepys after the Fire, was "prophesying destruction to the nation."[28] "Our native country is full of wastes, sadness, and murmurings," exclaimed one merchant.[29] To his friend Sir George Rawdon, Viscount Conway reported that "the next year is expected by all men to be a year of trouble and confusion."[30] Nearly all of Samuel Pepys's many and varied acquaintances were speaking the language of doom and gloom in the autumn of 1666. His cousin Roger Pepys, a country member of Parliament, was "confident we shall all be ruined very speedily."[31] Sir George Carteret, the Anglican Royalist treasurer of the navy, spoke "of the general complexion of matters ... with horror and gives us all for an undone people." The Presbyterian Denzil Hollis reputedly "wept to think in what a condition [we] are fallen."[32] The Anglican Royalist merchants Sir Richard Ford and Captain George Cocke, both of whom had been extremely confident of an absolute victory over the Dutch a few short months before, now were convinced "that we must be undone in a little time."[33]

It was no doubt this general malaise, this sense of inexorable decline, which provoked so many popular disturbances throughout the country.[34] Almost as

27 Giustinian to Doge and Senate, 18/28 September 1666, *CSPV*, p. 78. I hope to show below that, while the economic devastation wrought by the Fire should not be minimized, it was political considerations not economic ones which prevented the English from sending out a fleet in 1667. I am arguing that the real devastation engendered by the Fire was on the national psyche; it revealed deep ideological fissures hitherto submerged below an ostensible Anglican Royalist consensus.

28 Pepys, *Diary*, Vol. VII, 2 December 1666, p. 395. See also Pepys, *Diary*, Vol. VII, 12 November 1666, p. 366.

29 Thomas Lacherly to George Oxenden, 11 March 1667, BL, Add. 40713, ff. 4–5; see also James Oxenden to George Oxenden, 8 January 1667, BL, Add. 40713, f. 28v.

30 Edward Conway to Sir George Rawdon, 17 November 1666, HL, HA 14447. See his similar statement in Conway to Ormonde, 13 November 1666, Carte 35, f. 126v.

31 Pepys, *Diary*, Vol. VII 26 November 1666, p. 387.

32 Pepys, *Diary*, Vol. VII, 14 November 1666, pp. 369–370.

33 Pepys, *Diary*, Vol. VII, 18 November 1666 (Cocke), p. 375; Pepys, *Diary*, Vol. VII, 19 December 1666 (Ford), p. 416.

34 Paul Seaward has argued that the members of the Cavalier Parliament were obsessed with "their sense of decline." Paul Seaward, *The Cavalier Parliament and the Reconstruction of the Old Regime 1661–1667* (Cambridge, 1989), p. 326. This is certainly an apt description of popular as well as elite sentiment for much of the 1660s. I think, however, to understand fully the viciousness of the Parliamentary debates of 1666–1667 one needs to recall that, for brief periods both at the Restoration and during the Anglo-Dutch War, there were moments of heady optimism, moments in which the English were once again confident that they would achieve their rightful place in the world. Victory in the war, it must be remembered, was thought to bring with it economic prosperity and the destruction of both radical religious dissent and republicanism.

soon as the flames dissipated in London there were fears of "some distractions and disorders among us."[35] Sure enough, throughout the country people who had been willing and able to pay their stiff taxes throughout the early months of the war rioted against the hearth tax. In Newcastle, Lynn, and Hereford – as well as in many other places – the people who "were much discontented" began "to beat the collectors of the hearth money."[36]

This sudden descent from ecstasy to misery, from national exultation to national lamentation, from confidence of military victory to murmurings about a possible humiliating defeat, necessarily led to introspection. There was little doubting that the Fire had altered the national mood. But, why did the English think the Fire had happened? To this question, the Dean of St. Paul's, William Sancroft, noted, "every faction amongst us hath a revelation, hath an interpretation."[37] The immediate predisposition of Anglican Royalists was to blame the fire on the usual suspects – the fanatics and their European allies the Dutch.[38]

It soon became clear, however, that there was precious little evidence to sustain this interpretation, and, more importantly, very few were prepared to accept such an explanation. Before the ashes on the London streets had cooled, the government issued its official account of the Fire, an account which asserted that "the whole was an effect of an unhappy chance, or to speak better, the heavy hand of God upon us for our sins, showing us the terror of his judgment in thus raising the fire."[39] It was God's role in punishing London for its sins, particularly its most horrid sin of rebelling against its king, which Anglican Royalist polemicists and preachers

35 Pepys, *Diary*, Vol. VII, 30–31 October 1666, pp. 347–349.

36 Richard Forster (Newcastle) to Williamson, 7 December 1666, PRO, SP 29/180/127; Edward Bodham (Lynn) 5 December 1666, PRO, SP 29/180/85; Joseph Fitzherbert (Bristol) to Williamson, 1 December 1666, PRO, SP 29/180/5; Muddiman's newsletter, 24 November 1666, PRO, SP 29/179/41; Max Beloff, *Public Order and Popular Disturbances 1660–1714* (Oxford, 1938), pp. 92–93; Seaward, *Cavalier Parliament*, pp. 272–273.

37 William Sancroft, *Lex Ignea: Or, The School of Righteousness*, sermon preached before Charles II, 10 October 1666 (London, 1666), p. 23. See the similar statements by Richard Perrinchief, *A Sermon Preached before the Honourable House of Commons*, 7 November 1666 (London, 1666), pp. 21–23; James Oxenden to George Oxenden, 8 January 1667, BL, Add. 40713, f, 29r.

38 John Lysle (West Cowes) to Williamson, 5 September 1666, PRO, SP 29/170/102; Earl of Carlisle to Williamson, 8 September 1666, PRO, SP 29/170/152 (reporting a rumor he had heard); Thomas Neulin (translator) *Bishop Parker's History of his Own Time* (London, 1727), p. 117 (the only retrospective account blaming the Fire on "rebel fanatics"); Jo. Carlisle (Dover) to Williamson, 5 September 1666, PRO, SP 29/170/103; Luke Whittington (Hull) to Williamson, 8 September 1666, PRO, SP 29/170/159; intelligence to Ormonde, 21 September 1666, Carte 35, f. 94r; examination of Edward Taylor (age 10) by John Lord Lovelace, 9 October 1666, PRO, SP 29/171/11.

39 *A True Relation of that Sad and Deplorable Fire* [8 September] (York, 1666), broadside. See also Joseph Williamson's Memorial, September 1666, PRO, SP 29/173/132; Arlington to Ormonde, 7 September 1666, Carte 46, f. 363; Sir Heneage Finch to Lord Conway, 8 September 1666, HL, HA 14724; D. de Repas to Sir Robert Harley, 8 September 1666, BL, Add. 70010, f. 316r.

expatiated upon. "The dividers cried out," Richard Baxter wrote of the Anglican preachers, "it is God's just judgment on the City, that hath been so much against the king and the bishops, and God would not pardon them though the king did."[40] "Now loyal London has full ransom paid, / For that defection the disloyal made," rhymed the Anglican Royalist poet John Crouch after the Fire.[41] Charles II's chaplain Nathaniel Hardy thundered that the Fire was an occasion for "our wealthy citizens" to recall "how forward they were to part with their wealth for raising a rebellious war against their sovereign, which at last most tragically ended in his murder."[42]

It was a measure of a how far the Anglican Royalist consensus had deteriorated since 1664, however, that very few concluded that the Fire was in fact London's punishment for murdering Charles the Martyr. While radical Protestants and republicans, that "generation of fanatic vipers," blamed the Fire on the sins of the Restored Monarchy, most in England were convinced that the Fire had been set by the French in collusion with Papists.[43] Despite official denials it was "generally concluded from pregnant circumstances too large now to relate that this was not an accident but a design."[44] Early reports claimed both of England's foreign enemies had carried out the firing of the City.[45] Very quickly, however, popular fury focused on the French and the Papists. "The plot as is generally reported," Anthony Wood wrote to a friend from Oxford, "was laid and acted by the Papists and French."[46] Popular gossip in Pembroke reported "a great treason acted by the French" in burning London.[47] "The ignorant and

40 Matthew Sylvester, *Reliquiae Baxterianae* (London, 1696), Pt. III, p. 18; see also Ludlow, "A Voyce," Bod., English History MSS C487, p. 1132.

41 John Crouch, *Londiniensis Lacrymae: Londons Second Tears Mingled with her Ashes* (London, 1666), p. 9. The "defection" referred to is the spilling of "a Martyr's blood." See the similar views expressed in Nicholas Buckeridge to George Oxenden, 26 December 1666, BL, Add. 40713, ff. 1–2.

42 Nathaniel Hardy, *Lamentation, Mourning and Woe*, preached 9 September 1666 (London, 1666), p. 29. See also Sancroft, *Lex Ignea*, pp. 21–22; George Cartwright, "Upon the Deploreable Fire," 1666, BL, Add. 34363, f. 57r.

43 Richard Watts (Walmer) to Williamson, 6 September 1666, PRO, SP 29/170/114. For more on the radical claims see: Ludlow, "A Voyce," Bod., English History MSS C487, pp. 1131–1132; *Parker's History*, p. 118; John Fitzherbert (Bristol) to Williamson, 22 September 1666, PRO, SP 29/172/106.

44 Dr. Peter Barwick to Sancroft, 7 September 1666, Bod., Tanner MSS 45, f. 100r. See also Francis Bellott (Pendennis) to Williamson, 10 September 1666, PRO, SP 29/171/34; Pepys, *Diary*, Vol. VII, 6 September 1666, p. 277.

45 Examination of Anne English, 3 September 1666, PRO, SP 29/170/64; Silas Taylor (Harwich) to Williamson, 4 September 1666, PRO, SP 29/170/93; Pepys, *Diary*, Vol. VII, 5 September 1666, p. 277; Alexander Fleming to Daniel Fleming, 6 September 1666, Bod., Don MS C37, f. 8r; Evelyn, *Diary*, 7 September 1666, p. 462.

46 Anthony Wood to Dr. Richard Lower, 15 September 1666, Bod., Tanner MSS 45, f. 103v.

47 Francis Malory (Pembroke) to Williamson, 10 September 1666, PRO, SP 29/171/27. The same tale was told in the north. See Colonel Anthony Byerly to John Cosin, 8 September 1666, in George Ornsby (editor), *The Correspondence of John Cosin* Pt. II (Durham, 1872), p. 155.

deluded mob," the unsympathetic William Taswell remembered, "who upon the occasion were hurried away with a kind of frenzy, vented forth their rage against the Roman Catholics and Frenchmen; imagining those incendiaries (as they thought) had thrown red-hot balls into the houses."[48] The French, one broadside claimed, were "confidently believed" to be "the plotters of the ruin of this famous city."[49] Other reports, all over the kingdom, emphasized the role of Catholic and Jesuit conspirators. "it is generally believed, but not at court," Dr. William Denton informed his friend Sir Ralph Verney, "that the Papists have designed this and more, many and strong presumptions there are for it."[50] "The great talk of the time was, who were the burners of the city?" recalled Richard Baxter, "and there came in so many testimonies that it was the plotted weapon of the Papists, as caused the Parliament themselves to appoint a committee to inquire after it, and receive information."[51]

It was this Parliamentary committee, combined with the voluntary confession of a deranged Frenchman, which finally convicted the French and Papists of having set the Fire in the court of public opinion.[52] The committee proved, to the satisfaction of most, that "several persons, Papists, Irish and French spoke of it to their friends before the Fire began."[53] Within a short

48 George Perry Elliott (editor), "Autobiography and Anecdotes by William Taswell," in *The Camden Miscellany* Vol. II (1853), September 1666, p. 11; Pepys, *Diary*, Vol. VII, 5 September 1666, p. 275; Pepys, *Diary*, Vol. VII, 7 September 1666, p. 279; Hyde, *Life*, p. 351.

49 *London's Lamentation: Or its Destruction by a Consuming Fire* (1666). See also *The Late Apology in Behalf of the Papists Re-Printed and Answered in Behalf of the Royalists* (London, 1667), p. 37.

50 Dr. William Denton to Sir Ralph Verney, 8 September 1666, Firestone Library, Verney MSS Reel 21 (unfoliated).

51 Sylvester, *Reliquiae Baxterianae*, Pt. III, p. 18. For more on claims that Catholics set the Fire, see P. Manaton (Barnstaple) to Williamson, 11 September 1666, PRO, SP 29/171/56; Elizabeth Isham (Worcestershire) to Sir Ralph Verney, 12 September 1666, Firestone Library, Verney MSS Reel 21 (unfoliated); Ralph Hope (Coventry) to Williamson, 15 September 1666, PRO, SP 29/171/128; Anthony Thorold (Lyme) to James Hickes, 29 September 1666, PRO, SP 29/173/79; Muddiman's newsletter, 6 November 1666, PRO, SP 29/177/80; Robert Elborough, *London's Calamity by Fire* (London, 1666), p. 14; Simon Ford, *The Conflagration of London* (London, 1667), p. 27; *Tydings from Rome, or England's Alarm* (London, 1667), p. 6; Thomas Barlow (Oxford) to Francis Parry, 8 January 1668, Bod., English Letters MSS C328, f. 509v. Beloff has argued that the popular interpretation of the causes of the Fire was a significant turning point in the history of Restoration public opinion: "it marks the beginning of the period when all untoward accidents were ascribed to the mchinations of the 'papists', thus foreshadowing the outburst of national hysteria at the time of the Popish Plot." Beloff, *Public Order*, p. 37.

52 For the confession of Hubert see newsletter, 11 October 1666, PRO, SP 29/174/139; Sir Edward Harley to Lady Harley, 20 October 1666, BL, Add. 70010, f. 339v; Josselin, *Diary*, 11 November 1666, pp. 531–532.

53 Sir Edward Harley to Lady Harley, 20 October 1666, BL, Add. 70010, f. 339r. See also Committee's Report Concerning Firing of London, 1666, BL Sloane 970, f. 35r; St. Serfe's newsletter, 23 October 1666, LOC, 18124 Vol. I, f. 123r; Muddiman's newsletter, 27 October 1666, PRO, SP 29/176/62; Sir Edward Harley to Lady Harley, 27 October 1666, BL, Add. 70010, f. 341r; Pepys, *Diary*, Vol. VII, 5 November 1666, pp. 356–357;

time it was "believed by the most" that London was "purposely set on Fire by furious French ... for they are a malicious people."[54]

Why did the English public, which had two years previously been convinced that republicans and radical Protestants were the most significant – indeed the only – threat to their regime, turn so viciously against the French and Catholics in the autumn of 1666? Why was Charles II's government so singularly unsuccessful in channeling popular anger against the republican and heterodox Dutch? What had happened to shatter the Anglican Royalist political consensus?

Louis XIV's entry into the war on the Dutch side, beginning with his support of the United Provinces against the Bishop of Munster in the autumn of 1665 and culminating in his declaration of war against England in the winter of 1666, dramatically altered the English understanding of the nature of the conflict.

Over the course of 1665 it became increasingly apparent that France would soon honor its diplomatic obligations to the United Provinces and enter the war against England.[55] English Francophobia grew apace. Already in January, before war with the Dutch had officially been declared, there were "great rejoicings for the first news which made it visible that our king hath apprehensions of the arms of him of France."[56] The French ambassador's failure to celebrate the English victory at Lowestoft so provoked "the common people" that they "threw firebrands against his door and broke his glass windows."[57] By mid-summer there was so much "talk amongst the people against the French nation" that the Dutch ambassador Van Goch

Sylvester, *Reliquiae Baxterianae*, Pt. III, p. 18; Ludlow, "A Voyce," Bod., English History MSS C487, p. 1135.

54 An. Masters to George Oxenden, 15 January 1667, BL, Add. 40713, f. 28r. See also examination of Bellow and his wife, 31 July 1667, PRO, SP 29/211/111; "A Warning to Protestants," 21 April 1667, Carte 35, f. 386r; "Vox et Lacrymae Anglorum," January–February 1668, Bod., Don MSS E23, f. 33r. Of course, the most lasting testimony to this popular conviction is the inscription on the monument.

55 Hollis to Bennet, 4/14 February 1665, PRO, SP 78/120, f. 39r; Sir Ralph Verney to Edmund Verney, 18 May 1665, Firestone Library, Verney MSS, Reel 20 (unfoliated); Downing to Arlington, 19 May 1665, PRO, SP 84/176, f. 40r; Arlington to Fanshawe, 29 June 1665, in Thomas Bebington (editor), *The Right Honourable the Earl of Arlington's Letters* ... Vol. II, p. 82; Downing to Arlington, 7 July 1665, PRO, SP 84/177, f. 9r; Pepys, *Diary*, Vol. VI, 22 July 1665, p. 165; Hollis to Arlington, 9/19 August 1665, PRO, SP 78/121, f. 33; Samuel Tuke to John Evelyn, 12 August 1665, Christ Church, Evelyn In-Letters 1298; Hollis to Arlington, 12/22 August 1665, PRO, SP 78/121, f. 38r; Arlington to Ormonde, 22 August 1665, Carte 46, f. 198; Thomas Thynne to his father, 8/18 September 1665, Longleat House, Thynne MSS 12, f. 1r; Sir Thomas Osborne to Lady Osborne, 13 October 1665, Andrew Browning, *Osborne* Vol. II, p. 12; John Lord Berkeley to Ormonde, 23 October 1665, Carte 4, f. 450v.

56 Thomas Salusbury to Earl of Huntingdon, 9 January 1665, HL, HA 10663. See also Orrery to Ossory, 16 May 1665, *Orrery State Letters*, p. 193.

57 Ludlow, "A Voyce," Bod., English History MSS C487, p. 1072. See also M. Van Goch to States General, 16/26 June 1665, PRO, SP 84/176, f. 172v.

thought they were "no less hated than the Dutch."[58] By the time that Lord Chancellor Clarendon "with nervous eloquence stirred the people to wrath" against France, he was already preaching to the converted.[59] "The humor of England is grown much more crusty and rough toward that people, than a little while since it has been," Sir Robert Southwell wrote of the French.[60] English privateers began systematically seizing and pillaging French merchant ships, expressing their eagerness "for a rupture with the crown of France."[61] Colonel Walter Slingsby enthused that "our people are strangely eager after a French war like an empty hawk transported with the hopes of purchase."[62] One newsletter-writer claimed the English were "in a mutiny for a war with France."[63]

When Louis XIV finally declared war in Paris in late January 1666, Henry Oldenburg was convinced that it "will unite England as one man."[64] William Temple agreed that it was "the best way could have been found out to unite all his Majesty's subjects."[65] On 10 February heralds in London proclaimed war against France, eliciting spontaneous celebrations.[66] "Never was any declaration proclaimed with a more general satisfaction to the people than that of the war against France," Henry Muddiman announced proudly.[67] The Presbyterian secretary of state William Morrice was convinced there was "great animosity against the French and a national antipathy."[68] The English, it soon became clear, were willing to risk their lives in order to defend their country against the French. The London silk weavers "who are mixed of French and English [descent] offered their

58 Van Goch to States General, 20 July 1665, PRO, SP 84/177, f. 133r. See also Arlington to Henry Coventry, 7 July 1665, Longleat House, Cov. MSS LXIV, f. 184v; Dr. William Denton to Sir Ralph Verney, 27 July 1665, Firestone Library, Verney MSS Reel 20 (unfoliated).

59 Giustinian to Doge and Senate, 24 November/4 December 1665, *CSPV*, pp. 230–231 (reporting on the previous month's Parliamentary activity); Pepys, *Diary*, Vol. VI, 16 October 1665, p. 270.

60 Robert Southwell to Ormonde, 24 October 1665, Carte 34, f. 452v.

61 Sagredo to Doge and Senate, 14/24 November 1665, *CSPV*, p. 227; Colonel Walter Slingsby (Isle of Wight) to Williamson, 1 November 1665, PRO, SP 29/136/3; Giustinian to Doge and Senate, 16/26 January 1666, *CSPV*, p. 247.

62 Colonel Walter Slingsby (Isle of Wight) to Henry Muddiman, 30 October 1665, PRO, SP 29/135/109.

63 Newsletter from Oxford, 16 January 1666, Carte 72, f. 64r; see also Giustinian to Doge and Senate, 19/29 Janury 1665, *CSPV*, p. 249.

64 Henry Oldenburg to Robert Boyle, 27 January 1666, *Oldenburg Correspondence*, Vol. III, p. 33.

65 William Temple to Carlingford, 31 January/10 February 1666, *Memoirs of Taaffe*, p. 99. This was the view espoused in the official newsletter: Williamson's newsletter, 30 January 1666, Carte 222, f. 84r.

66 News from London, 12/22 February 1666, *CSPV*, p. 266. See also William Coventry to Ormonde, 10 February 1666, Carte 47, f. 436v.

67 Henry Muddiman to ?, 16 February 1666, PRO, SP 29/148/38.

68 William Morrice to Henry Coventry, 30 March 1666, Longleat House, Cov. MSS LXIV, f. 325r. See also Giustinian to Doge and Senate, 27 March/ 6 April 1666, *CSPV*, p. 281.

persons and fortunes for prosecution of this war."[69] In the north of Ireland "the major part" were "as forward and willing to fight in this war against the French as any men can be."[70] Many who had previously refused to fight in the war now came forward as volunteers.[71] On the Isle of Wight there was "much readiness to protect their king and country," the men were very much "animated ... against the French."[72] After the French Declaration of War, the Earl of Castlemaine recalled, "no body ... was daunted, but on the contrary we were the more penchantly animated by it."[73]

Why was there such popular enthusiasm for war against France? Why did a nation, convinced that its republican and religiously heterodox enemies were seeking universal monarchy, embrace so readily a war against the most absolute monarchy in Europe? Why, in short, were the English so eager to fight an enemy with none of the Netherlanders' ideological flaws?

Much of the explanation for this reaction lies in the widespread and growing belief that France had originally provoked, and was doing everything in its power to prolong, the war. It was not only the republican Algernon Sidney who believed that "the King of France has encouraged us to the war, that we may perish in it."[74] George Downing, in a rare endorsement of one of John De Witt's political assessments, agreed that the French "are mightily glad of this hopes and appearance of a breach between his Majesty and this country, for that they hope thereby not only to get a share of the trade, but to carry on their other designs without controls or hindrance."[75] It was the French, claimed William Temple, "whose work it was perhaps to begin the war and whose interest it is to continue it."[76] William Morrice opined in the spring of 1665 that it was Louis XIV's "proper end dictated by his interest to engage and embroil us and he hath

69 St. Serfe's newsletter, 10 February 1666, LOC, 18124 Vol. I, f. 28r.

70 J. T. to Ormonde, 12 March 1666, Carte 34, f. 628r.

71 See for example petition of John Tiler, March 1666, PRO, SP 29/152/77; D. de Repas to Sir Robert Harley, 4 July 1666, BL, Add. 70010, f. 314v.

72 R. Dillington (Knighton) to Williamson, 14 July 1666, PRO, SP 29/162/136.

73 Castlemaine, "History of the Dutch War," 1668, NMM, Clifford Papers, Dw130, p. 6.

74 Algernon Sidney, "Court Maxims," Warwickshire Record Office, f. 164. This was also apparently the radical William Say's view: Ludlow, "A Voyce," Bod., English History MSS C487, p. 1065.

75 Downing to Clarendon, 6 May 1664, Bod., Clar. 107, f. 196r. He restated this opinion the following year: Downing to Clarendon, 27 January 1665, Bod., Clar. 108, f. 195v. William Coventry shared Downing's opinion: William Coventry to Arlington, 9 August 1665, PRO, SP 29/128/75. Coventry elaborated these views in his "Essay of France," 1664, Longleat House, Cov. MSS CI, f. 25r. Apparently the view that France fomented the war was widely held in the United Provinces: see Boreel to States General, 29 April/9 May 1664, PRO, SP 84/170, f. 139v; De Bacquoy/Van Ruyven to Bennet, 26 August/5 September 1664, PRO, SP 84/172, f. 9v; newsletter from The Hague, 7 April 1665, PRO, SP 84/175, f. 82r.

76 William Temple to Ormonde, 21/31 December 1666, Carte 47, f. 314v. See also Temple to Arlington, 4/14 December 1666, PRO, SP 77/35, f. 310.

hitherto moved in such ways and with such pace as may rather bring things to extremities than reconcile them."[77] The scientist Henry Oldenburg thought that had the Dutch "not been assured by [the French] of sea and land-assistance, they had never begun the war."[78] The Anglican virtuoso John Evelyn was also convinced that "this terrible war" was "begun doubtless at secret instigation of the French."[79]

Not only did the English believe that the French had provoked the war, they were also convinced that Louis XIV's subtle diplomats did all in their power to preclude an Anglo-Dutch accommodation. Lord Ashley kept among his papers a letter, purportedly written by the French minister De Lionne, advising Louis XIV that "it would be a stroke of admirable prudence to let [the Anglo-Dutch War] go on" because both antagonists would then be "reduced to the point of being no more able to oppose those conquests which your Majesty has formed in your mind."[80] "The Italians generally" thought similarly of Louis XIV's strategy, claiming that the French will "do what possibly they can to keep us and the Dutch at wars and to ruin us both."[81]

After war between the English and the Dutch had begun, French duplicitous mediation ensured that no compromise would be concluded.[82] When the French began to fear that Dutch resolve would fail after the first year's campaign, they shored it up by entering the war. Arlington was certain that Louis XIV declared for the Dutch "to prevent their treating with us."[83] "The Dutch were upon thoughts of articles for peace," the East India merchant Sir William Ryder explained to George Oxenden, "but the French to prevent it furiously denounced war against us."[84] French hopes were immediately realized. "The Dutch are grown more audacious and obstinate," complained William Morrice after the French Declaration of War, "those seeds of peace which both sides were cultivating, are stifled and

77 William Morrice to Henry Coventry, 31 March 1665, Longleat House, Cov. MSS LXIV, f. 144r.

78 Oldenburg to Boyle, 21 November 1665, *Oldenburg Correspondence*, Vol. II, p. 616. Clarendon made almost an identical argument in his memoirs. See Hyde, *Life*, pp. 330–331.

79 John Evelyn, *Diary*, 5 April 1665, pp. 404–405.

80 De Lionne to Louis XIV, 1666, PRO, PRO 30/24/4, f. 137r.

81 George Legat (Genoa) to Williamson, 25 July/4 August 1666, PRO, SP 79/1, ff. 235–236. The Venetian ambassador in Paris agreed: Giustinian to Doge and Senate, 12/22 June 1666, *CSPV*, pp. 17–18; Giustinian to Doge and Senate, 31 July/10 August 1666, *CSPV*, p. 50.

82 William Temple to Ormonde, 18/28 September 1665, Carte 47, f. 258v; Hyde, *Life*, p. 271; News from The Hague, 31 August/10 September 1665, *CSPV*, p. 198.

83 Arlington to Henry Coventry, 2 February 1666, Longleat House, Cov. MSS LIII, f. 307r. See also Arlington to Ormonde, 12 December 1665, Carte 46, f. 229; Arlington to Ormonde, 20 January 1666, Carte 46, f. 294.

84 Sir William Ryder to George Oxenden, 1 March 1666, BL, Add. 40712, f. 45v. Similar views are expressed in Henry Coventry to Carlingford, 21 March 1666, Beinecke Library, Osborn Collection, Carlingford Papers, Box II.

mortified."[85] Having given their support to the Dutch, many thought, the French began to fear that the Dutch would emerge from the war victorious. As a result Louis XIV opted to support the Dutch as little as possible, he "chose rather to see the English and them weakening each other than to give any real assistance against their enemies."[86] When peace terms were again floated in the autumn of 1666 Louis XIV and his minions succeeded in preventing the Dutch from considering them. His policy, the English thought, was to "overawe the Dutch" so that "our peace will be strangely hindered."[87]

French duplicitous mediation, ambivalent aid of the Dutch, and diplomatic obstructionism were all of a piece. The English became convinced – and those less firmly committed to intolerant Anglicanism became convinced more quickly – that it was all part of the French grand strategy to achieve universal dominion. A war between Europe's two great maritime powers, a war in which Europe's two greatest navies were busily destroying each other and each other's merchant marines, gave France the perfect opportunity to seize control of the world's trade. "The clashing of those two trading nations laying trade asleep," the Presbyterian William Morrice wrote of the Anglo-Dutch War, France "could take this opportunity to get it into their hands."[88] The former radical preacher and Cromwellian George Downing complained to a member of the States General that "it was lamentable to see these two nations about to cut each other's throats ... while their neighbors would get all the profit out of it and laugh at their folly."[89]

Indeed in almost every commercial arena the French used the Anglo-Dutch conflict to seize upon their trade routes. French merchants merely

85 William Morrice to Henry Coventry, 12 February 1666, Longleat House, Cov. MSS LIII, f. 310r. Morrice is positing a causal connection between the French Declaration and the demise of the peace feelers. Thomas St. Serfe thought that the French intercepted the vital letters: St. Serfe's newsletter, 27 February 1666, LOC, 18124 Vol. I, f. 34r. John Evelyn intended to endorse this opinion in his "History," see his Notes for History of Second Dutch War, Christ Church, Evelyn MSS 134, f. 105.

86 Ludlow, "A Voyce," Bod., English History MSS C487, p. 1122. See also Carlingford to Reverend Burgate, 12/22 August 1666, *Memoirs of Taaffe*, p. 124; Giustinian to Doge and Senate, 31 July/10 August 1666, *CSPV*, pp. 50–51.

87 St. Serfe's newsletter, 8 November 1666, LOC, 18124 Vol. I, f. 129r; Oldenburg to Boyle, 15 November 1666, *Oldenburg Correspondence*, Vol. III, p. 282. See also William Temple to Arlington, 11/21 December 1666, PRO, SP 77/35, f. 328v; Muddiman's newsletter, 11 November 1666, PRO, SP 29/178/69; Arlington to Sir Robert Southwell, 3 January 1667, Bebington, *Arlington's Letters*, Vol. II, p. 215.

88 William Morrice to Henry Coventry, 14 April 1665, Longleat House, Cov. MSS LXIV, f. 156r. See also William Morrice to Henry Coventry, 12 May 1665, Longleat House, Cov. MSS LXIV, f. 163r. Many in the merchant community expressed similar sentiments: news from The Hague, 2/12 March 1665, *CSPV*, p. 89; Downing to Clarendon, 28 April 1665, Bod., Clar. 108, f. 229r.

89 News from The Hague, 2/12 March 1665, *CSPV*, p. 89. See the similar views in Downing to Clarendon, 28 April 1665, Bod., Clar. 108, f. 229r.

replaced Dutch ones in the European carrying trade.[90] In France every effort was made to sabotage the commercial endeavors of English merchants.[91] In the West Indies the French massacred the English at St. Kitts and then "made themselves masters of all the Caribee islands except Barbados."[92] "The French picked this quarrel," John Evelyn maintained, "out of affectation of sovereignty in the Mediterranean and to control the trade of other nations."[93] As soon as war broke out between the English and the Dutch the French set about terrorizing English merchants and enforcing their commercial claims with a powerful fleet.[94] By 1666, in the Mediterranean, the French "nation's shipping [was] carrying all the trade before them," and the Earl of Winchilsea was convinced "that in time they will obtain what they desire" in the Levant.[95] Even in Newfoundland, where De Ruyter had made one of his more spectacular descents in 1665, it was the French who were accused of attempting to possess the trade.[96] In fact, the French exploited the economic space generated by the Anglo-Dutch War to begin to gain a foothold in the East India trade.[97] While in early 1664 the English might well have feared the economic expansionism of the aggressive Dutch mercantile community, by late 1666 they had every reason to tremble at the

[90] Hollis to Arlington, 13/23 September 1665, BL, Althorp Papers Papers C13 (unfoliated); Robert Southwell to Ormonde, 24 October 1665, Carte 34, ff. 452–453.

[91] Edward Moor, John Holman, Benjamin Arundel, Andrew Stuckey, Thomas Preston, Andrew Whitley to Hollis, 21 May 1665, PRO, SP 78/120, f. 138r; Hollis to Arlington, 11/21 October 1665, PRO, SP 78/121, f. 111v; St. Serfe's newsletter, 24 November 1665, LOC, 18124 Vol. I, f. 6r.

[92] Samuel Tucker to William Johnson, 15/25 February 1667, PRO, SP 84/182, f. 44r. See also Toby Bonnell (Dublin) to John Johnson, 25 December 1666, CUL, Add. 1, f. 1r; Nicholas Buckeridge to George Oxenden, 26 December 1666, BL, Add. 40713, f. 2r. The massacre at St. Kitts was extremely well publicized in England, and elicited widespread popular fury. See Arlington to Carlingford, 27 July 1666, *Memoirs of Taaffe*, p. 152; Thomas Waade (Whitby) to Williamson, 12 July 1666, PRO, SP 29/162/91; Thomas Mayden (Amsterdam) to Joseph Hill, 8 July 1666, PRO, SP 29/162/60/V; Sir Robert Paston to his wife, 19 June 1666, NRO, Bradfer-Lawrence MSS IC/1; Pepys, *Diary*, Vol. VII, 18 June 1666, p. 171; Ludlow, "A Voyce," Bod., English History MSS C487, p. 1121; instructions to St. Albans, 1666, Bod., Clar. 84, f. 43r; *Current Intelligence*, 18–21 June 1666.

[93] John Evelyn, notes for history of second Dutch War, Christ Church, John Evelyn MSS 134, f. 100.

[94] Levant Company to Consul Cave, 20 November 1665, PRO, SP 105/113, f. 58; John Evelyn to Sir Richard Browne, 28 November 1665, Christ Church, Evelyn Out-Letters 1486; Allan Broderick to Ormonde, 2 December 1665, Carte 34, f. 490r; newsletter from Oxford, 5 December 1665, Carte 72, f. 58v.

[95] Arnold White and Arthur Bernardiston (Smyrna) to Winchilsea, 29 January 1666, LRO, DG7/Box 4963, Bundle VII; Winchilsea to Arlington, 20/30 May 1666, PRO, SP 97/18, f. 197r; Joseph Kent to Williamson, 15/25 September 1665, PRO, SP 85/8, ff. 28–29.

[96] "A Narrative Showing the Benefit of the Newfoundland Trade," 6 December 1667, PRO, SP 29/224/58.

[97] De Bacquoy/Van Ruyven to Bennet, 24 September/4 October 1664, PRO, SP 84/172, f. 93r; Downing to Clarendon, 9 September 1664, Bod., Clar. 108, f. 179; Downing to Arlington, 1 August 1665, PRO, PRO SP 84/177, ff. 51–52; Thomas Tyne to George Oxenden, 10 March 1666, BL, Add. 40712, f. 21r.

prospect of the world's trade being usurped and dominated by a newly commercially conscious French monarchy.

The diversion created by the Anglo-Dutch War, which the English were coming to believe the French had provoked, combined with the fortuitous death of King Philip IV of Spain, created a power vacuum in the Spanish Netherlands, a power vacuum which Louis XIV was all too happy to fill with his armies.[98] The implications of a French invasion of the Low Countries, so long perceived to be of pivotal strategic importance in European politics, was such that "even their allies the Hollanders grow very jealous of them on that side."[99] Without an Anglo-Dutch peace, Bishop Morley of Winchester feared, "it will be impossible to secure Flanders against the French or secure Holland itself if the French once become masters of Flanders."[100] "If France should master that country," Henry Coventry scribbled to Carlingford full of trepidation, "where, when, or by whom he will be stopped is more than I can guess."[101]

It was precisely such a French torrent, a torrent now fueled by the vast economic resources of a royally sponsored commercial empire, that all England was beginning to dread. "France tumbles about like the Leviathan," the religiously tolerant scientist Henry Oldenburg warned Lord Brereton, "and would be a terror to Europe."[102] "France is quiet within itself," observed the former Cromwellian Roger Boyle Earl of Orrery, "and governed by a young prince, ambitious absolute, and wealthy, and apt on any occasion to enlarge his dominions."[103] Denzil Hollis, the former

[98] One can track the growing realization that the French meant to invade the Spanish Netherlands in: newsletter from The Hague, 1/11 September 1665, PRO, SP 101/47, f. 233r; Arlington to Fanshawe, 17 December 1665, BL, Harleian MSS 7010, f. 465v; Sir Bernard Gascoigne to Arlington, 16/26 August 1666, PRO, SP 29/169/7; John Lysle (West Cowes) to Williamson, 20 October 1666, PRO, SP 29/175/117; Muddiman's newsletter, 11 November 1666, PRO, SP 29/178/69.

[99] Diary of Sir William Clarke, 19 May 1666, BL, Add. 14286, f. 31r. See also Marin Zorzi (Madrid) to Doge and Senate, 13/23 June 1666, *CSPV*, p. 22; Charles Molloy, *Holland's Ingratitude: Or, A Serious Expostulation with the Dutch* (London, 1666), pp. 13–14.

[100] George Morley to ? Sheldon, 30 September 1665, Bod., Tanner MSS 45, f. 31r.

[101] Henry Coventry to Carlingford, 17 February 1666, Beinecke Library, Osborn Collection, Carlingford Papers, Box II.

[102] Oldenburg to Lord Brereton, 16 January 1666, *Oldenburg Correspondence*, Vol. III, pp. 22–23. Oldenburg also told Robert Boyle that he feared that France's expanding commecial empire was designed "so they may keep their moneys at home and make conquests with it abroad." Oldenburg to Boyle, 28 September 1665, *Oldenburg Correspondence*, Vol. II, p. 533.

[103] Orrery to Ormonde, 14 December 1666, *Orrery State Letters*, Vol. II, p. 96. William Temple repeatedly voiced similar views: Temple to Arlington, 6/16 November 1666, PRO, PRO SP 77/35, f. 247; Temple to Arlington, 14/24 December 1666, PRO, SP 77/35, f. 333r; Temple to Ormonde, 2/12 February 1666, Carte 34, f. 601v; Temple to Arlington, 23 July/2 August 1666, PRO, SP 77/34, f. 398v; Temple to Arlington, 1/11 September 1666, PRO, SP 77/35, f. 111v. Haley has pointed out that Temple's August 1666 pamphlet meant for Dutch consumption, *Lettre d'un Marchand de Londres à son Ami d'Amsterdam*

Presbyterian leader and current ambassador in France, felt certain that the French aimed "to become the masters of the trade of Europe."[104] Edmund Verney, whose political and religious views were quite moderate, knew Louis XIV as "the dreadful hector of Christendom."[105] Thomas Sprat, the Duke of Buckingham's chaplain, was familiar with and excoriated Gallic claims making "France the seat of a universal monarchy."[106]

Soon many in England of all ideological stripes began to appreciate the danger from French expansionism, began to enunciate their belief that " 'tis our interest as well as of all Christian princes and republics to keep the [European] balance even ... for the peace and liberty of the rest of Christendom."[107] Louis XIV, the East India merchant Humphrey Gyfford knew, had "an exceeding treasure, vast armies, hath by purchase and building increased his shipping to a considerable number, very well enforced and provided, is an ambitious resolute prince of good counsel and conduct, who knows his interest and advantage to be in eternizing a war between the Dutch and us that he may pick the bone and get the marrow."[108] Sir Allan Broderick, a devout Anglican, observed that the French "doubt not (as the generality of their letters express) to become arbitrators of Christendom both by sea and land."[109] It was "apparent" to the Duke of Ormonde that "France aspires to umpire all the differences in Christendom."[110] Thomas St. Serfe made the same point in his newsletter when he informed his readers that Louis XIV intended "to debate the Empire of the Sea."[111] The sole aim and justification of Colbert's elaborate economic policies, Clarendon noted in his memoirs, was to make France the arbiter of Europe, to allow Louis XIV to "imitate the famous precedent of adjudging that to themselves that was in difference between their neighbors."[112]

The identification of Louis XIV as an aspiring universal monarch placed a great deal of pressure on the Anglican Royalist ideological nexus. While

Depuis la Dernière Bataille de Mer, highlighted the danger from the aspiring greatness of France. See Haley, *English Diplomat*, p. 96.

104 Hollis to Arlington, 18/28 October 1665, PRO, SP 78/121, f. 122.

105 Edmund Verney to Sir Ralph Verney, 20 February 1665, Firestone Library, Verney MSS Reel 20 (unfoliated, my translation). For a discussion of the political views of the Verneys, see my "From Butterboxes to Wooden Shoes," *Historical Journal* (June, 1995).

106 Thomas Sprat, *Observations of Monsieur de Sorbier's Vayage into England* (London, 1665), p. 37. See also Josselin, *Diary*, 21 January 1666, p. 524; Marin Zorzi (Madrid) to Doge and Senate, 2/12 January 1667, *CSPV*, p. 120 (reporting on conversations with the Earl of Sandwich, who was in Madrid in the capacity of ambassador).

107 MSS Pamphlet, 1665, NMM, Clifford Papers Vol. III, Dw100, f. 6.

108 Humphrey Gyfford to George Oxenden, 15 April 1667, BL, Add. 40713, ff. 54–55.

109 Allan Broderick to Ormonde, 9 December 1665, Carte 34, f. 506r. See also Broderick to Ormonde, 6 April 1667, Carte 35, f. 372r.

110 Ormonde to William Temple, 16 March 1667, Carte 47, f. 333r. Louis XIV's attempt to achieve universal monarchy was reportedly dramatized on an Oxford stage: Joseph Kent to Williamson, 3/13 February 1666, PRO, SP 85/8, f. 73.

111 St. Serfe's newsletter, 24 March 1666, LOC, 18124 Vol. I, f. 45r.

112 Hyde, *Life*, pp. 290–291.

English propagandists might excoriate Louis XIV for aiding and abetting the Dutch rebel state, no one could doubt that he was the most absolute monarch in Europe.[113] The author of one squib circulating at court argued, uncontroversially, that Louis XIV had reduced to virtual slavery "not only the queen, but the princes of the blood, the nobility, the religious, the soldiery, the courts of justice, the universities, the merchants, the citizens, and the people, and it is by these steps that [he] hopes to mount to the universal monarchy."[114] The French government "is monarchical to excess" observed another pamphleteer for "the king imposeth on his subjects what he lists."[115] It was a commonplace that the French people were in a state of virtual "slavery," were subjected to "an Egyptian bondage," were "slaves in body and in mind."[116]

Nor, of course, could France be categorized as a radical Protestant state. The French, like the Dutch, were widely suspected of meddling with the disaffected in the British Isles. But unlike the Dutch, whom Anglicans were convinced were working in alliance with their radical Protestant brethren, the French were thought, for the most part, to be plotting rebellion with Catholic priests. Well before France actually entered the war, concern began to mount that the French were laying the groundwork for Papist insurrection. One of the Duke of Ormonde's informants reported that Louis XIV was offering "his assistance in forwarding the Catholic cause."[117] The Irish Catholics, thought Clarendon, "want no malice to invite [the French] to do all the hurt they can."[118] Orrery, whose Cromwellian past may have made him more sensitive to Papist threats than his Anglican colleagues, "warmly apprehended danger from those of their religion," a danger which he was sure would not "possibly be neglected by the French, nor arms nor

[113] George Eliot, *A English Duel* (1666), broadside; *Hollands Representation: Or, The Dutchmans Looking-Glass* (London, 1665), broadside; Molloy, *Holland's Ingratitude* (1666), sig. A3v.

[114] "A Charitable Advice of France Lamenting the Deplorable Condition of the Netherlands," 16/26 April 1667, Sir William Haward's Collection, Bod., Don MSS B8, ff. 122–123. I am grateful to Rachel Weil for discussing this manuscript with me.

[115] *Europae Modernae Speculum: Or, A View of the Empires, Kingdoms, Principalities and Common-Wealths of Europe* (London, 1665), pp. 95–96.

[116] St. Serfe's newsletter, 10 February 1666, LOC, 18124 Vol. I, f. 28r; *Poor Robin's Character of France* (London, 1666), p. 30; [John Caryll], *The English Princess: Or, The Death of Richard the III* (London, 1667), p. 40 (first performed March 1667). For other endorsements of this political commonplace, see Samuel Tuke to John Evelyn, 28 October 1665, Christ Church, Evelyn In-Letters 1299; Sir Edward Nicholas to Williamson, 4 January 1666, PRO, SP 29/144/37; *The English French-Mans-Address* (1666), broadside.

[117] Intelligence to Ormonde, 27 April 1665, Carte 34, f. 180r. See also newsletter from The Hague, 22 September/2 October 1665, PRO, SP 101/47, f. 274r; Hollis to Arlington, 2/12 December 1665, PRO, SP 78/121, f. 171r; Giustinian to Doge and Senate, 19/29 June 1666, *CSPV*, p. 24; Richard Williams to Ormonde, 13 March 1666, Carte 34, f. 632r.

[118] Clarendon to Ormonde, 18 August 1666, Carte 47, f. 125v. In his memoirs Clarendon emphasized the desire of Louis XIV to give "life to some domestic rebellion in England and in Ireland." Hyde, *Life*, p. 290.

ammunition omitted to be sent to them."[119] William Temple got wind of Colbert's discussions with a series of Irish Catholic priests who were supplied "with instructions from France to dispose the Irish to a general revolt upon assurance of support in all kinds from France."[120] The Irish Catholic nobleman, and virulent Francophobe, the Earl of Carlingford was also convinced that the French were contributing vast sums to Catholic priests "as toward a war of religion."[121]

The English also suspected that Louis XIV was "laboring to stir up the kingdom of Scotland to an rebellion." The French strategy, it was claimed, was to "send disguised in apparel some seminaries, Jesuitical priests, and other factioners to stir them up" while at the same time convincing the "sectarians" that Charles II was "a Roman Catholic, as they say may be perceived clearly by the assistance his Majesty giveth to the Bishop of Munster for the destroying of the Protestant religion in Holland."[122]

French entry into the war in 1666, then, not only raised new military problems for the English, it also cast a great deal of doubt upon the Anglican Royalist understanding of the nature of the conflict. No longer was the Restored Monarchy threatened merely by its traditional enemies, radical Protestantism and republicanism. Now the English were also fighting an enemy associated with the old Parliamentarian bogeys of Popery and arbitrary government. For Charles II and his government to combat successfully these two very different enemies simultaneously required an ideological realignment, a redefinition of Englishness.

The magnitude of the ideological reorientation required quickly became evident. For most throughout Britain it was the absolutist French monarchy not the Dutch Republic which seemed to be the more dangerous enemy, the more serious claimant to the universal monarchy. The Dutch ambassador Van Goch, who might be accused of wishful thinking, reported to his superiors that "the commonalty are more incensed against the French than the Netherlanders."[123] His assessment, however, was seconded by Charles II who informed the French ambassadors at Salisbury that while Londoners had loaned him £100,000 "to continue the war with the United Provinces" they would offer "four times as much if he should choose to break with the

119 Orrery to Ormonde, 14 December 1666, *Orrery State Letters*, Vol. II, p. 96. Orrery apparently convinced Arlington of the danger: Arlington to Ormonde, 1 May 1666, Carte 46, f. 292r; Arlington to Ormonde, 26 June 1666, Carte 46, f. 323.

120 Temple to Ormonde, 21/31 December 1666, Carte 47, f. 315v. See also Temple to Arlington, 21/31 December 1666, PRO, SP 77/35, f. 342.

121 Carlingford to Ormonde, 29 January 1667, Carte 35, f. 285r; Carlingford to Ormonde, 26 February 1667, Carte 35, f. 323r.

122 Advice from Paris, April 1665, PRO, SP 78/120, f. 129r. Pepys also believed that Louis XIV was behind the 1666 rebellion in Scotland. Pepys, *Diary*, Vol. VII, 25 November 1666, p. 384.

123 M. Van Goch to States General, 12/22 June 1665, PRO, SP 84/176, f. 168v.

most Christian."[124] Robert Southwell was similarly persuaded that his compatriots "would be more fond to break with France, than they are resolute in continuing this war with the Dutch."[125] Dutch authorities, after interrogating a group of captured English fishermen, concluded "they hated the French more than the Dutch."[126] "A peace with Holland and the continuance of a war with France," argued the English diplomat William Temple, "are such infallible steps to his Majesty's and the kingdom's glory and greatness that nothing should be omitted that could contribute to them."[127] "All this kingdom," Robert Mein wrote from Scotland, wish "for a peace with the Dutch, but war with the French."[128] In Deal "our common people cry out peace with Holland, and war with the unworthy French."[129] "Contrary to what it was last year," summarized Arlington accurately in 1666, "everybody now cries to us have peace with the Dutch and war with France."[130]

At the same time that French entry into the war refocused English popular animosity onto an absolutist and Catholic state, the manifest suffering at home which accompanied the war led many in England to shift their domestic concerns from fears of fanatics and republicans to their government's own shortcomings. The speed and ease with which the Interregnum regimes had defeated the Dutch, the deep-seated belief in the superiority of the English navy, led many to ponder the inability of the Restored Monarchy to deliver the knockout blow.

High taxes, the economic devastation associated with a maritime war, and the horror and misery associated with the plague, all combined to create a sense of urgency during the war years. The optimistic Hollando-phobic propaganda, a body of literature which reminded its readers of the facility of the Cromwellian victory over the Dutch, created extremely high standards of military success. As a result, though the English proved victorious in the majority of the battles fought in the first two years of the war, there was a growing concern that victory had not yet been achieved. After the Bergen fiasco, Samuel Pepys heard current complaints of "a great deal of money being spent, and the kingdom not in a condition to spare, nor

124 Sagredo to Doge and Senate, 23 June/ 3 July 1665, *CSPV*, p. 147.

125 Robert Southwell to Ormonde, 12 October 1665, Carte 34, f. 431r; see also Warham Jennett (Dover) to Williamson, 31 January 1666, PRO, SP 29/146/72.

126 Relation of captured English fishermen, 5/15 August 1666, PRO, SP 101/50/138 (my translation).

127 Temple to Arlington, 21/31 August 1666, PRO, SP 77/35, f. 74.

128 Robert Mein (Edinburgh) to Williamson, 11 August 1666, PRO, SP 29/167/49. See also Robert Mein (Edinburgh) to Williamson, 7 August 1666, PRO, SP 29/166/116.

129 Richard Watts (Walmer) to Williamson, 17 August 1666, PRO, SP 29/168/9. See also Richard Watts (Deal) to Williamson, 12 December 1666, PRO, SP 29/181/83; Richard Watts (Deal) to Williamson, 24 February 1667, PRO, SP 29/192/87. For another example of this sentiment, see Edmund Verney (East Claydon) to Sir Ralph Verney, 4 May 1667, Firestone Library, Verney MSS Reel 21 (unfoliated).

130 Arlington to Ormonde, 17 February 1666, Carte 46, f. 256.

a Parliament, without much difficulty, to meet to give more."[131] Recriminations against the government's management of the war only accelerated when Parliament did meet. "The Dutch appearing on our coast, though to no effect in the world but their own damage," observed the Earl of Sandwich with a certain amount of ire, "hath given occasion to foolish discourses."[132] The infamous division of the fleet during the Four Days Battle the following summer convinced a still larger number of people that the war was being poorly managed. After the battle "there was nothing to be heard among the common seamen but complaints against dividing our fleet."[133] Samuel Pepys heard "that all the commanders, officers, and even the common seamen, do condemn every part of the late conduct of the Duke of Albemarle."[134] Ominously one of those seamen, Thomas Barlow, blamed the division of the fleet on "English Papists and traitors."[135]

Naturally such sentiments were episodic, and could often be assuaged by an ensuing naval victory. However, as English suffering became more profound and as the economic devastation became more general, so too did the belief in governmental incompetence become more widespread. Certainly the treatment of the country's seamen, "without whom the land would soon be brought under subjection," left ample scope for criticism.[136] In many ports could be heard the "sad cries of poor sick seamen which daily perish in the streets for want of quarters."[137] "In many ships," it was claimed, "there is not meat nor drink that men can eat."[138] Many sailors ran away for lack of clothes.[139] The most common, most bitter, and most dangerous grievance of the seamen was their lack of pay. This treatment of the country's seamen, John Evelyn thought, was "not frugality ... but madness and the very brink of confusion." The result, he felt certain, would be that Charles II would lose "all his interest in his seamen."[140] Sure enough, it became increasingly difficult to man the fleet, and those who did enlist frequently mutinied for lack of pay.[141] No wonder that the flamboyant country member of Parlia-

131 Pepys, *Diary*, Vol. VI, 31 August 1665, p. 208.

132 Earl of Sandwich to Sir Thomas Clifford, 28 October 1665, NMM, Clifford Papers, Vol. III, Dw99.

133 Arlington to Ormonde, 5 June 1666, Carte 46, f. 317r; Sir Thomas Clifford to Arlington, 6 June 1666, PRO, SP 29/158/46I.

134 Pepys, *Diary*, Vol. VII, 10 June 1666, p. 158.

135 Basil Lubbock (editor), *Barlow's Journal*, Vol. I (London, 1934), pp. 116, 119.

136 Barlow, *Journal*, p. 128.

137 Peter Pett (Chatham) to Pepys, 21 September 1665, PRO, SP 29/133/22.

138 Letter from a woman to Charles II, 30 June 1666, PRO, SP 29/160/104.

139 Captain Roger Jones to Navy commissioners, 25 September 1665, PRO, PRO SP 29/133/37. For all of these grievances, and Pepys's perception that they were being incompetently dealt with see Pepys, *Diary*, Vol. VI, 18 September 1665, p. 230.

140 John Evelyn to Sir Richard Browne, 23 October 1665, Christ Church, Evelyn In-Letters 1480. See also Williamson's notes, 6 November 1665, PRO, SP 29/136/71.

141 Ludlow, "A Voyce," Bod., English History MSS C487, pp. 1099–1100; Williamson's newsletter, 29 January 1667, Bod., Don MSS C37, f. 9r; Pepys, *Diary*, Vol. VI, 14 June 1667, p. 267; Davies, pp. 147–148.

ment Sir Richard Temple included the "non-payment of seamen whereby the great ships have been kept in port all the Winter long and the seamen utterly disheartened and discouraged from the king's service" among his list of grievances prepared for the Parliamentary session of 1667.[142]

Most believed it was not want of money but graft and corruption which kept the navy poorly supplied and the seamen in constant penury. The well-publicized revelations that the Earl of Sandwich had improperly seized prize goods after the 1665 campaign convinced many that such activity was the rule rather than the exception.[143] Many came to suspect that many members of government, including the most prominent, were sacrificing the lives and purses of good patriots in order to line their own pockets. It was not merely Samuel Pepys's crotchety friend George Cocke who believed that the Lord Chancellor and Lord Treasurer minded "getting of money and nothing else."[144] In January 1666, for example, "a turbulent crowd" gathered in front of Clarendon's new house – commonly called "Dunkirk House" since the Lord Chancellor was thought to have paid for the magnificent new dwelling from the sale of the Normandy town to Louis XIV – "to administer punishment for the venality which they suspected."[145] "Vox Populi," one of Arlington's intelligencers was forced to admit, had it that England was being handicapped by corruption in its war against France and the United Provinces. It was widely believed "that the tenth part of England's strength is not employed, though the fortune of all England lie at stake."[146] No wonder Edmund Verney doubted whether any sum "would suffice to vanquish the Hollanders, French, and Danes, considering how things have been managed till now."[147] "Too late grown wiser," one poet wrote of the English, "they their treasure see / Consum'd by fraud or lost by treachery."[148]

Increasingly the incompetent management of the war was understood to be symptomatic of a profound governmental malaise, a deeply imbedded cancer of the body politic. Republicans, of course, had known all along that any monarchy would prove to be arbitrary, would govern in a corrupt fashion.[149] Remarkably, over the course of the war – and with accelerated frequency during and after the campaign of 1666 – even many fervent

142 Sir Richard Temple, "General Heads of Grievances," 1667, HL, Temple Stowe STT Military Box 1 (50).

143 Pepys, *Diary*, Vol. VI, 11 October 1665, p. 261; Robert Southwell to Ormonde, 24 October 1665, Carte 34, f. 453r; Allan Broderick to Ormonde, 16 December 1665, Carte 34, f. 512r.

144 Pepys, *Diary*, Vol. VI, 9 September 1665, p. 218.

145 Giustinian to Doge and Senate, 9/19 January 1666, *CSPV*, p. 244; Pepys, *Diary*, Vol. VI, 20 February 1666, p. 39.

146 L. Hugh Squire (Westminster) to Arlington, 24 June 1666, PRO, SP 29/159/108.

147 Edmund Verney (East Claydon) to Sir Ralph Verney, 15 November 1666, Firestone Library, Verney MSS Reel 21 (unfoliated).

148 "The Fourth Advice to a Painter," 1667, *POAS*, p. 141.

149 This was Algernon Sidney's point in the "Court Maxims." See Scott, *Algernon Sidney*, pp. 190–204.

supporters of the Restored Monarchy could not deny the ubiquitous corruption at its core. John Evelyn, a committed Anglican Royalist, frequently complained to Samuel Pepys "of the vanity and vices of the court, which makes it a most contemptible thing."[150] The treasurer of the navy, Sir George Carteret, lamented "the baseness and looseness of the court."[151] The country gentleman Roger Pepys "doth by no means like the liberty of the court."[152] The dissoluteness of Charles II's court was hardly a well-kept secret. Charles II's relationship with Barbara Palmer Lady Castlemaine, for example, was not unknown in Oxford. One morning the king's mistress awoke to find written on her door: "The reason why she is not ducked / is because she is by Caesar ___ ."[153] Charles II's amours – and Charles merely set the example for the rest of his court – were thought to be outrageous because they were not so much a diversion from the rigors of political life as a replacement for it. "The whole nation" says "give the king the Countess of Castlemaine and he cares not what the nation suffer," claimed one of Charles II's angry female subjects.[154] Indeed a wide variety of Pepys's acquaintances complained that the king was ignoring the nation's pressing business.[155]

While the nation was reeling from the burden of heavy wartime taxation, the interruption of commerce, and the ravages of the plague, at court money was freely spent on the newest fashions and the most lavish luxuries. Even the Earl of Clarendon "doth confess our straits here and everywhere else arises from our outspending our revenue; I mean that the king doth do so."[156] Lady Ranelagh commented bitterly that while "scarcity of money is generally complained of ... it produces no abatement of excesses and those continued must increase the scarcity."[157] There was a widespread perception that governmental offices were mere sinecures, that no one was doing the work of government. Edward Howard, for example, pilloried the court

150 Pepys, *Diary*, Vol. VII, 29 January 1666, p. 29; Pepys, *Diary*, Vol. VII, 26 September 1666, p. 297; Pepys, *Diary*, Vol. VII, 26 April 1667, p. 181; Evelyn, *Diary*, 10 October 1666, p. 464.

151 Pepys, *Diary*, Vol. VI, 24 July 1665, p. 168. See also Pepys, *Diary*, Vol. VII, 26 February 1666, p. 57.

152 Pepys, *Diary*, Vol. VIII, 27 January 1667, p. 33. For Pepys's own sentiments, see Pepys, *Diary*, Vol. VII, 15 October 1666, p. 323. The previous year Pepys's patron, the former Cromwellian Earl of Sandwich, had condescendingly commented that "all the court are in an uproar with their loose amours." Pepys, *Diary*, Vol. VI, 17 November 1665, pp. 301–302.

153 Denis de Repas to Sir Robert Harley, 8 March 1666, BL, Add. 70010, f. 278r; see also Pepys, *Diary*, Vol. VII, 9 January 1666, p. 8.

154 Letter from a woman to Charles II, 30 June 1666, PRO, SP 29/160/104.

155 Pepys, *Diary*, Vol. VII, 7 July 1666, p. 197; Pepys, *Diary*, Vol. VII, 8 December 1666, p. 400; Pepys, *Diary*, Vol. VIII, 9 May 1667, p. 207.

156 Pepys, *Diary*, Vol. VIII, 20 February 1667, p. 75.

157 Lady Ranelagh to Earl of Burlington, 7 May 1667, BL, Althorp Papers B4 (unfoliated).

"about selling of places and doing everything for money," on the London stage in his popular play *The Change of Crownes.*[158]

It was because of this "sad, vicious, negligent court" that by the autumn of 1666 "all sober men" were becoming "fearful of the ruin of the whole kingdom this next year."[159] Indeed, Clarendon recalled, that as members of Parliament assembled for that autumn session "they did not conceal the very ill opinion they had of the court and the continual riotings there."[160] "Cries are now heard on every hand," reported one Venetian observer, "that since the House of Stuart came to the throne England has never enjoyed felicity but has suffered from incessant miseries."[161]

While the entry of France into the war had reminded the English of the political evils of absolutism, had enabled the enunciation of concerns that "the model of France" was being followed too closely in England, it also coincided with renewed concerns about the growth of Popery.[162] Fears of Popery, of course, were omnipresent in seventeenth-century England. In the early 1660s, however, most in England were far more concerned with the threat from radical Protestantism, Popery in disguise, than they were terrified of a renewed Roman Catholic menace.[163] Even England's alliance with the Bishop of Munster against the Protestant United Provinces – an alliance that Dutch propagandists claimed to be "a conspiracy of Papists" – did not raise much concern in Britain.[164] However, the ubiquitous rumors

158 F. S. Boas (editor), *The Change of Crownes* (Oxford, 1949); Williamson's journal, 22 April 1667, PRO, SP 29/231, f. 14v; Pepys, *Diary*, Vol. VIII, 15–16 April 1667, pp. 167–169.

159 Pepys, *Diary*, Vol. VII, 31 December 1666, p. 426.

160 Hyde, *Life*, p. 367; see also Pepys, *Diary*, Vol. VII, 26 September 1666, p. 298.

161 Giustinian to Doge and Senate, 18/28 September 1666, *CSPV*, p. 77.

162 Hyde, *Life*, p. 239. See also Sprat, *Observations*, pp. 75–76. For an early statement that the style of the Restoration court was "Frenchified" see *The Last Will and Testament of the Late Deceased French Jackanapes* (London, 1661), pp. 3–4. This fear was expressed in the Parliamentary motion against the importation of French luxury goods, and the reform of court fashion in the autumn of 1666.

163 Radical Protestants themselves continued to emphasize the threat from Roman Catholicism. See, for example, John Taylor to Hannah Booth, 2 May 1665, PRO, PRO SP 29/121/93 IV.

164 Newsletter from The Hague, 1/11 September 1665, PRO, PRO SP 101/47, f. 229 (my translation). See also Arlington to Carlingford, 7 October 1665, Beinecke Library, Osborn Collection, Carlingford Papers, Box II (unfoliated); Temple to Castel Rodrigo, 2/12 December 1665, *The Works of Sir William Temple* (London, 1814), Vol. I, p. 225; Temple to Arlington, 2/12 March 1666, PRO, SP 77/34, f. 102v; Ludlow, "A Voyce," Bod., English History MSS C487, p. 1076. This Dutch propaganda campaign does appear to have had a fair amount of success on the continent. See newsletter from The Hague, 26 Sepember/6 October 1665, PRO, SP 101/47, f. 281v; William Morrice to Henry Coventry, 9 November 1665, Longleat House, Cov. MSS LIII, f. 258r; newsletter from The Hague, 10/20 November 1665, PRO, SP 101/47, f. 311r; Moray to Oldenburg, 27 November 1665, *Oldenburg Correspondence*, Vol. II, p. 625. The English government was extremely concerned to combat this perception. See Clarendon to Henry Coventry, 4 October 1665, Longleat House, Cov. MSS LXIV, f. 239; MSS Pamphlet, 1665, NMM, Clifford Papers Vol. III, Dw100, ff. 5–7.

of French political conspiracy, the widely perceived court corruption, and the manifest proliferation of Catholic propaganda, all served to revive fears of a more traditional form of Popery in the autumn of 1666.[165] On the Isle of Wight it was rumored "as though the Romanists would have a design upon us that are Protestants."[166] The Hertfordshire-trained bands marched out of the exercise field when they heard they were to serve under Popish officers.[167] Dissenters in the West Country were said to "employ men and women to go up and down on purpose to inform that the mother queen doth intend to bring in Popery into this land and the king doth countenance it."[168] In Chester there were "of late many rumors of Papist plots," which the Anglican Royalist Sir Geoffrey Shakerley judged "to be the old Presbyterian design revived to disturb the peace of the kingdom once more through the Papists' sides."[169] One William Hopkins of Wedgbury in Staffordshire was reputed to have exclaimed that "the king and Duke of York are Papists, and the king hath been at mass underground within this week, or fortnight, and I can prove it."[170] Dr. Isaac Basire received a letter from William Prynne in which he ominously warned "style *veteri* of fears and jealousies of plots and designs of Jesuits and Romanists against our church and religion."[171] In Yorkshire the Nonconformists all claimed that there was "an absolute intention to bring in Popery."[172] Unsurprisingly in traditionally puritan Dorchester there was an anti-Popery riot provoked by an innkeeper changing his sign from that of the red lion to that of the pope.[173]

All over the country, and with alarmingly reminiscent intensity, then, English men and women were once again expressing their fears of Popish plotting in the autumn of 1666. Upon arriving in London for the Parliamentary session Sir Edward Harley discovered that "the members of the House from all parts are full of alarms concerning the Papists."[174] "Papists at this time very insolent in most parts of the nation," the Anglican Oxford scholar

165 *More News from Rome or Magna Charta, Discoursed of Between a Poor Man & his Wife* (London, 1666), p. 1; St. Serfe's newsletter, 29 November 1666, LOC, 18124 Vol. I, f. 135r.

166 John Lysle (West Cowes) to Williamson, 10 November 1666, PRO, SP 29/177/158. For fears of Popery in Bristol, see John Fitzherbert (Bristol) to Williamson, 19 November 1666, PRO, SP 29/178/135. See also John Fitzherbert (Bristol) to Williamson, 3 November 1666, PRO, SP 29/177/39.

167 Ludlow, "A Voyce," Bod., English History MSS C487, p. 1126.

168 Peter Crabb (Exeter) to Arlington, 11 August 1666, PRO, SP 29/167/68.

169 Sir Geoffrey Shakerley (Chester) to Williamson, 17 September 1666, PRO, SP 29/178/103. See also Shakerley to Williamson, 19 November 1666, PRO, SP 29/178/134.

170 Deposition of William Hopkins of Wedgebury, County Stafford, before Sir Robert Hall, 17 September 1666, PRO, SP 29/172/13.

171 Isaac Basire (Durham) to Williamson, 4 December 1666, PRO, SP 29/180/68.

172 Christopher Sanderson (Eggleston) to Williamson, 23 October 1666, PRO, SP 29/175/87.

173 C. Sawtell (Weymouth) to Edmund Sawtell, 5 June 1667, PRO, SP 29/203/77.

174 Sir Edward Harley to Lady Harley, 20 October 1666, BL, Add. 70010, f. 340r.

Anthony Wood confided in his diary that same month, they "appear in public, contrive the massacring of many hundreds."[175] These sentiments, this ubiquitous whispering about Catholic plotting, Pepys tellingly pointed out was "the very beginning of the late troubles."[176] John Fitzherbert of Bristol, while commenting on the proliferation of anti-Papist gossip, warned that "we have been cheated into twenty years of wars by the same artifices."[177]

Unlike the previous two years in which every effort had been made to discover and disarm Dissenters and republicans, the autumn of 1666 was marked by a crackdown on Roman Catholics. All over the country the houses of Roman Catholics were searched for arms.[178] In Parliament members "took occasion to fall upon the Papists," compelling Charles II to issue a proclamation enjoining enforcement of the Elizabethan recusancy laws.[179] The result was that "in many places of the country the common people, beyond what is intended, disarm the Papists."[180] The Duke of Albemarle and others strictly administered the oaths of supremacy and allegiance in order to purge the army of Catholics.[181]

The entry of France into the war – an absolutist and nominally Catholic power – opened up the field of political discourse. At the outset of the war, a war which was begun in a fit of Anglican Royalist enthusiasm, any criticism of the regime, any voice of dissent, would have been, and often was, labeled as yet another republican or fanatic attempt to overthrow the Restored Monarchy in collusion with the grasping imperialist Dutch. The French declaration of war, however, made it clear to English observers that it was not exclusively republican and religiously pluralist regimes which sought universal dominion. Indeed the reports of Dutch economic misery combined with their manifest military vulnerability convinced many that the French represented the greater threat. As long as Charles II and his government seemed poised to repeat the Cromwellian victories over the Dutch, it was extremely difficult to criticize the regime. However, when the Orangist political offensive collapsed, the Fire devastated England's metropolis and morale, while barely a blow had been struck against the aggressive and ambitious French, a barrage of political criticism was heard throughout

175 Anthony Wood, *Diary*, October 1666, Bod., Wood's Diaries MSS 10, f. 32r.

176 Pepys, *Diary*, Vol. VII, 27 October 1666, p. 343.

177 John Fitzherbert (Bristol) to Williamson, 19 November 1666, PRO, SP 29/178/135.

178 Thomas Rugge, "Mercurius Politicus Redivivus," 30 October 1666, BL, Add. 10117, f. 180r.

179 James S. Clarke, *The Life of James the Second* (London, 1816), Vol. I, , p. 424; Sir Edward Harley to Lady Harley, 3 November 1666, BL, Add. 70010, f. 349r; Ludlow, "A Voyce," Bod., English History MSS C487, p. 1136; Samuel Rolle, *The Burning of London in the Year 1666* (London, 1667), sig. A5–A6.

180 Ludlow, "A Voyce," Bod., English History MSS C487, p. 1136.

181 Pepys, *Diary*, 4 November 1666, pp. 353–354; Rugge, "Mercurius Politicus Redivivus," November 1666, BL, Add. 10117, f. 182r.

the kingdom. That most in England thought the Fire had been set by a French/Papist coalition rather than by an alliance between the Dutch and the radicals demonstrates the extent to which the center of English political discourse had shifted.

23

The rise of political opposition

This ideological shift in English popular opinion reflects the ambiguous nature of the Restoration itself. Presbyterians and Anglicans, moderate constitutionalists as well as those with more absolutist tendencies, had supported the Restoration of Charles II in 1660. All, of course, had been confident that their king would be everything that they had hoped for, would fit their own very different images of what a good English king should be. "The people in general desired a king," the republican Algernon Sidney was forced to admit during the Anglo-Dutch War, but they had hoped "to see an abolition of taxes, the nation established in happiness, riches, strength, security, and glory." Instead by the autumn of 1666 the English were overwhelmed with taxes, made miserable by economic hardship and the plague, and fearful of a French invasion. The hopes of moderates that "having been brought up in the school of affliction [Charles II] had there learned temperance in his prosperity; that the experience he had gained when he was abroad would so have armed him against the deceits and flatteries of courtiers that he would yield to nothing but reason and justice" were certainly not realized.[1] Instead many began to believe that Charles II and many of his courtiers had returned from France with an affection for the French style of government, the French religion, and – despite the war which Louis XIV had declared against his cousin Charles II – the French king.

In the end the English lost the war not so much because the government's economic infrastructure had collapsed – though the sheer extent of popular misery certainly fueled the criticism of the government – but because the government was no longer fighting the war that a large segment of the political nation wanted it to fight. While English radicals had always warned of the threats from Popery and arbitrary government, by the autumn of 1666 many moderates – Presbyterian Royalists and supporters of limited monarchy – were enunciating the same concerns. Moderates now insisted that the danger from Catholics and absolutists was as great as that

1 Algernon Sidney, "Court Maxims," 1666, Warwickshire Record Office, f. 4.

from republicans and religious radicals. Indeed the enormous size of the French army, the well-known ties between French and Irish Catholics, and the ubiquitous encroachments of French commercial endeavors into English economic preserves, convinced many that absolutist and religiously intolerant France represented the greater threat to English security, that France was the most serious aspirant to universal monarchy. In the autumn of 1666 these concerns were forcibly put in Parliament, forcibly put in such a way which called for a redefinition of the nature of the Restoration regime.

The ideological divisions in English political culture, in many ways submerged and muted since the outbreak of the war, reemerged with an explosion in the Parliamentary sessions of 1666–1667. Although no cohesive opposition party developed in this session, a fairly coherent ideological critique of Anglican Royalist conduct was powerfully and often vitriolically advanced in both the Commons and the Lords.[2] Observers of all political stripes knew that Parliament was deeply divided. The Anglican Royalist diarist Robert Milward referred to the divisions between "the old Parliament gang" and the "Royal party."[3] Early in the Parliamentary session Sir William Batten told Pepys that "they fall into faction;" several months later he noted "the great heart-burnings, one party against the other."[4] The Anglican Royalist merchant and naval supplier George Cocke described the heated debates between "the court" and "the other part."[5] Andrew Marvell, Nonconformist member of Parliament and former Cromwellian, advised his painter to "describe the Court and Country, both set right / On opposite points, the black against the white. / Those having lost the nation at trick-track, / These now advent'ring how to win it back."[6]

There could be no doubting the ill temper of Parliament.[7] The Anglican Royalist treasurer of the navy Sir George Carteret asserted that the Parliament is "in a bad humor," adding that the incompetence of the king's servants in the House of Commons "will put all in a fire."[8] Edward Conway thought the temper of Parliament was quite ominous indeed. To his friend George Rawdon he wrote that "there are as great discontents and parties in both houses, and as great expectations of trouble and confusion as ever there was in the year 40 or about those times."[9] The English radical

2 I agree with Seaward's lucid description of the ideological situation in this session. See Paul Seaward, *The Cavalier Parliament and the Restortion Crisis 1677–1683* (Cambridge, 1991) pp. 298–302.

3 Caroline Robbins (editor), *The Diary of John Milward* (Cambridge, 1938), 6 October 1666, p. 16.

4 Pepys, *Diary*, Vol. VII, 25 October 1666, pp. 341–342; Pepys, *Diary*, Vol. VIII, 8 February 1667, p. 49.

5 Pepys, *Diary*, Vol. VIII, 10 December 1666, p. 402.

6 Andrew Marvell, "Last Instructions to a Painter," 4 September 1667, *POAS*, p. 105.

7 Giustinian to Doge and Senate, 9/19 November 1666, *CSPV*, p. 103.

8 Pepys, *Diary*, Vol. VII, 14 November 1666, p. 370.

9 Conway to Sir George Rawdon, 10 November 1666, HL, HA 14445. See similar language

exiles in the United Provinces were confidently predicting "that a little time will bring forth a great alteration in England."[10] Allan Broderick reported after the Parliamentary session that a number of bishops "are very crazy, so that I doubt a short time may bring great alteration to the Church and state."[11]

So violent were disagreements in Parliament that a bill was brought in to prevent dueling.[12] Both of the most spectacular squabbles in Parliament involved the often flamboyant and always enigmatic Duke of Buckingham. In October the Earl of Ossory, one of the Duke of Ormonde's sons, challenged Buckingham to a duel as a result of his arguments in the Irish cattle debate.[13] The following month the two were at it again when Ossory saw fit to remind Buckingham's ally Lord Ashley of his Cromwellian past, and to call Buckingham himself a liar.[14] In December a hot debate over the Canary Company's patent – which Buckingham opposed – prompted the Marquis of Dorchester to come to blows with the belligerent duke.[15]

It was not only Buckingham's provocative personality which had made him the target of Anglican Royalist wrath. He had become the focus around which criticism of the conduct of the war could coalesce. Clarendon recalled bitterly that in this Parliamentary session a coalition was "begun and warmly pursued" between dissatisfied members of the House of Lords, led by the Duke of Buckingham, and "some members of the House of Commons who made themselves remarkable by opposing all thing which were proposed in that House for the king's service." Buckingham, Clarendon claimed, did all he could to "get an interest in all such persons, invited them to his table, pretended to have a great esteem of their parts, asked counsel of them, lamented the king's neglecting his business, and committing it to other people who were not fit for it; and thus reported all

in Conway to Ormonde, 27 October 1666, Carte 34, f. 459r; Conway to Rawdon, 8 March 1667, HL, MSS HA 14456. This was also the opinion of Roger Pepys: Pepys, *Diary*, 27 January 1667, pp. 32–33; Pepys, *Diary*, 27 February 1667, pp. 85–86.

10 Samuel Tucker to Arlington, 1/11 February 1667, PRO, SP 84/182, f. 19r. The previous year, after the less rancorous 1665 session of Parliament, the Northern radical Christopher Eyon thought England was faced with stark political choices: "it would be either a state and no king, or else a king and no state." W. Haglet (Durham) to Christopher Sanderson, 2 May 1666, PRO, SP 29/155/15.

11 Allan Broderick to Ormonde, 30 April 1667, Carte 35, f. 400r.

12 Newsletter, 11 October 1666, PRO, SP 29/174/139.

13 Thomas Rugge, "Mercurius Publicus Redivivus," 21 October 1666, BL, Add. 10117, f. 180r; Pepys, *Diary*, Vol. VII, 27 October 1666, pp. 342–343; Broderick to Ormonde, 27 October 1667, Carte 35, f. 111r; Arlington to Ormonde, 27 October 1666, Carte 46, f. 392r; Conway to Ormonde, 27 October 1666, Carte 34, f. 459v.

14 Pepys, *Diary*, Vol. VII, 19 November 1666, p. 376; Arlington to Ormonde, 20 November 1666, Carte 46, f. 402r.

15 Pepys, *Diary*, Vol. VII, 19 December 1666, pp. 414–415; Henry Coventry to Thomas Thynne, 21 December 1666, Longleat House, Thynne MSS 16, f. 449r; Arlington to Ormonde, 22 December 1666, Carte 46, f. 428; Denis de Repas to Sir Robert Harley, 22 December 1666, BL, Add. 70010, f. 355r.

the license and debauchery of the court in the most lively colors."[16] This was not the bitter revisionism of an exiled minister. Sir Allan Broderick informed Ormonde at the time that "my Lord of Buckingham behaves himself with great insolency and joins throughout with all the malcontents in the House of Commons."[17] The Earl of Orrery, who was rather more sympathetic to Buckingham, knew that he had become "the favorite of the House of Commons."[18] When the duke was arrested and stripped of his offices the following spring, ostensibly for having cast the king's horoscope, it was widely thought that his real crime was "his being of a cabal with some discontented persons of the late House of Commons, and opposing the desire of the king in all his matters in the House – and endeavoring to become popular."[19]

Although there had been persistent rumors of the revival of the Earl of Bristol's old faction, the criticism voiced in Parliament in the session of 1666–1667 had a much broader base than those previous opponents of the Earl of Clarendon.[20] This was not so much "the formed opposition" based on personal connections and a lust after power and place, described by Clayton Roberts, but rather a loose and very angry grouping based on ideological discontent.[21] The Duke of Buckingham facilitated cooperation and encouraged connections among many disparate groups and interests, all of which were becoming concerned about the increasingly intolerant and absolutist direction of the government's activity. This coalition included former Presbyterians and proponents of greater religious liberty like Lord

16 Hyde, *Life*, p. 369.

17 Broderick to Ormonde, 12 January 1667, Carte 35, f. 246v.

18 Orrery to Ormonde, 25 January 1667, *Orrery State Letters*, Vol. II, p. 137.

19 The phrase is Sir Hugh Cholmly's in Pepys, *Diary*, Vol. VIII, 3 March 1667, pp. 93–94. See also Marvell, "Last Instructions," 1667, *POAS*, p. 117; Thomas Rugge, "Mercurius Politicus Redivivus," 11 March 1667, BL, Add. 10117, f. 192v; Roger Morrice, "Eminent Worthies," Dr. Williams' Library, J, 1651(4). For his arrest and deprivation, see Sir Richard Browne to Evelyn, 26 February 1667, Christ Church, Evelyn In-Letters, 426; Pepys, *Diary*, Vol. VIII, 27 February 1667, p. 86; Joseph Williamson's Journal, 4 March 1667, PRO, SP 29/231, f. 1r; Henry Coventry to Thomas Thynne, 8 March 1667, Longleat House, Thynne MSS 16, f. 457r. For the astrological charge, see John Evelyn, notes for history of the second Dutch War, Christ Church, Evelyn MSS 134, f. 39; Arlington to Ormonde, 26 February 1667, Carte 46, f. 457. John Heydon, Buckingham's astrologer, proclaimed under threat of torture that "death shall close up the scene before I will be forced to damn my soul for a witness to their wicked designs, my last words shall be the duke is innocent, for I know nothing against him." Heydon to Stephen Mounteage, 13 March 1667, in Daniel Parsons (editor), *The Diary of Sir Henry Slingsby* (London, 1836), p. 368. Significantly the official newsletters publicized Heydon's former republican sentiments. See newsletter, 12 February 1667, Bodl., Don MSS C37, f. 10r; newsletter, 26 February 1667, Bod., Don MSS C37, f. 13v.

20 For the revival of the Bristolians, see Letter from Middleburgh, 3/13 December 1665, PRO, SP 101/47, f. 323v; newsletter from The Hague, 3/13 December 1665, PRO, SP 101/47, f. 325r; Pepys, *Diary*, Vol. VII, 26 August 1666, p. 261; Conway to Ormonde, 5 January 1667, Carte 35, f. 240v.

21 Clayton Roberts, *Schemes and Undertakings: A Study of English Politics in the Seventeenth Century* (Columbus, 1985), p. 63.

Ashley, Sir Robert Howard – who had become "no small man in that house, of which he is a member" – and Sir Richard Temple.[22] In addition to these "Presbyterian Switzers," Buckingham found support from "citizens and merchants" as well as from "a gross of English gentry, nobly born, / Of clear estates, and to no faction sworn."[23] In the Commons these country gentlemen included the well-respected John Vaughan, Sir Thomas Littleton – whom Sir William Penn described "as one of the greatest speakers in the House of Commons, and the usual second to the great Vaughan" – as well as William Garraway and Edward Seymour.[24]

These men were not held together by common political or religious backgrounds – they had fought on different sides in the 1640s and included Anglicans as well as Nonconformists – but had come to fear and despise the tenets of Anglican Royalist governance. They criticized the methods used to fight the war against the French and the Dutch, not the justice of the cause. They agreed with men like Buckingham and Sir Robert Howard that an intolerant baroque monarchy could not fight and win the war they thought they were fighting, that it was not a truly English style of government.

Buckingham attracted support precisely because he was perceived to be sympathetic to religious liberty and to oppose irresponsible and arbitrary government. Ironically it is possible that the very courtiers whom Buckingham did so much to frustrate in the Parliamentary session of 1666–1667 might have encouraged him to pose as a champion of Nonconformity. "The court doubting the issue of this second battle," heard Ludlow of the nervous month after the English defeat in the Four Days Battle, "think fit to promise liberty of conscience to the Presbyterians, to which end the Duke of Buckingham was sent to treat with the Lord Fairfax."[25] There can be little question that Buckingham was sympathetic to the cause. "We spurn not at opposite opinions," Buckingham wrote of the English nation, "a tree hath many branches which sprout from one body, so God hath many people

22 Conway to Ormonde, 13 November 1666, Carte 35, f. 126r; Conway to Ormonde, 29 December 1666, Carte 35, f. 197v. On Howard's importance and his commitment to liberty of conscience, see above and Orrery to Ormonde, 25 January 1667, *Orrery State Letters*, Vol. II, p. 137; Ruth Spalding (editor), *The Diary of the Bulstrode Whitelocke 1605–1675* (Oxford, 1990), 13 March 1663, pp. 663–664; John Finch to Conway, 17/27 July 1666, Carte 35, f. 52v. On Sir Richard Temple see Roberts, *Schemes and Undertakings*, p. 58.

23 Marvell, "Last Instructions," 1667, *POAS*, pp. 112–114.

24 See the valuable discussion of factional groupings in Seaward, *Cavalier Parliament*, pp. 94–96; St. Serfe's newsletter, 28 February 1667, LOC, 18124 Vol. I, f. 170r; Pepys, *Diary*, Vol. VII, 3 July 1666, p. 192; Pepys, *Diary*, Vol. VII, 18 July 1666, p. 210; Pepys, *Diary*, Vol. VII, 6 October 1666, pp. 310–311.

25 Ludlow, "A Voyce," Bod., English History MSS C487, p. 1126. It might well be this plan to unleash Buckingham which prompted Denis de Repas to inform the sympathetic Sir Robert Harley that "here is a talk of granting liberty of conscience." Denis de Repas to Sir Robert Harley, 4 July 1666, BL Add. 70010, f. 314v.

which worship several ways."[26] Two years later John Wilkins, who "was most openly and zealously for an accommodation or a comprehension of those that could be comprehended within the establishment and for an indulgence for others as the true interest of the Church," was preferred to the see of Chester "by the Duke of Buckingham's means."[27] Indeed Buckingham's sympathy for Nonconformity was known throughout the country. Among the fanatics it was reputedly known that "the duke said if the king had established the Presbyterian way, without bishops and common prayer, he had done well."[28] After Buckingham was sent to the Tower in early 1667, it was openly said in Coventry that "his chief offense was his activity against the Papists and in behalf of the Nonconformists."[29] Richard Bower claimed that the gossip in Yarmouth similarly ran "that the prosecuting of the Duke of Buckingham arises from his dispersing the Papists in Yorkshire."[30] In Yorkshire itself, where Buckingham was immensely popular with the justices of the peace, the deputy lieutenants as well as the Dissenters, one suspected fanatic praised the duke "for a true and brave statesman." Among the Dissenters in the North the general "discourse" held that Buckingham was "a well wisher of theirs."[31]

Buckingham, many were certain, was just as concerned about political liberty as he was about religious liberty. In his commonplace book he noted under the heading of government that "he that has hold of a glass may break it," presumably by holding it too tightly.[32] Buckingham claimed, Clarendon recalled, "that all his displeasure against the court proceeded from their declared malignity against the liberty of the subject, and their desire that the king should govern by the example of France."[33] He fumed quite publicly about the corruption implicit in the French style of government. He championed the "seamen's having their pay," remuneration which he said they were denied because of court

26 George Villiers, Duke of Buckingham, "A Field of Virtue," 1666, PRO, SP 29/187/184.

27 Roger Morrice, "Eminent Worthies," Dr. Williams' Library, Morrice MSS J, 1672(2). For more on Buckingham's commitment to toleration and his patronage of Wilkins, see Barbara Shapiro, *John Wilkins 1614–1672: An Intellectual Biography*. (Berkeley, 1969), pp. 170–171. Buckingham may well have been one of the "very many of the considerablest persons in England" whom William Say thought "do now apply to and court the phanatiques." Ludlow, "A Voyce," Bod., English History MSS C487, p. 1065.

28 William Leving's information, 12 February 1667, PRO, SP 29/191/91. See also L. W. to Sir George Lane, 7 February 1667, Carte 35, f. 302r.

29 R. H. (Coventry) to Williamson, 11 March 1667, PRO, SP 29/193/86.

30 Richard Bower (Yarmouth) to Williamson, 18 March 1667, PRO, SP 29/194/44.

31 William Haggert (Yorkshire) to Mr. Phillipson, 6 April 1667, PRO, SP 29/197/21I; Sir Philip Musgrave (Yorkshire) to Williamson, 2 May 1667, PRO, SP 29/199/28. For Buckingham's popularity in the north, see Thomas Osborne to Buckingham, 19 January 1665, BL, Egerton 3328, f. 12r; John Mascall (York) to Williamson, 21 July 1666, PRO, SP 29/164/24; Pepys, *Diary*, Vol. VIII, 7 April 1667, pp. 154–155.

32 Buckingham, "Commonplace Book," in C. Phipps (editor), *Buckingham: Public and Private Man* (New York, 1985), p. 202.

33 Hyde, *Life*, p. 370.

corruption.[34] More generally he pleaded, always with great panache, for "the ease and general burden of the nation."[35] The English, Buckingham insisted, were "oppressed with taxes" because they were being "cheated of their money by great officers."[36] No wonder that that most committed of absolutists, the Earl of Peterborough, detested the Duke of Buckingham.[37]

Buckingham and the loosely organized critics of the court, then, did not oppose the war which the government had initiated – indeed they loathed Dutch republicanism as passionately as any in England[38] – rather, they objected to the way in which it was being conducted. In fact, almost immediately upon their arrival in London the members of Parliament resolved "most unanimously" that "the king shall be supplied with what sums soever are necessary for the carrying on this war and are resolved most vigorously to prosecute it unless the Dutch will come to an honorable and just peace."[39] Although there were bitter debates over the means to supply the king in the subsequent months, commitment to the war never wavered. "How we shall raise the £1,800,000 voted yesterday, I cannot foresee," wrote Allan Broderick to Ormonde with a certain amount of concern, "but the House of Commons are very zealous in their resolutions of supporting the war or obtaining an honorable peace."[40]

It was precisely in the debate over the supply bill that the opponents of the government began to outline their case. The assault began when Buckingham introduced a bill in the House of Lords "to have all such as either has or hereafter shall embezzle his Majesty's treasure by cheats or any other fraudulent means to be punished as a felon."[41] Soon William Garraway "and those people" were complaining in the Commons about "the maladministration of things as to money."[42] The supply bill ground to a halt under the weight of bitter recriminations from a variety of discontented

34 "King Charles II's Discourse about Buckingham," 8 June 1667, Browning, Vol. II, p. 31; Information of Jeremy Bower of Bradford, April 1667, Parsons, pp. 375–376.

35 Intelligence from L. W., 7 February 1667, Carte 35, f. 304r.

36 Allan Broderick to Ormonde, 2 March 1667, Carte 35, f. 329.

37 Peterborough to Williamson, 11 April 1665, PRO, SP 29/117/96; Peterborough to Williamson, 16 April 1665, PRO, SP 29/118/55; Peterborough to Williamson, 20 April 1665, PRO, SP 29/118/95.

38 Clarendon claimed that Buckingham himself had promoted the war "all he could." Hyde, *Life*, p. 251.

39 Williamson's newsletter, 18 September 1666, Carte 72, f. 95r; Williamson's newsletter, 25 September 1666, Carte 72, f. 100r; Earl of Southampton to Winchilsea, 4 October 1666, LRO, DG7/Box 4984, Letters Folder; Giustinian to Doge and Senate, 9/19 November 1666, *CSPV*, p. 103.

40 Allan Broderick to Ormonde, 13 October 1666, Carte 35, f. 101r. See also newsletter, 8 November 1666, Carte 72, f. 110v; Arlington to Ormonde, 13 October 1666, Carte 46, f. 385v; Arlington to Ormonde, 10 November 1666, Carte 46, f. 396r.

41 St. Serfe's newsletter, 6 October 1666, LOC, 18124 Vol. I, f. 119r; Sir Thomas Clifford to Arlington, 6 October 1666, PRO, SP 29/174/85; Pepys, *Diary*, Vol. VII, 5 October 1666, pp. 308–309.

42 Pepys, *Diary*, Vol. VII, 10 October 1666, p. 317.

members of both houses. The Duke of York complained that "all must stand still till the king gets money." But, as Pepys recorded in his diary, the members were loath to do anything because they "are so dissatisfied with the king's management, and his giving himself up to his pleasures, and not minding the calling to account any of his officers."[43]

The tenor of the surviving discussions makes it clear that it was absolutism and not mere administrative incompetence which was the overwhelming fear. Supplying the king by means of a universal excise, for example, was objected to on the grounds that "it may make the king so rich as not to need a Parliament."[44] In early December William Garraway and Sir Robert Howard brought in a proviso to the supply bill – which "was carried against the court by 30 or 40 voices" – demanding that the government provide Parliamentary commissioners with an account of all the money received since the outbreak of he war.[45] "Such a distrust is fallen into the Parliament of the misapplication of money given to, and rising from the war," Arlington perceptively explained to William Temple, "that they are unwilling to finish the despatch of their new gift, till they are satisfied of the well expending of their former."[46] When Charles II rejected the proposed Parliamentary commission of inquiry in favor of a Royal commission, the Commons were furious. Arlington noted their "very ill temper," while George Mountagu informed Pepys that "all is like to go ill, the king's displeasing the House of Commons by evading their bill for examining accounts."[47] In the event the Poll bill was belatedly passed, and no full-scale inspection of the accounts took place until after the conclusion of the war. However, the debate over war finance revealed the deeply felt unease of many members of Parliament with the government's conduct of the war, the increasing concern that they were subject to an arbitrary government. The future Treasury commissioner Sir John Duncombe clearly understood the political implications of the increasing Parliamentary distrust of the ideological aspirations of those in government. He told Samuel Pepys that he doubted if the king "will ever make war again but [Parliament] will manage themselves."[48]

Many of the other issues around which Parliamentary discontent coalesced indicated the increasing fear of arbitrary government. "The grand particulars prosecuted by our patriots" included the impeachment of Lord Mordaunt, declaring the Canary patent a monopoly, and the suppression of

43 Pepys, *Diary*, Vol. VII, 31 October 1666, p. 349.

44 Edward Conway to Ormonde, 27 October 1666, Carte 34, ff. 459–460.

45 Pepys, *Diary*, Vol. VII, 8 December 1666, pp. 399–400; Arlington to Ormonde, 8 December 1666, Carte 46, f. 412r.

46 Arlington to Temple, 10 December 1666, Thomas Bebington (editor), *The Right Honourable the Earl of Arlington's Letters* ... (London, 1701), Vol. I, p. 111. See also Conway to Ormonde, 27 December 1666, Carte 35, f. 198r.

47 Pepys, *Diary*, Vol. VIII, 2 January 1667, p. 2; Arlington to Ormonde, 5 January 1667, Carte 46, ff. 434–435.

48 Pepys, *Diary*, Vol. VIII, 24 April 1667, p. 179.

Popery.[49] The governor of Windsor Castle Viscount Mordaunt had been a prominent Royalist conspirator in the 1650s, and was rewarded with his current post for his role in the Restoration. The impeachment proceedings against him were the result of some horrible accusations brought in by one his subordinates, William Tayleur. Even the sympathetic John Evelyn thought Mordaunt's conduct amounted to "tyranny during his government of Windsor Castle."[50] For many critics of the government, Paul Seaward has shown, Mordaunt's crime "was simply the most graphic illustration of a creeping corruption of the worst kind that was gradually engulfing the government."[51]

That the government had granted a patent to the Canary Company, many thought, was further proof of the arbitrary nature of the Restoration government. Edward Seymour, one of the leading members associated with Buckingham, insisted in a conference of the two Houses that "it was no wonder if patents of this nature were sometimes procured because importunity of ministers might prevail for grants that are uneasy."[52] This open castigation of government corruption coupled with the crescendo of complaints against Popery sounded extremely ominous to the historically minded. "Unless the king doth do something against my Lord Mordaunt and the patent for the Canary Company before the Parliament next meets,"

49 Broderick to Ormonde, 9 February 1667, Carte 35, f. 305r. See also Orrery to Ormonde, 18 January 1667, *Orrery State Letters*, Vol. II, p. 129; Arlington to Ormonde, 19 January 1667, Carte 46, f. 440; Broderick to Ormonde, 12 January 1667, Carte 35, f. 246. The Irish Cattle bill, which was frequently identified as part of the patriots' program, does reflect the growing economic discontent of the country. But while it was strongly opposed by Anglican Royalist Privy Councillors, it was also opposed by any who had Irish connections. Interestingly, however, some of the arguments advanced by the government's critics in favor of the bill also contained implied denunciations of absolutism. Sir Robert Howard, for example, defended the controversial "nuisance" clause in the bill on the grounds that "the king nor any king ever could do anything which was hurtful to the people" – the implication being that the prerogative was limited by the national interest. Pepys, *Diary*, Vol. VIII, 9 January 1667, p. 9.

50 Evelyn, *Diary*, 23 November 1666, p. 469. See similar statements in Pepys, *Diary*, Vol. VII, 26 November 1666, p. 386; Henry Coventry to Sir Thomas Thynne, 21 December 1666, Longleat House, Thynne MSS 16, f. 449r. The Mordaunt affair loomed large in the popular imagination. Pepys claimed that "many hundreds of people" crowded in to hear a conference between the two Houses over his impeachment. Pepys, *Diary*, Vol. VIII, 28 January 1667, p. 34.

51 Seaward, *Cavalier Parliament*, p. 287.

52 Quoted in Seaward, *Cavalier Parliament*, p. 285 (*Journal of the House of Lords*, Vol. 10, pp. 62–65). For discussion of the violent quality of the Parliamentary critique see Allan Broderick to Ormonde, 3 November 1666, Carte 35, f. 118r; Broderick to Ormonde, 29 December 1666, Carte 35, f. 191; Orrery to Ormonde, 11 January 1667, *Orrery State Letters*, Vol. II, p. 117. The Company was strongly supported by both Clarendon and Arlington: Sir Arthur Ingram (governor of the Canary Company) to Williamson, 2 October 1665, PRO, SP 29/134/12; Clarendon to Ormonde, 30 January 1666, Carte 47, f. 104v. It tended to irk the more politically radical London merchants, see petition of Samuel Wilson, November 1665, PRO, SP 29/137/113.

George Cocke believed "there will be a civil war before there will be any more money given."[53]

In the autumn of 1666, then, English political opinion underwent a dramatic transformation. While Sir Robert Holmes's dramatic and daring attack on the Dutch merchants in the Vlie had prompted celebrations and expectations of total victory throughout the British Isles, the Parliamentary session of 1666–1667 revealed a deeply divided and largely pessimistic political nation. The failure of the Orangist revolution in the United Provinces and the devastation wrought by the Fire of London had not so much transmogrified English political sentiment as revealed the tenuous nature of the ostensible Anglican Royalist consensus. Many groups besides Anglican extremists and ultra-Royalists had promoted the Restoration of the monarchy, but after the Northern Rebellion (1663) those other voices had been silenced. The Northern Rebellion had seemed to prove the Anglican Royalist case: religious dissent unleashed the most perverse of human passions, leading ineluctably to rebellion at home and ambitious imperialism abroad. The Dutch quest for universal dominion provided compelling evidence of the pernicious designs of a state governed along the principles of religious pluralism and political republicanism. French entry into the war, and the manifest universalist ambitions of Louis XIV, however, made it possible to voice an alternative set of political concerns. The French quest for universal monarchy, their duplicitous mediation between the English and the Dutch, their increasingly evident designs on the Spanish Netherlands, convinced many that an absolutist and intolerant state could be just as dangerous as a religiously radical and republican one. The evident governmental corruption, made manifest by the inability of the Restoration regime to defeat a foe quickly and easily despatched by the Interregnum regimes, led many to voice their now legitimated concerns about absolutism and intolerance in the domestic sphere. These were not merely the concerns of radicals – though many of the arguments made by Ludlow, Sidney, and their friends were now heard in Parliament – but of moderates who had never supported the Rump or Nominated Parliaments, who had enthusiastically welcomed the return of the king in 1660. For these people, and they existed throughout the kingdom, republicanism and absolutism were both dangerous threats from which England needed to be protected. They worried that while Charles II's government clearly appreciated the threat from the fanatics, they were seeking to emulate the French style of governance.

53 Pepys, *Diary*, Vol. VIII, 17 February 1667, p. 70.

24

The road to Chatham: the decision not to send out a battle fleet

The critics of the government "in whose hands we are yet entirely as to his Majesty's supply" were creating so much mischief in Parliament that "you will not wonder we make no more despatch in our preparations for the next year," complained Arlington to Sandwich who was now ambassador in Spain.[1] At the moment that the Dutch fleet was systematically burning his navy and terrifying the residents of his capital, Charles II fumed to Sir Thomas Osborne, one of the Duke of Buckingham's closest associates, that "we might thank those men" – those Parliamentary allies of Buckingham – for the Dutch fleet lying now upon our coast, for had the money been given in time "we had had a fleet in readiness."[2] So powerful was this analysis, so seemingly prophetic was Arlington after the devastating Dutch raid on the Medway in June 1667, that it has become the accepted explanation for the English failure to set out a fleet in the spring of 1667. Members of the House of Commons, whether out of a lust for personal power or because they knew the country was simply unable to finance another year's campaign, are said to have successfully obstructed the war effort.[3]

The enthusiasm with which members of the House of Commons had resolved to support their king with a generous supply for the war at the outset of the Parliamentary session, and the consistently anti-absolutist tone of much of the criticism of the conduct of the war, demand a reconsideration of the government's case. Was it Parliamentary intransigence and the consequent scarcity of financial resources which prompted the Privy Council to decide against preparing a full-scale battle fleet for the campaigning season of 1667?

1 Arlington to Sandwich, 13 December 1666, Thomas Bebington (editor), *The Right Honourable the Earl of Arlington's Letters* ... (London, 1701), Vol. II, pp. 211–212. See also Allan Broderick to Ormonde, 9 March 1667, Carte 35, f. 337r.

2 "King Charles II's Discourse about Buckingham," 8 June 1667, in Andrew Browning *Osborne*, Vol. II, p. 33.

3 See, for example, Hutton's argument that "men motivated primarily by a desire for personal power had almost crippled their country's capacity to fight, by playing with remarkable skill upon the prejudices and anxieties of back-benchers." Ronald Hutton, *The Restoration* (Oxford, 1985), p. 257.

The decision "of altering the manner of the war this year" was taken within weeks of the adjournment of the Parliamentary session.[4] Thomas St. Serfe immediately publicized and defended this strategic decision in his newsletter.[5] The news traveled just as quickly across the North Sea; De Witt and his friends quickly surmised that the English strategy "may facilitate their design."[6]

That the Dutch did have a design, that they intended to set out a battle fleet in conjunction with the French despite their economic difficulties was well known in England.[7] Letter after letter reached Williamson's office advising the English "not to flatter yourselves that the Hollander will not be soon ready."[8] By early April many throughout England thought the Dutch "will block up the very Thames and ride triumphant all the summer."[9] The government desperately sought to shore up naval defenses.[10] Lady Ranelagh announced to her brother Burlington that "if God restrain these enemies from pursuing the advantages they now have upon us, I shall think it fit to be a deliverance fit to be reckoned with '88 and the Gunpowder Treason."[11]

4 Pepys, *Diary*, Vol. VII, 6 March 1667, pp. 97–98; William Coventry to Ormonde, 12 March 1667, Carte 47, f. 476r; Pepys, *Diary*, Vol. VIII, 17 March 1667, p. 115. Though Arlington already predicted that it would be the strategy a month earlier: Arlington to Ormonde, 1 February 1667, Carte 46, f. 447v, it is quite likely that the decision to lay up the fleet was made informally well before the issue was debated openly in the Privy Council.

5 St. Serfe's newsletter, 16 March 1667, LOC, 18124 Vol. I, f. 177r. It is significant that St. Serfe, who might well have had close connections at court through Lauderdale, floated the strategy in his newsletter in early January: St. Serfe's newsletter, 12 January 1667, LOC, 18124 Vol. I, f. 152r.

6 William Temple to Arlington, 19/29 March 1667, PRO, SP 77/36, f. 145r. See also Benjamin Glanville to Williamson, 10/20 March 1667, PRO, SP 77/36, f. 127r.

7 For Dutch economic difficulties see, for example, Richard Watts (Deal) to Williamson, 21 December 1666, PRO, SP 29/182/79; William Davidson (Antwerp) to Williamson, 12/22 January 1667, W. del Court (editor), "Sir William Davidson in Nederland," in *Bijdragen voor Vaderlandsche geschiedenis en Oudheidkunde*, 4th series, Vol. 5 (1906), p. 393.

8 Davidson to Williamson, 2/12 March 1667, Del Court, "Sir William Davidson," pp. 396–397; D. S. to Williamson, 9/19 March 1667, PRO, SP 77/36, f. 123r. See also Giustinian to Doge and Senate, 26 February/8 March 1667, *CSPV*, p. 138.

9 Henry Oxenden to George Oxenden, 8 April 1667, BL, Add. 40713, f. 48; Davidson to Williamson, 30 March/9 April 1667, Del Court, "Sir William Davison," p. 405; Giustinian to Doge and Senate, 2/12 April 1667, *CSPV*, p. 147; Temple to Ormonde, 2/12 April 1667, Carte 35, f. 396v; Richard Watts (Deal) to Williamson, 5 April 1667, PRO, SP 29/196/89; Josselin, *Diary*, 7 April 1667, p. 535; John Carlisle (Dover) to Williamson, 7 April 1667, PRO, SP 29/196/118; Dr. William Denton to Sir Ralph Verney, 18 April 1667, Firestone Library, Verney MSS Reel 21 (unfoliated). The English were well aware of Dutch preparations for war throughout the spring. See Warham Jennett (Dover) to Sir Philip Froude, 20 April 1667, PRO, SP 29/197/146; Sir Jeremy Smith (Hull) to Williamson, 20 April 1667, PRO, SP 29/197/150; Arlington to Ormonde, 11 May 1667, Carte 46, f. 472v; Richard Watts (Dover) to Williamson, 16 May 1667, PRO, SP 29/201/9; John Smith (Margate) to Williamson, 1 May 1667, PRO, SP 29/201/15; Colonel Anthony Gilby (Hull) to Williamson, 19 May 1667, *CSPD*, p. 108.

10 Arlington to Burlington, 1 April 1667, BL, Althorp Papers B6 (unfoliated); Allan Broderick to Ormonde, 6 April 1667, Carte 35, f. 372r.

11 Lady Ranelagh to Burlington, 20 April 1667, BL, Althorp Papers B4 (unfoliated).

Though government finances were certainly limited, and many throughout England were reeling from the triple blow of plague, fire, and war, there is good reason to believe that money could have been raised to underwrite the fleet for one final campaign. The winter of 1666–1667 was not the first time that the naval administration had issued alarming reports of its inability to finance another campaign. "God knows what will become of all the king's matters in a little time," exclaimed the naval clerk Samuel Pepys in the autumn of 1665, "for he runs in debt every day, and nothing to pay them looked after."[12] It was not long before many came to their king's support. In late December 1665 "the bankers of the city" had advanced the crown "money for equipping the navy."[13] The East India Company and even the controversial Canary Company had followed suit.[14] Indeed as soon as Parliament had voted supply that year many throughout the kingdom advanced the king large sums.[15] Even after the disastrous Four Days Fight, at a time when Pepys thought the City merchants were "little pleased with the king's affairs," the City lent its king £100,000.[16]

Naturally another year of war, coupled with the economic devastation wrought by the Fire, further straightened mercantile finances. But there is no reason to believe that English merchants would not once again have rushed to support their government had they perceived the necessity, indeed had they been so much as approached. The Fire might have destroyed the merchants' houses and disrupted their trade, but it did not deprive them of their capital. George Cocke marveled that "never so great a loss as this was borne so well by citizens in the world as this," concluding that "not one merchant upon the Change will break upon it."[17] The merchants, concurred John Evelyn, "complied with their foreign correspondence as if no disaster at all had happened. Nor do we hear of so much as one that has failed."[18] The Exchange, temporarily displaced to Gresham College, was soon so

12 Pepys, *Diary*, Vol. VI, 16 October 1665, p. 268. Pepys's was not a lone voice. See Josselin, *Diary*, Vol. VI, 22 October 1665, p. 522; Allan Broderick to Ormonde, 23 December 1665, Carte 34, f. 514r; George Cocke in Pepys, *Diary*, Vol. VI, 3 September 1665, pp. 210–211; George Carteret in Pepys, *Diary*, Vol. VI, 27 November 1665, p. 311; Richard Povey in Pepys, *Diary*, Vol. VI, 15 October 1665, pp. 266–267.

13 St. Serfe's newsletter, 30 December 1665, LOC, 18124 Vol. I, f. 16r.

14 Williamson's newsletter, 24 April 1666, Carte 222, f. 99v; account of the battle, 7 June 1666, PRO, SP 29/158/48.

15 Williamson's newsletter, 23 January 1666, Carte 222, f. 87v. See, for example, the substantial sums recorded in "Lenders in Norfolk to the Crown," 14 April 1666, SRO, DW1744/7.

16 Pepys, *Diary*, Vol. VII, 18 June 1666, p. 171; Rugge, "Mercurius Politicus Redivivus," 21 June 1666, BL, Add. 10117, f. 166v; Pepys, *Diary*, Vol. VII, 21 June 1666, p. 174.

17 Pepys, *Diary*, Vol. VII, 15 September 1666, p. 287.

18 John Evelyn to Sir Samuel Tuke, 27 Septmber 1666, Christ Church, Evelyn Out-Letters. See similar statement in newsletter, 29 September 1666, Carte 72, f. 102r; Pepys, *Diary*, Vol. VIII, 25 September 1667, p. 450.

crowded with business that "there has hardly been any passage in or out for two hours together, though this place for the meeting of the merchants is rather more capacious than the former."[19] One newsletter-writer soon crowed that there was ten times more business being conducted in London than in Amsterdam.[20] No wonder, then, that the Dutch were reputedly astonished "that after the late ruin of London all men continue amongst us so merry and hearty, no sign of any such mischief, when they expected we should have been wholly ruined and lost."[21] There is every reason to believe that just as the Fire's disruption of commerce encouraged many to volunteer to serve in his Majesty's fleet, the narrowing of investment opportunities which was a necessary consequence of the Fire might well have made loans to the crown a more attractive investment.[22]

There is ample evidence to suggest that the English were still willing to dig into their depleted budgets to finance causes which they deemed worthy. After the Fire parish after parish throughout the country found it possible to raise "a very liberal contribution towards the relief of the City of London."[23] In addition, after the Chatham disaster, when no one could doubt the necessity for national defense, the City of London and many individuals again offered the king large sums.[24] Impoverished and weary the English might have been, but they could still summon the wherewithal to lend to a manifestly worthy cause.

It is not surprising, then, that most informed political observers thought the English would again send out a fleet for the campaign of 1667. Despite Parliamentary intransigence over the committee of accounts Allan Broderick could still confidently inform Ormonde that "we shall be able to set out as good a fleet as the last year (modestly speaking) if not a better, before the

19 Muddiman's newsletter, 11 November 1666, PRO, SP 29/178/69. See the similarly rosy economic picture painted in Thomas Flatman to Sancroft, 24 September 1666, Bod., Tanner MSS 45, f. 108r.

20 St. Serfe's newsletter, 18 December 1666, LOC, 18124 Vol. I, f. 142r.

21 Newsletter, 19 October 1666, Carte 72, f. 105v.

22 Giustinian to Doge and Senate, 25 September/5 October 1666, *CSPV*, 35, p. 81. See also Lady Gardiner to Sir Ralph Verney, 5 November 1666, Firestone Library, Verney MSS Reel 21 (unfoliated) (suggesting that merchants were searching for investment opportunities). I owe this point to Henry Roseveare.

23 Hugh Acland (Truro) to Williamson, 15 October 1666, PRO, SP 29/175/44. See also Josselin, *Diary*, 6 October 1666, p. 531; Thomas Holden (Falmouth) to James Hickes, 14 October 1666, PRO, SP 29/175/21; John Cosin (Durham) to Mayor of London, 14 December 1666, in George Ornsby (editor) *The Correspondence of John Cosin* Pt. II (Durham, 1872), pp. 163–164; Richard Izacke, *Antiquities of Exeter* (London, 1677), p. 172. For a typical sermon advocating donations for the relief of London see Edward Stokes, *A Sermon*, preached at Eton College, 10 October 1666 (Oxford, 1667).

24 Corportion of London Rep. Book, 21 June 1667, CLRO, Rep. 72, f. 124r; Duchess of Richmond and Lennox to Duke of Richmond, 2 July 1667, in Scott Robertson (editor), "Letters to the Duke of Lennox, A.D. 1667–1672," in *Archaeologia Cantiana* Vol. 17 (1887), p. 375; Pepys, *Diary*, Vol. VIII, 22 June 1667, pp. 283–284. For private donors, see Pepys, *Diary*, Vol. VIII, 23 August 1667, p. 397.

usual fighting time in June."[25] The naval supplier George Cocke was confident in February that if the king's council "were wise and the king would mind his business, he might do what he would yet."[26] "The new tax of poll money is well and cheerfully paid in everywhere and rises very high," reported the solicitor-general Heneage Finch, "so that God be praised we are in a good condition to make war."[27] William Temple was relieved to discover that "the slowness of your preparations this spring is rather from design to turn the course of the war upon another foot" than from "want of money."[28] After the Dutch success at Chatham Samuel Pepys and one of his fellow naval clerks – two of the men most qualified to comment upon the subtleties of naval finance – concurred "that it will hardly be want of money alone that will excuse to the Parliament the neglect of not setting out a fleet, it having never been (harbor) bound in our greatest straits; but how[ever] unlikely that it appeared, yet when it was gone about, the state or the king did compass it."[29]

It was this perceived capacity of the Restoration state to finance another campaign which provoked so many of the best-informed politicians to vilify those who had decided to lay up the fleet in 1667. Just days after the Dutch had broken through the chain in the Medway, the Earl of Anglesey concluded that the cost of hastily raising the militia to prevent a landing had put the government "to more charge than a fleet to have kept off our enemies would have done."[30] Significantly Anglesey, whose financial expertise subsequently won him the positions of treasurer of the navy and governor of the Royal Africa Company, claimed that nine months previously he had advised against the counsel taken "not to have a royal navy at sea sufficient to balance an enemy," warning "what the Dutch might and would do and is since partly accomplished."[31] Both the Earl of Carlingford, who had been Charles II's envoy in Germany, and the Duke of Ormonde advised, after the Parliamentary session, that "peace is best made with a good and ready sword in the hand."[32] John Evelyn, whose position as commissioner for sick and wounded seamen familiarized him with the complexities of naval wartime finance, exclaimed that "those who advised

25 Allan Broderick to Ormonde, 19 January 1667, Carte 35, f. 263r. It is significant that Broderick only changed his assessment after the Privy Council's strategic decision.

26 Pepys, *Diary*, Vol. VIII, 31 January 1667, p. 37.

27 Heneage Finch to Sir John Finch, 22 February 1667, LRO, DG7/Box4984, Letters Folder.

28 William Temple to Arlington, 2/12 April 1667, PRO, SP 77/36, f. 180v.

29 Pepys, *Diary*, Vol. VIII, 15 June 1667, p. 273.

30 Anglesey to Ormonde, 11 June 1667, Carte 47, f. 156r.

31 Anglesey to Ormonde, 15 June 1667, Carte 47, f. 158r. Anglesey's dating suggests that the proposal to lay up the fleet may have been accepted well before the vicious Parliamentary debates over the committee for accounts, and at about the time that the Earl of St. Albans began his negotiations with the French.

32 Ormonde to Anglesey, 23 February 1667, Carte 51, f. 30v; Carlingford to Ormonde, 16 February 1667, Carte 35, f. 313v; Carlingford to Ormonde, 26 February 1667, Carte 35, f. 323r.

his Majesty to prepare no fleet this spring, deserved I know not what!"[33] The Earl of Orrery, whose extensive political connections and close friendship with Charles himself allowed him to offer an informed opinion, complained to his brother Burlington that "we should either have been certain of peace and had it actually proclaimed, or else should have had the fleet in a body, especially when we knew the French and the Dutch were coming out stronger than ever."[34] The "disgrace" which Orrery bemoaned was a disgrace occasioned by a bad strategic choice, not necessitated by Parliamentary obstructionism.[35] Prince Rupert, who as admiral was intimately familiar with the conduct of the war and as a Privy Councillor was involved in the decision to lay up the fleet, announced in open Parliament that it was "none of the least miscarriages that have been observable in the late war, that no fleet was kept in a body the last summer."[36] Naturally many of these recriminations were attempts to evade blame for the disastrous outcome of the war; however, these arguments would have had little credibility had all agreed that the government had no choice but to lay up the fleet.

The desperate scramble to avoid responsibility began almost as soon as the Privy Council made its decision. By the second week of March the victualler of the navy Dennis Gauden reported that "our masters do begin not to like of their counsels in fitting out no fleet, but only squadrons and are finding out excuses for it."[37] Predictably enough, after the descent on Chatham the Council "were ready to fall together by the ears at the council-table, arraigning one another of being guilty of the counsel that brought us into this misery, by laying up all the great ships."[38] In his memoirs the Duke of York at various times blamed Clarendon, Southampton, Albemarle, and other ministers for the decision, while carefully absolving himself.[39] Southampton, who had opposed the war, had not played a significant role in any major decision since its outbreak, and who was in fact dying at the time, seems unlikely to have wielded the political muscle necessary to have pushed through such an important strategic decision. Albemarle, who was always in favor of force, was specifically absolved by Charles himself.[40] Indeed it was rumored that he had advised the king "in Council that whatever it should cost him to set forth his fleet once more ... but it was

33 Evelyn, *Diary*, Vol. VIII, 28 June 1667, p. 486; see also Pepys, *Diary*, Vol. VIII, 3 June 1667, pp. 248–249.

34 Orrery to Burlington, 1 July 1667, BL, Althorp Papers B4 (unfoliated).

35 Orrery to Ormonde, 25 June 1667, *Orrery State Letters*, Vol. II, p. 173.

36 Prince Rupert's Relation of the Affairs at Sea, 1667, Corpus Christi College MS 298, f. 91v. The speech is also summarized by Milward: Caroline Robbins (editor), *The Diary of John Milward* (Cambridge, 1938), 31 October 1667, pp. 106–107.

37 Pepys, *Diary*, Vol. VIII, 13 March 1667, p. 110.

38 Pepys, *Diary*, Vol. VIII, 14 June 1667, p. 269.

39 James S. Clarke, *The Life of James the Second* (London, 1816), Vol. I, p. 425.

40 ? to Viscount Conway, 15 June 1667, PRO, SP 29/205/78.

overruled by the good husbands of the Council."[41] Clarendon might at first glance seem to be one of those good husbands. But his close friend Allan Broderick opposed the decision at the time, and later insisted that Clarendon "had no share in the direction of the war, much less in detaining our first and second rate frigates in port to their destruction."[42] Indeed it is hard to imagine that a man who couldn't persuade the king to follow his advice on the Irish Cattle Bill in January could suddenly coerce him into taking such a radical military step. Another opponent of the war, and Clarendon's bitter enemy, Sir William Coventry was fingered for the decision by the Whitehall gossips.[43] However, Coventry's subsequent insistence that he "was never of opinion for making the war by parties" is supported by all the available evidence.[44] In February William Coventry had told the Duke of York that he "would not think [the Earl of Southampton] should offend God" by spending his Sundays raising loans for a war fleet rather than attending divine service.[45] In April he advised Pepys that "we shall soon have enough of fighting in this new way that we have thought on for this year."[46]

Many were quick to point out that the naval strategy of fighting in parties was originally proposed by the eminent Cromwellian seaman Sir John Lawson.[47] Henry Coventry went so far as to claim that "we make him a Privy Councillor in his grave."[48] However, it seems far more likely that it was the treasurer of the navy Sir George Carteret – along with Lawson one of the original proponents of making war with a "flying fleet"[49] – who, able to put his case before the Privy Council in both body and spirit, persuaded his colleagues to accept his naval strategy. Carteret's Francophilia and pathological hatred of Dissenters were very much the sentiments then in

41 R. Neville (Bellingham) to Sir Henry Neville, 21 June 1667, PRO, SP 29/206/116I. For corroboration of this rumor see Allan Broderick to Ormonde, 1 December 1666, Carte 35, f. 160.

42 Allan Broderick to Ormonde, [30] March 1667, Carte 35, ff. 356–357; Broderick to Ormonde, 2 July 1667, Carte 35, f. 522v.

43 Pepys, *Diary*, Vol. VIII, 14 June 1667, p. 270; Evelyn, *Diary*, 24 August 1667, p. 489.

44 William Coventry, "Notes," Longleat House, Cov. MSS XCVIII, f. 166r. For Coventry's opposition to the plan the first time it was floated see Coventry to Arlington, 5 May 1665, PRO, SP 29/120/68; Coventry to Arlington, 5 May 1665, BL, Add. 32094, f. 54v.

45 Pepys, *Diary*, Vol. VIII, 17 February 1667, pp. 66–67.

46 Pepys, *Diary*, Vol. VIII, 1 April 1667, p. 140. Additional circumstantial support is provided by Sir William's letter to his brother immediately after the descent on Chatham in which he averred that "all this is the consequence of our new way of making war by squadrons and not keeping a body of a fleet. God forgive them who advised it . . ." William Coventry to Henry Coventry, 14 June 1667, Longleat House, Cov. MSS LIV, f. 216r. This is hardly the language one would expect from a proponent of the pirating war strategy.

47 See for example, Castlemaine, "History of the Dutch War," 1668, NMM, Clifford Papers, Vol. III, Dw130, f. 14; St. Serfe's newsletter, 16 March 1667, LOC, 18124 Vol. I, f. 177r.

48 Henry Coventry to Thomas Thynne, 1 April 1667, Longleat House, Thynne MSS 16, ff. 461–462.

49 Allan Broderick to Ormonde, [30] March 1667, Carte 35, ff. 356–357.

vogue at court.[50] Indeed just at the time that the decision was taken to lay up the fleet George Cocke claimed that Carteret was "so great with the king that let the Duke of York and Sir William Coventry and his office do or say what they will, while the king lives, G[eorge Carteret] will do what he will."[51] Carteret had long bemoaned the state of the naval budget, suggesting that it would be impossible to set out a fleet for the previous year's campaign.[52] Very early in the Parliamentary session of 1666, long before criticism of the court's conduct of the war could have significantly delayed naval preparations for the 1667 campaign, Carteret was praying for "a good and speedy peace before it be too late."[53] The following month he told Pepys not only that "we shall not have a fleet at sea next year" but that it was "a thing expected by the king" and that "their matters were laid accordingly."[54] Often in the early months of the year he provoked William Coventry into violent outbursts because of his refusal to borrow money for the navy.[55] Indeed Carteret adamantly opposed having anything to do with the moneyed men in the City, calling all such proposals "dangerous discourse."[56] It is quite likely that Carteret believed, along with his fellow Anglican Royalist Daniel Fleming, that "most of our monied men" had "been anti-Royalists and still smattering ... somewhat thereof," and was therefore unwilling to put the kingdom literally in their debt.[57] No wonder "the people madly pursue[d]" Carteret after Chatham with all imaginable spite.[58]

Why had George Carteret and his supporters thought it best not to summon the nation's financial resources? What enabled them to persuade their colleagues that there was no need to prepare a fleet for the 1667 campaign? The difficult Parliamentary session, a session in which the Anglican Royalist agenda had come under bitter attack, convinced Arlington and many others that peace was "our most desirable object, all things that contribute to that are for the present best for us."[59] Clarendon

50 Pepys, *Diary*, Vol. VI, 6 November 1665, p. 291 (hatred of Dissenters); Pepys, *Diary*, Vol. VIII, 28 June 1667, pp. 299–300 (Francophilia).

51 Pepys, *Diary*, 17 February 1667, p. 69.

52 Pepys, *Diary*, Vol. VI, 6 November 1665, pp. 291–292. See also Pepys, *Diary*, Vol. VII, 26 January 1666, p. 24; Pepys, *Diary*, Vol. VII, 19 March 1666, p. 77.

53 Pepys, *Diary*, Vol. VII, 20 October 1666, pp. 334–335.

54 Pepys, *Diary*, Vol. VII, 25 November 1666, p. 383.

55 Pepys, *Diary*, Vol. VIII, 1 April 1667, p. 140; Pepys, *Diary*, Vol. VIII, 3 April 1667, pp. 143–144; Pepys, *Diary*, Vol. VIII, 12 April 1667, pp. 164–165.

56 Pepys, *Diary*, Vol. VII, 10 June 1666, p. 166.

57 Daniel Fleming (Rydal) to Williamson, 25 June 1666, PRO, SP 29/159/119. Gary De Krey informs me that similar reticence about borrowing from City Presbyterians was expressed in the 1670s.

58 Allan Broderick to Ormonde, 2 July 1667, Carte 35, f. 522v. Carteret was not previously popular with many members of Parliament, probably because of his perceived graft. See Pepys, *Diary*, Vol. VII, 13 October 1666, pp. 321–322; Pepys, *Diary*, Vol. VII, 5 November 1666, p. 356.

59 Arlington to Ormonde, 26 February 1667, Carte 46, f. 457r.

opined that Charles II opted for the defensive strategy precisely because he "was not without a reasonable hope of peace, which he resolved to cherish."[60] "Had there been the least suspicion" that the Dutch would not accede to a peace, Sir Andrew Riccard informed the East India Company's representatives at Breda, "they would have seen England in another posture, than they have now unluckily found it in."[61] It was a treaty, negotiated not with the Dutch but with Louis XIV, which allowed Carteret to persuade others of the Privy Council along with the king himself that there was no need to send out a fleet in 1667. The English government had allowed "the seamen to go trading voyagers," fumed Allan Broderick "whilst we trusted the promises of a faithless prince and the credulity of my Lord St. Albans."[62]

Many at court, including Charles II himself, had long wanted an alliance with Louis XIV, a king whose style of government they very much admired. Before the outbreak of the war Charles had been convinced that "a very fast friendship is good and necessary" for both he and his cousin Louis XIV.[63] In order to promote "a nearer union and firmer alliance" with France Charles had sent his dear friend Lord Fitzharding to Louis XIV with "private instructions."[64] Though Fitzharding's mission proved a failure, it did not put an end to English attempts at securing a French alliance. The Duke of York maintained a private correspondence with Louis XIV, a correspondence which encouraged him to assure Arlington that "the French will not fall out with us."[65]

Throughout the first summer of the war Arlington conducted negotiations with Louis XIV, using St. Albans as a go-between – a means of proceeding which infuriated Charles II's official ambassador Denzil Hollis.[66] It was this dallying with France which still rankled with Sir Richard Temple in 1667. He remained furious that "we should be deluded by French councils and

60 Hyde, *The Life of Edward Earl of Clarendon* (Dublin, 1760), p. 396. This sentiment is endorsed by the Earl of Arlington's biographer: see Violet Barbour, *Henry Bennet Earl of Arlington: Secretary of State to Charles II* (Washington DC, 1914), p. 105.

61 Andrew Riccard to Robert Thomson and Thomas Papillon, 14 June 1667, IOL, E/3/87, f. 40r. The author of the "New Instructions to a Painter," placed a rather less benevolent gloss on the government's negotiations: BL, Add. 28523, f. 71v.

62 Allan Broderick to Ormonde, 11 June 1667, Carte 35, f. 474v.

63 Charles II to Duchess of Orleans, 17 October 1664, Cyril Hartmann, *Charles II and Madame* (London, 1934), p. 117.

64 William Morrice to Henry Coventry, 11 November 1664, Longleat House, Cov. MSS LXIV, f. 29r; Charles II to Duchess of Orleans, 15 December 1664, Hartmann, *Charles II and Madame*, p. 134; Charles II to Duchess of Orleans, 5 January 1665, Hartmann, *Charles II and Madame*, p. 138.

65 Hollis to Bennet, 18/28 January 1665, PRO, SP 78/120, f. 17r; York to Arlington, 15 April 1665, PRO, SP 29/118/35.

66 St. Albans to Arlington, 15/25 July 1665, PRO, SP 78/121, ff. 9–10; St. Albans to Arlington, 22 July/1 August 1665, PRO, SP 78/121, f. 18v; St. Albans to Arlington, 25 July/4 August 1665, PRO, SP 78/121, f. 22; Hollis to Williamson, 14/24 October 1665, PRO, SP 78/121, f. 119v.

hanker so far after an alliance with the French so impossible and contrary to our interest as to neglect to set out any fleet till April following."[67] After the French declared war, Henrietta-Maria did everything in her power to prevent her son and nephew, Charles II and Louis XIV, from coming to blows.[68] Though the negotiations ultimately came to nothing – Arlington characterized the terms as "such as his Majesty might fairly have expected after the loss of a battle" – it is surely significant that Charles II and his government were still seeking means of accommodation with the French at the exact moment that his subjects were whipping themselves into a Francophobic frenzy.[69]

During the 1666 campaign St. Albans continually assured Arlington and Charles himself that Louis XIV was uninterested in supporting the Dutch in their war with England. He also insisted that while "the war with Holland is very good for you as long as you have no other enemies, when France comes to be declared with them in it, it will be no longer so."[70] It is unclear when the English government began to warm once again to the notion of a French alliance – it may well have been in the wake of the devastating Fire of London – but that they did so that autumn is certain.[71] Rumors of the Anglo-French negotiations soon began to leak. Many "suspected," Ludlow recalled, that there was "underhand treating of an agreement" between the French and English kings.[72] Thomas St. Serfe reported in his newsletter that there was "a whisper as if there were some underhand treaty with France."[73] Richard Cooling, Lord Chamberlain Manchester's secretary, informed Pepys "that he doth believe there are some things on foot for a peace between France and us."[74] In Paris,

67 Sir Richard Temple, general heads of grievances, 1667, HL, Temple Stowe STT Military Box 1 (50).

68 Newsletter from The Hague, 12/22 January 1666, PRO, SP 84/179, f. 11v; Hollis to Arlington, 3/13 March 1666, PRO, SP 78/122, f. 99r; William Temple to Arlington, 16/26 March 1666, PRO, SP 77/34, f. 126r; newsletter from The Hague, 30 March/9 April 1666, PRO, SP 101/48, f. 211; Letter from The Hague, 7/17 April 1666, PRO, SP 101/48, f. 238v; Arlington to William Temple, 10 April 1666, Bebington, *Arlington's Letters*, Vol. I, p. 73; St. Albans to Arlington, 10/20 April 1666. PRO, SP 78/122, f. 136v; newsletter from The Hague, 13/23 April 1666, PRO, SP 101/48, f. 260r.

69 Arlington to Temple, 27 April 1666, Bebington, *Arlington's Letters*, Vol. I, p. 75; diary of Sir William Clarke, 28 April 1666, BL, Add. 14286, f. 9r; Arlington to Ormonde, 28 April 1666, Carte 46, f. 290r; Charles II to Duchess of Orleans, 2 May 1666, Hartmann, *Charles II and Madame*, p. 181; diary of Sir William Clarke, 5 May 1666, BL, Add. 14286, f. 15v.

70 Arlington to Ormonde, 3 July 1666, Carte 46, f. 329; St. Albans to Arlington, 12/22 August 1666, PRO, SP 78/121, ff. 41–42.

71 Giustinian to Doge and Senate, 28 August/7 September 1666, *CSPV*, p. 63; Charles II to Duchess of Orleans, 18 October 1666, Hartmann, *Charles II and Madame*, pp. 184–185; St. Albans to Ormonde, 20 November 1666, Carte 35, f. 132v; K. H. D. Haley, *An English Diplomat in the Low Countries* (Oxford, 1986), p. 104.

72 Ludlow, "A Voyce," Bod., English History MSS C487, p. 1142.

73 St. Serfe's newsletter, 27 November 1666, LOC, 18124 Vol. I, f. 134r.

74 Pepys, *Diary*, Vol. VIII, 9 January 1667, p. 11.

Brussels, and The Hague diplomats were confidently predicting an Anglo-French accord.[75]

That there was no official confirmation of the negotiations was part of a well thought-out strategy. While the peace "overture is pleasing to his Majesty and those he principally trusts," Arlington explained to Ormonde, Charles II had no intention of acknowledging officially the negotiations then in progress for fear such an admission would provide the House of Commons with a pretext not to vote supply.[76] No wonder Pepys's Presbyterian stationer was convinced the "queen mother is about and hath near finished a peace with France," a peace which he feared "will be a means to introduce Popery."[77] No wonder Marvell later so successfully turned his venom on St. Albans, that man whom "age, allaying now that youthful heat, / Fits him in France to play at cards and treat." He was given "no commission lest the court should lie, / That disavowing treaty, ask supply."[78]

As soon as the Poll Bill had passed, the Earl of St. Albans was despatched back to Paris with instructions – official ones this time – to sound out "the reality of the French king's intentions for peace" and willingness to compel the Dutch to "agree to just and honorable conditions."[79] Clarendon was technically correct if substantively disingenuous, then, when he later claimed that it was "about the time when the Parliament was prorogued" that St. Albans informed Charles "that he was confident, if his Majesty would make any advance towards a peace, the queen would be able to dispose that king to hearken to it, and to be a mediator between England and Holland."[80]

The optimistic Francophile St. Albans was soon writing from Paris full of enthusiasm for the peace. Though "there is no certainty what will be done in order to peace," he scribbled to Ormonde upon his arrival in Paris, "but I am of judgment that they do here desire it enough to embrace it upon such terms as are good for us to wish it upon."[81] To Arlington and Charles St. Albans elaborated that Louis XIV promised "to satisfy entirely" the English demands as outlined in his instructions on the condition that Charles II offered "assurance of taking no engagement contrary to the interests of France in the space of one year."[82] Louis XIV wanted a guarantee that he

75 Giustinian to Doge and Senate, 11/21 December 1666, *CSPV*, p. 114; Giustinian to Doge and Senate, 18/28 December 1666, *CSPV*, p. 116; Letter from The Hague, 10/20 January 1667, PRO, SP 101/51/14; newsletter from Holland, 10 January 1667, PRO, SP 101/51/15.

76 Arlington to Ormonde, 18 December 1666, Carte 46, f. 426r; Haley, *English Diplomat*, p. 105.

77 Pepys, *Diary*, Vol. VII, 24 December 1666, p. 420.

78 Marvell, "Last Instructions," 4 September 1667, *POAS*, pp. 101–102.

79 Instructions to St. Albans, 1667, Bod., Clar. 84, f. 43r; Carlingford to Ormonde, 15 January 1667, Carte 35, f. 251r.

80 Hyde, *Life*, p. 400.

81 St. Albans to Ormonde, 6/16 February 1667, Carte 35, f. 300r.

82 St. Albans to Arlington, 6/16 February 1667, Bebington, *Arlington's Letters*, Vol. I, p. 125; St. Albans to Charles II, 6/16 February 1667, in F. A. M. Mignet, *Négociations Relatives a la Succcession d'Espagne Sous Louis XIV* (Paris, 1835), Vol. II, p. 42.

would have a free hand to pursue his designs in Flanders, to secure his wife's rights to the Spanish Netherlands.[83] In return he promised to use his "interest" with the Dutch to make "a good and honorable" peace with the English. As soon as this news reached London, Charles II signed the required letter to the queen mother and returned it by courier to Paris.[84]

While the English were at times concerned about the quality of the terms which the French would secure for them, they were confident that Louis XIV would guarantee a peace. St. Albans never wavered in his belief that there would be "a quick agreement."[85] When the English and Dutch ambassadors were about to sit down to the negotiating table along with the French, St. Albans wrote confidently of French support for the English demands, assuring Arlington that there was "no appearance that it can miscarry."[86] While Arlington occasionally doubted French sincerity, he announced in late February that "we begin to believe they are in earnest."[87] By early April St. Albans was congratulating Arlington for his resumed "confidence of this court."[88] To Ormonde Arlington wrote that "we may in all events conclude the peace will be made, the only question will be upon the goodness of the conditions."[89] During the peace treaty itself Arlington insisted "that the measures France hath taken will oblige them to press the conclusion of that negotiation."[90] That spring all at court were confident that the French would force De Witt and his political allies to a peace. "We have assurance from France of their real intention for a peace," William Morrice assured Thomas Thynne, though there was "pregnant reason to doubt that the governing party in Holland inclines not thereunto, but yet we suppose they will be carried about by the first mover, viz. France."[91]

83 Subsequent explications of this treaty make it clear that this was the intent, and that the English understood this. Ludlow, "A Voyce," Bod., English History MSS C487, p. 1144; Arlington to Ormonde, 18 May 1667, Carte 46, f. 476r; Allan Broderick to Ormonde, 3 August 1667, Carte 35, f. 595v.

84 Arlington to Ormonde, 12 February 1667, Carte 46, f. 450; Arlington to St. Albans, 12 February 1667, PRO, SP 78/123, f. 22r; Charles II to Henrietta Maria, 1667, Bebington, *Arlington's Letters*, Vol. I, pp. 139–140; Charles II to St. Albans, 1667, Mignet, *Négociations*, Vol. II, p. 43.

85 St. Albans to Ormonde, 28 March/7 April 1667, Carte 35, f. 364r; St. Albans to Ormonde, 10/20 April 1667, Carte 35, f. 366; St. Albans to Ormonde, 24 April/4 May 1667, Carte 35, f. 403r.

86 St. Albans to Arlington, 4/14 May 1667, PRO, SP 78/123, f. 82r; St. Albans to ?, 7 May 1667, HMC, *5th Report*, p. 315; St. Albans to Ormonde, 18/28 May 1667, Carte 35, f. 446r.

87 Arlington to Ormonde, 26 February 1667, Carte 46, f. 456; Arlington to Sandwich, 28 February 1667, Bebington, *Arlington's Letters*, Vol. II, p. 220. For Arlington's doubts, about the quality of the terms not the French desire for a peace, see Arlington to Ormonde, 9 March 1667, Carte 46, f. 461r.

88 St. Albans to Arlington, 10/20 April 1667, PRO, SP 78/123, f. 67r.

89 Arlington to Ormonde, 27 April 1667, Carte 46, ff. 470–471.

90 Arlington to Sandwich, 9 May 1667, Bebington, *Arlington's Letters*, Vol. II, p. 223.

91 William Morrice to Thomas Thynne, 19 April 1667, Longleat House, Thynne MSS 30, f. 40r.

William Coventry, Pepys noted, "seems to be sure of a peace."[92] Allan Broderick was convinced that "the K[ing] of France [is] more impatient than we of despatching the treaty."[93]

The diplomatic instructions drawn up for the ambassadors going to negotiate a peace with the Dutch reminded them "of all that hath privately passed between us and France," which explained "the great cause we have to promise ourselves all assistance from thence toward the peace."[94] Henry Coventry made it clear in his diplomatic correspondence with Clarendon that he was well aware that the French had obliged themselves in Paris to compel the Dutch to a reasonable peace.[95] During the descent on Chatham, Arlington reassured Henry Coventry that in exchange for the English promise "not to enter into any league against the interest of France for one whole year" the French vowed not only to "restore entire what they had taken from us in America" but also that they "would employ their credit with Holland to get us a good peace and upon the terms you already know."[96] It was in fact common court gossip that Louis XIV had told the French ambassador that "he is for the King of England's having an honorable peace."[97]

The Anglo-French negotiations were not a closely kept secret. Dr. William Denton informed Sir Ralph Verney within two days of the Anglo-French agreement that "here was a messenger from my Lord St. Albans who was despatched and returned the next day; his errand was thought to be peace."[98] Throughout the spring rumors circulated that the English and French had agreed. In Dover there was "nothing but a discourse of peace with France."[99] Sir Hugh Cholmley, one of the queen's gentlemen ushers, told Pepys that France "hath assured our king that if he will make a league with him, he will make a peace exclusive to the Hollander."[100] Henry Muddiman apparently circulated accounts of the treaty with the French in his newsletter.[101] "Many believe the particulars of the treaty are already adjusted," Carlingford told Sir Edward Dering, "whereof our making so

92 Pepys, *Diary*, Vol. VIII, 22 April 1667, p. 175. See also Sir William Coventry to Sir James Thynne, 3 May 1667, Longleat House, Thynne MSS X, f. 174r.

93 Allan Broderick to Ormonde, 30 April 1667, Carte 35, f. 400r.

94 Instructions to Henry Coventry and Denzil Hollis, 18 April 1667, Bod., Clar. 159, f. 68r. There is another copy of these instructions at PRO, SP 84/182, f. 101r.

95 Henry Coventry to Clarendon, 10/20 May 1667, Bod., Clar. 159, f. 2v.

96 Arlington to Henry Coventry, 7 June 1667, Longleat House, Cov. MSS XLIV, f. 37. See similar assurances from Clarendon to Hollis: Clarendon to Hollis, 27 May 1667, Bod., Clar. 159, f. 7.

97 Pepys, *Diary*, Vol. VIII, 18 April 1667, p. 170.

98 Dr. William Denton to Sir Ralph Verney, 14 February 1667, Firestone Library, Verney MSS Reel 21 (unfoliated).

99 John Carlisle (Dover) to Williamson, 5 March 1667, PRO, SP 29/193/45.

100 Pepys, *Diary*, Vol. VIII, 11 March 1667, p. 108. Cholmley repeated the story to Pepys on 24 March 1667, pp. 127–128.

101 Thomas Corie (Norwich) to Dr. John Crofts, 20 March 1667, PRO, SP 29/194/80. This may have been the basis of the story circulating in Lynn. See Edward Bodham (Lynn) to Williamson, 27 March 1667, PRO, SP 29/195/43.

little preparations for war is a proof."[102] Certainly George Cocke was one of those who knew the terms of the assurances from France, and was confident that "our peace is agreed on."[103]

By May "the peace between us and France is not now doubted by anybody."[104] One correspondent of the Earl of Huntingdon confidently predicted that "tomorrow or Thursday ... the peace with France will be proclaimed in this city."[105] Frederick Thynne reported that "vulgarly we say we have concluded a peace with France for two campaigns."[106] To Burlington Lady Ranelagh wrote that "here is a report grown current that we shall have a peace with the French and Swedes excluding the Dutch and Dane."[107] In Rydal, Deal, and Lyme "almost everybody says that peace is concluded on between us and France."[108] A newsletter-writer from Rotterdam, then, was not far wrong to claim that "the common opinion is there that England and France will agree without Holland."[109]

Gossip in diplomatic circles and merchant enclaves throughout Europe agreed unanimously that the English and French had come to an underhand agreement. William Temple informed Arlington that "De Witt and his party" knew well that a treaty was being concluded in Paris.[110] The Venetian ambassador in Paris confided to his superiors that a "good understanding" was "universally believed to be definitely established between England and this crown."[111] In Hamburg "the common discourse is an agreement betwixt France and England."[112] Similar reports were also current in the Spanish Netherlands.[113]

The English government, then, failed to prepare a battle fleet for the campaigning season of 1667 not because it was financially incapable of doing so, but because it had been assured by the French that this would not be necessary.[114] Carefully keeping the French negotiations in play, while

102 Carlingford to Sir Edward Dering, 20 April 1667, BL, Stowe MSS 744, f. 157.
103 Pepys, *Diary*, Vol. VIII, 22 April 1667, p. 176.
104 Sir Ralph Verney (London) to Edmund Verney, 2 May 1667, Firestone Library, Verney MSS Reel 21 (unfoliated).
105 Gervase Jacques to Earl of Huntingdon, 7 May 1667, HL, HA 7657.
106 Frederick Thynne to Thomas Thynne, 9 May 1667, Longleat House, Thynne MSS XXX, f. 54r.
107 Lady Ranelagh to Burlington, 11 May 1667, BL, Althorp Papers B4 (unfoliated).
108 Richard Watts (Deale) to Williamson, 30 May 1667, PRO, SP 29/202/90. See also Daniel Fleming (Rydal) to Williamson, 4 May 1667, PRO, SP 29/199/66; Anthony Thorold (Lyme) to James Hickes, 1 June 1667, PRO, SP 29/203/3.
109 Newsletter from Rotterdam, 21/31 May 1667, PRO, SP 101/51/56.
110 William Temple to Arlington, 15/25 March 1667, PRO, SP 77/36, f. 139r.
111 Giustinian to Doge and Senate, 30 April/10 May 1667, *CSPV*, p. 156. See also Giustinian to Doge and Senate, 23 April/3 May 1667, *CSPV*, p. 152.
112 E. Jollyvet (Hamburg) to Thomas Thynne, 14 May 1667, Longleat House, Thynne MSS 20, f. 29r.
113 Benjamin Glanville to Williamson, 26 May/5 June 1667, PRO, SP 77/36, f. 275r; newsletter from Haarlem, 10/20 May 1667, PRO, SP 101/51/28.
114 This seems to be the conclusion drawn by Haley, *English Diplomat*, p. 110.

scrupulously avoiding any official commitment, Charles II managed to secure Parliamentary supply for a war which he felt confident he would not have to fight. The most deeply committed Anglican Royalist ministers much preferred negotiating with the French than making concessions to their Parliamentary critics. Rather than fight a war or negotiate a peace with the republican and religiously pluralist Dutch, they seized the opportunity to procure an alliance with the most powerful monarch in Europe, with the assurance that he would compel the Dutch to accede to reasonable terms. Once the Earl of St. Albans had secured Louis XIV's assent to an agreement, Sir George Carteret had little difficulty in pushing his preferred naval strategy through the Privy Council. Unfortunately for Carteret and his colleagues, this strategy was widely publicized, creating popular expectations of an honorable and advantageous peace.

A peace guaranteed by France had become increasingly attractive to Charles II and his embattled ministers over the course of the Parliamentary session of 1666–1667. While more moderate councilors had advocated making concessions, almost any concessions, in order to procure a supply and continue the war, other ministers began to enunciate alarmingly absolutist prescriptions. Absolutism, of course, had long been suspected by the critics of the Restored Monarchy. Sir Hugh Cholmley told Pepys at the outset of the Parliamentary session that "there is reason to fear that as soon as the Parliament have raised this money, the king will see that he hath got all that he can get, and then make up a peace."[115] A few months later it was common gossip that "all our court are mightily for a peace, taking this [to] be the time to make one, while the king hath money, that he may have something of what the Parliament hath given him to put him out of debt, so as he may need the help of no more Parliaments as to the point of money."[116] "Yet draw these causers of the kingdom's woe," one poet advised her painter, "still urging dangers of the common foe / asking new aids for war, with the same face / as if (when given) they meant not to make peace."[117]

While there can be no question that Charles II and most of his ministers had originally been quite forthright about their commitment to the Anglo-Dutch War, in the autumn of 1666 – in the wake of the Fire and their discomfort over the French entry into the war – they do seem to have taken a turn toward a rather higher view of the royal prerogative. They did begin to favor a French style of government. After the Fire Baptist May, the

115 Pepys, *Diary*, Vol. VII, 15 October 1666, p. 323.
116 Pepys, *Diary*, Vol. VIII, 14 February 1667, p. 62. See also Pepys, *Diary*, Vol. VIII, 31 March 1667, p. 139.
117 "New Instructions to a Painter," 1667, BL, Add. 28253, f. 71r. For more extreme statements about a concerted absolutist program see Ludlow, "A Voyce," Bod., English History MSS C487, p. 1089; *The Happy Union of England and Holland* (London, 1689), pp. 14–15.

Keeper of the Privy Purse, enthused to the king "that this was the greatest blessing that God had ever conferred upon him, his Restoration only excepted," for now London "that rebellious city which was always an enemy to the crown" could never again be "a bit in his mouth and a bridle upon his neck." May concluded that there was "no other way to govern that rude multitude but by force."[118] This interpretation apparently received broad approval at court. According to Richard Baxter many courtiers "cried out rejoicingly: 'Now the rebellious city is ruined, the king is absolute, and was never king indeed till now.'"[119] The Anglican Royalist merchant George Cocke assured Pepys that the Fire "will make the Parliament more quiet than otherwise they would have been, and give the king a more ready supply."[120]

Parliament did not prove to be suppliant, did not at all acquiesce to the newfound enthusiasm for a more perfect monarchy at Whitehall. George Carteret lamented Charles II's compromise commission of accounts, claiming that by doing so he "is become but as a private man." "The king must," he urged, "if [Parliament] do not agree presently, make them a courageous speech; which he says he may do (the City of London being now burned, and himself master of an army) better than any prince before him."[121] In the face of the barrage of Parliamentary criticisms, Edward Conway wrote to the sympathetic Duke of Ormonde, that "if the king will be resolute to his own resolutions, 'tis certainly the best way of encountering such a calumniation."[122] He soon announced that Charles II was limited to two options: "either the kingdom will be reduced to a commonwealth or the king must dissolve this present [Parliament] and govern by some other medium."[123] "I wish we could hear of some overtures toward peace," Ormonde himself wrote to William Temple, "then would the king be freed from a necessity of consenting to unreasonable things" from Parliament.[124] The true danger to English government, in Ormonde's eyes, came from the unsettling demands of the newly organized opposition, not from anything the French might do. "I confess," he confided to Anglesey, "I am more disturbed with fear of misunderstandings in Parliament than with anything our enemies can do against us without it."[125] "Nothing can help us but the king's making a peace as soon as he hath this money," insisted the naval

118 Hyde, *Life*, pp. 355–356.
119 Sylvester, *Reliquiae Baxterianae* (London, 1696), Pt. III, p. 18; Hyde, *Life*, p. 356.
120 Pepys, *Diary*, Vol. VII, 15 September 1666, p. 286.
121 Pepys, *Diary*, Vol. VII, 4 October 1666, p. 307. Sir Richard Ford, who had been one of the court's most prominent mercantile advisors during the war, seemed to advise a similar solution when he lamented that "the House of Commons is a beast not to be understood." Pepys, *Diary*, Vol. VII, 19 December 1666, p. 416.
122 Conway to Ormonde, 29 December 1666, Carte 35, f. 197v.
123 Conway to Ormonde, 5 January 1667, Carte 35, f. 240v.
124 Ormonde to William Temple, 14 October 1666, Carte 47, f. 304.
125 Ormonde to Anglesey, 19 January 1667, Carte 51, f. 24r.

administrator, chancellor to the queen, and scientific virtuoso Viscount Brouncker, "thereby putting [the king] out of debt, and so becoming a good husband; and then he will neither need this, nor any other Parliament till he can have one to his mind."[126] Arlington, who had previously advised the use of force to eliminate the Nonconformist threat, now hoped that "we can get this succor complete and a tolerable peace after it" so that "his Majesty's affairs may pretend a good face."[127]

Clarendon, for all of his commitment to the law and political moderation, seems to have lost his nerve in the winter of 1666–1667. Conway was able to "perceive in his discourse" that the Lord Chancellor "hath a great mind to dissolve this Parliament."[128] This was certainly the popular perception. "What frosts to fruit, what ars'nic to the rat," rhymed Andrew Marvell in his famous portrait of Clarendon, "what to fair Denham mortal chocolate, / What an account to Cart'ret, that, and more, / A Parliament is to the Chancellor."[129] Clarendon's son-in-law the Duke of York, while he almost certainly advocated sending the fleet to sea in 1667, was hardly an opponent of sterner measures. He had long advised raising an army in the north, which he would lead in order to overawe Scotland, keep the north in line, and "in some degree balance London, and make them court more the favor of the crown."[130] Gilbert Burnet was not far wrong to claim that James felt deeply that "everything is to be carried on in a high way, and that no regard is to be had to the pleasing the people, and he has an ill opinion of any that proposes soft methods."[131] No wonder Charles reputedly told his brother that he had no fear of assassination since "they will never kill a lamb to have a lion rule over them."[132]

Anglican Royalists openly espoused a more elevated view of the prerogative at this time. Cortez, the hero of John Dryden's *Indian Emperour* performed in January 1667, asserted that "monarchs may err, but should each private breast / judge their ill acts, they would dispute their best." Against the notion that private citizens should criticize their rulers to further the public good, another of Dryden's heroes asserted that "what e're faults in princes time reveal, / none can be judge where can be no appeal."[133] "They that rule are God's substitutes, and no creatures of the people," preached Joseph Glanville on Charles the Martyr Day 1667, "for the people have no power to govern themselves, and consequently cannot devolve any

126 Pepys, *Diary*, Vol. VII, 16 December 1666, p. 411.
127 Arlington to Ormonde, 18 December 1666, Carte 46, f. 426v.
128 Conway to Ormonde, 2 February 1667, Carte 35, f. 290v.
129 Marvell, "Last Instructions to a Painter," 1667, *POAS*, p. 116.
130 Pepys, *Diary*, Vol. VI, 25 October 1665, p. 277 (reporting gossip from the Earl of Sandwich); Earl of Peterborough to Williamson, 12 August 1665, PRO, SP 29/129/15 (he is almost certainly referring to the same proposal).
131 Burnet, "History," BL, Add. 63057A, f. 77v.
132 Diary of Henry Townsend, 22 April 1661, BL, Add. 38490, f. 73r.
133 John Dryden, *The Indian Emperour* (London, 1667), pp. 50, 80.

upon another."[134] "Believe it," thundered Clarendon's chaplain Robert South; "it is a resolute tenacious adherence to well chosen principles, that adds glory to greatness, and makes the face of a governor shine in the eyes of those that see and examine his actions. Disobedience, if complied with, is infinitely encroaching and having gained one degree of liberty upon indulgence, will demand another upon claim."[135] In a pamphlet published with Gilbert Sheldon's imprimateur Sir Francis Theobald insisted that in England "we have ... absolute monarchy, and herein we differ from the Lacedaemonian-kings, who were subject to their ephori, which had a power above them: No, ours agree with the Persian-government; for their kings had plenary power in all things, not subject to be called to account by any person whatsoever; and so is ours ... So that it is an unquestionable truth, that the king is subject to no overruling power of man, and that he is free from all humane coercion and restraint."[136] Among Joseph Williamson's papers is a treatise by his friend from Queen's College days, John Brydall, asserting that "to do what he will without punishment, that is to be a king ... which dignity cannot indeed consist, if the peers of the realm, or the Commons, or both together in Parliament, or the people collectively, or representatively have any coercive power over the person of the King of England, from whom all authority is derived; and whose only presence doth silence and suspend all inferior jurisdiction and force." These powers meant, Brydall explained, that the king "is above all law," and that "the property of the subject shall not so exclude the dominion of the sovereign but that he may for the good of the Commonwealth deprive any of his subjects of their right."[137] No wonder so many of Charles II's advisors were attracted to a treaty negotiated by a man who hoped to build a new Versailles at Greenwich.[138]

Clearly it was not merely the paranoid imaginations of such diverse critics as Edmund Ludlow, Andrew Marvell, and Sir Richard Temple which perceived a "design of introducing an arbitrary government and standing army" being promoted by "some of the king's great officers to the jealousy

134 [Joseph Glanvill], *A Loyal Tear Dropped at the Vault of Our Late Martyred Sovereign* (London, 1667), preached 30 January 1667, pp. 6–7.

135 Robert South, *A Sermon Preached at Lambeth Chapel*, 25 November 1666 ([London], 1666), p. 29. In a clear reflection on the rhetorical strategies of the Parliamentary critics of the court South went on to ask "was not this method observed in the late most flourishing and successful rebellion? for how studiously did they lay about them, both from the pulpit and the press, to cast a slur upon the king's person, and to bring his governing abilities under a disrepute? And then, after they had sufficiently blasted him in his personal capacity, they found it easy work to dash and overthrow him in the political" (pp. 19–20).

136 Sir Francis Theobald, *A Discourse Concerning the Original and Basis of Government* (London, 1667), p. 16.

137 John Brydall, "Ius Maiestatis," 1665, PRO, SP 29/143/145.

138 St. Albans to Arlington, 19/29 July 1665, PRO, SP 78/121, f. 15r.

of his best subjects."[139] Arlington, after consultation with Charles himself, had already advised Ormonde to raise "a formed army" in Ireland.[140] In the spring of 1667 an official newsletter floated the idea of raising such an army in England.[141] So it was not merely the dire circumstances of the Chatham disaster which prompted Charles "to frame a land army."[142]

England failed to set out a fleet for the campaign of 1667 largely because the Anglican Royalist consensus had been shattered, because Charles II and his closest ministers had come to have a very different understanding of the war than a large segment of the population. While many now thought that the absolutist French king Louis XIV posed the most serious threat to achieve a universal monarchy, Sheldon, Carteret, Arlington, and the Duke of York continued to focus their animosity and their energies on the republican and religiously pluralist Dutch. As a result they understood the Parliamentary criticism of the conduct of the war not as a constructive attempt to ameliorate English naval policy, but as the seditious speeches of the Netherlanders' natural allies. In this context they sought to separate Louis XIV from his unnatural alliance with the Dutch, while attempting to emasculate their Parliamentary critics by mimicking his successful governmental style in England. No wonder one poet, writing of the nation's statesmen, was perplexed "which most, the Dutch or Parliament, they fear."[143]

It was with full confidence that they had secured a guarantee of a desirable peace from the ideologically sympathetic Louis XIV, then, that the English sought to reopen lines of communication with the Dutch. A peace treaty needed to be signed with the States General even if its terms had already been stipulated in Paris. After many feelers, both official and unofficial, Charles II proposed to the Dutch that their ambassadors meet at The Hague to treat for peace.[144]

A proposal to meet on the enemy's territory, rather than in one's own country or at a neutral site, normally implied concession of defeat. For the English, however, this was not a retreat but a final diplomatic offensive. Arlington, probably with the advice of a coterie of Orangist exiles, made the stunning offer of negotiation in the United Provinces because it offered a

139 Sir Richard Temple, "General Heads of Grievances," 1667, HL, Temple Stowe STT Military Box 1 (50); Marvell, "Last Instructions to a Painter," 1667, *POAS*, p. 122; Ludlow, "A Voyce," Bod., English History MSS C487, p. 1148.

140 Arlington to Ormonde, 15 May 1666, Carte 46, f. 298.

141 Newsletter, 2 April 1667, Bod., Don MSS C37, f. 19v.

142 Arlington to Sandwich, 10 June, 1667, Bebington, *Arlington's Letters*, Vol. II, p. 225; Arlington to Ormonde, 11 June 1667, Carte 46, f. 489r.

143 "The Fourth Advice to a Painter," 1667, *POAS*, p. 146.

144 St. Serfe's newsletter, 8 January 1667, LOC, 18124 Vol. I, f. 151r; Thomas Downton to Williamson, 10/20 January 1667, PRO, SP 77/36, f. 14r; Pepys, *Diary*, Vol. VIII, 16 January 1667, p. 17; Arlington to Ormonde, 1 February 1667, Carte 46, f. 447r; Henry Coventry to Thomas Thynne, 18 February 1667, Longleat House, Thynne MSS 16, f.451r.

last desperate chance to overthrow the Dutch republican regime.[145] Arlington had from the first advocated negotiating in the United Provinces where "the people of Holland who are fond of the peace will be judges."[146] A treaty at The Hague, he later explained to William Temple, will force the Dutch people to be "undeceived of the opinion they have ever had" – an opinion which he often claimed was drummed into the Dutch by De Witt and his faction – "that his Majesty was totally adverse to the peace."[147] Highlighting for the Dutch people the mendacity of republican propaganda, the English hoped, would infuriate them so much that they would revive the Orangist cause, a cause which the English ministers would then be in a position to promote.[148] By "assigning The Hague for the place," Allan Broderick informed Ormonde, Charles II could "undeceive the long abused people of those provinces of his readiness to embrace peace, the consequence whereof (if refused) we hope may beget an insurrection on De Witt and his party."[149] "It is obvious to every man," Thomas St. Serfe asserted confidently in his newsletter, that "during this transaction the interest of the Prince of Orange will be more advantageously managed, and if the States be too rational in their negotiation, that then the [Dutch] commons will be not so easily seduced."[150] Surely it was for this reason, as Haley has suggested, that Charles II made sure to have his invitation to negotiate at The Hague published and widely disseminated in the United Provinces.[151]

The design was so simple, and so attractive, that it did not escape the notice of the European diplomatic community. "In his choice of The Hague," wrote the Venetian Giustinian to his employers, "the British king had the intention ... of introducing suspicion and disputes among them, in which he might be able to profit through the adherents of Orange."[152] The French knew well that "the choice of The Hague for the place of treaty was resolved by his Majesty of Great Britain, not so much to accelerate the peace, as out of a close design to frame intrigues in the States of the United Republic."[153] Nor was De Witt unaware of the plot, a plot rendered all the

145 For Arlington's central role (which is supported by his dominance of the diplomatic correspondence) and his reliance upon De Witt, see Pepys, *Diary*, Vol. VIII, 17 February 1667, p. 69; William Temple to Arlington, 12/22 March 1667, PRO, SP 77/36, f. 131r.

146 Arlington to Ormonde, 5 January 1667, Carte 46, f. 435.

147 Arlington to Temple, 15 February 1667, Bebington, *Arlington's Letters*, Vol. I, pp. 115–116. This argument was often repeated. See newsletter, 19 February 1667, Bod., Don MSS 37, f. 12r; Joseph Williamson's Journal, 4 March 1667, PRO, SP 29/231, f. 1r.

148 Heneage Finch to Sir John Finch, 22 February 1667, LRO, DG7/Box 4984, Letters Folder.

149 Allan Broderick to Ormonde, 16 February 1667, Carte 35, f. 311r.

150 St. Serfe's newsletter, 14 February 1667, LOC, 18124 Vol. I, f. 165r.

151 Haley, *English Diplomat*, p. 110.

152 Giustinian to Doge and Senate, 19/29 March 1667, *CSPV*, p. 144.

153 Letter from France to Holland, 26 February 1667, Bebington, *Arlington's Letters*, Vol. I, p. 135; Giustinian to Doge and Senate, 19 February/1 March 1667, *CSPV*, p. 137. Political afficionados in Italy were well aware of the intent implicit in the English offer: Joseph Kent to Williamson, 16/26 March 1667, PRO, SP 85/8, f. 212r.

more plausible by the initial wave of Dutch popular enthusiasm for the treaty.[154] He and his party were suspicious that "the Prince of Orange and his party would try to secure some advantages" at The Hague.[155] "The interest of the Prince of Orange," confirmed Thomas Thynne, "is what makes Holland [desire] a garrison to treat in."[156]

After much wrangling, and amid fears that Dutch intransigence would scotch the entire treaty, De Witt managed to get his garrison to treat in. Breda, it seems, was acceptable to both the English and the Dutch because while it was a garrison, it was a traditionally Orangist garrison.[157] There can be no doubt that the English ambassadors were to "have acted the part that villain Downing did, of corrupting the people and drawing them to the party of the Prince of Orange."[158] But the Orangist game was played, and it had been lost. The citizens of Breda might have been sympathetic to the Orangist cause, but they were hardly in a position to spearhead a nation-wide Orangist insurrection as the inhabitants of The Hague – simultaneously the seat of the States General and the States of Holland – might have been. William Temple knew well there was now no hope of an Orangist revolution, leading him to muse that "perhaps plain direct words and blows are the true genius of our nation (as they have been of all lasting greatness in kingdoms and states) and when we go to refine too much in our business, we fall into a posture out of our force."[159]

At the same time that Charles proposed The Hague as the venue for treating with the Dutch, he and his Privy Council nominated Denzil Hollis and Henry Coventry to head the English delegation. Both men had diplomatic experience, but neither could have had the full confidence of those running affairs. Hollis might have been "wholly at the devotion of the Chancellor," but he had made his Nonconformist sympathies known during his residency at Paris and was reputed to be increasingly critical of the

154 William Temple to Arlington, 15/25 February 1667, PRO, SP 77/36, f. 79; Carlingford to Ormonde, 16 February 1667, Carte 35, f. 314r.

155 Giustinian to Doge and Senate, 26 February/8 March 1667, *CSPV*, p. 139; see also Pepys, *Diary*, Vol. VIII, 3 March 1667, p. 92; newsletter from The Hague, 21 February/3 March 1667, Carte 47, f. 328r.

156 Thomas Thynne to Arlington, 22 February/4 March 1667, PRO, SP 95/6, f. 148v.

157 Arlingon to Ormonde, 19 March 1667, Carte 46, f. 458r; Williamson's journal, 20 March 1667, PRO, SP 29/231, f. 5v; Pepys, *Diary*, Vol. VIII, 23 March 1667, pp. 125–126; newsletter, 26 March 1667, Bod., Don MSS 37, f. 18r; William Temple to Ormonde, 2/12 April 1667, Carte 35, ff. 368–369.

158 Ludlow, "A Voyce," Bod., English History MSS C487, p. 1147. For confirmation of this, see James Oxenden to George Oxenden, April 1667, BL Add. 40713, f. 48; Instructions to Hollis and Coventry, 18 April 1667, PRO, SP 84/182, ff. 94–95; Giustinian to Doge and Senate, 2/12 April 1667, *CSPV*, p. 146; Castlemaine, "History of the Dutch War," 1668, NMM, Clifford Papers Vol. III, Dw130, f. 13; "Narrative of What Hath Passed Between His Majesty , the Dutch &c.," 26 August 1667, IOL, E/3/87, f. 45v.

159 William Temple to Arlington, 8/18 March 1667, PRO, SP 77/36, f. 122.

Restoration regime.[160] Coventry was less ideologically suspect, but as George Cocke pointed out, "not so weighty as he should be."[161] But, if the real negotiation was taking place in Paris – no doubt under the close supervision of the queen mother and the Duchess of Orleans – the quality of the ambassadors at Breda made little difference. They, their splendid retinue, and the commercial team sent by the East India Company, existed largely for show.[162]

Initially the show they put on was quite splendid indeed. Upon the arrival of the English ambassadors on the Dutch coast they were greeted with "expressions of joy" and transferred to the Dutch yachts which escorted them to Breda.[163] After a few days for rest and preparation the English made their elaborate formal entry into Breda, where they were received "with very great civility."[164] "Had you been present at it," Dr. Mews gushed to Williamson, "I cannot tell which would have most pleased you, the order and splendor of it, or the joy which appeared in all people's looks arising from the hopes of enjoying that which they so much want and long for, peace." However, the procession was marred by the Grand Marshal Sir George Charnock's being thrown from his horse, an omen which had it not occurred in private would have led to "ominous conjectures and interpretations."[165]

The omen soon seemed prophetic indeed. While the English had initially been buoyed by the inclusion of a number of Orangists in the Dutch negotiating team,[166] they must have been disconcerted by the persistent rumors that the Dutch will "not hear of any satisfaction to be given to our king."[167] Each letter from the ambassadors at Breda revealed new difficulties, new Dutch demands. The Dutch insisted that all old commercial

160 [James Ralph], *The History of England* (London, 1744), Vol. I, p. 70 (relations with Clarendon); Hollis to Arlington, 25 April/5 May 1665, PRO, SP 78/120, f. 122r; Ludlow, "A Voyce," Bod., English History MSS C487, pp. 1126, 1147.

161 Pepys, *Diary*, Vol. VIII, 17 February 1667, p. 70.

162 The East India Company despatched John Joliffe, Robert Thomson, and Thomas Papillon. Newsletter, 14 May 1667, Bod., Don MSS 37, f. 24r; William Temple to Clarendon, 21/31 May 1667, PRO, SP 77/36, f. 260v; Sir William Ryder to George Oxenden, 16 April 1667, BL Add. 40713, f. 14v. These men were, as Dr. Peter Mews pointed out, "a sort of strange cattle, proud and schismatical." Dr. Mews to Williamson, 8/18 June 1667, PRO, SP 84/182, f. 153v.

163 Dr. Peter Mews to Williamson, 3/13 May 1667, PRO, SP 29/199/43; William Allestree to Williamson, 10/20 May 1667, PRO, SP 84/182, f. 112r.

164 "The Entry of their Excellencies," 14/24 May 1667, PRO, SP 84/182, f. 113r; Pepys, *Diary*, Vol. VIII, 16 May 1667, p. 218.

165 Dr. Mews to Williamson, 17/27 May 1667, PRO, SP 84/182, ff. 117–118.

166 Broderick to Ormonde, 6 April 1667, Carte 35, f. 372r; Williamson's journal, 27 April 1667, PRO, SP 29/231, f. 16r.

167 William Swan (Hamburg) to Thomas Thynne, 7 May 1667, Longleat House, Thynne MSS XXX, f. 50v. For other manifestations of this rumor see Pepys, *Diary*, Vol. VIII, 6 March 1667, p. 100; J. Paul (Elsinore, Denmark) to Thynne, 9 April 1667, Longleat House, Thynne MSS XXX, f. 29r; William Temple to Ormonde, 15/25 April 1667, Carte 35, f. 393r; Richard Browne (Aldborough) to Williamson, 15 April 1667, PRO, SP 29/197/74.

grievances, including the well-publicized reparations demanded for the ships *Bon Esperanza* and *Henry Bonaventura*, should "be silenced." The Dutch ministers baldly stated that "without a total annulling [of] all pretenses no peace could be."[168] They requested that the English repeal or dispense with the Navigation Act.[169] When the English ambassadors asked for the return of the island of Pula Run, the Dutch retorted that they would rather continue the war than accede to such a demand.[170] In such an atmosphere it is hardly surprising that the English began to despair of a peace. "By what we hear," Hollis and Coventry wrote to Clarendon, "Holland is not inclined to a peace on any equitable terms."[171] This pessimism soon permeated England. "I find it everywhere now to be a thing doubted whether we shall have peace or no," recorded Samuel Pepys.[172] Elizabeth Papillon informed her husband Thomas that "all the talk at London is that we shall have no peace."[173] "I find most at their wits' end," scribbled one courtier, "whither the Dutch fleet is designed and whether peace or war will be the consequence of it."[174]

These provocative Dutch demands it should be emphasized, do not prove the centrality of economic issues in the Anglo-Dutch struggle, but rather demonstrate the Dutch determination to receive an acknowledgment that they had won the war. "The States detaining Pula Run and denying justice in the case of the two ships were the chief reasons of the war on the king's side," Henry Coventry perceptively pointed out, "and should he quit them without recompense this consequence would necessarily follow: either he began the war wrongly or that though he had right he could not maintain it against the States."[175] Dutch diplomatic intransigence reflected not their economic aspirations, but their political position. For while the Dutch diplomatic team was quibbling over reparations for ships long ago seized, and the restoration of an island now rendered commercially useless, the Dutch navy was in the process of gathering its might for the most effective naval strike of the century. As affairs stood "at the first at Breda," the Presbyterian East India Company commissioner Thomas Papillon recalled,

168 Henry Coventry to Clarendon, 10/20 May 1667, Bod., Clar. 159, f. 1v; Henry Coventry to Clarendon, 24 May/3 June 1667, Bod., Clar. 159, f. 10r; William Swan to Williamson, 17 May 1667, PRO, SP 82/11, f. 57r.

169 Henry Coventry to Clarendon, 27 May/6 June 1667, Bod., Clar. 159, f. 13v.

170 St. Albans to Arlington, 6 March 1667, Bebington, *Arlington's Letters*, Vol. I, p. 144; William Morrice to Thomas Thynne, 12 April 1667, Longleat House Thynne MSS XXX, f. 34r; Allan Broderick to Ormonde, 20 April 1667, Carte 35, f. 382; Henry Coventry to Clarendon, 10/20 May 1667, Bod., Clar. 159, f. 1v; William Temple to Denzil Hollis, 19/29 May 1667, Carte 35, f. 434r.

171 Hollis and Coventry to Clarendon, 18/28 May 1667, Bod., Clar. 159, f. 3v. See also Henry Coventry to Thomas Thynne, 20/30 My 1667, Longleat House, Thynne MSS XVI, f. 467r.

172 Pepys, *Diary*, Vol. VIII, 20 May 1667, p. 225.

173 Elizabeth Papillon to Thomas Papillon, 31 May 1667, CKS, U1015/C14/1.

174 Edmund Cooke to Ormonde, 1 June 1667, Carte 35, f. 459r.

175 Henry Coventry to Clarendon, 10/20 May 1667, Bod., Clar. 159, f. 2r.

"there was not the least probability of an accord" because "the Dutch daily expected the success of their fleet according to which they might steer their course in the treaty."[176] The descent on Chatham and the burning of the greater part of the English navy could not but alter the diplomatic situation.

Initially the Dutch attack on Chatham provoked a wave of fury from the English Privy Councillors. Negotiations with such a perfidious nation could only be conducted with men-of-war, many reasoned. "We grow daily more obdure and inflexible by finding ourselves so perfidiously dealt with by some and insolently treated by others," secretary Morrice informed Henry Coventry. "His Majesty cannot be frighted into assent."[177] "The continuance of the treaty will be dishonorable," fumed Clarendon.[178] "We should have been willing to have made a fair peace," Arlington assured William Temple, "but we shall be very loath to give the world cause to say we are beaten into it."[179] The Privy Council went so far as to discuss recalling the English ambassadors from Breda.[180]

Most informed observers felt that the dramatic Dutch attack had sounded the death knell of the Breda negotiations. "I believe a few days will end this treaty," Henry Coventry confided to his cousin Thomas Thynne.[181] "The sad loss of his Majesty's ships at Chatham hath put a stop to all business and almost to all private conversation," reported Pierre Du Moulin from Breda.[182] William Morrice claimed the "treaty is becalmed."[183]

Naturally this feeling of English despair was reinforced by newfound Dutch diplomatic aggression. Confident that the English could do little to defend themselves – that "England can carry on the war no longer" – the Dutch raised the diplomatic stakes.[184] "It is not imaginable what a height of humor they are risen here upon finding themselves at sea and no fleet to control them," bemoaned Henry Coventry.[185] That humor led the Dutch to float some fairly lofty demands. They asked for the repeal of the Navigation Act, the revocation of English claims to the dominion of the seas, the

[176] Thomas Papillon's account of the negotiation, July 1667, CKS, U1015/O13.

[177] William Morrice to Henry Coventry, 10 June 1667, Longleat House, Cov. MSS XLIV, f. 41r.

[178] Clarendon to Henry Coventry, 7 June 1667, Bod., Clar. 159, f. 159r.

[179] Arlington to William Temple, 7 June 1667, Bebington, *Arlington's Letters*, Vol. I, p. 168.

[180] Anglesey to Ormonde, 11 June 1667, Carte 47, f. 156; Arlington to Ormonde, 11 June 1667, Carte 46, ff. 488–489; William Morrice to Henry Coventry, 14 June 1667, Longleat House, Cov. MSS XLIV, f. 43r; Williamson's journal, 24 June 1667, PRO, SP 29/231, f. 31v.

[181] Henry Coventry to Thomas Thynne, 6/16 June 1667, Longleat House, Thynne MSS XVI, f. 470v. See similar sentiments in Henry Coventry to Arlington, 10/20 June 1667, Longleat House, Cov. MSS LXXXI, f. 15r.

[182] Pierre Du Moulin to Arlington, 14/24 June 1667, PRO, SP 84/182, f. 150r.

[183] News from Ghent, 17/27 June 1667, PRO, SP 77/36, f. 327v. Even the formerly optimistic Lord Ogle now predicted that "we shall have no peace this year." Ogle to Sir George Savile, 13 June 1667, BL, Althorp Papers C1 (unfoliated).

[184] ? Tucker to Walter Tucker, 12/22 July 1667, BL Add. 21947, f. 107r.

[185] Henry Coventry to Clarendon, 14/24 June 1667, Bod., Clar. 159, f. 31r.

absolute forfeiture of Pula Run, and the elimination of "all pretensions before the war."[186] Unsurprisingly these demands were only magnified in popular discourse. "The Dutch impose beyond measure," complained Sir Nathaniel Hobart, "and will not hear of a peace but upon such conditions as would hardly be expected from absolute conquerors."[187] Upon hearing these reports, none in England thought their king would condescend to a peace. "We here have little expectation of peace," averred Jane Papillon.[188] "I am none of those that expect peace," concurred the court gossip Edward Cooke.[189] "My faith is not strong enough to believe we shall have any peaceable issue of the treaty," opined the naval supplier Silas Taylor, "the humor of that people is insolent and the little they have got certainly puffs them too high for them to comply with reason."[190]

But comply the English did within a fortnight. In early July Henry Coventry returned to England with the Dutch demands in hand. After a heated debate in the Privy Council, which seems to have been over whether it was possible to raise objections to various articles in the Dutch propositions rather than whether to agree to the peace, the English sent Coventry back to Breda with orders to sign. "The peace is concluded," a relieved Clarendon informed his friend Burlington.[191] Both ambassadors could soon confirm that the treaty was signed without a hitch. By the end of the month Sir John Coventry had brought the final documents to London, which were duly ratified.[192] The second Anglo-Dutch War was at an end.

There was little mystery in the Privy Council's change of heart. Reflection had convinced all that the English were in no position to continue the war. "The utility of peace (indeed the necessity)," wrote William Morrice, "preponderated all the objections against the terms and conditions, and it was resolved to acquiesce."[193] At the Council board Charles himself

186 Pierre du Moulin to Arlington, 14/24 June 1667, PRO, SP 84/182, f. 141v; Letter from Rotterdam, 17/27 June 1667, PRO, SP 84/182, f. 211r; Henry Coventry to Clarendon, 18/28 June 1667, Bod., Clar. 159, f. 35r; Hollis to Clarendon, 20/30 June 1667, Bod., Clar. 159, f. 37r; William Allestree to Williamson, 1/11 July 1667, PRO, SP 84/183, f. 2r.

187 Sir Nathaniel Hobart to Sir Ralph Verney, 26 June 1667, Firestone Library, Verney MSS Reel 21 (unfoliated). See also Sir Geoffrey Shakerley (Chester) to Williamson, 15 July 1667, PRO, SP 29/209/122.

188 Jane Papillon to Thomas Papillon, 3 July 1667, CKS, U1015/C11/7.

189 Edward Cooke to Ormonde, 5 July 1667, Carte 35, f. 529r.

190 Silas Taylor (Harwich) to Williamson, 6 July 1667, PRO, SP 29/208/113.

191 Clarendon to Burlington, 13 July 1667, BL, Althorp Papers B5 (unfoliated). See also Dr. William Denton to Sir Ralph Verney, 12 July 1667, Firestone Library, Verney MSS Reel 21 (unfoliated); Lawrence Hyde to Burlington, 13 July 1667, BL, Althorp Papers B5 (unfoliated); Allan Broderick to Ormonde, 13 July 1667, Carte 35, f. 537r; Dr. Mews to Williamson, 15/25 July 1667, PRO, SP 84/183, f. 32r; Dr. Mews to Williamson, 19/29 July 1667, PRO, SP 84/183, f. 35r; Pepys, *Diary*, Vol. VIII, 22 July 1667, p. 347.

192 Hollis and Henry Coventry to Clarendon, 22 July/1 August 1667, Bod., Clar. 159, f. 48r; Arlington to Ormonde, 27 July 1667, Carte 46, f. 513r.

193 William Morrice to Thomas Thynne, 12 July 1667, Longleat House, Thynne MSS 30, f. 103r.

admitted that "the forces of our enemies are grown too great for us."[194] Sir William Coventry agreed that "we are so ill prepared for war as may presently make an enemy contemn us."[195]

Did the Dutch, flush with victory and able to procure almost any concession from the English, demand an economically punitive treaty? Did they use their victorious fleet to coerce the capitulations concomitant to the victors in a trade war? Certainly they made no economic concessions. "We find ourselves to be excluded from satisfaction ... and all our concerns out of doors," lamented the governor of the East India Company.[196] "Though I was at the treaty," Thomas Papillon later insisted, "yet I say I had no hand in it."[197] That the Dutch did not grant any new advantages to the English after the war, however, does not prove that their struggle with England was a trade war; it merely demonstrates that they denied the justness of the English pretensions.

In fact, the advantages which the Dutch did gain by the treaty had little to do with trade. Each side kept what it had gained from the other during the war, in terms of both land and merchandise. The Dutch gained Pula Run, it is true, but that was granted them because they were able to demonstrate that they had returned it to the English in 1665, and then recaptured it during the war. In any event, the English had determined to

194 Pepys, *Diary*, Vol. VIII, 12 July 1667, pp. 329–330.

195 William Coventry to Ormonde, 13 July 1667, Carte 47, f. 494v. All of the surviving evidence suggests that this was a virtually unanimous assessment. See Pierre du Moulin to Arlington, 14/24 June 1667, PRO, SP 84/182, ff. 150–151; Anglesey to Ormonde, 15 June 1667, Carte 47, f. 158r; Pepys, *Diary*, Vol. VIII, 23 June 1667, p. 285; Henry Coventry to Thomas Thynne, 22 July/1 August 1667, Longleat House, Thynne MSS XVI, f. 471r; Ludlow, "A Voyce," Bod., English History MSS C487, p. 1152. This was also the assessment of the Venetian ambassador in Paris: Giustinian to Doge and Senate, 16/26 July 1667, *CSPV*, p. 174.

196 Andrew Riccard to Robert Thomson and Thomas Papillon, 5 July 1667, IOL, E/3/87, f. 42v.

197 Thomas Papillon to George Oxenden, 26 August 1667, BL Add. 40713, f. 6r. This is the point to note that the Nonconformists present at Breda were no less aggressive in pursuing England's interests than the Anglicans. Hollis denounced the "unworthiness of the Dutch." Thomas Papillon to ?, 23 June 1667, CKS, U1015/F16/1; St. Serfe's newsletter, 8 June 1667, LOC, 18124 Vol. I, f. 208r. And Papillon and his colleagues fought bitterly for their economic rights. Thomas Papillon's account of the negotiations, July 1667, CKS, U1015/O13. They were not, as Anglican Royalist propaganda predicted, betrayers of their country. While they did not sympathize with the religious program of the Anglican Royalists, and while they were far more ready to enunciate fears of French universal monarchy, moderate Nonconformists such as Papillon and Hollis (both had opposed Pride's Purge and welcomed the Restoration) despised republicanism. Hollis's political activities in the 1640s are well known. Sir Thomas Chamberlain, sometime governor of the East India Company, averred that "Thomas Papillon hath constantly upon all occasions manifested a cordial and loyal affection to King Charles the first, and martyr of ever blessed memory, and that for his endeavors to have restored his said most sacred Majesty he was by an order of the then pretended House of Commons committed to Newgate in about the month of February anno 1647." Certificate by Sir Thomas Chamberlain, 9 December 1662, HMC, *Various Collections*, Vol. III, p. 257.

surrender the island well before the descent on Chatham, since the island was "absolutely destroyed" and would require "great charge and at least seven years to produce any benefit."[198] Nor was the surrender of Pula Run unilateral. In exchange for the now economically inconsequential island and Surinam in South America, the English were allowed to keep Cape Corso on the West African coast and the New Netherlands in North America. Both sides were allowed to retain what they had captured during the war.

The Dutch also secured a clarification of the Navigation Act allowing them to import goods from Germany into England. This, however, did not represent an economic concession at all. "As to the Act of Navigation, you will hear much noise that it is repealed," Henry Coventry advised William Temple, "there is no such thing, neither doth the article about that matter give the States any more advantage than (as I conceive) the Act gave them before."[199] All who examined the treaty for its commercial content remarked on its mildness. The treaty, thought one of the onlookers at Breda, was "a very advantageous one for England considering our present condition."[200] The normally Hollandophobic St. Serfe confessed in his newsletter that "the truth is the articles are as full and rational as could be expected."[201] The terms were rational because they were virtually identical to those in the treaty negotiated in very different circumstances in 1662. After studying the terms of the treaty the Marquis of Dorchester concluded that he could "see nothing in them that any prudent man can reasonably except against, especially as the times then were. Those between us and the Dutch, as I remember, are much of the same nature with those in 1662."[202] "There is no variation from the treaty in 1662," Anglesey agreed, "but that Pula Run which we had by that being now out of our possession is left to the Dutch and we are to enjoy Cape Corso."[203] "The terms are very little different from that in 1662," chimed in one of the Duke of Richmond's

198 Instructions to Hollis and Coventry, 18 April 1667, PRO, SP 84/182, f. 98v. See also Arlington to Ormonde, 16 March 1667, Carte 46, f. 462r; Clarendon to Coventry and Hollis, 27 May 1667, Bod., Clar. 159, f. 7r; news from Holland, 8 July 1667, PRO, SP 29/208/153.

199 Henry Coventry to William Temple, 25 July/4 August 1667, Longleat House, Cov. MSS LXXXI, f. 24v. On the same point see also Allan Broderick to Ormonde, 6 July 1667, Carte 35, f. 530r. The only other economic concession made was to allow the Dutch to redefine contraband goods, which seems to have provided them with a negligible economic advantage. "An Account of What Articles are Demanded by the Treaters at Breda," 7 July 1667, Carte 46, f. 502v.

200 William Allestree to Williamson, 15 July 1667, PRO, SP 101/49/141.

201 St. Serfe's newsletter, 7 September 1667, LOC, 18124 Vol. I, f. 245r. See also St. Serfe's newsletter, 11 July 1667, f. 221r. This is Haley's assessment as well: Haley, *English Diplomat* pp. 129–130.

202 Dorchester to Williamson, 30 August 1667, PRO, SP 29/215/78.

203 Anglesey to Ormonde, 6 July 1667, Carte 47, f. 164r.

correspondents, "they to keep what they have taken, and we what we have taken."[204]

The significant concessions, however, were political. The English were forced to accept, as a modification to the terms of the treaty of 1662, the indemnification "now and at all times [of] all persons retiring into their countries for scruple of conscience."[205] Never again would the Dutch be by treaty compelled to return men like Corbet, Okey, and Barkstead to the likes of George Downing.

The final concession was not included in the treaty, but merely implicit in it. The English were compelled to abandon the Orangist cause. Before the ink from the Treaty of Breda had dried the States of Holland resolved "against ever having any Stadholder, and all men, as soon as admitted into the magistracy are to take their oaths never to give their consent for one."[206]

The Treaty of Breda said precious little about economic affairs, precisely because the second Anglo-Dutch War was not a trade war. The English had feared that a corrupt political culture would eventually achieve universal dominion. To prevent that, to overthrow the republican regime, and to sever the ties between the English and Dutch sectarian communities, the English had decided to go to war in 1664. The cost of having lost that war, then, was not punitive commercial measures but Dutch guarantees of protection for English religious and political exiles, and additional constitutional protection for the Dutch republican party. The Anglican Royalist foreign-policy gambit had been lost.

204 Captain Horton to Duke of Richmond, 5 July 1667, BL, Add. 21947, f. 81r. For similar assessments, see Ludlow, "A Voyce," Bod., English History MSS C487, p. 1153; William Temple to Arlington, 7/17 June 1667, PRO, SP 77/36, f. 307v – Temple is here analyzing the Dutch pretensions.

205 Arlington to Ormonde, 6 July 1667, Carte 46, f. 500v; see also Ludlow, "A Voyce," Bod., English History MSS C487, f. 1147; "An Account of the Articles in Difference," 7 July 1667, Carte 46, f. 502v; Anglesey to Ormonde, 13 July 1667, Carte 47, f. 166v; newsletter from Haarlem, 5/15 August 1667, PRO, SP 101/51/56; Pepys, *Diary*, Vol. VIII, 8 July 1667, p. 326. For the centrality of this issue to Dutch concerns see extracts from the resolutions of States General, 1/11 May 1667, Longleat House, Cov. MSS XLIV, ff. 14–16.

206 Henry Coventry to Clarendon, 29 July/8 August 1667, Longleat House, Cov. MSS LXXXI, f. 27r. See also Williamson's Journal, 20 July 1667, PRO, SP 29/231, f. 39r; *Parker's History of his Own Time*, pp. 248–249; Haley, *English Diplomat*, p. 128.

25

The demise of Anglican Royalist foreign policy

What were the political consequences of the defeat at Chatham and the subsequent concessions made at Breda? How did the English react to their government's failure to defend them against the wrath of the Dutch navy? How did they account for their defeat?

Certainly the end of the war was initially greeted as "good news" throughout the country.[1] In London the peace was announced "with trumpets and kettle drums, and the people shouting for joy,"[2] and villages throughout the country the rumor, and eventually the proclamation, of peace prompted huge celebrations: bells were rung, guns went off, fireworks were exploded. "The bells have hardly lain still in all the country about ever since the news of peace," reported one of Williamson's corespondents from Lyme.[3] In Weymouth the peace "raised the dead to life."[4]

This display of popular emotion largely reflected relief at the conclusion of a war which had proved devastating. The end of the war meant the possibility of economic revival. Throughout the country people expected the peace to reinvigorate sagging commerce. From Truro Hugh Acland reported

1 Charles Lord Clifford to Burlington, 27 July 1667, BL, Althorp Papers B5 (unfoliated); Evelyn, *Diary*, 24 August 1667, p. 492.

2 Jo. Copleston to Duke of Richmond, 27 August 1667, BL Add. 21947, f. 140r.

3 Anthony Thorold (Lyme) to Williamson, 28 August 1667, PRO, SP 29/215/55.

4 Christopher Sawtell (Weymouth) to Edmund Sawtell, 27 August 1667, PRO, SP 29/215/28. For reports from other parts of the country. see Dr. Peter Mews (Oxford) to Williamson, 26 September 1667, PRO, SP 29/217/174; Richard Bower (Yarmouth) to Williamson, 4 September 1667, PRO, SP 29/216/56; Thomas Holden (Falmouth) to James Hickes, 10 July 1667, PRO, SP 29/209/39; Richard Watts (Deal) to Williamson, 29 July 1667, PRO, SP 29/211/61; John Carlisle (Dover) to Williamson, 1 September 1667, PRO, SP 29/216/9; John Clarke (Plymouth) to Williamson, 27 August 1667, PRO, SP 29/215/30; Jo. Trelawney (Exeter) to Williamson, 24 July 1667, PRO, SP 29/210/121; John Fitzherbert (Bristol) to Williamson, 3 August 1667, PRO, SP 29/212/43; Jo. Baskerville (Bristol) to Williamson, 7 September 1667, PRO, SP 29/216/86; John Man (Swansea) to Williamson, 5 August 1667, PRO, SP 29/212/66; Charles Whitington (Hull) to Williamson, 26 August 1667, PRO, SP 29/215/20; Edward Bodham (Lynn) to Williamson, 4 September 1667, PRO, SP 29/216/48; John Smith (Margate) to Williamson, 3 September 1667, PRO, SP 29/216/37; John Bower (Bridlington) to James Hickes, 14 July 1667, PRO, SP 29/209/109; Richard Forster (Newcastle) to James Hickes, 11 July 1667, PRO, SP 29/209/52; John Maurice (Minehead) to James Hickes, 6 August 1667, PRO, SP 29/212/96.

that "many people" were convinced that "if the treaty take effect" they would "be in better condition for the future."[5] In Bridgewater "trade advances in hope of a successful treaty."[6] "If a peace follow," predicted Sir Andrew Riccard the Presbyterian governor of the East India Company, "the East India Company purpose to renew their trade, to attend it with as much or more vigor than ever."[7] Secretary Morrice captured the national sentiment when he advised Henry Coventry that "the hopes of peace have quickened trade and our spirits also."[8]

Far from proving economically disastrous, the result one would expect from a punitive peace concluding a lost trade war, all of the economic expectations of the nation's traders were fulfilled. One ballad proclaimed the peace by announcing that "the plenipotentiaries signed the peace / That our bound up trading might have a release."[9] And a release English trade did enjoy. In town after town the news of peace "put life into trade again."[10] The economic revival in London made it finally possible to commence the reconstruction of the City after the Fire.[11] "God be thanked the storms of war are blown over," a relieved James Oxenden wrote to his brother George in Surat, "and our halcyon days restored and now a little trading would set the nations to rights again, which hath been very much decayed by our late contentions."[12] The Levant Company similarly enthused that the "long desired peace" would finally enable them to resume their trade.[13] English merchants in Italy were also confident that with the conclusion of the peace "trade may open and flourish again."[14]

5 Hugh Acland (Truro) to Williamson, 28 March 1667, PRO, SP 29/195/56. Similar hopes were expressed by others: see Sir Ralph Verney to Edmund Verney, 30 May 1667, Firestone Library, Verney MSS, Reel 21 (unfoliated); Ormonde to Anglesey, 28 May 1667, Carte 51, f. 48v.

6 William Symons (Bridgwater) to James Hickes, 25 May 1667, PRO, SP 29/202/1.

7 Andrew Riccard to George Oxenden, April 1667, BL, Add. 40713, f. 38r.

8 William Morrice to Henry Coventry, 17 May 1667, Longleat House, Cov. MSS XLIV, f. 24r.

9 "The Triumphs of Four Nations," July 1667, in John Holloway (editor), *The Euing Collection of English Broadside Ballads* (Glasgow, 1971), p. 580.

10 Edward Bodham (Lynn) to Williamson, 2 August 1667, PRO, SP 29/212/29; Richard Forster (Newcastle) to Williamson, 2 August 1667, PRO, SP 29/212/30; Antony Thorold (Lyme) to James Hickes, 26 August 1667, PRO, SP 29/215/26; Christopher Sawtell (Weymouth) to Edmund Sawtell, 31 August 1667, PRO, SP 29/215/80; Ma. Anderton (Chester) to Williamson, 11 September 1667, PRO, SP 29/216/144; John Clarke (Plymouth) to Williamson, 13 September 1667, PRO, SP 29/217/10; M. Scott (Berwick) to Williamson, 15 September 1667, PRO, SP 29/217/40; William Symons (Bridgwater) to Williamson, 18 October 1667, PRO, SP 29/220/71.

11 Anglesey to Ormonde, 14 September 1667, Carte 47, f. 172r; St. Serfe's newsletter, 27 August 1667, LOC, 18124 Vol. I, f. 240r.

12 James Oxenden to George Oxenden, 30 September 1667, BL Add. 40713, f. 8v. See also John Mascall to George Oxenden, 4 October 1667, BL, Add. 40713, f. 12r; An. Masters to George Oxenden, 13 October 1667, BL Add. 40713, f. 23; East India Company to Consul Lannoy, 26 August 1667, IOL, E/3/87. f. 45v.

13 Levant Company to Winchilsea, 2 September 1667, PRO, SP 105/113, f. 85r.

14 Joseph Kent to Williamson, 21 September/1 October 1667, PRO, SP 85/9, f. 23r.

Long the English did for the end of the war, but precious few were happy with the way in which it was concluded. While "the rejoicings of peace are general" admitted one newsletter-writer they "were not so transporting as might be imagined."[15] On the day the peace was proclaimed Pepys reported that though the "bells rung" there were "no bonfires that I hear of anywhere."[16] Instead of wild celebrations, scurrilous poems were scattered on the streets complaining that the Dutch "treat with rod in hand, our buttocks bare; Judge what the issues of such treaties are."[17] "Draw coats of pageantry and proclamations, / Of peace concluded with one, two, three nations," one poet advised yet another painter, "Canst thou not on the 'change make merchants grin, / Like outward smiles while vexing thoughts within?"[18] Indeed upon visiting the Exchange Roger and Samuel Pepys found "all the merchants sad at this peace" – sad, clearly, not because they stood to lose economically, quite the contrary, but because it was a peace gained "with buttocks bare."[19]

This was the sentiment of more than the merchant community. "Many now condemn it," Carlingford wrote of the peace.[20] Pepys thought "nobody pleased with the peace; and yet nobody daring to wish for the continuance of the war."[21] "The populace seem to be for nothing less now they have it," concluded another observer.[22] Dr. Mews heard from his English correspondents that there was little popular enthusiasm for the treaty concluded at Breda.[23] The explanation for this popular displeasure was not dissatisfaction with the actual terms of the treaty – these left the English no worse off than they had been before – but rather that it was a "snarling peace."[24] "The peace is generally very acceptable," explained Colonel Anthony Gilby from Hull, "yet some begin already to declare their suspicion that it is not an honorable one."[25] Indeed fears that English honor, rather than English profits, had been sacrificed at the negotiating

15 Newsletter, 17 August 1667, Bod., Don MSS C37, f. 38v; newsletter, 17 August 1667, Carte 72, f. 131v.

16 Pepys, *Diary*, Vol. VIII, 24 August 1667, p. 399.

17 "Vox et Lacrimae Anglorum," Bod., Don MSS E23, f. 32r. Another "knavish pamphlet" was distributed entitled "Peace, peace and we shall catch a mouse." Jo. Copleston to Duke of Richmond, 20 August 1667, BL Add. 21947, f. 121v.

18 "The Fifth Advice to a Painter," 1667, *POAS*, p. 147.

19 Pepys, *Diary*, Vol. VIII, 29 July 1667, p. 362. For earlier mercantile dissatisfaction with the English style of negotiation see Williamson's journal, 17 June 1667, PRO, SP 29/231, f. 29v.

20 Carlingford to Ormonde, 13 August 1667, Carte 35, f. 634r.

21 Pepys, *Diary*, Vol. VIII, 29 July 1667, pp. 361–362.

22 William Griffith to Thomas Thynne, 3/13 August 1667, Longleat House, Thynne MSS 30, f. 118r.

23 Dr. Mews to Williamson, 2/12 August 1667, PRO, SP 84/183, f. 61r; Dr. Mews to Williamson, 5/15 August 1667, PRO, SP 84/183, f. 63r.

24 William Temple to Sir John Temple, 30 September/10 October 1667, in *The Works of Sir William Temple* (London, 1814) Vol. I, p. 292.

25 Colonel Anthony Gilby (Hull) to Williamson, 31 July 1667, *CSPD*, p. 344.

table permeates almost all of the critiques of the treaty. "The people hereabouts are very joyful to hear some good hopes of a peace betwixt Holland and us," revealed one of Williamson's Berwick contacts, "yet not so greedy, but that they will venture all their lives and fortunes ere it were upon any other ground but honorable terms."[26] The Hull seamen similarly swore that "rather than we should have peace on dishonorable terms, they would venture their lives and fortunes."[27]

If the Treaty of Breda was dishonorable, the English knew quite well who was to blame for the submissive style of the English negotiation. "The discontents of the people, I fear, will not be moderated by" the peace, Carlingford told Ormonde, "the subject of whose discourse is in calumniating the government, with reflection on particular persons."[28] Pepys "did not find the Change at all glad of [the peace], but rather the worse, they looking upon it as a peace made only to preserve the king for a time in his lusts and ease."[29]

An essential element of the royal strategy of political independence, of course, had been the forging of the covert French alliance, an alliance widely suspected and now universally vilified. Presbyterians and political moderates, those least likely to appreciate the ideological attraction of an alliance with absolutist France, were the first to enunciate warning against French duplicity in the spring of 1667. The Nonconformist merchant James Houblon was sure from the first that "we shall be abused by the King of France."[30] "The French are thought to play a forced game and to come with intentions to entangle rather than treat, and stifle that in the cradle which they could not in the birth," warned that quintessential Restoration moderate William Temple.[31] Delay, Temple pointed out, "imports so much greatness to France" because it kept pinned down the only two nations capable of arresting the French advance in Flanders.[32] The Presbyterian secretary of state William Morrice, who had earlier warned of French aspirations to universal monarchy, told Sir Hugh Cholmley that "we are, and shall be, only fooled by the French."[33]

Slowly others began to perceive the depths of the French perfidy. While

26 M. Scott (Berwick) to Williamson, 14 July 1667, PRO, SP 29/209/108.

27 Charles Whittington (Hull) to Williamson, 31 July 1667, PRO, SP 29/211/106. See also Samuel Barnardiston to George Oxenden, 20 April 1667, BL, Add. 40713, f. 62r; Ma. Anderton (Chester) to Williamson, 13 July 1667, PRO, SP 29/209/74; Robert Mein (Edinburgh) to Williamson, 16 July 1667, PRO, SP 29/209/136; Edward Bodham (Lynn) to Williamson, 17 July 1667, PRO, SP 29/210/7.

28 Carlingford to Ormonde, 24 August 1667, Carte 35, f. 657r.

29 Pepys, *Diary*, Vol. VIII, 27 July 1667, p. 355.

30 Pepys, *Diary*, Vol. VIII, 5 April 1667, p. 151.

31 William Temple to Ormonde, 2/12 April 1667, Carte 35, f. 370v. See also his earlier unheeded warnings: Temple to Arlington, 19/29 March 1667, PRO, SP 77/36, f. 145r; Temple to Williamson, 19/29 March 1667, PRO, SP 77/36, f. 147r.

32 Temple to Ormonde, 21/31 May 1667, Carte 35, f. 450r.

33 Pepys, *Diary*, Vol. VIII, 31 May 1667, p. 244.

Clarendon held out hopes for the French until the last, Henry Coventry gradually began to perceive that conclusion at Breda was not in the French interest.[34] "The truth is (but this to yourself) the King of England relied on France," Henry Coventry confided in his cousin Thomas Thynne, and it had become clear that "France hath abused us sufficiently, I believe, and dexterously endeavored to put jealousies between us and our friends."[35] Even Clarendon, ever loath to ascribe any duplicity to the part of the French, averred that had the French "deal[t] infamously with us" it "must shut out all confidence in us towards them to the end of the world."[36]

The profundity of French duplicity, the extent of the infamy of their dealings with the English, soon became manifest. While the Dutch navy, under the command of the Holland Grand Pensionary's brother Cornelius, prowled the North Sea terrifying inhabitants of English coastal towns, an English seaman managed to intercept a pacquet boat delivering messages from the Dutch flag ship. On it was a letter from Cornelius De Witt to the States General making it clear that the French had not only been privy to, but had planned to participate in, the Dutch descent on Chatham.[37] The contents of the letter were immediately publicized in Williamson's newsletter, hinting that this explained why "the French hold off the treaty all they can and incite the Dutch to insist upon a difficulty of their raising."[38]

Unsurprisingly such revelations prompted both anger and despair. "The French have but juggled with us all this winter and are in close conjunction with the Dutch," seethed Anglesey, "I wish ... we could charge them home with falsehood and breach of promise."[39] Mary Elmes knew quite well that Louis XIV had promised "that he would do what lay in his power to make the Dutch stand to the agreement made with us in 62." "God grant," she prayed in a letter to her relative Sir Ralph Verney after these newest revelations, "he does not back from all this now we are in so ill a condition."[40] The interception of the letter proved to Sir Thomas Gower "that the French cheat, abuse the king, dissemble in the whole, and treat without intention of peace."[41] Louis XIV "hath not in any measure

34 Clarendon to Hollis, 27 May 1667, Bod., Clar. 159, f. 7v; Clarendon to Henry Coventry, 31 May 1667, Bod., Clar. 159, f. 11r; Henry Coventry to Clarendon, 27 May/6 June 1667, Bod., Clar. 159, f. 14r.

35 Henry Coventry to Thomas Thynne, 6/16 June 1667, Longleat House, Thynne MSS XVI, f. 470.

36 Clarendon to Henry Coventry, 7 June 1667, Bod., Clar. 159, f. 17r.

37 Cornelius De Witt to the States of Holland, 6/16 June 1667, PRO, SP 84/182, f. 172r.

38 Williamson's newsletter, 10 June 1667, Bod., Don MSS C37, f. 28; Williamson's Journal, 11 June 1667, PRO, SP 29/231, f. 28r.

39 Anglesey to Ormonde, 11 June 1667, Carte 47, f. 156r. Lady Ranelagh to Burlington, 15 June 1667, BL, Althorp Papers B4 (unfoliated). See the similar sentiments of the Catholic Carlingford: Carlingford to Ormonde, 15 June 1667, Carte 35, f. 476r.

40 Mary Elmes (Covent Garden) to Sir Ralph Verney, 18 June 1667, Firestone Library, Verney MSS, Reel 21 (unfoliated).

41 Sir Thomas Gower to Viscount Fauconberg, 13 June 1667, HMC *Various Collections*,

performed his promises to the queen mother and my Lord St. Albans," seethed Allan Broderick, promises which "led us to believe our 1st, 2nd, and 3d rate ships useless whilst we were assured of a firm peace ere the Dutch had equipped their fleet."[42] Cornelius De Witt's letter merely proved, Broderick informed Ormonde, that "the King of France laughs at my Lord St. Albans and never intended to keep faith with him," leading Broderick along with many others to question the English "giving too easy faith to that supercilious prince."[43] Even Arlington soon conceded that the English had "too much cause to believe all [the French] capitulations were but amusements."[44] French duplicitous mediation coupled with the their evident martial prowess confirmed most in England in the conclusion enunciated in the Baron de Lisola's runaway best-seller: French "ambition" would settle for no less than "the universal monarchy."[45]

Not only did the events of the spring and summer of 1667 undermine the Anglican Royalist case for the trustworthiness of absolutist allies, they also cast doubt on the association between Dissent and rebellion, on the necessary alliance between the English Nonconformist community and the religiously pluralist Dutch. The plague, the Fire, and ultimately the descent on Chatham had placed great pressure on the ability of the English government to police the English Nonconformist community. Communication links were severed, Anglican ministers fled from their pulpits,[46] and

Vol. II, p. 125. See also Basil Lubbock (editor), *Barlow's Journal*, Vol. I (London, 1934), p. 134.

42 Allan Broderick to Ormonde, 8 June 1667, Carte 35, f. 465.

43 Broderick to Ormonde, 11 June 1667, Carte 35, f. 474r; Broderick to Ormonde, 15 June 1667, Carte 35, f. 478v.

44 Arlington to Ormonde, 11 June 1667, Carte 46, f. 488v; Temple naturally expressed the same concerns. Temple to Arlington, 18/28 June 1667, PRO, SP 77/36, f. 328.

45 [François Baron de Lisola], *The Buckler of State and Justice Against the Design Manifestly Discovered of the Universal Monarchy* (London, 1667), sig. A6r. In this pamphlet, published almost certainly in September, Lisola argued that the Anglo-Dutch War was "raised by the French practices, and fomented by their industry, giving the counterpoise to him who for the time appeared the weaker" in order to "depress all powers which are capable of obstructing the torrent of their enterprises" (p. 13). In a later section Lisola marveled that the French "always held a negotiation open by the means of the Earl of St. Albans," a negotiation which eventually resulted in "a secret treaty of peace with [the English] without the consent, nay without the knowledge, of their allies, without making any mention of them or their interests, and without any reservation of or relation to the general peace." "But that which is more astonishing," Lisola concluded along with much of English popular sentiment, "that after this peace was concluded, notwithstanding the promise made to the English not to use any hostility against them, France used all its endeavors with the States of the United Provinces to put out their fleet speedily to sea, binding themselves to join their own fleet with it, and agreeing with them upon all the conditions necessary for this effect. If this proceeding doth not open the eyes of all Europe, they'll have no cause to complain of the calamities which they are to suffer by France, which takes so much pains to undeceive them" (pp. 296–298).

46 *A Pulpit to Let* (London, 1665); Arlington to Humphrey Henchman Bishop of London, July 1665, PRO, SP 29/127/136; Hester Strype to John Strype, 29 July 1665, CUL, Add 4, f. 35r; Gilbert Talbot to Henry Coventry, 24 August 1665, Longleat House, Cov. MSS

local militia were drawn to the coasts to protect against foreign incursions. No greater opportunity for rebellion could have been imagined than that presented in the months following the Fire. Yet, instead of joining the triumphant Dutch fleet and its accompanying small band of English radical allies in a choreographed reinstitution of the English Commonwealth, the Nonconformist community flocked to support King and country with an incredible degree of unanimity.

Despite the notorious prominence of radicals like Algernon Sidney, William Say, and Joseph Bampfield, who were quite happy to plot with the Dutch and French to overthrow the English government, the vast majority of English Nonconformists were eager to aid their native land in any way they could. Far more typical than Sidney and his coterie were people like the Nonconformist Low Countries-based Jeffrey Elatson who upon hearing "of the likelihood of a breach between England and Holland" thought it not "convenient to live in a nation in hostility to the land of my nativity." If his inability to conform made it impossible for him to return to England he hoped he "might possibly procure liberty to go to some foreign plantation where I might have some hopes to employ myself and family."[47] William Coventry similarly knew of "one Ravens an English shipwright who went into Holland for Nonconformity" who refused a generous offer of employment from the Holland Admiralty in the hopes that he could instead do service for his native country.[48]

In this context it is hardly surprising that nothing ever came of the various attempts by the Dutch to foment a rebellion in England during the war. One of Arlington's informers reported that he knew well what "is promoted from Holland" but assured the secretary of state that "there is nothing really in action."[49] Letter after letter from all over the country assured the government that among the Nonconformists there was "a general disposition to quietness."[50] Those in England who did maintain

XXV, f. 103r; J. W., *A Friendly Letter to the Flying Clergy*, 6 September 1665 (London, 1665), p. 1; John Tillotson to William Sancroft, 14 September 1665, BL, Harleian MSS 3785, f. 35r; Oldenburg to Robert Boyle, 31 October 1665, in Rupert A. Hall and Marie Boas Hall (editors), *The Correspondence of Henry Oldenburg*, Vols. II–IV (Madison, 1966–1967), Vol. II, p. 586; Dr. Peter Barwick to William Sancroft, 9 December 1665, Bod., Tanner MSS 45, f. 44r.

47 Jeffrey Elatson to Mr. Progers, 27 October 1664, PRO, SP 29/103/137.

48 William Coventry (York) to Arlington, 28 August 1665, PRO, SP 29/131/46.

49 Leonard Williams to Bennet, 9 February 1665, PRO, SP 29/112/61.

50 Quotation from intelligence from London Meetings, 22 July 1665, PRO, SP 29/127/61. See also: William Coventry (York) to Arlington, 7 August 1665, PRO, SP 29/128/53; G. Phillips (Rickmansworth) to Arlington, 22 October 1665, PRO, SP 29/135/37; Earl of Carlisle (Naworth) to Williamson, 1 January 1666, PRO, SP 29/144/2; Sir Philip Musgrave to Arlington, 15 January 1666, PRO, SP 29/145/36; Robert Lord Brooke (Warwick Castle) to Deputy Lieutenants of Warwickshire, 19 January 1666, William Salt Library, SMs 565/103; Christopher Sanderson (Eggleston) to Williamson, 27 February 1666, PRO, SP 29/149/43; Thomas Osborne (Yorkshire) to Buckingham, 17 March 1666, BL, Egerton MSS 3328, f. 31r.

contacts with the exiles in the United Provinces were almost universally described as "contemptible."[51] One government informant described the plotting to have been between "some inconsiderable persons fugitives on the other side of the water [and] some less considerable here."[52] "I dare confidently affirm," wrote another, "that there is not one single person amongst all the sects, that is any tolerable measure considerable, either for wisdom or estate, that doth in the least meddle in this business." "I believe," he concluded, "they will never have to do either with the French or Hollanders."[53] The government should be far more concerned about the possibility of "a tumultuous insurrection of the poor" concluded another spy, in an assessment seconded by the Bishop of London himself, than a religious rebellion. There was "not any grounds to suspect the least disturbance from any of the religious sects."[54]

Far from leading insurrections in concert with Dutch invasions led by religious exiles, most English Nonconformists were ostentatious in their loyalty to the regime, in their support for the war against the nation's enemies.[55] Ralph Josselin, who was at best an occasional conformist, prayed for the English navy in its battles with the Dutch.[56] The loyalty of many Nonconformists went much farther than prayers and good wishes. William Temple was confident that "the whole people in general [were] spirited in the pursuit of this quarrel."[57] Upon rumors of a French landing in Devon in June 1666 "those we call fanatics were very forward to take up arms and to defend their country."[58] While it was true that many Nonconformists did "reflect upon their disappointment of that indulgence to their consciences which they promised themselves from his Majesty's public declaration [at Breda]," admitted one of Arlington's agents, "yet I cannot see but that they are lovers of their country and would be sorry to see it made a prey to foreigners, and I do verily believe upon very reasonable

51 William Morrice to Henry Coventry, 30 March 1666, Longleat House, Cov. MSS LXIV, f. 325r.

52 Letter to Arlington, 17 June 1665, PRO, SP 29/124/98.

53 Letter to Arlington, 26 February 1666, PRO, SP 29/149/42.

54 Intelligence from London Meetings, 22 July 1665, PRO, SP 29/127/61; Humphrey Henchman to Arlington, 19 August 1665, PRO, SP 29/129/63.

55 I take this support not to be unqualified endorsement of the justifications for the war – they would hardly support a war against religious liberty – but as a manifestation of a sense of national identity. Most Nonconformists despised republics as much as most of their Anglican brethren. It is important to recall the deep antipathy which men like Denzil Hollis and Thomas Papillon had for the Rump.

56 Josselin, *Diary*, 11 June 1665, 3 June 1666, pp. 518, 528. In Edinburgh the Protestant Dissenters were ostentatiously supportive of the war effort: Robert Mein (Edinburgh) to Henry Muddiman, 10 June 1665, PRO, SP 29/124/14.

57 William Temple to Arlington 8/18 May 1666, PRO, SP 77/34, f. 217v.

58 Thomas Holden (Falmouth) to James Hickes, 27 June 1666, PRO, SP 29/160/25. The same phenomenon was witnessed elsewhere in the country: see Richard Watts (Walmer) to Williamson, 30 June 1666, PRO, SP 29/160/117; Anthony Thorold (Lyme) to Williamson, 30 June 1666, PRO, SP 29/160/121.

terms they might be engaged to venture their all to prevent it."[59] In Oxford "our very Anabaptists declare, if permitted, to engage against Dutch and French."[60] Sir Roger Bradshaigh, no friend to Dissent, conceded that "the fanatic and Presbyterian will be as ready as any to take commission."[61] "We find in these parts little cause to suspect those we call disaffected," reported another Anglican Royalist Sir John Reresby from York, "but rather a general willingness to serve their king and country should there be any invasions."[62] "We have had less trouble and alarms from the discontented party than ever we had in any year since it hath pleased God to restore his Majesty," admitted the ever-suspicious Arlington in 1666, "the suspected party ... have as frankly observed their estates and persons in opposition to any invasion from abroad, or insurrection at home, as if they did not differ in any degree from us in their zeal to serve the king."[63]

The devastating effects of the Fire, and the concurrent disillusionment with the government's conduct of the war, did nothing to diminish the loyalty of the Nonconformist community. "As to risings and rebellions," Thomas Thynne was instructed to inform his Swedish hosts, "had any considerable part of the people been disposed to such crimes, they would without doubt have laid hold of the opportunity."[64] "It was not the least observable thing in the time of the Fire and after," chimed in Richard Baxter, "considering the late wars, and the multitude of disbanded soldiers, and the great grief and discontent of the Londoners, for the silencing and banishing of their pastors, that yet [the Nonconformists] were heard in the time of their calamity, no passionate words of discontent or dishonor against their governors, even when their enemies had so oft accused them of seditious inclinations, and when extremity might possibly have made them desperate."[65]

59 Letter to Arlington, 2 July 1666, PRO, SP 29/161/24.

60 George Liboni (Oxford) to Williamson, 15 July 1666, PRO, SP 29/163/11.

61 Sir Roger Bradshaigh (Haigh) to Williamson, 17 July 1666, PRO, SP 29/163/64.

62 Sir John Reresby (York) to Williamson, 28 July 1666, PRO, SP 29/165/50.

63 Arlington to Sandwich, 23August 1666, in Thomas Bebington (editor), *The Right Honourable the Earl of Arlington 's Letters* ... (London, 1701), Vol. II, p. 193. For other evidence of loyalty prior to the Fire see Arlington to Temple, 6 July 1666, Bebington, *Arlington Letters*, Vol. I, p. 87; Lieutenant Edward Suckley (Landguard Point) to Williamson, 7 July 1666, PRO, SP 29/161/128; John Maurice (Minehead) to James Hickes, 13 July 1666, PRO, SP 29/162/102.

64 Instructions for Thomas Thynne, November 1666, PRO, SP 95/6, f. 106v. The author of the instructions pointed out that, in view of the Dutch dalliances with Sidney and his friends, "none could better refute this objection than the Hollanders themselves." See also Mark Scott (Berwick) to Williamson, 26 September 1666, PRO, SP 29/173/29. Of course, the situation was rather different in Scotland, but this merely proves the great degree of distance between the two political cultures.

65 Matthew Sylvester, *Reliquiae Baxterianae* (London, 1696), Pt. III, p. 18. See the similar view expressed in *Observations Both Historical and Moral Upon the Burning of London* (London, 1667), pp. 6–7.

The descent on Chatham only fortified Nonconformist resolve. Even the Quakers were said to have offered Charles II 6,000 men to help in the nation's defense.[66] "All sorts of people seem very willing and forward to hazard their lives and fortunes for their king and country," Richard Forster wrote from Newcastle, which was not atypical.[67] It was this obvious loyalty, a loyalty which was merely a reaffirmation of the sentiments implicit in their previous "vigorous actings for the restitution of his Majesty that now is," which led John Corbet to insist that far from detracting from "kingly power and dignity" the Nonconformists are "well satisfied, as none more, in the ancient fundamental constitution of this kingdom."[68] "Is there never a drop of English blood in the veins of the sectary?" asked another proponent of religious liberty rhetorically. "How shall that thing you call obstinacy and faction, when they suffer the violence of your laws, and are unmoved, appear to be the most undaunted courage of the English spirit when it shall show itself in the field?"[69]

Developments in foreign affairs, then, in the final year of the Anglo-Dutch War invalidated the central assumptions of the Anglican Royalist credo. Louis XIV's political perfidy demonstrated that monarchs, even the most absolute of monarchs, were no more trustworthy, no less likely to seek universal monarchy, than republics. The remarkable loyalty of the English Nonconformist community during the most disastrous phase of the war, by contrast, made it clear that they were not closet republicans, that they were not Papists in disguise.[70] Instead Cornelius De Witt's triumphant assault on the undefended English navy convinced most in England that their govern-

66 Newsletter, 18 June 1667, Bod., Don MSS C37, f. 29r.

67 Richard Forster (Newcastle) to Williamson, 21 June 1667, PRO, SP 29/206, 123. See also Ma. Anderton (Chester) to Williamson, 6 July 1667, PRO, SP 29/208/114; Hugh Acland (Truro) to Williamson, 22 July 1667, PRO, SP 29/210/81; Richard Forster (Newcastle) to Williamson, 12 July 1667, PRO, SP 29/209/70.

68 [John Corbet], *A Discourse of the Religion of England* (London, 1667), p. 40.

69 *A Proposition for the Safety and Happiness of the King & Kingdom both in Church and State*, 18 June 1667 (London, 1667), p. 44. It is true, of course, that many continued to believe in the ineluctable link between religious dissent and political rebellion. See, for example, Joseph Williamson to Thomas Thynne, 5 April 1667, Longleat House, Thynne MSS 30, f. 42; Sir John Birkenhead, 4 March 1668, in Anchitell Grey, *Debates of the House of Commons From the Year 1667 to the Year 1694* (London, 1763), Vol. I, p. 105; Richard Bower (Yarmouth) to Williamson, 9 December 1667, PRO, SP 29/224/77; Richard Allestree, *A Sermon Preached Before the King at Whitehall*, 17 November 1667 (London, 1667), p. 22; George Morley, *A Sermon Preached before the King at Whitehall*, 5 November 1667 (London, 1683), pp. 13–14, 18. I am merely claiming that this was no longer the only respectable political assessment, that the Anglican Royalist consensus had been shattered.

70 Thus I disagree with Richard Greaves's claim that it was "the end of the Dutch War" and the consequent diminution of the risk from their "plotting with the enemy" which gave "new hope to the nonconformists in 1667." Richard L. Greaves, *Enemies Under His Feet: Radicals and Nonconformists in Britain, 1664–1667* (Stanford, 1990), p. 142. Rather it was the Nonconformist community's spectacular loyalty to king and country during the war which gave them hope.

ment was both incompetent and corrupt, that the national interest had been sacrificed to some other end.

It was precisely concern about the ulterior motives of the Restoration government which interested men and women throughout England after the Medway debacle. Why, the English asked themselves, had their government failed to set out a fleet after Parliament had voted an ample supply? Why had it been more concerned with rounding up loyal, if religiously heterodox, subjects than fighting malevolent and ambitious foreign enemies? Why had the English allowed themselves to be duped by the French? The answer, an increasingly large segment of the political nation came to suspect, was that their governors were seeking to rule in a new way; they were hoping to establish a French style of government.

Initially the news that the Dutch were in the Medway provoked shock, disbelief, and panic. "The dismay that is upon us all in the business of the kingdom and navy at this day is not to be expressed," scribbled Pepys, "nobody knowing which way to turn themselves."[71] "I found things here in such confusion that nobody knew what to say or do," concurred Charles Lord Clifford.[72] When he returned to London with the Dutch terms, Henry Coventry thought he had never seen the capital in "greater disorder."[73] Soon the shock turned to anger. While Edward Cooke thought "Whitehall is the most melancholy place I ever saw," he knew London was "the most discontented."[74] Allan Broderick observed that "dejection" had come to mix "with animosity in the minds of men."[75]

People from a wide variety of ideological outlooks began to vent their anger at their governors. The "fanatics" or those who "would fain have the king lower and themselves higher" circulated rumors throughout the country that "the success of the Dutch in burning some of our ships" was the result of "treachery above and that some of our great persons were guilty."[76] Radical Dissenters were, however, by no means unique in arriving at this assessment. Pepys's apothecary told him that "the world says all over that less charge than what the kingdom is put to, of one kind or other, by this business, would have set out all our great ships."[77] Sir Allan Broderick, no radical, exclaimed that "so stupendous a negligence in all sorts of officers no story mentions."[78] "There is a general consternation and wonder that we were in no readiness to receive the enemy," wrote Williamson's

71 Pepys, *Diary*, Vol. VIII, 14 June 1667, p. 268.
72 Charles Lord Clifford to Burlington, 22 June 1667, BL, Althorp Papers B5 (unfoliated).
73 Henry Coventry to Thomas Thynne, 1/11 August 1667, Longleat House, Thynne MSS 16, f. 473r.
74 Edward Cooke to Ormonde, 9 July 1667, Carte 35, f. 534r.
75 Allan Broderick to Ormonde, 25 June 1667, Carte 35, f. 496r.
76 Richard Browne (Aldborough) to Williamson, 18 June 1667, PRO, SP 29/206/47; J. Bentham (Lowich) to Williamson, 16 June 1667, PRO, SP 29/205/117.
77 Pepys, *Diary*, Vol. VIII, 14 June 1667, p. 268.
78 Allan Broderick to Ormonde, 15 June 1667, Carte 35, f. 478r.

Bedfordshire correspondent Dr. Jeremy Bentham. Two days later Bentham himself mused "how strangely were all our counselors lulled into a dead sleep of security that nothing less than so mortal a blow and irreparable loss should awaken them."[79] From Deal Richard Watts reported that "the common people and almost all other men are mad, some crying out we were sold, others that there were traitors in the Council."[80] "The moderate and sober people" in Minehead were convinced "that there was a great deal of negligence and treachery in this last business."[81] In short, there was everywhere what the Earl of Carlingford called "malice inveterate, incorrigible detraction of court."[82]

Carlingford was not exaggerating. Stories and myths of the debauchery of Charles II's court were in everyone's mouths. A Quaker stripped naked and ran through Westminster Hall comparing the court to "Sodom and Gomorrah."[83] His sentiments found an unusual second in the king's chaplain Dr. Creighton who preached "against the sins of the court, and particularly against adultery, over and over instancing how for that single sin in David, the whole nation was undone. And of our negligence in having our castles without ammunition and powder when the Dutch came upon us."[84] Pepys's diary in this period is filled with conversations with a variety of people who all expressed the belief that "the king and court were never in the world so bad as they are now for gaming, swearing, whoring, and drinking and the most abominable vices that ever were in the world – so that all must come to naught."[85] Rumors even circulated that while the Dutch were burning the King's ships he was dining with his mistress Castlemaine and the Duchess of Monmouth who "were all mad in hunting of a poor moth."[86] No wonder one poem published that summer compared Charles II to Nero.[87] No wonder indeed that "nobody hath so good opinion of the king and his Council and their advice, as to lend money, or venture their persons or estates or pains upon people that they know cannot thrive with all that we can do, but either by their corruption or negligence must be undone."[88]

These were not sentiments expressed merely by political insiders. Nor

79 Jeremy Bentham to Williamson, 14 June 1667, PRO, SP 29/205/63; Jeremy Bentham to Williamson, 16 June 1667, PRO, SP 29/205/117.

80 Richard Watts (Deal) to Williamson, 15 June 1667, PRO, SP 29/205/77.

81 John Maurice (Minehead) to Williamson, 18 June 1667, PRO, SP 29/206/43.

82 Carlingford to Ormonde, 13 August 1667, Carte 35, f. 635r. These fears of official treachery were even stated in print: *City and Countrey Mercury*, 13–17 June 1667.

83 Ferdinando Davys to Earl of Huntingdon, 30 July 1667, HL, HA1952.

84 Pepys, *Diary*, Vol. VIII, 29 July 1667, pp. 362–363.

85 Pepys, *Diary*, Vol. VIII, 27 July 1667, p. 355. See also Pepys, *Diary*, Vol. VIII, 24 June 1667, p. 286; Pepys, *Diary*, Vol. VIII, 29 July 1667, p. 361; Pepys, *Diary*, Vol. VIII, 8 August 1667, p. 377.

86 Pepys, *Diary*, Vol. VIII, 21 June 1667, p. 282.

87 Sir John Denham, *Directions to a Painter* (London, 1667), p. 34.

88 Pepys, *Diary*, Vol. VIII, 11 July 1667, pp. 328–329.

were they fears which died out as soon as the flames were no longer visible from Chatham. Instead broadsheets, ballads, libels, and gossip criticizing and denigrating the government's conduct in the war were widely circulated throughout the summer of 1667. It was a summer, Sir Philip Musgrave thought, in which "every man speaks his fancy as he fears or wisheth."[89] In Minehead "a great many false reports" were spread "reflecting upon his Majesty and his government."[90] Gossip and rumor were supplemented by poetry and written libels. Such writings, such "lusty libels" said to be "strangely insolent," were "thrown about" London and in Whitehall itself.[91] Ludlow heard that during that summer "libels run throughout city and country without control, casting dirt upon king, court and Parliament."[92] Although only a small fraction of these rhymes and reproaches survive, the available evidence substantiates Ludlow's claim. One poem found over the privy stairs at Whitehall entitled "Carolus Rex Secundus" read "Hobbes his religion, Hyde his morals gave / To God and man, a most ungrateful knave."[93] "Plague, fire, and war have been the nation's curse / But to have these our rulers is a worse," averred another.[94]

It was also during the summer that an unofficial account of the Parliamentary inquest into the causes of the Fire, an inquest which concluded that the Fire was "designed by the Papists, executed by the Frenchmen and their Jesuits, countenanced and approved by the whole court," was circulated throughout the country.[95] Nonconformist book-sellers, including the notorious religious radical Elizabeth Calvert, were said to have disseminated the pamphlets in Bristol, Bedfordshire, Westmoreland, Yorkshire, as well as in London.[96] While the pamphlet's distribution certainly reflects the

89 Sir Philip Musgrave to Williamson, 24 June 1667, PRO, SP 29/206/177.

90 John Maurice (Minehead) to Williamson, 27 August 1667, PRO, SP 29/215/34.

91 Allan Broderick to Ormonde, 23 July 1667, Carte 35, f. 562r; Dr. William Denton (London) to Sir Ralph Verney, 5 September 1667, Firestone Library, Verney MSS, Reel 22 (unfoliated).

92 Ludlow, "A Voyce," Bod., English History MSS C487, p. 1147. There were sporadic attempts to check this dissemination of scurrilous material, exemplified by the arrest of Henry Oldenburg, but they proved to be ineffectual. Henry Oldenburg to Seth Ward, 15 July 1667, *Oldenburg Correspondence*, Vol. III, p. 448. For circulation of the "Advice to a Painter" poems see Pepys, *Diary*, Vol. VIII, 1 July 1667, p. 313; Pepys, *Diary*, Vol. VIII, 16 September 1667, p. 439; Allan Broderick to Ormonde, 23 July 1667, Carte 35, f. 569r.

93 "Carolus Rex Secondus," in Sir William Haward's Collection, Bod., Don MSS B8, f. 183.

94 "New Instructions to a Painter," 1667, BL Add. 28253, f. 71r. See another aspersion on the nation's governors in "A Ballad," BL Add. 34362, f. 18v. The author of *The Answer of Mr. Wallers Painter to his Many New Advisers* (London, 1667) claimed that the prevailing style of poetry attempted "to hang up order in effigy" (p. 6). See also *News from the Stage* (London, 1668), broadside.

95 Jeremy Bentham (Loddington) to Williamson, 15 July 1667, *CSPD* Addenda 1660–1685, pp. 205–206.

96 Information of Susannah Moore, bookseller in Bristol, 12 July 1667, PRO, SP 29/209/75 II; Sir Thomas Langton and Sir John Knight (Bristol) to Arlington, 13 July 1667, PRO, SP 29/209/75; information of George Clarke (Bristol), 12 July 1667, PRO, SP 29/209/75 II; Sir Philip Musgrave (Yorkshire) to Williamson, 19 August 1667, PRO, SP 29/214/27;

industriousness of the suppliers, there can be little doubt that it sold so well precisely because it encapsulated popular fears.

In this mood, it was hardly surprising that many radicals confidently expected a revival of the Good Old Cause. The exiles in Rotterdam offered "hearty prayers and supplications" that the success of the Dutch fleet "may open a way for the restoration of those saints to their former dignities."[97] Similar sentiments were expressed in England. In Rochester one John Groscomb was heard to say "that within three months" there would be "an army brought from all places against London and should take it and turn out the present Parliament, and put in the old one, and then they would take the king and try him as they did his father."[98] In London a woman loudly proclaimed and repeated three times that "she wished the king hanged at the highest tree in England."[99] The virtuoso John Beale was certain that "the leading sectaries" intend to "strike at king and Church."[100]

More remarkable was that in the summer of 1667 more sober heads, those much closer to the ideological center of the political nation, were also convinced that the Restoration regime was in desperate trouble. "I am so troubled to see the uncontrolled madness and disorders of the people in all these parts, that I am almost weary of living," wrote Joseph Glanville from Bath; "they still grow in numbers and insolence, and openly denounce judgments and damning sentences against all that come to the public."[101] "The government is hated and the people desire a change," thought the Venetian ambassador Giustinian.[102] Sir Hugh Cholmley declared to Pepys that "he expects that of necessity this kingdom will fall back again to a commonwealth."[103] Pepys soon felt that "most people I meet with" were convinced "that we shall fall into a commonwealth in a few years, whether we will or no; for the charge of a monarchy is such as the kingdom cannot be brought to bear willingly."[104] Even Arlington admitted that "there is a

Daniel Fleming (Rydal) to Williamson, 16 August 1667, PRO, SP 29/213/118; Pepys, *Diary*, Vol. VIII, 16 September 1667, p. 439; John Fisher (Gray's Inn) to John Hobart, 2 August 1667, Bod., Tanner MSS 45, f. 205r.

97 John Smyth (Rotterdam) to Samuel Cottington, 14/24 June 1667, PRO, SP 29/205/73. This was no doubt the source of the predictions in the *Rotterdam Gazette*: Letter from The Hague, 25 July/4 August 1667, PRO, SP 77/37, f. 51r; extract from *Rotterdam Gazette*, 14 July 1667, PRO, SP 29/209/101.

98 Information of Dorcas, wife of John Comber (Rochester), 5 July 1667, PRO, SP 29/209/150 I.

99 Sir John Robinson to Williamson, 2 August 1667, PRO, SP 29/212/32.

100 John Beale to John Evelyn, 31 August 1667, Christ Church, Evelyn In-Letters 63.

101 Joseph Glanville (Bath) to Dr. John Beale, 10 September 1667, PRO, SP 29/216/133.

102 Giustinian to Doge and Senate, 25 June/5 July 1667, *CSPV*, p. 171. See also Giustinian to Doge and Senate, 16/26 July 1667, *CSPV*, p. 174.

103 Pepys, *Diary*, Vol. VIII, 9 August 1667, pp. 377–378.

104 Pepys, *Diary*, Vol. VIII, 19 August 1667, pp. 390–391. There was a great upsurge in Cromwellian nostalgia at this time: Charles Whittington (Hull) to Williamson, 16 June 1667, PRO, SP 29/205/128; Pepys, *Diary*, Vol. VIII, 11 August 1667, p. 382. Pepys noted that "everybody doth nowadays reflect upon Oliver and commend him, so brave things he

fear and discontent in the generality of men's minds."[105] "I should take this for the year '41," Richard Bower wrote ominously from Yarmouth, in "which I well remember the same game being now a playing and the people as insolent in their speeches against those that govern and command, making it a pastime to speak evil of them."[106] Lady Hollis reputedly claimed "that there were such divisions at home that a civil war could not be avoided."[107]

The danger was so great, the fears were so pervasive, because the criticisms of the government were so precise and so generally enunciated. Throughout the country there were fears of "French and Papist," of "the French invasion, then the Papists rising."[108] "People make nothing of talking treason in the streets openly," Pepys complained, "as, that we are bought and sold and governed by Papists and that we are betrayed by people about the king and shall be delivered up to the French."[109] Throughout England the Anglican Royalist regime was being accused of Popery and French governance.

Fears of Popery were rife throughout the summer. In many regions of the country there were rumors that the Papists were firing towns and villages.[110] Ludlow knew of "great fears" commonly expressed "of some bloody and Popish designs being put in speedy execution."[111] Significantly many thought the court was complicit in these plans. Some "have been very busy in possessing the people that the government grow Popish and hope to play their game by their new levies."[112] It was "not only whispered but publicly discoursed" among "the ignorant common people" in Carlisle "that the king is a Papist and intends to set up the Popish religion."[113] "Since Popery

did and made all the neighbor princes fear him; while here a prince, come in with all the love and prayers and good liking of his people, and have given greater signs of loyalty and willingness to serve him with their estates than ever was done by any people, hath lost all so soon, that it is a miracle what way a man could devise to lose so much in so little time." Pepys, *Diary*, Vol. VIII, 12 July 1667, p. 332.

105 Arlington to Ormonde, 30 July 1667, Carte 46, f. 516v. See also Arlingon to Henry Coventry, 2 August 1667, Longleat House, Cov. MSS XLIV, f. 163v. Ludlow, who shared none of Arlington's political outlook, reported the same level of political unrest: Ludlow, "A Voyce," Bod., English History MSS C487, p. 1150.

106 Richard Bower (Yarmouth) to Williamson, 5 August 1667, PRO, SP 29/212/74.

107 Thomas Papillon to ?Jane Papillon, 1 July 1667, CKS, U1015/F16/1.

108 Christopher Sawtell (Weymouth) to Edmund Sawtell, 6 July 1667, PRO, SP 29/208/111; Josselin, *Diary*, 7 July 1667, p. 536. See also Sir Geoffrey Shakerley (Chester) to Williamson, 17 June 1667, PRO, SP 29/206/12; Arlington to Northumberland, June 1667, PRO, SP 29/207/142; Orrery to Ormonde, 25 June 1667, *Orrery State Letters*, Vol. II, pp. 176–177; Silas Taylor (Harwich) to Williamson, 5 July 1667, PRO, SP 29/208/82.

109 Pepys, *Diary*, Vol. VIII, 14 July 1667, pp. 269–270.

110 Jane Papillon to Thomas Papillon, 3 July 1667, CKS, U1015/C11/7; Richard Watts (Deal) to Williamson, 4 July 1667, PRO, SP 29/208/79 (reporting a story that Bristol was burned); Williamson's journal, 2 July 1667, PRO, SP 29/231, f. 33v.

111 Ludlow, "A Voyce," Bod., English History MSS C487, p. 1158.

112 Sir Jonathan Trelawney (Fowey) to Williamson, 3 July 1667, PRO, SP 29/208/47.

113 Sir Philip Musgrave (Carlisle) to Williamson, 22 August 1667, PRO, SP 29/214/80.

hath been the noise," lamented Dr. John Beale, "all mouths do join the queen mother, and St. Albans, Monmouth, all great favorites, Lord Secretary in the list ... 'tis the great alarm and generally indulged."[114] These fears provoked some very uncomfortable comparisons. "There is a general fear amongst the many that they are in danger of no less than a massacre by the Papists," Dr. Bentham informed Joseph Williamson, "our late miseries and confusions thus began."[115] "Our gentry help on the cry of Popery," complained John Beale; "we are apparently and irrevocably back to 42."[116]

Along with fears of court Popery came concerns that the government hoped to rule in an arbitrary way, that it hoped to mimic Louis XIV's style of governance. The political theory which had become fashionable at court in the spring of 1667, convinced many that they were now to be ruled by standing armies rather than by Parliament. Rumors were widespread that the Duke of York, the Earl of Clarendon, and Charles II himself were in favor of "bringing things to be commanded by an army."[117] This gossip, of course, was given some substance by the government's need to raise troops to defend the country after the descent on Chatham. But even these troops, so manifestly necessary for defense, were denounced as "Papist, the scum of Goring, and trepanners of poor people."[118] It was said "that our own soldiers are far more terrible to those people of the country-towns than the Dutch themselves."[119] At the short Parliamentary session of July 1667, Sir Thomas Thompkins, an old ally of the Earl of Bristol but also "an old Cavalier and sequestered in Cromwell's time," thundered that "since our last meeting the king had raised an army, and the people are afraid and talk aloud that he intends to govern by a standing army."[120] Thompkins was

114 John Beale to John Evelyn, 24 August 1667, Christ Church, Evelyn In-Letters, 62. Sir Edward Spragg was also accused of Popery. See John Maurice (Minehead) to Williamson, 18 June 1667, PRO, SP 29/206/43. The story that "we are betrayed by Papists and others about the king" was also spread by Pepys's apothecary Walter Pelling. See Pepys, *Diary*, Vol. VIII, 13 June 1667, p. 264.

115 Dr. Jeremy Bentham (Loddington) to Williamson, 15 July 1667, *CSPD* Addenda 1660–1685, p. 206.

116 John Beale to John Evelyn, 31 August 1667, Christ Church, Evelyn In-Letters, 63. See also John Beale (Yeovil) to Williamson, 31 August 1667, PRO, SP 29/215/89. Significantly the bishops were also vilified as violently "as ever in the year 1640." Pepys, *Diary*, Vol. VIII, 21 December 1667, p. 585. See also Jeremy Bentham to Williamson, 14 June 1667, PRO, SP 29/205/63; Pepys, *Diary*, Vol. IX, 1 January 1668, pp. 1–2.

117 Pepys, *Diary*, Vol. VIII, 27 July 1667, p. 355; Pepys, *Diary*, Vol. VIII, 29 July 1667, pp. 366–367.

118 Sir Jonathan Trelawney (Dartmouth) to Williamson, 6 August 1667, PRO, SP 29/212/58. On the decision to raise the troops for defense, see Arlington to Ormonde, 15 June 1667, Carte 46, f. 491r; Allan Broderick to Ormonde, 15 June 1667, Carte 35, f. 478v.

119 Pepys, *Diary*, Vol. VIII, 30 June 1667, p. 309. For other complaints of standing armies in localities see John Fisher (Gray's Inn) to John Hobart, 2 August 1667, Bod., Tanner MSS 45, f. 205r.

120 ? to Michael Boyle Archbishop of Dublin, 10 August 1667, Carte 35, f. 649. On Thompkins, see Paul Seaward, *The Cavalier Parliament and the Reconstruction of the Old Regime 1661–1667* (Cambridge, 1989) p. 88.

quickly seconded by Sir Thomas Littleton and William Garraway, members of Parliament who in the last session had worked closely with Buckingham. Despite Sir William Coventry's assurance, an assurance which was almost certainly honest, that the government had no intention of maintaining the army, the House of Commons voted an address that the army be disbanded.[121] It was no doubt the profundity of this fear of governance by a standing army which prompted both Sir Richard Temple and Sir Edmund Waller to comment on its long history of political subversion.[122]

Fears of a standing army were accompanied by a concern that the government intended to abandon Parliament. "Many doubt of a standing army and say it's under debate if the Parliament shall meet or not," Sir Ralph Verney was advised.[123] Rumors abounded, rumors which were not unrelated to political reality, that there were fierce divisions within the Privy Council as to whether it was necessary or desirable to summon Parliament during the national disaster. It was said that Carteret, York, Clarendon, and especially Sheldon – always supported by the vast majority of the episcopacy – were "afeared of a Parliament." This coalition was ably opposed in Council by Sir William Coventry and the Earl of Anglesey.[124] "There is one great gown man against it," was John Rushworth's gloss on the government's debate over the utility of Parliament in the present circumstances, "and all the bishops and Papists and all those who have cozened and cheated the king."[125]

Ralph Josselin's comment that "our fears are of a standing army, Papists,

121 Pepys, *Diary*, Vol. VIII, 25 July 1667, pp. 352–353; Giustinian to Doge and Senate, 13/23 August 1667, *CSPV*, p. 180; Arlington to Ormonde, 27 July 1667, Carte 46, f. 513v; Caroline Robbins (editor), *The Diary of John Milward* (Cambridge, 1938), 25 July 1667, p. 83; Lady Ranelagh to Burlington, 25 July 1667, BL, Althorp Papers B4 (unfoliated); Roger Pepys to John Hobart, 25 July 1667, Bod., Tanner MSS 45, f. 204r. For evidence that the government no longer hoped to rule by a standing army, see Carlingford to Ormonde, 2 July 1667, Carte 35, f. 520r; Arlington to Sandwich, 25 July 1667, Bebington, *Arlington's Letters*, Vol. II, p. 231; Anglesey to Ormonde, 27 July 1667, Carte 47, f. 170r; Ferdinando Davys to Earl of Huntingdon, 30 July 1667, HL, HA 1952; Arlington to Ormonde, 30 July 1667, Carte 46, f. 517.

122 Sir Richard Temple, "An Account of Government," 1667, Bod., English History MSS C201, ff. 13–14; Waller 29 October 1667, Grey, *Debates*, Vol. I, p. 13; Waller, 9 November 1667, Grey, *Debates*, Vol. I, pp. 29–30.

123 John Cary to Sir Ralph Verney, 20 June 1667, Firestone Library, Verney MSS, Reel 21 (unfoliated).

124 Sir Nathaniel Hobart to Sir Ralph Verney, 20 June 1667, Firestone Library, Verney MSS, Reel 21 (unfoliated); Arlington to Ormonde, 18 June 1667, Carte 46, f. 492; Pepys, *Diary*, Vol. VIII, 18 June 1667, p. 277; Pepys, *Diary*, Vol. VIII, 21 June 1667, p. 282; Pepys, *Diary*, Vol. VIII, 25 June 1667, pp. 292–293; Pepys, *Diary*, Vol. VIII, 28 October 1667, pp. 305–306.

125 John Rushworth to Lady Ranelagh, 15 June 1667, PRO, SP 29/205/76. It is a telling measure of the government's ideological shift in 1667 that Rushworth became the secretary of Sir Orlando Bridgeman, the man who became Lord Keeper after Clarendon was compelled to surrender the seals. Ludlow, "A Voyce," Bod., English History MSS C487, p. 1160.

and persecution," then, were typical of the political climate in the summer of 1667.[126] There was great concern among the memers of Parliament gathered in London in July that the king "and the Duke of York do what they can to get up an army, that they may need no more Parliaments." The common gossip was that Lady Castlemaine had told Charles "that he must rule by an army or all would be lost," while Bab May had advised his master to "crush the English gentleman."[127]

It was these concerns which prompted some to engage in profound thinking about the nature of the English constitution. Sir Richard Temple insisted that "there was never any state well founded but what was mixed; and that never any government hath been just, where the authority was placed otherwise than in such hands which had a check of power in other hands to keep them from exceeding it quite contrary to the balance." Such a mixed constitution, he claimed, was in place in "all the lawful governments in Europe."[128] Throughout his essay, an essay in which he emphasized the dangers from standing armies, reason of state thinking, and of rule without Parliament, Temple made it clear that he thought the English constitution was in grave danger from recent developments. It was more than theoretical musing, then, when he noted that the English people "have never been provoked against their governors under other notion, than that their governors or favorites had a design to change [the constitution] and introduce an absolute monarchy."[129] It was these same concerns which provoked John Locke to warn against "some that tell us that monarchy is *jure divino*." These men who asserted that "the sole, supreme, arbitrary power and disposal of all things is and ought to be by divine right in a single person," Locke exclaimed, "have forgot what country they are born in, under what laws they live, and certainly can not but be obliged to declare Magna Charta to be downright heresy."[130] Moderate Anglicans as well as Nonconformists, country gentlemen as well as future Whigs, were convinced in the summer of 1667 that Charles II was being counseled to govern in an un-English way. "The design is," Sir Hugh Cholmley was convinced, "to have a land army, and so to make the government like that of

[126] Josselin, *Diary*, 4 August 1667, p. 537. See his similar fears the previous month: Josselin, *Diary*, 14 July 1667, p. 536.

[127] Pepys, *Diary*, Vol. VIII, 29 July 1667, p. 361.

[128] Sir Richard Temple, "An Essay Upon Government," 1667, Bod., English History MSS C201, f. 2r.

[129] Sir Richard Temple, An Account of Government," 1667, Bod., English History MSS C201, f. 20r.

[130] John Locke, "An Essay on Toleration," 1667, in Carlo Augusto Viano (editor), *John Locke: Scritti Editi E Inediti Sulla Tolleranza* (Turin, 1961), pp. 81–82. The same concerns about Magna Carta cropped up in the late 1667 Parliamentary session in which Lord Chief Justice Keeling was accused of calling "the privilege of Magna Charta … Magna Farta." Pepys thought that the accusations that Keeling and his ilk were bringing in "arbitrary government … very high language, and of the same sound with that in the year 1640." Milward, *Diary*, 11 December 1667, p. 163; Pepys, *Diary*, Vol. VIII, 12 December 1667, p. 577.

France."[131] "When I was in London men did speak out," the country member of Parliament Roger Pepys claimed, that "the supine negligence" of not setting out the fleet in 1667 "was done by design to make the nation poor that thereby the standing army might the sooner be raised and when [done] let it be a means to bring us under arbitrary power as it is in France."[132]

While there were clearly ubiquitous fear that the events of the 1640s were being repeated, the situation was actually quite different. Almost no one in England besides the bishops, the Duke of York, and a few Francophilic courtiers – those who had had the king's ear in the spring – in fact entertained such an elevated view of prerogative after the Chatham disaster. Nonconformists and moderate Anglicans – and it is significant that men like Sir William Coventry, Sir George Savile, and Lord Buckhurst openly criticized absolutist policies – all advocated a Parliamentary solution to the nation's ills. Ideological divisions were certainly not drawn along confessional lines. Just as significant was the fact that Charles II was not so deeply committed ideologically to Anglican Royalist policies. Instead of digging in his heels in defense of the policies pursued in the latter half of the war, he abandoned them.

By the end of June 1667 Charles II had decided to convene Parliament, a decision which immediately "revived the city of London."[133] Every effort was made to treat the previous session's court critics with "more than ordinary kindness."[134] Sir George Carteret was compelled to exchange his office of treasurer of the navy with the Earl of Anglesey. Significant pressure was put on Viscount Mordaunt – whose exercise of "arbitrary power" still provoked the extreme rage of many moderates – and the Canary Company to capitulate to its critics.[135] Charles II soon insisted on the enforcement of measures against Papists which led the Nonconformist community to look upon him with "a kindness more than common or usual."[136] All of this led

131 Pepys, *Diary*, Vol. VIII, 12 July 1667, pp. 331–332.

132 Roger Pepys to John Hobart, 2 July 1667, Bod., Tanner MSS 45, f. 202r.

133 Roger Pepys to John Hobart, 2 July 1667, Bod., Tanner MSS 45, f. 202r; Arlington to Ormonde, 25 June 1667, Carte 46, f. 496v; Allan Broderick to Ormonde, 25 June 1667, Carte 35, ff. 494–495.

134 Allan Broderick to Ormonde, 17 June 1667, Carte 35, f. 484r.

135 Roger Pepys to John Hobart, 2 July 1667, Bod., Tanner MSS 45, f. 202r; James Thurston (London) to Conway, 29 June 1667, *CSPD*, p. 296; Lady Ranelagh to Burlington, 29 June 1667, BL, Althorp Papers B4 (unfoliated); Allan Broderick to Ormonde, 29 June 1667, Carte 35, f. 502r; Allan Broderick to Ormonde, 2 July 1667, Carte 35, f. 522v; Dr. Mews to Williamson, 9/19 July 1667, PRO, SP 84/183, f. 11r. Mordaunt ultimately sought a pardon under the Privy Seal, while the Canary Company submitted itself to the judgment of the Privy Council. Williamson's journal, 1 July 1667, PRO, SP 29/231, f. 33r; Seaward, *Cavalier Parliament*, p. 319.

136 James Baskerville (Bristol) to James Hickes, 18 September 1667, PRO, SP 29/217/75; James S. Clarke, *The Life of James the Second* (London, 1816), Vol. I, pp. 429–430; Anglesey to Ormonde, 14 September 1667, Carte 47, f. 172r; Ronald Hutton, *The Restoration* (Oxford, 1985), p. 278.

Lord Brouncker to comment correctly that unlike his father Charles II "is resolved ... to do all possible to please the Parliament."[137]

Charles II's ultimate concession to popular opinion was his sacrifice of the Earl of Clarendon. Clarendon, it must be emphasized, was vilified and despised not for his actions and beliefs, but for those of the Anglican Royalist regime. Indeed, the English political nation blamed him for many decisions which he had opposed.[138] Immediately after Chatham Clarendon "was affronted by persons of quality in Westminster Hall, his house in James's fields, commonly called Dunkirk House ... was forced by the women, his windows broken, and his trees planted before it peeled."[139] The mob was convinced, incorrectly, as were a wide variety of contemporary poets that it was Clarendon's advice which "hounds us on the Hollander," that it was "perfidious Clarendine" who caused England to "pick quarrels with our neighbor nations," that it was the Lord Chancellor who so that "his friends in the navy wou'd not be ingrate / to grudge him timber" for his new house "fram'd 'em the war."[140]

It was widespread popular anger against the conduct of the war, an anger which had a voice in the Privy Council to be sure, not merely a newly reinvigorated Presbyterian party which brought Clarendon down.[141] The

137 Pepys, *Diary*, Vol. VIII, 8 September 1667, pp. 424–425.

138 It was this political reality which explains Buckingham's initial attempt to court Clarendon, and Colonel Birch's insistence upon defending him in Parliament. Pepys, *Diary*, Vol. VIII, 26 August 1667, p. 402; Seaward, *Cavalier Parliament*, pp. 318–319. The Presbyterian William Morrice also defended Clarendon in Parliament. Milward, *Diary*, 23 October 1667, p. 97. These were all men who had first-hand knowledge of Clarendon's actual policies and beliefs. Edmund Verney, no friend of absolutism, worried that Clarendon would be condemned merely by popular opinion. Edmund Verney (East Claydon) to Sir Ralph Verney, 18 November 1667, Firestone Library, Verney MSS, Reel 22 (unfoliated).

139 Ludlow, "A Voyce," Bod., English History MSS C487, pp. 1150–1151. This story is substantiated in Pepys, *Diary*, Vol. VIII, 14 June 1667, p. 269; ? to Viscount Conway, 15 June 1667, PRO, SP 29/205/78; Giustinian to Doge and Senate, 8/18 July 1667, *CSPV*, p. 172; Giustinian to Doge and Senate, 10/20 September 1667, *CSPV*, p. 184.

140 *Directions to a Painter*, p. 5; "Vox et Lacrimae Anglorum," Bod., Don MSS E23, f. 36v; "A Housewarming to Chacellor Hyde," Victoria and Albert Museum, Forster and Dyce Collection D25F37, ff. 2–3; "The Downfall of the Chancellor," Victoria and Albert Museum, Forster and Dyce Collection D25F37, f. 6; "On the Earl of Clarendon," 1667, Bod., Don MS b8, f. 218.

141 Paul Seaward (in *Cavalier Parliament*) has shown that Clarendon in fact made an approach to the Presbyterians before his fall, pp. 318–319; see also ? to Michael Boyle, 10 August 1667, Carte 35, f. 650r. William Coventry, sympathetic to Dissent, but not a Presbyterian, led the charge within the Privy Council against Clarendon, and was supported by Arlington. George Evelyn to John Evelyn, 30 August 1667, Christ Church, Evelyn In-Letters 579; Pepys, *Diary*, Vol. VIII, 30 August 1667, p. 409; Pepys, *Diary*, Vol. VIII, 31 August 1667, p. 410; John Coppleston to Duke of Richmond, 31 August 1667, BL, Add. 21947, f. 141v; Pepys, *Diary*, Vol. VIII, 2 September 1667, pp. 414–415; Henry Oxenden to George Oxenden, 2 September 1667, BL, Add. 40713, f. 25v; Sir William Coventry to Sir George Savile, 3 September 1667, BL, Althorp Papers C4 (unfoliated); Clarke, *Life of James the Second*, p. 431. The result of the broad based opposition to Clarendon was that by December "even those that are against my Lord Chancellor and the court in the House do not trust or agree with one another." Pepys, *Diary*, Vol. VIII, 6 December 1667, p. 568.

articles for impeachment, which were brought into Parliament against Clarendon in October 1667, brought in by moderate Anglicans rather than Nonconformists, had a great deal to do with the government's conduct during the war.[142] Two of the most damaging charges reflected the prevailing popular concern with arbitrary governance, that England lost the war because the government had opted to ally covertly with the French in Europe, and to mimic their governmental style in England. Clarendon was said to have "abused the king in all his treaties, especially in those of France, making the king believe that he was certain of a peace with the French king, which was the cause that the preparations for our war and defense were neglected until the King of France came out and joined with the Dutch."[143] There can be no question that Clarendon was popularly perceived to be a Francophile. After Clarendon's demise there were "great hopes that England will not be long misled by France."[144] A Venetian observer was convinced that his sympathy for France was the most significant cause of his demise.[145] But there is no evidence that he was behind the negotiations conducted in Paris under the supervision of his lifelong political enemy the queen mother. Nor is there evidence to substantiate the gossip circulated in England and on the continent by the Baron de Lisola that Clarendon was "a dependent of France."[146] Clarendon was being blamed for a policy which he probably did not initiate, and which was almost certainly supported by the king and the Duke of York.

Similarly Clarendon was accused of having advised the king to "dissolve this Parliament and set up a standing army."[147] The charge of rule by military force, of course, was unfounded, and in any event would have been anathema to a man so deeply committed to the rule of law.[148] Instead these were charges which more nearly applied to the men who were actually designing England's war policy in the winter and spring of 1667, men like York, Arlington, and Sir George Carteret. It was Anglican Royalist policy, not Charles II's Lord Chancellor, which was being condemned.

Of course, the decision to strip Clarendon of the seals and award them to Sir Orlando Bridgeman was ultimately the king's. The precise reasons for Charles II's dismissal of his Lord Chancellor are now impossible to recover. But there can be no doubt that he supported the Commons's impeachment of the fallen leader in the expectation that it would make him a popular

142 For a list of the articles and the men who brought in each individual charge, see "Articles against the Earl of Clarendon," 1667, Carte 36, f. 86.

143 Milward, *Diary*, 26 October 1667, p. 100.

144 Newsletter from Holland, 13/23 September 1667, PRO, SP 101/51/160.

145 Giustinian to Doge and Senate, 17/27 September 1667, *CSPV*, p. 185.

146 William Temple to Arlington, 6/16 September 1667, PRO, SP 77/37, f. 109r; Giustinian to Doge and Senate, 10/20 September 1667, *CSPV*, p. 184.

147 Milward, *Diary*, 26 October 1667, p. 99; "The Heads of the Charges against Clarendon," 26 October 1667, Carte 35, f. 800.

148 Seaward, *Cavalier Parliament*, pp. 18–22.

king. "There can be nothing advanced in the Parliament for my advantage," Charles informed his sister, "till this matter of my Lord Clarendon be over."[149] In this assessment he was almost certainly right. Many members of Parliament praised the dismissal of the Lord Chancellor as "an act of transcendental goodness."[150] One poet averred the people were as happy as when they roasted the Rump.[151] Arlington only exaggerated slightly when he claimed the dismissal gave "a great deal of satisfaction to the world."[152]

Exactly paralleling Clarendon's fall, and confirming the complete rejection of Anglican Royalist governance, was the meteoric rise of the Duke of Buckingham. Buckingham, who had been stripped of all of his offices and outlawed for his Parliamentary activity, probably at Arlington's behest, in the spring, finally surrendered himself in late June.[153] While a London mob had viciously attacked Clarendon House less than a fortnight previously, Buckingham basked at the Sun Tavern in Bishopsgate in popular adulation.[154] "Gazed on by numerous spectators," graciously accepting "the applause of the vulgar," many of whom were purportedly "praying for him as their patriot," Buckingham dined and tasted the wines at the tavern ostentatiously accompanied by Lord Rivers, Lord Buckhurst, Lord Vaughan, and the Duke of Monmouth on his way to the Tower.[155] Buckingham's submission proved to be only nominal. With "many of the discontented Parliament," including Sir Robert Howard and Sir Thomas Meres, at his side Buckingham quietly answered the Privy Council's charges, denying to the last that he had cast the king's horoscope.[156] Perhaps at Castlemaine's request, but more probably as part of Charles's

149 Charles II to Duchess of Orleans, 30 November 1667, Cyril H. Hartmann, *Charles II and Madame* (London, 1934), p. 196. For evidence that Charles II encouraged the impeachment see Cornbury to Ormonde, 8 December 1667, Carte 36, f. 84v; Williamson's newsletter, 15 October 1667, Carte 72, f. 40r; Conway to Ormonde, 15 October 1667, Carte 35, f. 764r; Conway to Ormonde, 22 October 1667, Carte 35, f. 778r.

150 Williamson's newsletter, 15 October 1667, Carte 72, f. 139r.

151 "On Chancellor Hyde," 1667, BL, Add. 34362, f. 18r; see another copy with slight variation in Beinecke Library, Osborn Collection B52/1, f. 158.

152 Arlington to Sandwich, 5 September 1667, Bebington, *Arlington's Letters*, Vol. II, pp. 234–235. See also Richard Bower (Yarmouth) to Williamson, 2 September 1667, PRO, SP 29/216/28.

153 Williamson's journal, 27 June 1667, PRO, SP 29/231, f. 32v.

154 Pepys, *Diary*, Vol. VIII, 28 June 1667, pp. 299–302.

155 Richard Graham to Burlington, 29 June 1667, BL, Althorp Papers B6 (unfoliated); Richard Graham to Burlington, 9 July 1667, BL, Althorp Papers B6 (unfoliated); Allan Broderick to Ormonde, 29 June 1667, Carte 35, f. 502; Mary Elmes to Sir Ralph Verney, 29 June 1667, Firestone Library, Verney MSS, Reel 21 (unfoliated); Orrery to Ormonde, 9 July 1667, *Orrery State Letters*, Vol. II, p. 226. This list of Buckingham's guests neatly encapsulates the breadth of his appeal: Rivers was a Catholic at the time, Vaughan a Quaker, Monmouth later became a Nonconformist martyr, and Buckhurst who had served under the Duke of York in the campaign of 1665 was widely known for his patronage of the arts and his moderate but vigilant political views.

156 Carlingford to Ormonde, 2 July 1667, Carte 35, f. 520v; Pepys, *Diary*, Vol. VIII, 12 July 1667, pp. 330–331; Pepys, *Diary*, Vol. VIII, 17 July 1667, p. 342.

program of concessions to public opinion, Buckingham was soon released.[157] Buckingham's brief incarceration only magnified his popularity. He "is cried up to be the best man in the world," wrote one of the Archbishop of Dublin's correspondents.[158] "People do speak kindly of the Duke of Buckingham, as one that will inquire into faults, and therefore they do mightily favor him," noted Samuel Pepys with a certain degree of trepidation.[159] Lady Stanley observed that it was "now the fashion to admire [Buckingham] for everything."[160]

Soon his resuscitation was complete, receiving again all of his offices, his place at the Council board, and ultimately the king's kindness[161] Buckingham had not sacrificed his principles in order to be restored to the king's good graces; rather Charles II had jettisoned his Anglican Royalist policies and some of his ministers in order to bask in the reflected glory of a wildly popular statesman. Instead of conforming to the policies of his opponents, Buckingham continued to pursue his principles of the previous winter. He employed the republican John Wildman as his secretary and showered favors upon the radical merchant and former Rump naval administrator, Colonel George Thomson.[162] Former Cromwellians like Orrery, Anglesey, and Ashley were known to be Buckingham's close allies.[163] He also continued to pursue two lines of policy which confirmed the popular perception that he was the protector of "the people's interest against tyranny and popery."[164]

That Buckingham would support greater leniency for Nonconformists,

[157] For the Castlemaine story, see Pepys, *Diary*, Vol. VIII, 12 July 1667, p. 331; Pepys, *Diary*, Vol. VIII, 17 July 1667, p. 342. For Buckingham's release: Mr. Ross to Richmond, 9 July 1667, BL 21947, f. 85r; Lady Ranelagh to Burlington, 9 July 1667, BL, Althorp Papers B4; St. Serfe's newsletter, 16 July 1667, LOC, 18124 Vol. I, f. 224r; Williamson's journal, 16 July 1667, PRO, SP 29/231, f. 37r; Allan Broderick to Ormonde, 16 July 1667, Carte 35, f. 549r.

[158] ? to Michael Boyle, 10 August 1667, Carte 35, f. 650r.

[159] Pepys, *Diary*, Vol. VIII, 22 July 1667, p. 349.

[160] Lady Henrietta-Maria Stanley to Countess of Burlington, 31 July 1667, BL, Althorp Papers B6 (unfoliated). Buckingham was so popular that after he had scuffled with Henry Killegrew at a playhouse it was feared that had Charles II not banished Killegrew "the people would have stoned him." ? to Michael Boyle, 10 August 1667, Carte 35, f. 650r; Dr. William Denton to Sir Ralph Verney, 25 July 1667, Firestone Library, Verney MSS Reel 21 (unfoliated); Williamson's journal, 20 July 1667, PRO, SP 29/231, f. 38v.

[161] Lord Ogle to Sir George Savile, 20 September 1667, BL, Althorp Papers C1 (unfoliated); Carlingford to Ormonde, 28 September 1667, Carte 35, f. 737r; Orrery to Ormonde, 1 November 1667, *Orrery State Letters*, Vol. II, p. 314.

[162] Anglesey to Ormonde, 10 December 1667, Carte 47, f. 174r; Pepys, *Diary*, Vol. VIII, 7 December 1667, pp. 570–571; Pepys, *Diary*, Vol. VIII, 12 December 1667, p. 577; H. W. to Sir Philip Musgrave, 19 December 1667, PRO, SP 29/225/40; Sir Ralph Verney to Edmund Verney, 12 December 1667, Firestone Library, Verney MSS, Reel 22 (unfoliated); Sir Ralph Verney to Edmund Verney, 19 December 1667, Firestone Library, Verney MSS, Reel 22 (unfoliated).

[163] See, for example, Clarke, *Life of James the Second*, p. 434.

[164] Ludlow, "A Voyce," Bod., English History MSS C487, p. 1160.

either through proposal of comprehension or toleration, would have surprised no one.[165] More startling was the breadth of support such proposals received both among politicians and in the country at large. The Earl of Anglesey, whose influence at court skyrocketed after Chatham, was said to have advocated "toleration of all religions here."[166] Sir Orlando Bridgeman, the new Lord Keeper, was widely and correctly perceived to be sympathetic to plans for comprehension.[167] Charles himself was rumored to have again voiced his support for toleration.[168]

It was clear that outside the confines of Whitehall the failure of the Anglican Royalist conduct of the war, coupled with the Nonconformist loyalty during the ultimately disastrous struggle, had created the ideological space necessary to initiate a new and vigorous debate over the merits of religious liberty. Upon reviewing the recent effusions of the press, John Beale observed that "the stationers have taught us all to give advices for some kind of toleration or relaxation of the conforming acts."[169] "The question of liberty of conscience," agreed John Locke, has been "much bandied about us."[170] Dr. John Owen confessed to be "a little surprised" at the "multiplication at this time" of discourses "about indulgence and toleration."[171] Nonconformists all over England were jubilant at the prospect of legal relief.[172]

165 For Buckingham's agitation along these lines see John Hacket, Bishop of Lichfield and Coventry, to Sheldon, 15 February 1668, Bod., Tanner MSS 45, f. 278r; H. W. to Sir Philip Musgrave, 19 December 1667, PRO, SP 29/225/40; Pepys, *Diary*, Vol. VIII, 21 December 1667, pp. 584–585.

166 Allan Broderick to Ormonde, 22 June 1667, Carte 35, f. 489r.

167 Sir Orlando Bridgeman to Sir Ralph Verney, 13 January 1665, Firestone Library, Verney MSS, Reel 20 (unfoliated); Pepys, *Diary*, Vol. VIII, 31 August 1667, p. 410; Dr. William Denton to Sir Ralph Verney, 5 September 1667, Firestone Library, Verney MSS, Reel 22 (unfoliated); Ma. Anderton (Chester) to Williamson, 11 September 1667, PRO, SP 29/216/144; Sir Philip Warwick to Sir Orlando Bridgeman, 1 December 1668, SRO, D1287 MSS 183/1; Greaves, *Enemies under His Feet*, p. 144.

168 John Fitzherbert (Bristol) to Williamson, 14 August 1667, PRO, SP 29/213/95; Pepys, *Diary*, Vol. IX, 31 January 1668, pp. 45–46 (reporting a conversation with Colonel Birch); Edward Hyde, *The Life of Edward Earl of Clarendon* (Dublin, 1760), p. 360.

169 John Beale to John Evelyn, 24 August 1667, Christ Church, Evelyn In-Letters 62.

170 Locke, "An Essay," Viano, *John Locke*, p. 81.

171 [John Owen] *Indulgence and Toleration Considered* (London, 1667), p. 3. There were in fact numerous contributions to the religious liberty debate in 1667: see besides the works by Owen and Locke previously cited [John Humphrey], *A Proposition for the Safety and Happiness of the King & Kingdom both in Church and State* 18 June 1667 (London, 1667); Sir Richard Temple, "An Essay Upon Government," 1667, Bod., English History MSS C201, esp. f. 10; [J. Corbet], *A Discourse of the Religion of England*; *Omnia Comesta a Belo* (1667); [John Owen], *A Peace-Offering in an Apology and Humble Plea for Indulgence and Liberty of Conscience* (London, 1667); *The Inconveniencies of Toleration* (London, 1667). This is not the place to analyze the debate over toleration, which continued well into 1668 in the press and in Parliament, and of course was periodically renewed throughout the later seventeenth century. My point is merely that the Dutch War shattered the Anglican Royalist consensus, making such a debate possible.

172 Richard Bower (Yarmouth) to Williamson, 28 July 1667, PRO, SP 29/211/55; Joseph Glanvill (Bath) to John Beale, 10 September 1667, PRO, SP 29/216/133; Dr. Peter Mews

More significantly it was widely thought that the majority of the political nation supported some form of concession to the Nonconformists. Roger Pepys was convinced in Cambridge "by our university men" that religious liberty is "to be granted."[173] From Bedfordshire Dr. Jeremy Bentham reported that "a toleration and liberty of conscience is looked on as the only panpharmacon."[174] Samuel Pepys, drawing upon his wide range of acquaintances, felt certain that "most of the sober party be for some kind of an allowance to be given."[175] "Most people here," concurred the scientist Henry Oldenburg, "look for an act of Comprehension."[176] That the Comprehension bill failed, that it "was thrown out of the House with ignominy," had far more to do with the lobbying skill of the episcopacy and the composition of a Parliament elected in 1662, than it did with contemporary popular sentiment or the ideological profile of the men now in favor at court.[177] The failure of the bill, thought one well-informed observer, was a "great blow" because it was "so much desired by much the greater part of the nation."[178]

The natural result of such a profound ideological shift in the nation's political outlook, an ideological transformation directly resulting from the failure of the Anglican Royalist war effort, was a new foreign-policy orientation. The widespread conviction that the French had successfully played a double game, had seduced both English and Dutch while they marched through the Spanish Netherlands without resistance, only magnified English Francophobia.[179] "The French are more cried out against

(Oxford) to Williamson, 26 September 1667, PRO, SP 29/217/174; Charles Honeywood (Portsmouth) to Williamson, 29 October 1667, PRO, SP 29/221/72; Richard Bower (Yarmouth) to Williamson, 18 December 1667, PRO, SP 29/225/39; Richard Bower (Yarmouth) to Williamson, 8 January 1668, PRO, SP 29/232/70; Letter from Staffordshire, 3 February 1668, PRO, SP 29/234/35; Mr. Saltmarsh (Great Ellington) to Sancroft, 8 February 1668, Bod., Tanner MSS 45, f. 276r.

173 Roger Pepys to John Hobart, 2 July 1667, Bod., Tanner MSS 45, f. 202r.

174 Dr. Jeremy Bentham to Williamson, 15 July 1667, *CSPD*, Addenda 1660–1685, p. 206.

175 Pepys, *Diary*, Vol. IX, 20 January 1668, p. 31.

176 Henry Oldenburg to Robert Boyle, 1 October 1667, *Oldenburg Correspondence*, Vol. III, p. 504.

177 Sir Richard Browne to John Evelyn, 12 February 1667, Christ Church, Evelyn In-Letters 428. See also Edward Conway to Sir George Rawdon, 29 December 1666, HL, HA 14452 (on the episcopate's opposition); Allan Broderick to Ormonde, 11 February 1668, Carte 36, f. 155; Letter to the Duchess of Ormonde, 21 April 1668, *Orrery State Letters*, Vol. II, p. 350; Roger Morrice, "Eminenent Worthies," Dr. Williams' Library, J1684(4).

178 Pepys, *Diary*, Vol. IX, 10 February 1668, p. 60.

179 For this belief, already outlined above, see also Lady Ranelagh to Burlington, 25 May 1667, BL, Althorp Papers B4 (unfoliated); Orrery to Ormonde, 21 June 1667, *Orrery State Letters*, Vol. II, p. 169; William Temple to Arlington, 25 June/5 July 1667, PRO, SP 77/36, f. 340r; Arlington to Ormonde, 25 June 1667, Carte 46, f. 496; Orrery to Burlington, 1 July 1667, BL, Althorp Papers B4 (unfoliated); William Temple to Sir John Temple, 30 September/10 October 1667, in *The Works of Sir William Temple* (London, 1814), Vol. I, pp. 290–291; Ludlow, "A Voyce," Bod., English History MSS C487, pp. 1156–1157.

than the Dutch," Dr. Peter Mews was informed, "having lulled us asleep with a treaty."[180] Thomas Papillon, no friend of republicanism and certainly cognizant of the reality of Dutch economic competition, concluded that the French "are much the worst enemies."[181] Orrery encapsulated English popular sentiment when he declared to Ormonde that "I had much rather (under God) trust to our swords, than to the French promises."[182]

The English were becoming increasingly convinced that the French perfidy was long thought out, that they had a deep and dark design. Concern for the well-being of Flanders was reinforced by persistent rumors that the French were about to invade England.[183] Dominance of the Low Countries and subjugation of England were widely perceived to be central elements of the French grand strategy to achieve universal dominion. "People say here publicly, and it is the language of many," reported the French ambassador Ruvigny with remarkable acuity, that they "should rationally have the same fear and same thoughts of the French" as they formerly had of Charles V and Philip II, the same fears of "universal monarchy."[184] Indeed fear of French universal monarchy was ubiquitous. The Irish Catholic Earl of Carlingford warned his friend Ormonde that "the King of France has a hopeful prospect of being universal monarch."[185] The French, thought the moderate Thomas Thynne, "turn all stones to embroil Christendom, that they may find the less opposition."[186] Joseph Williamson's Weymouth correspondent John Pocock heard that after the French conquered the Spanish Netherlands, "England and Holland are but a

180 Dr. Peter Mews to Williamson, 21 June/1 July 1667, PRO, SP 84/182, f. 212r.

181 Thomas Papillon to ?, 4 June 1667, CKS, U1015/F16/1.

182 Orrery to Ormonde, 3 July 1667, *Orrery State Letters*, Vol. II, p. 200.

183 Evidence for English concern about the Spanish Netherlands is ubiquitous. For some early examples, see Carlingford to Sir Edward Dering, 20 April 1667, BL, Stowe MSS 744, f. 157v; Anglesey to Ormonde, 27 April 1667, Carte 47, f. 146r; Caterin Belogno (Madrid) to Doge and Senate, 24 April/4 May 1667, *CSPV*, pp. 154–155 (reporting on Sandwich's assesment of English public opinion); Gervase Jacques to Huntingdon, 30 April 1667, HL, HA 7655; Sir Ralph Verney to Edmund Verney, 23 May 1667, Firestone Library, Verney MSS, Reel 21 (unfoliated); Henry Coventry to Arlington, 24 May/3 June 1667, Longleat House, Cov. MSS LXXXI, f. 6v; William Temple to Arlington, 31 May/10 June 1667, PRO, SP 77/36, f. 290v; Arlington to Ormonde, 1 June 1667, Carte 46, ff. 484–485; John Coventry to Sir James Thynne, 10 June 1667, Longleat House, Thynne MSS X, f. 176r; Carlingford to Ormonde, 30 July 1667, Carte 35, f. 582r. On fears of French invasion, see Marvell, "Last Instructions," 1667, *POAS*, p. 119; Pepys, *Diary*, Vol. VIII, 18 June 1667, p. 277; Richard Bower (Yarmouth) to Williamson, 1 July 1667, PRO, SP 29/208/8; Anglesey to Ormonde, 13 July 1667, Carte 47, f. 166v; Pepys, *Diary*, Vol. VIII, 31 December 1667, p. 602; Pepys, *Diary*, Vol. IX, 10 January 1668, p. 18; Arlington to Ormonde, 15 February 1668, Carte 46, f. 598v; Conway to Ashley, 28 February 1668, PRO, 30/24/4, f. 154v; Ludlow, "A Voyce," Bod., English History MSS C487, p. 1159.

184 Ruvigny to de Lionne, 9/19 September 1667, in F. A. M. Mignet, *Négociations Relatives à la Succession d'Espagne Sous Louis XIV* (Paris, 1835), Vol. II, pp. 513–514 (my translation).

185 Carlingford to Ormonde, 2 July 1667, Carte 35, f. 520.

186 Thomas Thynne to Arlington, 3/13 November 1667, PRO, SP 95/6, f. 237v.

breakfast for them."[187] "The French king appears more and more to have vast designs," Oldenburg wrote to Robert Boyle full of trepidation.[188] Edmund Verney referred to the French as "our arch-enemies." He insisted that the French invasion of Flanders was against "the interest of the House of Austria, of Germany in general, of Denmark, of Holland and of our country." This was because Louis XIV aimed at making the Netherlanders his "slaves" as a key step towards his achievement of "the universal monarchy."[189] His father Sir Ralph, possibly convinced by Lisola's polemics, as well as his son's urgent warnings, also feared that "the King of France aims beyond imagination."[190] Pepys eagerly read Lisola's *Buckler* which he thought "very good and solid." Just prior to that he had perused Fulke Greville's *Life of Sidney*, which described the Spanish designs on universal monarchy and the necessity of an Anglo-Dutch alliance, declaring his "prophesying our present condition here in England in relation to the Dutch" to be "very remarkable."[191]

By far the most eloquent, most persistent, and most important expositor of the French designs was the English envoy in the Spanish Netherlands, Sir William Temple. Temple, who thought he had "seldom met with a better sort of man" than Lisola, was convinced that Louis XIV sought "by division amongst his neighbors to pick up and bring them all at last under his dominion, as universal monarch over Christendom."[192] He repeatedly warned that should Flanders fall prey to the arms of Louis XIV the rest of Europe would soon fall like so many neatly aligned dominoes, that the "French greatness will grow by that means past all restraint of treating with any of their neighbors as with equals."[193] He thought the time to act was quickly passing. He prayed that "we shall avoid the reproach I have heard

187 John Pocock (Weymouth) to Williamson, 21 December 1667, PRO, SP 29/225/109.

188 Oldenburg to Robert Boyle, 1 October 1667, *Oldenburg Correspondence*, Vol. III, p. 504.

189 Edmund Verney to Sir Ralph Verney, 4 May 1667, Firestone Library, Verney MSS, Reel 21 (unfoliated, my translation); Edmund Verney to Sir Ralph Verney, 16 December 1667, Firestone Library, Verney MSS, Reel 22 (unfoliated, my translation); Edmund Verney to Sir Ralph Verney, 5 January 1668, Firestone Library, Verney MSS, Reel 22 (unfoliated, my translation).

190 Sir Ralph Verney to Edmund Verney, 28 November 1667, Firestone Library, Verney MSS, Reel 22 (unfoliated); Sir Ralph Verney to Edmund Verney, 12 (unfoliated) (Lisola). Lisola's *Buckler* appeared in late May, see newsletter, 28 May 1667, Bod., Don MSS C37, f. 26r; Williamson's journal, 28 May 1667, PRO, SP 29/231, f. 24r.

191 Pepys, *Diary*, Vol. IX, 16 February 1668, p. 61 (Lisola); Pepys, *Diary*, Vol. IX, 1 January 1668, p. 1 (Greville); Pepys, *Diary*, Vol. IX, 2 January 1668, p. 2 (Greville).

192 On his friendship and sympathy with Lisola see Temple to Arlington, 23 October/2 November 1666, PRO, SP 77/35, f. 214v; Temple to Arlington, 2/12 November 1666, PRO, SP 77/35, f. 234v; Temple to Arlington, 14/24 May 1667, PRO, SP 77/36, f. 247r; Temple to Williamson, 28 May/7 June 1667, PRO, SP 77/36, f. 280r. For his declaration that Louis XIV sought universal monarchy see: Temple to Orlando Bridgeman, 30 November 1667, SRO, D1287/18/3/2.

193 Temple to Arlington, 12/22 November 1667, PRO, SP 77/37, f. 202r; Temple to Arlington, 21 June/1 July 1667, PRO, SP 77/37, f. 10r; Temple to Sir John Temple, 30 September/10 October 1667, *Works*, Vol. I, p. 291.

so often, and I think so reasonably made against our last great minister," that having "the offer of what alliance and where he pleased" he "made none." "To be neutral in the quarrels of neighbors," Temple declared, "is a counsel which an esteemed wise man I remember says no wise prince ever took."[194] Only an immediate Anglo-Dutch alliance, which was clearly in their "common interest," could prevent Flanders from being "swallowed up."[195]

Unlike the previous year in which the English government had continued to pursue an Anglican Royalist foreign policy, a foreign policy in which the Dutch Republic rather than the French monarchy was perceived to be the more serious aspirant to universal dominion, Charles II and his ministers did act upon the profound popular fear of French aggrandizement. While the English ambassadors were still at Breda, De Witt had dropped hints that he desired "a league between England and Sweden and Holland."[196] The Dutch were apparently so convinced of French perfidy that they "now lay the fault on the French as the authors of the late wars betwixt them and England."[197] After much prodding from the Dutch, goading by the Spanish, and pleading from Lisola, the English despatched William Temple to The Hague armed with the assurance that Charles II still felt "all possible kindness" for the Prince of Orange, "yet the considerations of his interests at this time shall not at all interfere with, or disturb the great interest betwixt the nations, which must ever be superior to that particular one."[198]

While historians have traditionally credited the English Secretary of State Arlington with having promoted the negotiations which resulted in the Triple Alliance, this seems intrinsically unlikely.[199] Not only was Arlington

194 Temple to Arlington, 1/11 October 1667, PRO, SP 77/37, f. 145v. This proverb, I think, should be read as much as a reproach to Arlington as to Clarendon.

195 Temple to Bridgeman, 30 November 1667, SRO, D1287/18/3/2. See also Temple to Arlington, 1/11 October 1667, PRO, SP 77/3, f. 145v; Temple to Arlington, 12/22 November 1667, PRO, SP 77/37, f. 201v; Temple to Arlington, 19/29 November 1667, PRO, SP 77/37, f. 208; Temple to Ormonde, 31 December 1667, Carte 36, f. 61v; Temple to Bridgeman, 17/27 January 1668, *Works*, Vol. I, pp. 313–314.

196 Henry Coventry to Clarendon, 16/26 August 1667, Bod., Clar. 159, f. 62v; Carlingford to Ormonde, 13 August 1667, Carte 35, f. 634v; Henry Coventry to Clarendon, 19/29 August 1667, Longleat House, Cov. MSS LXXXI, f. 34r; Silas Taylor (Harwich) to Williamson, 26 August 1667, PRO, SP 29/215/23; Temple to Arlington, 27 August/6 September 1667, PRO, SP 77/37, f. 101v; Arlington to Ormonde, 31 August 1667, Carte 46, f. 542v.

197 Silas Taylor to Williamson, 3 September 1667, PRO, SP 29/216/38.

198 Instructions to William Temple, 25 November 1667, PRO, SP 77/37, f. 218v. For the decision, see Giustinian to Doge and Senate, 17/27 September, 1667, *CSPV*, p. 185; Arlington to Sandwich, 26 September 1667, Bebington, *Arlington's Letters*, Vol. II, pp. 257–258; Lisola to Arlington, 26 June/6 July 1667, PRO, SP 77/36, f. 342r; K. H. D. Haley, *An English Diplomat in the Low Countries* (Oxford, 1986), p. 157.

199 This is largely because Arlington himself took credit for the achievement, a view which was also supported by the French diplomat Ruvigny. See Haley, *English Diplomat*, p. 175; Violet Barbour, *Henry Bennet Earl of Arlington: Secretary of State to Charles II*

political predispositions were fortified by the reports of the English ambassadors from Breda, especially those of his political protégé Sir Henry Coventry. Arlington allowed that the ambassadors confirmed reports that "the current of the country" favored the English "joining with them in the defense of Flanders," but he pointed out that it was the politicians who made the decisions, and these the ambassadors "do very much suspect ... are not inwardly of the same mind."[200] Indeed report after report from Henry Coventry suggested that, while it was clear to most in the United Provinces as well as in England that the French sought "the universal monarchy by sea as well as land," De Witt was "yet French in his heart."[201] Joseph Williamson's newsletter, despatched from Arlington's office, belittled the proposals for an Anglo-Dutch alliance, insisting that "Holland aims to have us do their work at our costs."[202] "We, on our side," proclaimed Arlington himself, "are afraid the Dutch affect this declaration [of support for Flanders] from us, only to enable them to make better conditions with France."[203] As late as December Arlington thought the Dutch "are likelier to go in for their share of the prey than to assist [the Spanish] and we shall think ourselves happy if we be not attacked."[204]

Arlington, in fact, supported the isolationist policies so long associated with the Earl of Clarendon. The Dutch, he explained to Temple, "must speak closer to us before they will be able to engage us in a quarrel that does not only concern them more than us; but for ought I see more than Spain itself."[205] "The king must settle his own affairs," Arlington lectured Ormonde, "before he meddles with his neighbors."[206] "And the truth is," the increasingly vociferous Francophobe Sandwich was advised, "though the peace be made with our enemies abroad, there is such a fomentation of ill humors at home, that no good counselor can advise his Majesty to any

also supported by the French diplomat Ruvigny. See Haley, *English Diplomat*, p. 175; Violet Barbour, *Henry Bennet Earl of Arlington: Secretary of State to Charles II* (Washington DC, 1914), pp. 118–136; Ruvigny to Louis XIV, 20/30 January 1668, Mignet, *Négociations*, Vol. II, p. 562.

200 Arlington to Ormonde, 14 September 1667, Carte 46, f. 550v.

201 Henry Coventry to Thomas Thynne, 5/15 September 1667, Longleat House, Thynne MSS XVI, f. 475. For the persistence of Coventry in this view throughout the summer, see Henry Coventry to Clarendon, 10/20 May 1667, Bod., Clar. 159, f. 2v; Coventry to Clarendon, 24 May/3 June 1667, 24 May/3 June 1667, Bod., Clar. 159, f. 9v; Coventry to Clarendon, 31 May/10 June 1667, Bod., Clar. 159, f. 15v; Coventry to Clarendon, 14/24 June 1667, Bod., Clar. 159, f. 32v; Hollis and Coventry to Clifford, August 1667, Longleat House, Cov. MSS XLIV, f. 177. Unfortunately Coventry's correspondence with Arlington has not been located, though evidence from his other letters indicates that it it did exist.

202 Williamson's newsletter, 22 October 1667, Carte 72, f. 141r. Earlier in the Summer Williamson "suspected the French and Dutch are treating about the dividing of Flanders." Williamson's journal, 20 July 1667, PRO, SP 29/231, f. 39r.

203 Arlington to Temple, 22 November 1667, Bebington, *Arlington's Letters*, Vol. I, p. 190.

204 Arlington to Ormonde, 7 December 1667, Carte 46, f. 578v.

205 Arlington to Temple, 4 October 1667, Bebington, *Arlington's Letters*, Vol. I, p. 183.

206 Arlington to Ormonde, 31 August 1667, Carte 46, f. 542v.

new hazards or costly designs."[207] Finally, Arlington relied upon a financial argument, the same argument which he had almost certainly supported when the decision was made not to send out the fleet earlier in the year. "The necessities of the kingdom after such a war," he insisted, meant that an alliance against France "cannot be maintained but by the Parliament's giving his Majesty yet more money than they are either able, or willing to do."[208] Earlier he had advised Ormonde that "the war hath been too heavy for his Majesty hastily to enter into a new one."[209] Arlington, then, opposed alliance with the Dutch both as a result of his continued distrust of their intentions and because he felt that England was politically and financially unable to support such an alliance. Significantly he did not even accept the strategic analysis upon which the alliance was based. "Keeping the balance even between the two crowns" might be an argument advanced by "witty men" and "talked out of doors," but, Arlington emphasized, it was not his.[210] It is difficult indeed to believe that a man imbued with such deeply held beliefs, to say nothing of his precarious political position, was the architect of the Triple Alliance.

A more likely candidate was the man who was so widely credited with leading the assault on the Anglican Royalist regime, the man who had so often and so vocally criticized the conduct of the war against the Dutch and the new French style of government. Unlike Arlington, who every day had to fear new aspersions on his character and his policies, it was widely thought, at exactly the critical juncture when the decision was taken to pursue an alliance with the Dutch, that "the Duke of Buckingham doth rule all now."[211] The government clerk John Gregory was convinced that "Buckingham and Bristol are [Charles II's] only Cabinet Council."[212] Conway warned Ormonde that his enemy "Buckingham governs all."[213] The court doctor Pierce reported that "the king is now fallen in and become a slave to the Duke of Buckingham, led by none but him."[214] Buckingham, as befitted a man so deeply interested in international affairs, did not limit his influence to domestic matters. It soon became widely known that he, along with the two secretaries whose official responsibility it was, "do all

207 Arlington to Sandwich, 8 August 1667, Bebington, *Arlington's Letters*, Vol. II, p. 232. Temple had received an almost identical assessment the previous week: Arlington to Temple, 2 August 1667, Bebington, *Arlington's Letters*, Vol. I, p. 179.

208 Arlington to Sandwich, 31 October 1667, Bebington, *Arlington's Letters*, Vol. II, pp. 264–265.

209 Arlington to Ormonde, 18 May 1667, Carte 46, f. 476.

210 Arlington to Temple, 4 October 1667, Bebington, *Arlington's Letters*, Vol. I, p. 183.

211 Pepys, *Diary*, Vol. VIII, 30 December 1667, p. 597. This belief was so widely held in diplomatic circles that Charles II felt compelled to assure his sister that he still retained his political independence: Charles II to Duchess of Orleans, 5 March 1668, Hartmann, *Charles II and Madame*, p. 204.

212 Pepys, *Diary*, Vol. VIII, 16 November 1667, p. 532.

213 Conway to Ormonde, 22 October 1667, Carte 35, f. 778.

214 Pepys, *Diary*, Vol. VIII, 27 November 1667, p. 550.

foreign business" and "managed" the "present treaty with the Dutch."[215] While Buckingham's complicity in the Cabal's ill-fated foreign adventures has predisposed historians to view him as a Francophile,[216] all of the available evidence suggests that in 1667 he was committed to putting a halt to the French advance in Flanders. In October he was meeting clandestinely with Lisola and the Spanish ambassador Molina. The previous month he had informed the French ambassador that "all in England are against France, because of a furious jealousy that they had conceived against the power of the king." Ruvigny concluded despondently that Buckingham "is persuaded of this just like the others."[217] So manifest was the duke's fear of French puissance, so powerful was his sway over the king known to be, that contemporaries knew immediately who was responsible for the Triple Alliance. "Our chief minister," Sir Nathaniel Hobart advised Sir Ralph Verney, has "made a peace abroad."[218]

It was Buckingham, rather than the isolationist and committed Orangist Arlington, who was far more likely to appreciate the increasingly optimistic reports from Temple. In September Temple, who throughout the spring concurred with Arlington in the belief that there was little to be hoped for from the Frenchified and thoroughly committed republican De Witt, reported sympathetically on the gossip common in Brussels. There it was said, Temple revealed approvingly, that Charles II "cannot better divert his people's thoughts and humors from working inward than by busying them upon some easy war abroad, nor make the ill success of our late war forgotten, but by the success of another." "And," the gossip ran, "if [Charles II] can enter into a common league with the emperor, the Swede, and the Dutch for preserving these countries and thereby checking the ambition of France and restoring a firm and general peace of Christendom, no war can be of more justice and honor, nor in such a conjuncture more easy or certain of success."[219] At the same time that Arlington was busily

215 Conway to Ormonde, 30 November 1667, Carte 35, f. 373v; Sir Ralph Verney to Edmund Verney, 28 November 1667, Firestone Library, Verney MSS, Reel 22 (unfoliated).

216 Even this, I think, is a misreading of his foreign vision in the 1670s. Buckingham thought that the Dutch were the only real threat to England because he felt that naval power was the only real source of strength. Given the intractability of the Dutch republican government, he thought it best to make a temporary alliance with France to cow the Dutch into their natural position of dependence on England, and then he hoped to demolish the French monarchy. This position is described elliptically in *A Free Conference Touching the Present State of England Both at Home and Abroad: In Order to the Designs of France*, imprim., Joseph Williamson 21 January 1668 (London, 1668).

217 Ruvigny to de Lionne, 9/19 September 1667, Mignet, *Négociations*, Vol. II, p. 513 (my translation).

218 Sir Nathaniel Hobart to Sir Ralph Verney, January 1668, Firestone Library, Verney MSS, Reel 22 (unfoliated).

219 William Temple to Arlington. 6/16 September 1667, PRO, SP 77/37, f. 110v. The Governor of the Spanish Netherlands, the Marquis of Castel Rodrigo, frequently assured Temple that De Witt himself was "grown now more a Spaniard than ever he was thought a Frenchman." Temple to Arlington, 13/23 September 1667, PRO, SP 77/37, f. 119r.

denouncing De Witt to all who cared to listen, Temple visited the Holland Grand Pensionary. Not only did he discover that the Dutch "seemed already to have forgotten all the enmity which three years' war had been raising between the nations," but he found De Witt and his party "hearty in the point of defending Flanders."[220] Temple was clearly convinced, like so much of the English political nation, that Louis XIV had to be stopped and that an alliance with the Dutch – even with De Witt – was the best means to do it.

Once the decision was taken in England to go ahead with a league to bridle the power of France, there was little to prevent the conclusion of an agreement. Despite the delays normally associated with the Christmas season Temple and De Witt had hammered out an agreement less than two months after Temple's instructions were drafted. Unsurprisingly the "league of mediation" – a league in which the United Provinces and England, with the possible inclusion of others, guaranteed France's military gains on the condition that they would put an end to their attacks – was not greeted with glee in France. The French were said to be "extremely scandalized" at it, while Louis XIV was known to be "nettled."[221] Despite the scrupulously neutral wording of the league, Heneage Finch observed, it was "looked on at Paris as a league made against them, for so it will prove in effect if the desires of the Great Monarch can not be circumscribed."[222] It was indeed an agreement, Samuel Parker recalled, aimed at throttling the ambition of Louis XIV, a monarch quite "capable of universal empire."[223]

The new foreign policy, this complete reorientation away from the Anglican Royalist preference of war with the Dutch and alliance with the French, was greeted with unbridled enthusiasm in England and throughout Europe. In Lynn "all people" were "highly pleased with the conclusion of the late treaty with the Dutch."[224] The news "gives at present more satisfaction [in] general" in East Anglia than the Treaty of Breda.[225] The Bishop of Lincoln pronounced that the league with the Dutch "pleases everybody."[226] Sir John Hobart could not imagine "a more pleasing prospect toward the stopping the impetuosity that too probably threatens a desolation to the neighboring countries."[227] Pepys thought it "the first good act that hath been done a great while, and done secretly and with great

[220] Temple to Arlington, 19/29 September 1667, PRO, SP 77/37, f. 121r; Temple to Arlington, 25 September/5 October 1667, PRO, SP 77/37, ff. 133–134; Temple to Ormonde, 1/11 October 1667, Carte 35, f. 752.

[221] Dr. William Denton to Sir Ralph Verney, 23 January 1668, Firestone Library, Verney MSS, Reel 22 (unfoliated); Arlington to Ormonde, 21 January 1668, Carte 46, f. 587.

[222] Heneage Finch to Daniel Finch, 23 January 1668, LRO, DG7/Box 4984 Letters Folder.

[223] Thomas Newlin (translator), *Bishop Parker's History of his Own Time* (London, 1727), p. 131.

[224] Edward Bodham (Lynn) to Williamson, 29 January 1668, PRO, SP 29/233/113.

[225] John Hobart to Sir John Hobart, 27 January 1668, Bod., Tanner MSS 45, f. 264r.

[226] Pepys, *Diary*, Vol. IX, 23 January 1668, p. 35.

[227] Sir John Hobart to John Hobart, 2 January 1668, Bod., Tanner MSS 45, f. 258r.

seeming wisdom."[228] London, which had received the news of the peace at Breda with more resignation than enthusiasm, now seemed transported with pleasure. Margaret Elmes reported that this peace, which she heard Buckingham "hath had a great hand in making," "pleaseth most." Indeed it was extremely popular among the City's merchants who "talk of sending out ships apace and hope to have trading pretty good."[229] The Venetian Marc Antonio Giustinian concurred that the proposed "union of England, Sweden and Holland for peace between the two crowns has been received with no ordinary pleasure by the people of London."[230] Sir William Temple had good reason to take pride in having "had the good fortune to please at once the king and kingdom."[231]

Outside of France, all Europe seemed to share England's enthusiasm for the Anglo-Dutch agreement. The first reports of the union "mightily pleased" the inhabitants of the Spanish Netherlands.[232] In the United Provinces "the joy and wonder" was "hardly imaginable."[233] Significantly these sentiments were shared not only among Protestants and those whose territory was immediately threatened by the young and powerful Louis XIV. The Catholic convert and former Queen of Sweden Christina whispered to the English resident in Hamburg that "it would be a great and wise thing for England and Holland now to join both by sea and land to fall upon the French [king] and damp his pride."[234] Opinion in Rome suggested just how much European culture had changed since the days of the Thirty Years War. Far from cheering on the conquests of a great Catholic power, all in Rome were "very sensible of the French progress in Flanders," hoping against hope for an Anglo-Dutch union, a union between two Protestant powers.[235] When news of "the league betwixt England and Holland" reached Rome it touched off an "extraordinary jubilee."[236] "The Pope and court" could not have been happier at this alliance "to give some bound to the unlimited exorbitance of the French whom they say are the plague and perplexity of Christendom."[237]

With such universal acclamation both at home and abroad, then, it was no small wonder that the news of the Anglo-Dutch league significantly altered the mood in Parliament. Temple, Arlington, and Ormonde all rightly predicted that the agreement would bring "the Parliament together in good

228 Pepys, *Diary*, Vol. IX, 20 January 1668, p. 30.
229 Margaret Elmes (Covent Garden) to Sir Ralph Verney, 23 January 1668, Firestone Library, Verney MSS, Reel 22 (unfoliated).
230 Marc Antonio Giustinian to Doge and Senate, 11/21 February 1668, *CSPV*, p. 215.
231 Temple to Arlington, 31 January/10 February 1668, PRO, SP 84/183, f. 177r.
232 J. W. to Williamson, 19/29 January 1668, PRO, SP 77/38, f. 15r.
233 Temple to Ormonde, 14/24 January 1668, Carte 36, f. 121v.
234 Sir William Swann to Williamson, 8 June 1667, PRO, SP 82/11, f. 63v.
235 Francis Bayllardy to Arlington, 7/17 September 1667, PRO, SP 85/9, f. 13.
236 Joseph Kent to Williamson, 21 February/3 March 1668, PRO, SP 85/9, f. 119r.
237 Joseph Kent to Williamson, 8/18 February 1668, PRO, SP 85/9, ff. 117–118.

humor."[238] By the middle of February Arlington was convinced that "both [parties] will agree in succoring his Majesty for the support of his union with Holland," a sentiment echoed by the country member of Parliament Roger Pepys.[239] Indeed it was widely said in Parliamentary circles that "the league" was "the only good public thing that hath been done since the king came into England."[240] It was with good reason as well as a sense of a job well done which prompted the Lord Keeper, who might well have strongly supported Buckingham in advocating the Anglo-Dutch union, to reflect that the result of the Anglo-Dutch War "even the most inglorious part of it" might have been ironically to pave the way for a league which will promote "peace, honor, and strength to his Majesty and his people."[241]

That an Anglo-Dutch league was the outcome of the war was indeed ironic. It was never the intended result of the Anglican Royalist promoters of the war, men and women who hoped to overthrow the republican and religiously liberal regime in the United Provinces. But the voices of men like Sir George Carteret, Sir Richard Ford, and the Duke of York were discredited; Buckingham, Anglesey, and merchants like the Presbyterian Thomas Papillon now received sympathetic audiences from the king. These new advisors, it must be emphasized, were not supporters of the Good Old Cause, were not sympathizers with De Witt's regime; but they were willing to accept that at the moment French-style government at home and French expansionism in Europe represented a far greater threat to English political life than republicanism. Anglican Royalists did not lose the force of their convictions, rather they lost their political monopoly because moderate political sentiment in England no longer believed that religious Nonconformity ineluctably led to political treason, that monarchies were inevitably virtuous. Patriotism, moderates now concluded, meant defense of a peculiarly English culture not commitment to a particular religious position or a purely monarchical form of government. Attempts at achieving universal dominion, attempts which most in England knew they had to sacrifice everything to prevent, could be made by either republicans or absolutists. In either case overweening ambition, rather than a particular theological position, was the driving force. Most in England by the later 1660s knew that it was their duty to keep political ambition within bounds, both abroad and at home.

238 Temple to Arlington, 12/22 November 1667, PRO, SP 77/37, f. 202; Ormonde to Anglesey, 29 January 1668, Carte 51, f. 84r; Arlington to Ormonde, 28 January 1668, Carte 46, f. 589r.

239 Arlington to Ormonde, 18 February 1668, Carte 46, f. 600v; Roger Pepys to John Hobart, 20 February 1668, Bod., Tanner MSS 45, f. 280r.

240 Pepys, *Diary*, Vol. VIII, 14 February 1668, p. 70.

241 Sir Orlando Bridgeman to Arlington, 11 July 1668, SRO, D1287/18/3/1. For Bridgeman's role see William Temple to Sir John Temple, 13 December/2 January 1667, *Works*, Vol. I, p. 295.

Conclusion

The three Anglo-Dutch Wars of the seventeenth century have never caused much concern for historians content to separate domestic and foreign policy. Whether ideology or factional squabbles accounted for domestic political turmoil, England's foreign involvements could always be explained by geopolitical considerations. Since contemporaries thought of England and the United Provinces as the two great commercial states of seventeenth-century Europe, it seemed perfectly reasonable to assume that both sides understood themselves to be economic rivals. The long lists of commercial disputes placed on the negotiating table by the trading companies from each side provides ample confirmation for scholars predisposed towards an economic account of these wars. The willingness of both the English Commonwealth and the Restored Monarchy to fight the same enemy appears to clinch the argument: the English fought the Dutch, it is said, because their economic interest demanded it. England's emergence from these struggles as the great trading power of the eighteenth and nineteenth centuries, coupled with the United Provinces' resubmergence into the watery bogs from which they had unnaturally sprung, has overshadowed English defeats in the second and third Anglo-Dutch Wars. The English might have lost the military battle, but they won the economic war.

A close examination of the first two of these Anglo-Dutch confrontations, however, reveals that these all-too-plausible hypotheses have little basis in the contemporary evidence. Neither war was an English attempt to capture trade routes from a chief economic rival. The first war occurred because members of the Rump Parliament and their political supporters were furious that the Dutch, whom they had long admired as the ideal Protestant and republican state, proved to have been hopelessly corrupted by their long vassalage to the House of Orange. The godly and republican in England, though long aware of the absolutist intentions of the descendants of William the Silent, had expected that with God's merciful elimination of William II, the Netherlands would be restored to its original virtuous republican constitution. The Rump Parliament's leading politicians, infused with this Protestant and republican understanding of the Dutch polity, opted to send two of their most eminent statesmen, Walter Strickland and Oliver St. John, to the United Provinces. However, rather than gratefully accept the sincere proposals of union presented by Walter Strickland and Oliver St. John, the Orangist crowds in The Hague verbally insulted and physically assaulted the English ambassadors. The party of Orange, the English political nation learned, had not expired with its leader in November 1650.

Although the good Dutch patriots made every effort to make up the breach, the Orangists did everything to make war unavoidable. Even as the republicans sent a diplomatic team to London, ostensibly to beg forgiveness, the Orangists were busily building up their navy. Then, just as the Dutch deputies prepared to sign a treaty committing the two states to a firm alliance, the Orangist admiral Martin Van Tromp launched an attack on the English navy. Tromp, with Orangist flags prominently displayed, claimed that Admiral Blake and his navy had no authority in the British seas since his commission derived not from the hereditary monarch and proprietor Charles II, but from an illegitimate and usurping political entity. Rump politicians and their supporters quickly concluded that the recent republican revolution in the United Provinces had not offset decades of political corruption promoted by the absolutist Princes of Orange. Until the Lord had shown them the rod, many in England reasoned, the Dutch people would follow the sinful Orangist policies of material self-interest and alliance with the Antichristian House of Stuart. The English were compelled to fight the Dutch in the 1650s to defend their own state against the assaults of monarchy and irreligion, against Orange and Mammon.

Not surprisingly, when the Dutch republicans had tamed the power of their Orangist enemies, English enthusiasm for the war waned. Only after the Dutch republicans, under the leadership of the young Grand Pensionary John De Witt, had reestablished control of the navy, the Province of Holland, and ultimately, the States General, could any English political grouping contemplate the possibility of peace. After months of ineffectual negotiations, the English deputies finally began to retreat from their intransigent positions as they witnessed town after town in the United Provinces replace the bloody ensigns of the House of Orange with the red, white, and blue of the republican States General. The English could be confident that a restoration of Dutch republicanism would bring with it a return to virtue; there was no longer any reason to fear Dutch materialism. The English negotiating team that concluded that war in April 1654, then, provided against the recurrence of hostilities not by seizing Dutch economic assets, but by political means: the exclusion of the Prince of Orange from his traditional offices and the reorientation of English foreign policy against the international menace represented by the alliance of Spain and the Papacy. The materialism and absolutism of the Orangist party, the English now knew, were the outward marks of covert agents of the aspiring universal monarch, the King of Spain. The surest means to prevent future Dutch corruption was to strike at the font of corruption itself: the Habsburg monarchy.

The Restored Monarchy, rather than continuing the Protestant and republican foreign policy of the Commonwealth and Protectorate, pursued its mirror opposite after 1660. Since Anglican Royalists were convinced that the twin sins of republicanism and religious fanaticism had precipitated the Great Rebellion, they were determined to stamp out those evils both at home and abroad. While supporters of the Rump, the Nominated Parliament, and, ultimately, the Protectorate had realized that aid for the Stuarts from their Orangist Dutch allies would always threaten their regimes, the Anglican Royalist members of Parliament and courtiers concluded that the Dutch republican pipeline to their radical English brethren would make rebellion endemic in England. After all, the Dutch republicans were committed to religious toleration – irreligion in Anglican Royalist eyes – and had welcomed the most extreme of the Commonwealth's supporters with open arms. Not coincidentally when the Anglican Royalists turned their attention to the economic woes of the Restored Monarchy, they persuaded themselves that Dutch unfair trading practices and Nonconformist obstructionism had debilitated England's trade. Presbyterians and fanatics, Anglican supporters of the Restored Monarchy knew quite well, would do everything to hinder the economic well-being of those who were not members of their dangerous tribe. The solution to this problem – and for the Anglican Royalists the Northern Rebellion and the Dutch seizure of the Malabar coast were emphatically different manifestations of the same problem – was to humble the Dutch.

As long as the war went well and public opinion remained focused on Dutch universalist aspirations, the Anglican Royalist political consensus held firm. However, French entry into the war on the Dutch side and English military defeats made the Anglican Royalist explanation of the war – that it was a struggle of rational government against republicanism and religious toleration – untenable. For enthusiastic supporters of the Restored Monarchy there could have been no more obvious ally for Charles II than that most absolute of monarchs, Louis XIV. Hence, when France made common cause with the republican Dutch, the English were forced to examine their own ideological assumptions and reconsider the political intentions of the French. The military power, and growing economic might, so ostentatiously displayed by the young French monarch, convinced many that he was "as likely to be Universal Monarch, as Spain was," that he was in fact a more serious aspirant to universal dominion than the republican United Provinces.[1] English political moderates were reminded that political

[1] Henry Marsh, *A New Survey of the Turkish Empire* (London, 1664).

liberty could be threatened not only by republics but by ambitious absolute monarchies as well. This revitalized fear of absolutism abroad was reinforced on the domestic front when these moderates came to analyze England's military defeat. Financial embezzlement, corrupt appointments, and covert dealings with the French, political moderates and many radicals concluded, not English military impotence explained their naval shortcomings. Many in the Parliamentary session of 1666–1667, following Buckingham's lead, insisted that the war be fought in a more efficient, in a more English, fashion. Instead the government chose to conclude a secret treaty with the French, and conserve the supply which Parliament had voted to continue the war. The king and his government had decided to adopt absolutist political strategies. While much of the political nation had come to see the French as a more significant political and ideological threat than the Dutch, Charles II's government increasingly embraced the French as their natural brethren. The spectacular raid on the Medway, planned jointly by the Dutch and the French, made it impossible any longer to deny the extent of French perfidy. While very few in England were willing to embrace the Dutch republican government, most perceived it to be less dangerous than that of France. By the end of the year Charles II had been compelled to eschew both his long-desired alliance with his cousin Louis XIV and any thought of attempting to imitate his political style in England.

Not only was Anglican Royalist confidence in absolute monarchy called into question, but the events of 1666–1667 invalidated the Anglican Royalist identification of religious dissent with political rebellion as well. The English Nonconformist community, which Anglican Royalists had persistently described as Papists in disguise, as political untouchables sure to rebel at every opportunity, had proved remarkably loyal despite the myriad disasters which beset the nation. While a few incorrigible radicals had indeed maintained contacts with their government's enemies, most paid their taxes, volunteered to serve in the navy or the local militia, and sought to sever previous ties with their nation's enemies. They had demonstrated beyond all doubt that they would die for their country before they would rebel to attain religious liberty; they were English first and Nonconformists second.

The willingness of both the Restored Monarchy and the Rump Parliament to go to war against the Dutch, then, demonstrates not a continuity in foreign policy but a radical discontinuity. Both regimes agreed that the Dutch polity was ideologically divided between Orangists and republicans; but the Restored Monarchy found its natural allies in the supporters of the House of Orange, while the Rump knew its friends were the republican supporters of John De Witt and the States of Holland. It was a reflection of the complete ideological reversal represented by the Restoration that while the Interregnum regimes had fought to prevent the establishment of monarchy in the United Provinces, the Restored English Monarchy struggled to transform the Dutch Republic into an Orangist monarchy.

This close, and at times microscopic, study of Anglo-Dutch relations in the middle of the seventeenth century has done more than revise the accepted interpretations of the first two Anglo-Dutch Wars; it has pointed to several fundamental transformations in English political culture.

While English popular opinion could disapprove and block foreign-policy initiatives in the late sixteenth and early seventeenth centuries – preventing Elizabeth's proposed marriage with the Duke of Anjou and making Charles Stuart's alliance with the Spanish Infanta well nigh impossible[2] – the two Dutch Wars were the first occasions when activism outside the confines of the court had actually pushed the nation into war. Much evidence suggests that J. R. Jones has gone too far in claiming that "public opinion whether spontaneous or in the shape of pressure groups seems to have had very little effect on those who made the major decisions."[3] In fact, popular anti-Dutch sentiment, fueled by a wide variety of pamphlets, sermons, and broadsides, pushed the Rump into war in 1652. The widespread belief among the officers of the Commonwealth's navy that God demanded belligerence against the apostate Dutch raised the political temperature to such a scalding height that even the cooling effect of the Dutch diplomatic mission was unable to prevent the outbreak of hostilities. The popular conviction that the Dutch had reformed by late 1653 placed immense pressure on the Protectorate to put an end to the hostilities and commence a war against the real enemies, the Spanish and the Jesuits. Despite the Earl of Clarendon's plea for a return to the "blessed condescension and resignation of the people ... to the crown" in Queen Elizabeth's time, the outbreak of the second Anglo-Dutch War soon proved that in the England to which Charles II returned "everyman is now become a statesman."[4] Although authors of court memoranda had been advising Charles II to go to war against the Dutch since the moment he returned to English soil in 1660, only when the Anglican Royalist reaction of 1663–1664 demanded action against Dutch perfidy did war become inevitable.

Similarly, popular fears of French political dominion and English absolutism made it increasingly difficult for Charles II's regime to continue the

2 Wallace T. MacCaffrey, *Queen Elizabeth and the Making of Policy, 1572–1588* (Princeton, 1981), pp. 243–266; Thomas Cogswell, "England and the Spanish Match," Ann Hughes and Richard Cust (editors), *Conflict in Early Stuart England* (London, 1989), pp. 107–133.

3 J. R. Jones, *Britain and the World 1649–1815*, p. 53.

4 *His Majesties Most Gracious Speech, Together with the Lord Chancellors, To the Two Houses of Parliament, At their Prorogation On Monday the Nineteenth of May, 1662* (London, 1662), pp. 10–11; Marquis of Newcastle, "Treatise," Bod., Clar. 109, p. 65. These sentiments were also expressed in Restoration newspapers. See for example, *Intelligencer*, 31 August 1663, pp. 1–3; *Newes*, 21 April 1664, p. 257.

Anglican Royalist crusade. Acutely aware of his financial vulnerability after the disastrous conclusion of the war, Charles II felt compelled to accede to the popular demand for an Anglo-Dutch alliance against the aspiring universal monarch Louis XIV. In both cases the political nation proved to be both interested in, and well informed about, foreign affairs. As much as many courtiers may have wished to restore the royal prerogative in foreign affairs, the ferocious and voluminous political discourse of the 1640s and 1650s guaranteed that there could be no turning back. There were now powerful segments of the political nation, motivated more by an understanding of domestic and international affairs than by any particular and selfish interest, which insisted on impressing their views on the makers of English foreign policy. "Foreign policy became of necessity a new thing from the moment the Monarchy was removed," Sir John Seeley observed long ago, "and the change thus made could not be undone by the Restoration of the Monarchy."[5]

Although the wars fought against the Dutch do not represent the simple replacement of a religious by an economic foreign policy, they do suggest a profound shift in the content of English political culture. When members of the Rump discovered, to their surprise and dismay, that appeals to a common Protestantism and republicanism were insufficient for the Dutch to unite with them in a common crusade against the Whore of Babylon and monarchical tyranny, they were forced to rethink seriously their own ideological presuppositions. The broad spectrum of English Protestant opinion now aligned itself along a line marked by two well-defined poles. Some Englishmen and women – predominantly the religious radicals – determined that, since God had demonstrated by innumerable and irrefutable signs that the world was in its last days and that the godly in England were certainly among those who would lead the way in the final struggle against the Antichrist, all those who put up the least resistance to their designs would be but stubble unto their swords. The Dutch, by rejecting the proposed union and by attacking the English in the British seas, had demonstrated that they were now to be counted among the forces of the Beast.

Others, though they were also committed Protestants, were not convinced that the millenium was so near at hand. For these men and women the Lord had not clearly demonstrated a single way to godliness. It was enough, for the present, for the godly to have the root of the matter in them. The essential concern was to prevent demonstrable Popery and arbitrary govern-

[5] This is not to deny the success of Roger L'Estrange's censorship. However, after the Restoration subversive political discussion continued in coffee houses, conventicles, in the theater, and in the underground (and overseas) press. Sir J. R. Seeley, *The Growth of British Policy* (Cambridge, 1922), Vol. II, p. 1. For a more detailed analysis of the Restoration public sphere, see my "'Coffee Politicians Does Create': Coffee Houses and Restoration Political Culture," in *Journal of Modern History* (December 1995).

ment. But instead of pointing to specific forms or practices as their more radical antagonists did, these moderates suggested that Popery was tyranny and the destruction of magistracy. These men and women were convinced that demands that all governors be godly – demands common to Jesuits and Anabaptists – would lead inevitably to anarchy. In short, they suggested that Popery consisted of religious enthusiasm and political tyranny. They knew quite well from studying recent history that both of these evils sprang from the Spanish court and its religious servants, the Jesuits. When the Nominated Parliament resigned and the religious radicals were defeated, then, much more was decided than the fate of an illegitimate Parliament. A language which appealed exclusively to the Bible and divine inspiration was forever banished from the center of the political stage. While the radicals had demanded the destruction of the Whore of Babylon and the fulfillment of the prophecies of the Book of Revelation, the Cromwellian moderates adopted a foreign policy aimed at obstructing the political machinations of the aspiring universal monarch Philip IV of Spain. In so doing, they were concerned above all to protect the English national interest.

This secularizing trend in political ideology continued after the Restoration.[6] Adopting and adapting the political conclusions of the Cromwellian moderates, Anglican Royalist polemicists attacked their opponents as fanatics intent on subverting magistracy. The Dutch, they argued, were Papists in disguise not because they performed mass in secret but because they followed Suarez and Bellarmine in condoning resistance to magistrates. The Dutch Republic, after all, had been formed in an act of resistance to a legitimate monarch, Philip II of Spain. Nor did those Nonconformists who criticized Anglican Royalist policies and who became increasingly convinced that their government's Hollandophobic policies were misguided, reach these conclusions because of their ecclesiology or their theology. Rather these men and women determined that real Popery was not so much resistance to magistrates as it was the establishment of arbitrary government in Church and state. The true danger to England, they concluded, was from the intolerant and politically powerful Anglican Church and the absolutist and clericist King of France.

The Civil War years and the Interregnum, then, brought decisive changes in the content of English political vocabulary. After the Treaties of Westphalia, Munster, and the Pyrenees had put an end to the universalist pretensions of the Habsburgs and the Roman Catholic Church, English men and women were free to define the new Popery and identify the new

6 For other parallel discussions of secularization see Steven N. Zwicker, "England, Israel and the Triumph of Roman Virtue," in Richard H. Popkin (editor), *Millenarianism and Messianism in English Literature and Thought 1650–1800* (Leiden, 1988), pp. 37–64; Blair Worden, "Introduction" to his edition of Edmund Ludlow's *A Voyce from the Watch Tower* (London, 1978), especially pp. 5–16, 51–55.

universal monarch. Popery, one Anglican divine noted with a degree of disgust, "is now a word of very dubious signification, and means rather what everyone dislikes, than what is so indeed."[7] Though differences between Protestants and Papists "be mostly managed on the side of religion," William Penn noted, "the great point is merely civil, and should never be otherwise admitted or understood."[8] "The difference between the Papist and the Protestant," agreed one of Penn's polemical adversaries, "is not precisely religious, nor chiefly such; 'tis a civil empire, and a secular interest consequent thereto, which the Church of Rome aims at."[9] Anti-Popery remained a powerful rallying cry after the Restoration, but one with a significantly altered meaning: Popery was now a civil rather than a spiritual issue. Similarly, the meaning of universal monarchy had changed: aspirations for universal dominion were no longer attributed to the Most Catholic King of Spain. Anglican Royalists identified the republican and pluralist United Provinces as the new threat; while Nonconformists and political moderates pointed to the absolutist and intolerant French king Louis XIV.

Naturally there were both religiously enthusiastic Royalists and millenarian Nonconformists after the Restoration; but neither of these groups had a political future. The plague, the Fire, and ultimately the successful Dutch raid on the Medway invalidated the early religious glosses on the Restoration. It was exceedingly difficult to believe that Charles II was the new David, or Moses, if God so manifestly wished to punish him. In addition, the loyalty of the Nonconformists in these difficult times shattered the association between Protestant dissent and political rebellion. Conversely the rebellions and plots of the religious extremists, such as Thomas Venner and Edmund Ludlow,[10] all ended in failure. Instead the foundation of successful political opposition to the new Stuart absolutism was laid by the former Cromwellian moderate Anthony Ashley Cooper in alliance with the moderate Royalist Duke of Buckingham. These men and their followers appealed to right reason and England's interest rather than to divine inspiration and Israelite precedents.

The secularization of the language of English political culture made possible an equally fundamental transformation: the addition of an economic discourse to considerations of English national interest. Although members of the English political nation had conceived of their foreign policy in terms of opposition to universal monarchy since at least the reign

7 Luke De Beaulieu, *Take Heed of Both Extremes* (London, 1675), sig. A4r.
8 [William Penn], *One Project for the Good of England* (1679), p. 7.
9 *A Seasonable Corrective to the One Project for the Good of England* (London, 1680), p. 4.
10 Venner was a fifth monarchist. That Ludlow was a committed Christian republican; a man who derived his politics from his interpretation of the Bible should be clear from the extensive citations from his correspondence and memoirs throughout this monograph. See also Worden, "Introduction" to his edition of *A Voyce from the Watch Tower*, pp. 5–9.

of Queen Elizabeth, prior to the middle of the seventeenth century the universal monarch was expected to wield his power almost exclusively through the deployment of massive land armies and a repressive religious inquisition. The late sixteenth- and early seventeenth-century universal monarch was simply the most powerful Roman Catholic prince in political and military terms. The transformation of the nature of warfare apparent in the Dutch struggle for independence and in the Thirty Years War, however, had significantly altered Englishmen's understanding of the basis of power. By 1654 it was clear to most English observers that for a universal monarch to succeed in compelling the rest of the world to submit to his will, he would have to control the world's trade. The fantastic wealth of the Indies – both East and West – allowed the aspiring universal monarch to maintain large armies, to bribe and corrupt foreign politicians, and, if necessary, to bring entire states to their knees by means of economic warfare. So when the Protectorate decided to launch a defensive war to prevent Philip IV from achieving his goal of universal hegemony, it attacked the source of Spanish revenue, the West Indies, rather than the Iberian peninsula.

This alteration of the rhetoric of universal monarchy, the addition of mercantile power to the number of the universal monarch's attributes, vastly broadened the field of potential aspirants. Potentially, any great economic power could be interpreted as aiming at universal monarchy. The hegemony of the universal monarch, in this scenario, need not be overt. The universal monarch could exert as much power by pressuring his allies into action or inaction as by conquering them. Significantly the Dutch Republic, though it had no large standing army and was not even a monarchy, could be seen as aspiring to universal dominion. The Dutch, as Anglican Royalist polemicists were quick to point out, might look like small and insignificant merchants in Europe, but in the East Indies they were known as Lords of the South Seas. They might not look as if they could defend themselves from Europe's great military powers, but they had defeated the previously invincible Spanish tercios by wreaking havoc upon the Spanish economy.

By the later seventeenth century most political observers believed the age of religious wars had passed.[11] One polemicist during the second Anglo-Dutch War insisted that "wars for religion" were "but a speculation, an imaginary thing," religion was a pretext "which wise or rather cunning men make use of to abuse fools." "In truth," this polemicist concluded, "there never was nor ever will be any" wars of religion.[12] William Temple, an important Restoration moderate, also doubted "whether there was ever yet

11 Here I am in disagreement with the conclusions advanced by J. C. D. Clark and Linda Colley. See J. C. D. Clark, *Revolution And Rebellion.* (Cambridge, 1986), p. 65; J. C. D. Clark, *The Language of Liberty 1660–1832* (Cambridge, 1994), *passim*; Linda Colley, *Britons: Forging the Nation 1707–1837* (New Haven, 1992), p. 3 and *passim.*

12 MSS pamphlet, 1665, NMM, Clifford Papers, Vol. III, Dw100, f. 5.

any war of religion or ever will be."[13] These observers did not doubt that England's was a Protestant foreign policy, but they were defining that policy in increasingly Erastian terms. A Protestant foreign policy was above all one which sought to protect national laws, and by consequence religions established by those laws.[14] The universal monarchy of the later seventeenth century, like the universal monarchy of the later sixteenth century, would necessarily be Papist. But in the later seventeenth century that Popery would be measured less by the amount of incense the universal monarch burned in his churches than by the amount of money the universal monarch spent in overthrowing his rivals' regimes or in repressing alternative modes of religious worship – in short, by his international commercial and cultural influence.

While Anglican Royalists and Nonconformists agreed about precious little after the Restoration, they did concur that England's foreign policy should primarily aim to prevent any state from attaining a universal monarchy. "The interest of every nation," Algernon Sidney asserted uncontroversially, "is to keep others from attaining [universal monarchy], and maintain its own freedom and independence [of] any for protection."[15] The difference was that Anglican Royalists were certain that it was the United Provinces who were seeking universal dominion, while Nonconformists were equally convinced that the real menace was Louis XIV.

The first two Anglo-Dutch Wars, then, represent a crucial turning point in English foreign policy. While medieval English kings went to war to defend their patrimonies; kings and their councils of the sixteenth and early seventeenth centuries went to war to defend their religion and their political ideology; the wider political nation of the later seventeenth century went to war to defend the national interest. The English Republic waged war against the Dutch to defend Protestantism and republicanism against the international threat of absolute monarchy. The Restored Monarchy fought the United Provinces to protect England from the unbridled economic ambition of a republican and religiously pluralist state. Though there can be no doubt that Englishmen and women from the accession of Elizabeth were certain they were part of *an* elect nation, that elect nation was only a part of the wider elect nation of European Protestant believers. The nation that was defended from the Spanish Armada, and from the onslaught of the great armies of the House of Austria was the nation of the "Saints and Witnesses of Jesus Christ" who were "but one body politic, or one common-wealth, for they are all united into one common interest in what part of the world

13 William Temple to Arlington, 29 September/9 October 1665, PRO, SP 77/33. f. 294v.

14 I have argued this case at greater length in "Britain and the World in the 1650s," in John Morrill (editor), *Regicide to Restoration: The Consequences of the English Revolution* (London, 1992).

15 Algernon Sidney, "Court Maxims," 1664–1665, Warwickshire Record Office, f. 152.

soever they be."[16] The nation defended from universal monarchy in the later seventeenth century was conceived in very different terms – it was both geographically delimited and necessarily of this world. It was a nation with its own political institutions, its own church, its own economy, and its own traditions of liberty which would ally with other nations, if need be, to confound "any family or state that set upon the ... design of enslaving all the rest unto their wills."[17] English politicians of all stripes agreed after 1654 that war should be fought to protect the national interest; the controversy lay in defining the national interest.

England did not become a first-rate international power between 1650 and 1668. But England did undergo during that period crucial and dramatic transformations which made Marlborough's and Wolfe's great victories possible. The mid-seventeenth-century alterations were primarily ideological and political in character. Englishmen and women were willing to suffer through the extension of state power and the infringements on their personal liberties so carefully detailed by John Brewer[18] because they knew that they were defending their religious and political liberties against a universal monarch. Englishmen and women rallied around Queen Elizabeth in the 1580s and 1590s in the struggle against Philip II to prevent that Spanish king from conquering the world for the forces of Antichrist. Supporters of the Rump began fighting the United Provinces in 1652, because under the spell of the House of Orange the Dutch had joined the legions of the Whore of Babylon. But after the fierce and critical discussions of 1653, both inside and outside of Parliament, Englishmen were convinced that the eschatological struggle would be a war of attrition rather than a frontal assault. A vastly expanded and politically well-informed nation now knew that Popery and universal monarchy were ideologies with economic and political as well as religious programs. Cromwellian moderates waged war against Spain to prevent it from consolidating the economic hegemony that would finally make Tomasso Campanella's intolerant and absolutist universal monarchy a real possibility. Anglican Royalists, from Whitehall to Yorkshire, desired a war against the Dutch to prevent that republican and

16 M[ary] Cary, *The Resurrection of the Witnesses and England's Fall from (The Mystical Babylon) Rome* (London, 1653), Thomason: 14 November 1653; Patrick Collinson, *The Birthpangs of Protestant England* (London, 1988), pp. 14–17; Paul Christianson, *Reformers and Babylon: English Apocalyptic Visions from the Reformation to the Eve of the Civil War* (Toronto, 1978), pp. 41–46; Katherine Firth, *The Apocalyptic Tradition in Reformation Britain 1530–1645* (Oxford, 1979), pp. 106–110. All of these are, of course, refinements of William Haller's classic *Foxe's Book of Martyrs and the Elect Nation* (London, 1963).

17 Sidney, "Court Maxims," Warwickshire Record Office, f. 154. The argument against universal monarchy in the later seventeenth century is best summarized by Istvan Hont, "Free Trade and the Economic Limits to National Politics: Neo-Machiavellian Political Economy Reconsidered," in John Dunn (editor), *The Economic Limits to Modern Politics* (Cambridge, 1990), pp. 41–120.

18 John Brewer, *The Sinews of Power* (London, 1989).

religiously pluralist state from acquiring the universal dominion which it believed it had inherited from Spain. The wars of the Augustan age were so different from those of the Elizabethan age not because the vocabulary of politics had changed, but because the same words – Popery and universal monarchy – had radically different meanings.

The traditional historiographical separation of domestic and foreign policy, this book has attempted to show, obfuscates more than it explains. Diplomatic and economic historians have been able to describe the seventeenth-century Anglo-Dutch Wars as trade wars only by ignoring the rich cultural contexts in which those conflicts took place. Commercial concerns and diplomatic interests were functions of ideological orientation, just as were commitments to ecclesiologies or political forms. Similarly, domestic political disputes did not occur in isolation from European developments. The English in the seventeenth century were constantly writing and gossiping about the continent; they placed their own histories in a European context. Their ultimate frame of reference was neither localist nor British, but European and universal. When the English went to war in the seventeenth century, they knew why they were risking their fortunes and their lives. They knew, as they had always known, that England's proper role was to prevent universal dominion. Local and domestic politics was so powerfully charged precisely because of this larger significance. By examining that larger significance, by attending to the rich seventeenth-century discussions about affairs beyond the British Isles – about the nature of universal monarchy – historians of Britain gain a deeper understanding of the ideological significance of the political and cultural developments in an age of revolution.

BIBLIOGRAPHY

The contours of my indebtedness to modern scholarship are delineated in the footnotes. The bibliography is devoted exclusively to seventeenth-century materials.

I. MANUSCRIPT SOURCES

ALL SOULS COLLEGE, OXFORD

309 Letters from Sir George Downing and Sir William Temple to Arlington
317 Autobiography and Verses of Sir William Trumbull

BEINECKE LIBRARY, YALE UNIVERSITY

Osborn Collection

Carlingford Papers

BODLEIAN LIBRARY, OXFORD

Additional Manuscripts

C267 Pengelly Letterbook (East India merchant)
C304A Sheldon Letterbook

Aubrey Manuscripts

12–13 Aubrey Correspondence

Carte Manuscripts

24–36, 46–49, 51 Ormonde's Papers 72 Newsletters to Ormonde 1660–1685
73 Sandwich Papers
77 Correspondence of the Earls of Huntingdon 1569–1643, 1661–1678
79–81 Papers on Public Affairs of Lord Wharton 1640–1699
103 Correspondence on Public Affairs 1625–1680
222 Newsletters on English and European Affairs 1662–1684

Clarendon Manuscripts

41–48, 75–85, 92, 154–155 Clarendon's Letters and Papers
100–101 Notes Passed at the Privy Council

104–108	Downing Letters to Clarendon
109	Marquis of Newcastle's Treatise of Advice
159	Treaty of Breda Correspondence

Dep. C171N

Nalson Papers

Don Manuscripts

B8 Sir William Haward's Collection
C37 Le Fleming Newsletters
E23 Political Poetry

Douce Manuscripts

357 English Political Poems 1640–1685

English History Manuscripts

C37	Letters to Ormonde
C44	Letters received by Sir John Shaw (merchant at Antwerp)
C201	Sir Richard Temple Papers
C487	Edmund Ludlow's "Voyce from a Watch Tower"
C710–712; E308–314	Notebooks of Roger Whitley

English Letters Manuscripts

C5 Joseph Williamson Letters
C210 Rev. John Palmer Letters
C328 Sir Frances Parry Papers

English Miscellaneous Manuscripts

E118 Diary of George Starkey
F381 Diary of Samuel Woodforde

North Manuscripts

North Family Papers

Rawlinson Manuscripts

A1–14	Thurloe's Papers
A130	Henchman Diary of House of Lords March 1664–19 December 1667
A195	Pepys Papers
A207	Minutebook of the Commissioners of the Navy 1650–1653
A225–226	Journal of the Orders of the Admiralty Committee 1650–1652
A227	Copybook of Admiralty Letters 1652–1653
A315	T. Mundy's Letters, Papers, and Journals
C129	Journal of Walter Strickland and Oliver St. John 8 March–28 June 1651
C556	Poems on State Matters 1660s
C734	Lieuwe Van Aitzema, "Selections"
D204	Letterbook of Sir John Reresby 1661–1679

Letters 52	Wharton Letters 1640–1662
Letters 64	Letterbook of Henry Appleton 1661–1662
Letters 104	Letters to Lord Wharton 1649–1691
Letters 113	John Cooke–Charles Beale Letters 1663–1671
Poet. 26	Political Poems
Poet. 30	Satire Against Cromwell
Poet. 37	Songs Religious and Political 1650–1660
Poet. 84	Miscellaneous Poems and Songs 1650–1670

Tanner Manuscripts

45–55	Letters and Papers 1651–1667
296	Journal of Sir Thomas Allin 1660–1667

Wood's Diaries MSS

6–12	Diaries of Anthony Wood 1662–1668

BRITISH LIBRARY

Additional Manuscripts

4156–4157	Birch Collection (Thurloe Papers)
4158	Downing Letters
4159	Miscellaneous Letters and Papers 1650s and 1660s
4211	Draft Anglo-Dutch Treaty 1652
4992	Bulstrode Whitelocke's *Annals*
5488–5489	Hill Papers
5810	Cambridgeshire Collections
10114	Diary of John Harrington 1646–1653
10116–10117	Thomas Rugge's Diurnall
12184–12186	Sir Richard Browne Correspondence 1641–1651
14286	Diary of Sir William Clarke
15857–15858	Richard Browne and John Evelyn Letters
16272	Letterbook of Sir Walter Vane
21947	Richmond Correspondence
22919–22920	Downing Papers
25283–25285	Commonplace Books of Oliver St. John
27447	Paston Letters
27999–28009	Oxenden Correspondence
29550–29551	Hatton Family Correspondence 1660–1668
31984	Bulstrode Whitelocke's *Annals*
32093–32094	Malet Collection
32679	Denzil Holles Letters 1663–1665
34362–34363	Seventeenth-Century Poetry
35838	Hardwicke Papers
37345	Bulstrode Whitelocke's *Annals*
37346–37347	Bulstrode Whitelocke's Swedish Embassy
38490	Diary of Henry Townshend April 1660–April 1663
40696–40699	Correspondence of Sir George Oxenden
40705–40707	Sir George Oxenden's Letters from Surat
40710–40713	Sir George Oxenden's Letters from England
41254	Letterbook of 2nd Viscount Fauconberg 1665–1684

46374	Diary of Sir John Harrington
54322	Oxenden Commonplace and Memorandum Books
58444	Joshua Moore's Life of Lord Belasyse
61483–61485	Papers of the 2nd Earl of Bristol
6305	A Gilbert Burnet's History
63081	Townshend Letters
70010–70011	Harley Correspondence
70081	Harley Papers 1611–1750
70095	Harley Verses

Althorp Papers

B5	Correspondence of Boyle Family 1664–1682
B6	General Correspondence 1632–1689
C1	Letters to Halifax 1661–1686
C13	Letters to William Coventry 1665–1671
C18	Copies of Letters 1664–1669

Egerton Manuscripts

997	Bulstrode Whitelocke's Lectures
2534, 2537–2539	Edward Nicholas Papers
2560	Poem on Second Dutch War
2620	Oliver Cromwell Letters

Harleian Manuscripts

3785	Letters to William Sancroft
7010	Fanshawe Letters

Loan Manuscripts

29/176–179	Harley Correspondence 1647–1666
29/235	Vere and Cavendish Papers
29/236	Cavendish Papers 1661–1695
29/240	Miscellaneous Letters and Papers 1540–1706
29/241	Navy Papers 1640–1696
29/275	Edward Harley's Dunkirk Letterbook 1660–1661
57/1	Bathurst Papers

Sloane Manuscripts

970	Report Concerning Firing of London

Stowe Manuscripts

142	Includes Letters from Charles II and James on Dutch War
185	Includes Thurloe's Analysis of Foreign Affairs
744	Dering Papers

Thomason Manuscripts

(read on microfilm)

TT: E705(10)	"A New Ballad to the Tune of Coo-Land," Thomason: 12 July 1653

TT: E710(13). "Mr. Feake's Hymn," Thomason: 11 August 1653
TT: E714(7). "Proclamation by the Supreme Lord the Free Born People of England." Thomason: late September 1653

Trumbull Manuscripts

(not yet catalogued)

Microfilm

M636 Verney papers

CAMBRIDGE UNIVERSITY LIBRARY

Additional Manuscripts

1, 4, 7 Strype Correspondence
40 Miscellaneous Letters and Historical Documents
42 Poetry
79 Cambridge Poetical Commonplace Book
5872 Dr. Williams Papers
7091 Household Book of James, Duke of York 1662–1664
8499 Diary of Isaac Archer

Dd.9.43 Letterbook of Sir Anthony Oldfield
Dd.9.51 Catalogue of Marquis of Halifax's Books

CENTRE FOR KENTISH STUDIES, MAIDSTONE

U1007 Dering Papers
U1015 Papillon Papers

CHRIST CHURCH, OXFORD

Edward Nicholas Letters

Richard Browne Letters

John Evelyn Manuscripts

In-Letters (incompletely numbered)
Out-Letters (incompletley numbered)

10 Edward Hyde–Richard Browne Letterbook
39 Evelyn's Outletters 1655–1679
134 Notes for History of Second Dutch War
164 Sir Samuel Tuke Collections

CORPORATION OF LONDON RECORD OFFICE

Journals

J41 1649–1660
J45 1660–1664
J46 1664–1669

Remembrancia

R9 1660–1665
Repertory Books of the Court of Aldermen

CORPUS CHRISTI COLLEGE, OXFORD

176 Poems and Songs
298, 302, 307, 310, 332 William Fulman Papers

DOCTOR WILLIAMS' LIBRARY, LONDON

Roger Morrice's "Eminent Worthies"

DOWNING COLLEGE, CAMBRIDGE

George Downing Letterbook/Diary

FIRESTONE LIBRARY, PRINCETON UNIVERSITY

Verney Manuscripts (on microfilm)

FOLGER SHAKESPEARE LIBRARY, WASHINGTON DC

Va300 Henry Oxenden's verses to his friends
Xd483 Colonel Robert Bennet(t) Papers

GUILDHALL, LONDON

25,200 Letters Regarding St. Paul's
5570/4 Court Minutes of the Fishmongers Company
11588/4 Court Minutes of the Grocers Company

HOUGHTON LIBRARY, HARVARD UNIVERSITY

fMS Eng. 1343 Mrs. Donald F. Hyde Collection
Gay Collection

HUNTINGTON LIBRARY, SAN MARINO, CALIFORNIA

Hastings Manuscripts

Huntington Miscellaneous Manuscripts

Temple Stowe Manuscripts

INDIA OFFICE LIBRARY, LONDON

East India Company Correspondence

E/3/22 27 March 1650–20 March 1652
E/3/23 31 March 1652–21 March 1654
E/3/24 27 March 1654–15 March 1656
E/3/26 26 March 1659–23 March 1661
E/3/27 26 March 1661–2 March 1663

E/3/28 30 March 1663–27 February 1665
E/3/29 25 March 1665–22 March 1669
E/3/84 Despatch Book 1626–23 February 1660
E/3/86 Despatch Book 6 February 1661–12 January 1666
E/387 Despatch Book 7 March 1666–27 June 1672

Factory Records

G/21 Java
G/21/3 Pt. III 1650–1671
G/21/4 1664–1676
G/21/5 1664–1670
G/36 Surat
G/36/2 1660–1668
G/36/104 Letters Received 1663–1666
G/36/105 Letters Received 1668–1671
G/40 Miscellaneous
G/40/2 1663–1672
G40/3 1664–1681

Home Miscellanies

H/40 Miscellaneous Material 1650s and 1660s
H/42 Miscellaneous Material relating to the Dutch 1660s

Foreigners

T/2/6 Letters Regarding Dutch in East Indies 1617–1674

LEICESTERSHIRE RECORD OFFICE, LEICESTER

DG7 Finch Papers

LIBRARY OF CONGRESS, WASHINGTON, DC

18124 Vol. I Thomas St. Serfe Newsletters

LONGLEAT HOUSE, WARMINSTER, WILTSHIRE

Coventry Manuscripts
Thynne Manuscripts
Whitelocke Manuscripts

NATIONAL LIBRARY OF SCOTLAND

Adv. MSS. 19–1–26 Bennet Papers

NATIONAL MARITIME MUSEUM, GREENWICH

Clifford Papers (3 Volumes)

AGC/ Letters

AGC/L/1 Sir John Lawson Letters
AGC/L/2 Charles Longland Letters

WYN/Penn Papers

NEW YORK PUBLIC LIBRARY

John Bowne Diary

NORFOLK RECORD OFFICE, NORWICH

Bradfer–Lawrence Manuscripts

Ic/Sir Robert Paston Correspondence

Ketter–Cremer Manuscripts

7/66 Miscellaneous Papers

Raynham Hall Manuscripts

(read at Norfolk Record Office)
Horatio Viscount Townshend Personal Papers Boxes

PEPYS LIBRARY, MAGDALENE COLLEGE, CAMBRIDGE

2265 Notes on Naval Actions 1654–1676; Lists of Merchants serving in First Anglo-Dutch War.
2554 Pepys's Defence of Second Dutch War
2589 Expenses of Second Dutch War
2611 William Penn's Naval Collection
2698 Journals of Robert Holmes
2866 Collections of Pepys's History of the Navy
2888 The Political Grounds and Maxims of Holland 1669 – translated by Toby Bonnel

PUBLIC RECORD OFFICE, CHANCERY LANE, LONDON

C109/23 Pt. II William Atwood Papers
HCA 30 High Court of Admiralty Prize Papers
PC 2/ Privy Council Registers
SP 9/16 Joseph Williamson's Spy Book
SP 18/ Letters and Papers, Interregnum
SP 25/ Order Books, Letterbooks and Committee Books, Interregnum
SP 29/ Letters and Papers, Charles II
SP 30/Shelf F Pamphlets and Papers, Charles II
SP 44/ Entering Books, Charles II
SP 46/ Supplemental Domestic State Papers
SP 75/ State Papers, Foreign, Denmark
SP 77/ State Papers, Foreign, Flanders
SP 78/ State Papers, Foreign, France
SP 79/ State Papers, Foreign, Genoa
SP 80/ State Papers, Foreign, German Empire
SP 82/ State Papers, Foreign, Hamburg
SP 84/ State Papers, Foreign, Holland
SP 89/ State Papers, Foreign, Portugal

SP 94/ State Papers, Foreign, Spain
SP 95/ State Papers, Foreign, Sweden
SP 97/ State Papers, Foreign, Turkey
SP 98/ State Papers, Foreign, Tuscany
SP 99/ State Papers, Foreign, Venice
SP 101/47–51 Newsletters from the United Provinces 1627–1668
SP 101/96 Miscellaneous Foreign Newsletters 1619–1669
SP 101/122 Intercepted Dutch Letters 1664–1668
SP 103/46 Dutch Treaty Papers 1651–1665
SP 105/98 Diary of Negotiations with Dutch Deputies 1653
SP 105/141 Diary of Treaty Negotiations with Swedish Ambassador 1653
SP 105/112 Levant Company Outletters 1617–1662
SP 105/113 Levant Company Outletters 1662–1665
SP 105/144 Levant Company Register Book 1648–1668
SP 105/151 Levant Company Court Minutes 1648–1660
SP 105/152 Levant Company Court Minutes 1660–1671
PRO 30/24/ Shaftesbury Papers
PRO 31/3/ Baschet Transcripts

PUBLIC RECORD OFFICE, KEW GARDENS, LONDON

CO 1/ State Papers Colonial General Series
CO 77/ State Papers, Colonial Series, East Indies
T.70/75 Minute Book of the Royal Adventurers for Africa
T.70/309 Journal of Accounts 1662–1663 of Royal Africa Company

SOCIETY OF ANTIQUARIES, LONDON

203 Meredith Papers

STAFFORDSHIRE RECORD OFFICE, STAFFORD

D593 Leveson-Gower Collection

D593//P/8/2/2 John Langley Letters

D868 Gower Letters

D1287 Bradford Manuscripts

D1287/10/1 Miscellaneous Bridgeman Papers
D1287/18/3 Orlando Bridgeman Correspondence

Dw1721 Bagot of Blithfield Papers

Dw1721/3/231B Lieutenancy Papers 1660–1666
Dw1721/3/246 Seventeenth-Century Poems

Dw1744 Shrewsbury Manuscripts

Dw1744/60 Lieutenancy Papers 1664–1690
Dw1744/71 Norfolk Memorandum on Supply 1665–1666

VICTORIA AND ALBERT MUSEUM, LONDON

Forster and Dyce Collection

D25F37–38	Odes, Songs and Satyrs of the Reign of Charles II
F47A39	Ormonde Papers
F47A45	Orrery Correspondence
F48G2/1	Miscellaneous Papers

WARWICKSHIRE RECORD OFFICE, WARWICK

Algernon Sidney's "Court Maxims"

WILLIAM SALT LIBRARY, STAFFORD

SMs 454/Swynfen Family Papers
SMs 565/Chetwynd Lieutenancy Papers

WORCESTER COLLEGE, OXFORD

Clarke Manuscripts

NEWSPAPERS

Brief Relation of Some Affairs and Transactions, Civil and Military Both Forreign and Domestick, A.
City and Country Mercury, The.
Current Intelligence.
Daily Proceedings, The.
Diary, The.
Dutch Intelligencer, The.
Dutch Spy, The.
Faithful Post, The.
Faithful Scout, The.
Flying Eagle, The.
French Intelligencer, The.
French Occurrences, The.
Great Brittain's Post.
Impartial Intelligencer.
Intelligencer, The
Loyal Intelligencer, The.
Loyal Messenger, The.
Mercurius Aulicus.
Mercurius Bellonius.
Mercurius Britannicus.
Mercurius Cinicus.
Mercurius Classicus.
Mercurius Elencticus.
Mercurius Heraclitus.
Mercurius Poeticus.
Mercurius Politicus.
Mercurius Pragmaticus.
Mercurius Publicus.

Mercury.
Moderate Intelligence.
Moderate Intelligencer.
Moderate Messenger.
Moderate Occurrences.
Moderate Publisher, The.
Newes Published for Satisfaction of the People, The.
Newes, The.
Perfect Account of the Daily Intelligence from the Armies in England, Scotland, and Ireland, the Navy at Sea, and other transactions of, and in relation to this Common Wealth, A.
Perfect Diurnall of Some Passages and Proceedings of, and in relation to, the Armies of England, Ireland, & Scotland, A.
Perfect Diurnall, The.
Perfect Occurrences.
Perfect Passages of Every Daies Intelligence From the Parliaments Army, under the Command of his Excellency the Lord General Cromwell.
Politique Informer.
Politique Post, The.
Severall Proceedings in Parliament.
True and Perfect Dutch Diurnall, The.
True and Perfect Informer, The.
Weekly Intelligencer of the Commonwealth, The.

PAMPHLETS

J. A. (Fellow, King's College). *Upon the Lamentable Fire in London* [1666].
Abstract of Several Letters and Choice occurrences ..., An (London, 1653). Thomason: 28 January 1653.
Ad Populum: Or, A Low Country Lecture to the People of England. (London, 1653). Thomason: 27 August 1653.
Adams, Edward. *A Brief Relation of the Surprizing Several English Merchants Goods, by Dutch Men of War* (London, [May] 1664).
Additional Discourse, An (London, 1653). Thomason: 2 August 1653.
Afflictions of the Afflicted, The (London, 1653). Thomason: 6 October 1653.
Aitzema, Lion. *Notable Revolutions: Beeing a True Relation of What Hap'ned in the United Provinces of the Netherlands* (London, 1653).
Allestree, Richard (Chaplain to Charles II). *A Sermon Preached Before the King at Whitehall.* 17 November 1667 (London, 1667).
[Allison, John.] *Upon the Late Lamentable Fire in London* (London, 1666).
Ames, William. *The Saints Security, Against Seducing Spirits* (London, 1652). Thomason: 30 November 1651.
Amsterdam, and her Other Hollander Sisters put out to Sea, By Van Trump, Van Dunck, & Van Dumpe (London, 1652). Thomason: 12 July 1652.
Andrews, William. *Newes from the Starrs: Or an Ephemeris for the Year of Man's Redemption by Jesus Christ, 1665* (London, 1665). 29 August 1664.
Anglia Liberata: Or, The Rights of the People of England Maintained Against the Pretences of the Scottish King, as They Are Set Forth in an Answer to the Lords Ambassadors Propositions of England (London, 1651). Thomason: 4 October 1651.
Another Bloody Fight at Sea Between the English and the Dutch upon the Coast of Flanders (London, 1652). Thomason: 15 June 1652.

Another Bloudy Fight at Sea Between the English and the Dutch (London, 1652). Thomason: 30 July 1652.
Another Bloudy Fight at Sea Upon the Coast of Cornwal, on Saturday the 13 of this instant June (London, 1652). Thomason: 21 June 1652.
Another Declaration: Wherein is Rendered a Further Account of the just Grounds and Reasons of the Dissolving the Parliament (London, 1653). Thomason: 3 May 1653.
Answer of Mr. Wallers Painter to his Many New Advisers, The (London, 1667).
Answer of the Parliament of the Commonwealth of England, to Three Papers Delivered in to the Council of State by the Lords Ambassadors Extraordinary of the United Provinces . . ., The (London, 1652). Thomason: 17 June 1652.
Answer to the Declaration of the Imaginary Parliament of the Unknowne Commonwealth of England . . ., An (Rotterdam, 1652). Thomason: 10 October 1652.
Answer to the French Declaration, An (London, 1666).
Answer to the Pope's Letter, An (1680).
Army No Usurpers, The (London, 1653). Thomason: 20 May 1653.
Aron-bimnucha: Or An Antidote to Cure the Calamities of their Trembling For Fear of the Ark (London, 1663).
Articles of Peace, Union and Confederation Concluded and Agreed between his Highness Oliver Lord Protector . . . and the Lords the States General of the United Provinces of the Netherlands (London, 1654).
Articles of the Perpetual Peace, The (London, 2 May 1654).
Aspinwall, William. *A Brief Description of the Fifth Monarchy, or Kingdome that Shortly is to Come into the World* (London, 1653). Thomason: 1 August 1653.
An Explication and Application of the Seventh Chapter of Daniel (London, 1654). Thomason: 20 March 1654.
[Ayleway, William.] *The Royal Solemnity: Or, The Crown Triumphant* (London, 1662).
A. B. *A Brief Relation of the Beginning and Ending of the Troubles of the Barbados* (London, 1653). Thomason: 29 July 1653.
Bacon, Sir Francis. *True Peace: Or a Moderate Discourse* (London, 1663).
Bagshaw, Henry. *A Sermon Preacht in Madrid.* 4 July 1666 (London, 1667).
[Bakewell, Thomas.] *A Brief Answer to the Objections of All Sorts, Against Presbyterian Churches and their Goverment* (London, 1650). Thomason: 23 December 1650.
Banks, Noah. *Gods Prerogative Power* (London, 1650). Thomason: 8 November 1650.
Beacon Set on Fire, A (London, 1652). Thomason: 21 September 1652.
Beacons Quenched: Or The Humble Information of Divers Officers of the Army, and Other Wel-affected Persons, to the Parliament and Commonwealth of England, The (London, 1652). Thomason: 8 October 1652.
Bellamy, Thomas. *Philanax Anglicus* (London, 1662).
Bellum Belgicum Secundum (London, 1665).
[Bethel, Slingsby.] *An Account of the French Usurpation upon the Trade of England* (London, 1679).
The World's Mistake in Oliver Cromwell (London, 1668).
Bill, Edward. *Certain Propositions Sent by the States of Holland to the Lords Embassadors of the Common-wealth of England* (London, 1651). Thomason: 15 April 1651.
[Birkenhead, Sir John.] *A New Ballad.* (1666).

Cabala: Or an Impartial Account of the Noncomformists Private Designs, Actings and Wayes (London, 1663).
Black Dutch Almanack, The (London, 1651). Thomason: 4 December 1651.
Black Munday: Or, A Full and Exact Description of That Great and Terrible Eclipse of the Sun Which Will Happen on the 29. Day of March 1652 ... (London, 1651). Thomason: 5 September 1651.
Bloody Almanack, The (London, 1653). Thomason: 31 October 1653.
Bloudy Almanack: Or Englands Looking Glass, The (London, 1650).
Bloudy Fight Between the Two Potent Fleets of England and Holland, A (London, 1653). Thomason: 4 June 1653.
Bloudy Newes from Holland (London, 1652). Thomason: 17 March 1652.
Bloudy Newes from Sea (London, 1652). Thomason: 6 July 1652.
Bloudy Newes from Sea (London, 1652). Thomason: 21 September 1652.
Booker, John. *Coelestiall Observations: Or an Ephemeris* (London, 1652). Thomason: 15 November 1651.
Telescopium Uranicum (London, 1664), 16 September 1663.
[Bourne, Nehemiah.] *The Copy of a Letter of the Reare-Admiral of the English Fleet for the Common Wealth of England, to an Eminent Merchant in London* (London, 1652).
Boyle, Roger, Earl of Orrery. *The History of Henry the Fifth's And The Tragedy of Mustapha, Son of Solyman the Magnificent* (London, 1668).
Boys, Edward. *Sixteen Sermons Preached Upon Several Occasions* (London, 1673).
Brayne, John. *The New Earth: Or, The True Magna Charta* (London, 1653). Thomason: 3 October 1653.
Brief Description of the Future History of Europe from Anno 1650 to An. 1710, A (1650). Thomason: 23 November 1650.
Brief Narration of the Mysteries of State carried on by the Spanish Faction in England ..., A (The Hague, 1651). Thomason: 10 July 1651.
Britaine, William De. *The Dutch Usurpation* (London, 1672).
The Interest of England in the Present War with Holland (London, 1672).
Britania Triumphalis (London, 1654). Thomason: 28 April 1654.
Brokeman, J. *The Tradesman's Lamentation: Or the Mechanicks Complaint* (London, 1663).
Brome, Alexander. *A Congratulatory Poem on the Miraculous and Glorious Return of that Unparallel'd King Charles the II* (London, 1660).
[Brown, David.] *The Naked Woman: Or a Rare Epistle Sent to Mr. Peter Sterry* (London, 1652). Thomason: 23 November 1652.
[Brydall, John.] *Jus Majestatis Anglicanae: Or a Treatise of the King's Sovereignty* (1665) MSS treatise at PRO SP 29/143/145.
Burnet, Gilbert. *The Life and Death of Sir Matthew Hale* (London, 1682).
W. C. *Coffo Philo: Or The Coffyhouse Dialogue* (Hamburg, January 1673).
Cade, William. *The Foundation of Popery Shaken* (London, 1678).
Campanella, Tho[mas]. *A Discourse Touching the Spanish Monarchy* (London, 1653). Thomason: 29 November 1653.
Canne, John. *A Second Voyce from the Temple to the Higher Powers* (London, 1653). Thomason: 15 August 1653.
A Voice from the Temple to the Higher Powers (London, 1653). Thomason: 13 June 1653.
Carpenter, Richard. *Rome in her Fruits*. Preached 5 November 1662 (London, 1663).
Cary, M[ary]. *The Resurrection of the Witnesses and England's Fall from (The Mystical Babylon) Rome* (London, 1653). Thomason: 14 November 1653.

Caryl, Joseph. *The Moderator* (London, 1652). Thomason: 11 May 1652.
The Oppressor Destroyed. Sermon delivered at St. Paul's 21 September 1651 (London, 1651). Thomason: 6 October 1651.
[Caryll, John.] *The English Princess: Or, The Death of Richard the III* (London, 1667).
Cat May Look Upon a King, A (London, 1652).
Certain Considerations Relating to the Royal African Company of England (1680).
[Chamberlayne, Edward.] *Englands Wants* (London, 1667).
Chappel, Samuel. *A Diamond or Rich Jewel, Presented to the Commonwealth of England, for the inriching of the Nation* (London, 1650). Thomason: 4 January 1651.
Character of Coffee and Coffee Houses, A (London, 1661).
Character of a Phanatique, The (London, 1661). Thomason: 26 March 1660.
Character of France, A (London, 1659).
[Chenell, Francis.] *The Beacon Flaming with a Non-Obstante* (London, 1652). Thomason: 15 December 1652.
Child, Josiah. *A Treatise* (London, 1681).
Chilmead, E. (translator). *Thomas Campanella An Italian Friar and Second Machiavel His Advice to the King of Spain for Attaining the Universal Monarchy of the World* (London, 1660). Preface by William Prynne.
Christian and Brotherly Exhortation to Peace, A (London, 1653). Thomason: 30 December 1653.
[Clavell, Robert.] *His Majesties Propriety and Dominion on the British Seas Asserted* (London, 1665).
Cliffe, E[ward]. *An Abbreviate of Holland's Deliverance By, and Ingratitude to the Crown of England and House of Nassau* (London, 1665).
Cobbertt, Thomas. *The Civil Magistrate's Power In Matters of Religion* (London, 1653). Thomason: 15 February 1653.
Codrington, Robert (translator). *The Life and Death of Alexander the Great*. From Quintus Curtius Rufus (London, 1661).
Coffee Scuffle, Occasioned by a Contest Between a Learned Knight and a Pitiful Pedagogue, The (London, 1662).
Coffo-Philo. *An Occasional Dialogue at a Coffee-House* (1667).
Coke, Roger. *A Treatise Wherein is Demonstrated That the Church and State of England Are in Equal Danger With the Trade of It* (London, 1671).
Collings, John. *Vindiciae Ministerii Evangelici* (London, 1651). Thomason: 6 June 1651.
Responsoria ad Errotica Pestoris, sive, Vindiciae Vindiciarum, ID East, The Shepherds Warning discovered in a Revindication of the great Ordinance of God: Gospel Preachers and Preaching (London, 1652). Thomason: 28 July 1652.
Confusion Confounded: Or, A Firm Way of Settlement Settled and Confirmed (London, 1654). Thomason: 18 January 1654.
Cook, John. *Monarchy No Creature of Gods Making* (Waterford, 1652).
Cooper, Edm[und]. *The Asse Beaten for Bawling* (London, 1661).
Coppie of the Anti-Spaniard made at Paris by a French Man, a Catholique, The (London, 1590).
Coppin, Richard. *Saul Smitten for not Smiting Amalek According to the Severity of the Command*. Sermon delivered at Somerset House 1 May (London, 1653). Thomason: 20 August 1653.
[Corbet, John.] *A Discourse of the Religion of England* (London, 1667).

Corraro, Angelo. *A Relation of the State of the Court of Rome* (London, 1664).
[Court, Pieter de la.] *The True Interest and Political Maxims of the Republick of Holland and West-Friesland* (London, 1702).
C[oventry], W[illiam]. *Trades Destruction is Englands Ruine: Or Excise Decryed* (London, 1659).
Cowley, Abraham. *The Second and Third Parts of the Works*. 6th edition (London, 1689).
Crouch, John. *Belgica Caracteristica: Or The Dutch Character* (London, 1665).
Flowers Strowed by the Muses (London, 1662).
Londiniensis Lacrymae: Londons Second Tears Mingled with her Ashes (London, 1666).
London's Bitter-Sweet-Cup (London, 1666).
The Dutch Embargo (London, 1665).
Cry for A Right Improvement, A (London, 1651). Thomason: 22 October 1651.
Culpeper, Nicholas. *An Ephemeris for the Year 1651* (London, 1651). Thomason: 9 January 1651.
An Ephemeris for the Year 1652 (London, 1652). Thomason: November 1651.
An Ephemeris for the Year of Our Lord, 1653 (London, 1653). Thomason: 16 November 1652.
Catastrophe Magnatum: Or The Fall of Monarchie (London, 1652). Thomason: 31 March 1652.
Cup of Coffee: Or, Coffee in its Colours, A (London, 1663).
I. D. *Concordia Rara Sonorum: Or a Poem Upon the Late Fight at Sea* (London, 1653). Thomason: 26 March 1653.
L. D. *An Exaxt Relation of the Proceedings and Transactions of the Late Parliament* (London, 1654). Thomason: 14 February 1654.
R. D. *Sir Francis Drake Revived: Who is or may be a Pattern to Sterre up all Heroicke and Active Spririts of these Times, to Benefit their Countrey and Eternize their Names by the Noble Attempts* (London, 1653). Thomason: 8 November 1652.
T. D. *England's Anathemy* (London, 1653). Thomason: 11 October 1653.
Dangerous and Bloudy Fight Upon the Coast of Cornwall Between the English and the Dutch, On Thursday last, A (London, 1652). Thomason: ca. 24 October 1652.
Darell, John. *A True and Compendious Narration: Or (Second Part of Amboyna)* (London, 1665).
[Davenant, Charles.] *Essays Upon I. The Ballance of Power II. The Right of Making War, Peace, and Alliances. III. Universal Monarchy* (London, 1701).
De Beaulieu, Luke, *Take Heed of Both Extremes* (London, 1675).
Declaration and Full Narrative of the proceedings of Admirall Vantrump with the Dutch Fleet at Sea, A (London, 1651). Thomason: 24 November 1651.
Declaration and Message Sent from the Queen of Bohemia, Lord Craven Lord Goring, And Divers Other English Gentlemen Resident at The Hague in Holland, on Friday Last, November 5 1652, The (London, 1652). Thomason: 5 November 1652.
Declaration and Narrative of the Proceedings of the Parliament of England, Touching the Message and Letters of Credence, Sent From the Estates General of the United Provinces; and Presented to the Parliament of the Lord Ambassador Cats, A (London, 1651). Thomason: 29 December 1651.
Declaration and Resolution of the States of Holland, Touching the Parliament and Commonwealth of England . . . , The (London, 1652). Thomason: 28 May 1652.

Declaration and Speech of the Lord Admiral Vantrump and his Setting up the Great Standard of Broom for the States of Holland, for the clearing of the Narrow Seas of all Englishmen, The (London, 1653). Thomason: 9 March 1653.

Declaration Concerning the Government of the Three Nations, A (London, 1653). Thomason: 21 December 1653.

Declaration from the General and Council of State, A (London, 1653). Thomason: 12 June 1653.

Declaration of Divers Elders and Brethren of Congregationall Societies, in and about the City of London, A (London, 1651). Thomason: 1 November 1651.

Declaration of his Excellency the Lord Admiral Vantrump Touching the Royal Fort of Monarchy …, A (London, 1652). Thomason: 21 July 1652.

Declaration of the Cardinal Mazarini, The (London, 1652). Thomason: 24 August 1652.

Declaration of the Further Proceedings of the English Fleet upon the Coast of Holland, A (London, 1653). Thomason: 9 June 1653.

Declaration of the Generals at Sea, A (London, 1653). Thomason: 27 April 1653.

Declaration of the High and Mighty Lords, The States of Holland, Concerning the Parliament and Commonwealth of England …, A (London, 1652). Thomason: 5 April 1652.

Declaration of the Hollanders, The (London, 1652). Thomason: 9 July 1652.

Declaration of the Hollanders Touching the Late King, and the Commonwealth of England, A (London, 1652). Thomason: 23 July 1652.

Declaration of the L. Admiral Vantrump Concerning The King of Scots, and the Parliament of England …, A (London, 1652). Thomason: 25 June 1652.

Declaration of the Lord General and his Councel of Officers: Shewing the Grounds and Reasons for the Dissolution of the late Parliament, A (London, 1653). Thomason: 23 April 1653.

Declaration of the Nobility and Gentry that Adhered to the Late King, Now Residing In and About the City of London, A (London, 1660). Thomason: 20 April 1660.

Declaration of the Parliament of the Commonwealth of England, Relating to the Affairs and Proceedings Between this Commonwealth and the States General of the United Provinces of the Low Countreys, and the Present Differences occasioned on the States part, A (London, 1652). Thomason: 9 July 1652.

Declaration of the Present Proceedings of the French, Danes, and the Hollanders, touching the King of Scots, A (London, 1653). Thomason: 4 March 1654.

Declaration of the Proceedings of Major General Massey, Sir Marmaduke Langdale, and Lieut. Col. John Lilburne Touching the King of Scots …, A (London, 1652). Thomason: 22 December 1652.

Declaration of the States of Holland, Concerning the King of Scots, The (London, 1653). Thomason: 16 June 1653.

Declaration of the States of Holland Concerning the Parliament of England, A (London, 1651). Thomason: 8 March 1652.

Declaration or Manifest of the High and Mighty Lords The States Generall of the United Netherland Provinces, A (Amsterdam, 1652).

Dell, William. *The Tryal of Spirits* (London, 1653). Thomason: December 1653.

Denham, Sir John. *Directions to a Painter* (London, 1667).

Description of Tangier, A (London, 1664).

Discourse of the Religion of England, A (London, 1667).

Dolben, John. *A Sermon Preached before the King On Tuesday 20th June 1665* (London, 1665).

A Sermon Preached before His Majesty on Good Friday. 24 March 1665 (London, 1665).

Dominium Maris: Or, the Dominion of the Sea. Expressing the Title, which the Venetians Pretend unto the Sole Dominion, and Absolute Sovereigntie of the Adriatick Sea, Commonly called The Gulph of Venice (London, 1652). Thomason: 15 May 1652.

Douglas, James. *A Strange and Wonderful Prophesie* (London, 1651). Thomason: 22 January 1651.

Downing, Sir George. *A Discourse* (London, 1664). 16 December 1664.

Dr. Dorislaus Ghost, Presented by Time to Unmask the Vizards of the Hollanders; And Discover the Lions Paw in the Face of the Sun, in this Juncture of Time: Or, a List of XXVII Barbarous and Bloody Cruelties and Murthers, Massacres and Base Treacheries of the Hollanders against England and English Men ... (London, 1652). Thomason: 29 June 1652.

Dryden, John. *Amboyna: A Tragedy* (London, 1673).

Astraea Redux: A poem on the Happy Restoration and Return of His Sacred Majesty Charles the Second (London, 1660). Thomason: 19 June 1660.

The Indian Emperour (London, 1667).

To His Scared Majesty. A Panegyrick on his coronation (London, 1661).

Du Moulin, Peter. *A Vindication of the Sincerity of the Protestant Religion in the Point of Obedience to Sovereigns* (London, 1664).

Dutch Bloudy Almanack, The (London, 1653). Thomason: 19 October 1652.

Dutch Nebuchadnezzar: Or, a Strange Dream of the States General, The (London, 1666).

Dutch Remonstrance, The (London, 1672). 30 August 1672.

Dutch-mens Pedigree: Or A Relation, Shewing How They Were First Bred, and Descended from a Horse-Turd, Which Was Enclosed in a Butter-Box, The (London, 1653). Thomason: 8 January 1653.

Elborough, Robert. *London's Calamity by Fire* (London, 1666).

Eliot, George. *An English Duel* (1666).

Ellis, Clement. *To the King's Most Excellent Majesty: On His Happie and Miraculous Return* (London, 1660). Thomason: 11 June 1660.

Elslyot, Tho[mas]. *The True Mariner, and his* Pixis Nautica: *Or, The Expert Navigator, with his Metaphorical and Hieroglyphical Ship, Described and Platformed; to Demonstrate the way to Paradise* (London, 1652). Thomason: 18 March 1652.

Englands Appeal from the Private Cabal at White-Hall to the Great Council of the Nation (1673).

England's Joy for London's Loyalty (London, 1664).

England's Warning: That is, Three Remarkable Visions of Stephen Melish, An Inhabitant of Breslaw (London, 1664).

English French-Mans-Address, The (1666).

Erbery, William. *A Monstrous Dispute: Or, The Language of the Beast* (London, 1653). Thomason: 18 October 1653.

The Sword Doubled to Cut Off both the Righteous and the Wicked (London, 1652). Thomason: 21 July 1652.

Essay: Or, a Narrative of the Two Great Fights at Sea, An (London, 1666).

Establishment: Or, a Discourse Tending to the Settling of the Minds of Men, about some of the Chief Controversies of our Times, The (London, 1653). Thomason: 20 November 1653.

Europae Modernae Speculum: Or, A View of the Empires, Kingdoms, Principalities and Common-Wealths of Europe (London, 1665).

Evangelium Armatum (London, 1663).
Evans, Arise. *Light for the Jews* (London, 1664).
Evelyn, John. *A Panegyric to Charles the Second* (London, 1661).
Navigation and Commerce, Their Original and Progress (London, 1674).
A Parallel of the Antient Architecture with the Modern (London, 1664).
The Pernicious Consequences of the New Heresy of the Jesuits Against the King and the State (London, 1666).
A Character of England (London, 1659).
Tyrannus or the Mode (London, 1661).
Exact and True Relation of the Great and Mighty Engagement between the English and Dutch Fleets, An (London, 1653). Thomason: 6 September 1653.
Examiner Defended, In a Fair and Sober Answer To the Two and Twenty Questions Which Lately Examined the Author of Zeal Examined, The (London, 1652). Thomason: 14 September 1652.
R. F. *The Scot Arraigned, and at the Bar of Justice, Reason, and Religion, Convinced, Convicted, and Condemned of a most Horrid and Odious Conspiracy and Rebellion against the Native Liberty and Birth-right of the Church and Free State of England* (London, 1651). Thomason: 16 June 1651.
Fair Warning: Or, XXV Reasons Against Toleration and Indulgence of Popery (London, 1663).
Fair-Warning: The Second Part: Or XX Prophecies Concerning the Return of Popery (London, 1663).
Faithful Advertisement to all Good Patriots of the United Provinces, In the Present Conjunctures Since the Death of the Prince of Orange, A (London, 1650). Thomason: 18 December 1650.
Faithful Discovery of a Treacherous Design of Mystical Antichrist Displaying Christ's Banners, A (London, 1653). Thomason: 12 June 1653.
False Brother: Or A New Map of Scotland, Drawn by an English Pencil, The (London, 1650).
[Farnsworth, Richard.] *A Tolleration Sent Down from Heaven to Preach* (1665).
Festa Georgiana: Or the Gentries & Countries Joy for the Coronation of the King, on St. Goerge's Day (London, 1661). Thomason: 19 April 1661.
[Flatman, Thomas.] *A Panegyricke to his Renowned Majestie Charles the Second* (London, 1660). Wood: May 1660.
Ford, Simon. *Folly in Print: Or a Book of Rymes* (London, 1667).
Londini quod Reliquum or Londons Remains (London, 1667).
The Conflagration of London (London, 1667).
The Lords Wonders in the Deep. Preached in Northampton 4 July 1665 (Oxford, 1665).
Foulis, Oliver [pseudonym for David Lloyd, according to Wood]. *Cabala: Or, The Mystery of Conventicles Unveil'd* (London, 1664).
Free Conference Touching the Present State of England Both at Home and Abroad: In Order to the Designs of France, A (London, 1668).
French Dancing-Master and the English Soldier, The (London, 1666).
Full and Perfect Relation of the Great Plot, A (London, 1654). Thomason: 18 February 1654.
Full Particulars of the Last Great and Terrible Sea-Fight between the two Great Fleets of England and Holland ..., The (London, 1653). Thomason: 4 August 1653.
Fullwood, Francis. *The Churches and Ministry of England, True Churches and True Ministery*. Sermon delivered 4 May 1652 (London, 1652). Thomason: 18 July 1652.

J. G. *Dis-satisfaction Satisfied* (London, 1653). Thomason: 22 December 1653.

Gadbury, John. *Ephermeris: Or a Diary Astonomical and Astrological For the Year Of Grace 1665* (London, 1665).

Ephemeris (London, 1664).

Gallus Castratus (London, 1659).

Garment, Joshua. *The Hebrews Deliverance at Hand* (London, 1651). Thomason: 23 August 1651.

Gataker, Thomas. *Antinominianism Discovered and Confuted: and Free-Grace As It Is Held Forth in Gods Word ...* (London, 1652). Thomason: 20 July 1652.

Gayton, Edm[und]. *The Glorious and Living Memory of the Cinque Ports* (Oxford, 1666).

Gearing, William. *God's Sovereignty Displayed.* 27 March 1667 (London, 1667).

Gerbier, Sir Balthazar. *A Discovery of Certain Notorious Stumbling-Blocks Which the Devill, the Pope, and the Malignants Have Raised to Put Nations at Variance* (London, 1652). Thomason, 12 March 1652.

[Glanville, J.] *A Loyal Tear Dropped at the Vault of Our Late Martyred Sovereign* (London, 1667).

Gloria Britanica (London, 1661).

Glorious and Living Cinque-Ports of our Fortunate Islands, The (Oxford, 1666).

Golden Coast, or a Description of Guinney, The (London, 1665).

Good Newes from General Blakes Fleet (London, 1652). Thomason: 20 September 1652.

Goodman, William. *Filius Heroum, The Son of Nobles Set Forth in a Sermon Preached at St. Mary's in Cambridge before the University, on Thursday the 24th of May 1660* (London, 1660).

Goodwin, John. *The Apologist Condemned* (London, 1653). Thomason: 19 April 1653.

Goodwin, Tho[mas]. *Christ The Universall Peace-Maker* (London, 1651). Thomason: 10 March 1651.

Grand Catastrophe: Or the Change of Government, The (London, 1654). Thomason: 18 January 1654.

Grateful Non-Conformist: Or, A Return of Thanks to Sir John Baber knight, and Doctor of Physick who sent the Author Ten Crowns, The (London, 1665).

[Graunt, John.] *The Shipwrack of all False Churches: And the Immutable Safety and Stability of the True Church of Christ* (London, 1652). Thomason: 31 August 1652.

G[raunt], J[ohn]. *Truths Defender, and Errors Reprover: A Briefe Discoverie of Feigned Pesbyterie ...* (London, 1651). Thomason: 2 July 1651.

Great and Bloudy Fight at Sea on Monday 16 August, Neere Plimouth: Between Sir George Ayscue and the Holland Fleet, A (London, 1652). Thomason: 20 August 1652.

Great and Famous Sea-Fight Between the English and Dutch, A (London, 1652). Thomason: 30 November 1652.

Great and Famous Victory Obtained by the Parliaments Navy Near the Isle of Wight, A (London, 1652). Thomason: 2 November 1652.

Great & Terrible Fight at Sea Near the Coast of Holland, A (London, 1653). Thomason: 9 May 1653.

Great and Terrible Fight in France, A (London, 1652). Thomason: 12 November 1652.

Great Victory Obtained By his Excellency the Lord Gen: Blake ..., A (London, 1652). Thomason: 1 July 1652.

Great Victory Obtained by the English Against the Dutch, A (London, 1652). Thomason: 28 September 1652.

Greville, Sir Fulke (Lord Brooke). *The Life of the Renowned Sir Philip Sidney* (London, 1652).

Grotius, Hugo (translated by T. Manley). *De Rebus Belgicus: Or, The Annals, and History of the Low-Countrey Warrs* (London, 1665).

E. H. *A Scriptural Discourse of the Apostasie and the Antichrist, by way of Comment, Upon the First Twelve Verses of 2 Thess.* 2 (1653). Thomason: 21 June 1653.

G. H. *Two Speeches Delivered on the Scaffold at Tower Hill on Friday Last, by Mr. Christopher Love, and Mr. Gibbons* (London, 1651). Thomason: 23 August 1651.

[Hall], George. *A Fast Sermon Preached to the House of Lords.* 3 October 1666 (London, 1666).

Hall, John. *Poems* (Cambridge, 1646).

Hall, John (translator). *Hierocles upon the Golden Verses of Pythagoras: Teaching a Vertuous and worthy Life* (London, 1657).

[Hall, John.] *A Letter Written to a Gentleman in the Country Touching the Dissolution of the late Parliament and the Reasons Thereof* (London, 1653). Thomason: 16 May 1653.

A True Relation of the Unjust, Cruel and Barbarous Proceedings against the English at Amboyna In the East-Indies, by the Netherlandish Governour and Council There (London, 1651). Thomason: 29 November 1651.

Confusion-Confounded (London, 1654). *Lusus Serius: Or, Serious Passe-Time* (London, 1654).

H[all], J[ohn]. *The Grounds and Reasons of Monarchy* (Edinburgh, 1651).

Hamilton, William. *The Life and Character of James Bonnell Esq.* (Dublin, 1703).

Happy Union of England and Holland, The (London, 1689).

Hardy, Nathaniel. *Lamentation, Mourning and woe.* 9 September 1666 (London, 1666).

[Harvey, Chris.] *Faction Supplanted: Or, A Caveat against the Ecclesiastical and Secular Rebel* ([London], 1663).

Haughty Frenchmens Pride Abased, The. 30 September 1661 (London, [1661]).

Heath, James. *Flagellum: Or The Life and Death, Birth and Burial of Oliver Cromwell The Late Usurper* (London, 1663).

[Heylin, Peter.] *Augustus* (London, 1666).

Hickes, Thomas. *A Letter or Word of Advice to the Saints* (London, 1653). Thomason: 2 December 1653.

Higgins, Thomas. *A Panegyrick to the King* (London, 1660). Thomason: 10 June 1660.

His Majesties Declaration Against the French. 9 February 1666 (London, 1666).

His Majesties Declaration to his City of London. 13 September 1666 (London, 1666).

His Majesties Gracious Speech to Both Houses of Parliament on Thursday, November 24 1664 (London, 1664).

His Majesties Most Gracious Speech to Both Houses of Parliament. 21 September 1666 (London, 1666).

His Majesties Most Gracious Speech to Both Houses of Parliament on Monday the One and Twentieth of March, 1663/4 (London, 1664).

His Majesties Gracious Speech to Both Houses of Parliament Together with the Lord Chancellor's. 10 October 1665 (Oxford, 1665).

His Majesties Gracious Speech to Both Houses of Parliament Together with the Speech of Sir Edward Turnor Kt Speaker of the Honourable House of Commons, On Tuesday May 17 1664 at their Prorogation (London, 1664).
His Majesties Most Gracious Speech, Together with the Lord Chancellors, To the Two Houses of Parliament, At their Prorogation On Monday the Nineteenth of May, 1662 (London, 1662).
Holland, Samuel. *The Phoenix Her Arrival & Welcome to England* (London, 1662).
Hollands Representation: Or, The Dutch-mans Looking-Glass (London, 1665).
Honour of the English Soldiery, The (London, 1651). Thomason: 31 July 1651.
Howard, Edward. *A Panegyrick to his Highness the Duke of York on his Sea-Fight with the Dutch June 3d 1665* (London, 1666).
Howell, James. *Dodona's Grove: Or the the Vocal Forest* (London, 1645).
A German Diet (London, 1653).
The Parly of Beasts (London, 1660).
A Discourse of Dunkirk (London, 1664).
Hudibras. *On Calamy's Imprisonment, and Wild's Poetry* (1663).
Hue and Cry after the Dutch Fleet, A (London, 1666).
Hughes, W. *Magistracy God's Ministry: Or, A Rule for the Rulers and Peoples due Correspondence* (London, 1652). Thomason: 17 May 1652.
Humble Remonstrance of the General Councel of Officers Met at Dalkeith the fifth of May 1653, The (London, 1653). Thomason: 14 May 1653.
"Humble Representation of Several Aldermen, Aldermen's Deputies, Common Councilmen & Many Others, The." MSS. pamphlet. Thomason: [20] May 1653. TT: E697(18).
Hunt, Lieutenant-Colonel Robert. *The Island of Assada* (London, 1650). Thomason: 12 August 1650.
H[unton], S[amuel]. *The Army Armed and Their Just Powers Stated* (London, 1653). Thomason: 8 September 1653.
Hyde, Edward. *The Life of Edward Earl of Clarendon* (Dublin, 1760).
Inconveniencies of Toleration, The (London, 1667).
Iter Boreale His Country Clown (1665).
Izacke, Richard. *Antiquities of the City of Exeter* (London, 1677).
P. J. *Tyrants and Protectors Set Forth in their Colours* (London, 1654). Thomason: 9 June 1654.
Jenkins, William. *A Sermon Preached at Mary Aldermanbury, on the Fifth Day of November, 1651 ... Being the First Sermon he Preached since his Releasement* (London, 1652). Thomason: 14 November 1651.
Jenner, Thomas. *Londons Blame if not its Shame* (London, 1651). Thomason: 18 February 1651.
Jesuits Grand Design Upon England, The (1660).
Jesuites Reasons Unreasonable, The (London, 1662).
Johnson, William. *Deus Nobiscum* (London, 1664).
Joyful Newes from Holland (London, 1651). Thomason: 7 April 1651.
Justification of the Present War against the United Netherlands, A (London, 1672).
Kerswel, John. *Speculum Gratitudinis: Or David's Thankfulness unto God for all his Benefits. Expressed in a Sermon on the 29th of May 1664* (London, 1665).
Keymore, John. *Observations Made Upon the Dutch Fishing About the Year 1601* (London, 1664).
Killigrew, Henry. *A Sermon Preach'd Before the King.* 2 December 1666 (London, 1666).

[King], Henry. *A Sermon Preached at the Funeral of the Right Reverend Father in God Bryan Lord Bishop of Winchester . . . April 24 1662* (London, 1662).
King of Denmark's Message to the States of Holland, The (London, 1652). Thomason: 11 November 1652.
King of Scots Letter to the States of Holland Concerning Their Present Design and Engagement against England, The (London, 1652). Thomason: 7 July 1652.
King of Spain's Cabinet Counsel Divulged: Or, A Discovery of the Prevarications of the Spaniards With All the Princes and States of Europe, for Obtaining the Universal Monarchy, The (London, 1658). Thomason: 1 October 1657.
Knavery in all Trades: Or, The Coffee-House (London, 1664).
G. A. L. *The Court's Apology* (London, 1663).
J. L. *A Poem Royal* (London, 1662).
P. L. *The Shepherds Prognostication, Fore-TellingThe Sad and Strange Eclipse of the Sun, which Wil Happen on the 29 of March this Present Year 1652* (London, 1562). Thomason: 16 January 1652.
L'Estrange, Roger. *A Memento Directed to All Those That Truly Reverence the Memory of King Charles the Martyr* (London, 1662).
Considerations and Proposals In Order to the Regulation of the Press (London, 1663). 3 June 1663.
Interest Mistaken, or the Holy Cheat (London, 1661).
Toleration Discussed (London, 1663).
Laeophilus Misotyrannus. *Mene Tekel: Or, the Downfall of Tyranny* ([London], 1663). Printed on 30 January 1663.
Laney, Benjamin. *Five Sermons Preached Before His Majesty at Whitehall* (London, 1669).
Last Bloudy Fight at Sea, Between the English and the Dutch, on Tuesday last, The (London, 1652). Thomason: 27 July 1652.
Last Great and Bloudy Fight Between the English and the Dutch, The (London, 1652). Thomason: 6 July 1652.
Last Great and Terrible Sea-Fight Between the English and the Dutch, On Tuesday and Wednesday last, upon the Western Sound neer Cornwall . . . , The (London, 1652). Thomason: 24 August 1652.
Last Will and Testament of the Late Deceased French Jackanapes, The (London, 1661).
Late Apology in Behalf of the Papists Re-Printed and Answered in Behalf of the Royalists, The (London, 1667).
Lee, Richard. *Cor Humiliatum & Contritum. A Sermon Preached at S. Pauls Church London, Nov. 29 1663* (London, 1663).
Lereck, Joseph. *A True Accompt of the Late Reducement of the Isles of Scilly* (London, 1651). Thomason: 28 July 1651.
Letter from Admiral Vantrump to the Lords and Burgamasters of Amsterdam . . . , A (London, 1653). Thomason: 15 March 1653.
Letter from General Blakes Fleet, A (London, 1652). Thomason: 5 October 1652.
Letter from the Fleet, A (London, 1653). Thomason: 13 June 1653.
Letter Sent from his Excellency General Blake To the King of Denmark, A (London, 1652). Thomason: 29 July 1652.
Letter Sent from the States of Holland to the King of Scots, A (London, 1652). Thomason: 27 July 1652.
Letter to a Baron of England, Relating to the Late Bill, Concerning His Royal Highnesse, A (London, 1679).
Letter Written to a Friend in Wilts, A (London, 1666).

Lilburne, John. *L. Colonel John Lilburne Revived* (March 1653). Thomason: 27 March 1653.

Lily, William. *Annus Tenebrous: Or the Dark Year* (London, 1652).

Merlini Anglici Ephemeris (London, 1651). Thomason: 18 November 1650.

Merlini Anglici Ephemeris (London, 1653). Thomason: 16 November 1652.

Merlini Anglici Ephemeris (London, 1664). 16 September 1663.

Merlini Anglici Ephemeris: Or Astrological Judgements for the Year 1665 (London, 1665).

Monarchy: Or No Monarchy in England (London, 1651). Thomason: 6 August 1651.

Lin, Francis. *A Sharp, But Short Noise of Warr: Or, The Ruine of Antichrist by the Sword of Temporall Warr* (London, 1651). Thomason: 21 January 1651.

[Lisola, François Baron de.] *The Buckler of State and Justice against the Design Manifestly discovered of the Universal monarchy* (London, 1667).

London Undone: Or, A Reflection on the Late Disasterous Fire (London, 1666).

London's Lamentation: Or its Destruction by a Consuming Fire (1666).

Lord Merlins Prophecy Concerning the King of Scots, The (London, 1651). Thomason: 22 August 1651.

[Lupton, Donald.] *England's Command on the Seas* (London, 1653).

Luke, John. *A Sermon Preached before the Right Worshipful Company of the Levant Merchants* (London, 1664).

E. M. *Protection Perswading Subjection* (London, 1654). Thomason: 13 February 1654.

[Mackenzie, Sir George.] *Religio Stoici* (Edinburgh, 1665).

Mad Designe: or, A Description of the King of Scots Marching in his Disguise, After the Rout of Worcester, A (London, 1651). Thomason: 6 November 1651.

Maidens Complaint against Coffee: Or, the Coffee-House Discovered, The (London, 1663).

Markland, Abraham. *Poems on his Majesties Birth and Restauration* (London, 1667).

[Marsh, Henry.] *A New Survey of the Turkish Empire* (London, 1664).

Marshall, Stephen. *A Sermon Preached To The Right Honourable the Lord Mayor, the Court of Aldermen of the City of London, at their Anniversary Meeting on Easter Monday April 1652* (London, 1653). Thomason: 11 May 1653.

Matthew, Edward. *Karolou ... or the Most Glorious Star* (London, 1664).

May, Henry. *XXX Christian and Politick Reasons Wherefore England and the Low-Countries May Not Have Warres With Each Other* (London, 1652). Thomason: 15 June 1652.

Mede, Joseph. *Diatribiae Pars IV: Discourses on Sundry Texts of Scripture* (London, 1652). Thomason: 6 October 1652.

Memento for Holland: Or a True and Exact History of the Most Villainous and Barbarous Cruelties Used on the English Merchants Residing at Amboyna, A (London, 1653). Thomason: 2 July 1653

Mene Tekel to Fifth Monarchy, A (London, 1665).

Mercer, Richard. *A Further Discovery of the Mystery of the Last Times ...* (London, 1651). Thomason: 24 July 1651.

Mercurius Cambro-Britannicus: Or, News from Wales, Touching the Glorious and Miraculous Propagation of the Gospel in Those Parts (London, 1652). Thomason: 4 September 1652.

Mercurius Heliconicus: Or, A Short Reflection on Moderne Policy (London, 1651). Thomason: 12 February 1651.

Message Sent to the L. Admiral Vantrump, A (London, 1652). Thomason: 16 July 1652.

Miller, Robert. *The English-French-Mans Address Upon His Majesties Late Declaration* (London, 1666).

Milton, John. *A Defence of the People of England* (24 February 1651), in Don M. Wolfe (editor), *Complete Prose Works of John Milton*, Vol. IV (New Haven, 1966).

Molloy, Charles. *Holland's Ingratitude: Or, A Serious Expostulation with the Dutch* (London, 1666).

More Hearts and Hands Appearing for the Work (London, 1653). Thomason: 7 June 1653.

More News from Rome or Magna Charta, Discoursed of Between a Poor Man & his Wife (London, 1666).

More, Henry. *A Modest Enquiry into the Mystery of Iniquity* (London, 1664).

Morley, George. *A Sermon Preached before the King at Whitehall.* 5 November 1667 (London, 1683).

Mun, Thomas. *England's Treasure by Forraign Trade* (London, 1664).

Mutatus Polemo Revised by Some Epistolary Observations of a Country Minister, a Freind of the Presbyterian Government (London, 1650). Thomason: 14 November 1650.

Nedham, Marchamont (translator and compiler). *Of the Dominion or Ownership of the Sea* (London, 1652).

[Nedham, Marchamont.] *The Case Stated Between England and the United Provinces in this Present Juncture* (London, 1652).

A True State of the Case of the Commonwealth (London, 1654). Thomason: 8 February 1654.

New Hue and Cry after Major General Massey and Some Others, Who by the Help of Peters Keyes, Escaped from the Tower of London, August the 30, and is Thought to be Fled into Holland, A (London, 1652). Thomason: 6 September 1652.

New Relation of Rome, A (London, 1664).

New Remonstrance of the Free-Born People of England, A (London, 1651). Thomason: 14 November 1651.

News from Newcastle (London, 1651). Thomason: 3 February 1651.

News from the Stage (London, 1668).

Newton, George. *A Sermon Preached the 11. of May 1652 in Taunton* (London, 1652). Thomason: 16 July 1652.

Nicholson, Ben[jamin]. *Some Returns to a Letter Which Came From a General Meeting of Officers of the Army of England, Scotland, and Ireland Sitting at Saint James's Westminster* (London, 1653). Thomason: 12 March 1653.

No King but the Old King's Son (London, 1660). Thomason: 23 March 1660.

Norwood, Captain Robert. *A Pathway Unto England's Perfect Settlement* (London, 1653). Thomason: 27 July 1653.

Observations Both Historical and Moral Upon the Burning of London (London, 1667).

Ogilby, John. *The Fables of Aesop* (London, 1665).

The Relation of His Majesties Entertainment Passing through the City of London (London, 1661).

Old Sayings and Predictions Verified and (Fulfilled, Touching the Young King of Scotland and his gued Subjects (London, 1651). Thomason: 14 July 1651.

Omnia Comesta a Belo (1667).

One Broad-Side More for the Dutch: Or, The Belgick Lion Couchant (London, 1665).
Onely Right Rule for Regulating the Lawes and Liberties of the People of England, The (London, 1653). Thomason: 28 January 1653.
Owen, [David]. *Herod and Pilate Reconciled: Or the Concord of Papists, Anabaptists, and Sectaries against Scripture, Fathers, Councils, and other Orthodoxal Writers, for the Coercion, Deposition, and Killing of Kings* (London, 1663).
Owen, John. *A Sermon Preached to the Parliament, Octob. 13. 1652* (Oxford, 1652). Thomason: 30 October 1652.
The Advantage of the Kingdome of Christ in the Shaking of the Kingdomes of the World. Sermon Preached to Parliament 24 October 1651 (Oxford, 1651).
A Peace-Offering in an Apology and Humble Plea for Indulgence and Liberty of Conscience (London, 1667).
Indulgence and Toleration Considered (London, 1667).
H. P. and B. G. *The Next Way to France: Or, A Short Dialogue Between Two Zealous Well-Wishers of the Kingdom of Christ* (London, 1651). Thomason: 11 November 1651.
T. P. *Hickledy-Pickledy: Or, The Yorkshire Curates Complaint* [1665].
Palmer, Roger, Earl of Castlemaine. *An Account of the Present War Between the Venetians and the Turk* (London, 1666).
Parker, Robert. *The Mystery of the Vialls Opened* (London, 1650). Thomason: 21 August 1650.
Parliament of England's Message to the Queen of Sweden . . . , The (London, 1652).
Parliament Routed: Or Here's a House to Let, The. [1653] Thomason: 3 June 1653.
Particulars of all the Late Bloody Fight at Sea, The (London, 1653). Thomason: 6 June 1653.
Peace-Maker, The (London, 1653). Thomason: 16 December 1653.
[Penn, William]. *One Project for the Good of England* (1679).
Pennington, Isaac. *A Considerable Question About Government* (London, 1653). Thomason: 9 May 1653.
The Fundamental Right, Safety and Liberty of the People ... Briefly Asserted (London, 1651. Thomason: 15 May 1651.
Perrinchief, Richard. *A Sermon Preached before the Honourable House of Commons.* 7 November 1666 (London, 1666).
The Workes of King Charles I Defender of the Faith with the History of his Life (London, 1662).
Perfect Occurrences (London, 1653). Thomason: 3 February 1653.
Perswasive to A Mutuall Compliance Under the Present Government: Together with a Plea For a Free State Compared with Monarchy, A (Oxford, 1652). Thomason: 18 February 1652.
[Peter, Hugh.] *A Dying Fathers Last Legacy to an Only Child* (London, [1665]).
P[eter], H[ugh]. *Good Work for a Good Magistrate* (London, 1651). Thomason: 17 June 1651.
Peters, Thomas, *A Remedie Against Ruine: A Sermon Preached at the Assizes in Lanceston Cornwall, March 17 1651* (London, 1652). Thomason: 17 July 1651.
[Petyt, William]. *Britannia Languens: Or, A Discourse of Trade* (London, 1680).
Philanax Protestant (London, 1663).
Philanglus. *One Project for the Good of England* (1679).
Philolaus: Or, Popery Discovered to the People (London, 1663).
Philpot, Thomas. *The Original and Growth of the Spanish Monarchy* (London, 1664).

Pierce, Thomas. *The Primitive Rule of Reformation: Delivered in a Sermon Before His Majesty at Whitehall Feb. 1 1662 [1663]* (London, 1663).

Plot of the Jesuites. The (London, 1653). Thomason: 1 November 1653.

Poor Robin 1664: An Almanack After a New Fashion (London, 1664).

Poor Robin's Character of France (London, 1666).

Porter, Tho[mas]. *Spiritual Salt: Or, A Sermon on Matth. 5. 13*. Preached 20 February 1649 (London, 1651). Thomason: 3 June 1651.

Presbytery Displayed (London, 1663).

Proclamation for a Thanksgiving for the Late Victory for His Majesties Naval Forces against the Dutch, A (London, 1666).

Procul Este Prophani: The Pulpit Vindicated From, and Against a Sacraligious Pamphlet Entitled the Pulpit to Let. (London, 1665).

Proposition for the Safety and Happiness of the King & Kingdom both in Church and State, A. 18 June 1667 (London, 1667).

Propositions for Peace (London, 1653). Thomason: 14 June 1653.

Prynne, William. *The Second Tome of an Exact Chronological Vindication*. 29 May 1665 (London, 1665).

Pulleston, Hamlet. *Monarchie Britannicae Singularis Protectio* (London, 1661).

Pulpit to Let, A (London, 1665).

Quaeries: Or, a Dish of Pickled-Herring Shread, Cut and Prepared according to the Dutch Fashion (London, 1665).

Quarles, John. *Rebellion's Downfall* (London, 1662).

Qui Chetat Chetabitur: Or Tyburne Cheated (London, 1661).

J. R. *An Answer For Mr. Calamie to a Poem Congratulating his Imprisonment in Newgate* (1663).

N. R. *The Belgick Lyon Discovered* (London, 1665).

S. R. *The Blind Man's Folly Discovered* (London, 1666).

[Ralph, James.] *The History of England*. (London, 1744).

Ramesey, William. *Vox Stellarum: Or, The Voice from the Starres* (London, 1652). Thomason: 25 November 1651.

Ramsey, James. *Bloudy Newes from the East-Indies* (London, 1651). Thomason: 12 December 1651.

Reasons Why the Supreme Authority of the Three Nations (For the Time) Is Not in the Parliament But in the new Established Councel of State ... (London, 1653). Thomason: May 1653.

Recreation for Ingenious Head-Pieces: Or, a Pleasant Grove for their Wits to Walk In (London, 1663).

Remarkable Observations of Gods Mercies towards England (London, 1651). Thomason: 29 September 1651.

Remonstrance from Holland, A (London, 1652). Thomason: 24 December 1652.

Resolution of the Hollanders, The (London, 1652). Thomason: 20 July 1652.

Resolution of the Noble and Great Mighty Lords, the States of Holland and West-Friesland (The Hague, 1665).

Reynell, Carew. *The Fortunate Change: Being a Panegyrick to His Sacred Majesty* ... 23 April 1661 (London, 1661).

Reynolds, Edward. *A Sermon Preached Before the Peers*. 7 November 1666 (London, 1666).

[Robinson], [Henry]. *Liberty of Conscience: Or the Sole Means to Obtaine Peace and Truth, Not Onely Reconciling His Majesty with His Subjects, but all Christian States and Princes to One Another, with the Freest passage for the Gospel* (1643) [1644]. Thomason: 24 March [1644].

Rod for the Fools Back: Or, An Answer to a Scurrilous Libel, Called the Changeling, A (1663).

Rogers, John. *Sagrir: Or Doomes-Day Drawing Nigh* (London, 1653). Thomason: 7 November 1653.

Rolle, Samuel. *The Burning of London in the Year 1666* (London, 1667).

Roman History of Lucius J. Florus, The (London, 1669).

Routing of De Ruyter: Or the Barbadoes Bravery, The (London, 1665).

Royal Victory, The. 2–3 June 1665 (London, 1665).

L. S. *Natures Dowrie: Or, the Peoples Nature Libertie Asserted* (London, 1652).

St. Serfe, Thomas. *Tarugo's Wiles: Or, The Coffee-House* (London, 1668)

Sancroft, William. *Lex Ignea: Or, The School of Righteousness.* Sermon Preached Before Charles II 10 October 1666 (London, 1666).

Satyr on the Adulterate Coyn Inscribed The Common-Wealth (London, 1661).

Saunders, Richard. *Apollo Anglicanus* (London, 1664).

Plenary Possession Makes a Carefull Power or Subjection to Powers That Are in Being Proved to be Lawfull and Necessary, In a Sermon Preached Before the Judges in Exeter 23 March 1650 (London, 1651). Thomason: 28 July 1651.

Sclater, William *Civil Magistracy by Divine Authority.* Preached at Southampton Assizes 4 March 1652 (London, 1653). Thomason: 30 October 1652.

[Scott, Thomas.] *The Belgick Pismire* (London, 1622).

The Spaniards Cruelty and Treachery to the English in the Time of Peace and War, Discovered (London, 1656). Thomason: 15 August 1653.

Seasonable Corrective to the One Project for the Good of England, A. Thomason: 24 July 1680.

Seasonable Expostulation with the Netherlands, A (Oxford, 1652). Thomason: 12 June 1652.

Second Beacon Fired by Scintilla, A (London, 1652). Thomason: 4 October 1652.

Second Character of Mercurius Politicus, The (1650). Thomason: 23 October 1650.

Second Discovery of Hind's Exploits: Or a Fuller Relation of his Ramble, Robberies, and Cheats in England, Ireland, Scotland with his Voyage to Holland, A (London, 1652). Thomason: 19 November 1651.

Second Narrative of the Signal Victory, A. 3 June 1665 (London, 1665).

Second Part of the Tragedy of Amboyna, The (London, 1653). Thomason: 8 August 1653.

Sedition Scourg'd (London, 1653). Thomason: 20 October 1653.

Several Proposals for the Generall Good of the Commonwealth with the Grounds and Reasons Thereof (London, 1651). Thomason: 19 February 1651.

Sharp, John. *A Sermon Preached on the Day of Public Fast.* 11 April 1679 (London, 1679).

Short and Serious Narration of London's Fatal Fire, A (London, 1667).

Smith, Edward (translator). *The King of Denmark His Declaration Concerning the English Merchant Shiops Lying in Copenhagen* (London, 1653). Thomason: 23 May 1653.

Smith, Nicholas (Shoemaker at Tillington, Sussex). *Wonderful Prophecyes Revealed* (London, 1652). Thomason: 30 November 1652.

[Smith, William.] *Ingratitude Reveng'd: Or, A Poem Upon the Happy Victory of his Majesties Naval Forces Against the Dutch; June 3 and 4 1665* (London, 1665).

Sorbiere, Samuel. *A Voyage to England* (London, 1709).

South, Robert. *A Sermon Preached at Lambeth Chapel.* 25 November 1666 ([London], 1666).

Twelve Sermons, Preached Upon Several occasions (London, 1692).

Speech and Confession, of Sir Henry Hide (Embassadour for the King of Scotland, to the Emperour of Turkie), The (London, 1651). Thomason: 5 March 1651.

Speech of Sir Edward Turnor, The (London, 1666).

Speech of Sir Ellis Leighton Kt At the Tholsell of Dublin April the 4th 1672, The (Dublin, 1672).

Speeches and Prayers of John Barkstead, John Okey, and Miles Corbett . . . With Some Due and Sober Animadversions On the Said Speeches, The (London, 1662).

Spittlehouse, John. *A Warning-Piece Discharged* (London, 1653).

An Explanation of the Commission of Jesus Christ (London, 1631). Thomason: 22 September 1653.

The Army Vindicated In their late Dissolution of the Parliament (London, 1653). Thomason: 24 April 1653.

The First Addresses (London, 1653). Thomason: 5 July 1653.

Sprat, Thomas. *Observations on Monsieur de Sorbier's Voyage into England* (London, 1665).

Spurstowe, William. *The Magistrates Dignity and Duty: Being a Sermon preached on October 30 1653 at Paul's Church* (London, 1654). Thomason: 24 January 1654.

Sterry, Peter. *England's Deliverance From the Northern Presbytery Compared with its Deliverance from the Roman Papacy*. Preached at St. Margaret's Westminster, 5 November 1651 (London, 1651).

Stillingfleet, Edward. *A Sermon*. 10 October 1666 (London, 1666).

Stokes, Edward. *A Sermon*. Preached at Eton College 10 October 1666 (Oxford, 1667).

Strange and Terrible News, from Holland, and Yarmouth (London, 1651). Thomason: 11 March 1651.

Streater, J. *A Glympse of that Jewel, Judicial, Just, Preserving Libertie* (London, 1653). Thomason: 31 March 1653.

Strena Vavasoriensis, A New-Years Gift for the Welch Itinerants (London, 1654). Thomason: 30 January 1654.

Stubbe, Henry. *A Further Iustification of the Present War Against the United Netherlands* (London, 1673).

Summary Narration of the Signal Victory . . . 3d of June 1665, A (London, 1665).

Swadling, T. *Two Letters: The One to a Subtile Papist: The Other to a Zealous presbyterian* (London, 1653). Thomason: 31 August 1653.

Tanner, John. *Angelus Britannicus: An Ephemeris for the Year of Our Redemption 1664* (London, 1664).

Tatham, John. *Aqua Triumphalis: Being a True Relation of the Honourable the City of London's Entertaining Their Sacred Majesties upon the River of Thames . . . the 23 day of August 1662* (London, 1662).

[Tatham, John.] *Neptunes Address to his Most Sacred Majesty Charles the Second*. 22 April 1661 (London, 1661).

Temple, William. *Lettre d'un Marchand de Londres à Son Ame d'Amsterdam Depuis la Dernière Bataille de Mer* (1666).

"Ten Queries by a Friend of the New Dissolved Parliament" (MSS. pamphlet). ca. 25 April 1653. TT: E693(5).

Terrible and Bloudy Fight at Sea between the English and the Dutch, A (London, 1652). Thomason: 23 July 1652.

Terrible and Bloudy Newes From Sea (London, 1652). Thomason: 6 August 1652.

Testis-Mundus Catholicus. *Lingua Testium* (London, 1651). Thomason: 1 July 1651.

Theaureajohn. *Theousori Apokolipikak: Or, Gods Light Declared in Mysteries* (London, 1651). Thomason: 13 August 1651.
[Theobald, Francis.] *A Discourse Concerning the Original and Basis of Government* (London, 1667).
To His Excellency The Lord General Cromwell and all the Honest Officers and Souldiers in the Army for the Commonwealth of England: The Humble Remonstrance of Many Thousands in and about the City of London, on the behalf of all the Free-Commoners of England (1653). Thomason: 21 April 1653.
To His Royal Highness the Duke of Yorke: On our Late Sea-Fight (Oxford, 1665).
[Tomkins, Thomas]. *The Modern pleas* (London, 1675).
Troubles of Amsterdam, The. Printed in Dutch Translated into English by L. W. (London, 1650). Thomason: 12 November 1650.
True and Exact Character of the Lowe Countreys; Especially Holland: Or, The Dutchman Anatomized and Truly Dissected, A (London, 1652). Thomason: 15 March 1652.
True and Exact Relation of the Most Dreadful and Remarkable Fires, A (London, 1666).
True and Perfect Narrative of the Great and Signal Success of a Part of his Majesties Fleet, A [9 August 1666] (London, 1666).
True Narrative of the Cause and Manner of the Dissolution of the late Parliament, A (London, 1653). Thomason: 19 December 1653.
True Relation of that Sad and Deplorable Fire, A [8 September] (York, 1666).
True Relation of the Last Great Fight. A (London, 1653).
True Relation of the Last Great Fight at Sea, A (London, 1653).
True Relation of the Unjust, Cruel, and Barbarous Proceedings Against the English at Amboyna, A. 3rd edition (London, 1665).
Tryall of Mr. Love, The (London, 1651). Thomason: 22 June 1651.
Th. Tw., *An Elegiack Memoriall of General Deane* (London, 1653). Thomason: 24 June 1653.
Two Letters From the Fleet at Sea Touching the Late Fight (London, 1653). Thomason: 4 June 1653.
Two Royal Acrosticks on the Dutch in the Ditch [1666].
Two Terrible Sea-Fights (London, 1652). Thomason: 2 November 1652.
Tydings from Rome, or England's Alarm (London, 1667).
[Ufflet, John]. *A Caution to the Parliament, Council of State, and Army* (London, 1653). Thomason: 2 September 1653.
Upon His Royal Highness His Late Victory Against the Dutch [1665].
Upon the Present Plague at London and His Majesties Leaving the City [Oxford, 1665].
Vertues of Coffee, The (London, 1663).
Victory over the Fleet of the States General, The (27 July 1666) (London, 1666).
[Villiers, George, 2nd Duke of Buckingham.] *A Letter to Sir Thomas Osborn* (London, 1672).
Voice of a Cry at Midnight: Or, An Alarme to Churches & Professors Speedily to Revive their Temple Worke, or Open-Workship, The (1664).
Voice of the Shepherd Through the Clouds to his Lambs on Earth, The (1663).
Votivum Carolo (1660).
Vox Plebis: Or, The Voice of the Oppressed Commons of England Against their Oppressors (London, 1653). Thomason: 18 April 1653.
Vox Veritatis. Thomason: 16 November 1650.

G. W. (Lincoln's Inn). *Anglo-Tyrranus, or the Idea of a Norman Monarch* (London, 1650). Thomason: 3 December 1650.

J. W. *A Friendly Letter to the Flying Clergy*. 6 September 1665 (London, 1665).

J. W. *A Mite to the Treasury of Consideration in the Commonwealth* (London, 1653). Thomason: 5 May 1653.

Brandy-Wine in the Hollanders Ingratitude ([London], 1652). Thomason: 30 July 1652.

W. W., *Britannia Iterum Beata* (London, 1662).

The English and Dutch Affairs Displayed to the Life (London, 1664).

[Waller, Edmund.] *Instructions to a Painter* (London, 1665).

Upon Her Majesties New Building at Somerset-House (London, 1665).

Ward, Seth. *A Sermon Preached Before the Peers*. 10 October 1666 (London, 1666).

Seven Sermons (London, 1674).

Warning Seriously Offered to the Officers of the Army, and Others in Power, A (London, 1653). Thomason: 18 May 1653.

Welsh Narrative, Corrected, And Taught to Speak True English, and some Latine: Or, Animadversions of an Imperfect Relation in the Perfect Diurnal ..., A (London, 1652). Thomason: 20 September 1652.

Western Wheele Turned Round to the Last Spoke. The. Wood: February 1660 (London, 1660).

Wharton, George. *Calendrium Carolinum: Or, A New Almanack After the Old Fashion For the Year of Christ 1664* (London, 1664).

Calendrium Carolinum: Or, A New Almanack After the Old Fashion For the Year of Christ 1665 (London, 1665)

Wheel of Time turning Round to the Good Old Way: Or The Good Old Cause Vindicated, The. 24 March 1662.

Homeroscopeion (London, 1652). Thomason: November 1651.

[White, Thomas.] *An Exact and Perfect Relation of the Terrible, and Bloody Fight: Between the English and Dutch Fleets in the Downs, on Wednesday the 19 of May 1652* (London, 1652). Thomason: 25 May 1652.

Whitfield, Thomas. *The Extent of Divine Providence*. (London, 1651). Thomason: 8 May 1651.

Whole Manner of the Treaty, The (London, 1654). Thomason: 11 March 1654.

[Wild, Robert.] *An Essay Upon the late Victory Obtained by His Royal Highness the Duke of York Against the Dutch, upon June 3 1665* (London, 1665).

The Recantation of a Penitent Proteus: Or the Changeling (1663).

Wing, Vincent. *An Almanack and Prognostication For The Year of our Lord God, 1664* (London, 1664).

Wither, George. *British Appeals, with Gods Merciful Replies, On the Behalfe of the Commonwealth of England* (London, 1651).

Parellelogrammaton (1662). 3 May 1662.

The Dark Lantern (London, 1653).

Three Private Meditations (1665).

Tuba-Pacifica (1664).

[Womock, Lawrence.] *Pulpit Conceptions, Popular Deceptions* (London, 1662).

Wood, Seth. *The Saints Entrance into Peace and Rest by Death* (London, 1651). Thomason: 23 June 1651.

Woofe, Abraham. *The Tyranny of the Dutch Against the English* (London, 1653).

Worlds Wonder: Or Joyful Newes from Scotland and Ireland Comprised in the ensuing Predictions, and Monethly Observations, for the Present Year, 1651, The (London, 1651). Thomason: 20 February 1651.

[Worsley, Benjamin.] *The Advocate* (London, 1652). Thomason: 11 February 1652.
Wren, Matthew. *Monarchy Asserted* (Oxford, 1659).
Yonge, William. *Englands Shame: Or the Unmasking of a Politick Atheist* (London, 1663).

PRINTED COLLECTIONS, DIARIES AND MEMOIRS

Abbott, Wilbur Cortez (editor). *The Writings and Speeches of Oliver Cromwell.* Vol. II (Cambridge MA, 1939).
Bachrach, A. G. H. and Collmer, R. G. (editors and translators). *Lodewijck Huygens' The English Journal 1651–1652* (Leiden, 1982).
Bebingon, Thomas (editor). *The Right Honourable the Earl of Arlington's Letters* ... (London, 1701).
Birch, Thomas (editor). *A Collection of the State Papers of John Thurloe, Esq.* (London, 1742).
Boas, Frederick S. (editor). *The Change of Crownes* (London, 1949).
Browning, Andrew (editor). *Memoirs of Sir John Reresby.* 2nd edition (London, 1991).
Burnet, Gilbert. *History of My Own Time.* Vol. I (Oxford, 1823).
Chappell, Edwin (editor). *Shorthand Letters of Samuel Pepys* (Cambridge, 1933).
Clarendon, Edward Hyde, Earl of. *The History of the Rebellion and Civil Wars in England* (Oxford, 1843).
Clark, Andrew (editor). *The Life and Times of Anthony Wood.* Vol. I (Oxford, 1891).
Clarke, James Stanier (editor). *The Life of James the Second.* Vol. I (London, 1816).
Coate, Mary (editor). *The Letter-Book of John Viscount Mordaunt* (London, 1945).
Collections Relating to the Family of Crispe (privately published, 1882–1896).
Courthorpe, E. J. (editor). *The Journal of Thomas Cunningham of Camphere 1640–1659* (Edinburgh, 1928).
Dalton, Charles (editor). *English Army Lists and Commission Registers 1661–1714.* Vol. I 1661–1685 (London, 1892).
De Wicquefort, Abraham. *Histoire des Provinces Unies des Pais Bas* (Amsterdam, 1864).
Del Court, W. (editor). "Sir William Davidson in Nederland," in *Bijdragen voor Vaderlandsche Geschiedenis en Oudheidkunde.* 4th series, Vol. 5 (1906), pp. 375–425.
Del Court, W. and Japikse, N. (editors). "Brieven van Sylvius en Buat," in *Bijdragen en Mededeelingen van het Historische Genootschap.* Vol. 27 (1906), p. 536–591.
Dictionary of National Biography.
Donno, Elizabeth Story (editor). *Andrew Marvell: The Complete English Poems* (London, 1972).
Elliott, George Perry (editor). "Autobiography and Anecdotes by William Taswell," in *The Camden Miscellany.* Vol. II (1853).
Elrington, C. M. and Todd, James (editors). *The Whole Works of James Ussher with a Life of the Author.* Vol. XVI (Dublin, 1864).
Ffarington, Susan Maria (editor). *The Farington Papers* (Manchester, 1856).
Firth, C. H. (editor) *The Memoirs of Edmund Ludlow* (Oxford, 1894).
Geyl, Pieter (editor). "Stukken Betrekking Hebbende op den tocht naar Chatham," in *Bijdragen en Medeelingen van het Historisch Genootschap* Vol. 38 (1917), pp. 358–435.

Goodison, R. R. (editor). "Further Correspondence Relating to the Buat Affair," in *Bijdragen en Medeelingen van het Historisch Genootschap*. Vol. 57 (1936), pp. 1–61.

Grey, Anchitell. *Debates of the House of Commons From the Year 1667 to the Year 1694* (London, 1763).

Hall, A. Rupert and Hall, Marie Boas (editors). *The Correspondence of Henry Oldenburg*. Vols. II–IV (Madison, 1966–1967).

Hartmann, Cyril Hughes. *Charles II and Madame* (London, 1934).

Heath, Helen Truesdell (editor). *The Letters of Samuel Pepys and His Family Circle* (Oxford, 1955).

Historical Manuscripts Commission, *5th Report.*

6th Report.

De Lisle.

Finch.

Kenyon.

Leyborne-Popham.

Ormonde.

Various Collections.

Holloway, John (editor). *The Euing Collection of English Broadside Ballads* (Glasgow, 1971).

Hooker, Edward Niles and Swedenberg, H. T. Jr. (editors). *The Works of John Dryden*. Vol. I: *Poems 1649–1689* (Berkeley, 1956).

Journal of the House of Commons.

Journal of the House of Lords.

Laughton, J. K. (editor). "A Letter from Sir John Lawson to Sir Henry Vane, 1652," in *Notes and Queries* 6th series. Vol. 8 (July–December 1883), pp. 3–4.

Lettres et Négociations [de] Mr. Jean De Witt. Vol. I (Amsterdam, 1725).

Lomas, S. C. (editor). *The Letters and Speeches of Oliver Cromwell with Elucidations by Thomas Carlyle* (London, 1904).

Lubbock, Basil (editor). *Barlow's Journal.* Vol. I (London, 1934).

MacPherson, James (editor). *Original Papers: Containing the Secret History of Great Britain from the Restoration to the Accession of the House of Hanover* 2nd edition (London, 1776).

Macray, W. Dunn (editor). *Edward Hyde's History of the Rebellion and Civil Wars in England* (Oxford, 1888).

Notes Which Passed at Meetings of the Privy Council (London, 1896).

Mahoney, John L. (editor). *An Essay of Dramatic Poesy and Other Critical Writings by John Dryden* (New York, 1965).

Mayer, Joseph (editor). "Inedited Letters of Cromwell, Colonel Jones, Bradshaw, and other Regicides," in *Transactions of the Historic Society of Lancashire and Cheshire*. New series, Vol. 1 (1861), pp. 177–300.

Middleton, W. E. Knowles (editor and translator). *Lorenzo Magalotti at the Court of Charles II His "Relazione d'Inghilterra" of 1688* (Waterloo, Ontario, 1980).

Mignet, F. A. M. *Négociations Relatives à la Succession d'Espagne Sous Louis XIV.* Vols. II, III (Paris, 1835, 1842).

Newlin, Thomas (translator). *Bishop Parker's History of his Own Time* (London, 1727).

Original Letters of his Excellency Sir Richard Fanshaw (London, 1701).

Ornsby, George (editor). *The Correspondence of John Cosin.* Pt. II (Durham, 1872).

Parsons, Daniel (editor). *The Diary of Sir Henry Slingsby* (London, 1836).

Powell, J. R. (editor). *The Letters of Robert Blake* (London, 1937).

Poynter, F. N. L. (editor). *The Journal of James Yonge* (Hamden, CT).
Raine, James (editor). *Depositions from the Castle of York* (London, 1861).
Riden, Philip (editor). *George Sitwell's Letterbook 1662–1666* (Derby, 1985).
Robbins, Caroline (editor). *The Diary of John Milward* (Cambridge, 1938).
Robertson, Scott (editor). "Letters to the Duke of Lennox, AD 1667–1672," in *Archaeologia Cantiana*. Vol. 17 (1887), pp. 373–391.
Routledge, F. J. (editor). *Calendar of the Clarendon State Papers*. Vol. V (Oxford, 1970).
Rutt, John Towill (editor). *Diary of Thomas Burton*. Vol. III. (London, 1828).
Sachse, William (editor). *The Diary of Roger Lowe* (New Haven, 1938).
Salwey, Thomas. *Occasional Poems* (privately published, 1882).
Simmons, J. (editor). "Some Letters from Bishop Ward of Exeter, 1663–1667," in *Devon and Cornwall Notes and Queries* Vol. 21 (1940–1941).
Spalding, Ruth (editor). *The Diary of Bulstrode Whitelocke 1605–1675* (Oxford, 1990).
Steckley, George F. (editor). *The Letters of John Paige, London Merchant, 1648–1658* (London, 1984).
Steig, Margaret F. (editor). *The Diary of John Harington, M.P. 1646–1653*. (Somerset Record Society, 1977).
Sylvester, Matthew. *Reliquiae Baxterianae* (London, 1696).
Symonds, E. M. (editor). *The Diary of John Green (1635–1657)*. Pt. III in *English Historical Review*. Vol. 44 No. 173 (January 1929), pp. 106–117.
Taaffee, Karl (editor). *Memoirs of the Family of Taaffe* (Vienna, 1856).
Tanner, J. R. (editor). *Further Correspondence of Samuel Pepys* (London, 1929).
The Works of Sir William Temple. Vol. I (London, 1814).
Viano, Carlo Augusto (editor). *John Locke: Scritti Editi e Inediti Sulla Tolleranza* (Turin, 1961).
Warner, George F. (editor). *The Nicolas Papers*. Vol. I. 1641–1652 (London, 1886)
Whitelocke, Bulstrode. *Memorials of the English Affairs*. Vol. III (Oxford, 1853).
Worden, Blair (editor). *Edmund Ludlow: A Voyce from the Watch Tower* (London, 1978).

Index

absolutism
  Dutch 15–16, 108–109, 182–183, 190, 441–442
  English 183–184, 233, 369, 372, 376–378, 379, 393–396, 424–425, 444, 445, 448
  French 275, 353, 357, 359, 361, 365, 367, 370, 378, 397, 410, 412, 416, 440, 443, 448
  Spanish 451
Acland, Hugh 289, 407
Act of Uniformity (1662) 214, 216, 217, 227
Actium 302
Acts and Monuments, Foxe 59
Adams, Edward (East India merchant) 244–245, 263–264
Admiralty courts
  English 63
  Dutch 70
Africa 195, 204, 222, 237, 238, 245–248, 260–261, 263–264, 267, 294, 300, 302, 303–304, 320, 405
Africa Company 294, 300, 302, 303–304, 320, 405
Agincourt 1
Agrigentum 258
Aleppo 302
Alexander the Great 301
Algerian the Great 301
almanacs 42, 61, 79, 90, 92, 95, 97, 232, 234
Alva, Duke of 62
Amalia of Orange (Princess Dowager of Orange) 199, 204
Amboyna 23, 51, 56, 59–60, 64, 92–93, 181, 202, 263–264
Ames, William 23
Amsterdam 147, 199, 264, 283, 382
  William II's attack on 15, 109–110, 112, 334
  attitude toward England 29, 32, 57, 65–66, 67, 142
  and Navigation Act 50–51
  English grievances against 60, 62, 73, 88, 212, 304
  English merchants in 73–74, 99
  Orangism in 109–110, 144, 334, 340–341
  republicanism in 111–112, 210, 338, 339
  irreligion and sedition in 204, 206, 212
  English Dissenters in 228
Amsterdam and her Other Hollander Sisters 88
Anabaptists 115, 124, 153, 163, 165–166, 187, 228, 415, 447
Anglican Royalists 213
  views of the Dutch 198, 204, 256, 258, 260–268, 302, 309, 216, 325, 330, 443, 445, 447–448, 449, 450, 451–452
  Restoration as victory of 214
  newsletters 216, 220
  fear of Dissent and rebellion 225, 230–236, 330, 366, 378, 386, 393–394, 395, 443
  and English trade policy 237, 238, 240, 242, 243, 245, 247–255
  attempts to purge trading companies 326–328
  pessimism of 347–348
  interpretations of the Great Fire 348–349
  ideological consensus attacked and undermined 349–351, 358–360, 363–364, 367–368, 370–373, 378, 386, 397, 406, 412, 416, 421, 431, 440, 443–444, 446
  Charles II abandons policies of 425–426, 427–430, 434, 436
Anglo-Dutch War, third 243
Anjou, Duke of 445
Annesley, Arthur, Earl of Anglesey 249, 383, 394, 405, 411, 423, 425, 429, 430, 440
Antichrist 46, 61, 76, 78, 118, 129, 132, 164–165, 442, 446, 451
Antigua 46
Anti-Popery 6, 7, 366, 448
Antwerp 251
Appleton, Henry (English naval commander) 173, 212
Apsley, Colonel James 30–31

Armada, Spanish (1588) 450
army, Dutch 16, 189, 263
army, English
political role of New Model 13, 114, 115, 117, 122, 124, 183, 190, 228, 420
tool of absolutism 16, 233, 393–395, 396–397, 422–427
newsletters of 75, 94, 115, 134, 146, 188
of Charles I 250
purge of Catholics in 367
army, French 275, 370
army, Scottish 83
army, Spanish 90
Army Plot 252
Ascham, Anthony 119
Ashburnham, William 249, 252
Ashe, Edward 43
Assada 49
Atkinson, Robert 225, 229
Avery, Samuel 45
Ayscue, Sir George 101, 319

Babylon 97, 127, 131–132, 165
Babylon, Whore of 128, 131, 164, 191, 232, 446, 447, 451
Ball, Andrew 127
ballads 215, 224, 279, 280, 284, 286, 287, 301, 306, 308, 408, 419
Baltic (Eastland) trade 85, 93, 127, 174, 184, 283, 295, 300
Bampfield, Joseph 154, 218, 227, 229, 413
Banks, Noah 19, 23
Bantam 299, 304
Barbados 46, 68, 356
Barkstead, John 212, 406
Barlow, Thomas 362
Barnard, Edward 127
Barnstaple 176
Basire, Dr. Isaac 366
Bastide, de la Croix 199
Bath 287, 420
Batten, William 272, 370
Baxter, Richard 325, 349–350, 394, 415
Beale, John 420, 422, 430
Bedfordshire 417–419, 430
Behn, Aphra, spy and dramatist 312, 341
Bellarmine, Cardinal Robert 310, 447
Bellievre, French ambassador to the Netherlands 30
Bellings, Richard 223
Bellamy, Edward 202
Bellasys, John, Lord Fauconberg, Governor of Tangier 215, 233, 248
Bence, James, Presbyterian Royalist 150
Bence, John, Restoration alderman 249
Bendish, Thomas, English ambassador to Constantinople 42
Bennet, Henry, Earl of Arlington and secretary of state
associates and correspondents of 154, 203, 224, 238, 271, 278, 281, 295, 314, 318, 322, 325, 338, 345–346, 363, 413–414
observations, opinions of 217, 219, 226, 234–235, 237, 264, 271–272, 276, 283, 285, 291, 295, 298–299, 323, 332, 337–339, 344–345, 354, 361, 376, 379, 386, 397, 415, 420, 428, 439
publication of *England's Treasury by Foreign Trade* 257
marital ties to House of Orange 322
contacts with Orangist agents 343
and negotiations with France 387–392, 412
advocation of force against Dissenters 395, 397, 427
and negotiations with Dutch 397–398, 402
and outlawing of Duke of Buckingham 428
unlikely to have initiated Triple Alliance 434–437
Bennet, Colonel Robert 17, 178, 190
Bentham, Jeremy 418, 422, 430
Bergen, naval battle off 283, 361
Berkel 202
Berkeley, John Lord, sub-governor of Africa Company 248–249
Bermuda 46
Bernhard, Israel 178
Berwick 282, 286, 410
Bethel, Slingsby 90, 170, 182
Beverning, Dutch ambassador to England
republicanism of 120
negotiations in England (1653) 121–122, 132–134, 138–140, 142, 147, 149–150, 152–153, 169
observations on English political scene 131, 153
Restoration regime distrust of 200, 202
Beverweert, Mademoiselle de 322
Bicker 111
Bideford 287
Biddolph, Theophilius 238
Binnenhof 191
Birkenhead, John 266, 301, 305
Bishop, George 20, 23
Bishopsgate 428
Blackborne, Robert 83, 116
Blake, Admiral Robert 57, 64, 69, 72, 74, 77, 97, 101–103, 127, 135, 169, 442
Blake, William, merchant 292
Blakestone, William 229
Blenheim, battle of 1
Bloudy Almanack: Or Englands Looking Glass, The 42
Bludworth, Thomas 238, 242

Bombay 243, 245, 305
Bon Aventura 220, 320, 401
Bona Esperanza 220, 320, 401
Bond, Dennis 52–53, 72, 74, 105
Bonnel, Toby, merchant 105, 346
Bordeaux 122, 295
Bordeaux, French ambassador to England 115, 120–121, 123, 152, 191
Boreel 141
Boroughs, John 70, 72
Boston 296
Bourne, Nehemiah 77, 127, 177, 228
Bower, Richard 282, 374, 421
Boyle, Richard, Duke of Burlington 297, 380, 384, 392, 403
Boyle, Robert 433
Boyle, Roger, Earl of Orrery 258, 297, 306, 315, 326, 357, 359, 372, 384, 429, 432
Bedford, Thomas 277
Bradshaigh, Roger 415
Bradshaw, Richard 180
Bramston, John 272
Breda 335, 399, 414
Breda, negotiations at 387, 399–403, 434
Breda, Treaty of 274, 405–407, 409–411, 438–439
Brenner, Robert 12–13 and n. 10, 32 n. 91, 40 n. 1, 43 n. 14, 44 and nn. 19, 21, 45 n. 23, 46 n. 30, 47, 52 n. 54, 97, 102 n. 3, 119
Brereton, Lord 357
Brest, pirates from 177
Brewer, John 1 and n. 1, 451 and n. 18
Bridgeman, Orlando 247, 427, 430
Bridgewater 407
Bristol 58, 96, 280, 296–297, 367, 419
Broderick, Allan 358, 371–372, 375, 382, 385, 387, 391, 398, 412, 417
Brouncker, Henry 249, 251
Brouncker, Viscount William 329, 395, 425
Browne, Richard 117, 133
Brussels 389, 437
Brydall, John 396
Buckeridge, Nicholas 245
Buckhurst, Lord 425, 428
Buckinghamshire 282, 284
Buckler 433
Buckworth, John 242
Burghley, Lord Cecil 256
Burgoyne, Roger 342
Burnet, Gilbert 227
Burnham 296
Bussara 245
Butler, James, Duke of Ormonde 371
  commentary of 36, 358, 383, 394, 439
  associates, correspondents of 150, 216–217, 219, 222, 226, 234–235, 237, 272, 285, 295, 328, 332, 339, 359, 372, 375, 382, 389–390, 394, 397–398, 410, 412, 432, 435–436
Butler, Thomas, Earl of Ossory 371

Cabal 437
Cadiz 292
Calvert, Elizabeth 419
Calvin, John 266
Cambridge 430
Campanella, Tommaso 185, 451
Canary Company 371, 376–377, 381, 425
Cannae, battle of 287
Canne, John 97, 118, 129
Cape Bon Esperance 246, 264
Cape Corso 405
Cape Verde 246
Capp, Bernard 22 n. 37, 25 n. 53, 53 and n. 58, 64 and nn. 108, 109, 100 n. 43, 103 n. 7, 128 n. 30, 173 n. 17, 186 n. 49
Caribbean 65, 259, 292, 356
Carleton, Dean Guy 215, 226
Carlisle 422
Carlisle, John 224, 299
Carpenter, Richard 265
Carteret, George, treasurer of the navy 321, 347, 364, 370, 385–387, 393–394, 397, 423, 425, 427, 440
Carthage 92, 258, 267, 301–302, 311
Cary, Mary 165
Cat May Look Upon A King, A 21
Catherine of Braganza 222, 243
Catholics
English 223, 249–251, 350–351, 359–360, 365–367, 369
Irish 51, 359–360, 370, 432
(See also Papists)
Cats, Lord Jacob 50, 54
Cavalier Parliament 196, 214, 216, 226
  parochialism of 4–5
  factional strife in (1663) 222–223
  royalism of (1664) 235–236
  and the April 1664 trade resolutions 237–239, 247, 254–255
  and circulation of news 277
  and granting of supply for fleet 274, 379–384, 386, 393, 417
  Clarendon's speeches to 262, 303, 307, 311, 35, 325
  enthusiasm for war with Dutch 291, 331
  and crackdown on Dissent 326, 329
  and fear of Papists 350, 366–367
  criticism of court in (1666–1667) 362–363, 365, 369–373, 376–378, 393, 422–424
  court distrust of 386, 389, 393–397, 423–424, 436

radical criticism of 419–420
Charles II's decision to placate 425–428
failure of Comprehension bill in 429
reaction to Triple Alliance 439–440
Cavaliers/Royalists 18, 93, 204, 209, 218, 248, 377
ties with Orangists 28, 34, 46, 58, 87, 108–109, 146
attacks on Commonwealth representatives in Netherlands 29–30
newsletters and reports of 40, 83, 102, 118, 121–122, 124, 133, 161, 163
pirates 42, 87, 173–174, 176
fears of Anglo-Dutch rapprochement 104, 113–114, 150, 152, 154–155
reaction to end of first Anglo-Dutch War 169–170
scrutiny of Restoration regime policies 222
clamor for war against Dutch 238
non-Anglican 330, 369
(See also Anglican Royalists)
Challoner, Thomas 24, 47–48, 52
Chamberlain, Thomas, Governor of the East India Company 220, 260
Change of Crownes, The, Howard, 365
Charlemagne 256
Charles I, King of England 16, 20, 28, 83, 87, 158, 183, 250–251, 349, 445
Charles II, King of England
during the Interregnum 15, 35–36, 42, 49, 58–59, 71, 88, 107–109, 111–112, 114, 118, 154, 157, 169, 183, 442
visit to the United Provinces (1660) 195, 198
continuities with Cromwell's foreign policy 196
support for Orangist cause 196–204, 206–207, 220, 322, 324–325. 330, 333, 335–337, 343
and court adventurism 197
and Franco-Dutch accord (1662) 208
and negotiations with the Dutch 209, 212, 220, 321
Presbyterians and Restoration of 214
and fears of rebellion 217–219, 224, 226–227, 229–231, 233–234, 349
marriage to Catherine of Braganza 222
Parliamentary and popular discontent with (1663) 222, 224
and Parliamentary loyalism (1664) 235
and trading companies 243, 247, 251, 253–254, 327
and naval power 258, 271
desire for alliance with France 260, 387–390, 393, 397, 443–444
and fear of Dutch imperialism 262, 299, 302, 305, 318–320, 330
and laying up of fleet before Dutch attack on Chatham 274, 379, 384, 387, 393
and Four Days Fight 284
fears of Dutch aid to Nonconformists 309, 311, 313–316, 330
and popular discontent with anti-Dutch policy 351, 360
and neglect of navy 362
dissoluteness of 364, 418
and revival of anti-Popery laws 367, 425
absolutist tendencies of 369, 376, 378, 393–395, 397, 422, 424, 444
and proposed negotiations in Netherlands 397–399
and conclusion of peace 403–404
Nonconformist loyalty to 415
concessions to public opinion 425, 427–428, 430, 434, 436–437, 445–446
fading of religious enthusiasm for 448
Charles V, Holy Roman Emperor 256, 432
Carnock, George 400
Chatham, destruction of English fleet at 272–275, 312, 343, 379, 382–384, 386, 391, 397, 402, 405, 407, 411–412, 415–417, 419, 422, 425–426, 430, 444, 448
Chauran, De 210
Chelmsford 272
Chester 282, 287, 297, 366, 374
Chichester 225
Chichester, Bishop of 231
Child, Josiah 44
China 173, 264
Cholmley, Hugh, queen's usher 391, 393, 410, 420, 424
Chowne, Henry, East India trader 305
Christina, Queen of Sweden 50, 439
Churchill, John, Duke of Marlborough 451
Cinque Ports 72, 74, 296
Civil War, English 4, 6, 214, 216, 231, 313, 447
Clarges, Thomas 271
Clarke, Francis 242, 293
Clarke, Sir William, Duke of Albemarle's secretary 16, 332
Clergy
Dutch 16, 37, 108, 110, 121, 142, 310, 333–334
English 16, 95, 103, 117–118, 125–126, 131, 163, 168, 187, 232–233, 277, 279–280, 288, 313, 326, 349
Scottish 38
Cley 296
Cliffe, Edward 170, 182, 201–202, 266
Clifford, Charles Lord 417
Clifford, Thomas 238
coal, price and supply of 175–176, 297–298

Cockayne, George 53, 129, 224
Cocke, Captain George 238, 249–250
coffeehouses 276, 279–280, 292
Cogswell, Thomas 6 and n. 24
Coke, Roger 263
Colbert, Jean-Baptiste 254, 358, 360
Comenius 259
Comminges, French ambassador 235, 239
committee of trade 240, 242, 244, 247
Comprehension bill 430–431
"Considerations Regarding the Dutch" 201
Constantinople 173, 294, 328
Conventicle Act 236, 253, 255
Conway, Viscount Edward 95, 253, 271, 346–347, 370, 394–395, 436
Cook, John, solicitor-general at trial of Charles I 20
Cooke, Edward 403, 417
Cooling, Richard 388
Cooper, Lord Anthony Ashley, later Earl of Shaftesbury 248, 251, 354, 371, 372–373, 429, 448
Cooper, John 276
Cooper, J. P. 40 n. 1, 41 nn. 2, 3, 4, 42 n. 6, 47–48 and n. 33, 48 n. 38
Coppin, Richard 116
Corbet, Miles, regicide 212, 206
Corbet, John 416
Cornwall 289
Cortez, Hernan 395
Coulan, Henri Fleury de, Sieur de Buat 323, 343–345
Council of State (English)
  and diplomatic mission to Netherlands (1651) 15, 23–25, 28, 31–32, 34–35, 38
  ideology of 21, 124–125
  and trade policy 42, 44–46, 98–99, 172–173
  and negotiations with Netherlands (1652) 52, 54–55
  and popular Hollandophobia 59, 61, 63, 79
  reaction to battle of the Downs (1653) 70, 72–75
  and renewal of negotiations with Dutch (1653) 105, 108, 119, 121, 123, 125, 133–136, 148, 152, 161
  new elections for (1653) 163
Council of Trade (English) 46–49, 240
Council of Trent 153
Courland, Duke of 320
court (English)
  early Stuart 3–4, 6
  avarice/ambition of factions at 5, 7, 197, 273
  opinion at 198, 201–202, 208, 211, 217, 226, 234, 238, 272, 281, 300, 310, 350, 359, 373, 385–386, 390–391, 393–394, 401, 403, 443
  and trading companies 238–241, 246, 248–252, 254, 293
  criticism of corruption at 364–366, 369, 372, 374–375, 418–419
  emulation of France at 369, 374, 385–387, 422, 425
  conflict with "Country" party in Parliament 370, 373, 375–376
  Popery at 419, 421–422
  ideological shift at 430–431, 436
  affected by popular opinion 445–446
Court, Peter de la, Dutch republican theorist 205
"Court Maxims", Sidney, 259
Covent Garden 329
Coventry 218, 287, 374
Coventry, Henry 225, 262, 299–300, 320, 331, 357, 385, 391, 399–403, 405, 408, 410–411, 417, 434–435
Coventry, John 403
Coventry, William 204, 217, 239, 242, 244–247, 249, 251–253, 257, 268, 271–272, 277, 281, 285, 298, 318–320, 385–386, 391, 404, 413, 423, 425
Cowley, Abraham 300
Craddock, Richard 124, 260–261
Creighton, Dr. Robert 233, 418
Crofton, Zachary 215
Cromwell, Colonel Henry 132
Cromwell, Oliver
  and England as great power 1–2
  ideology of 4, 23, 76, 184, 189–191
  associates and correspondents of 18, 20, 23, 25, 38, 45–46, 53, 55, 88, 101, 200
  inquiry into battle of the Downs 72, 74
  attitude toward first Anglo-Dutch War 84–86, 121–123, 126–127, 129, 131–132
  and popular attitudes toward the war 96
  and dissolution of Rump 114, 115–116, 118
  and renewed negotiations with Dutch (1654) 132, 136, 139, 141, 149–150, 152–153, 158, 162–163
  conflict with radicals and dissolution of Nominated Parliament 141, 162–164, 166, 168
  and conclusion of Treaty of Westminster 168, 170–171, 173, 179–182, 184, 202, 211, 323, 330
  regime compared to Charles II's 203, 209, 253, 361, 367
  and Nonconformists 232, 330
  John De Witt compared to 306
  and sequestration of Thomas Thompkins 422

Cromwellians (moderates) 86, 133, 143, 147, 161, 164–165, 180, 185–186, 189–191, 447, 451
former, during Restoration 195, 24, 234, 254, 313–314, 319, 355, 357, 359, 370–371, 385, 448
Crouch, John, Anglican Royalist publicist and poet 264, 300, 302, 349
Croullé 17, 23
Cubitt, Captain Joseph 128
Culpeper, Cheney 48
Culpeper, Nicholas 61–62, 76, 92
Cumberland 325
Cuneus, Dutch secretary 226
Cust, Richard 5, 5 n. 22, 6 n. 26

Dalkeith 116
Daniel, Book of 95
Danvers, John 52
Darrell, John, East India merchant 260, 262, 264
Dartmouth 282
Davenant, Charles 238, 308
Davenant, William 238
Davenport, George 276
David, Biblical king of Israel 233, 418, 448
Davidson, William 311–312
De Britaine, William 202, 264, 267
De Bruyn 153
De Groot, Peter 120, 150, 157, 321
De Lionne, French minister 354
De Ruyter, Michiel, Dutch admiral 197, 263, 290, 294, 301, 339, 345
De Wicquefort, Abraham 204, 207, 212
De Witt, Cornelius 272, 411–12, 416
De Witt, John, Pensionary of Holland 111, 114, 196–197, 353
and peace negotiations with England 119–120, 138, 142, 161
correspondents of 131, 134, 152
and domestic struggles with Orangists 144, 146–147, 154–155, 207, 333, 336, 338–339, 341, 442
and Treaty of Westminster 182
opposition to restoration of William III 200–202, 205, 210, 323, 330
hostility to English monarchy 203, 206, 208–211, 220, 308
pursuit of alliance with France 207–208, 337–338
sheltering of English dissidents 230
compared to Mark Antony 302
affinity with English Dissidents/republicans 305, 310–312, 444
offers to English of generous terms 321–322, 324
and exposure of English/Orangist agent 343–345
and English courtship of France 380, 390, 392
English support for insurrection against 398–399
and negotiations for Triple Alliance 434–435, 437–438, 440
De Witt, Witte 91, 111
Deal 277, 361, 392, 418
Deane, Richard 17
Declaration of the Nobility and Gentry that Adhered to the Late King, The 251
Defence of the People of England, A, Milton, 21
Delft 67, 161, 212, 228–229
Dell, William 164
Denmark/the Danes 1, 165, 174, 180–181, 242, 264, 283, 363, 392, 433
Denton, Dr. William 340, 350, 391
Derbyshire 286
Dering, Edward 391
Desborough, Colonel John 136, 169, 228
Deventer 336
Devon 297, 414
Diary, The 59
Dickens, Charles 2 and n. 10
Digsby, George, Earl of Bristol 223, 372, 422, 436
Discourse of Dunkirk, A, Howell, 219
Dixon, William Hepworth 2 and n. 6
Dolman, Lieutenant-Colonel 104, 106, 132, 139, 147, 272
Dolman, Thomas 225, 233
Dominium Maris 72
Doncaster 234
Donne, John 63, 95
Dorchester 366
Dordrecht/Dort 67, 144
synod of 17
Dorislaus, Dr. Isaac 15–16, 23, 51, 78, 119
Douglas, James 19
Dover 287, 299, 391
Downing, George 173, 186, 200–213, 218–220, 227–228, 239, 246, 258–259, 261, 263–264, 267, 278, 281, 291–292, 298, 302, 311, 319–323, 331–332, 336, 353, 399, 406
Downing, George 355
Downs, battle of the 57, 69, 71–72, 74–75, 77–78, 101, 135, 148
Drake, Francis 48
Dryden, John 198, 301, 303, 395
Du Moulin, Peter 265, 402
Dublin 276, 280, 286, 297, 315, 345, 429
Dublin Castle 223
Dunbar, battle of 11, 19, 38

Dunckin, William 59
Duncombe, John 376
Dungeness, battle off (30 November 1652) 102
Dunkirk 189, 214, 250, 275
  sale of 219, 222, 363, 426
  pirates operating out of 212
Durham 117, 276, 314
Dury, John 53
Dutch, English views of
  false Protestantism of 14, 37–38, 50, 58, 76–79, 88–89, 93, 129–130, 179–180, 190–191, 204, 265–267, 305, 309–311
  materialism, ambition of 14, 36–38, 46, 75, 78–79, 88–93, 96, 100, 190, 262–264, 303–305
  monarchism of 14, 36, 38, 46, 50, 58–59, 62, 70–71, 75, 76–79, 87–88, 93, 100, 108–110, 112, 135, 179–180, 190–191
  rebelliousness, anti-monarchism of 202–203, 265, 305–309
Dutch Drawn to the Life, The 203–204, 261
Dutch Intelligencer, The 129

East Anglia 438
East Claydon 284
East India Company, Dutch 32, 99, 172, 331
East India Company, English
  political influence of 40–41
  attitude toward first Anglo-Dutch War 43–44, 98
  impact of first Anglo-Dutch War 172–173, 179
  and Anglo-Dutch negotiations 213, 220
  attitude toward second Anglo-Dutch War 243–245, 262, 267. 292–2292, 305
  African posts seized by Africa Company 246
  Dissenters in 248, 327–328
  and Richard Ford 249
  impact of second Anglo-Dutch War 293
  financial support for war effort 381
  and negotiations at Breda 387, 400–401, 404
  reaction to the conclusion of peace 408
East India Company, French 244, 320
East Indies 93, 159, 172, 184, 243–245, 260–264, 267–268, 292–293, 299–300, 304–305, 320, 449
Edgeman, William 102, 133
Edinburgh 276, 286–287, 297
Edward, Prince 29–30
Egypt 116, 130, 359
Eighty Years War 13, 257
Elatson, Jeffrey 413
Elizabeth I 2, 11, 90, 184–185, 188–189, 191, 259, 367, 445, 449, 450–452
Elizabeth, Queen of Bohemia 29
Elmes, Margaret 439
Elmes, Mary 411
Enckhuysen 143–144, 155, 341
England's Treasure by Foreign Trade, 257
English Channel 122, 173, 195, 222, 262–263, 296, 298–299
(See also Narrow Seas)
Ephraim, Biblical figure 95, 156–157
Escorial 191
Establishments, The 187
d'Estrades, French ambassador to the Netherlands 338
Eternal League (1605) 51
Evangelium Armatum 231–232
Evans, Arise 203–204, 230
Evelyn, John 20, 117, 258, 263, 267, 271–272, 284, 300, 303, 310, 325, 354, 356, 362, 377, 381, 383
Everard, Richard 223
Everitt, Alan 3 and n. 11
Evertsen, Jan, Dutch vice-admiral 63
Evertson, Cornelius, Dutch sea captain 324
Exchange, the London 279–281, 284, 381, 409
Exclusion Crisis 251
Ezekiel, Book of 78, 91

Fairfax, Thomas Lord 373
Fair Warnings: Or XXV Reasons Against Toleration and Indulgence of Popery 266
Faithful Post, The 112
Faithful Scout, The 60, 63, 66, 131, 189
Faithfull Advertisement to all good Patriots, A 15–16, 23
Fanshawe, Richard, English ambassador to Spanish 258–259, 268, 271, 298
Farnell, J. E. 12, 13 n. 9, 44 and n. 21, 45 n. 23, 49
Farnsum, Rippenda Van 199
fast days 95–96, 216, 277
Feak, Christopher 129, 131, 163, 167
Feiling, Keith 196 and n. 4, 199 n. 3, 221 n. 18, 273 and nn. 20, 21, 274 and n. 29, 321 n. 21
Ferdinand III, Holy Roman Emperor 189
fifth monarchists/fifth monarchy 49, 53, 86, 119, 131, 164, 186, 225
Finch, Heneage, Earl of Winchester 277, 294, 31, 327–328, 346, 356, 383, 438
Finch, John 203, 241
Fitzharding, Lord 387
Fitzherbert, John 367
Five Mile Act 326
Flanders 357, 390, 410, 432–435, 437–439

Fleming, Daniel 325, 386
Fleming, Oliver 123, 126, 152
Fletcher, George 276
Florence 240–241
Flower, Stephen 299
Flushing 62, 67, 211, 340
Ford, Richard 225, 238, 247–250, 252, 257, 290, 300, 303, 347, 440
Ford, Simon 258, 264–265
Forster, Richard 416
Foulis, Oliver 228, 230–231, 266
Four Days Battle/Four Days Fight (1–4 June 1665) 283–285, 339, 362, 373, 381
Foxcroft, George 292, 327
Foxe, John 59, 227
France/the French 1–3, 55, 134, 150, 222, 263, 267, 273, 345
  reports by diplomats, agents, and newsletters 17, 23, 42, 79, 103, 115–116, 120–121, 137, 141, 152, 159, 161, 191, 199, 223, 235, 239, 335
  the godly in 22, 157
  hostility toward Commonwealth 30, 107
  compared to Dutch 38
  privateering and English reprisals 42–43, 60, 63–64, 98, 173, 176, 241–242
  as trade competitor 98, 242, 244, 246, 254
  negotiations with Dutch 119
  English assistance to Frondeurs 122
  as outwork of Antichrist 131–132, 165
  alliance with Netherlands 199, 207–208, 250
  sale of Dunkirk to 219
  Court pursuit of alliance with 254, 320, 324, 387–393, 397, 410, 426–427, 444
  as aspirant to universal monarchy 258–260, 357–360, 370, 432–440, 443–444
  role in war between England and United Provinces 275, 283, 294–296, 302, 315, 326, 335, 337–339, 351–357, 357, 360–361, 363, 365, 367, 380, 384, 413–414, 443–444
  as model for English absolutism 275, 365, 369, 374, 387, 393, 424–425–426, 440, 444, 447
  duplicity of 275, 410–412, 427, 431–432
  English trade with 295
  blamed for Great Fire of London 349–351, 419
Francophobia 254, 275, 351, 431
Frederick III, King of Denmark 264
Frederick William I, Elector of Brandenburg 207, 323
Fredericksburg 246
French Intelligencer, The 64, 68
French Occurences, The 71, 73, 87, 90, 110
Friesland 28, 106, 109, 120, 200, 206, 211, 335
Frost, Joseph 16

Gambia River 320
Gardiner, Samuel Rawson 13, 14 n. 13, 45 n. 27, 51 n. 49, 57 n. 80, 63 nn. 105, 106, 65 n. 112, 70 n. 129, 71 nn. 130, 132, 133, 73 n. 138, 74 n. 143, 75 n. 144, 77 n. 6, 85 and n. 7, 40 n. 60
Garraway, William 373, 375–376, 422
Gathered Churches 96, 119, 187
Gauden, Dennis, navy victualler 384
Gazette, The 277
Gelderland 28, 109, 200, 211, 336
Genoa 242
Gerbier, Balthazar 48, 61–62, 102, 104
Germany 22, 26, 30, 181, 189, 327, 336, 383, 405
Geyl, Pieter 196–197 and n. 7, 200 n. 6, 204 n. 18, 211 n. 41
Giavarina, Francesco, Venetian ambassador to England 212
Gilby, Anthony 296, 409
Giustinian, Marc Antonio, Venetian ambassador to England 287, 340, 398, 420, 439
Glanville, Joseph 395, 420
Glasgow, Archbishop of 315
Glorious Revolution 274
Gloucester 58, 217
Goch, Van, Dutch ambassador 281, 293, 352, 360
Golden Coast, The 204
Goodman, William 265
Goodwin, John 95
Gower, Thomas 224, 229, 411
Grand Catastrophe, The: Or the Change of Government 183
Gravesend 143, 180
Greaves, Richard 225 n. 6, 227 n. 11, 235, 236 n. 34, 314 n. 191, 417 n. 70, 430 n. 167
Greece, classical 140
Greene, Henry 60, 64
Greene, John 78
Greenland Company (English) 40, 174
Greenwich 396
Gregory, John 436
Gresham College 381
Greville, Fulke, Lord Brooke 186, 256, 433
Grey, Thomas, deputy governor of Africa Company 248–249
Groenveld, Simon 13 and n. 11, 15 n. 1, 22 n. 40, 24 n. 50, 51 n. 47, 63 and n. 103, 72 n. 135
Groningen 18, 24, 28, 200, 335

Groscombe, John 420
Grotius 265
Guernsey 93
Guicciardini, Francesco 21
Guildford 329
Guinea 197, 246–247, 261–263, 268, 290, 292, 298, 300, 304
Gunpowder Plot 380
Gyfford, Humphrey, East India merchant 233, 358

Haarlem 144, 341
Habsburg, House of 256, 433, 443, 447
The Hague 50, 120, 153, 188, 434
  negotiations in (1651) 11–12, 26, 28–29, 31–34, 36, 38, 44, 442
  murder of Dr. Dorislaus in 15, 51
  English royalist exiles in 18
  news reports from 58, 65, 120, 122, 133, 141, 259, 389
  Orangist riots in 67, 144–145
  return of Dutch ambassadors to 141, 152, 180
  Charles II's visit to 195, 198
  negotiations in (1662) 200, 208
  conflicts between Orangists and republicans in 334, 339–341, 399
  Charles II's proposal to negotiate in (1667) 397–399
Hall, John 20, 59–50, 117, 165
Hamburg 174, 242, 295, 327, 392, 439
Hampden 222
Hannibal 287, 302
Hanseatic cities 174, 295
Hardy, Nathaniel, Charles II's chaplain 394
Harley, Edward 366
Harley, Robert 162
Harper, L. A. 44 and n. 20, 47 and nn. 32, 34
Harrison, Thomas 22, 74, 124, 131, 136, 153, 162–163, 166–168, 191
Hartlib, Samuel 25, 49, 59
Harwich 280, 287
Hastings, Theophilius, Earl of Huntingdon 298, 324, 392
Hatsell, Henry 99
Hatton, Lady 188
Hawkins, John 48
Heath, James 170
Hemskerke, Captain Van 287
Henrietta Anne, Duchess of Orleans, sister of Charles II 324, 400, 428
Henrietta Maria, mother of Charles II 49, 389–390, 400, 411, 422, 427
Henry V 258
Herbert, Philip, Earl of Pembroke 52, 248
Hereford 58, 348
Hertfordshire 366
Hibbard, Caroline 6 and n. 25
Hickes, James 273
Hickman, William 38
Hill, Christopher 84 and n. 4, 123 n. 20
Hind, James 61
Hinton, R. W. K. 41 nn. 4, 5, 48, 48 n. 37, 174 n. 19
Hobart, Nathaniel 285, 403, 437
Holland (province)
  opposition to House of Orange 15–17, 67, 109, 113, 200–201, 207, 406
  support for peace with English Commonwealth 18, 24, 29–31, 54, 57, 66–67, 104–109, 111–114, 119–120, 128, 150–151, 153
  animosity toward English Commonwealth 37, 67, 110
  ambassadors to England from 120
  opposition to proposed merger of English and Dutch sovereignty 136–137, 142
  struggle between Orangists and republicans in 143–146, 154–156, 340–341, 344–345, 399
  in the eyes of English radicals 165
  and Act of Seclusion 182, 202–203
  reception for Charles II 195
  friction with Restoration Monarchy 200–207, 210–213, 217
  and English dissidents 212, 227, 342
  economic pretensions of 260, 263
  perfidy of 305–306
Hollandophobia 50, 63, 97, 102, 187, 246, 292, 304, 361, 405, 447
Hollis, Denzel 262, 281, 295, 320, 323, 335, 339, 347, 357, 387, 399, 401
Hollis, Lady Esther 421
Holmes, Clive 5, 6 n. 23
Holmes, Robert 246, 261, 287, 289, 339, 342, 347, 378
Hooke, William 88
Hoorn 144, 341
Hopkins, William 366
Houblon, James, merchant 410
Howard, Edward 364
Howard, Robert 373, 378, 428
Howard, William 25
Howell, James 72, 219
Hughes, Ann 5, 6 nn. 23, 26
Hughes, William 19
Hugly 305
Huguenots 254
Hull 286, 289, 296, 329
Hungary 2
Hunt, Lieutnant-Colonel Robert 49
Hutton, Ronald 197 and n. 10, 273 n. 23, 274 and n. 27, 277 and n. 14, 326 n. 54, 330 and n. 82, 342 n. 86, 379 n. 3

Hyde, Edward, Earl of Clarendon
analysis of events under Commonwealth 26, 44, 69, 83, 102, 104–105, 109–110, 112–113, 121, 123, 133, 137, 145, 149–150, 157, 162–163, 169
associates and correspondents of 32, 182, 201, 203, 205, 209–211, 216, 239, 259, 298, 321, 391, 396, 401
and Charles II's passage through Netherlands 195, 198
and efforts to prevent Anglo-Dutch war 196–197
and negotiations with Dutch 199–202, 204–205, 208–209, 212–213, 218
assessment of domestic situation under Restoration 216, 218–220, 226, 315, 325–326, 328, 395
and sale of Dunkirk to France 219, 222, 363
confrontation with Bristol in Parliament 223
view of Dutch 228, 262, 304, 307, 311
on trade and trade resolutions 239, 252–253, 303–304, 319
addresses to Parliament 262, 277, 303, 307, 311, 315, 325–3326
after defeat at Chatham 273, 402–403
and negotiations with France 324, 389, 410–411
on English defeats of Dutch 340
and Sieur de Buat 343, 345
and Great Fire of London 346
and war with France 352, 358–359
and court excesses 364–365
and Parliamentary opposition 371–372, 374
and decision to lay up fleet 384–387
criticism and downfall of 422–423, 426–428, 434–435
and popular opinion 445
Hyde, Lord Cornbury 223
Hyde, Robert 233

Iceland 174
Independent Brotherhood 49
Independents 95, 115, 124, 166, 214, 227–228, 230
Indian Emperour, The, Dryden, 395
Infanta 445
Intelligencer, The 224, 232
Intercursus Magnus (1495) 34–35, 45, 50
Ipswich 176, 277
Ireland 51, 55, 94, 109, 111, 130, 141, 240, 254, 263, 265, 297, 299, 314–315, 350, 353, 359–360, 370, 385, 397
Irish Cattle Bill 223, 371
Irish Sea 176
Isaiah, Book of 95
Israel/Israelites 19, 21, 77, 94, 117, 130, 144, 156, 184, 265, 448
Israel, Jonathan 13 and n. 12, 85 and n. 6, 196 and n. 6, 242 and n. 14, 243 and n. 17, 245 and n. 22, 273–274 and nn. 23, 26
Italy 2, 140, 227, 241, 257, 259, 271, 294, 354, 408

James I 22
James II, earlier Duke of York
hostility toward Dutch republicans 27, 220–221, 304, 397
and reprisals by Orangist merchants 65
and English trade objectives 197
associates of 204, 217, 233, 239, 249, 251, 318, 385
suspected plot against 216
and royal succession 222
attitude toward political dissent 226, 329, 375–376, 395, 422–423, 425
and Africa Company 246, 248
as admiral 271, 283, 301, 319
as instigator of second Anglo-Dutch War 293
Catholicism of 366
and decision to lay up fleet 384, 395
influence of 386, 440
and negotiations with Louis XIV 387, 427
Japan 173, 264
Jessey, Henry 166
Jesuits 130, 186–191, 266, 268, 310, 350, 360, 366, 419
Jews 88–89, 118, 203, 334
John of Austria 258
Johnson, Captain 70
Joliffe, John 24, 253
Jones, Elizabeth, Lady Ranelagh 272, 364, 380, 392
Jones, Giles, English resident in Venice 324
Jones, Colonel John 118, 124
Jones, J. R. 4 and n. 18, 5 n. 20, 14 and n. 14, 197 and n. 9, 198 n. 11, 273–274 and nn. 22, 25
Jongstall, Dutch ambassador to England 120–121, 137, 142, 149, 156, 211
Josselin, Ralph, Essex clergyman 16, 20, 22, 56, 59, 78, 83, 95, 115, 117, 177, 214, 224, 296, 414
Joyce 228
Judah 95, 157

Kent 297
Kent, John 109
Kent, Joseph 227, 271
Kenyon, Roger 275
Kermesse 143, 145

Kersies 297
Keysar 111
Kievet, John 324, 344
Knachel, P. A. 43 and n. 15
Knight, John 26–297
Knighton 282
Knox, John 230
Korr, Charles 85, 86 n. 8

Lagoe, Waldine 275
Lake, Peter 6 and n. 26
Lambert 215
Lancashire 215, 277, 329
Laney, Benjamin, Bishop of Lincoln 309, 438
Langley, John 242
Launceston 286
Lawrence, John 228
Lawson, John 117, 241, 385
Leeds 234, 314
Leicester, Earl of 78
Leiden 334
Leighton, Ellis, Africa Company secretary 249
Leith 175
Leopard, The 244
Leopold I, Holy Roman Emperor 437
Lepanto, battle of 83
L'Estrange, Roger 224, 230–231, 233, 255, 263, 326
Levant Company 40, 42–43, 98, 173–174, 179, 240–243, 248, 293–294, 319, 328, 356, 408
Life of Sidney, The, Lord Brooke, 186, 256, 433
Lilburne, Colonel Robert 117, 164
Lilly, William 61–62, 67, 77, 90, 93, 95, 129, 232
Limerick, Bishop of 283
Lincolnshire 277, 314
Lisle, John 52–3
Lisola, Baron de 412, 427, 433–434, 437
Littleton, Thomas 238, 373, 422
Livorno 240, 295
Locke, John 424, 430
London 58, 64, 99, 104, 187, 264, 290, 303, 314, 366, 375, 390, 403, 417, 423
  merchants/trade in 41–43, 47, 78, 84, 127, 177, 237–238, 241, 249–250, 253, 293, 295, 297, 326–327, 382, 408
  foreign diplomats in 56, 75, 18, 142, 151, 156, 160, 169, 442
  clergy in 91, 187–188, 326
  distribution of news/popular opinion in 92, 96, 116, 126, 129, 131, 147, 160, 168–169, 173, 178, 185, 250, 253, 276, 279–282, 285–287, 304, 352, 360–361, 365, 382, 401, 407, 419, 424–425, 428, 439
  Dutch community in 99
  shortage of coal in 176, 297
  Dissent, fears of rebellion in 215–217, 224–225, 234, 259, 415, 417, 420
  smuggling into 229–230
  Francophobia in 254
  Great Fire of 285, 346–351, 378, 382, 388, 393–394
  court plans to intimidate 395, 420
London, Bishop of 255, 414
Loughead, Peter 41 and nn. 2, 3, 4, 49 and n. 42, 245 and n. 22, 321 n. 21
Louis XIV 5, 226, 239
  and Fronde 122
  and treaty with United Provinces (1662) 208
  and sale of Dunkirk 219, 363
  and French East India Company 244
  as aspiring universal monarch 258–259, 275, 358, 378, 397, 432–433, 438–439, 446, 448, 450
  and Great Fire of London 347
  intervenes on side of Dutch (1666) 351–352
  playing off England against Dutch 353–355, 357
  absolutism of 359, 422, 443, 447
  support for British Catholics 359–360
  Charles II's pursuit of alliance with 320, 369, 387–391, 393, 397, 444
  English opposition's distrust of 410–412, 416, 427
Louis of Nassau, Heer of Beeverweert and Dutch ambassador to England 199, 210, 217
Loevesteen Party 111, 150, 201, 338, 340
  (See also Republicans/Republicanism, Dutch)
Love, William 328
Lovelace, John Lord 233
Lowestoft, battle of 281–282, 301, 308, 314, 321, 325, 251
Loyal Messenger, The 179
Loyola, Ignatius 266–267
Ludlow, Edmund 44, 170, 181, 222, 224, 229, 235, 239, 290, 311, 329, 333, 373, 378, 388, 396, 419, 421, 448
Lupton, Donald 87, 101
Lyme 287, 329, 392, 407
Lynn 288, 296, 314, 348, 438

Machiavelli, Niccolo 21, 37, 61, 89, 310
MacDowell, William, Royalist minister 18, 23, 71
Madagascar 49, 244

Malabar coast 260
Mallory, Francis 299
Manasseh, Biblical figure 157
Manchester 96, 275
Mare Clausum 70, 92
Mardyke 189
Mariana, Juan de 310
Mark Antony 302
Marshall, Stephen 166
Marten, Henry 19, 52, 105
Marvell, Andrew 89, 92, 322, 370, 389, 395–396
Mary I 227
Mary of Orange, Princess Royal 28, 156
Mascall, John 293
Masham, William 55
May, Bab 424
May, Baptist, Keeper of the Privy Purse 393–394
May, Henry 74
Mazarin, Jules, Cardinal 17, 79
McKeon, Michael 198 n. 11, 240 and n. 8, 248 and n. 29
Medemblick 144
Mediterranean Sea 13, 85, 90, 93, 98, 100, 173, 222, 242, 282, 294, 356
Medway, Dutch raid on (see Chatham)
Mein, Robert 276, 286, 297, 361
"Memorial Concerning De Witt and His Cabal, A" 203
merchant adventurers 45, 49, 90, 249, 295, 327
merchant interlopers 13, 41, 46, 119
Mercurius Bellonius 42, 78
Mercurius Britannicus 88
Mercurius Elencticus 36
Mercurius Politicus 11, 15, 17–18, 21, 28–29, 31, 37, 54, 57–58, 61–62, 64, 68, 77, 88–89, 93–94, 106–108, 110–111, 113, 125, 133, 136–137, 146, 153, 157, 169, 185–186, 188
Mercurius Pragmaticus 36
Meredith, William, merchant 179
Meres, Thomas 428
Mews, Dr. Peter 306, 400, 409, 431
Middleburgh 67, 145
Middlesex 297
Middleton, John 156
Middleton, Thomas 290
Mildmay, Henry 47, 52
Miller, John 4–5 and n. 19, 218 and n. 10
Milton, John 16, 21–22, 52, 59, 89, 118
Milward, Robert 370
Minehead 418–419
Moderate Intelligencer 131, 142, 146
Moderate Occurrences 129
Moderate Publisher, The 130, 168, 184
Modyford, Sir Thomas, Governor of Jamaica 254
Molina, Spanish ambassador 437
Molloy, Charles 306–307, 310
Monck, George, Duke of Albemarle 216, 283, 300, 305, 318, 329, 332, 342, 3362, 367, 384
Montagu, Robert, Earl of Manchester, Lord Chamberlain 303, 388
Moray, Robert 337
Mordaunt, Henry, Earl of Peterborough 233, 294, 375
Mordaunt, John Viscount 376–377, 425
Morgan, Isaac 296
Morley, George, Bishop of Winchester 216, 357
Morley, Herbert 52
Morosini, Michiel, Venetian diplomat 69
Morrice, William, secretary of state 208, 216, 239, 262, 278, 281, 302, 304, 322, 325, 352–355, 390, 402–403, 408, 410
Moses 94, 448
Mountagu, Edward, Earl of Sandwich 195, 217, 282–283, 362–363, 379, 435
Mountagu, George 376
Moyle, John 17
Muddiman, Henry 247, 261, 278–279, 283, 328, 352, 391
Mun, Thomas 84, 257, 260
Munster, Bishop of 335–337, 339, 351, 360, 365
Munster, Treaty of 447
Muscovy Company/Russia trade 243, 300
Musgrave, Philip 419
Mustapha, The Tragedy of, Boyle, 306

Narrow Seas 91, 102, 132, 171, 179, 262, 302
(See also English Channel)
national interest 447–448, 450–451
Natures Dowrie, L. S. 5, 22
Navigation Act 12–14, 40–41, 43–48, 50–51, 55, 57–58, 68, 79, 139, 159, 199, 243, 320, 401–402, 405
navy, Dutch 331, 333, 401, 412
  ideological character of 14, 70–71, 84, 110–112, 154–156, 339, 345, 442
  clashes with English 57, 70, 263, 272, 285, 299, 303, 339–340, 442
  States General's decision to expand (1652) 68–69
  cooperation with Royalist pirates 87
  recruitment for 143
  proposed merger with English navy 153
  fleet damaged in storm 164
  disruption of English economic life 174–176, 294, 296–298, 411

navy, Dutch (*cont.*)
proposed limitations on 180, 191
Price of Orange excluded from control of 189
fleet sent to Indies 172
and English Nonconformists 312–314, 413, 420
destruction of English fleet at Chatham 272, 275, 343, 379–380, 401–402, 407, 416
use of after Chatham 404
navy, English 73, 190, 216, 271, 315, 329, 426
ideological character of 14, 64, 69, 77, 117, 123, 127, 445
clashes with Dutch 57, 68, 69–70, 74, 85, 93–94, 97, 102–103, 135, 281, 283, 285–287, 299, 303, 314, 339–340
prayers for 89, 414
and interests of English merchants 99–100, 171, 173, 177, 318–320
reforms and urges of 94, 103
blockade of Dutch coast 100, 134
proposed merger with Dutch navy 153
strength of 271–272
laying up of/assault on at Chatham 272, 274–275, 379–388, 392, 395, 397, 416–417, 424, 436
volunteers for 290, 444
expectations of success for 325, 341–342, 361
officials of 321, 347, 364, 370, 425
complaints about management of 361–363
navy, French 43, 356
Nedham, Marchamount 11, 18, 21–22, 70, 88–89, 92, 105, 183
Nero, Roman Emperor 418
New Netherlands 322, 405
Newcastle 282, 286–287, 297–298, 348, 416
Newcastle, Duke of 230, 233, 258, 266
Newfoundland 174, 263, 356
newsbooks/newspapers 11, 17, 24, 42, 59–60, 79, 87, 90, 94–97, 107, 132–133, 146, 168, 234, 277–280
(See also individual newspapers)
newsletters 36, 95, 123–124, 137, 146–147, 156–157, 160, 162, 176, 223, 224–225, 260, 263, 278–280, 314, 341, 352, 382, 392, 409
Royalist (during Interregnum) 40, 121, 163
in army 75, 94, 115, 188
French 79
Dutch 206
official (Anglican Royalist) 216, 220, 234, 247, 253, 261, 275–276, 278–280, 300, 306, 341–342, 358, 380, 388, 391, 397–398, 405, 411, 435
circulation of during Restoration 278–280
Newton, George 125
Nicholas, Sir Edward 30, 65, 104, 113, 149, 169, 182, 204, 214–217, 255, 267
Nicholls, Anthony 178, 190
Nieupoort, Lord 106, 120, 122, 140–142, 149–150, 156, 159, 169
Nominated (Barebones) Parliament 86, 91, 99, 131, 171, 180, 183, 191, 443
ideological divisions in 84, 123–125, 126, 147, 162–164, 166
dissolution of 85–86, 123, 167–168, 178, 180, 447
calling of 118
Nonconformists/Dissenters 215, 218, 223–227, 229–235, 242–244, 248, 250–251, 253–255, 259, 266, 268, 280, 314–316, 325–326, 328–329, 342, 366–367, 373–374, 378, 385, 412–417, 424–426, 429–430, 444–445, 447–448, 450
Norfolk 277
North Allerton 234
North America 93, 405
North Sea 208, 212, 297, 331, 380, 411
Northern Rebellion 224–227, 229, 231, 233–236, 242, 254, 378
Northampton 217
Northampton, Earl of 215, 277
Norwich 99, 277, 279, 282
Nottinghm 280
Nye, Philip 166

Octavian 302
Okey, Colonel John, regicide 212, 406
Oldenbarnevelt, Johan van 68, 334
Oldenburg, Henry 278, 352, 354, 357, 431, 433
O'Neill, Daniel 217, 222
Orangists/Orangism 14, 71, 87, 249, 267
hostility to English Commonwealth 15, 23, 28, 58, 66–68, 75, 107–109, 442–443
apparent decline of 17
continued provincial strength of 28–30, 33, 36, 109–110
in Dutch navy 71, 110–112, 339–340
and Dutch corruption 78–79
struggles with Dutch republicans 113–114, 143–148, 153–156, 205–207, 332–340
and negotiations with England 120–121, 134–135, 137, 142, 150–151, 158
as viewed by English moderates and radicals 125, 128
and Popery 188
Restoration monarchy's cooperation with 200–201, 204–205, 210–211, 213, 218, 273, 287, 322–324, 397–400, 406, 445

defeat and purge of 343–346, 367, 378
and Arlington 434, 437
Osborne, Thomas 313, 325, 379
Overijssel 28
Overton, Robert 118
Owen, Bishop David 266
Owen, John 78, 94–95, 124, 126, 166
Oxenden, George, President of Surat 213, 245, 260, 293, 305–306, 316, 327, 337, 354, 408
Oxenden, Henry 328
Oxenden, James 408
Oxford 280, 282, 289–291, 349, 364, 366, 414–415

Paige, John 42, 46, 56, 78, 83, 100, 127, 160, 174, 190
Palmer, Barbara, Lady Castlemaine 285, 364, 418, 424
Palmer, Roger, Earl of Castlemaine 332, 353
pamphlets 11, 42, 83, 94–96, 137, 279–280, 300, 303
Dutch 15–16, 23, 58, 205, 307, 310–311
anti-monarchical 20, 6
anti-Dutch 59, 62, 77, 79, 88–89, 92–93, 201–202, 204, 228, 263, 267, 303, 307
religious radical 164, 166
anti-Spanish 186
Anglican Royalist 219, 232, 234, 396
anti-court 215, 224, 231, 234, 253, 313, 419
anti-French 359, 420
"Paper Concerning the Dutch" 186
Papillon, Elizabeth 401
Papillon, Jane 403
Papillon, Thomas 254, 401, 404, 431, 440
Papists 188, 223, 232, 265–266, 313, 326, 349–350, 359, 362, 365–368, 374, 416, 419, 421–423, 425
Paris 352, 438
foreign diplomats in 56, 64, 100, 109, 122, 138, 153, 160–161, 235, 258, 324, 388, 392, 399
news reports to/from 158, 169, 178
Anglo-French negotiations in 208, 389–392, 397, 400, 427
Parliament (before, during Civil War) 14, 25, 31, 202, 216, 222, 360
(See also Rump, Nominated, Cavalier Parliaments)
Parker, Edward 178
Parker, Ralph 178
Parker, Robert 23
Parker, Samuel 291, 308, 311, 314, 329, 438
Paston, Robert 284, 315
Paulet, Robert 51, 54
Paulucci, Lorenzo, Venetian resident 57, 96, 100–101, 103, 105, 109, 121–123, 125–126, 152, 157, 160, 163, 167, 169, 176
Pauw, Adrian 63, 74–75, 78, 104, 106, 111, 181
Peace-Maker, The 168
Pearl, Valerie 12 n. 7, 25 and n. 53
Pearle, Thomas, Levant merchant 294
Pembroke 286, 349
Penn, William 117, 126–127, 373, 448
Penning, Nicholas 242
Pepys, Roger 374, 364, 424, 430
Pepys, Samuel
observations of 195, 215–216, 233, 235, 237, 239, 241, 249, 260, 272, 275–276, 284–287, 291, 295–296, 347, 367, 376, 381, 383, 391, 401, 409–410, 417–418, 420–421, 429, 431, 433, 438
comments made to 217, 222, 226–227, 238, 244, 246–247, 249, 260, 285, 321, 347, 361–364, 370, 376, 385–386, 388–389, 391, 393–394, 417, 420
Perfect Account, A 18, 31–32, 43, 56, 63, 93, 144, 161, 166, 179, 185
Perfect Diurnall, A 37, 65, 185
Perfect Passages 51, 67, 78
Persia 292, 299, 303, 396
Peter, Hugh 51, 101, 126, 168
Pett, Peter 128
Phelips, Edward 216
Philanax Protestant 256, 265
Philip II, King of Spain 256, 309, 432, 447, 451
Philip IV, King of Spain 185, 187–189, 357, 443, 447, 449
Pickering, Gilbert 136
Pierce, Thomas, court doctor 436
Pierrepont, Henry, Marquis of Dorchester 371, 405
plague 275, 342, 361, 364, 369, 381, 412, 448
Plymouth 282, 286
Pocock, John 432
Poleron 244
Poll bill 376, 383, 389
Poor Robin 1664: An Almanack After a New Fashion, 232
Poortmans, John 116
Pope, the 61, 76, 189, 223, 225, 232, 256, 265, 271, 366, 349
Popery 189
pre-civil War fears of 4, 6
as defining problem of seventeenth-century England 5
conflicting definitions of 6–7, 223, 446–448, 450–452

Popery (*cont.*)
  Dutch opposition to 17, 23
  Dutch collusion with 37–38, 77, 88, 129, 266, 268
  English radicals accused of encouraging 166, 365
  advancement of in Germany 190
  English fears of revived after Restoration 223, 360, 365–366, 369, 377, 389, 421–422, 429
  Nonconformists as agents of 232
Popham, Colonel 43
Porter, Charles, merchant 232
Portland, battle of 83, 90, 94, 103–104, 108, 110
Portsmouth 60, 290
Portugal 219, 222, 243, 246, 248, 300
Powell, Vavasor 115, 167
Presbyterians 249, 278, 325, 347, 352, 355, 357–358, 389, 401, 408
  Whitelocke on 53
  sympathy for peace with the Dutch 105
  viewed by religious radicals 129
  Royalists 150, 369
  Dutch as 204, 2265–266, 310
  Act of Uniformity and disaffection of 214–216, 218, 223, 225
  cooperation with Dutch 227, 230, 313, 315
  as anti-monarchical and Papist 230–231, 266, 310, 313, 366
  influence in merchant community 255, 327–328, 440, 443
  intensified repression of 329
  as supporters of Duke of Buckingham 372–374
  distrust of France 410
  loyalty during second Anglo-Dutch War 415
  and downfall of Clarendon 426
Presbytery Displayed 230
Price, J. L. 197, 198 n. 11, 202 n. 10
Priestley, Margaret 254 and n. 47
Privy Council 237, 241, 294, 322, 326, 337, 379, 384–385, 387, 393, 399, 402–403, 423, 426, 428
Protestant Cause
  failure of Charles I to lead 4
  enthusiasm for among Commonwealth leaders 22, 24–26, 35, 37, 47–53, 58, 74, 148
  Dutch abandonment of 50, 79, 88, 148, 446
  attempts to divide 61, 186
  Dutch support for 67, 133
  revival of prospects for 153, 157
  and Treaty of Westminster 181, 183
  ideological foundations for 185–186, 188–189
  and Triple Alliance (1688) 439
  abandonment by Restoration regime 443
  shifting definitions of 450
Providence Island Company 4
Prynne, William 366
Pula Run 401, 403–405
Purefoy, William 52
puritans 309
Pym, John 222
Pyrenees, Treaty of the 258, 447

Quakers 228, 234, 329, 415, 418

Ralegh, Walter 48
Raleigh, Carew 47
Ralph, James 292
Rawdon, George 271, 347, 370
Rawkins, Thomas 315
Read, Morgan 242
Reading 95
reason of state 89
De Rebus, Grotius 265
reparations 202, 209, 401
republicans/republicanism, English 14, 74, 429, 431
  classical and apocalyptic influences 14, 18–19, 21–22, 24–25, 77
  and desire for union with Dutch 14, 18, 25–27, 40, 444
  and disillusionment with Dutch 14, 35, 44, 50, 58–60, 77, 79, 87–89, 100, 180, 190–191, 441–442, 446, 450
  in the navy 64
  and dissolution of Rump 117
  divided attitudes toward Dutch 125, 128, 132
  criticism of Treaty of Westminster 170–171, 181
  Cromwell continues foreign policy of 183
  cooperation with Dutch republicans 198, 272, 307, 311–312
  dissatisfaction with Restoration 214, 363, 369
  as threat to Restoration regime 226, 351, 360–361, 367, 370
  blame of Great Fire on Restoration regime 349
  Francophobia among 353
  Dissenters and 416
republicans/republicanism, Dutch
  desire for peace with England 67–68, 104, 106, 113, 147, 150
  struggles with Orangists 68, 108, 112, 143–147, 150, 153–156, 331–334, 338–340, 342, 344–345, 442, 444

on diplomatic mission to England (1653) 120–121, 133, 149, 442
as viewed by English religious radicals 129
rejection of English plans for union 140–141
as threat to Restoration regime 198–206, 208, 211, 213, 217, 220, 229–230, 250, 256, 275, 305–309, 311–312, 317, 324, 330, 351, 353, 367, 375, 378, 393, 397–398, 406, 437, 440, 443, 448, 450–451
cooperation with France 337–338, 443
Reresby, John 415
Resolution of the Hollanders, The 91
Restoration 53, 170, 217, 238, 253, 281, 302, 320, 377, 383, 394, 410, 416, 420
continuity/change in English foreign policy after 4, 196, 447–450
and English views of international politics 4, 256–257, 446
Dutch republican opposition to 112
political factionalism after 197
views of Dutch after 200–201, 204, 213, 229
contemporaries compare with Commonwealth 209, 378
as victory of Anglican Royalists 214, 444
criticism of 224, 399–400
and merchant community 240, 248–252
circulation of news under 276, 279
ambiguous nature of 369–370, 378
Revelation, Book of 447
Riccard, Andrew, governor of East India Company 387, 408
Rich, Robert, Earl of Warwick 48
Richardson, Edward 229
Richmond 225
Riggs, Edward 225, 229
Rivers, Lord 428
Roberts, Clayton 372
Robinson, John 250
Rochester 420
Rogers, John 164–165
Rome
classical 18, 21, 73, 92, 140, 256, 258, 267, 287, 301–302, 306–307, 333
Papal 96, 128–129, 131–132, 165, 167, 190, 223, 232, 256, 266, 439
book of 124
Rotterdam 65, 67, 99, 161, 169, 228–229, 249, 334, 339–340, 344, 392, 420
Rowen, Herbert 110 n. 28, 140 n. 60, 154 nn. 15, 18, 171 n. 7, 267 n. 39, 181–182, 197 and n. 8, 199 n. 3, 200 n. 6, 221 n. 18, 333 n. 15, 335 n. 34, 338 n. 56, 343 n. 1
Royal Society 276
Rugge, Thomas 216
Rump Parliament 378
and merchant interests 7, 32, 41, 43, 50, 57, 84–85, 98–99
and overtures to Netherlands for union 11–17, 23–27, 32, 54, 441–442
and Navigation Act 2, 11–14, 40, 44, 46–47, 50
and disillusionment with the Dutch 14, 31, 33, 35–36, 38, 51–52, 72–75, 77, 89, 91, 94, 179, 441–443, 446
ideology of 19–21, 25, 48–50, 52–54, 76, 79, 89, 97, 126, 183, 444, 451
Dutch hostility toward 37, 58–59, 65, 88
war aims of 84–85, 171
dissolution of 85, 114–117, 119, 121, 122, 124, 132, 168
renewed interest in negotiating with Dutch 101–107, 112, 114
Dutch republicans compared to 129, 305, 314, 341
attempt to regulate coal supplies 176
individuals formerly employed by 212, 346, 429
popular hostility toward 222, 428
compared to Papists 310
impact of public opinion on 445
Rupert, Prince 42, 283, 304, 318, 384
Rushworth, John 272, 423
Russell, Conrad 3 and n. 12
Rutherford, Lord 250, 266
Ruvigny, French ambassador 432, 437
Rydal 392
Ryder, William, naval supplier 248–250, 252, 305, 354

Sa, Emmanuel 310
Sagredo, Giovanni, Venetian ambassador to France 100, 122, 153
Sagrir 164
St. Alban's, Earl of 208, 324, 387–391, 393, 411–412, 422
St. Anne's, Blackfriars 115, 117–118, 124, 131–132, 163–164, 168
St. Dunstan in the East 49
St. George, Fort 292, 327
St. James's Day, battle of (25 July 1665) 285, 339–340, 344
St. John, Oliver
mission to Hague (1651) 11, 15, 18, 26–27, 29–36, 55, 138, 153, 184, 442
profile of 24–25
bitterness after failure of mission 38–40, 44–45, 50, 58, 63
role in passing Navigation Act 44–45, 47, 49
associates of 49, 104
exile in United Provinces 228

St. Kitts 356
St. Paul's 166, 252, 276, 348
St. Peter-le-Poer 91
St. Serfe, Thomas, newsletter-writer 275, 278–279, 300, 306, 340–341, 358, 380, 388, 398, 405
Salibury 360
Salisbury, Earl of 52
Salmasius 22
Salusbury, Thomas 298, 324
Salwey, Richard 48–49
Sambrooke, Jeremy 172
Samuel, Book of 20–21
Sancroft, William 276, 348
Sandys, Colonel 277
Saunders, Richard 232
Savile, George 425
Say, William, regicide 311, 413
Schaep, Dutch agent 31, 50
Scheveling 195, 198, 203
Scipio 302
Sclater, William 91, 187
Scot, Thomas 51–53, 105, 186, 190
Scotland/Scots 50, 229–230
  Dutch compared to 14, 37–38, 45, 61, 78–79, 137, 141
  Dutch aid to 15–16, 34–36, 109, 111, 130, 146, 156, 161, 202, 311–312, 315
  agents at Hague 30, 71
  support for Charles I 83
  circulation of news in 94, 96, 341
  support for Parliament during Civil War 216
  and repression of Dissent 227, 395
  dependence on trade 297, 299
  French attempt at subversion in 360
  Francophobia in 361
Scott, James, Duke of Monmouth 422, 428
Scott, Jonathan 5 and n. 21, 18–19 and n. 36, 22 n. 35, 25 and n. 54, 48 and 38, 200 n. 6, 311 and n. 173, 363 n. 149
Scudamore, James 290
Seas Magazines Opened: Or, The Hollander Dispossessed 91, 126
Seaward, Paul 198 n. 11, 214 n. 1, 235, 236 n. 34, 238 and n. 5, 240 and n. 8, 257 n. 2, 274 nn. 24, 27, 326 nn. 54, 47, 347 n. 34, 348 n. 36, 370 n. 2, 373 n. 24, 377 and nn. 51, 52, 423 n. 120, 426 n. 135, 427 n. 141, 428 n. 148
Seclusion, Act of 182, 202
Sedition Scourged 165
Seeley, John 2 and n. 8, 446 and n. 5
Selden, John 70, 72
sermons 20, 53, 79, 90, 94–97, 115–116, 122, 126, 164, 187, 224, 230, 232, 234, 282, 287–288, 309
Several Proceedings of State Affairs 125, 133, 157, 169, 185
Severus, Roman Emperor 233
Seymour, Edward 247, 373, 377
Shakerley, Geoffrey 310, 366
Shaw, John 238, 249, 251
Sheldon, Gilbert, Archbishop of Canterbury 285, 326–328, 396–397, 423
Sidney, Algernon 18–19, 25, 75, 105, 224, 239, 259, 312, 353, 369, 378, 413, 450
Sidney, Philip 90, 186, 256
Sidney, Philip, Viscount Lisle 24, 52–54, 91
Simpson, John 49, 129
Sitwell, George 286
Slingsby, Colonel Walter 225, 352
Smith, George, merchant 213, 242
Smith, Hugh 215
Smith, Captain 64
Smith, Thomas, naval commissioner 128
Smyrna 241, 328
Sodom and Gemorrah 418
Somerset House 115–116, 166
Sound, Danish 32, 50, 111, 154, 283
South, Robert 396
Southampton 187
Southwell, Robert 352, 361
Soveraignty of the British Seas, The, Boroughs, 70
Spain
  Cromwell's aggression against 1–22, 85, 445
  Elizabethan antagonism toward 3
  viewed by English republicans
  diplomats based in 40, 189, 271, 379
  merchants trading with 42, 175, 179, 295
  as aspirant to universal monarchy 48, 185–191, 256–257, 265, 433, 442–443, 449–451
  Dutch hatred of 73, 108
  Dutch revolt against 88, 90, 96, 140, 202, 309
  Dutch atrocities compared to those of 93
  treaties with 134
  Portuguese revolt against 219
  ports of closed to East India Company 243
  Richard Ford supports peace with 250
  continued conflict with England in West Indies 254
  decline of 258–259
  Dutch as successors to 260, 263, 267–268, 300, 304, 452
  and coalition against France 434–437
  and Popery 447
Spanish Monarch 185
Spanish Netherlands 251, 357, 378, 390, 392, 431–433, 439
Spiritual Brotherhood 47–48

Spittlehouse, John 129–131
Sprat, Thomas, Duke of Buckingham's chaplain 272, 358
Spurstowe, William 187
Staffordshire 366
Stanley, Lady 429
States General (Netherlands)
  and St. John-Strickland mission 12, 18, 27–28, 30–33, 39
  and Dutch popular opinion 14, 65, 332, 334, 336
  and recognition of English Commonwealth 15, 24
  republicans gain control of 17
  Princess Royal's influence in 28
  sending of ambassadors to England 50
  Anglophobia in 67, 88
  decision to equip large fleet 68
  calls for removal of Orangist symbols 71
  refusal to punish Admiral Van Tromp 73
  renewed negotiations with England 101, 105, 114, 119–120, 122, 135, 142, 149, 151, 158, 161, 166, 346
  ideological struggles in 107–111, 114, 143, 147, 150–151, 156, 201
  stepping up of war preparations 161
  order of attacks on English in East Indies 172
  reception for Charles II 195, 198
  George Downing and 200, 213
  and restoration of Prince of Orange 204
  and alliance with France 208, 411
  and negotiations with England 210, 213
  sheltering/recruiting of English dissidents 230, 312
  and Dutch imperial pretensions 264, 304
  compared with Rump 305–306
  commercial disputes with English 320, 322
  discovery of Orangist plot 343–345
  and English fears of France 355
  and peace negotiations 397, 399
Stellingswerf 111, 143
Stephens, Philamon 185
Sterry, Peter, minister 163
Stevens, John 305
Stone, Lawrence 1 and n. 2
Stone, Robert 137
Straits of Gibraltar 241, 292, 298
Strickland, Thomas 238
Strickland, Walter 105, 127, 136
  mission to Hague (1651) 11, 15, 18, 23–27, 29, 32–36, 40, 45, 50, 55, 58, 63, 138, 153, 184, 442
Strong, William
Stuart, House of 4–6, 11, 15, 34, 48, 58, 77, 87, 108–110, 112, 114, 146–147, 182–184, 197, 200, 202–203, 207–208, 249, 251, 305, 312, 365, 442–443, 448
Stuart, Charles, Duke of Richmond 405
Stubbe, Henry 171
Suarez, Francesco 447
Sun Tavern 428
supply, Parliamentary grants of 274, 375–376, 379, 381, 389, 393–394, 417
Surat 327, 408
Surinam 405
Surrey 297
Sussex 175
Swann, William, Anglican resident in Hamburg 327
Swansea 286
Sweden/Swedes 49–50, 91, 181, 242, 246, 300–302, 320, 392, 415, 434, 437, 439
Switzerland 53, 140, 181, 373
Sylvius, Gabriel 323, 336

Taaffe, Theobald, Earl of Carlingford 301, 357, 360, 383, 391, 409–410, 418, 432
Tacitus 21
Taiwan 264
Talbot, Gilbert 283, 331
Tartars 303
Taswell, William 350
Taunton 125
taxation 129, 156, 295–296, 331–332, 348, 361, 364, 369, 375, 383, 444
Tayleur, William 377
Taylor, Silas 403
Temple, Richard 223, 363, 373, 387, 396, 423–424
Temple, William 283, 287, 323, 331, 333, 337–338, 346, 352–353, 360–361, 376, 383, 392, 394, 398–399, 402, 405, 410, 414, 433–435, 437–439
Ter Goes 145
Ter Veer 211
Texel 143, 153
battle off 94, 96, 111, 124, 128, 130
Thames 102, 154, 329, 380
Theobald, Francis 396
Thirty Years War 4, 6, 257, 439, 449
36 Articles 55, 57, 121, 152
Thompkins, Thomas 422
Thompson, Maurice 12, 41, 49, 98, 119
Thompson, Colonel Robert 98, 119, 122
Thomson, Colonel George 429
Three Days Battle (2–4 June 1653) 94, 97, 118, 120–121, 127–128, 130
Thurloe, John 32–33, 36–38, 40, 45, 74, 113, 118, 128, 140, 154, 165–167, 178–180, 183–184

Thynne, Frederick 392
Thynne, Thomas 302, 390, 399, 402, 411, 415, 432
Tiberius, Roman Emperor 224
Tichborn, [?]Robert, alderman 166
Tiel 336
trade
  depressions in 12, 41, 218–219, 252–253, 287, 331
  rivalries as cause of Anglo-Dutch War 12–14, 84–85, 96–97, 99, 190, 196–197, 210–211, 274, 291, 404, 406, 443, 452
  Dutch interest in union with England limited to 26, 34, 36–37, 57, 127–128, 133, 138
  English offer of concessions in 32, 139, 159–160, 320
  and merchant interlopers 41
  threatened by France, Venice 42–43
  effect of war on 42, 78, 97–100, 172–178, 246–247, 291–299, 318–319, 331–332
  Navigation Act as attempt to punish Dutch via 44–47, 56
  Dutch efforts to monopolize 48, 70, 91–93, 260–262, 299–301, 303–305
  English assaults on Dutch 74
  and Treaty of Westminster 171–171, 178–181
  Dutch idolatry of 204, 306
  Dutch fear English assault on 206
  with enemies of English and Dutch regimes 210
  in English woollens 228
  April trade resolution (1664) 237–240, 244, 252, 255, 322
  complaints of obstacles to 240–247, 252–254, 443
  as components of universal monarchy 257–265, 267, 299–301, 304, 358, 449
  and Nonconformity 326
  Dutch harassment of English trade 333
  French seizure of during Anglo-Dutch War 353, 355–357
  and Great Fire of London 381
  improvement with news of peace 407–408
Trapnel, Anna 131
Travers, Walter, merchant 268
Trelawney, John 223
Triennial Act, repeal of 235, 237, 255
Trinity House 47, 173
Triple Alliance 434, 436–437
Troubles of Amsterdam, The 15
True State of the Case of the Commonwealth, The, Nedham, 183
Truro 288, 407
Townshend, Horatio Lord 296
Tuke, Samuel 271
Turner, Edward 231
Turkey/Turks 88–89, 98, 173, 185, 231–232, 240–242, 259, 261, 264, 293
Tyre 78, 91, 130

Ulster 315
Underdown, David 53 and n. 59
universal monarchy 256, 450–452
  pursued by Spain/Habsburgs 48, 185, 191, 256, 258–259, 432–433, 442–443, 447
  maritime trade and 257–258, 263, 267–268, 449
  pursued by France/Louis XIV 259–260, 275, 302, 358–360, 370, 378, 397, 410, 412, 416, 432–433, 435, 443, 446
  pursued by the Dutch 260–263, 265, 267–268, 302, 304, 330, 353, 360
  and religion 448–450
Ussher, James 25, 49
Utrecht 29, 211, 335

Valkenburg, John, director of North Coast of Africa/Dutch West India Co. 261
Van Aitzema, Lieuwe 28, 138, 213
Van Horn, Simon, Dutch ambassador to England 199
Van de Perre, Paulus 50, 120, 138, 147, 152–153
Van Ruyven, Dirk 206–207, 218, 267
Van Tromp, Cornelius 241, 339–341, 344, 346
Van Tromp, Martin 57, 69–74, 83, 87, 101–102, 110–111, 122, 134–136, 148, 153–155, 175, 442
Vandeputt, Peter 337
Vane, Henry 19, 24–25, 55, 74, 118, 215
Vane, Walter, diplomat 137, 163, 323, 336–337
Vaughan, John 373
Vaughan, Richard Lord 428
Venice
  as a European power 2
  diplomatic reports of 40, 56–57, 64, 66, 69, 73, 75, 85, 96, 100–101, 103, 105, 109, 121–123, 125–126, 152–153, 157, 160, 163, 167, 169, 176, 189, 212, 216–219, 235, 247, 272, 287, 290, 295, 297, 301, 321, 324, 332, 340, 344, 346, 365, 392, 398, 420, 427, 439
  as trade competitor 42, 98, 240–241
  and *Dominium Maris* 72
  foreign diplomats in 109, 310, 324
  as republican model 140
Venner, Thomas 448
Vere, Francis 90
Vermuyden, Sir Cornelius 186

Verney, Edmund 358, 363, 433
Verney, Ralph 285, 296, 340, 350, 391, 411, 423, 433, 437
Vernon, Thomas 242
Versailles 396
Villaflore, Conde de 258
Villiers, George, second Duke of Buckingham 226, 272, 358, 371–375, 377, 379, 423, 428–429, 436–437, 439–440, 444, 448
Virginia 46
Vlie, English raid on the 287, 289, 339–340, 347, 378
Vox Plebis 129

J. W. pamphlet author 88
Wall, Thomas, Guinea merchant 52
Waller, Edmund 300–302, 423
Wallis, John 289
Walsh, Robert 229
Walwyn, William 40
Ward, Seth, Bishop of Exeter 297
Warwick 277
Warwick, Philip 222
Wase, Christopher 303
Wassenaer, Jacob van (Lord of Opdam, Dutch naval commander) 153–155
Watts, Richard 277, 418
Waynright, James 180
Webster, Charles 47
Webster, John 262
Wedgbury 366
Weekly Intelligencer of the Commonwealth, The 12, 67, 76, 78, 83, 107, 146, 155, 169, 176
Wells 296
Wentworth, Peter 52
Wentworth, Thomas Lord 150
West Indies 93, 100, 159, 184, 189–190, 247, 254, 257, 259–263, 267–268, 300, 356, 449
Westminster, negotiations in 31, 51–58, 64–65, 69–70, 75, 101, 119, 121, 141, 208
Westminster Hall 166, 418, 426
Westminster, Treaty of 85–86, 179–181, 184, 330
Westmorland 419
Westphalia, Treaty of 447
Weymouth 407, 432
Whalley, Colonel Edward 166
Wharton, George, almanac writer 234
White 228
Whitehall 208, 248, 313, 385, 394, 417, 419, 430, 451
Whitelocke, Bulstrode 24–25, 36, 38, 46, 65, 69, 103, 105, 116, 134, 137, 145
  profiled 52–53
  and treatise on English sovereignty of the sea 72
  on avarice 91–92, 97
  friends, correspondents of 102, 106–107, 128, 178, 183, 224
Whittington, Luke 289
Wight, Isle of 225, 353, 366
Wildman, John 429
Wilkins, John, Bishop of Chester 374
William I (the Silent), Prince of Orange 441
William II, Price of Orange 11, 15–17, 28–29, 31, 34, 51, 68, 108–110, 112, 334, 441
William III, Prince of Orange
  struggle over restoration of (1650s) 17, 28–29, 68, 107–108, 110–113, 120, 123, 135–136, 139, 143–147, 154–156
  struggle over restoration of (1660s) 201, 207, 212, 332–336, 338–341, 343, 345
  Anglo-Dutch agreement to exclude from power 158–159, 182, 189, 442
  English efforts to restore 196–200, 203–208, 210–211, 213, 221, 239, 309, 322–325, 330, 398–399
  temporary English abandonment of 218, 220, 434
William Frederick 137
Williamson, Joseph 206–207, 210, 212, 215, 228, 234, 237, 247, 251, 253, 273, 277–278, 282, 286, 325, 328, 338, 342, 380, 396, 400, 407, 410–411, 417, 422, 432, 435
Williamson, William 214, 216
Willoughby, Francis Lord 46, 128
Wilson, Charles 12 and n. 8, 84 and n. 5, 97, 110 n. 28, 171 and n. 7, 172 n. 9, 196 and nn. 5, 6, 220 n. 16, 273 and n. 19, 274 and nn. 26, 28
Winchilsea, Earl of, ambassador in Constantinople 241, 255, 294, 301, 328, 346, 356
Winter, Edward 327–328
Wise, Lawrence 129
Wither, George 16
Wolfe, General James 451
Wolstenholme, John 249, 251–252
Womock, Lawrence 232–233
Wood, Anthony, Anglican Oxford scholar 282, 349, 366–367
woollen industry 228, 238, 240
Woolrych, Austin 86 and nn. 9, 10, 118 n. 5, 123, 124 n. 22, 140 n. 60, 149 n. 2, 153 n. 12, 162 n. 40, 163 and nn. 45, 46
Woolters, Captain John 127
Worcester, battle of 52, 58–59, 61
Worden, Blair 18 and nn. 19, 20, 19 n. 22, 21 n. 35, 40 n. 1, 41 and n. 5, 44 n. 20, 47

Worden, Blair (*cont.*)
n. 3, 48 n. 38, 49 n. 39, 53 and nn. 58, 59, 61, 74 n. 140, 78 n. 8
Worsley, Benjamin 12, 43, 47–50, 59
Wriothesley, Thomas, Earl of Southampton 244, 384–385

Yarmouth 99, 175
York, city of 178, 234, 252, 415
Yorkshire 314, 325, 329, 366, 374, 419

Zeeland 17–18, 24, 28–29, 63, 65–68, 109, 111–113, 120, 138, 145–147, 153, 165, 188, 200, 207, 211, 227, 334–335, 340–341
Ziereckzee 145
Zwoll 336

Titles in the series

*The Common Peace: Participation and the Criminal Law in Seventeenth-Century England**
CYNTHIA B. HERRUP

Politics, Society and Civil War in Warwickshire, 1620–1660
ANN HUGHES

*London Crowds in the Reign of Charles II: Propaganda and Politics from the Restoration to the Exclusion Crisis**
TIM HARRIS

*Criticism and Compliment: The Politics of Literature in the England of Charles I**
KEVIN SHARPE

Central Government and the Localities: Hampshire, 1649–1689
ANDREW COLEBY

John Skelton and the Politics of the 1520s
GREG WALKER

Algernon Sidney and the English Republic, 1623–1677
JONATHAN SCOTT

Thomas Starkey and the Commonwealth: Humanist Politics and Religion in the Reign of Henry VIII
THOMAS F. MAYER

*The Blind Devotion of the People: Popular Religion and the English Reformation**
ROBERT WHITING

The Cavalier Parliament and the Reconstruction of the Old Regime, 1661–1667
PAUL SEAWARD

The Blessed Revolution: English Politics and the Coming of War, 1621–1624
THOMAS COGSWELL

Charles I and the Road to Personal Rule
L. J. REEVE

George Lawson's 'Politica' and the English Revolution
CONAL CONDREN

Puritans and Roundheads: The Harleys of Brampton Bryan and the Outbreak of the English Civil War
JACQUELINE EALES

An Uncounselled King: Charles I and the Scottish Troubles, 1637–1641
PETER DONALD

*Cheap Print and Popular Piety, 1550–1640**
TESSA WATT

The Pursuit of Stability: Social Relations in Elizabethan London
IAN W. ARCHER

Prosecution and Punishment: Petty Crime and the Law in London and Rural Middlesex, c. 1660–1725
ROBERT B. SHOEMAKER

Algernon Sidney and the Restoration Crisis, 1677–1683
JONATHAN SCOTT

Exile and Kingdom: History and Apocalypse in the Puritan Migration to America
AVIHU ZAKAI

The Pillars of Priestcraft Shaken: The Church of England and its Enemies, 1660–1730
J. A. I. CHAMPION

Stewards, Lords and People: The Estate Steward and his World in Later Stuart England
D. R. HAINSWORTH

Civil War and Restoration in The Three Stuart Kingdoms: The Career of Randal MacDonnell, Marquis of Antrim, 1609–1683
JANE H. OHLMEYER

The Family of Love in English Society, 1550–1630
CHRISTOPHER W. MARSH

*The Bishops' Wars: Charles I's Campaigns against Scotland, 1638–1640**
MARK FISSEL

*John Locke: Resistance, Religion and Responsibility**
JOHN MARSHALL

Constitutional Royalism and the Search for Settlement, c. 1640–1649
DAVID L. SMITH

Intelligence and Espionage in the Reign of Charles II, 1660–1685
ALAN MARSHALL

The Chief Governors: The Rise and Fall of Reform Government in Tudor Ireland, 1535–1588
CIARAN BRADY

Politics and Opinion in Crisis, 1678–1681
MARK KNIGHTS

Catholic and Reformed: The Roman and Protestant Churches in English Protestant Thought, 1604–1640
ANTHONY MILTON

Sir Matthew Hale, 1609–1676: Law, Religion and Natural Philosophy
ALAN CROMARTIE

Henry Parker, the Public's 'Privado': The Political Writer and the English State in Civil War
MICHAEL MENDLE

Protestantism and Patriotism: Ideologies and the Making of English Foreign Policy, 1650–1668
STEVEN C. A. PINCUS

* *Also published as a paperback*